25.00

1228

001228   TELEPEN

D0298300

M
LIBRARY

Don

National Children's Bureau series

Editor: Ronald Davie

This series examines contemporary issues relating to the development of children and their needs in the family, school and society. Based on recent research and taking account of current practice, it also discusses policy implications for the education, health and social services. The series is relevant not only for professional workers, administrators, researchers and students but also for parents and those involved in self-help movements and consumer groups.

Combined Nursery Centres
Elsa Ferri, Dorothy Birchall,
Virginia Gingell and Caroline Gipps

Growing Up in Great Britain: Papers from the National Child Development Study
Ken Fogelman (editor)

Children in Changing Families: a Study of Adoption and Illegitimacy
Lydia Lambert and Jane Streather

Caring for Separated Children
R. A. Parker (editor)

A Fairer Future for Children
Mia Kellmer Pringle

Unqualified and Underemployed: Handicapped Young People and the Labour Market
Alan Walker

The editor

Ken Fogelman is Assistant Director (research), National Children's Bureau.

The book

Since 1958, the 16 000 children in Britain born in one week that year have been the subjects of a long-term, multidisciplinary research study known as the National Child Development Study. At regular intervals throughout their childhood, data have been collected through educational tests, questionnaires from schools, medical examinations, and interviews with parents. Many of the findings from this unique study have been published in articles and papers in learned journals. This book brings together a selection of papers with a new introduction and overview to give a comprehensive insight into the experience of growing up in Britain today. The book is essential reading, and an indispensable reference-point, for all those concerned with the study of child development.

THE ST. HELENS COLLEGE OF TECHNOLOGY

DC 305.23
3 - 053.7

43258

-- OCT 1983

LIBRARY

Growing Up in Great Britain

Papers from the
National Child Development Study

Edited by
Ken Fogelman

M

Macmillan for the
National Children's Bureau

© National Children's Bureau 1983

All rights reserved. No part of this publication may be reproduced or transmitted, in any form or by any means, without permission.

First published 1983 by
THE MACMILLAN PRESS LTD
London and Basingstoke
Companies and representatives throughout the world

ISBN 0 333 34394 8

Typeset by
Cambrian Typesetters,
Farnborough, Hants

Printed in Hong Kong

Foreword

MIA KELLMER PRINGLE

Founder-Director of the National Children's Bureau and now a Vice-President

Its origin and aims

In 1958, for the purpose of a perinatal mortality survey, Professor Neville Butler, on behalf of the National Birthday Trust, gathered information on virtually every baby (some 98 per cent) born in England, Scotland and Wales during the week 3—9 March. This group of children — numbering some 17 000 births in all — is therefore a completely representative national cross-section. A vast amount of social, obstetric and medical information was collected concerning the mother, the course of her pregnancy and labour. In addition, a great deal of detailed information was amassed on her baby at the time of birth and within the first week of life.

The National Child Development Study (1958 cohort)

In 1964 the opportunity arose to trace and study these children again, the hope being that it would become a long-term, multidisciplinary investigation of all the children in this birth week. In this project — called the National Child Development Study (1958 cohort) — there have so far been four follow-ups when the subjects were respectively 7, 11, 16 and 23 years old. From the outset I had two hopes for the study.

The first was to continue studying the growth and development of the children well into adulthood, because the project provides an unrivalled opportunity to find some answers to many important questions — answers which are neither known nor easy to discover by other means. By looking at a large representative group at various ages it becomes possible to describe and make generalisations about the health, physical development and home environment as well as about the behaviour and educational attainment of the subjects. This provides a base-line against which the parent, teacher, doctor or psychologist can judge the development and needs of a particular child; while the policy-maker and administrator can judge the effectiveness and adequacy of existing services in the light of the conditions which are revealed.

My second hope was that, in addition to the regular follow-ups of the entire cohort, the NCB would make more detailed and intensive studies of children with special needs and compare their long-term, all-round development with that of the whole cohort; in this way factors affecting their health, adjustment and performance, both adverse and beneficial, could be identified. To ensure that there would be sufficient numbers in the various groups to be studied, it was considered necessary to follow up the entire cohort rather than a stratified sample. These linked or related studies have so far covered the following groups: physically and mentally handicapped children; those living in care, socially disadvantaged children; children born to unmarried mothers; adopted children; those in one-parent families; children who have a step-parent; those belonging to ethnic minorities; and gifted children.

The longitudinal nature of the project makes it possible to unravel some of the interrelationships between social, medical and obstetric factors in the mother, the baby's birth history and antenatal development on the one hand, and the child's subsequent all-round growth and adjustment on the other. For example, a picture can be built up of the long-term relationship between parental social background, low birth weight and the child's level of educational achievements; or it can be established how many children who showed behaviour difficulties at the age of 7 still do at 11 and 16, and in what ways they and their environments differ from those of children who have 'outgrown' them in the intervening years, as well as from those who developed behaviour difficulties only at the later ages; or the development of adopted children can be compared with those who remained with their own mothers or came into care, as well as with other children in the whole cohort who had a similar social-class background.

Thus each successive follow-up provides valuable descriptive and normative material about a representative group of British children at a particular age, while the multidisciplinary, longitudinal nature of the whole project makes it possible to see changes in development of the same children and young people over a period of years, albeit with a rather broad brush; in contrast, the more intensive and detailed investigations of children with special needs can explore more qualitative aspects of growth and development.

Looking back, my early hopes and intentions for the study have to a considerable extent been fulfilled. Inevitably there have been problems and difficulties, many of them related to the availability of funds. Also with hindsight it is possible to see that certain aspects of the work might well have been handled differently. But, overall, it has proved to be a challenging and most worthwhile venture, made all the more so by the generous help and support given by many professional workers completely of their own volition, by the co-operation of local education and social services as well as health authorities; by a great number of colleagues who managed, in their busy professional lives, to spare time for the giving of advice and criticism; and, perhaps, above all, by the willing co-operation over the years of both the parents and the children, now adults themselves. Without these the project could never have been mounted, nor could it have been so productive and seminal.

Continuity of staffing and funding

While inevitably there has been staff turnover, for a study of this magnitude and duration there has been remarkable stability and continuity over the past twenty years: Professor Neville Butler, who directed the original perinatal study and co-directed the first and second follow-ups, remained an Honorary Consultant. Dr Ronald Davie, who was senior research officer at the time of the first follow-up and then co-director as well as deputy director of the Bureau, remained Honorary Consultant when he took up a chair at the University of Cardiff, and now has returned as director of the Bureau; Professor Harvey Goldstein was part-time statistician during the first follow-up, then became the Bureau's principal statistician, and on taking up a chair at London University remained an Honorary Consultant; Peter Wedge was senior research officer at the time of the second follow-up and continued to be closely involved as deputy director of the Bureau in the third and beginning of the fourth follow-up; the present writer has been closely involved with the study since its inception right up until the end of 1981; Ken Fogelman has been involved in the second, third and current follow-up, now in his capacity as assistant director (research); and Professors Michael Healey, Jim Tanner and Bill Wall have throughout acted as Honorary Consultants to the study.

With regard to sponsorship and funding, the opposite has been the case. Each follow-up has had a different group of sponsors. which made forward planning from one sweep to the next, and also long-term security, quite serious problems. Funds for each major follow-up have come mainly from public sources, in particular central government departments; whereas the related projects, dealing with children who have special needs, have mainly come from charitable foundations.

This continued confidence in the study and the NCB as the organisation with overall responsibility for its direction is much appreciated. It is based, I would hope, on both the quality of work which has resulted and also on its continued productivity. Also, the study has now built up a storehouse of information which can be tapped by special interests; for example, a request to look into the development and academic achievement of children from service families could be met because there were a sufficient number of children to make a special analysis viable.

Success — how to judge it?

This is always a very difficult question, but three criteria might go some way towards providing an answer. The first is that most of the major findings have implications for policy, both at local and central government level. Also these findings have influenced professional organisations as well as the practice of individual professional workers, such as teachers, health visitors and paediatricians. Of course, it is always difficult to point directly to the effectiveness of research findings in relation to policy changes, because many other influences always play a part. Clearly the climate of the time as well as economic, social and political circumstances all make their impact on changes in thinking and practice. However, quite a number of examples could be given of the impact the findings have had, not only on academic knowledge but also on professional practice and policy issues.

The second criterion for success is, I feel, the productivity of the study. During its nineteen years' existence, one book and eight chapters or articles have been produced on average every year. Moreover, the NCB has explored innovative means of disseminating the findings, making as much use as possible of the media as well as of 'popular presentations' in addition to the more traditional academic reports.

The present volume is itself a new departure. Rather than produce a final volume, it was decided at the outset of the third follow-up that papers would be produced as quickly as possible, bearing in mind, of course, the priorities of the sponsors. Thus the delay between data collection and publication would be reduced. However, because these articles have appeared in a wide range of journals, it has been felt desirable to collect them together under two covers, to be, as it were, a source and reference book. Whether our initial decision was correct or not only time will tell.

Perhaps the third criterion is the most convincing, because it is the judgement of independent researchers in the World Health Organisation. The book *Prospective Longitudinal Research* (ed. S. A. Mednick and A. E. Baert), published by Oxford University Press in 1981, reviews sixty-five longitudinal studies carried out in Europe. From among these three projects are singled out, one of which is the National Child Development Study. The editors then conclude as follows:

The three studies reviewed above are first rate. They have enormous potentialities that are untapped. These projects, and others of similar calibre, deserve continued attention and support. The results of the British National Child Develop-ment Study illustrate the advantages which can be gained from a well conceived longitudinal study carried out on a large population base . . . Yet the diverse and important results presented so far by the National Children's Bureau represent only a fraction of the information which could be gleaned from the data already collected. Furthermore, the next follow-up wave of the survey could enrich the data base along a whole new dimension by providing information on the children of the original cohort. These possibilities make the National Child Development Survey an invaluable resource for medicine and social science, a resource which can produce new information at relatively low unit costs; its maintenance costs, therefore, should be looked at in light of the speed with which questions can be answered if studies are based on this population.

December 1982 M.K.P

Contents

Acknowledgements

The papers included in this collection were prepared by members of the National Child Development Study research team. I should like to thank them for both their contribution and their stimulating and enjoyable company. I am also grateful to all my colleagues at the National Children's Bureau, to the study's consultants and to representatives of the sponsors for their advice and support.

The work described in the following pages was funded by a grant from the Department of Education and Science and the Department of Health and Social Security. The preparation of this book and its publication at an advantageous price was made possible by a further generous grant from the DES.

This was supplemented by a kind donation from Mr and Mrs E. Gummer, in memory of their late son Giles, a member of the cohort of young people about whom the book is written.

I am grateful to the editors of all the journals in which these papers were originally published for their permission to include the edited versions in this book.

Above all, I wish to thank the young people in the study, their parents and the teachers, doctors, health visitors and many others in local authorities who gave so generously and freely of their time to make the study possible.

K. F.

Introduction

The year 1972 saw the publication of *From Birth to Seven*, a comprehensive report of the 7-year stage of the National Child Development Study. Since then, despite there having been two further stages of the study, at 11 and 16, it has not been possible for anyone interested in the study's results to find them between a single pair of covers. Although several more books have been published, these have been about specific sub-groups of children such as the gifted, the socially disadvantaged, and those living with a single parent. Other results from the study are to be found in papers in journals — over eighty such articles have been based on the data collected since the work described in *From Birth to Seven* was carried out.

This reflects a quite deliberate strategy. First, a book of the scope of *From Birth to Seven* inevitably takes a considerable time to prepare and to publish — particularly when those responsible for it are largely occupied by further stages of the same study — whereas individual papers can often make the results publicly available more quickly. Second, a study of this size entails the efforts of a large team of researchers, who can all have the satisfaction of seeing their own specific contributions acknowledged through their authorship of individual papers, rather than obscured in a single large volume.

However, it cannot be denied that a comprehensive report is more convenient to the reader and gives a better picture of the range and output of the study. Hence it has always been intended to produce such a publication as soon as it proved possible.

At the time of writing, preparations are in hand for the continuation of the National Child Development Study into adulthood. It therefore seems timely to bring together the work which has been completed, exploring growth and development during the school years. This book is based on the papers which incorporated data collected at the 11- and 16-year stages of the study (and which of course in many cases relate these to the information which was collected at birth and at age 7).

What follows is not a straightforward reproduction of the original articles. For example, each of the originals had to be readable in its own right and therefore contained a historical and methodological account of the study. As such an account is to be found in this introduction, there is no need to repeat it in each paper. Second, some of the original material, particularly that which first appeared as chapters in other books, is too long to include in full, so summaries only are given. Third, there are instances where a particular paper refers to or summarises earlier or complementary work published elsewhere. Since this latter work is itself sometimes included in this book then, again, such repetition has been avoided. Such considerations, together with other minor alterations, amount to a considerable quantity of editing. The editor hopes that the various authors will feel that justice has been done to the content and spirit of their original work.

This book is intended primarily for an academic audience. We hope that it contains enough technical detail for other researchers to be able to judge its competence, and it is, in places, heavily statistical. It is extremely unlikely that anyone will set out to read this book from cover to cover. Further, we hope it will serve as a reference work and a source for those who wish to know in detail what the study has found on a particular topic.

However, we appreciate that there is a large audience among professionals and the general public who are also interested in the findings of the study. For that reason we are preparing a more succinct account of all the major findings from the study from birth to the age of 16.

CONTENT

The sheer number of publications from the NCDS in the past few years makes it impossible to attempt to include them all here and so some choices have had to be made. It will be seen that the papers are grouped thematically, and at least some material from each paper relevant to that theme has been included. Within this structure, the editor must acknowledge that the final selection has had to be dependent on his judgement and taste, and should not be taken as having any implications for the perceived quality or importance of those papers which have been omitted.

Before turning to the papers themselves, the remainder of this introduction provides a historical account of the study; a detailed description of the study and its tracing and data-collection methods; a discussion of response rates and patterns; and a brief consideration of some other methodological issues.

At the end of the book will be found an overview which attempts, first, to pick up some general threads drawing on material in several papers and, second, to identify some of the practical implications of the findings.

THE NATIONAL CHILD DEVELOPMENT STUDY

Origins

In 1958 a study was mounted by Professor Neville Butler, for the National Birthday Trust Fund, of all births in England, Scotland and Wales in the week 3—9 March 1958. At that time the British perinatal mortality rate, i.e. the proportion of babies who were either stillborn or died within seven days of birth, was 35 per 1 000 births. The main purpose of the study was to examine social and obstetric factors associated with such deaths. To this end, the study successfully obtained information on some 98 per cent of the total births (about 17 000) registered as occurring during that week.

By investigating the factors related to mortality risk and the well-being of the new-born baby, this research demonstrated many facts which are now commonplace and was able to give numerical precision to often observed relationships. It showed, for example, that the risk of a perinatal death was 50 per cent higher than average if the mother was having her fifth or subsequent baby; and was 30 per cent higher in mothers who smoked heavily during pregnancy compared with non-smokers.

Twelve years previously, in 1946, a team led by J. W. B. Douglas had also studied children born in Britain during the same week, and subsequently has followed up about a third of the sample at regular intervals. The success of this study prompted interest in the possibility of following up the 1958 'cohort' of births.

Strong representations were made to the Plowden Committee and, in 1964, the Department of Education and Science agreed to commission the National Children's Bureau to collect information on all these children when they were aged 7. This follow-up study of all the surviving children became known as the National Child Development Study (NCDS), and the first major publication appeared both as an Appendix to the Plowden Committee report and as a book (*Eleven Thousand Seven-Year-Olds*). At the time the study was instituted the aims were summarised as follows:

Short-term

1. To study the educational, behavioural, emotional, social and physical development of a large and representative group of British children in order to gather normative data; to investigate the complex interrelationships between the many facets, both normal and deviant, of children's development; and to report the incidence of handicaps and the provision currently being made.
2. To utilise the uniquely comprehensive perinatal data, already available, in an evaluation of the relationships between conditions during pregnancy and at birth, both medical and social, and the development of children in all its aspects at the age of 7 years.

Long-term

1. To explore the constancy and change in the pattern of children's development longitudinally, and to investigate the associated educational, environmental and physical factors.
2. To follow the progress — over a long period — of those children who at birth might be considered 'at risk' in order to evaluate possible latent effects; and also to examine any postnatal factors, environmental, educational or medical, which may minimise a handicap.
3. To identify and follow the progress of children who at 7 years of age are already handicapped or showing signs of difficulty; those who because of adverse social or other circumstances might be considered 'at risk' of becoming educationally backward or socially deviant; and those who display talent or aptitude.
4. To evaluate the efficiency of medical and educational provision for handicapped, deviant and exceptional children.
5. To identify groups of children of special interest, including many of those identified under (3) and (4) above, so that intensive studies may be mounted by expert teams. This would permit much more detailed and comprehensive investigation of the factors involved against a backcloth of the necessarily cruder data gathered in the follow-up of the whole cohort.

The three follow-ups

There have, at the time of writing, been three full follow-ups of the entire cohort. As already mentioned, the first took place in 1965, when the children were aged 7. To a certain extent this date was dictated by circumstances in that it coincided with the interest of the Plowden Committee and thus with the availability of finance. However, it does also coincide with an important stage in the progress of British schoolchildren: the majority of the NCDS children would be in their final year of infants' schooling and about to transfer to a new department or new school.

The second follow-up was planned to coincide with the next major change in most British children's schooling, and took place in 1969 when the children were aged 11, and therefore, for the majority, in their final year of junior schooling. This stage of the study was funded by the Social Science Research Council.

The third follow-up, funded jointly by the DES and the DHSS, took place in 1974, when the children were aged 16 and thus in their final year of compulsory schooling. They were, in fact, part of the first year group to be required by new legislation to stay at school until 16.

At each follow-up, information was obtained from four main sources: the children themselves, their parents, local authority medical officers, and schools.

A detailed description of those variables used in the course of analyses will be found in the relevant papers, but the overall pattern was as follows:

1. At each age, the parents (in fact most commonly the mother alone) were interviewed in the home by a local authority health visitor, who completed a pre-coded form during the interview.
2. At each age, each child received a full medical examination from a local authority medical officer, who again completed a pre-coded form, additionally using some information available from medical records to help in compiling a medical history.
3. At each age, the schools [usually the headteacher and class teacher(s)] completed a questionnaire providing information on the school and on the study child.
4. At 11 and 16, the study child completed a questionnaire (a relatively brief one at the earlier age) and the following tests were administered:

At age 7: Southgate Reading Test — a test of word recognition and comprehension particularly suited to identifying backward readers; 'Copying Designs' Test — to obtain some assessment of the child's perceptuomotor ability; 'Drawing a Man' Test — as an indication of the child's general mental and perceptual ability; Problem Arithmetic Test.

At age 11: General Ability Test — containing verbal and non-verbal items; Reading Comprehension Test — constructed by the National Foundation for Educational Research in England and Wales (NFER) specifically for use in this study; Arithmetic/Mathematics Test — also provided by the NFER for use in this study.

At age 16: Reading Comprehension Test — same test as used at 11; Mathematics Test — a test devised at the University of Manchester and originally intended for use in the NFER's study of comprehensive schools.

To have provided a complete set of those instruments as an appendix to this volume would have increased its size (and cost) unacceptably. For those readers who wish to see them, copies are available from: The Supplementary Publications Scheme, British Library (Lending Division) Boston Spa, Yorkshire LS23 7BO, quoting reference no. SUP 81013.

Tracing and the collection of data

The basic methods of tracing the children have been the same for all three follow-ups. The first stage of the tracing took advantage of the fact that all the children in the study were born in one week. It was therefore possible to write to every school in the country which might contain children of the relevant age, with a request for them to list all children on their register born in the week. The great majority of children were traced in this way.

Naturally, a disproportionate effort was then required to trace the remaining few. Once the lists supplied by schools had been matched with the study's records, and those yet untraced identified, then various strategies were used to find the remainder: the local authority in which the child was last known to live was contacted, including health authorities and social service departments where these were known to have been responsible for the care of the child; last-known addresses were written to; appeals were mounted on radio and in local newspapers; in a few cases the NHS Executive Councils, though understandably unwilling to provide us directly with addresses, were able to pass on a letter which requested people to make contact with us; and when supplied with a list of the final few whom we had not been able to trace the Central Health Register was able to inform us of those who had emigrated or died.

Of course, such a brief summary gives little indication of the detailed work often necessary — the misspelt names, the uncertainties about dates of birth, the difficulties of identifying with certainty which of the children with identical names and birth dates is the correct one to match with earlier information when both have changed their addresses and schools frequently, and the inevitable reminder letters. This is just one of the stages at which a project of this kind is crucially dependent on the expertise and enthusiasm both of its own technical and clerical staff and of those in local authorities.

Throughout the study we have considered it

important that those taking part should do so willingly. Therefore, once the study members were traced, the next step, at each follow-up, has been to send a letter to the parents, via the school, in order to explain what we should be doing to enlist their cooperation — but to give them the opportunity to opt out totally or in part, if they so wished. Few took this opportunity at the 7- and 11-year stages, but rather more did so at 16, and this is discussed further below.

At the same time as tracing was taking place the various interview schedules and questionnaires were being designed and piloted. Once finalised and printed, these were then despatched to local health authorities, who organised their distribution to medical officers and health visitors who were to carry out the medical examinations and parental interviews, and to local education authorities, who distributed the school-based material.

There were two significant departures from this general method for the 16-year follow-up. First, there were the independent schools, with whom we corresponded directly. Second, there was the impact of local government reorganisation which came about during the period when local authorities were dealing

with our material. Many authorities were still able to take responsibility for distributing and returning the forms but in other cases this was taken over by the research team.

Response

It will be seen that there are several points in the above procedure at which it is possible to lose the opportunity of obtaining information. A child might not be traced, or having been traced, the parents might decide not to take part, or after that, through the child's absence or the parents' unwillingness, or even the occasional administrative slip-up, no or partial data may be obtained.

Table I.1 provides the relevant figures to describe response patterns throughout the study. It can be seen that the overall response rate, of those known to be alive and still in the country, has remained satisfactorily high throughout, though declining slightly from just over 91 per cent at 7 to just over 87 per cent at 16.

The explanation for this slight reduction seems to reside largely in the increasing number of refusals. As there was no obligation to offer any reasons for

TABLE I.1   *Basic distributions (percentages)*

	Age	Total	Some data	Refusal	No data*	Untraced*	Emigrant at sweep†	Deaths since and including previous sweep
(a)	Birth All children	100.0 (N = 17 733)	98.2		1.8		—	—
(b)	7 years All children (excluding	100.0 (N = 18 118)	85.0	0.5		7.7	2.3	4.5
	deaths and emigrants)	100.0 (N = 16 883)	91.3	0.5		8.3	—	—
(c)	11 years All children (excluding	100.0 (N = 18 365)	83.3	4.5		3.9	3.8	4.5
	deaths and emigrants)	100.0 (N = 16 835)	90.9	4.9		4.1	—	—
(d)	16 years All children (excluding	100.0 (N = 18 578)	79.5	6.2	2.3	3.1	4.3	4.7
	deaths and emigrants)	100.0 (N = 16 915)	87.3	6.7	2.5	3.4	—	—

* At the ages of 7 and 11 years, for technical reasons, the separate figures for 'no data' and 'untraced' are unavailable.
† Some of the emigrants at earlier ages return later and are included in the above figures. In all 1013 children had ever emigrated by the age of 16 (5.5 per cent of the 16-year-old total).

opting out, we cannot be certain why this happened, but two reasons were mentioned by significant numbers at 16. First, there were those parents who referred to the fact that their child would be preparing for public examinations in the period concerned and they did not wish anything to interfere with this. Second, we were unfortunate in that the 1971 Census had received some considerable adverse publicity not long before we were contacting parents. It was clear that for a small minority this was the cause of animosity to surveys in general.

Of course, the above account of response is not quite the whole story, as it refers to children who were traced and for whom some information was obtained. As has been described, there were several sources of information at each follow-up — schools, parents, medical officers and the children themselves — and it may also be possible for one or more of these to be incomplete. For example, at 16, the numbers for each instrument used were as follows:

Medical examination forms	11 686
Parental interview forms	11 642
Educational questionnaires	12 764
Individual questionnaires	12 101
Test booklets	12 015
Total with some information	14 761

Potential problems of response

Generally satisfactory as the response figures are, any element of non-response could introduce problems. There are three main possible effects which need to be considered:

(1) Numbers could become too small for valid generalisations to be made. Given the size of the NCDS this is not likely to be a general problem, but certainly needs to be borne in mind when small sub-groups of children are under consideration. However, this is really only a special case of the need for care in any study when carrying out complex analysis, to ensure that results are not presented when individual cell sizes are too small to justify them.

(2) One of the major characteristics of the NCDS is that it provides a group which is representative of people of about the same age. Clearly it is possible that non-response could lead to bias in ways which would make this no longer true. This is discussed further below.

(3) The most important kinds of findings to emerge from the study are concerned with relationships; for example, between aspects of social and family background and children's development, and about changes over time. Even if there were a problem about overall representativeness, it would not necessarily follow that such relationships were also biased. This is something which needs to be considered quite separately.

It is a rarely stressed advantage of longitudinal studies that they can use their earlier data to explore issues such as (2) and (3) above. For example, in the NCDS, it is possible to check whether those children for whom no information was obtained at 16 differed significantly from other children in terms of their characteristics at birth, 7 and 11. It is also possible to recalculate analyses examining relationships at, say, 11, or between 7 and 11, omitting children who were missed at 16, in order to assess what effect, if any, this has on results.

The first paper reproduced in this book originally appeared as an appendix to *Britain's Sixteen-Year-Olds* (Fogelman, 1976) and describes a very detailed set of such analyses, which were carried out following the 16-year follow-up.

In general, the results are reassuring. In terms of their parents' occupation and education, for example, the differences between those with and without data are small, and indices of physical development do not show any bias.

There were found to be small differences in test scores, those children without data at 16 having slightly lower average reading, mathematics and general-ability scores at 11. However, this does not appear to have any significant effect on analyses which compare average test scores for different groups.

Evidence was found of a moderate bias in relation to certain 'disadvantaged' groups which appear to be underrepresented by a factor of no more than 10 per cent. These include children receiving special education at 11, children who were illegitimate and children who had been in care by the age of 7.

Generally satisfactory as this pattern is, it does not dispose of the problem altogether since those analyses check for differences between those with some data and no data at all. The same pattern cannot necessarily be expected to appear in relation to responses to a particular questionnaire or question. Furthermore, in the course of some of the more complex, longitudinal analyses, drawing on data from more than one source over several ages, numbers with complete data can be reduced quite dramatically. There is therefore a need for continuous monitoring for the presence of any bias, particularly in the specific context of analyses where national representatives is important. This has been done and is referred to in many of the papers. In a few cases some evidence of small bias has appeared, but in none so far has this proved to be sufficient to invalidate the analysis.

The exploitation of longitudinal data

One unique contribution which longitudinal studies offer is in their ability to identify change, and its timing, in the characteristics of an individual or group. Nevertheless, it is often said that, whatever the potential of longitudinal studies, they do not in fact capitalise on this and carry out analyses which could have been done just as well with a single cross-sectional survey.

It is inevitable that a study such as the NCDS which obtains such a wide range of information in the course of a single follow-up will offer attractions to sponsors and others in the forms of data which are of immediate interest and do not require treating longitudinally.

There is no reason why such work should not be carried out, provided that it does not upset the overall balance and divert efforts from that work to which a longitudinal study is best suited. Furthermore, where cross-sectional analysis has been carried out this is often of relevance to issues of importance in early adulthood and thus likely to form the basis of longitudinal analyses when the NCDS continues to study the young people in the future.

Turning to the techniques which have been used in the remainder of the work, treating the data longitudinally and exploiting the unique characteristics of such studies, there are four basic models of analysis which can be identified as permeating our work. Each of them answers questions and tests hypotheses in a way which is open only to longitudinal studies.

The first approach is the most straightforward and obvious. In its general form it investigates the extent to which certain characteristics are stable, or to which children move in and out of certain categories across the stages of the study. Perhaps its clearest application is in some of the studies of physical health. In the investigation of children with asthma and wheezy bronchitis, for example, we examined the changing reports at 7, 11 and 16 and were thus able to identify the proportions of children experiencing this condition throughout most of their childhood, and the likelihood that a child with asthma or wheezy bronchitis at 7 would still be suffering from this at 16. Other examples of this approach, outside the field of physical health, include an examination of changes in children's levels of attainment.

A second method of analysis can be seen in the study of differences which develop between social groups in school attainment. Essentially, this method is equivalent to analysis of covariance, examining differences between groups of interest on a dependent variable (such as an attainment test score) after adjusting for values on an independent variable similar to the dependent variable (such as an earlier attainment test score). In this way it is possible to describe differences between groups not simply at a single point in time, but after allowing for pre-existing differences, thus identifying changes in differences (or 'progress'). This method was also appropriate for, say, the studies of school characteristics and of ability grouping in the secondary school.

The third approach arises where one wishes to identify whether differences in the characteristics of children in different groups existed before they became members of those groups. For example, it was possible to describe the behaviour ratings of children who were later to come into care and demonstrate the extent to which contrasts with those children never received into care (by 11) were already apparent, thus showing the extent to which the poor behaviour in school of children in care is not due to that experience as such, but to other aspects of their environment.

Fourth, there is the obvious case where one wishes to relate the early circumstances of a child to a later outcome. This can be extended to examine the contrasts in association with the same circumstances coming into effect at different ages, as has been done, for example, in the work on children in one-parent families.

The edited papers which follow include examples of all these various analytical approaches and, we hope, give an indication of the breadth of work which is possible with such a rich body of data as those now held by the National Child Development Study.

A note on the presentation of results

Many of the papers which follow contain the results of analysis of variance or covariance. It may be helpful to provide some brief explanatory note on their presentation, some aspects of which may not be familiar to all readers. A more detailed consideration of these and other statistical issues can be found in the Statistical Appendix (pp. 359—60).

(1) *Transformation.* In many of the analyses, a test score, most commonly reading or mathematics, has been used as the dependent variable. Where necessary these scores have been transformed in order to provide an approximate normal distribution and to satisfy the assumptions of the method. Scores are then usually presented on a scale which has a mean of zero and a standard deviation of one. For scores on tests given at 7 and 11, results are sometimes presented in terms of very approximate age equivalents. Although these can be seen as helping to make the results more readily comprehensible, they should be interpreted with caution. This approach was not felt to be appropriate for the tests at 16.

(2) Results are presented (sometimes graphically) in terms of fitted constants, which are calculated from unstandardised regression coefficients, or, less frequently, adjusted means. Although fitted constants and adjusted means are not equivalent in terms of their absolute values, differences can be considered as equivalent. A fuller account of the general method can be found in the statistical appendix to *From Birth to Seven* (Davie *et al.*, 1972).

(3) In samples of the size involved in NCDS analyses, the χ^2-test is equivalent to an F-test, and is preferred because of its simplicity.

I

A Study of the Response Rates of 16-Year-Olds in the National Child Development Study*

Introduction

It is well known that the subjects of a survey who fail to provide any information are usually atypical (Moser and Kalton, 1971). The characteristics which distinguish them from the rest, however, vary with the reason for the failure to provide information, and four causes for such failure can be distinguished.

First, there are those who refuse to co-operate. A letter was sent to the NCDS child's parents or guardians which explained the nature of the study, reminded them of its earlier stages and invited their co-operation in the 16-year-old follow-up. A decision to refuse may often have been taken in response to the wishes of the child. Second, there are those children born during the survey week who could not be traced. Third, there are children who were traced, whose parents or guardians did not refuse at the time of initial contact, but from whom no data could be obtained subsequently. Fourth, there are those children who died or emigrated and so were excluded from the study's terms of reference.

Biases due to non-response

Although mainly concerned with biases in the 16-year-old data, we shall also devote some space to biases at earlier ages. There are two reasons for this. First, although response rates were studied to some extent for earlier ages (see, for example, Davie *et al.*, 1972), this was not as comprehensive as the enquiry which is reported here for the 16-year-olds. It was felt at the time that the overall response was sufficiently high (91 per cent at 7 and 11 years and 98 per cent at birth) to have confidence in the analyses based on the data available. To place the results of the analysis of the 16-year-olds in better perspective, however, it is useful to study comparable data for the earlier ages. Second, the major part of the present analysis of the 16-year-old data uses the

data available at 11 years and to a lesser extent at 7 years to compare with the 16-year response categories. If the available data at these ages are biased, then we may be underestimating some of the 16-year-old biases.

Response rates

Table 1.1 on p. 4 gave the basic response rates at birth, 7, 11 and 16 years. The appropriate figures on which subsequent analyses are based are those which exclude deaths and emigrants. We see that the 16-year response rate of 87.3 per cent results from a somewhat higher percentage of refusals and no data or untraced than at 11. Between 7 and 11 years, however, although the overall responses are very similar, the non-response at 7 was almost entirely due to those untraced or with no data, whereas over half the non-response at 11 was due to refusals. To a certain extent the differential response at the different ages reflects the somewhat different strategies used to collect the data — as outlined in the preceding section. It may be, for example, that the increasing percentage of parents who refused to co-operate is partly related to exposure to the study itself and partly also to the reluctance of parents of some 16-year-olds for their children to take part in the medical examination. A reason given by some of the parents was their fear that the time taken to provide information for the study might interfere with their children's public examination prospects. Also, adverse publicity concerned with confidentiality in the 1971 Census may have contributed to parental unwillingness to take part.

16-year-old responses in terms of birth, 7- and 11-year variables

Since the best response rate is at birth, it is natural to compare the response categories at 7, 11 and 16 years in terms of birth factors. This has been done for birth weight, which has one of the strongest

*By Harvey Goldstein.

associations with subsequent development of any of the measurements made at birth (Goldstein and Peckham, 1976). There are no statistically significant differences in mean birth weight between the response categories at either 7, 11 or 16 years.

A study of the differences between 16-year-old response categories in terms of measurements at previous ages will indicate the variables at 16 which are likely to suffer from bias. This may enable us in subsequent analyses to make appropriate corrections to estimates, or at least to suggest caution in interpretation. The absence of a difference at earlier ages, however, does not necessarily imply a similar absence at 16 years. For example, the mean value of a measurement at 11 years for those who refuse at 16 years may have the same value as for those with data, but there may have been a greater change in the mean value between 11 and 16 for the refusals, and this is something we cannot know. All we can do in this case is to study the average rate of change in the same or a similar measurement between 7 and 11 years, supposing that different rates of change between those ages are likely to be reflected also between 11 and 16 years. Finally, we can study the effect on analyses at 7 and 11 years of including and excluding the non-responders at 16, and in this way obtain an estimate of the likely effect of non-response on a typical set of analyses using the 16-year data.

The Appendix tables (pp. 13—18) present comparisons between the four categories at 16 years: some data, refusals, no data and untraced. In order to estimate bias we are interested in the comparison between those with some data and the remainder, and it is these comparisons which are commented on mainly.

Categorised variables at 7 and 11 years

From the variables measured at 7 and 11 years a number were chosen to represent typical educational, social, demographic and medical characteristics of the children and their families. These included the classification of children into particular categories which have been used to define participants in special related studies, such as that on adopted children (Seglow *et al.*, 1972). Section A of the statistical analyses (p. 12) lists those variables for which no significant differences between the four response categories emerged, and those where significant differences were found between the four response categories but where no overall significant differences between those with data and the remainder were found. Full details are given for those analyses where overall significant differences were found. We summarise here the main pattern of findings.

The children identified as belonging to certain

'disadvantaged' groups at 7 and 11 years are less likely to provide information at 16 years. These comprise illegitimate children, those receiving special education and those who exhibit 'anti-social' behaviour in schools, between 3 and 6 per cent of children falling into each of these categories. The proportion of those children among the no-data or untraced group is up to about twice that amount those with data and, with the exception of the illegitimate children, the refusals tend to have a slightly lower proportion.

We have summarised the overall bias in percentage terms. Thus, for example, among those with data at 16 years, 3.90 per cent were receiving or waiting for special educational provision or had a decision pending. This compares with an overall estimate of 3.24 per cent, a percentage bias of −4.6 per cent. The figures given for percentage bias, however, do depend on the particular categorisations adopted. For example, if we study only the percentage of children from 1—2 child households, this bias is −1.9 per cent compared with 0.5 per cent for children from 5+ child households. This implies some caution in the interpretation of results but may also suggest ways in which variables should be categorised in subsequent analyses of the 16-year-olds data.

Of the remaining variables analysed, relatively large overall biases (more than 1.0 per cent), which were also statistically significant, were found for country of residence, number of children in the household, and type of household accommodation. For other variables, there were significant differences but smaller biases (between 0.5 per cent and 1.0 per cent). These were whether the child goes to clubs out of school, whether he or she had ever been admitted to hospital overnight, and the degree of crowding in the home. The direction of the bias is such that the proportion of children in categories typically associated with slower development, lower school attainments, etc., tends to be underestimated when only those with some data at 16 years are considered. There are, however, some exceptions to this. One is place of residence, where, for example, there are relatively more children with some data from Scotland and Wales compared with England. Another is the number of children in the household, where the small families are underrepresented among those with data. Likewise, those ever admitted to hospital are overrepresented among those with data.

Some general patterns emerge from a study of Section A (p. 12). One is that the indices of physical development tend to be unrelated to the response categories at 16 years. Parents' education, occupation, attitudes and aspirations for the child also tend to be unrelated to the response categories. Children's leisure activities are related to response but do not lead to much overall bias. The physical circumstances of the home tend to give rise to larger biases, and the largest biases of all are found among certain categories of 'disadvantaged' children.

Where the biases are relatively large a certain amount of caution needs to be used in interpreting findings based on similar variables measured at 16 years. The values of the percentage biases at 7 and 11 years will probably be underestimates of the true 16-year bias since some movement between categories will have taken place in the intervening five years. The greatest bias found has an absolute magnitude no greater than 6 per cent and most are much less.

Another complication concerns the composition of the 11-year-old sample who have some data. As pointed out earlier, comparisons between 16-year response categories exclude those for whom data were unavailable at 11 years. If substantial biases exist at 11 years, then there may be a cumulative effect which the above analysis has failed to detect. In view of the similar overall response rates at 7 and 11 years and the increased uncertainty associated with making comparisons with 7-year information, we have not attempted systematically to study the same 7-year variables as we have the above 11-year variables. Tentative as the present results are, however, they do present a fairly encouraging picture for most variables, and it would seem reasonable to regard a 16-year-old relative bias of 10 per cent as an upper limit. A further problem arises when we wish to study the biases for sub-groups of the data, for example within social classes. If the biases are sufficiently different, then comparisons between subgroups may become distorted. We discuss this problem in the next section.

Continuous variables at 7 and 11 years

We have carried out two types of analysis relating response at 16 years to test scores, social adjustment and height. One type of analysis studies the average difference between 16-year response categories before and after adjusting for other factors, and the detailed results are presented in Section B of the statistical analyses (pp. 16—17). The other studies of the effect on analyses of variance carried out using 7- and 11-year data, of excluding those without 16-year data, and the detailed results are given in Section C of the statistical analyses (p. 18).

Differences between 16-year response categories

In terms of 11-year measurements of reading, mathematics, height and social adjustment, the differences in mean values between response categories are relatively small. For the mental test scores it is about 0.1 years, which is small when compared with the social-class difference (about 1.5 years) and that between children from 1 or 2 compared with 4 or more child households (0.8 to 1.4 years). The difference for the social adjustment score is relatively somewhat greater, though still only about one-fifth of the corresponding differences for social class and number of children in the household. The height difference is very small indeed (0.2cm) and not statistically significant. For the corresponding variables at 7 years, only the differences for reading and social adjustment are appreciable, being about one-quarter of the social class and number of children differences. It is also of interest to note that the refusals tend to have rather higher attainments, to be better adjusted and taller than the other nonresponders, and also to a lesser extent do better than those with data at 16 years. Section A indicates that the refusals tend to come from smaller families with better living conditions who are more affluent and generally more 'privileged'. It is therefore not surprising that these children have higher average attainments, etc. A similar finding is described in a study by Labouvie *et al.* (1974).

For reading and mathematics attainment, differences in 16-year response categories in terms of 11-year attainment have been analysed, after allowing for 7-year attainment. For mathematics, but not for reading, there are differences between the response categories after allowing for 7-year scores. For a given 7-year mathematics score there is an average of 0.2 years difference in 11-year mathematics between those with data at 16 and those without. This suggests a slightly higher rate of change of mathematics attainment between 7 and 11 years for the former group, which amounts to about 0.05 years of mathematics attainment per year of age. If this is extrapolated to 16 years of age, we might expect an overall difference between those with and without data of about 0.3 to 0.4 years. This would imply an overall bias of about 0.05 years of mathematics attainment at 16 years.

It is of some interest to note that for the mental test scores at 11 years (and to a smaller extent for social adjustment), the bias increases after adjusting for the number of children in the household and social class. This is largely due to a relatively lower score for the refusals, and to a relatively higher score for those with no data and results from the adjustment for number of children rather than from the adjustment for social class. This can be seen from the table in Section A (p. 14) which shows that there is a much higher refusal rate from 1- and 2-child households. Also, children from these households tend to have higher than average scores and we would expect an adjustment for this factor to reduce the difference between those with data and the refusals. In all there are three times as many refusals as there are children with no data and the net effect on the total non-responders is to lower their mean value further below that for those with some data. Thus, because of the particular numbers in the different response categories and the associated mean values, an overall narrowing of differences leads to increased overall bias. It seems, therefore, that simply to adjust analyses for those variables which show some bias will not necessarily lead to a reduction in overall bias. However, the biases we have demonstrated are small, and in the following section we study the direct effect of excluding non-responders upon some analyses of variance.

The effects of excluding the non-responders at 16 years from analyses of 11-year test scores

Section C shows the effect of excluding 16-year-olds without information on certain analyses of variance (p. 18). For both reading and mathematics attainment the main effect is to increase the differences between the constants fitted to the social classes. The differences between the non-manual children and those from social class V, after adjusting for 7-year score, are increased by 3 and 2 per cent respectively. This is relatively small and certainly much smaller than the effect of adjusting for the unreliability of 7-year test scores (Fogelman and Goldstein, 1976). (See pp. 27–36.) The effect of excluding children without 16-year information on the difference between children from 1- and 2-child households and those from 5- or more child households, is to increase it by 1 per cent in the case of reading and to leave it unchanged in the case of mathematics. As with social class, the effect seems to be acceptably small.

Conclusions

The longitudinal nature of the National Child Development Study permits detailed comparisons of the children who do and do not respond at each age, in terms of data at previous ages. At 16 years the comparisons are largely in terms of the data collected at 11 years of age, and to a smaller extent at 7 years. This procedure depends upon assumptions about the unbiasedness of the data at these previous ages, and presents a problem which cannot be entirely resolved within the present study.

Taking these reservations into account, it seems that we may draw the following conclusions. Children who have previously belonged to 'disadvantaged' groups are less likely to provide any information at

16 years, and for estimates of the proportions of children with particular characteristics an upper limit for the relative bias at 16 years is about 10 per cent. Hence, where such estimates are made, this figure can be used to provide upper or lower corrected estimates. For mental test scores at 11 years, the differences between the extreme categories of variables such as social-class and family-size ratings have small biases of up to about 3 per cent. The differences between those with and without 16-year-old data are also small for both mental and behavioural test scores at 11 years, and the resulting overall biases are very small indeed. In the case of height any differences appear to be negligible. There is evidence in the case of mathematics attainment of a higher rate of change in attainment between 7 and 11 years for those with data at 16 compared with those without. A simple extrapolation of this difference to 16 years gives an overall bias in mathematics attainment of about 0.05 years, which would seem to be acceptably small.

Statistical analyses

In the following tables, significance levels are indicated thus:

* * *	$p < 0.001$
* *0.001	$< p < 0.01$
*0.01	$< p < 0.05$
Otherwise 0.05	$< p$

Multiple comparisons (Gabriel, 1966) between the four response categories have been carried out with a view to detecting dissimilar categories consistent with an overall significance level of 5 per cent. The detailed results of these are not reported here but are commented upon in the text.

Tests for a linear trend in the proportions of the dichotomy in a $2 \times k$ contingency table across the ordered levels of the other factor have also been carried out (Bhapkar, 1968).

The tables in Section A are for those factors which might have shown a difference in the proportions in each category of response status at 16 years, which is significant at the 5 per cent level. Emigrants and deaths are excluded.

Section A

I. The following 11-year variables, categorised into dichotomies indicated, were studied but differences were not significant at the 5 per cent level:

1. Whether mother stayed at school beyond the minimum leaving age.
2. Social class (Non-Manual, Manual).
3. Social class (III Manual and IV, V).

4. Multiple births (singleton, multiple).
5. Child often or sometimes bored (parental opinion).
6. Time off school (one week in past year).
7. Doctor's assessment of vision (any defect).
8. Doctor's assessment of hearing (any abnormal loss).
9. Boy's pubic hair (stage 1).
10. Girl's pubic hair (stage 1).
11. Abnormalities at medical examination (any abnormalities).
12. Any abnormalities of ear, nose, throat, palate, at medical examination.
13. Ever had asthma.
14. Whether father stayed at school after minimum leaving age.
15. Whether parents wanted child to leave school as soon as possible.
16. Whether mother very satisfied with play amenities 10—15 minutes from home.

II. For the following 11-year and 7-year variables, categorised as indicated, significant differences (at the level indicated) were found between the four response categories, but no significant differences were found between those with data at 16 years and the remainder:

1. Sex**.
2. Whether or not in care by 7 years*.
3. Whether or not had severe reading difficulty at 7 years***.
4. Whether or not child borrows books from a library at 11 years***.
5. Whether or not child had a congenital condition at 11 years*.
6. Whether or not there was family financial trouble at 11 years***.
7. Whether or not the child had free school meals at 11 years***.
8. Tenure at 11 years (owned, rented, tied to occupation)***.
9. Position of front door at 11 years (At or below street level, above street level)***.
10. Number of home moves between birth and 11 years (0—1, 2—4, 5+)***.
11. Whether or not mother satisfied with home, at 11 years*.

III. *Response categories at 16 years (percentages in brackets)*

Percentage biases are calculated as the percentage increase in the first row of the table (except where stated) for the 'some data' compared with the 'total'.

Factor		Some data		Refusal		No data		Untraced		Total	
(i) *Special education*	Pending, waiting, or receiving	354	(3.1)	19	(3.0)	16	(6.7)	19	(7.4)	408	(3.2)
	None	11 119	(96.9)	614	(97.0)	223	(93.3)	239	(92.6)	12 195	(96.8)
	Total	11 473	(100.0)	633	(100.0)	239	(100.0)	258	(100.0)	12 603	(100.0)

χ^2 (3 df) = 18.4***   Some data *vs* Remainder χ^2 (1 df) = 8.9**
Percentage bias = —4.6

Factor		Some data		Refusal		No data		Untraced		Total	
(ii) *Illegitimate with data at 7 years*	Yes	419	(3.2)	53	(5.3)	10	(3.0)	19	(5.9)	501	(3.4)
	No	12 859	(96.8)	951	(94.7)	324	(97.0)	302	(94.1)	14 436	(96.7)
	Total	13 278	(100.0)	1 004	(100.0)	1 004	(100.0)	334	(100.0)	14 937	(100.0)

χ^2 (3 df) = 16.9***   Some data *vs* Remainder χ^2 (1 df) = 14.0***
Percentage bias = —5.7

Table III *continued*

Factor		Some data		Refusal		No data		Untraced		Total	
(iii) *Region at 11 years*	North-West	1 700	(12.5)	88	(10.7)	51	(15.0)	63	(18.4)	1 902	(12.6)
	North	981	(7.2)	46	(5.6)	13	(3.8)	16	(4.7)	1 056	(7.0)
	East and West Riding	1 164	(8.5)	69	(8.4)	39	(11.8)	14	(4.1)	1 286	(8.5)
	North-Midlands	1 034	(7.6)	84	(10.2)	18	(5.3)	27	(7.9)	1 163	(7.7)
	East	1 138	(8.4)	100	(12.1)	22	(6.5)	26	(7.6)	1 286	(8.5)
	London and South-East	2 404	(17.7)	169	(20.5)	94	(27.7)	75	(21.9)	2 742	(18.1)
	South	855	(6.3)	43	(5.2)	10	(2.9)	33	(9.6)	941	(6.2)
	South West	868	(6.4)	48	(5.8)	11	(3.2)	28	(8.2)	955	(6.3)
	Midlands	1 273	(9.3)	88	(10.7)	38	(11.2)	24	(7.0)	1 423	(9.4)
	Wales	750	(5.5)	30	(3.6)	23	(6.8)	10	(2.9)	813	(5.4)
	Scotland	1 457	(10.7)	60	(7.3)	20	(5.9)	26	(7.6)	1 563	(10.3)
	Total	13 624	(100.0)	825	(100.0)	339	(100.0)	342	(100.0)	15 130	(100.0)

χ^2 (30 df) = 138.2***   Some data *vs* Remainder χ^2 (10 df) = 79.4***
Percentage bias; England = −0.6; Scotland = 3.4; Wales = 2.4

Factor		Some data		Refusal		No data		Untraced		Total	
(iv) *No. of children in household at 11 years*	1–2	5 117	(41.5)	410	(58.6)	117	(41.5)	99	(36.4)	5 743	(42.2)
	3–4	5 135	(41.6)	221	(31.6)	92	(32.6)	114	(41.9)	5 562	(40.9)
	5+	2 089	(16.9)	69	(9.8)	73	(25.9)	59	(21.7)	2 290	(16.8)
	Total	12 341	(100.0)	700	(100.0)	282	(100.0)	272	(100.0)	13 595	(100.0)

χ^2 (6 df) = 107.2***   Some data *vs* Remainder (linear trend over number of children categories) χ^2 (1 df) = 17.1***
Percentage bias: 1–2 child households = −1.9; 5+ child households = 0.5

Factor		Some data		Refusal		No data		Untraced		Total	
(v) *Goes to clubs out of school at 11 years*	Often or sometimes	5 875	(49.0)	304	(42.2)	136	(48.8)	135	(50.0)	6 450	(48.7)
	Hardly ever or never	6 114	(51.0)	416	(57.8)	143	(51.2)	135	(50.0)	6 808	(51.3)
	Total	11 989	(100.0)	720	(100.0)	279	(100.0)	270	(100.0)	13 258	(100.0)

χ^2 (3 df) = 12.8**   Some data *vs* Remainder χ^2 (1 df) = 6.1*
Percentage bias = 0.7

Factor		Some data		Refusal		No data		Untraced		Total	
(vi) *Ever admitted overnight to hospital up to 11 years*	Yes	5 602	(45.5)	277	(39.6)	125	(44.6)	123	(45.9)	6 127	(45.2)
	No	6 713	(54.5)	422	(60.4)	155	(55.4)	145	(54.1)	7 435	(54.8)
	Total	12 315	(100.0)	699	(100.0)	280	(100.0)	268	(100.0)	13 562	(100.0)

χ^2 (3 df) = 9.3*   Some data *vs* Remainder χ^2 (1 df) = 5.1*
Percentage bias = 0.7

Factor		Some data		Refusal		No data		Untraced		Total	
(vii) *Type of household accommodation at 11 years*	Whole house	11 135	(90.1)	644	(91.7)	237	(84.0)	216	(79.7)	12 232	(89.8)
	Other	1 231	(9.9)	58	(8.3)	45	(16.0)	55	(20.3)	1 389	(10.2)
	Total	12 366	(100.0)	702	(100.0)	282	(100.0)	271	(100.0)	13 621	(100.0)

χ^2 (3 df) = 36.9***   Some data *vs* Remainder χ^2 (1 df) = 8.4**
Percentage bias (other accommodation) = −2.5

Table III *continued*

Factor		Some data		Refusal		No data		Untraced		Total	
(viii) *Crowding at 11 years*	Persons per room										
	≤1.0	7 436	(60.2)	503	(71.8)	159	(56.2)	155	(57.0)	8 253	(60.6)
	− 1.5	3 423	(27.7)	149	(21.2)	73	(25.8)	65	(23.9)	3 710	(27.3)
	>1.5	1 492	(12.1)	49	(7.0)	51	(18.0)	52	(19.1)	1 644	(12.1)
	Total	12 351	(100.0)	701	(100.0)	283	(100.0)	272	(100.0)	13 607	(100.0)

χ^2 (6 df) = 62.2***   Some data *vs* Remainder (linear trend over crowding categories) χ^2 (1 df) = 5.9*
Percentage: ≤1.0 persons per room = −0.7; >1.5 persons per room = 0.0

Factor		Some data		Refusal		No data		Untraced		Total	
(ix) *Anti-social behaviour at school at 11 years*	Delinquent, rebellious or easily led	728	(5.8)	46	(6.1)	30	(9.7)	42	(14.1)	846	(6.1)
	None of the above	11 806	(84.2)	712	(93.9)	278	(90.3)	256	(85.9)	13 052	(93.9)
	Total	12 534	(100.0)	758	(100.0)	308	(100.0)	298	(100.0)	13 898	(100.0)

χ^2 (3 df) = 42.3***   Some data *vs* Remainder χ^2 (1 df) = 16.9***
Percentage bias = −5.4

SECTION B　*Analyses of variance: fitted constants for main effects models*

χ^2 values are adjusted for the other factors. Fitted constants in brackets are unadjusted for the other factors. (Social class and number of children in the household are measured at the same ages as the dependent variable.)

Dependent variable		*11-year reading score in years*				*11-year mathematics score in years*			
Mean score		11.0				11.0			
Sample size		11 781				11 778			
Total variance		8.17				5.29			
Independent variables		Fitted constant	se	df	χ^2	Fitted constant	se	df	χ^2
Overall		11.1　(10.7)				11.0　(10.8)			
Some data		0.3　(0.3)				0.3　(0.3)			
Refusal		0.5　(0.7)		3	40.3*** (45.0***)	0.4　(0.5)		3	43.7 *** (44.4***)
No data		−0.2　(−0.4)				−0.2　(−0.3)			
Untraced		−0.6　(−0.6)				−0.5　(−0.5)			
Number of	1	0.6				0.1			
children in	2	0.4				0.4			
household	3	−0.1		3	596.1***	0.0		3	330.9***
	4+	−0.9				−0.5			
Social class	1.7		0.05	1	1 119.0***	1.4	0.04	1	1 139.0***
Non-Manual − Manual									
Response contrast　Some data − Remainder		0.12　(0.04)	0.05	1	5.6* (0.4)	0.09　(0.04)	0.04	1	5.3* (1.0)
Residual mean square		6.97				4.62			
Interactions (adjusted separately for main effects only)									
Response x no. of children				9	11.6			9	11.4
Response x social class				3	10.5*			3	6.4
No. of children x social class				3	21.9***			3	26.9***

Dependent variable		*11-year height in centimetres*				*Transformed social adjustment score at 11 years: $(x + 3/8) 1/2$*			
Mean score		144.4				2.55			
Sample size		11 672				11 783			
Total variance		53.4				2.07			
Independent variables		Fitted constant	se	df	χ^2	Fitted constant	se	df	χ^2
Overall		144.7　(144.3)				2.66　(2.73)			
Some data		0.1　(0.1)				−0.20 (−0.19)			
Refusal		0.3　(0.7)		3	4.6*** (9.3)*	−0.22 (−0.27)		3	36.8*** (39.4)***
No data		−0.8　(−1.1)				0.18　(0.22)			
Untraced		0.4　(0.3)				0.24　(0.24)			
Number of	1	1.1				−0.06			
children in	2	0.9				−0.14			
household	3	−0.2		3	321.0***	−0.08		3	194.6***
	4+	−1.8				0.28			
Social class	Non-Manual −	1.7	0.14	1	144.7***	−0.40	0.03	1	214.0***
	Manual								
Response contrast　Some data − Remainder		−0.1　(−0.2)	0.1	1	0.2 (1.9)	−0.08 (−0.06)	0.03	1	9.0** (4.8)*
Residual mean square		51.1				1.99			
Interactions (adjusted separately for main effects only)									
Response x no. of children				9	8.3			9	10.1
Response x social class				3	7.1			3	2.5
No. of children x social class				3	4.1			3	7.5

Dependent variable		*11-year reading score in years*				*11-year mathematics score in years*			
Mean score		11.0				11.0			
Sample size		9 777				9 741			
Total variance		7.94				5.22			
Independent variable		Fitted constant	se	df	χ^2	Fitted constant	se	df	χ^2
Overall		11.8				12.9			
Some data		0.1				0.2			
Refusal		0.1				0.3			
No data		−0.1		3	3.0	−0.3		3	19.2***
Untraced		−0.1				−0.2			
7-year score in years (measured about 7.0 years)		0.86	0.01	1	6 524.0**	0.68	0.01	1	4 509.0***
Response contrast:　Some data − Remainder		0.1	0.06	1	2.2	0.2	0.06	1	13.6***
Residual mean square		4.75				3.56			
Interactions (adjusted separately for main effects only)									
Response x 7-year score				3	4.5			3	2.9

(SECTION B — CONTINUED)

Dependent variable

	7-year reading score (transformed sin⁻¹ √x/30 in years)	7-year arithmetic score (transformed sin⁻¹ √x/10 in years)

	7-year reading score	7-year arithmetic score
Mean score	7.0	7.0
Sample size	9 761	9 730
Total variance	3.52	2.06

Independent variable		Fitted constant	se	df	χ^2	Fitted constant	se	df	χ^2
Overall		7.0				7.1			
	Some data	0.2	(0.2)			0.0	(0.0)		
	Refusal	0.4	(0.4)	3	27.5*** (31.6)***	0.1	(0.1)		
	No data	−0.2	(−0.2)			0.0	(0.0)	3	3.8 (4.9)
	Untraced	−0.4	(−0.4)			−0.1	(−0.1)		
Number of	1	0.3				0.0			
children in	2	0.2				0.1			
household	3	0.0		3	289.0***	0.0		3	37.7***
	4+	−0.5				−0.1			
Social class	Non-Manual — Manual	0.8	0.04	1	442.3***	0.5	0.03	1	291.2***
Response contrast	Some data — Remainder	0.2 (0.2)	0.05	1	20.4*** (19.9)***	0.0 (0.0)	0.01	1	1.5 (1.5)
Residual mean square				3.23				1.99	

Interactions (adjusted separately for main effects only)	df	χ^2	df	χ^2
Response x no. of children	9	11.4	9	21.4*
Response x social class	3	2.7	3	7.1
No. of children x social class	3	12.0**	3	1.4

Dependent variable

	7-year height in centimetres	7-year social adjustment score (x + 3/8) 1/2
Mean score	122.4 cm	2.60
Sample size	9 368	9 735
Total variance	35.31 cm²	1.95

Independent variables		Fitted constant	se	df	χ^2	Fitted constant	se	df	χ^2
Overall response		123.0				−2.63			
	Some data	−0.2	(−0.2)			−0.10	(−0.09)		
	Refusal	0.5	(0.8)			−0.18	(−0.19)		
	No data	−0.3	(−0.6)	3	7.2 (12.4)**	−0.04	(0.01)	3	12.6** (14.1)**
	Untraced	0.0	(0.0)			0.32	(0.27)		
Number of	1	1.2				−0.05			
children in	2	0.6				−0.11			
household	3	−0.2		3	257.7***	−0.03		3	80.9***
	4+	−1.6				0.19			
Social class	Non-Manual — Manual	−1.3	0.13	1	93.5***	−0.34	0.03	1	125.3***
Response contrast	Some data — Remainder	0.0 (0.0)	0.18	1	0.0 (0.0)	−0.11 (−0.11)	0.04	1	7.8** (7.9)**
Residual mean square				33.85				1.90	

Interactions (adjusted separately for main effects only)	df	χ^2	df	χ^2
Response x no. of children	9	5.4	9	11.1
Response x social class	3	3.3	3	3.7
No. of children x social class	3	14.7**	3	10.5*

SECTION C   *Analyses of variance: fitted constants for main effects models*

χ² values are adjusted for the other factors. Fitted constants in brackets are for the analyses confined to the children who only have have 16-year data.

Dependent variable		11-year reading score in years				11-year reading score in years			
Mean score		11.0	(11.0)			11.0	(11.0)		
Sample size		9 824	(8 909)			9 911	(8989)		
Total variance		7.91	(7.99)			7.91	(7.99)		
Independent variables		Fitted constant		se	df	χ²	Fitted constant	se	df	χ²
Overall		11.7	(11.7)				10.7	(10.7)		
7-year score in years (measured about 7.0 years)		−0.79	(0.79)	0.01 (0.01)	1	5 517.0*** (4 932.0)***				
Social class at 7 years	Non-Manual	0.83	(0.85)							
	Manual + IV	−0.19	(−0.20)		2	500.0*** (480.0)***				
	V	−0.64	(−0.65)							
Number of children in household at 7 years	1−2						0.98	(0.99)		
	3−4						0.17	(0.17)	2	706.8*** (638.1)***
	5+						−1.15	(−1.16)		
Residual mean square		4.51	(4.56)				7.39	(7.46)		

Dependent variable		11-year mathematics score in years				11-year mathematics score in years			
Mean score		11.0	(11.0)			11.0	(11.0)		
Sample size		9 907	(8 985)			9 788	(8 873)		
Total variance		5.21	(5.18)			5.21	(5.19)		
Independent variables		Fitted constant	df	χ²		Fitted constant	se	df	χ²
Overall		10.7	(10.7)			12.74	(12.73)		
7-year score in years (measured about 7.0 years)						0.62	(0.62)	0.01 (0.01)	1	3 981.0*** (3 560.0)***
Social class at 7 years	Non-Manual					0.94	(0.95)			
	III manual + IV					−0.16	(−0.17)		2	860.6*** (805.8)***
	V					−0.78	(−0.78)			
Number of children in household at 7 years	1−2	0.62	(0.62)						
	3−4	0.15	(0.15)	2	440.1*** (400.6)***				
	5+	−0.77	(−0.77)						

II

Social Background and Development

1 Social Class and Family Size*

DEVELOPMENTAL CORRELATES OF FAMILY SIZE

Introduction

Virtually all research studies that have investigated the relationship between family size and children's development have pointed to an adverse association between being in a large family and educational attainment, social adjustment and health. This paper will briefly examine these findings, and their possible explanations, and will then describe the research on family size that has been carried out as part of the National Child Development Study.

Findings from other studies

The disadvantages of coming from a large family appear to start at birth, and continue throughout childhood. The chance of a child being born alive and surviving the first week of life is greater for earlier-born children than for those children who are fourth or later born and who, by definition, enter a larger family (Butler and Alberman, 1969; Russell et al., 1963). For school-age children there is considerable evidence of an association between small family size and above-average ability and educational attainment (Douglas, 1964; Nisbet and Entwistle, 1967; Davie et al., 1972). The chances of staying on at school beyond the age of 15 are much less for the child from a large family (Robbins Report, 1963). In addition, a number of studies have demonstrated the relationship between family size and children's physical growth (Grant, 1964; Douglas and Simpson, 1964; Davie et al., 1972) and between family size and psychological and social adjustment (Tuckman and

* Original sources: Fogelman, K.R., 'Developmental correlates of family size', *British Journal of Social Work*, 5, 1, 1975; Fogelman, K. R. and Goldstein, H., 'Social factors associated with changes in educational attainment between 7 and 11 years of age', *Educational Studies*, 2, 2, 1976; Fogelman, K., Goldstein, H., Essen, J. and Ghodsian, M., 'Patterns of attainment', *Educational Studies*, 4, 2, 1978; Richardson, K., 'Reading attainment and family size: an anomaly', *British Journal of Educational Psychology*, 47, 1977; Tibbenham, A., Gorbach, P., Peckham, C. and Richardson, K., 'The influence of family size on height', previously unpublished.

Regan, 1967; Davie et al., 1972). For a review of these and other research studies see Prosser (1973).

Various hypotheses have been put forward to explain the apparent disadvantages suffered by children from large families. For example, a number of researchers have advanced what might be called the 'shared resources' hypothesis. Other things being equal, the large family has to spread its available resources more thinly than the small family. Perhaps the most obvious resource which has to be shared is the family income. One result of this is that children from large families are likely to have less nutritious diets than those from small families (Lambert, 1964).

In terms of ability and attainment as well as social adjustment, the most important resource in this context may well be 'adult time per child'. Nisbet's (1953) finding that children from large families were more adversely affected in tests of verbal than of non-verbal ability led him to suggest that their relative lack of verbal interaction with their parents could be an important factor. Davie et al. also advanced this explanation and went on to suggest that there was a parallel to be drawn in social adjustment: 'It can be argued that since social adjustment in school is in one sense a measure of conformity to school (i.e. adult) standards of behaviour, those children who have to share their parents' time with more brothers and sisters have less opportunity to learn and to adapt to adult standards' (p. 179).

Floud (1961), however, pointed out that there is some evidence that the educational disadvantages of a large family are less marked for the children of Catholic parents, even at the bottom of the social scale. If generally true, this finding would cast doubt on the notion that the significance of a small family for educational performance should be sought in some distinctive quality of educational value in the environment it provides. It would lend support to the suggestion that for children at a given social level, relative size of family is, generally speaking, symptomatic of parental attitude and family pressures favourable to a child's educational progress.

Floud's hypothesis is also in effect advanced by

Davie *et al.*: 'The parents who opt for a large family will have a different set of priorities; priorities which perhaps are less likely to be achievement oriented, and less concerned with higher attainment at school or with conformity to school norms than those of other parents.'

There is no firm evidence at present as to the validity or relative importance of the hypotheses outlined above, but it is likely that all have a part to play in explaining the disadvantages suffered by children from large families.

The present study

The measure of family size used for the follow-up at 11 and in the analyses reported here is related to the number of children in the family, rather than the total number of persons. It is taken to be 'the number of children under 21 who normally live in the study child's household' — this excludes children in the household who, for example, were at home only for holidays. The age limit of 21 years is an arbitrary one, but was imposed because it was felt that the influence of children in the household who were very much older was likely to be of a different nature from that of children nearer to the age of the study children.

At the age of 7 children from large families were found to be at a disadvantage compared with children from small families in all the measures examined — reading attainment, arithmetic attainment, social adjustment and height. Children from families containing five or more children were found to be as much as twelve months on average behind children from families with only one or two children in reading score, after allowance had been made for social class, region and sex. The association between arithmetic attainment and family size was, however, much less marked; this may support the suggestion that children from large families suffer in verbal skills in particular, though it also reflects the smaller total variance on this test. The remainder of this discussion presents and discusses the associations found between family size and other relevant variables at the age of 11.

Family size and social class

First, families tend to be larger where the father is in a manual occupation. This is shown in Table 1.1.

There is little difference between the professional groups (I and II) and the other non-manual group (III Non-Manual), but there is then a steady increase in average family size through the skilled and semi-skilled manual groups to the unskilled group at the extreme. In this last group more than one-third of the children are in families with five or more children, a proportion which is over four times as great as that for the children of fathers in professional occupations.

TABLE 1.1   *Number of children in the household by social class (percentages)*

| No. children | Social class | | | | | |
	I and II	III Non-Manual	III Manual	IV	V	Total
1	12	13	11	10	8	11
2	40	39	32	27	20	33
3	28	27	25	24	14	25
4	13	12	16	17	19	16
5	4	5	8	10	15	8
6+	3	4	9	12	19	8
Total	100	100	100	100	100	100
$N =$	3 077	1 198	5 549	2 245	774	12 843

Family size and crowding

As one might expect, large families are more likely to live in overcrowded home conditions than small families. This is shown in Table 1.2. The crowding index here is obtained by dividing the total household size (adults and children) by the number of rooms in the family's accommodation.

TABLE 1.2   *Number of children in the household by crowding (percentages)*

| No. children | Crowding (persons per room) | | | | | |
	≤1.0	−1.5	−2.0	>2.0	Total	N
1	97	2	1	0	100	1 530
2	88	11	1	0.1	100	4 506
3	65	24	5	0.7	100	3 473
4	25	67	7	1	100	2 122
5	10	53	31	6.1	100	1 061
6+	2	23	53	21	100	1 102
$N =$	8 348	3 770	1 306	357		13 781

It can be seen from the table that a crowding density of 1.0 persons per room or lower is associated with smallest family size and that crowding increases with increasing family size. The NCDS data also allowed an examination of other aspects of housing which can only be reported briefly here. It was, however, found that the smaller the size of the family, the more likely it is that the family will have the sole use of three basic amenities — indoor lavatory, bathroom and hot water supply. Also, smaller families are more likely to be housed in owner-occupied property than in council rented property or unfurnished rented property. Council tenants are likely to have larger families than those in unfurnished rented property.

Family size and region

Table 1.3 shows a general tendency for families to be slightly larger in Scotland than in England, and within England there are more families with two or three children and less with five or more children in the South. In Wales there are slightly more single-child families, but also the largest proportion of families with six or more children.

TABLE 1.3   *Number of children in the household and region (percentages)*

| No. children | National and regional groups | | | |
	North* England	South* England	Scotland	Wales
1	11	11	10	14
2	32	35	28	33
3	25	26	23	24
4	15	15	18	13
5	4	7	10	6
6+	9	6	10	11
Total	100	100	100	100
N =	6 148	5 439	1 446	759

*The 'North' of England is a combination of the five standard regions used by the Registrar-General: Northern, N. Western, E. and W. Ridings of Yorkshire, N. Midlands and Midlands. The 'South' of England consists of all remaining regions.

Family size and parental interest in education

It was suggested earlier that a possible explanation for the associations between family size and different aspects of children's development was that parents with small families might in general have somewhat different attitudes in other respects, too; and that these attitudes might be relevant to children's abilities, attainments and adjustment to school. It is worthy of note, then, that, in general, the smaller the family size, the more likely were the parents to have taken the initiative to visit their child's school. The relationship between family size and this measure is shown in Table 1.4.

These figures are, however, also compatible with the 'shared resources' hypothesis since parents of large families will have less time and opportunity to visit schools.

TABLE 1.4   *Number of children in the household by discussion at school at parents' initiative (percentages)*

No. children	Father only	Mother only	Both parents	Neither	Total	N
1	6	34	23	38	100	1 364
2	5	32	28	35	100	1 155
3	5	32	24	40	100	3 183
4	5	31	19	46	100	1 945
5	4	31	14	52	100	972
6+	3	28	9	60	100	1 010

Finally, the relationship between family size and parental education was examined — the index of parental education being whether the parents had stayed on at school beyond the minimum school-leaving age or not. For both mothers and fathers, continued education is associated with smaller family size.

Family size and children's development at 11 years

It is apparent that the different factors considered so far in relationship to family size are themselves inter-related. For example, there are regional differences in social-class distribution and this may be reflected in the regional differences in family size. Thus if we are to attempt to identify the relationships between family size and aspects of children's development, we must allow for the extent to which these other important variables are related to family size and the measure of development used.

To achieve this, analyses of variance have been carried out which include all those variables considered above and which calculate their separate associations with the dependent measures — reading, mathematics, social adjustment and height.

A brief word of explanation about these analyses will make the discussion below clearer.

In presenting the results relating to reading and mathematics attainment it is possible to relate scores to their rate of increase with a child's age. Thus it is possible to describe the results in terms of 'months of reading and mathematics age'. In interpreting the findings of an analysis of variance such as those on which the following figures are based it should always be borne in mind that the precise findings are specific to the particular analysis carried out. A different test of reading or mathematics might have produced different results. Also the omission of any of the independent variables or the inclusion of new ones or their categorisation in different ways could affect the results obtained. In the last resort it is a matter of judgement as to whether all the important, relevant factors have been included in an analysis.

In Figures 1.1—1.4 we have omitted variables which do not show a relationship with the dependent measure at the 5 per cent level of significance. The full list of variables included in each of these analyses and their definitions is as follows:

1. *Sex.*
2. *Social class*, five categories: I and II, III Non-Manual, III Manual, IV, V.
3. *Household amenities*, four categories: indoor lavatory, bathroom and hot water supply combined as follows:
   (a) sole use of all three amenities
   (b) sole use of two
   (c) sole use of one
   (d) sole use of no amenity
4. *Tenure*, three categories: owner-occupier or tied to occupation, private rented, council.
5. *Region*, four categories: Scotland, Wales, North England, South England.
6. *Mother's education*, two categories: stayed on at school after the minimum school-leaving age, did not stay on.
7. *Father's education*, two categories — as for mother.
8. *Parental initiative to discuss child with teacher*, four categories: father only, mother only, mother and father, neither.
9. *Crowding*, four categories: ≤1.0, −1.5, −2.0, >2.0 persons per room.
10. *Number of older children under 21 in the household*, four categories: 0, 1, 2, ≥3.
11. *Number of younger children in the household*, four categories: 0, 1, 2, ≥3.
12. *Number of children under 21 in the family but not living in the household*, three categories: 0,1, ≥2.

To turn to the results shown in the illustrations, it will be seen that instead of using merely the total number of children in the household under the age of 21 years as an index of family size, a distinction has been made between the number of children in the household who are older than the study children and the number who are younger. The number of older children is taken from the child's position in the family; the number of younger children refers to births to the study child's mother since that of the study child. (In addition, the relationship between the number of children not in the household, e.g. those away at boarding school, and the outcome measures was examined, but in no case was this statistically significant.)

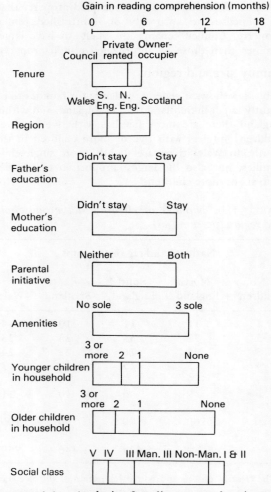

FIGURE 1.1   *Analysis of reading comprehension and home factors (N = 9 789)*

Family size and reading and mathematics attainment

The difference in reading attainment between those children with no older children in the household and those with three or more was equivalent to a gain of fourteen months. Between those with no younger children in the household and those with three or more there was a difference of twelve months. The overall difference between children with no other children under the age of 21 in the household and those with three or more younger *and* three or more older was, therefore, equivalent to a gain of twenty-six months in reading age, in the context of this particular analysis. The comparable figure for gain in mathematics age was a little under twelve months.

The comparison between the family size and the social-class 'effects' is noteworthy — the average

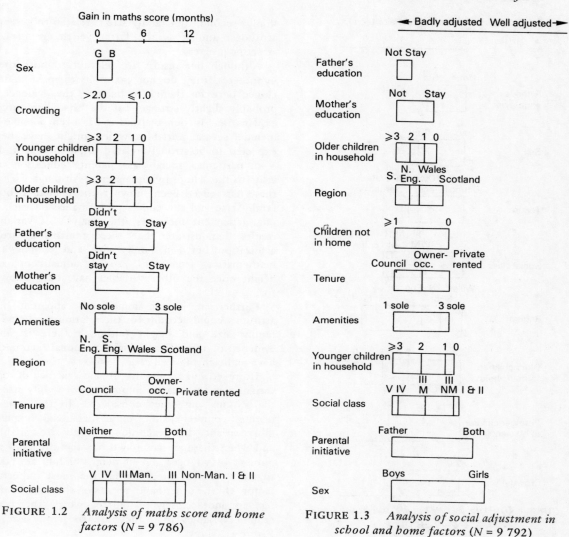

FIGURE 1.2 *Analysis of maths score and home factors (N = 9 786)*

FIGURE 1.3 *Analysis of social adjustment in school and home factors (N = 9 792)*

differences between family size groups, as defined, are bigger than between social-class groups for both reading and mathematics attainment.

Family size and social adjustment

The same variables as in the above analyses were included in an analysis which used the Bristol Social Adjustment Guides (Stott, 1966) score as the outcome measure (Figure 1.3). The BSAG is completed by teachers, giving descriptions of a child's behaviour in school, and scores on it give an indication of the child's adjustment to the school situation.

Figure 1.3 shows that the average difference in social adjustment score between those children with no older children in the household and those with three or more is well under half the size of the average difference in score between boys and girls; it

is well over half the social-class difference. The average difference in score between those children with no younger children in the household and those with three or more is the same as the social-class difference, in the context of this analysis. The overall combined effect of three or more younger children in the household and three or more older children compared with none is the same as the average difference in social adjustment score between boys and girls at this age.

Family size and height

Figure 1.4 shows the relationship between the children's height at the age of 11 years and the variables included in the above analyses. After allowance for other variables, the differences in height associated with having three or more older children and with

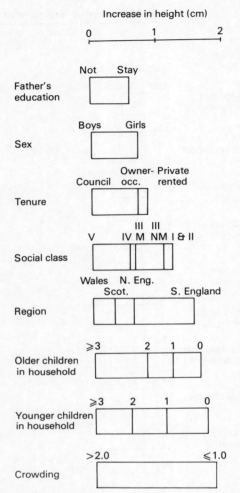

Increase in height (cm)

FIGURE 1.4   *Analysis of height and home factors*
(N = 9 208)

thinly; second, that family size is related to parental attitudes, and it is the latter which are in fact affecting progress.

Although our results are relevant to both these hypotheses, they do not enable us to make a firm choice between them. On balance, the evidence is probably slightly stronger for the 'shared resources' explanation. In our analyses it has been possible to include several variables which might have been expected to be strongly related to parental attitudes — in particular, social class, parents' education and visits to the school by the parents. Although each of these has indeed been shown to be related to both family size and the child's performance on each of our dependent measures, the analysis of variance results demonstrate that there remains a strong association between family size and reading and mathematics attainment, social adjustment and height once the other variables have been allowed for.

Further, it is not immediately apparent how attitudes could account for the relationship between family size and height (although there is some evidence of the effects which emotional factors can have on height: Powell *et al.*, 1967).

However, our results do provide evidence of some variation in the relative importance of family size to the various outcomes considered. In the case of reading comprehension, only social class explains more variance than each of the family-size variables, and when these are combined, i.e. the effects of the number of younger and of older children are taken together, this becomes by far the most important factor. On the other hand, results on the mathematics test are more closely related to several other background variables than they are to family size, as Figure 1.2 shows.

If 'shared resources' were the crucial determinant of the relationship between family size and development, it might have been expected that the number of older children would have a greater influence than the number of younger children, since the 11-year-old will have been 'sharing' with the former all his life, but with the latter for only a part of it. In fact this proves to be the case only for social adjustment in school.

For reading, mathematics and height there is little or no difference in the proportions of variance explained by these two variables.

In summary, it would seem that the NCDS data give some support for each of these two hypotheses and that both may give partial explanations of the relationship between family size and development.

The existence and extent of this relationship is demonstrated by the results reported here. If we take the most extreme comparison, then we should expect

having three or more younger children in the household are of similar magnitudes and the combined effect is an average difference of 3.9cm. This compares with a difference of 1.3cm between children in social classes I and II and those in social class V.

Discussion

The results from a study such as this one cannot give direct evidence of causality. However, the findings presented here do reveal a number of interesting associations between such outcomes as school attainment, school adjustment and height, and several environmental variables. Of these, family size appears to be one of the most influential.

Two alternative hypotheses were described in the earlier section of this paper: first, that the poorer performance of children in large families is due to the necessity of the family's resources being shared more from our figures to find that the average differences at this age between only children and those having three younger and three older children in the household amount to twenty-six months in reading, just under twelve months in mathematics and 3.9cm in height. There is also a significant difference in adjustment to school values as measured by the BSAG.

Of course, there may be other measures which were not used in this study, particularly perhaps in such areas as sociability and adaptability, on which the results may have been very different, but it is apparent that in the areas of conventional school attainment and in physical growth, as measured by height, the child in a large family is significantly behind his peers at the age of 11.

SOCIAL FACTORS ASSOCIATED WITH CHANGES IN EDUCATIONAL ATTAINMENT BETWEEN 7 AND 11 YEARS OF AGE

Ample evidence now exists about the relationship between social factors and children's attainment at school. A number of studies, both nationally and locally based, have shown differences between children from different family sizes and social classes at a variety of stages in their school career. Much of the early work in this area is summarised by Floud, *et al.* (1956) and Wiseman (1964); more recent perspectives are provided by Craft (1970) and Byrne *et al.* (1975).

The National Survey of Health and Development, a study of a sample of children born in one week of 1946, demonstrated differences associated with different family sizes and father's occupation on tests of reading vocabulary and intelligence at the age of 8 and additionally in arithmetic at age 11 (Douglas, 1964). Furthermore, these differences were found to persist through secondary school to the age of 15 (Douglas *et al.*, 1967).

Similar findings have emerged from the National Child Development Study. A decade after Douglas's findings, social class and family size are still associated with large differences in school attainment at the age of 7 (Davie *et al.*, 1972) and 11 (Fogelman, 1975).

A question which arises naturally from such findings is whether the differences between these groups change as the children progress through school. Do children of low social class and large families show a once-and-for-all difference which is stable throughout their education or does the gap between them and their peers become wider or narrower?

Douglas (1964) did investigate this question by examining change in test performance between the ages of 8 and 11. Concerning social class he concluded that the average test scores of children in four social classes differed more widely at 11 than they did at 8. However, with regard to family size, there was 'no evidence that children from large families deteriorated in their test performance . . . [showing] that the influence of family size on the level of test score has exerted its full effect by eight years'.

The purpose of the analyses reported here is to ascertain whether similar patterns are present for the period covered by the NCDS data, namely 1965 to 1969. In addition we have introduced a new factor into the analyses, that of changes in these variables between 7 and 11.

The specific variables considered are as follows.

7-year-old data (1965)

1. *Sex*.
2. *Social class*. The father's occupation was ascertained during the course of the parental interview. These occupations have been categorised according to the Registrar General's (1960) classifications of occupations into the following groups:

   I   higher professional
   II   other professional and technical
   III (non-manual); other non-manual
   III (manual); skilled manual
   IV   semi-skilled manual
   V   unskilled manual
        no male head of household

   In the analyses reported below the group with no male head of household (3 per cent of the total sample) has been omitted, as have all adopted and illegitimate children.
3. *Number of children in the household*. During the course of the parental interview the total number of children under the age of 21 in the household was obtained, and has been subdivided into the number who are older and younger than the study child.
4. *Reading attainments*. As measured by the Southgate reading test (Southgate, 1962), a standardised test of word recognition.
5. *Arithmetic attainment*. As measured by a problem arithmetic test constructed for use in this study by the National Foundation for Educational Research (NFER).

11-year-old data (1969)

1. *Sex*, *social class* and *number of children in the household* as at age 7.
2. *Reading attainment*. As measured by a test constructed by the NFER to be parallel with the

Watts—Vernon test of reading comprehension.
3. *Mathematics attainment*. As measured by a test constructed by the NFER for this study and combining a mixture of problems and mechanical items.

It should be noted that the reading and mathematics tests used at 7 and 11 are not the same with regard to the kinds of behaviour elicited. Thus we are in effect comparing one component of performance with another at the different ages. The 7- and 11-year reading scores have a correlation of 0.63 (0.66 after correction for attenuation), and the correlation for the 7- and 11-year mathematics scores is 0.56 (0.59 after correction).

Method of analysis

Douglas's (1964) findings mentioned above have been subject to certain statistical criticisms (Carter, 1964) based on his failure to take account of the 'measurement error', or unreliability, of the tests used when the children in the National Survey were aged 8. To take account of this we have formulated the problem in the following way.

Instead of attempting to measure change in score directly we explored whether for a given initial (i.e. at 7) test score the average scores at 11 are different for the various categories of social class and other variables considered. The advantage of this approach is that it avoids the problem of separately standardising the two test score distributions and does not make the assumption that the simple difference in standardised scores is the most relevant aspect of change to measure. Since, in practice, the difference between final and initial score is usually not independent of the initial score, more information is provided by considering the detailed relationship between the two. Thus the problem has been formulated in terms of the linear regression relationship of 11-year score on 7-year score (see the Appendix, pp. 35—6).

Categorisations of variables used

The variable categories were chosen on the basis of previous evidence and a preliminary exploration of the relationships within the present study. Thus the categories for older and younger children were chosen to provide as much detail as possible while retaining sufficient cell numbers for reliable estimates to be made. In the case of social class, previous evidence has suggested that the boundary between non-manual and skilled manual and that between semi-skilled and unskilled manual are both relatively more difficult for people to cross and coincide with

marked changes in test scores. This was confirmed by our preliminary analysis of the relationship between 7- and 11-year scores.

Presentation of results

Because it is desirable for results to indicate relative progress it has become conventional to relate test scores to their rate of increase with the reference group's age. We have therefore described the differences between groups in terms of 'years of reading (or mathematics) age'; and the axes on the diagrams below are scaled in this way. These values must not be interpreted too rigidly, however, since they are specific to the tests used and are strictly applicable only within a narrow range of ages.

For the 11-year reading test the estimate for the Watts—Vernon test (Start and Wells, 1972) has been used, since the NCDS 11-year reading test was derived from that test with very minor modifications which leave the distributional properties unaltered. For the mathematics test a sample of 239 children, some in their last year of primary school and some in their first year of secondary school, were given the test to provide an estimate of the mean change in score per year of age.

The estimate for the reading test is 2.2 points per year and for the mathematics test 4.5 points per year. Similar age-related scales are used for the 7-year tests and are reported in Davie *et al.* (1972).

Results

The findings of the first set of analyses are summarised in Table 1.5. For each dependent variable (i.e. reading and mathematics score), analyses have been carried out fitting, in addition to the 7-year test score, just one of the independent variables with which we are concerned (i.e. social class, sex or older and younger children in the household) and a fourth analysis fits all the independent variables simultaneously.

Social class

Figure 1.5a depicts a clear separation of the social classes between the ages of 7 and 11 in reading attainment and this is confirmed by the first analysis of variance summarised in Table 1.5. For a given 7-year score the children whose fathers were in non-manual occupations are, at 11, about 1 year ahead of social classes III Manual and IV, who in turn are about 0.4 years ahead of social class V. This of course, is additional to the pre-existing differences at the age of 7, which were respectively 0.9 years and 0.7 years (see Davie *et al.*, 1972). Thus the overall differences at 11 have increased to 1.9 years and 1.1 years respectively.

TABLE 1.5 *Summary of analysis of variance findings (fitted constants; standard errors in brackets)*

Independent variables	Categories	11-year reading score in years (N = 9 374) (total variance = 7.92)				11-year mathematics score in years (N = 9 363) (total variance = 5.19)			
Overall constant		10.9 0.8	11.0 0.9	10.7 0.8	10.7 0.8	10.9 0.6	11.0 0.7	10.7 0.7	10.7 0.6
7-year score	Per year	(0.01)	(0.01)	(0.003)	(0.01)	(0.01)	(0.01)	(0.01)	(0.01)
Social class	Non-Manual III Man + IV V	0.8 −0.2 −0.6			0.8 −0.2 −0.5	0.9 −0.2 −0.8			0.9 −0.2 −0.7
Sex	Boys—Girls		0.05		0.4 (0.04)	−0.0 (0.04)			0.0 (0.04)
No. of younger children	0 1 2 3 +			0.4 0.1 −0.1 −0.4	0.4 0.1 −0.1 −0.3			0.3 0.1 −0.1 −0.4	0.2 0.1 0.0 −0.3
No. of older children	0 1 2 3 +			0.4 0.1 −0.1 −0.4	0.4 0.0 −0.1 −0.3			0.5 0.2 −0.1 −0.6	0.4 0.1 −0.1 −0.4
Residual mean square		4.52	4.71	4.61	4.39	3.26	3.56	3.43	3.19
	Interactions significant at 0.05 level	Social class x 7-year score**		No. of older children x 7-year score*	Social class x 7-year score*** Sex x 7-year score***	Sex x 7-year score*		No. of younger children x no. of older children ***	Sex x 7-year score* No. of younger children x no. of older children** No. of younger children x social class*

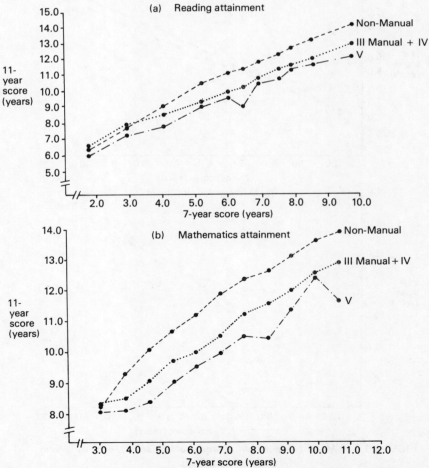

FIGURE 1.5 *Mean 11-year reading and mathematics scores for three social class groups at 7 years*

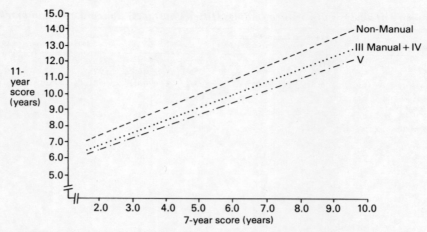

FIGURE 1.6   *Estimated regression of 11-year reading score on 7-year reading score for three social class groups at 7 years*

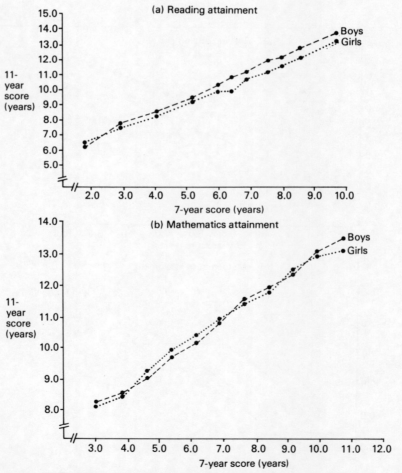

FIGURE 1.7   *Mean 11-year reading and mathematics scores by 7-year scales for each sex*

A similar result is found for arithmetic (Figure 1.5b), where the average difference associated with each 7-year score is 1.1 years between the Non-Manual and III Manual and IV group, and 6.6 years between the latter and social class V.

Additionally, interactions are present in the reading analysis, namely the regression lines for the social classes are not parallel. Figure 1.6 shows the fitted regression lines, indicating a slight divergence of the lines with increasing 7-year score. It is difficult to draw particular inferences from this finding which are not related to the scale of measurement of the 11-year score. By a suitable non-linear monotone transformation of this scale it may be possible to eliminate this interaction, and since the choice of scale transformation will be arbitrary, at least with respect to psychological or educational considerations, this imposes a limitation on the kind of inference to be drawn. The fact that the observed 11-year reading score for non-manual children is below that for III Manual and IV for low 7-year scores might suggest

an important interaction, but the number of cases is too small to draw firm conclusions. What can be inferred from Figures 1.6 and 1.5a, however, is that for all 7-year scores there are approximately constant differences between the three social classes, and in particular that the ordering of these differences is unaffected by transformation (see the Appendix). Where interactions occur in the following analyses they will be referred to only where their presence may have implications for any conclusions concerning such order relationships, but they are reported in the tables.

Sex

At the age of 7 it was found that girls were significantly ahead of boys in their reading-test scores. Figure 1.7a and the analysis of variance show that for given 7-year scores the boys' average 11-year score is 0.5 years ahead of the girls. The result of this is that there is no overall difference in reading attainment between boys and girls at 11.

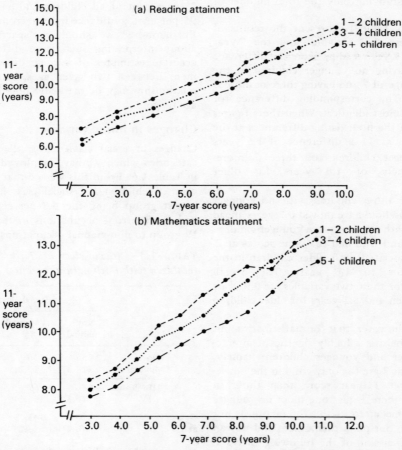

FIGURE 1.8   *Mean 11-year reading and mathematics scores for three 'number of children in household' groups*

For mathematics, on the other hand, there is no average difference between the sexes in the 11-year score for a given 7-year score. There is an indication of interaction, but any interaction effect that exists will be small and Figure 7b presents no clear pattern. At the age of 7 the boys were 0.2 years ahead of the girls and at the age of 11 the overall difference is 0.1 years. There is therefore no evidence of a change in the relatively small average difference between boys and girls.

Number of children in the household

Figures 1.8a and 1.8b show the average 11-year scores on the two tests for given 7-year scores for different total numbers of children in the child's household at the age of 7. For both reading and mathematics the greater the number of children in the household, the lower is the mean 11-year score for a given 7-year score. The total number of children in the household can be subdivided into those older than the study child and those younger. This provides more detailed information than studying only the total number of children.

The analyses in Table 1.5 present the results of jointly fitting these two variables and the 7-year score. For a given 7-year reading score the difference at 11 between having no younger children in the household at the age of 7 and having three or more is about 0.8 years. The corresponding difference for older children is almost identical. When these figures are combined with the pre-existing differences at the age of 7, we find at 11 a difference of 1.6 years between no younger children and three or more, and correspondingly of 1.8 years for older children.

In mathematics those children with no younger children in the household have moved 0.7 years ahead of those children with three or more younger children in the household and who had the same scores at 7. The difference associated with older children in the household amounts to 1.0 years. The overall differences at 11 for these two variables are 0.9 years for younger children and 1.2 years for older children in the household.

It will be seen, however, that for mathematics, but not for reading, there is a highly significant interaction between older and younger children; namely, that children who at 7 are the only child in the household have a lower 11-year score than those in households where there is just one older or younger child. While of some interest, this interaction is not directly relevant to our main theme here and we can ignore it in the discussion of the following analyses. We note, however, that it is still present in the more extensive analyses, though smaller in size.

Joint effects

Two of the variables considered — social class and the number of children in the household — are not independent of each other. For example, when these children were 7 the proportion of non-manual households with only one child was 8.8 per cent whereas the proportion in social class V was 5.7 per cent (Davie *et al.*, 1972). It is therefore of interest to study the joint and partial effects of these variables and sex on the 11-year-old scores.

The fitted constants do not differ substantially from those in the separate analyses, though the contrasts between categories are somewhat reduced. Since the effects are additive we can estimate differences between combinations of categories. To take an extreme contrast, a child from a non-manual home with no older or younger children in the household at the age of 7 is, at the age of 11, about 2.7 years ahead in reading of the child who obtained the same score at 7 but is from social class V and has three or more older and younger children in the household. However, this contrast involves only 2.3 per cent of all children and has an approximate 95 per cent confidence interval from 2.4 to 3.0 years. Furthermore, we should be particularly cautious about interpreting such large differences as being accurate estimates of average differences in attainment between two given ages, since the age–score relationship may be markedly non-linear over a wide age range.

Changes in home variables

Changes in social class, across the combinations of categories which we have employed, are summarised in Table 1.6. From this we see that for about 16 per cent of children the social class had changed, the largest group being the 6.3 per cent whose fathers had moved from occupations in the III Manual and IV group to non-manual occupations.

TABLE 1.6   *Social class at 7 by social class at 11 (children with both natural parents)*

		Social class at 11			
		Non-manual	III Manual + IV	V	Total
Social class at 7	Non-manual	2 958 (27.3)	346 (3.2)	15 (0.1)	3 349 (30.9)
	III Manual + IV	686 (6.3)	5 867 (54.1)	270 (2.5)	6 823 (62.9)
	V	20 (0.2)	343 (3.2)	317 (2.9)	680 (6.3)
	Total	3 694 (34.0)	6 556 (60.4)	602 (5.6)	10 852 (100.0)

Changes in household size are shown in Tables 1.7 and 1.8. At least 17 per cent of the children had at least one extra younger child entering the household between 7 and 11 and about 13 per cent had one less older child in the household by 11. Because of our definition of children this last figure will be explained mainly by those siblings who reach the age of 21 between the two follow-ups.

We have included these changes as additional variables in the analyses of variance, the results of which are shown in Table 1.9. There are two reasons for utilising the 11-year information by adding a measure of change rather than including the same variable measured at 11 years. First, we are interested in the changes themselves and it is natural to specify them directly in the analyses. Second, the high association between the 7- and 11-year variables could result in some instability in the fitted constants.

For younger children we have excluded those cases where there was a recorded decrease (1.6 per cent of all cases), since these are likely to be, in part, errors in recording. Similarly, we have excluded cases where an increase in older children has been recorded (0.9 per cent). Turning to the results, we find that the addition of the change variable slightly reduces the differences between the categories of the 7-year

TABLE 1.7   *Number of younger children at 7 by younger children at 11 (children with both natural parents)*

		Younger children at 11				
		0	1	2	3 +	Total
	0	4 275 (34.7)	590 (4.8)	68 (0.6)	20 (0.2)	4 953 (40.3)
	1	85 (0.7)	3 421 (27.8)	695 (5.6)	127 (1.0)	4 328 (35.2)
Younger children at 7	2	15 (0.1)	39 (0.3)	1 424 (11.6)	537 (4.4)	2 015 (16.4)
	3 +	7 (0.1)	7 (0.1)	32 (0.3)	962 (7.8)	1 008 (8.29)
	Total	4 382 (35.6)	4 057 (33.0)	2 219 (18.0)	1 646 (13.4)	12 304 (100.0)

TABLE 1.8   *Number of older children at 7 by older children at 11 (children with both natural parents)*

		Older children at 11					
		0	1	2	3	4 +	Total
	0	4 082 (37.0)	45 (0.4)	4 (0.0)	2 (0.0)	0 (0.0)	4 133 (37.5)
	1	310 (2.8)	3 401 (30.8)	23 (0.2)	5 (0.1)	1 (0.0)	3 740 (33.9)
Older children at 7	2	99 (0.9)	385 (3.5)	1 224 (11.1)	5 (0.1)	2 (0.0)	1 715 (15.6)
	3	27 (0.2)	102 (0.9)	235 (2.1)	446 (4.0)	6 (0.1)	816 (7.4)
	4 +	6 (0.1)	25 (0.2)	111 (1.0)	166 (1.5)	320 (2.9)	628 (5.7)
	Total	4 524 (41.0)	3 958 (35.9)	1 597 (14.5)	624 (5.7)	329 (3.0)	11 032 (100.0)

TABLE 1.9   *Summary of analysis of variance findings (fitted constants; standard errors in brackets)*

Independent variables	Categories		11-year reading score in years (N = 9 374) (total variance) = 7.92)	11-year mathematics score in years (N = 9 363) (total variance 5.19)
		Dependent variables		
Overall constant			10.7	10.5
7-year score	Per year		0.8 (0.01)	0.6 (0.01)
Social class at 7	Non-manual		0.8	0.9
	III Man. + IV		−0.3	−0.2
	V		−0.6	−0.7
Change in social class between 7 and 11	At 7	At 11		
	V	I–IV	0.0	0.0
	III Man. + IV	Non-Man.	0.5	0.5
	I–IV	V	−0.6	−0.5
	Non-Man.	III Man. + IV	−0.7	−0.6
		No change	0.0	0.0
Sex	Boys—Girls		0.4 (0.04)	0.0 (0.04)
No. of younger children at 7	0		0.3	0.2
	1		0.1	0.1
	2		−0.1	0.0
	3+		−0.3	−0.2
Increase in younger children between 7 and 11	0		0.2	0.2
	1		−0.1	0.0
	2+		−0.1	−0.2
No. of older children at 7	0		0.4	0.3
	1		0.0	0.1
	2		−0.1	−0.1
	3+		−0.4	−0.4
Decrease in older children between 7 and 11	0		−0.2	0.0
	1		0.2	0.0
	2+		0.0	−0.1
Residual mean square			4.34	3.15
	Interactions significant at 0.05 level		Social class x 7-year score*** No. of older children x 7-year score* Sex x 7-year score**	Sex x 7-year score* Younger children x older children*** Social class x younger children**

Significance tests. In the main body of the table, the independent variables are all significant at the 0.001 level, apart from sex and decrease in older children on the mathematics test, which are not significant at the 0.05 level. For the interactions: $*p < 0.05$; $**p < 0.01$; $***p < 0.001$.

variables. There are also comparatively large differences associated with the changes. In the case of social class, those moving from non-manual to skilled or semi-skilled groups had an average 11-year reading score 0.6 years behind those who stayed in the non-manual group for a given 7-year score. By contrast, those who moved in the other direction, from social class III Manual or IV into the non-manual group, were 0.5 years ahead in reading of those whose fathers remained in skilled or semi-skilled occupations. In the case of other children in the household the difference between having no further younger children in the household and having two or more was, though significant, small, being 0.4 years. Those children where two or more older children had moved out of the household were, by age 11, just 0.2 years ahead of those with the same number of older children at the two ages.

Arithmetic scores show a similar pattern. Those moving from the skilled and semi-skilled groups to the non-manual group show a gain of 0.5 years compared with those whose social class has not changed, and a move in the other direction is associated with a loss of 0.6 years. The effect of a change in the number of children in the household was small, an increase of two or more younger children being accompanied by a loss of 0.3 years and the difference associated with a decrease of two or more children failed to reach statistical significance.

Discussion

The National Survey children (Douglas, 1964) were 11 years old in 1957. Our data, twelve years later, confirm Douglas's findings on social class and additionally show that family size exhibits a changing association with attainment test scores between the ages of 7 and 11. We have also shown that social mobility and increase in family size influence test scores in the expected directions.

It is not the purpose here to pursue in detail any theoretical explanations for our findings, but one or two points are worth noting.

With regard to the family-size results, we need to be cautious in making comparisons between older and younger children since we know only the number of such children and not their ages. It is clear, however, that the greater the number of older or younger children in a child's household, the worse becomes the attainment of that child, and this is so after allowance has been made for social class. Furthermore, where older children 'leave' the household by passing the age of 21, and where there are no further younger children entering, there is a relative gain in attainment. This in part may reflect the effect of a longer spacing interval between the study child and other children in these households.

In the case of social class we find that in addition to the well-known difference between the children of manual and non-manual groups, those from 'upwardly' mobile families improve their attainment scores relative to those from static families, who in turn improve relative to those from 'downwardly' mobile families. The twelve years which separate the results of the National Survey and those of the present study have seen an increased apparent egalitarianism in educational provision, despite which this effect still appears.

Finally, we would like to stress that we are measuring the average differences which actually exist among children, and straightforward cause—effect relationships cannot be deduced from these.

Appendix: transformation of test scores

The relationship between the mean 11-year mathematics score and the 7-year arithmetic score is adequately described by a straight line, whereas that for reading becomes markedly non-linear for high 7-year scores. This, at least in part, reflects the fact that the 7-year reading test discriminated poorly between good readers and resulted in nearly one-third of children obtaining the top scores of 29 and 30. In order to simplify the analysis, the scale of the 7-year reading test has therefore been transformed to give an approximately linear relationship in Figure 1.5a. This figure and Figure 1.5b also show that the relationship remains linear within social-class groups, and this is also true for the categories of the other variables used in the analyses. The scales for the test scores are expressed in years, obtained by dividing each score by an estimate of the average change in score over a period of one year (see Goldstein and Fogelman, 1974).

It is a common practice to transform the distribution of 'raw' scores on mental tests to a Gaussian distribution. The distributions of the 11-year test scores have been studied within categories of social class and older and younger children and found to have near-Gaussian distributions without transformation. We have studied variance-stabilising transformations and have found no discernible improvement over the use of raw scores. We have therefore not carried out transformations for either of these two purposes. A third reason for transforming the dependent variable is to simplify the mathematical model. Although we have produced approximate linearity of regression through the transformation of the 7-year score in the case of reading, there is still the possibility of interactions occurring which could possibly be eliminated or substantially altered by a change of 11-year scale. For given 7-year scores we have compared the distributions of 11-year scores between categories of each variable used. If these distributions were to have different shapes, then it might be possible to find a non-linear but monotone transformation of the variable which would alter the relative ordering of the mean values of the three categories, and correspondingly alter our inferences. We find, however, that the distributions approximate closely to a Gaussian distribution and differ only in respect of their mean values. Similar results hold for the other 7-year variables and for the mathematics test scores. We can accept, therefore, that our inferences about order relationships between location parameters will be unchanged under monotone transformation, though of course the relative differences between means may alter.

Measurement error

It is a well-known result in simple linear regression (see, for example, Kendall and Stuart, 1961) that the presence of 'measurement error' in the independent variable leads to inconsistency in the estimation of the regression slope, namely that the expected value of the observed slope is always too small. In the present case, one of the independent variables, the 7-year score, is measured with error and we must make appropriate adjustment to obtain estimates of the fitted constants in the linear models.

The reported reliability of the 7-year reading test (Southgate, 1962) is 0.95. Since the transformation may have reduced this value, we have carried out our analyses using values of 0.90 and 0.80. No estimate for the 7-year mathematics test is available and we have also tried values of 0.90 and 0.80. We have studied the effect of correcting for measurement error by subtracting the variance of the 'errors' thus obtained (assuming independence of the measurement error and the other independent variables) from the variance of the 7-year score in the variance—covariance matrices of independent variables used in the analyses. This provides an unbiased estimator of the population covariance matrix involving the true variable, and leads to consistent estimates of coefficients and tests of significance, which, because of the large sample size, are ensured of a negligible bias (see Warren *et al.*, 1974).

This procedure, when carried out for the reliability values of 0.80 and 0.90, had little effect on the estimates and inferences. It is not until the reliability falls below about 0.6 that marked differences occur, for example the differences between the social-class groups approach zero. Hence, for simplicity, in the text all the basic findings are presented in terms of uncorrected observed scores.

In the tables we present fitted constants and significance tests for the variables in the linear models. For particular contrasts between variable categories and combinations of categories the standard errors may be relatively large. There are very many possible contrasts, however, and we present standard errors only for two-category and continuous variables, apart from one case in the text involving a contrast between category combinations involving small extreme groups.

PATTERNS OF ATTAINMENT

Introduction

In the previous paper, the relationship between changes in relative attainment of children between the ages of 7 and 11 and certain social factors was examined. In general it was shown that the gap in attainment among children of different social class and family size increased between the two ages. The purpose of the present paper is to extend this analysis, again using National Child Development Study data, to the age of 16 and to increase the number of social factors investigated.

The background factors on which we shall be concentrating are: sex, social class, family size and region. The overall question which we hope to answer is whether differences between groups of children defined by these factors, which are known to appear early in their school careers, are relatively stable, or

whether they increase or diminish during the time which children are attending school.

Such questions can only be answered adequately by large longitudinal studies. It is not surprising, therefore, that previous work is limited to the National Survey of Health and Development (NSHD), a study of a sample of children born in one week of 1946 (see, for example, Douglas, 1964; Douglas *et al.*, 1968), and to the National Child Development Study (NCDS).

The National Survey children were tested at the ages of 8, 11 and 15 with a range of tests. We shall, however, concentrate on reading and mathematics since these are the areas which were covered in the NCDS.

In relation to each of the background factors listed above, Douglas *et al.* (1968) report the following findings from the NSHD:

1. *Sex*. Girls obtained higher test scores than boys in both reading and mathematics up to the age of 11, but at 15 boys had moved ahead on both tests.
2. *Social class*. An increasing divergence among the social classes was found on both tests with the social-class gap in attainment greatest at 15.
3. *Family size*. At the age of 8 children from larger families obtained lower test scores than children from smaller families. However, there was no further increase in this gap at either of the later ages. Furthermore, for working-class children separately, the smallest differences in attainment among children of different-sized families were found at 15.
4. *Region*. At the age of 8 Scottish children did better on the two tests, particularly in reading. By 11 the English and Welsh children had caught up in their reading, but the Scottish children were still ahead in mathematics and remained so at 15.

The previous paper presented comparable findings (apart from regional differences) from the National Child Development Study, based on tests carried out at the ages of 7 and 11.

These analyses produced similar patterns to the National Survey with respect to social class. There were contrasts, however, in the findings in relation to sex and family size. At the age of 7, although girls had had higher mean reading test scores than boys, there was only a very small difference (and that in favour of the boys) in the arithmetic test means. By 11 the boys had caught up with the girls in reading and there continued to be little average difference in mathematics attainment between the sexes.

Whereas Douglas *et al.* concluded that the attainment differences associated with family size did not increase after the age of 8 and were 'determined by factors which exert their effect before the age at which they start school', the NCDS children exhibited an increase in the differences among children of different-sized families between the ages of 7 and 11.

In this paper, then, we shall be examining how such patterns of attainment have developed now that the National Child Development Study Children have been tested again, at the age of 16.

Data

The specific variables incorporated in the analyses reported here are as follows:

7-year data (1965)

1. *Sex*.
2. *Social class*. Fathers' occupations were ascertained in the course of the parental interviews, and have been categorised according to the Registrar-General's (1960) classification of occupations into the following groups: I, higher professional; II, other professional and technical; III NM, other non-manual; III M, skilled manual; IV, semi-skilled manual; V, unskilled manual. Children with no male head of household, or whose father's occupation could not be classified have been excluded from the analyses.
3. *Number of children in the household*. This is the number living in the household who are under the age of 21, subdivided in our analyses into the number of older and younger than the study child.
4. *Reading attainment*. Measured by the Southgate reading test (Southgate, 1962), this is a standardised test of word recognition.
5. *Arithmetic attainment*. Measured by a problem arithmetic test constructed for use in this study with the help of the NFER.

11-year data (1969)

1. *Sex, social class* and *number of children in the household* as at 7.
2. *Region*. Based on the following Registrar-General's Standard Regions: North England (Northern, N. Western, E. and W. Ridings of Yorkshire, N. Midlands and Midlands), South England (remaining regions of England), Scotland and Wales.
3. *Reading attainment*. Measured by a test constructed by the NFER to be parallel with the Watts–Vernon test of reading comprehension.
4. *Mathematics attainment*. Measured by a test constructed by the NFER for this study and containing a mixture of problem and mechanical items.

16-year data (1974)

1. Background variables as at the earlier ages.
2. *Reading attainment*. Measured by the same test as at 11.
3. *Mathematics attainment*. Measured by a test constructed by the NFER for use with this age group.

Method

As in the earlier analyses, we attempt to answer our questions by examination of the relationship of the 16-year test scores to the earlier test scores allowing for the relevant background factors. Preliminary analyses demonstrated that, for both tests, there was a relationship with the 7-year score, even after taking the 11-year score into account. Test scores at both the earlier ages have therefore been included in the analyses as independent variables. Our analyses can therefore be interpreted as showing whether for given 7- and 11-year scores, the average scores at 16 are different for the various categories of social class and other variables considered.

Two analyses have been carried out for each of the two 16-year tests. Each has 7-year and 11-year test scores as independent variables. The first analysis is concerned with social class and family size and includes social class at 11 and number of older and younger children at 11 as further independent variables. Additionally we wished to investigate the association with test scores of changes in these variables across the three ages, so two 'change in social-class' variables (7 to 11 and 11 to 16) and analogous 'change in family-size' variables were also incorporated. In the event the changes in family size did not prove to be significantly related, when adjusted for the other factors in the analysis, with 16-year test scores. Thus they have been omitted from the final reported analyses.

The second pair of analyses is primarily concerned with regional differences. However, in order to allow for differences among regions in their social-class composition, social class has again been included in these analyses as an independent variable. Because they are independent of any of the other background variables, sex differences could have been investigated by inclusion in either set of analyses and have in fact been included in the second.

Results

The results of the analyses of covariance examining social class and family size are summarised in Table 1.15 below (p. 41). It is not appropriate, because of an interaction, to present the regional analyses in the same form (see Figures 1.9 and 1.10 and Discussion below). In presenting the results we shall consider each variable in turn and in relation to the unadjusted differences shown in Tables 1.10–1.14.

Raw scores on the two 16-year tests have been transformed to have a normal distribution which has a mean of zero and a standard deviation of one. Thus the means and standard errors in Tables 1.10–1.14 and the fitted constants in Table 1.15 and the figures are in terms of standard deviation units.

The unadjusted comparisons are not limited to those children who could be included in the analyses of covariance by virtue of having information on all relevant variables at all ages. Further checks have been carried out to ensure that no bias is introduced into these analyses through the exclusion of children with incomplete data at any age, as well as those with no data at 16 discussed above.

Social class

To make any comparisons between the unadjusted means in Tables 1.10–1.14 and the fitted constants in Table 1.15 and Figures 1.9 and 1.10 clearer, it should be borne in mind that the latter are not the actual mean scores of the groups concerned. It is the differences between the fitted constants, rather than their absolute values, which are of interest and which can be compared with the differences between the unadjusted means.

In Table 1.10 we find the expected large average differences between the social classes. On both tests the difference in means between the extreme groups as categorised (i.e. between children of fathers in non-manual occupations and those of fathers in unskilled manual occupations) is greater than one standard deviation. Our question then concerns whether there is evidence that the differences represent an increase over the pre-existing differences between these groups.

TABLE 1.10   *16-year test scores by social class*

	Reading			Mathematics		
	Mean	se	N	Mean	se	N
Non-manual	0.53	0.016	3 241	0.50	0.017	3 236
III M + IV	−0.15	0.012	5 764	−0.16	0.012	5 732
V	−0.63	0.040	527	−0.52	0.039	517

The fitted constants in Table 1.15 demonstrate that this is the case. After adjusting for 7- and 11-year scores, there are still relatively large mean differences between the social-class groups. Again taking the extreme comparisons, they amount to just over one-third of a standard deviation for reading and a little less for mathematics.

Thus the pattern over all three ages is of a widen-ing gap between children of different social classes. Of course, this does refer to means, and the standard deviations within each social class are fairly large — virtually as large as the overall sample standard deviation. Even so, the figures in Table 1.10 imply that at 16 only about 15 per cent of the social-class V children could be expected to score above the mean of the non-manual children. It would be interesting in the future to examine how these differences relate to the public examination of these children.

Family size

A less clear-cut picture emerges in relation to family size. As already mentioned, we have divided this variable in order to look separately at the number of children older and younger than the study child. Tables 1.11 and 1.12 show the relationship of test scores to these two factors.

TABLE 1.11   *16-year test scores by number of older children (under 21) in the household*

	Reading			Mathematics		
	Mean	se	N	Mean	se	N
0	0.21	0.015	4 291	0.15	0.015	4 275
1	−0.07	0.016	3 550	0.07	0.016	3 528
2	−0.17	0.026	1 421	−0.15	0.026	1 410
3+	−0.51	0.033	878	−0.44	0.032	871

TABLE 1.12   *16-year test scores by number of younger children (under 21) in the household*

	Reading			Mathematics		
	Mean	se	N	Mean	se	N
0	0.17	0.016	3 540	0.10	0.016	3 520
1	0.11	0.017	3 359	0.09	0.017	3 347
2	−0.02	0.023	1 847	0.02	−0.023	1 834
3+	−0.34	0.028	1 386	−0.26	0.028	1 375

The contrasts in the two tables are fairly large, though less so than those associated with social class. Generally the differences in reading are a little greater than those in mathematics, and the differences associated with the number of older children greater than those for the number of younger children.

The relationship after allowing for test scores and social class is to be seen in Table 1.15. When these are taken into account the contrasts are inevitably much reduced, but remain statistically significant for the number of older children.

On both tests, those with no older children in the house have moved about one-seventh of a standard deviation further ahead of those with three or more older children in the household.

In relation to younger children in the household, however, the differences among the fitted constants are smaller, only just reaching statistical significance for the reading test, and not doing so for the mathematics test.

Thus it would appear that the gap in attainment related to the number of older children in the household is one which develops throughout the compulsory school years, but the further differentiation in relation to the number of younger children is extremely small, and may be non-existent for mathematics attainment.

Region

The simple differences at 16 among the four broadly grouped regions can be seen in Table 1.13. Once again, the pattern of results is similar for each test. There are, however, immediate contrasts with the results obtained by Douglas *et al.* (1968), mentioned above, for the cohort examined twelve years earlier. Among 16-year-olds in 1974 the Welsh children do relatively poorly on the reading test and, contrary to Douglas's findings, the Scots are certainly not ahead in mathematics.

TABLE 1.13   *16-year test scores by region*

	Reading			Maths		
	Mean	se	N	Mean	se	N
North England	0.01	0.015	4 294	0.02	0.015	4 268
South England	0.16	0.016	3 685	0.11	0.017	3 664
Wales	−0.13	0.041	577	−0.07	0.041	572
Scotland	−0.06	0.028	1 192	−0.05	0.029	1 188

Regional differences which take into account earlier scores are shown in Figures 1.9 and 1.10. In all the analyses reported in this section, tests have been carried out for the presence of interactions, i.e. whether the differences associated with one variable hold true for each category of another variable. For example, are the social-class differences reported equal for boys and girls, or do they vary according to sex? In general, such interactions have been found to be non-significant or trivial in size with no apparent implications for our findings. With only one exception they lead to no changes in the order relationships.

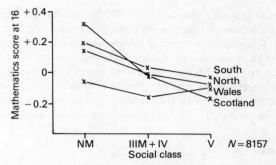

FIGURE 1.9   *16-year mathematics score for given 7- and 11-year score: region and social class*

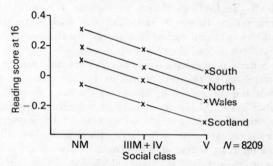

FIGURE 1.10   *16-year reading scores for given 7- and 11-year score: region and social class*

The exception is for the mathematics test in relation to social class and region, where the relationships among the regions are markedly different according to the social class of the children concerned. The pattern which emerges is shown in Figure 1.9, and it can be seen that the overall figures would mask a very different situation for each of the two extreme social-class groups.

In the relatively large skilled and semi-skilled manual group, the differences among the regions are extremely small (apart from the Welsh children), as indeed they are between the North and South of England for the other two social-class groups. In the, also large, non-manual group it is the Scots who have made the greatest average progress between 11 and 16, and the Welsh have done relatively poorly, while among the relatively small unskilled manual groups, these positions are reversed (but the differences are relatively small).

The fitted regression lines for the reading test, where no significant interactions were found, can be seen in Figure 1.10. It is clear that for each social-class group children in the south of England have made relatively good progress between the ages of 11 and 16, while the opposite is true for Scotland. At the age of 7, Scottish children were on average notably ahead of other areas of the country in their reading scores (Davie *et al.*, 1972), but by 16 they have been overtaken by children in England.

While it is interesting to speculate on the reasons for these intriguing findings relating to region — for example, might they be related to selection policies, or methods of ability grouping within schools or parental interest in their children's education — none is immediately convincing without further evidence.

Sex

As already mentioned, sex differences were examined in the course of the same analyses as those from which the findings shown in Figures 1.9 and 1.10 were taken. It was found that, for both tests, for children of equal earlier test scores, by the age of 16 boys have moved ahead of girls.

Since, as we have said, there were minimal sex differences in the test results at 11, the outcome at 16 is the difference in favour of the boys shown in Table 1.14. Although statistically significant it can be seen that the average differences at 16 between the sexes are not very large, particularly on the reading test, where it amounts to only about one-twentieth of a standard deviation. The small difference in mathematics raises the question of whether it is compatible with the considerably larger number of boys who enter and, among those who enter, who pass public examinations in mathematics (DES, 1976). It may be that there is still much female ability in this area which is not fully developed by our schools.

TABLE 1.14   *Mean 16-year test scores by sex*

	Reading			Mathematics		
	Mean	se	N	Mean	se	N
Boys	0.03	0.012	6 132	0.08	0.013	6 106
Girls	−0.02	0.012	5 858	−0.09	0.013	5 818

Changes in social class and family size

As already mentioned, changes over the three ages in each child's social class or family size were also examined in the course of the analyses presented in Table 1.15. As can be seen, the difference in 16-year scores for given earlier scores reached statistical significance only in the case of the mathematics test and for children whose social class changed between 7 and 11. In fact, even here the actual size of the difference is rather small.

It is interesting to note that on both the mathematics test and on the reading test, where the effect does not reach significance, children whose families are upwardly socially mobile between the ages of 7 and 11 show a relative deterioration in their performance by the age of 16, which might be taken to suggest that it is the social class earlier in the child's life that is of first importance. However, the pattern is reversed in relation to change in social class between 11 and 16 and these differences are in any case very small. Given also the lack of significance on the reading test, it would be wrong to place too great an emphasis on this result.

As mentioned, change in family size is not included in the final analysis reported in Table 1.15, as preliminary analyses showed there to be no relationship between this variable and the 16-year test score after allowance for earlier test scores.

Discussion

Before discussing our findings further, consideration must be given to a more general point concerning their overall validity. Following the publication of our earlier findings it has been suggested (Douglas, 1976; Richardson, personal communication) that the implication of our using different tests at different ages may be greater than we appreciated. That is, that different tests may have contrasting relationships with, for example, social class which would produce results such as these even if, say, the two tests had been given at about the same time. If this were the case, one could not argue that our findings indicated a widening gap, only that the gap is greater in some content areas than others.

This problem is not in fact disposed of by using the same tests on the two occasions. Given the large difference in ages, it would not be possible to find a single test where discrimination among children resulted from the same items within that test. In practice, the older children would answer correctly the majority of items on which younger children varied, and would themselves vary on a group of (harder) items which most younger children had got wrong, or had not attempted.

It is not possible to resolve this dilemma in a clear-cut fashion. However, we would argue that what is of first importance is the appropriateness of the test to the age group concerned. Does the test content sample from those skills which are important, which teachers are trying to teach, and which will subsequently be built upon, at the age in question? Nevertheless, one must acknowledge that different tests might produce different results. However, it can be noted that the general pattern of a widening gap in relation to social class, which is likely to be the most problematic variable in this context, appears for both reading attainment (where the same tests were used at 11 and 16) and for mathematics attainment

TABLE 1.15 *Summary of analysis of covariance: social class and family size*

Independent variable	Categories		16-year reading score (N = 4 332) (total variance = 0.90)			16-year mathematics score (N = 4 360) (total variance = 0.96)		
			Fitted constant	χ^2	(df)	Fitted constants	χ^2	(df)
7-year score	Per year		0.05	99.31	(1)***	0.04	47.7	(1)***
11-year score	Per year		0.24	3 671.01	(1)***	0.29	2 606.0	(1)***
Social class at 11	Non-Man.	(a)	0.16			0.16		
	III M + IV	(b)	0.02	63.3	(2)***	−0.02	54.4	(2)***
	V	(c)	−0.18			−0.14		
Older children at 11	0		0.07			0.08		
	1		0.02	22.5	(3)***	0.01	22.9	(4)***
	2		−0.02			−0.03		
	3 +		−0.07			−0.06		
Younger children at 11	0		0.04			0.01		
	1		0.01	9.5	(3)	0.02	1.8	(3)*
	2		−0.03			−0.01		
	3 +		−0.02			−0.02		
Change in social class 7–11	7	11						
	c	a + b	−0.02			−0.02		
	b	a	−0.06			−0.10		
	a + b	c	0.02	4.5	(4)	0.04	12.9	(4)*
	a	b	0.05			0.02		
	No change		0.01			0.06		
Change in social class 11–16	11	16						
	c	a + b	0.04			0.01		
	b	a	0.07	0.6	(4)	0.04	7.6	(4)
	a + b	c	−0.11			−0.01		
	a	b	−0.01			0.01		
	No change		0.02			0.00		
Residual mean square			0.30			0.42		

Significance tests: $p < 0.001$***; $p < 0.01$**; $p < 0.05$*; otherwise $p > 0.05$.

(where different tests were used at each age). Furthermore, this pattern also resembles that found in the NSHD, though none of these tests was common to both studies. Such evidence would seem to suggest that differences due to using different tests are not likely to be dramatic.

Turning to the findings, our results in relation to social class and family size show a continuation to the age of 16 of the patterns found earlier to the age of 11. That is, that the relatively advantaged children, of middle-class parents and small families, continue to show an increasing superiority in their reading and mathematics attainments.

Although we should not claim that our analyses incorporate an adequately detailed study of social mobility, our findings suggest that the association between children's progress and changes in social class is slight and contradictory.

Concerning family size, interesting differences have emerged when this is divided according to whether the other children in the household are older or younger than the child being studied. Between the ages of 11 and 16 it would appear that it is the number of older children which has the greater association with progress.

In the past, two kinds of explanations have been

offered for the relationship between family size and children's development. The first kind assumes a rather direct effect, resulting from, for example, shared physical resources (e.g. Lambert, 1964), or reduced access to parents' time (e.g. Davie *et al.*, 1972). The second suggests a less direct relationship, family size simply being associated with parental attitudes, which in turn are related to a child's progress (e.g. Floud, 1961).

If, as our results indicate, a change in family size does not have any implication for a child's educational progress, then this would seem to lend more support to the second of the above kinds of explanation.

On the other hand, our findings do not seem immediately compatible with the 'confluence model' proposed by Zajonc and Marcus (1975). Under this model the intellectual development of a child is related to the absolute (i.e. age-related) average level of the rest of its family. This model works well in explaining the relationship between development and family size and birth order at a single point in time. However, it would seem to predict that changes in a child's rate of progress would be related to changes in family size and equally to numbers of older and younger children. Neither of these predictions is supported by our data.

The relationship between progress and the other variables which we have examined, sex and region, has proved not to be so straightforward. Higher average scores of a group at one age cannot be taken to predict a similar position at the later age, there being considerable contrasts in such groups' relative progress between any two ages. Particularly interesting are the regional differences in mathematics attainment, with the Scottish and Welsh children showing contrasting rates of progress, not only during different periods, but also for different social class.

Finally, it is worth noting that, in addition to their possible social relevance, the results reported here would appear to have important methodological implications, particularly for educational researchers. In so-called 'quasi-experimental designs', for example, where children are matched according to their initial ability, differences may subsequently develop between groups which could be interpreted as treatment effects, but which might in fact be the result of differing social composition of the two groups. If such studies are to be adequately controlled, they must take account of children's social background — in particular their social class and family size — in addition to measured ability on one particular occasion.

READING ATTAINMENT AND FAMILY SIZE: AN ANOMALY

Introduction

The association between family size and school attainment is a long-established finding of developmental research. In Britain it has drawn further support from two well-known longitudinal studies, the National Survey of Health and Development (e.g. Douglas, 1964) and the National Child Development Study (Davie *et al.*, 1972; Fogelman, 1975: see pp. 21–7; Fogelman and Goldstein, 1976: see pp. 27–36). Two explanations for the relationship have commonly been adopted (see below). The present communication is restricted to a consideration of reading attainment. It illustrates the relationship between family size and reading attainment and draws attention to two sets of collateral data which, in juxtaposition with the former, may subserve an additional or alternative form of explanation.

The subjects were 520 11-year-old boys and girls, comprising a randomly selected sub-sample from the National Child Development Study. The present data were collected during the second follow-up study when the children were 11 years old. Reading attainment was tested using a sentence-completion reading comprehension test which was constructed as a parallel version of the Watts–Vernon test by the National Foundation for Educational Research. Examples of items are:

1. 'When the speaker asked if there were any questions he was [involved, immured, inundated, implied, instructed] with queries.'
2. 'As we both come from the same town, my wife and I have a great many [typical, mutual, friable, arable, viable] friends.'

The test was administered by teachers in schools under strict instructions regarding circumstances and timing. After completion of this test, the children were asked to write a composition on what they imagined their life to be like at the age of 25 years. Thirty minutes were allowed for this task.

We concentrated on two aspects of interest in the analysis of these compositions. First, it seemed important to know the volume of children's writing; we thus used 'composition length in words' as a measure of writing productivity. Second, indication of the syntactic richness or structural complexity of the language written was wanted. Syntax is a major aspect of linguistic development; for example, it has been shown how schoolchildren use progressively more sentence-combining transformations in their speech and writing (Hunt, 1970). Moreover, this trend would seem to be part of a more general cognitive capacity, namely 'the ability to pack a greater density of ideas into a single sentence by embedding one sentence in another' (Cazden, 1972). A major problem, however, is how this ability can be represented meaningfully and quantitatively. We have adopted the T-unit devised by Hunt (1970). The T-unit, which is the length in words of units consisting of each main clause together with attached subordinate clauses and non-clausal structures, inevitably conceals a lot of interesting information.

However, it has the advantage of exhibiting an increase in length as a direct function of syntactic complexity (Hunt, 1970). (For full details of data collection and analysis, see Richardson *et al.*, 1971a, to be found at pp. 341–8 of this book.)

Results

For some children not all details of the data were available, so that the numbers in each family size

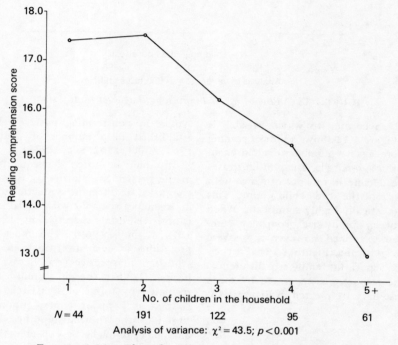

N = 44   191   122   95   61

Analysis of variance: $\chi^2 = 43.5$; $p < 0.001$

FIGURE 1.11   *Plot of reading test score against family size*

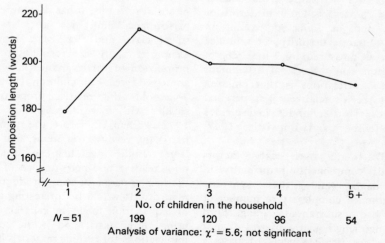

N = 51   199   120   96   54

Analysis of variance: $\chi^2 = 5.6$; not significant

FIGURE 1.12   *Plot of composition length against family size*

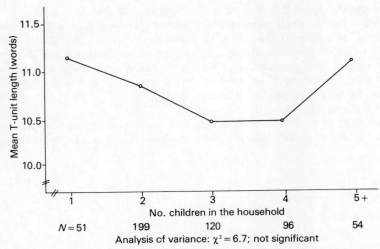

FIGURE 1.13   *Plot of mean T-unit length against family size*

group vary slightly according to which variable is being considered. Figure 1.11 shows a plot of reading comprehension score against number of children in the household for this sub-sample. The plot illustrates the typical average decline in test performance with increasing family size of the study child's home. This relationship was statistically highly significant. When the difference between family-size groups on composition length were examined, however, those were not found to be significant (Figure 1.12). Furthermore, there were no significant family-size differences on use of syntactic resources as measured by mean T-unit length. These data are plotted in Figure 1.13.

Discussion

The anomaly emerging in the analysis described is that children from larger families (on average 'poorer readers') perform as well as those from smaller families (on average 'better readers') in terms of writing productivity and, in doing so, exhibit an equivalent level of syntactic maturity, or sentence complexity, at least as measured by T-unit length. The usual explanation for the verbal attainment family-size (negative) correlations is that children from larger families receive relatively less parental verbal stimulus and/or suffer under inauspicious parental attitudes (Nisbet and Entwistle, 1967; Prosser, 1973).

Bormuth (1966) found over sixty factors contributing towards comprehension difficulty in reading test performance. Among these, syntactic elements such as sentence complexity or number of subordinate clauses had a substantial loading. Word difficulty and sentence length in themselves do not always seem to be significant aspects of passage readability, among children. However, the role of syntax in constraining passage reliability has been established in a number of studies (e.g. Epstein, 1961; Miller, 1962; Siler, 1973).

It should be noted that equality of T-unit length in the present sample does not preclude their being composed of different syntactic structures. Syntactic divergency associated with social class, for example, is now well established (Harms, 1963; Callary, 1971, 1974; Labov, 1969). The most prominent interpretations of such divergency are those based on a Whorfian perspective (e.g. Bernstein, 1972), which posits: (i) that speech systems are generated and regulated by forms of social relations, and (ii) that context is a major control upon syntactic usage. In so far as the Whorfian hypothesis has a level of generalisability, it might be expected that differentiation of syntactic usage might occur on the basis of family size; for example, it seems quite likely that families of different size will tend to generate different kinds of social relations. It has been noted that the reading-performance/family-size correlation holds within social class, and that of a number of measures examined family size accounts for by far the largest proportion of total variance in reading performance among 11-year-old children (Fogelman, 1975). In 7-year-olds this relative proportion is very much smaller with a word-recognition test (Davie *et al.*, 1972). Perhaps, therefore, the syntactic idiosyncrasies of (i) the reading test items, and (ii) children from larger families, will help account for the relatively poor reading test performance of the latter in spite of their apparent writing productivity and syntactic maturity. It would be interesting to know if this sort of explanation might be generalised to other studies using other tests, and if, in consequence, it has implications for reading materials in schools as well as selection of reading test items. Verifying it would, of course, demand a relatively thorough syntactic analysis of the language production of children from different-sized families, perhaps of the sort used by Callary (1971) or, on the basis of T-units, by Peltz (1973).

THE INFLUENCE OF FAMILY SIZE ON HEIGHT

It is well established that during childhood and up to the age of 14 or 15 there is a clear association between family size and height, with those from larger families tending to be shorter (e.g. Christiansen *et al.*, 1975; Fogelman, 1975: see pp. 21–7; Grant, 1964; Miller *et al.*, 1974; Ministry of Health, 1968; Moyes, 1976; Scott, 1961; Topp *et al.*, 1970; Yudkin, 1944). As one of these researchers (Grant, 1964) concludes: 'it seems clear that the larger the family the slower the rate of growth in it and this is established by the age of six years or perhaps even earlier if births follow closely together'. However, as Grant also points out, 'it remains to be considered whether the children in larger families fall still further behind during their later growth period'.

Doubt about whether the family influence on height continues into adulthood is rooted in the role that pubertal development plays in the relationship. It is well known that stage of puberty and height are themselves linked (Douglas and Simpson, 1964; Lindgren, 1976; Miller *et al.*, 1972; Miller *et al.*, 1974; Scott, 1961; Tanner, 1962), so that among children of the same age those at a more advanced stage of sexual maturity tend to be taller. Given also that children from small families tend to be taller, and additionally that children from small families reach sexual maturity earlier (Tanner, 1962; Douglas and Simpson, 1964; Grant, 1964; Scott, 1961), there are clearly grounds for reasoning that the family-size effect on height found prior to adulthood may be largely explained by the link with stage of puberty. In line with such a view, Tanner (1962) argues that 'one would expect, or at least hope, that at adulthood the [family size] differences will have disappeared. It is not known whether they disappear or persist in the United Kingdom data.'

It would seem that only a study of children with data available before and beyond sexual maturity — or with data making possible allowance for the independent effect of stage of puberty on height — can provide any real insight on this issue. Reports from previous British studies such as those of Douglas and Simpson (1964), Scott (1961) and Grant (1964) only trace children up to age 15 (although the Newcastle 'Thousand Family Study' retraced 442 children and measured them at age 22, height was only measured for different birth order, not family

sizes — Miller *et al.*, 1972). In the current study, data are available on a large nationally representative sample of children at ages 7, 11 and 16. That data are available at 16 is particularly useful since at this stage the vast majority of girls and approximately half the boys have reached sexual adulthood,* and presumably therefore, final height. Additionally, and of course, closely related to this point, we can see whether trends apparent in other studies at 14 and 15 are maintained, particularly the lessening of the family size influence on girls' height at those ages, in comparison with that at the age of 12 or 13. If this change in the family size influence is due to the majority of girls having reached maturity at this age, the family size influence should have virtually disappeared at age 16 when nearly all have reached this stage. If on the other hand, family size differences in height apparently persist beyond puberty it would seem to be evidence that there are factors other than stage of puberty involved in the family size-height relationship, such as different levels of nutrition or illness (although of course, such factors may themselves also be associated with stage of puberty).

The data

At each NCDS follow-up, height was measured by a school medical officer or nurse during a medical examination. At 7, instructions were merely to measure height 'without shoes to the nearest inch'. At 11 and 16 the instruction was to 'position the child against a wall or door, bringing a hard bound book or triangular piece of wood down on the child's head, mark the position of the lower edge with a pencil and then measure its height from the ground with a wood or steel measure to the nearest quarter inch'.

During the examination at age 16 medical officers were also asked to make an assessment of pubertal development including an assessment of the stage of breast development of girls, of facial, axillary and pubertal hair of boys, of whether boys' voices had broken and, additionally, girls were asked if menstruation had commenced. The child's social class was assessed at all ages according to the Registrar-General's Classification of Occupations (1960 at 7, 1966 and 11 and 16) from data obtained during a parental interview. From the same source information about parity (obtained at age 7) was obtained. Because slightly different questions were

* In our own study, by the age of 16, boys' pubic hair was considered 'adult' in 50 per cent of cases; 98 per cent of those girls on whom data were available had reached menarche (Fogelman, 1976). According to a mixed longitudinal study of English children (Marshall and Tanner, 1969 and 1970) mean age of menarche is 13½, with 95 per cent of girls commencing menstruation by around 15½.

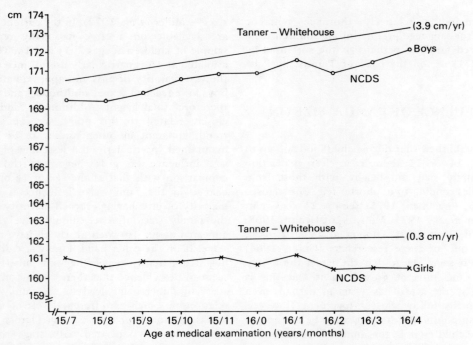

FIGURE 1.14   *Mean height from NCDS and Tanner—Whitehouse standards by age (all means have greater than 20 observations)*

asked at each age, we have no single measure of family size comparable at all three ages. At ages 7 and 11 we have data on those in the extended household under the age of 21, i.e. the child's brothers and sisters together with the relatively small number of young lodgers or other family members currently living in the household and any other children normally living in the household but currently away (i.e. those away at school in term time). At 16 we have information on the number of people in the household under 21 (but not the number in the extended household) and also on the number of siblings the study child had, including those living away from home.

In some later analyses we have partially resolved these difficulties by separating members of the family according to parity — which in the great majority of families is constant — and the number of younger children in the household. For convenience household size is usually referred to as 'family size' and number of younger children in the household as number of 'younger siblings'.

Results

1.   Height at 16

Whether or not children have reached sexual maturity and/or adult stature is clearly a crucial issue in our study of family-size influences on height. In Figure 1.4, therefore, we present the height of our 16-year-old study children according to the age at which they were measured, around 16, in years and months. It can be seen that in the case of boys, those who were in the older age range when measured (i.e. about 16 years 4 months) were on average about 2½ centimetres taller than those measured when eight or nine months younger. In the case of girls, final height has clearly been reached by the vast majority, with the mean height of those examined at over 16 no greater than that of those measured before 16. It can also be seen that our findings very closely resemble the Tanner—Whitehouse standards for the ages covered.

2.   Analysis by simple family size

Figures 1.15 and 1.16 present the crude differences in height in centimetres between boys and girls, and between children with small and large numbers of siblings at 16. The data are compared with those available from other British studies which present data separately at different ages for each sex: the results of the National Survey of Health and Development (NSHD — Douglas and Simpson, 1964), a study of London County Council schoolchildren (Scott, 1961) and of London children rehoused in Hertfordshire (Grant, 1964). Small differences in findings at any one age are probably best ignored due to small anomalies between the studies regarding criteria of 'family size'. Furthermore, family-size trends are not strictly linear, only children being no taller and

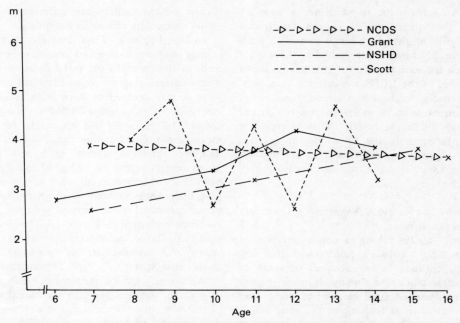

FIGURE 1.15   *Difference in height between boys of one-child families and boys of greater than four-child families (> three in the NSHD)*

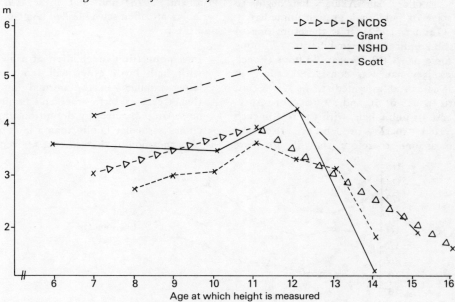

FIGURE 1.16   *Difference in height between girls of one-child families and girls of greater than four-child families (> three in the NHSD)*

sometimes marginally shorter than those of two-child families, in all four studies, particularly at the later ages (see Belmont *et al.*, 1975).

Despite these qualifications, there does seem to be clear evidence (Figure 1.15) from all the studies that family size has a clear influence on boys' height and that indeed it exerts a fairly constant effect on height

from the age of 6 until the age of 16, when the final NCDS measurement was taken. In the case of the NCDS, the difference in height between boys of one-child families and those of four or more was 3.5 centimetres at 16 compared with 3.8 at 11 and 3.9 at 7. Figure 1.16 suggests, however, that in the case of girls the picture is rather different. The NCDS finding at 16 confirms the trend shown at ages 14 and 15 in the other studies — the family-size influence on girls' height which seems to reach a peak at about 11 or 12 is much diminished at those later ages, by which the vast majority of girls have reached sexual maturity. In the NCDS the difference in girls' height between the smallest and largest families fell from 4.1 centimetres at 11 to 1.8 centimetres at age 16 (3.1 at age 7). In the NSHD the difference fell from 5.3 centimetres at age 11 to 2.1 at age 15. Nevertheless, there is no evidence that the family-size influence totally ceases to exist once puberty has been reached.

3.   *Analysis by birth order, younger siblings and state of sexual maturity*

Naturally, any study taking account merely of differences in height between children of large and small families without taking account of stage of puberty is rather crude. As already shown in Figure 1.14 girls have reached final height but there does seem to be a clear need to look at the analyses of boys' height separately for mature and immature boys. We did this using as our criterion stage of development of axillary hair. Axillary hair begins to grow at the stage of pubic hair growth immediately before adult (Tanner, 1962). It is therefore one of the latest possible indices of sexual maturity. Among the whole sample of NCDS 16-year-old boys (Fogelman, 1976) axillary hair was considered 'adult' in 29 per cent of cases and 'intermediate' in 32 per cent compared with figures of 50 and 39 per cent respectively in the case of pubic hair, with the rest in each case being rated 'sparse' or 'absent'. It seems reasonable to assume therefore that if boys are

mature on the axillary-hair criterion, they are likely to be 'mature' by almost any standard.

In fact, Figure 1.17 demonstrates that axillary-hair ratings separate mature and immature boys extremely well. In the case of boys rated in both the adult and intermediate stages of axillary-hair development, final stature seemed to have been attained in most cases since boys measured at different ages in months around 16 years do not appear to be of different mean height. On the other hand, those whose axillary hair was rated as 'absent' or 'sparse' were clearly much shorter regardless of age of examination and in both cases those so rated who were measured when past their 16th birthday were on average taller than those measured at a slightly younger age. On the evidence presented in Figure 1.17, we felt justified in classifying boys whose axillary hair was rated in the 'adult' and 'intermediate' categories as 'mature' and those rated 'sparse or absent' as 'immature'.

Analysis by family size need not only take account of state of puberty but also the fact that the child's birth order, like family size, has a strong relationship with height (Belmont *et al.*, 1975; Grant, 1964; Goldstein, 1971; Miller *et al.*, 1974; Neligan and Prudham, 1976) and that these two independent variables are themselves linked. As Goldstein (1971) points out:

In a population of children at a given age, those with high birth order will tend to come from larger families. In the normal family situation, the effects of birth-order and family-size cannot be separated, since, by definition, the oldest child enters a smaller family than a later-born child. . . It is meaningful therefore at a given age, only to

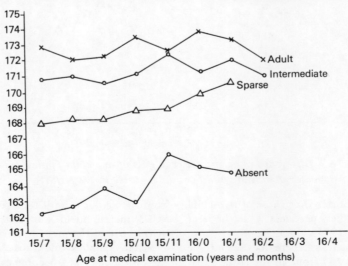

FIGURE 1.17   *Mean height by ratings of boys' axillary hair (all means have greater than twenty observations)*

separate the effect of younger siblings from that of birth-order.

In view of this problem the independent influence on height of birth order and younger siblings have been analysed at each age by means of analysis of variance. A third factor taken into account in these analyses is *social class*. This latter variable is included not only because it is associated with height (e.g. Douglas and Simpson, 1964; Goldstein, 1971; Miller *et al.*, 1972);

Neligan and Prudham, 1976; Tanner, 1962; Topp *et al.*, 1970) — an influence that is possibly declining as and where social conditions improve (e.g. Tanner, 1962; Lindgren, 1976; Moyes, 1976) — but also because it is strongly related to family size (e.g. Douglas and Simpson, 1964; Fogelman, 1975: see pp. 21–7). We have in fact used parity as our measure of birth order. This has the disadvantage that 'birth order' will include in a small number of cases still births and deaths but it has the advantage that it gives us a

TABLE 1.16   *Analysis of children's height at age 7 by social class, parity and number of younger children in the extended household*

Source	Height at 7 — boys (cm)				Height at 7 — girls (cm)			
	$N = 6585$ Total variance = 34.853 Residual mean square = 31.383				$N = 6212$ Total variance = 37.717 Residual mean square = 33.869			
	Fitted constant	se	df	χ^2	Fitted constant	se	df	χ^2
Overall constant	120.34				119.47			
Age coefficient (gain per year measured about 7.0 years)	5.11	0.27	1	346.3***	5.70	0.28	1	407.6***
Father's occupation								
I + II	1.37				1.01			
III + IV NM	0.48				0.53			
III M	−0.24		4	120.5***	−0.41		4	78.0***
IV M + V	−0.85				−0.80			
No male head of household (NMH)	−0.76				−0.33			
Parity 0	1.12		3	128.6***	0.94		3	98.1***
1	0.34				0.53			
2	−0.21				−0.32			
3 +	−1.25				−1.15			
No. of younger children in extended household								
0	1.21		3	111.6***	1.17		3	97.7***
1	0.38				0.49			
2	−0.21				−0.40			
3 +	−1.38				−1.26			

Test of interactions
Father's occupation x parity, $\chi^2 = 22.4$* (12 df) $\chi^2 = 13.8$ ns (12 df)
Father's occupation x no. younger, $\chi^2 - 7.8$ ns (12 df) $\chi^2 = 13.4$ ns (12 df)
Parity x no. younger, $\chi^2 = 17.0$* (9 df) $\chi^2 = 12.1$ ns (9 df)

Significance tests: $p < 0.05$ = *; $p < 0.01$ = **; $p < 0.001$ = ***; ns = non-significant.

TABLE 1.17   *Analysis of children's height at age 11, by social class, parity, and number of younger children in the extended household*

Source		Height at 11 — boys (cm) N = 5 872 Total variance = 47.504 Residual mean square = 43.905				Height at 11 — girls (cm) N = 5 631 Total variance = 54.826 Residual mean square = 51.161			
		Fitted constant	se	df	χ^2	Fitted constant	se	df	χ^2
Overall constant		140.90				141.58			
Age coefficient (gain per year measured about 11.0 years)		5.52	0.47	1	136.5***	6.02	0.52	1	134.3***
Father's occupation	I + II	1.25				1.19			
	III + IV NM	0.76				0.67			
	III M	−0.24		4	86.6***	−0.37		4	60.7***
	IV M + V	−1.01				−0.73			
	NMH	−0.76				−0.76			
Parity	0	1.15				1.04			
	1	0.44		3	90.2***	0.54		3	84.0***
	2	−0.26				0.02			
	3+	−1.33				−1.60			
No. of younger children in extended household	0	1.49				1.41			
	1	0.44		3	142.1***	0.60		3	103.6***
	2	−0.10				−0.47			
	3+	−1.83				−1.54			

Test of interactions
Father's occupation x parity, $\chi^2 = 11.1$ ns (12 df) $\chi^2 = 20.8$ ns (12 df)
Father's occupation x no. younger, $\chi^2 = 8.6$ ns (12 df) $\chi^2 = 11.2$ ns (12 df)
Parity x no. younger, $\chi^2 = 20.9$ ns (9 df) $\chi^2 = 19.1$* (9 df)

measure comparable at all three ages (see also Goldstein, 1971).

Tables 1.16–1.19 present the figures relating to the individual effects of each of parity, number of younger siblings in the household, social class, and age in years and months, at date of examination, while controlling for the other three variables at each of the three follow-ups.

Table 1.20 summarises the data in Tables 1.16–1.19 in a more simple form by looking at adjusted differences in height between the extremes of parity, number of younger siblings and social class. Again caution is required in interpretation as trends are not all linear. Figures 1.18–1.20 demonstrate graphically the differing influence parity and number of younger siblings have for each sex at each age.

At age 7 (Table 1.16) differences in height associated with parity and number of younger siblings are similar for boys and girls so that in each case children with three or more younger siblings and two or more previous live births are about 5 centimetres shorter than those of zero parity and with no younger siblings. There were significant interactions in the case of boys between social class and parity ($p < 0.05$) and parity and number of younger siblings ($p < 0.05$). In the latter case, boys of parity 2 with two younger siblings are slightly shorter than those with three younger siblings while among those with two younger siblings those of parity 3 or more are marginally taller than those of parity 2. Figure 1.21 illustrates this interaction, suggesting perhaps that its importance should not be exaggerated. There was also an inter-

TABLE 1.18 *Analysis of children's height at age 16 by social class, parity and number of younger children in the extended household*

Source		Height at 16 — boys (cm)				Height at 16 — girls (cm)			
		$N = 4\,465$ Total variance = 64.7 Residual mean square = 61.704				$N = 4\,257$ Total variance = 40.721 Residual mean square = 39.440			
		Fitted constant	se	df	χ^2	Fitted constant	se	df	χ^2
Overall constant		170.35				160.91			
Age coefficient (gain per year measured about 16.0 years)		3.24	0.65	1	25.0***	1.00	0.52	1	3.7 ns
Father's occupation	I + II	1.25				1.32			
	III + IV NM	0.82		4	50.2***	0.60		4	76.4***
	III M	−0.49				−0.43			
	IV + V M	−0.88				−1.05			
	NMH	−0.70				−0.44			
Parity	0	0.93				0.58			
	1	0.61		3	48.0***	0.25		3	28.4***
	2	−0.05				0.19			
	3 +	−1.49				−1.02			
No. of younger children in household	0	1.34				0.61			
	1	0.32		3	79.7***	0.21		3	17.7***
	2	0.33				−0.30			
	3 +	−1.99				−0.52			

Test of interactions
Father's occupation x parity, $\chi^2 = 16.6$ ns (12 df) $\chi^2 = 8.5$ ns (12 df)
Father's occupation x no. younger children = 6.5 ns (12 df) $\chi^2 = 6.6$ ns (12 df)
Parity x younger children = 12.8 ns (9 df) $\chi^2 = 15.0$ ns (9 df)

action between these variables at age 11 in the case of both sexes. Although the effects of parity and younger children were for the most part independent, there were several instances in which adjacent parity categories overlapped.

At age 11 the results were broadly similar to those at 7 but at the age of 16 the parity effect for girls is much diminished, while among boys it remains similar to that at the earlier ages. Similarly the effect of having younger siblings is also much less among girls than at previous ages and less than that among boys. It seems, therefore, that the influence of having competing older and younger siblings, as reflected in the family-size situation presented in Figure 1.16, is still present among girls at 16, but much diminished. Among boys, on the other hand, the individual and combined effect of older and younger siblings remains fairly constant, as in the case of the overall family-size influence.

If stage of puberty is, as suggested, the main determinant of the influence on height of factors associated with family size, we may anticipate that in the case of mature boys the influence of parity and number of younger siblings will be similar to that operating in the case of (mature) girls. Table 1.19 does provide some evidence to support such a belief: the parity effect is similar for mature boys and girls (although only slightly less than for immature boys) and the younger sibling effect much less among mature boys than among immature boys, though still almost twice that which exists in the case of girls.

Another point of interest in these analyses is that

(continued p. 54)

TABLE 1.19   *Separate analysis of height at age 16 by social class, parity and number of younger children in the household, for mature and immature boys*

Source		Height at 16 — mature boys (cm)				Height at 16 — immature boys (cm)			
		N = 2 718 Total variance = 51.873 Residual mean square = 50.448				N = 1 704 Total variance = 68.676 Residual mean square = 65.516			
		Fitted constant	se	df	χ^2	Fitted constant	se	df	χ^2
Overall constant		172.18				167.74			
Age coefficient (gain per year measured about 16)		1.88	0.73	1	6.6***	3.79	1.13	1	11.2***
Father's occupation	I + II	1.09				1.24			
	III + IV NM	0.66		4	28.6***	0.73		4	19.7***
	III M	−0.44				−0.70			
	IV + V M	−0.80				−1.01			
	(NMH)	−0.51				−0.26			
Parity	0	0.50				0.93			
	1	0.49		3	18.9***	0.59		3	14.8***
	2	0.28				−0.35			
	3+	−1.27				−1.17			
Younger children in the household	0	0.86				1.29			
	1	0.27		3	20.9***	0.28		3	40.3***
	2	0.03				0.81			
	3+	−1.16				−2.38			

Test of interactions
Father's occupation x parity, χ^2 = 9.5 ns (12 df) χ^2 = 19.1 ns (12 df)
Father's occupation x no. younger, χ^2 = 10.6 ns (12 df) χ^2 = 8.2 ns (12 df)
Parity x no. younger, χ^2 = 15.2 ns (9 df) χ^2 = 16.4 ns (9 df)

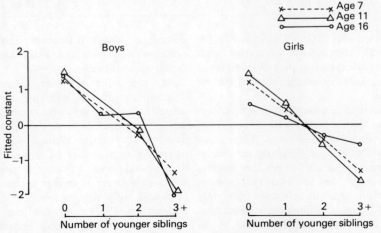

FIGURE 1.18   *Fitted constants for height (cm) at 7, 11 and 16: number of younger siblings adjusted for age, father's occupation and parity*

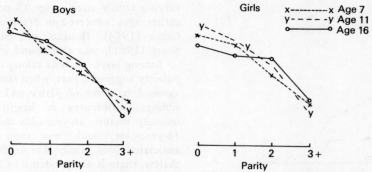

FIGURE 1.19 *Fitted constants for height (cm) at 7, 11 and 16: parity adjusted for age, father's occupation and number of younger siblings*

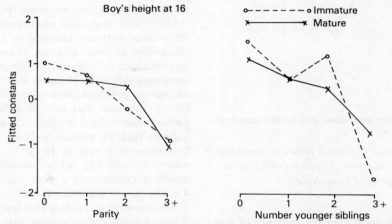

FIGURE 1.20 *Fitted constants for boys height (cm) at 16: parity and number of younger siblings adjusted for each other and for age and father's occupation*

TABLE 1.20 *Summary table: adjusted difference in height in centimetres between children of the extreme of parity, number of younger siblings and father's occupation*

	Girls			Boys			Mature boys 16	Immature boys 16
	Age 7	11	16	7	11	16		
Between children of 0 parity and children of ≥ 3	2.1	2.6	1.6	2.4	2.5	2.4	1.8	2.1
Between children with 0 and 3 + younger siblings	3.0	3.0	1.1	2.6	3.3	2.6	2.0	3.7
Combined effect* of the above 2	5.1	5.6	2.7	5.0	5.8	5.0	3.8	5.8
Between children of social class I and II and those of IV and V Manual	1.8	1.9	2.4	2.2	2.3	2.1	1.9	2.2

* Ignoring interactions (see p. 50).

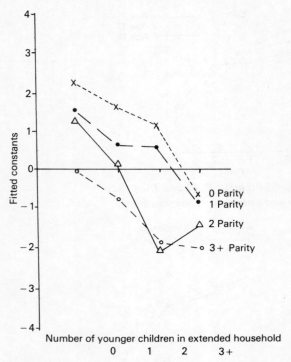

FIGURE 1.21   *Fitted constants for boys' height at 7 (cm): parity by number of younger children in extended household*

varying family sizes at age 14 or 15, compared with earlier ages, observed in previous British studies by Grant (1964), Douglas and Simpson (1964) and Scott (1961), was also found in the current study.

Among boys, analysis taking into account stage of puberty suggested that, when family-size factors were assessed in terms of parity and number of younger siblings, differences in height were less among sexually mature 16-year-olds than among immature 16-year-olds, and less than those differences associated with family size at the earlier age. Nevertheless, there is also evidence in Tables 1.18 and 1.19 that there are differences in height between boys and girls from differing family sizes which exist beyond puberty. In this respect, therefore, it is perhaps true that we should be no more positive than Scott (1961), who suggested that '*part, at least*, of the differences between children in the various family size groups at these ages can be accounted for by the varying ages of maturity', though some of the remaining influence of parity and number of younger siblings on girls and mature boys could be accounted for by the fact that not all girls or 'mature' boys have attained final height. Tables 1.18 and 1.19 indicate that, on average, girls are still growing about 1 centimetre a year at 16 (compared with 6 centimetres at age 11), while mature boys are gaining nearly 2 centimetres a year (compared with about 4 in the case of immature boys).

On the other hand, it is also true that there is some evidence from earlier studies that factors associated with family size do exist beyond puberty. Scott, for example, found that when the height of 13-year-old girls with varying numbers of siblings was analysed separately for those who had and had not attained menarche, differences were reduced, but there remained a 'pronounced family size gradient'. (It is true, of course, that 'menarche is only a single event in the combination of physical changes which constitute puberty' — Marshall and Tanner, 1969.) Topp *et al.* (1970), in a study of Kent schoolchildren, found that there was still a difference in height between girls from differing sizes of family in the 14—17 age range, by when the large majority should have commenced menstruation. Belmont *et al.* (1975) found that among 19-year-old Dutch men height was negatively correlated with family size at all levels of birth order within social class. The family-size effect was also identified among 20-year-old French army recruits (Trémolieres and Boulanger, 1950). The 1 000 family study in Newcastle found that, among girls but not boys, there were differences in height according to birth order of those measured at 22 years of age, but these differences were much less marked than at 15. (The authors claim that trends by family size 'are very similar to those by

the data apparently contradict the evidence of some recent foreign studies (e.g. Lindgren, 1976; Moyes, 1976; Christiansen *et al.*, 1975) by suggesting there is, in Britain, a significant difference in height between children from differing socio-economic backgrounds at all ages. In the current study we found, after allowing for age of measurement, differences in height between boys of social class I and II and boys of social class IV or V, of 2.7, 2.9 and 2.8 centimetres at ages 7, 11 and 16 respectively. Among girls the comparable figures were 2.3, 2.7 and 2.7 centimetres. Differences after also making allowance for parity and number of younger siblings are slightly reduced, but still significant (see the summary in Table 1.20).

Summary and discussion

Data available from a nationally representative longitudinal study suggest that whether we look at family size directly, or in terms of the number of previous live births and of younger siblings, there is some evidence that, among sexually mature children, the influence of family-size factors on height is less than among sexually immature children. An apparent lessening of differences in height between girls of birth rank'.) Hence the evidence of our own study, like previous studies, is not wholly conclusive. It does suggest that, while family-size differences in height are strongly linked to family-size differences in age of puberty, they may also be associated with economic and/or environmental factors such as different levels of diet, nutrition and illness. The relationship between family size, height and diet is, as a government report put it, 'a matter of some uncertainty' (Ministry of Health, 1968), though there was in fact a suggestion in the same report that height of children could possibly be associated with milk consumption. Similarly, a study of Kent schoolchildren by Cook *et al.* (1973) suggested that family-size differences in height discovered by an earlier study of the same children (Topp *et al.*, 1970) did not appear to be associated with differences in total nutrient intake, but may have had some link with the poorer *quality* of diet of those from large families, as assessed by nutrient intake per 1 000 kcal. Grant (1964) suggested that poorer growth of children from larger families could have an association with a greater risk of infection among larger families.

All these findings are highly tentative, and we have no evidence as to which, if any, of these factors influence the relationship between family size and height, and to what degree. None the less it does seem apparent from our study that since differences in height linked with family size persist at least into early childhood, the association of stage of puberty with height and family size may not wholly explain why children from larger families tend to be shorter.

2 Housing*

HOUSING FOR CHILDREN: FURTHER FINDINGS FROM THE NATIONAL CHILD DEVELOPMENT STUDY

Several studies have examined the housing situation in Britain (Donnison, 1967; Cullingworth, 1965) and have described the changes taking place in the pattern of housing tenure and in the types and size of household, at a national level. These studies did not, however, concentrate on the specific housing needs of any particular groups of people, such as the old, or families with children. The National Child Development Study provides an opportunity to look at the conditions and recent changes in housing as they affect children.

The importance of housing conditions for children at the age of 7 was considered in the report on the first follow-up of the NCDS (Davie *et al.* 1972), where it was shown that unsatisfactory housing conditions were related to the child's educational attainment. In addition to this, it seems inevitable that a child's housing situation will affect his opportunities for play, likelihood of undisturbed sleep, and his health, all of which are important factors in contributing to a child's happiness.

* Original sources: Essen, J. and Parrinder, D., 'Housing for children: further findings from the National Child Development Study', *Housing Review*, vol. 24, no. 4, 1975; Essen, J. and Fogelman, K., 'Childhood housing experiences', *Concern*, no. 32, 1979; Essen, J., Fogelman, K. and Head, J., 'Childhood housing experiences and school attainment', *Child: Care, Health and Development*, 4, 1978, 41—58; Essen, J., Fogelman, K. and Head, J., 'Children's housing and their health and physical development', *Child: Care, Health and Development*, 4, 1978, 357—69; Tibbenham, A., 'Housing and truancy', *New Society*, 10 March 1977.

Using data from the NCDS we are able to examine the extent to which the prevalence of overcrowding, the lack of basic amenities in the household and the availability of play facilities vary in different regions of Britain and between different tenure groups and social classes. We can also describe some of the changes which took place between 1965, when the children were 7, and 1969, when they were 11.

Overcrowding

Overcrowding is defined here as in the 1961 Census: a household is considered overcrowded if it has more than 1.5 persons per room. This is not a generous measure, and many households not falling in this category might consider themselves to be short of space.

The proportion of children in the study living in overcrowded conditions is high, namely 14.7 per cent at the age of 7, reducing only slightly to 12.1 per cent at the age of 11. The question to be considered here is whether some children are more likely than others to be overcrowded.

Overcrowding is strongly related to the family's social class — defined according to the Registrar-General's (1966) classification of the father's occupation. For example, at the age of 11, children whose fathers have unskilled manual jobs are more than ten times as likely to come from an overcrowded home as children whose fathers are in professional and managerial jobs.

There are also considerable regional differences. Table 2.1 shows proportions of children who were living in overcrowded homes in different parts of the country. The most striking figure in this table is for

TABLE 2.1   *Crowding among 11-year-olds by Regions*

	North	Midlands	London and South-East	South and South-West	Wales	Scotland	All
% overcrowded	11.7	8.6	10.4	6.7	9.5	32.0	12.1
% not overcrowded	88.3	91.4	89.6	93.5	90.5	68.0	87.9
			N = 13 797				

Scotland, where nearly one-third of children were overcrowded at age 11.

It is to be expected, given the present housing stock and its slow rate of change (Donnison, 1967), that large families are more likely to be overcrowded than small families. This was found to be so, with only 3.8 per cent of 11-year-olds from families with one to four children overcrowded, as against the alarmingly high figure of 57.2 per cent of children from families with five or more children. (Differences are only quoted in the text if they are statistically significant at the 5 per cent level or above.)

Poor housing conditions are often assumed to occur predominantly in privately rented accommodation, so it is not surprising to find the highest prevalence of overcrowding (38 per cent) in the furnished private rented sector. However, if we consider the unfurnished private rented sector, overcrowding is not as common in this tenure group as in council housing: some 20.1 per cent of children from council houses live in overcrowded homes, compared with 16 per cent of children from the unfurnished private rented sector. As a high proportion of 11-year-old children lives in council housing (43.8 per cent), the inadequate supply of housing suitable for larger families can be seen most acutely in the council-rented sector, which houses as many as 70 per cent of all children from overcrowded homes.

As was stated above, the prevalence of overcrowding at the age of 11 was slightly less than when the children were 7, and Table 2.2 enables us to look at this in more detail. Although approximately 18 per cent of children were in an overcrowded home either at 7 or 11, only about 8 per cent were in that situation at both 7 and 11. Nearly twice as many children had ceased to be overcrowded by 11 as had become so between 7 and 11. The percentages quoted here differ slightly from the corresponding figures quoted earlier due to incomplete data.

TABLE 2.2   *Crowding at 7 and 11*

	Overcrowded at 11	Not overcrowded at 11
Overcrowded at 7	7.9%	6.5%
Not overcrowded at 7	3.4%	82.2%

N = 11 842

The reasons for this overall reduction in overcrowding are probably twofold. The 'housing cycle' (Cullingworth, 1965; Donnison, 1967) may account for some of this. After the birth of the first child a family needs more space; however, they often cannot

afford it or find it for some years, so they are more likely to be overcrowded, and the necessary improvement in their housing does not take place until the children are older, when their income or their savings may be greater. The second reason could be that there has been a general improvement in children's housing. This was shown in an earlier paper (Parrinder, 1972) which compares NCDS findings with both the 1966 Census figures and the results from the National Survey of Health and Development which followed through a sample of children born in one week of March 1946 (Douglas, 1964).

Amenities

A second measure of housing conditions used in the present study is the availability in the home of basic amenities — an indoor lavatory, a hot water supply, and a bathroom. These three amenities are considered separately below as well as being combined into a single amenity scale. Once again it was found that a considerable number of the children suffered from such deficiencies in their housing (see Table 2.3).

TABLE 2.3   *Children in households which share or lack amenities at age 11*

Use of amenity	Indoor lavatory	Bathroom	Hot water	Share or lack at least one of these
% shared	1.3	1.4	0.7	12.3
% lacked	9.4	5.3	3.5	

N = 12 711

Certain groups of children can be identified who are particularly likely to share or lack these basic amenities. For example, there was a clear social-class trend. Just over one in five of children whose fathers had unskilled manual jobs but only about one in twenty-five of children with fathers in professional or managerial jobs shared or lacked one or more of these amenities.

Considerable regional differences were also apparent. Whereas Scottish children have a higher chance of being overcrowded than children from Wales or England, they are the least likely to share or lack amenities. Both these findings are to be expected to some extent because of the relatively high numbers of children in council housing in Scotland. It was the Welsh children, with 18.9 per cent from homes which were deficient in amenities, who were the worst placed on this measure.

There was some improvement in the availability of amenities between the ages of 7 and 11, though the proportion of children having to manage without some amenities in 1969 was still high, at 12.3 per cent, the figure in 1965 having been 18.5 per cent.

This improvement mainly took place in the owner-occupied and private rented sectors, though there were still great shortages of amenities in the private rented sector in 1969. Table 2.4 shows the proportion of children in each tenure group who had to share or lacked some of the basic amenities at either the age of 7 or 11.

TABLE 2.4   *Household amenities by tenure**

Amenity scale	Owner-occupied	Council rented	Private rented	Total
% shared or lacked — 1965	14.5	9.5	57.6	17.6
% shared or lacked — 1969	8.7	8.6	48.7	11.7

N = 12 081

* These tenure groups are not exhaustive, as 'rent free', 'tied to occupation' and 'other' categories have been excluded.

The table shows that as the improvement in the owner-occupied sector was not matched by a corresponding improvement in the council sector, by 1969 the two tenure groups had similar shortages of amenities. However, these apparent improvements for the 11-year-old children partly reflect moves from one tenure group to another, particularly moves out of the poorly equipped private rented sector as well as improvements within each type of tenure.

Bed sharing

There were some 17 per cent of children in the study who were sharing a bed at the age of 11. As might be expected, bed sharing is more common when the home is overcrowded. However, Table 2.5 shows that children who came from homes which were not overcrowded were more likely to share a bed if those homes were deficient in amenities. On the other hand, if the home were overcrowded, the likelihood of the child sharing a bed was equally high whether or not the house was well supplied with basic amenities.

Housing quality

The frequency with which children are found to be living in poor housing conditions leads to particular

TABLE 2.5   *Percentages of children sharing a bed at 11 within each crowding-by-amenity group*

Amenity scale	Crowding (persons/room)				Total proportion
	≤1.0	≤1.5	≤2.0	>2.0	
Sole use of	7.1	24.0	41.7	62.7	15.6
Not sole use of all	12.7	35.7	41.2	64.2	28.5
Total proportion	7.6	25.6	41.6	63.3	17.2

N = 13 532

concern about the effect of low-quality housing on the child. Table 2.6 shows the proportions of children living in poor-quality housing (defined by combining the overcrowding index with the amenities index) in 1965, or 1969, or both.

TABLE 2.6   *Percentages of children in three categories of housing quality* at 7 and 11*

		Housing quality at 11 years			
		A	B	C	Total
Housing	A*	1.3	1.4	1.7	4.5
quality at	B*	0.8	11.9	9.9	22.6
7 years	C*	0.4	4.4	68.1	72.9
	Total	2.5	17.7	79.8	100.0

N = 11 621

* Housing quality groups defined as:
A >1.5 persons per room and not sole use of the three basic amenities.
B >1.5 persons per room or not sole use of the three basic amenities.
C ≤1.5 persons per room and sole use of the three amenities.

The table shows that although only 1.3 per cent of children lived in poor-quality housing at both 7 and 11, a further 1.4 per cent lived in housing that was either overcrowded or deficient in amenities at both ages.

Play facilities

In addition to the physical quality of the home itself, a further important factor in a consideration of the quality of the child's environment is the play facilities which are available in the area.

According to the parents' reports, 8.1 per cent of the 11-year-old children had access to neither a park nor a recreation ground, and less than 60 per cent of the children had access to both these kinds of play space. Unlike the other measures of housing conditions used in the study, there was no social-class trend in the reported availability of outdoor play space. This does not mean that working-class children are as well placed for play outside as middle-class children. At the age of 7 (there are no comparable data at the age of 11) there was a highly significant social-class trend in the possession of gardens and yards, with middle-class children being the most likely to have these facilities (Davie *et al.*, 1972).

When the regional distribution of outdoor play space was examined, it was found that a similar proportion (about 9.5 per cent) of children from the Northern area of England (defined by combining the first two groups in Table 2.1) and from Scotland and Wales had access to neither a park nor a recreation ground. However, in the South of England the provision was considerably better; only 5.9 per cent of the children did not have access to either amenity.

This absence of play facilities is particularly serious when the households concerned are over-crowded, and have no back gardens, as these children must be in danger of having nowhere suitable to play at all. There are clearly great inadequacies in the provision of play amenities, and this is felt strongly by the parents, one-third of whom reported being dissatisfied with the play amenities in the area. The level of satisfaction showed a clear relationship with the availability of amenities.

However, the parents were also asked if they were satisfied with their housing conditions, and only 12.1 per cent reported that they were dissatisfied. This seems a very low proportion in view of the poor conditions that so many families are suffering from. The reasons for this have been discussed before (Wedge and Prosser, 1973), where it was suggested that comparisons with neighbours and the need for self-esteem tended to reduce the numbers who were prepared to admit that their homes were unsatisfactory.

Summary

In summary, the National Child Development Study shows that the quality of the environment in which considerable numbers of children live is unsatisfactory in several respects. In particular, one-fifth of the children were suffering from a lack of amenities in the household, or cramped conditions, or both, in 1969.

Taking the data collected in 1965 and 1969 into account we find that nearly one-third of the children were reported as living in such inadequate conditions on at least one of these occasions. This is in fact likely to understate the number of children who experienced these conditions by the age of 11, since our figures cannot include those who did so before the age of 7 or between the ages of 7 and 11, but who did not happen to fall into this category at the times our information was collected.

CHILDHOOD HOUSING EXPERIENCES

Publication of the Shelter report *No Place to Grow Up* (Fairbairns and Wintour, 1977) highlighted the particular concern for the housing conditions of children. There is now a considerable body of research demonstrating the special problems experienced by families with children, and showing the link between inadequate housing and, for example, poor school performance and health.

However, the great majority of this work has been concerned with young, pre-adolescent children. The data collected for the third follow-up of the National Child Development Study have enabled us to examine whether the relationships found among younger children also hold among 16-year-olds, and, more interestingly, whether there is one age during childhood at which housing conditions are most crucial for later development (see later papers). This paper will set these findings in perspective by finding out how many children are involved and identifying the amount of change and constancy in children's housing experiences during their years in school. We shall also compare the 16-year findings with those of a national sample born twelve years earlier.

The information with which we are concerned here is taken from the pre-coded form completed by health visitors in the course of interviewing the child's parents (usually the mother). Among the questions asked, several related to the family's home including the availability of basic amenities, namely bathroom, hot water supply and indoor lavatory, and the type of accommodation, for example whether the family lived in a house or a flat. From information provided on the number of people in the household and the number of rooms available it was possible to calculate a 'crowding ratio', and the usual convention has been followed of considering homes with a ratio greater than 1.5 persons per room as crowded.

Regional differences

The first striking finding which emerges from the 16-year information is the contrast among the three home countries. Table 2.7 demonstrates this for a number of measures.

The major contrast is between Scotland and the rest. People in Scotland were considerably more likely to be living in accommodation rented from the council, and to be in flats rather than houses or bungalows. Council housing is likely to be well provided with the amenities of bathroom, hot water supply and indoor lavatory, so the Scots are relatively well off in this respect, but is often less likely to provide space for larger families, and hence the difference in crowding.

TABLE 2.7   *Housing situation of 16-year-olds*

	England (%)	Wales (%)	Scotland (%)	Overall (%)
In council house	39	39	71	41
In houses or bungalows	93	97	69	90
In flats	7	2	30	9
Crowded	7	4	22	8
Without sole use of 3 amenities	2	11	4	6
N	9 602	607	1 307	11 516

Of course, not all those in flats are in 'high-rise' blocks: 8 per cent of the Scots live in buildings with four or more floors compared with 3 per cent of the English. Flat-dwelling of any kind is relatively rare among the Welsh children.

Historical comparisons

How do the housing circumstances of adolescents compare with those of the previous decade? It is possible to answer this question by comparing NCDS figures with those obtained by the National Survey of Health and Development, a longitudinal study of children born in Britain in one week in March 1946. The two samples are not exactly comparable, but can be made so, by producing weighted population estimates from the 1946 study — which the researchers on that study have kindly done, and supplied us with their results — and by excluding the illegitimate children, twins and immigrants from the 1958 cohort. Both studies collected their data during the children's last compulsory year at school, but this of course means at the age of 15 for children born in 1946.

The major differences which appear between the two studies are summarised in Table 2.8. That there has been some change in the types of dwellings which families with adolescents inhabit is shown by the last two pairs of figures in the table. A greater proportion of the later-born cohort lived in a house or bungalow, with a corresponding reduction in those in flats or 'rooms'. This has been accompanied by a marked improvement in amenities. Almost one in five of 15-year-olds in 1961 did not have a bathroom available, whereas by 1974 the figure for 16-year-olds is one in fifty. There has been a similar reduction in crowding, where the difference (although statistically significant) is relatively small. On the other hand, there has been a large reduction in the proportion actually having to share a bed.

These comparisons suggest that in some respects

TABLE 2.8   *Adolescents' housing in 1961 and 1974*

	NSHD — age 15 in 1961 (%)	NCDS — age 16 in 1974 (%)
Crowded	11	8
Sharing a bed	20	7
Without available bathroom	18	2
In house or bungalow	84	91

there have been considerable improvements in the housing of adolescents. However, even among the later-born cohort there are large numbers of children in conditions of discomfort. Furthermore, the overall improvement may, as we have seen, hide substantial regional variations.

Housing standards over time

In considering the situation at age 16 it is important to know whether the current circumstances reflect a situation which the child has experienced throughout its life or for only a relatively short period. By presenting a picture of adverse housing circumstances at one age, one may be substantially underestimating the extent of problems if there are large numbers who have had equal difficulties at an earlier stage in their lives.

To a large extent this question can be answered using NCDS data, since, as has already been mentioned, the children have been studied at the ages of 7, 11 and 16. Even here it should be borne in mind that the total proportion ever experiencing poor housing conditions between 7 and 16 will be underestimated, since no account is taken of the situation between follow-ups.

The figures for the main two indices of housing standard with which we have been concerned, crowding and amenities, can be seen in Table 2.9.

TABLE 2.9   *Crowding and amenities at three ages*

	Crowded (%)	Sharing or lacking amenities (%)
At all three ages	4	3
At 7 and 11, but not 16	4	5
At 11 and 16, but not 7	1	1
At 7 and 16, but not 11	1	1
At 7 only	6	8
At 11 only	2	2
At 16 only	1	2
Total at 7, 11 or 16	19	22

The first pattern which emerges is not unexpected in view of what is known about the 'housing cycle' (Donnison, 1967), namely that children's circumstances generally improve as they get older. For example, as can be calculated from Table 2.9, 15 per cent were crowded at the age of 7, 11 per cent at age 11 and 7 per cent at age 16.

Thus there are considerable changes in the course of the child's life mostly in the direction of improvement. Indeed, with respect to both crowding and amenities, the largest group in Table 2.9 is that which had poor housing at 7, but at neither of the later ages. Change in the other direction is relatively infrequent, though it should be pointed out that since there are some 800,000 16-year-olds in Britain even 1 per cent represents a by no means negligible number.

The overlap of crowding and amenities

An obvious question concerning Table 2.9 is whether the children shown as crowded all lacked amenities and vice versa. In fact, the overlap is quite small. For example, of the children known to have been crowded, 35 per cent had also lacked amenities at some time. Thus one-third of the children will have experienced one or other aspect of poor housing by the age of 16.

Taken together, the figures in Tables 2.8 and 2.9 confirm both that there have been considerable changes in housing circumstances in the twelve years between the NSHD and the NCDS, and also that individual families within which children are growing up have generally seen an improvement in their circumstances. However, as far as the overall housing stock is concerned, the combination of a marked decrease in bed-sharing by adolescents, but a smaller decrease in bed sharing by adolescents, but a smaller partly the result of families being better able to equip their homes, whereas the availability of suitably sized homes has not necessarily shown so much improvement.

Conclusions

Whatever the extent of overall improvement, the present situation can hardly be considered satisfactory when at least one in five of children who reach school-leaving age have experienced an overcrowded home, and a similar proportion has at some time in their school years not had the basic amenities of a bathroom, hot water supply and indoor lavatory. Furthermore, there are clearly parts of Great Britain where the situation is even worse. In times of economic recession it may be unrealistic to make generalised pleas for improvement, but if priorities must be determined then, where housing is concerned,

children are, as Parrinder has shown, relatively disadvantaged, at least in some respects. The likely adverse consequences may have long-term implications both for the children themselves and society. At the very least, it is important to continue to monitor the situation to ensure that the special circumstances of children are not hidden by the overall figures presented by the Census.

CHILDHOOD HOUSING EXPERIENCES AND SCHOOL ATTAINMENT

Introduction

The considerable numbers of households in housing difficulties in the population as a whole have often been the subject of study (Donnison, 1967; Cullingworth, 1965; Department of the Environment, 1975), in the course of which some attention has been paid to the very different types of housing problems which families with children experience (Parrinder, 1972; Davie *et al.*, 1972). However, only a few studies have considered the development of children who live in unsatisfactory homes, and the work that has been done in this area has been concerned with young, pre-adolescent, children.

Among these, the studies of 7-year-olds (Davie *et al.*, 1972; Wedge and Petzing, 1970), primary school-age children (Plowden, 1967) and 10- or 11-year-olds (Douglas, 1964; Rutter *et al.*, 1970; Fogelman, 1975; see pp. 21–7) showed that children in poor housing conditions had lower scores on tests of school attainment than children in more adequate housing conditions. The purpose of the first part of this paper is to find out whether this relationship between housing and school attainment also holds among 16-year-olds. The question then considered is whether children differ in their attainment at school at 16 according to their experiences of housing conditions throughout childhood, and whether there is any evidence for a particular age at which housing circumstances are most crucial for eventual attainment.

The final part is concerned not only with attainment at 16, but also with progress during the secondary school years, i.e. 16-year attainment after allowing for pre-existing differences at 11.

The general question of whether home and family circumstances continue to be associated with progress in school has been considered before for 11-year-olds (Douglas, 1964; Fogelman and Goldstein, 1976; see pp. 27–36), and, in the context of variables other than housing circumstances, for adolescents (Ross and Simpson, 1971; Douglas *et al.*, 1968; Fogelman *et al.*, 1978b: see pp. 36–42). Ross and Simpson (1971) considered two environmental factors, family size and parental education, and found that these factors were related to the children's rate of progress from 8 to 15. In agreement with these results, Fogelman *et al.* (1978b) found that family size, sex, social class and region were each associated with the children's progress in school between 11 and 16.

Data

A pre-coded form eliciting information about the children's family and housing situation was completed by a health visitor in the course of an interview with the child's parents. Three aspects of the children's housing circumstances have been used here:

1. Crowding in the household (as defined in the 1961 Census): households with more than one and a half persons per room have been considered crowded.
2. Access to basic amenities: adequate amenities defined as sole use by the household of a bathroom, hot water supply and an indoor lavatory.
3. Tenure: owner-occupied, rented from council, privately rented.

Method

The technique used to investigate the relationship between housing and attainment, after adjusting for other factors, was analysis of variance. The relative progress in school of children with different housing patterns was analysed by means of an analysis of covariance, allowing for each child's 11-year score.

Response levels

The level of response in the study as a whole was high, and an analysis of the representativeness of the responders to the 16-year-old follow-up showed that the extent of bias was small, except in a few minority groups (see pp. 9—20). However, as the present study involved consideration of housing conditions at each of three follow-ups, the numbers in the sample are considerably reduced, as only children with almost complete data could be included. A further study of bias in the children included in these analyses was therefore carried out, but this showed that although those without complete data had slightly lower mean scores overall this did not affect the difference in test scores between children in different housing conditions.

Results

Housing and attainment at 16

Earlier analyses of housing at age 11 showed that children in unsatisfactory housing conditions tend to come from the manual backgrounds and from large families, and to have other characteristics that are themselves related to school attainment. Therefore, in relating performance at school to housing conditions, allowance was made for these factors, by means of analysis of variance. Apart from the housing variables, the factors included in the analysis were: region of the country (North, Midlands or South of England, Wales or Scotland); family size (the number of children under 21 in the household); sex; social class (the occupation of the male head of household, categorised according to the Registrar-General's Classification of Occupations, 1966); parents' educational level (indicated by their age of leaving school); and, as an indication of parental attitudes to education, teachers' reports of whether the parents had visited the school during the current year to discuss the child's progress.

Table 2.10 shows that, after allowing for these factors, crowding, amenities and tenure at 16 all remained significantly related to both reading and maths attainment at 16. Children in crowded homes and those lacking amenities had lower scores than other children, as did those living in council homes. The average differences associated with these variables were fairly similar, in terms of standard deviation score, for the two tests. They range from about one-sixth of the overall standard deviation (the contrast on the maths test between those with and without the sole use of amenities) to one-third of a standard deviation (between children of owner-occupiers and the other groups, on the same test).

There were no significant interactions between the housing variables, which means that the difference in test score associated with each housing characteristic was independent of the other characteristics.

Comparisons with preliminary analyses of mean test scores of children in different housing conditions showed that by allowing for background factors the differences in test scores between the children in crowded and not-crowded homes were reduced by just over 20 per cent for both reading and maths, and the differences between children in owner-occupied and council-rented homes were reduced by about one-half on each test. The differences between children with and without amenities were not greatly affected by allowing for other family circumstances.

Patterns of housing conditions

School attainment has been shown above to be related to current housing conditions for 16-year-olds as well as for 11-year-olds and 7-year-olds.

The question which these findings together lead to is whether the relationship with attainment varies

TABLE 2.10 *Analyses of variance*

Independent variables at 16 yrs		Reading score at 16 (transformed) $N = 7\,225$ Total variance = 0.975				Maths score at 16 (transformed) $N = 7\,190$ Total variance = 0.970			
		Fitted constant	se	df	χ^2	Fitted constant	se	df	χ^2
Overall constant		−0.348				−0.261			
Crowding (<1.5 ⩾1.5)		0.274	0.042	1	41.6***	0.217	0.043	1	25.6***
Amenities (Sole − not sole)		0.219	0.046	1	22.3***	0.154	0.047	1	10.7***
Tenure:	owner	0.135		2	118.3***	0.166		2	153.2***
	council	−0.138				−0.147			
	private rent	0.003				−0.200			
Region:	North	−0.026		4	28.8***	−0.049		4	79.6***
	Midlands	−0.043				−0.058			
	South	0.021				−0.010			
	Wales	−0.083				−0.127			
	Scotland	0.131				0.244			
Family size (⩽3 − >3)		0.243	0.027	1	83.5***	0.136	0.027	1	25.3***
Sex (boy−girl)		0.056	0.021	1	7.3**	0.188	0.021	1	80.5***
Social class:	Non-Manual	0.384		3	333.3***	0.364		3	373.2***
	III M	0.001				−0.015			
	IV	−0.075				−0.057			
	V	−0.310				−0.292			
Parental education:	both left before 15	−0.133		2	93.4***	−0.143		2	107.8***
	one left before 15	0.013				0.011			
	both left after 15	0.120				0.132			
Parental visits (yes−no)		0.233	0.040	1	113.5***	0.190	0.022	1	73.9***

Notes: For both tests, interactions non-significant between each of crowding, amenities and tenure and each other + social class. Residual mean square = 0.772. Significance levels: $p > 0.05$ (not significant); $p < 0.05$*; $p < 0.01$**; $p < 0.001$***.

with the pattern of housing circumstances experienced throughout childhood, in particular with the age at which the children were in unsatisfactory conditions. Data presented in the preceding paper demonstrated how large proportions of children did change in their experience of overcrowding and access to amenities. Furthermore, there was considerable overlap between these two variables. Just over a third (34.6 per cent) of the children who were at one time or another crowded also lacked amenities at some time, and just under a fifth (17.9 per cent) of those never crowded lacked amenities at some time. This means that although four-fifths of children had not experienced each disadvantage when considered separately, only two-thirds (66.6 per cent) had not experienced either disadvantage.

There was also considerable movement between tenure categories (Table 2.11). As there are many different ways (twenty-seven) of moving between three tenure groups at three different ages, all the children who moved from one tenure group to another have been combined regardless of whether they moved before or after they were 11. The small number (forty-eight) of children who lived in each of the three tenure groups have been excluded.

It is likely that changes in housing conditions will

TABLE 2.11 *Change in tenure*

Owner-occupied at each of three ages	42.2
Council-rented at each of three ages	36.1
Private-rented at each of three ages	3.0
Moved from: owner to council	2.0
owner to privately rented	0.9
council to owner	6.9
council to privately rented	0.6
privately rented to owner	3.6
privately rented to council	4.6
Total ($N = 8\,318$)	100.0%

accompany changes in other respects, for example a new occupational level, or increase or decrease in size of family, which could themselves be related to attainment. These variables were therefore allowed for in initial analyses relating housing patterns to attainment. However, the only significant relationship was that between change in social class between 7 and 11, and mathematics attainment at 16, so the other variables have been omitted in the final analyses which are reported.

Housing patterns and 16-year attainment

The results of these analyses are summarised in Tables 2.12 and 2.13. In both the analyses of reading and mathematics attainment, differing patterns of crowding, amenities and tenure experienced by the children have been included. The other independent variables in the analyses, taken from 11-year data, are: social class, family size, sex, region of the country, parental educational level and parental visits to school.

TABLE 2.12   *Analysis of variance: reading score at 16 (transformed)*

Independent variables (11-year unless otherwise specified)	Fitted constant	se	df	χ^2
Crowded				
at 7, 11 and 16	−0.171		7	43.7***
at 7 and 11 only	0.065			
at 7 and 16 only	−0.253			
at 7 only	0.085			
at 11 and 16 only	0.070			
at 11 only	0.047			
at 16 only	−0.045			
never	0.202			
Sole use of amenities				
at 7, 11 and 16	0.140		7	29.0***
at 7 and 11 only	0.041			
at 7 and 16 only	0.069			
at 7 only	−0.004			
at 11 and 16	0.008			
at 11 only	−0.052			
at 16 only	−0.009			
never	−0.193			
Tenure				
owner all ages	0.214		8	114.5***
council rent all ages	−0.108			
private rent all ages	0.176			
owner to council	−0.096			
owner to private	−0.079			

Table 2.12 *continued*

Independent variables (11-year unless otherwise specified)	Fitted constant	se	df	χ^2
council to owner	0.030			
council to private	−0.251			
private to owner	0.137			
private to council	−0.023			
Social class				
Non-Manual	0.331		2	186.9***
III + IV Manual	−0.015			
V Manual	−0.316′			
Family size (⩽3 − >3)	0.216	0.029	1	53.1***
Sex (boys−girls)	0.060	0.023	1	6.5*
Region				
North England	0.012		4	30.6***
Midlands	−0.037			
South England	0.042			
Wales	−0.161			
Scotland	0.144			
Parents' education				
both parents left before 15 years	−0.108		2	47.5***
one parent left before 15 years	0.011			
both parents left after 15 years	0.097			
parental visits (yes−no)	0.182	0.035	1	52.4***

Residual mean square = 0.745. Significance levels: $p < 0.05$*; $p < 0.001$***. N = 5 395. Total variance = 0.945. Overall constant = −0.376.

TABLE 2.13   *Analysis of variance: maths score at 16 (transformed)*

Independent variables (11-year unless otherwise specified)	Fitted constant	se	df	χ^2
Crowded				
at 7, 11 and 16	−0.142		7	30.2***
at 7 and 11 only	0.007			
at 7 and 16 only	−0.201			
at 7 only	0.040			
at 11 and 16 only	0.139			
at 11 only	0.027			

Table 2.13 *continued*

Independent variables (11-year unless otherwise specified)	Fitted constant	se	df	χ^2
at 16 only	−0.034			
never	0.164			
Sole use of amenities				
at 7, 11 and 16	0.138		7	29.0***
at 7 and 11 only	0.087			
at 7 and 16 only	0.081			
at 7 only	0.183			
at 11 and 16	−0.047			
at 11 only	−0.283			
at 16 only	−0.023			
never	−0.136			
Tenure				
owner all ages	0.254		8	117.3***
council rent all ages	−0.069			
private rent all ages	0.171			
owner to council	−0.083			
owner to private	−0.283			
council to owner	0.104			
council to private	−0.231			
private to owner	0.130			
Social class				
Non-Manual	0.319		2	138.9***
III + IV Manual	−0.040			
V Manual	−0.279			
Family size (⩽3−>3)	0.141	0.030	1	22.0***
Sex (boys−girls)	0.176	0.024	1	53.9***
Region				
North England	−0.029		4	70.6***
Midlands	−0.070			
South England	−0.004			
Wales	−0.166			
Scotland	0.269			
Parents' education				
both parents left before 15 years	−0.141		2	66.1***
one parent left before 15 years	0.010			
both parents left after 15 years	0.131			
parental visits (yes−no)	0.167	0.026	1	42.3***

Table 2.13 *continued*

Independent variables (11-year unless otherwise specified)	Fitted constant	se	df	χ^2
Change in social class between 7 and 11				
V to I−IV	−0.105		4	19.7***
III and IV M to Non-Manual	−0.146			
I−IV to V	0.035			
Non-Manual to III and IV M	0.175			
no change	0.041			

Residual mean square = 0.761. Significance levels: $p < 0.001$***. N = 5 318. Total variance = 0.955. Overall constant = −0.360.

It was expected that when crowding and amenities changed at the same time, this could indicate major differences in living conditions which could therefore be associated with a disproportionate change in attainment. However, this interaction was tested in a preliminary analysis and found to be non-significant.

Each change-in-housing variable was significantly related to each measure of attainment after allowing for all the other factors in the analysis. In almost all cases the children who were never crowded, who always had the sole use of the basic amenities or who were always in owner-occupied homes clearly had higher average test scores in both reading and mathematics than any of the other groups. Also, although there were some exceptions, those always in poor conditions tended to have among the lowest scores. Among the groups who were in poor conditions at one or two follow-ups the differences in test scores were quite small.

In carrying out these analyses, the general hypotheses anticipated finding consistent relationships between housing difficulties and attainment according to the age at which unsatisfactory housing was experienced. However, it is apparent from the fitted constants that no patterns appear that are consistent across different ages, tests or housing variables, so that it is not possible to draw general conclusions of this kind.

It is nevertheless possible to make certain interesting, but limited, comparisons between specific groups. In relation to crowding and amenities it does not appear that there is a particular age at which temporary poor conditions are more important. Only very small differences were found among those groups which were crowded or lacked amenities at only one follow-up.

Although we have not examined changes in tenure at specific ages, some indication of the association between tenure patterns and attainment could be gained. Those children who were always in owner-occupied homes and those always in privately rented homes had higher average test results than those always in council-rented homes, with owner-occupiers' children having the highest average scores on both tests. It is interesting that children who moved from owner-occupied homes to council-rented homes only differed slightly in their average test scores from those always in council homes, but those who moved in the opposite direction, from council into owner-occupied homes had higher scores than those always in council homes. However, although this could suggest that conditions at the later ages are more important than earlier ages, this is not confirmed by other results.

The overall impression from these analyses is therefore that the differences tend to be between extreme groups. The children who were never in housing difficulties had the highest average attainment test scores, but among the groups who were at one time or another crowded or lacked amenities no systematic differences appeared.

Housing patterns and progress in school from 11 to 16
The previous analysis considered the eventual (16-year) attainment of children with different housing experiences. This stage of the analysis examines the children's progress through the secondary school, by investigating what differences in 16-year attainment remain after pre-existing differences in 11-year test scores have been taken into account. In particular, two interesting questions arise: first, whether changes in relative attainment are related to changes in housing circumstances during the same period; and second, whether early (i.e. at 7) adverse housing experiences remain associated with later educational progress, irrespective of later housing experiences.

These questions can be answered by analysis of covariance, which essentially repeats the analysis reported in Table 2.12, but with the addition of 11-year attainment score as a further independent variable. The results of these analyses are summarised in Tables 2.14 and 2.15.

For the first question considered above, our hypothesis was that an improvement in housing circumstances would be accompanied by an improvement in test scores. The results cannot be said to offer any consistent support for this expectation. In the first place, only the differences among the crowded groups on the reading test reached statistical significance; although the differences on the mathematics test, and for the amenities groups on both tests, appeared to be of a similar size, they did

TABLE 2.14   *Analysis of variance: reading score at 16 (transformed) for given 11-year score*

Independent variables (11-year unless otherwise specified)	Fitted constant	se	df	χ^2
Crowded				
at 7, 11 and 16	−0.054		7	14.8*
at 7 and 11	0.005			
at 7 and 16	−0.109			
at 7 only	0.072			
at 11 and 16	0.030			
at 11 only	−0.022			
at 16 only	0.006			
never	0.072			
Sole use of amenities				
at 7, 11 and 16	0.019		7	7.5 ns
at 7 and 11	0.030			
at 7 and 16	0.052			
at 7 only	−0.002			
at 11 and 16	0.014			
at 11 only	−0.018			
at 16 only	0.009			
never	−0.104			
Tenure				
owner at all ages	0.081		8	34.8***
council at all ages	−0.014			
private at all ages	0.071			
owner to council	−0.115			
owner to private	−0.115			
council to owner	0.046			
council to private	−0.062			
private to owner	0.056			
private to council	0.052			
Social class				
Non-Manual	0.113		2	47.7***
III + IV Manual	0.022			
V Manual	−0.135			
Family size (≤3 − >3)	0.056	0.019	1	26.7***
Sex (boys−girls)	0.078	0.015	1	28.7***
Region				
North England	0.035		4	26.5***
Midlands	0.027			
South England	0.050			
Wales	−0.125			
Scotland	0.013			

Table 2.14 *continued*

Independent variables (11-year unless otherwise specified)	Fitted constant	se	df	χ^2
Parents' education				
both left before 15	−0.046		2	17.6***
one left before 15	0.024			
both left after 15	0.022			
11-year reading score	0.118	0.001	1	7689.0***
Sig. interaction: crowding × 11 yr reading			7	23.4***

Residual mean square = 0.313. Significance levels: $p > 0.05$ ns; $p < 0.05$*; $p < 0.001$***. $N = 5\,534$. Total variance = 0.940. Overall constant = −2.040.

TABLE 2.15 *Analysis of variance: maths score at 16 (transformed) for given 11-year score*

Independent variables (11-year unless otherwise specified)	Fitted constant	se	df	χ^2
Crowded				
at 7, 11 and 16	−0.065		7	10.0 ns
at 7 and 11	0.008			
at 7 and 16	−0.023			
at 7 only	−0.050			
at 11 and 16	0.116			
at 11 only	−0.040			
at 16 only	0.014			
never	0.040			
Sole use of amenities				
at 7, 11 and 16	0.035		7	7.4 ns
at 7 and 11	0.077			
at 7 and 16	0.021			
at 7 only	0.074			
at 11 and 16	−0.020			
at 11 only	−0.095			
at 16 only	−0.016			
never	−0.076			
Tenure				
owner at all ages	0.092		8	34.2***
council at all ages	−0.022			
private at all ages	0.086			
owner to council	−0.066			
owner to private	0.190			
council to owner	0.052			
council to private	0.046			
private to owner	0.023			
private to council	−0.401			
Social class				
Non-Manual	0.087		2	25.5***
III + IV Manual	−0.016			
V Manual	−0.071			
Family size ($\leqslant 3 - > 3$)	0.055	0.022	1	6.3*
Sex (boys–girls)	0.157	0.017	1	81.7***
Region				
North England	−0.008		4	47.1***
Midlands	0.031			
South England	0.062			
Wales	−0.180			
Scotland	0.095			
Parents' education				
both left before 15	−0.055		2	24.4***
one left before 15	0.001			
both left after 15	0.054			
11-year reading score	0.691	0.010	1	4839.0***
Sig. interaction: none				

Residual mean square = 0.409. Significance levels: $p > 0.05$ ns; $p < 0.05$*; $p < 0.001$***. $N = 5\,454$. Total variance = 0.958. Overall constant = 0.132.

not reach significance, and, as for the previous analyses, the patterns of the fitted constants differ according to the test and housing measure being considered.

In order to answer the second question, comparisons can be made between those in unsatisfactory housing at 7 only and those never in unsatisfactory housing. However, as neither crowding nor amenities was significantly related to change in maths-test results, and access to amenities was not significantly associated with progress in reading, there were clearly no significant differences in these respects between the two relevant groups. Although crowding was significantly related to progress in reading between 11 and 16, the fitted constant for those crowded only at 7 was the same as for those who were never crowded, so clearly the former group showed no relative disadvantage in their progress.

These non-significant findings together show that any difference in attainment between those who were only crowded at 7 and those who were never crowded had already appeared by the time they were 11, and there was no evidence of additional differences in their reading or mathematics attainment after that time. It is interesting to note that, other than crowding and amenities, each of the other variables in the analysis which give some indication of the child's home environment, namely region, social class, family size and parental education, as well as tenure, was significantly related to the children's 16-year attainment after allowing for 11-year attainment.

Discussion

We have shown that, at 16, as at earlier ages, children in crowded conditions without certain basic amenities or in council homes had lower score on tests of school attainment than children from similar social backgrounds without these housing difficulties or in owner-occupied homes.

Clearly, as housing conditions at each of the ages of 7, 11 and 16 were related to attainment at the same age, children with different housing experiences throughout their childhood were expected to, and found to, differ in their attainment at 16. These differences mainly emerged between extremes, though it should be remembered that each aspect of housing was related to attainment separately, after adjusting for other aspects of housing. Since, as we have seen above, there were no significant interactions between housing variables, this means that children who experienced a combination of these disadvantages, even at only one follow-up, will have had correspondingly lower test scores (the extent of which can be calculated by simple addition of the fitted constants in each table).

From these analyses it was also possible to consider whether the relationship between poor housing and 16-year attainment varied with the age at which the inadequate housing conditions were experienced. However, there was no evidence of any clear, consistent differences in eventual school performance among the children according to the age they were in housing difficulties.

The final question which we wanted to answer was whether the children's housing experiences were associated with their rate of progress through secondary school. There were slight differences overall between children according to their experiences of crowding and their access to amenities, though the difference only reached significance in the relationship between crowding and reading.

Tenure was more closely related to rate of progress, with children in owner-occupied homes showing a greater rate of progress in reading and mathematics than most of the groups, in particular those in council homes, even after allowing for other social factors.

These analyses also enabled a consideration to be made of whether early childhood experiences of housing are related to later progress in school. For given 11-year attainment, the 16-year attainment of children who had only experienced housing difficulties early in their childhood (at 7) did not differ significantly from those who were never reported as in these difficulties. This means that there is no evidence of any additional differences between these groups' attainment after the age of 11.

The cross-sectional results suggest that in comparing children of similar family circumstances it is mainly between groups who have experienced extremes of housing conditions (in terms of crowding and amenities) that differences in attainment emerge.

However, in addition to considering those housing conditions which describe the home itself, the analyses also included variables reflecting the environment in which the home was situated, namely tenure and region. There were significant differences in 16-year attainment between children in council homes and those in owner-occupied homes, as well as between children living in different regions. The children's progress through the secondary school was also related both to tenure and to region. These findings suggest that in addition to the home conditions themselves the area in which the child lives is of importance in terms of school attainment.

Previous studies have found differences in children's development related to their environment. For example, Miller *et al.* (1974), in their study in Newcastle upon Tyne, compared IQ scores of 14-year-olds in different districts of the town, and found that within each social class the children in poorer districts had relatively low IQ scores.

Douglas (1964) related children's progress in school to their housing conditions, after adjusting for family size, parental interest and the school's academic record. He concluded that, although manual working-class children showed less progress than average between the ages of 8 and 11 if they were in unsatisfactory home conditions, those from non-manual social-class homes of this standard, although they had lower 8-year test scores, showed greater progress than the rest of their class, with the result they were not so behind at 11 as they had been at 8. On the assumption that the working-class but not the middle-class children were living in a poor area, Douglas suggested that it was the type of area rather than the standard of housing which was of importance in the children's progress through primary school.

Robinson and Gorbach (1977) studied regional differences in the attainment of 11-year-olds in the NCDS. They also considered the importance of the type of area in which the children lived, areas being grouped according to their pattern of urban development, such that they were also of similar socio-economic characteristics, for example in terms of the housing market and the proportion of the work-force in non-manual occupations. Robinson and Gorbach concluded that children's attainment was related to social factors in the child's own family, but, additionally, there were some differences related to socio-economic factors in the area in which the child lived.

The implications of our findings on housing and attainment together with these studies of the environment are twofold: children who at one time or another experience poor housing conditions, especially if this occurs throughout their childhood, clearly have lower attainment by the end of their compulsory school years. However, it makes little difference how old they are when they experience these conditions. In addition, children will also have relatively low attainment if the area in which they live, as distinct from their own family, is at a disadvantage in terms of socio-economic characteristics.

CHILDREN'S HOUSING AND THEIR HEALTH AND PHYSICAL DEVELOPMENT

Introduction

The housing conditions in which children live are important in themselves for humanitarian reasons, but are of additional importance if children in inadequate housing are likely to be retarded in their development or to have poor health. Previous research in this area has been scarce, particularly recently, but in general has concluded that there is an association between health and crowding (Martin, 1967). In particular, Pond (1957) and Wilner *et al.* (1962) found a higher frequency of colds, bronchitis, respiratory diseases, tuberculosis and digestive conditions among children in poor housing, and Miller *et al.* (1974) found both more accidents and diarrhoeal illnesses in overcrowded homes. More tentative evidence was presented by Schmidt (1966), who found that ill health was associated with crowding, though to a smaller extent than with population density, and by Fairbairns and Wintour (1977), who found slightly more non-asthmatic chest complaints in homes without basic amenities, though not in all social classes. Wedge and Prosser (1973) found that 'socially disadvantaged' children (defined in part by the quality of their housing) had more

accidents and missed more school for reasons of ill-health than 'ordinary children'.

There has been even less research on the relationship between housing and physical development (Christiansen *et al.*, 1975; Jackson, 1955), though considerable attention has been given to the relationship between other environmental factors and physical development (e.g. Douglas and Simpson, 1964; Davie *et al.*, 1972; Tanner, 1962; Acheson and Hewitt, 1954).

Using a nationally representative sample of schoolchildren provides an opportunity to examine the relationships between housing conditions and both children's health and their height, the latter being generally regarded as a good indicator of physical development.

The housing variables used here are taken from the 16-year-old follow-up and are: crowding (number of persons in the household per room), access to amenities (whether the household has a bathroom, hot water supply and indoor lavatory) and tenure (owner-occupied, rented from the council or privately rented).

From the range of health variables available to us, we wished to choose:

(a) those which were likely to be indicative of general health rather than, for example, a single acute episode; and
(b) those which applied to a sufficiently large proportion of children to be sensitive to our analyses.

These requirements led us to use the following variables, taken from the medical history supplied by the parents when the study child was 16:

1. Whether the child had had asthma or wheezy bronchitis in the previous year.
2. Whether the study child had had migraine or recurrent sick headaches in the previous year.
3. How much time the child had missed from school in the previous year for ill health.
4. Reasons (pre-coded) for absence of more than a week.

These reasons were supplied by the child's parents and therefore give a general indication of the kind of illness the child suffered from, rather than providing a strict medical diagnosis.

Response levels

The general level of response at each follow-up has been satisfactorily high for a study of this kind. However, the analysis of height required fairly full data to be available, so an additional check was made for bias due to the resultant reduction in sample size.

The result was satisfactory in that the respondents at 16 were of a similar average height at 11 to the non-respondents.

Results

Health

The proportion of children in different housing conditions is reported more fully elsewhere (see pp. 59–61). Here the indices of poor housing used are crowding and access to amenities, as these are likely to be of importance in themselves in a consideration of children's health and also may be indicators of housing which is sub-standard in other respects, such as being damp or poorly constructed (Committee on Housing in Greater London, 1965). Altogether 8 per cent of children were in homes with more than 1.5 persons per room, and 6 per cent were in homes without sole use of the three basic amenities.

Table 2.16 shows the relationship between crowding and absence from school for medical reasons for each of three social classes. The reason for allowing for social class is to prevent any differences in absence from school due to social reasons from affecting the results. There is a clear tendency for children to be reported by their parents as missing more school the more their homes were crowded in the non-manual and manual social classes, though for those with no male head of household there is no clear trend. The results have been presented for all those absent from school for more than one week together, regardless of how much school they missed, as the relationship between

crowding and absence was similar whether they were absent for a relatively short time (less than a month) or for longer (e.g. over three months), and the number who were absent for a long time was too small for more detailed analyses.

TABLE 2.16   *Crowding and absence from school for medical reasons by social class**

	Percentage absent more than 1 week in the year†					
	Non-Manual (%)	(N)	Manual (%)	(N)	No male head of household (%)	(N)
Crowding (persons per room)						
⩽1.0	35.7	3 080	46.4	3 830	55.4	654
1.0–1.5	43.6	553	51.7	1 937	55.2	134
1.5–2.0	49.0	100	53.6	645	56.8	37
2.0+	58.8	17	57.1	119	41.7	12

*Social class is defined by the occupation of the male head of household, using the Registrar General's Classification of Occupations, 1966.

†Percentage absent by crowding: Non-Manual χ^2 = 22.4 (3 df) $p < 0.001$; Manual χ^2 = 26.6 (3 df) $p < 0.001$; no male head of household not significant.

Table 2.17 shows the proportions of the whole cohort who were reported as missing school for more than a week in the year for each of the reasons given. The pre-coded question included other reasons, but they have not been presented if there were no reason to expect an association with crowding and there was no such association.

TABLE 2.17   *Crowding and reason for absence from school of more than one week in the year*

Reasons* for absence of more than one week*	Crowding (persons per room)					
	Non-Manual		Manual		No male head of household	
	⩽1.5 (%)	>1.5 (%)	⩽1.5 (%)	>1.5 (%)	⩽1.5 (%)	>1.5 (%)
Colds or influenza	27.1	32.5	33.4	34.9	36.9	26.5
Bronchitis or chest infections	2.0	5.1 (N = 6)	3.4	5.5	5.7	4.1 (N = 2)
Headaches	3.7	6.8 (N = 8)	7.3	7.7	8.6	16.3 (N = 8)
Bilious attacks, diarrhoea	3.0	2.6 (N = 3)	5.1	3.5	6.1	12.2 (N = 6)
Infectious diseases	1.9	6.8 (N = 8)	1.9	1.3	2.5	—
Accidents	3.0	4.3 (N = 5)	4.3	4.6	5.2	2.0 (N = 1)
N (all children)	3 633	117	5 767	764	788	49

*More than one reason could be given.

Reason/crowding
Bronchitis: Non-Manual χ^2 = 3.9 (1 df) $p < 0.05$; Manual χ^2 = 8.2 (1 df) $p < 0.01$.
Infectious diseases: Non-Manual χ^2 = 11.4 (1 df) $p < 0.001$.
All other comparisons non-significant.

Overall, absence due to each of the reasons in the table, except infectious diseases and bilious attacks, was more common among crowded children. However, after allowing for social class (apart from the eight crowded children with infectious diseases in the non-manual social classes), only absence for bronchitis was significantly more commonly reported for children in crowded homes, though this was not the case for those with no male head of household. There was also a tendency for headaches to be more common among children in crowded homes, but this did not reach significance level, possibly due to the small numbers involved.

A similar analysis of children in homes lacking basic amenities revealed only a slight association with time absent from school, which became even smaller and no longer significant after allowance was made for social class.

Although there was no increase in the total time away from school, it was expected that some medical reasons for absence would be more common among children in homes without amenities. For example, infectious diseases and bilious attacks could be expected to occur in families with inadequate sanitary arrangements (Wilner *et al.*, 1956). Table 2.18 shows that, in each social class, absence from school because of bilious attacks and also bronchitis was more common if the children's home lacked amenities, though perhaps due to small numbers these differences only reached significance among the manual social classes. Infectious diseases were rare altogether and were no more common among those in homes without amenities, and nor were colds or headaches. There was an inexplicable tendency for

more children in households with no male head to miss school because of an accident if they lacked amenities, but the numbers in this group are too small for much importance to be attached to this finding. There was barely any tendency in this direction in the other social classes.

The prevalence of asthma and migraine among children in poor housing conditions was also examined, but neither those in crowded homes nor those in homes without amenities were more likely to have suffered from either asthma or migraine in the previous year than those in more satisfactory housing.

In general, therefore, these results provide very little evidence of absence attributable to any particular illness, apart from chest infections, being consistently more common among children who were living in unsatisfactory housing conditions, though the crowded children were more likely to have more time off school. However, the analysis above only describes the situation when the children were 16, and does not take account of how long children had been living in particular conditions. It is therefore possible that children who had experienced poor conditions for several years would show more evidence of ill health. Data were available on the children's housing situation when they were 7 and 11 as well as 16. The health of the children in poor housing conditions at all three of these ages was compared with those always reported as in satisfactory homes, but the differences between them were barely greater than when only one age was considered. For example, 56 per cent of the children who were crowded at each of the three ages missed more than

TABLE 2.18   *Use of amenities and reason for absence from school for more than a week in the year*

Reasons* for absence of more than one week	Non-Manual		Manual		No male head of household	
	Sole use 3 amenities	Not sole use 3	Sole use 3 amenities	Not sole use 3	Sole use 3 amenities	Not sole use 3
	(%)	(%)	(%)	(%)	(%)	(%)
Colds	27.3	24.0	33.4	34.4	36.6	35.1
Bronchitis or chest infection	2.1	3.3 (4)	3.5	5.3	5.4	7.4 (7)
Headaches	3.7	5.8 (7)	7.2	8.8	8.5	12.8
Bilious attacks or diarrhoea	3.0	4.0 (5)	4.7	6.8	6.4	8.5 (8)
Infectious disease	2.0	1.7 (2)	2.0	0.6 (3)	2.6	1.1 (1)
Accidents	3.0	3.3 (4)	4.3	5.5	4.1	10.6
N (all children)	3 633	121	5 982	488	740	94

*More than one reason could be given.
Reason/crowding: bronchitis Manual χ^2 = 4.0 (1 df) $p < 0.05$; bilious attacks Manual χ^2 = 4.1 (1 df) $p < 0.05$; accidents: no male head χ^2 = 7.5 (1 df) $p < 0.01$. All other results non-significant.

a week of school for health reasons, which was similar to the corresponding figure for the children who were crowded at 16 (54 per cent).

Height

Table 2.19 shows that for both boys and girls there are differences in mean height at 16 according to their housing situation. There is some variation in the size of the differences, with only 1 cm between those with and without amenities, while the differences related to crowding are larger, and nearly twice as great for boys (3.7 cm) as girls (2 cm).

Housing conditions and height are both related to other socio-economic factors, so the children's height was analysed by means of an analysis of variance after allowing (simultaneously) for such factors (region of the country in which the child lived, social class, parental educational level (indicated by their age of leaving school) and family size (the number of children under 21 in the household), as well as other housing variables.

The analysis was carried out separately for boys

TABLE 2.19 *Mean height of children in different housing situation*

| | Mean height (cm) at 16 | | | |
	Girls		Boys	
Crowded (1.5 persons/room)	159.1	(313)	167.5	(315)
Not crowded (1.5 persons/room)	161.1	(3 589)	171.2	(3 777)
Not sole use of 3 amenities	160.0	(207)	169.9	(238)
Sole use of 3 amenities	161.0	(3 695)	170.9	(3 854)
Owner-occupied	161.7	(2 169)	171.8	(2 273)
Council rented	159.9	(1 545)	169.6	(1 617)
Privately rented	160.8	(188)	170.5	(202)

and girls, as at 16 they are at different stages of development, girls having in general reached their final height (Tanner, 1962). Clearly, in a large study

TABLE 2.20 *Height* at 16 and housing conditions*

Independent variables at 16 years	Height of boys (cm): N = 4 092; variance = 63.8; RMS = 60.8				Height of girls (cm): N = 3 902; variance = 40.5; RMS = 38.7			
	Fitted constant	se	df	χ^2	Fitted constant	se	df	χ^2
Overall constant	169.0				159.6			
Crowding ($\leqslant 1.5 > 1.5$)	1.6	0.5	1	9.4**	0.5	0.4	1	1.6 ns
Amenities (Sole − not sole)	0.4	0.5	1	0.7 ns	0.6	0.5	1	1.7 ns
Tenure: owner	0.6		2	12.9**	0.3		2	9.5**
council rented	−0.4				−0.4			
private rented	−0.2				0.1			
Region: North	−0.2		4	11.7*	−0.1		4	45.4***
Midlands	0.2				0.5			
South	0.7				1.2			
Wales	−0.7				−0.9			
Scotland	0.0				−0.7			
Social class: Non-manual	1.0		3	17.0***	1.1		3	29.4***
III manual	−0.1				0.1			
IV	0.0				−0.4			
V	−0.9				−0.8			
Family size ($\leqslant 3 - > 3$)	1.9	0.3	1	35.2***	0.8	0.3	1	9.6**

Interactions between each housing variable and each other and social class all non-significant.

Parental education − non-significant.

*Corrected for age of testing.

Significance levels: $p > 0.05$ ns, $p < 0.05$*, $p < 0.01$**, $p < 0.001$***.

such as the NCDS, medical examinations are made over a period of several months, so allowance has been made for the gain in height of those measured later.

Table 2.20 summarises the results of these analyses of variance. The small differences between those with and without amenities have been reduced to non-significance after adjusting for social factors. The differences between children in owner-occupied and council-rented homes remain significant but have been reduced from 1.8cm (girls) and 2.2cm (boys) to 0.7cm (girls) and 1cm (boys). The differences relating to crowding have also been reduced such that for girls it is non-significant (0.5cm), in comparison with 1.6cm for boys.

The assumption that 16-year-old girls, but not boys, have reached their final height is borne out by the relative variances in the height of the two sexes. The variance is much greater for boys, suggesting that it includes differences in stage of development as well as variation in adult height. It is therefore interesting that the difference in height related to crowding is so much greater for boys than girls, which could indicate that crowding is related to rate of growth rather than to ultimate height. It is notable that family size is also more clearly related to boys' height than girls' height at the age of 16, which could be reflecting a similar phenomenon.

As the above analyses only considered the housing situation when the children were 16, these small average differences could be masking more marked variations if the children had lived in inadequate conditions for a long time. Therefore, as for the health findings presented above, the height of the children in poor housing at all three follow-ups (at 7, 11 and 16) was contrasted with those never in poor housing, again by means of an analysis of variance. However, the pattern which emerged was essentially the same as the analysis shown in Table 2.20 and therefore has not been presented separately. This showed that, after allowing for social factors, girls' 16-year-old height was significantly related to tenure, but not crowding or amenities. For boys, amenities was barely related to height, and the difference between boys always in owner-occupied homes and those always in council houses was 1.2cm, hardly greater than the 1cm reported in the cross-sectional analysis. The difference in height between boys in crowded homes at all three and none of the follow-ups was 3.4cm, the only difference which was substantially increased by examining all three ages.

Discussion

The general conclusion that can be made here is that the relationship between housing conditions and either health or physical development is fairly weak, the only illness consistently more often reported for children in sub-standard housing being bronchitis. This is a somewhat unexpected result, particularly in view of the previous research described above, together with Schorr's (1964) theory that a causal relationship between poor housing and ill-health can be accepted when 'correlations are demonstrated and the mechanisms that are operating are well understood'. Also, Wilner *et al.* (1956) discusses the processes involved, for example the ill health that can result from lack of sleep as a consequence of crowding, the increased frequency of accidents expected in crowded or inadequate kitchens, and the minor digestive diseases which are likely to occur in homes with inadequate washing and toilet facilities. (Wilner *et al.*, however, also suggest that the poor health found in slum dwellings could be confounded by socio-economic factors, such as low incomes.)

There seem to be two possible explanations for the only slightly increased likelihood of ill health among the NCDS children in unsatisfactory housing. The first possibility concerns the measures used to determine ill health. First, in so far as the variable used for the most part to indicate poor health involved absence from school, there may be other factors in the child's background (which could affect the results) that determine whether they miss school. However, the lack of association between housing and asthma or migraine implies that the results are not peculiar to the question of absence from school. Second, the responses to each question will clearly reflect parents' perceptions of their child's health rather than being a purely objective measure of health. Differences in perception, and in whether ill health is reported, could be related to the family's social background, but as comparisons have been made between children of similar social class, the results presented here are unlikely to be affected by such variations.

The alternative explanation relates to the degree of inadequacy of the housing. We attempted to look at those children in the very poorest conditions, both (in the analyses of health) by selecting children at the extremes (only 1.3 per cent of the whole cohort were in homes with more than two persons per room, and 1.7 per cent did not have sole access to any basic amenities) and also, in a separate analysis, by considering children in inadequate conditions for a long time. However, it may be that although children in unsatisfactory housing circumstances do have more illnesses, this is only the case for highly unsatisfactory homes, and the scarcity of differences in the NCDS could indicate either that conditions in Britain are not so markedly inadequate as to affect children's health or that the few children who are so affected are hidden even in the small percentages selected for examination. The scarcity of illnesses more frequently reported among children in poor housing in the NCDS, together with the more marked relationship between housing and health found in earlier studies in both America and Britain (Pond, 1957; Wilner *et al.*, 1962; Martin, 1967), could reflect a relatively small variation in the quality of housing in Britain in the 1960s and 1970s.

Previous studies of the relationship between housing and physical development have been inconclusive. Jackson (1955), in a study in Baltimore, found that children who moved from slums to public (i.e. council) housing grew less than children who remained in the slums, though in all other respects, for example educational and social, they showed more progress. On the other hand, Wedge and Prosser (1973) found that 'socially disadvantaged' children were shorter than those who were not disadvantaged.

Acheson and Hewitt (1954) discussed the question of whether rate of growth necessarily affects final height. They argued that if both rate of growth and rate of maturation are retarded to the same extent, for example by a poor environment, then final height may not be affected, though clearly it will be reached later. This provides a possible explanation for the finding in this study that boys, but not girls, in crowded homes, are relatively short at the age of 16, as it shows how crowding could be related only to rate of growth and not to eventual height.

Conclusion

We have shown that within the existing range of British housing conditions there is only a weak relationship between housing and ill-health. However, this should not lead to complacency while there are children experiencing the discomfort of cramped, sub-standard homes. In addition, other research has found associations between housing and school attainment (see pp. 61–9), between housing and truancy (Tibbenham, 1977; see pp. 74–6) and between housing and delinquency (West and Farrington, 1973), and this should continue to cause concern until the inequalities in the housing market are further reduced.

HOUSING AND TRUANCY

What is the background of children who are truants? Studies consistently suggest that the lower the social class, the higher the rate of truancy — or at least the rate of non-attendance at school. However, it is likely that the broad social-class trends mask the effect of other influences at work. The research discussed here

suggests that there is a strong correlation between standard of housing and both truancy and non-attendance; and that this link between housing and truancy does not exist merely because more children of the lower social classes live in poor conditions.

Few previous studies have explored the relationship between truancy and living conditions, though the possibility of such an association has been raised in two Scottish studies. A study of truancy and non-attendance in Aberdeen (Blythman, 1975) recorded that truants 'tended to live in deprived neighbourhoods' and that over a third of the truants compared with only 17 per cent of non-truants lived in 'low-status, high delinquency areas marked by a concentration of sub-standard housing'.

A report on school absence in Glasgow, by the Institute for the Study and Treatment of Delinquency (ISTD, 1974), noted that the common element linking the three comprehensive schools that showed the highest rates of truancy and non-attendance was the type of housing area in which they were located. These localities were characterised by old and decayed housing, redevelopment and municipal housing of a pre-war type. This finding is particularly interesting in that the ISTD team argue that children in those schools with low rates of truancy came from 'good' housing areas with many owner-occupiers.

The study reported here has attempted to analyse the situation within the individual child's home, using clearly defined criteria of the housing conditions, as well as attempting to distinguish the relationship with social class.

Information on truancy and attendance came from a questionnaire filled in by staff at the child's school, and the data on housing and social class from a questionnaire answered by the child's parents.

The indices of household characteristics employed are overcrowding, as defined by the 1971 Census (an 'overcrowded' household being one where there are more than 1.5 persons per room), and access to basic amenities: whether the child's family has sole use of hot water, toilet and bathroom or whether they have no use of, or have to share, one or any. Social class is based on father's occupation and defined according to the Registrar-General's Classification of Occupations, 1966. The measure of truancy is the teacher's estimate of whether the pupil 'truants from school', with three possible responses: 'doesn't apply', 'applies somewhat' and 'certainly applies'. In this article 'truants' are those said to fit either of the latter two categories. While teachers' estimates are clearly rather subjective, and their value the source of much debate, they are probably the best measure of truancy available.

We calculated each child's school attendance rate as the ratio of his or her actual half-day attendances

in the autumn term 1973 to the total possible attendances in that term. Of course, truancy accounts for
only a part of non-attendance, and it seems likely
that rates of illness are also higher among children
living in poor housing conditions. However, our
initial findings revealed that, for example, only one in
ten children with an attendance rate of over 80 per
cent ('good attenders') is described as a truant,
compared with three in five children who have
attendance rates of 80 per cent or below ('poor
attenders'). It should also be stressed that the
children were, by chance, the first year-group
required to remain in school until the age of 16.
Hence the overall total of truants and their distribution between sub-groups will not necessarily be
representative of subsequent year-groups who would
never have expected to leave school at an earlier age.

It can be seen from Figure 2.1a that not only does
the rate of reported truancy increase with a lowering
of social class, but that there is also a significant
increase in truancy within each social-class grouping
where the child lives in overcrowded conditions.
Figure 2.1b demonstrates the existence of a similar
relationship between overcrowding and 'poor'
attendance. As well as there being poorer attendance
in the lower social-class groupings, within each class
there is a marked tendency for lower attendance to be
associated with overcrowding. Our findings also suggest that within non-manual groups there is a similar
link between both truancy and non-attendance and
the sharing of amenities. However, access to basic
amenities appears not to be related to truancy or
non-attendance in social classes IV and V.

It is not clear at this stage why children in social
classes IV and V who live in overcrowded conditions
appear to be more likely to be truants than others in
this grouping when the same does not apply to those
living where amenities are shared or lacking. Even in
the higher socio-economic groups, sharing amenities
seems to have a less strong association with truancy
and non-attendance than does overcrowding. It seems
apparent that overcrowding and sharing amenities are
not interchangeable as indicators of those housing
circumstances which predict a comparatively high
level of truancy and non-attendance. This clearly
suggests that reference to the general state of housing
in an area is rather inadequate in a discussion of home
factors associated with truancy.

Further research is needed to establish more
precisely the nature of the relationship between sub-
standard living conditions and truancy. The ISTD
team do offer one argument for a fairly direct link
between truancy and overcrowding: 'Overcrowding
can and does lead to bad sleeping habits; the children
are unable to go to sleep until the household finally
settles down with the consequence that they are too

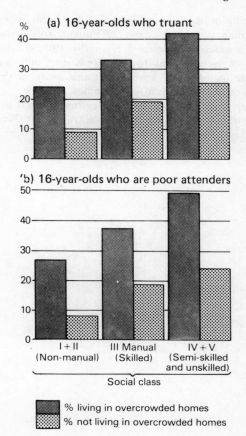

FIGURE 2.1

tired to go out in the morning.' If such a direct
association were to be established, it would offer a
possible explanation of the stronger relationship of
truancy with overcrowding than with poor amenities,
since sharing or lacking amenities would have little
direct connection with sleeping habits. Another
possibility is that the stress of living in overcrowded
conditions subjects families of any social class to such
pressures that encouraging children in their schooling
becomes a minor consideration. Other NCDS research
has linked overcrowding to poor educational attainment. It could be that a vicious circle is at work.

David Reynolds has suggested ('Schools do make a
difference', *New Society*, 29 July 1976) that after
studying children from relatively homogeneous social
backgrounds, thereby partially offsetting the
influence of class, it seemed apparent that individual
schools had an effect on rate of attendance. This is
despite the fact that all the schools studied were
secondary moderns.

Our argument about living conditions being
associated with the rate of truancy does not deny this
possibility. Indeed it could be that young people who

are badly housed are at high-truancy schools because high-truancy schools have catchment areas where there is much poor housing. Naturally, the alternative point of view is that these schools may only have become high-truancy schools because many of their pupils came from overcrowded homes.

Even if we leave aside school factors and look only at the home factors associated with truancy, it should be stressed that the material presented here is intended to complement, not contradict, previous studies. Thus there is no denial of a relationship between class background and truancy but rather an assertion that a consideration of class alone is inadequate, and that there is a need to include other background factors such as the housing conditions of pupils — especially the degree of overcrowding in the home.

3 Immigrants*

CHILDREN OF IMMIGRANTS: SOCIAL AND HOME CIRCUMSTANCES

Introduction

Although the literature on the immigrant population as a whole is quite extensive, that on immigrant children is heavily biased towards aspects of acculturation and education (e.g. Townsend and Brittan, 1972; Oakley, 1968; Taylor, 1974). Relatively little is written about their demographic characteristics, material conditions and home circumstances, and what there is tends to be concerned with subgroups of the immigrant population. For example, Rutter *et al.* (1975b), as part of a large investigation, studied these aspects for 10-year-old West Indian children in a London borough. Hood *et al.* (1970) also conducted an inquiry into the social conditions, health and use of services of 1-year-old West Indian children, again in a London borough.

To provide more information on these and other immigrant groups in Great Britain this paper — using a national sample of 16-year-olds — presents some findings on their social and home circumstances. Both children who were born here and those who moved to Britain after their birth are looked at and compared with children born here to parents also born in Britain.

The data

The characteristics examined in this report refer to when the children were aged 16. From information obtained from parents at 11 and 16 and the children at 16, four 'immigrant' groups were identified according to the following countries of origin:

1. India and Pakistan (referred to as the Asian group). Included in this group are a few children from other Asian countries as well as those from Africa who belonged to an Asian ethnic group.
2. West Indies and Caribbean (referred to as the West Indian group, WI).

3. Northern Ireland and Eire (referred to collectively as the Irish group).
4. Europe (including the USSR, but not Cyprus, Gibraltar and Malta — which were excluded) plus a few from America (North and South), Australia and New Zealand (referred to as the European group).

As important differences were expected between children born in Great Britain and those who arrived during their childhood, these four groups were further divided according to whether the children were born in the country mentioned (to parents one of whom at least was also not born in Great Britain) or whether they were born in Great Britain (to parents one of whom, at least, was born in the countries mentioned). The former are referred to as 'first-generation immigrants' and the latter as 'second-generation immigrants'. If the mother and father were from countries in two different groups, the father's country of birth was chosen rather than that of the mother.

It should be appreciated that the above groupings are very broad and that each group contains people from quite different backgrounds. In a study such as this we are only able to look at general trends and cannot allow for the numerous differences within each group. Indeed, as becomes clear later, the first-generation European group prove to be so heterogeneous as to make any conclusions meaningless. Although the small size of this group also contributes to this conclusion, they are nevertheless included to illustrate this point as well as for symmetry of presentation.

In addition to the above eight groups a further group of children were defined as those who were born abroad to parents born in Great Britain. These would include, for example, children of members of the armed forces, the diplomatic service, etc. A tenth group — the indigenous children, i.e. those born in Great Britain to parents born in Great Britain — constituted the majority.

It must be remembered that the data presented relate to a national sample of children. Thus the findings are not representative of all immigrant families but only those which included a 16-year-

*Original sources: Ghodsian, M. and Essen, J., 'Children of immigrants: social and home circumstances', *New Community*, 1980; Essen, J. and Ghodsian, M., 'Children of immigrants: school performance', *New Community*, 1979.

old in 1974. Furthermore, our second-generation immigrant groups contain both 'long-' and 'short-' term immigrants. That is, we could not distinguish between those intending to live here permanently or for a shorter period.

Results*

Table 3.1 presents the regional distribution of the groups. The first- and second-generation immigrants have been combined, as the distributions across regions were similar and some cell sizes were small.

*For the sake of clarity in the presentation of results, we have not included the results of statistical tests. Differences noted in the text are significant at least at the 5 per cent level (after adjustment to take into account multiple comparisons in each table), unless stated to the contrary. In a few instances where a difference does not reach statistical significance (perhaps due to small cell sizes) but is marked enough to merit comment these are offered in a tentative fashion while noting their statistical non-significance.

While there were generally equal proportions of each group in the North of England (except for the West Indians), proportionately more of the immigrants than the indigenous group could be found in the southern region. There were relatively fewer immigrants in Wales and Scotland (except for the Europeans in Wales). There was also a preponderance of West Indians and Irish groups in the Midlands.

The sex distribution of the second-generation groups closely resembles that of the indigenous group, with perhaps a slightly larger number of boys in the Asian group (Table 3.2). The latter is also true of first-generation Asian and Irish groups. On the other hand, there seems to be a slightly higher proportion of girls in the first-generation West Indian group. However, none of the differences was statistically significant.

Table 3.2 also shows the percentage of children in each group from non-manual backgrounds. It is apparent from this table that the sample size is

TABLE 3.1   *Regional distribution of the groups (first- and second-generation groups combined)*

Country of origin of parents and/or child	Region					Total (100%)
	North	Midlands	South	Wales	Scotland	
Asia	24.6	24.1	47.3	2.0	2.0	203
West Indies	12.3	38.5	45.1	2.5	1.6	122
Ireland	23.4	33.9	31.3	1.8	9.5	495
Europe	22.2	24.2	41.3	4.3	8.0	351
Indigenous children born abroad	25.5	28.6	38.8	3.1	4.1	98
Indigenous children born GB	27.9	25.9	26.9	5.9	13.4	8 517
Total	27.1	26.4	28.5	5.5	12.5	9 586

TABLE 3.2   *Percentage of boys and of children from non-manual backgrounds in each group*

		% boys	Total	% non-manual	Total
1st-generation immigrant children	Asia	55.9	152	33.0	103
	West Indies	44.7	76	2.2 (1)	45
	Ireland	61.3	62	28.9	38
	Europe	(49.2)	63	(52.2)	23
2nd-generation immigrant children	Asia	55.1	107	72.0	75
	West Indies	52.5	80	12.0	50
	Ireland	52.7	547	24.1	399
	Europe	47.3	383	36.0	275
Indigenous children born abroad		53.1	113	61.0	82
Indigenous children born GB		50.8	9 794	37.8	7 584
Total		50.9	11 377	37.2	8 674

reduced on this variable and that the reduction is generally greater for the immigrant groups. Part of the reason for this is that the social-class grouping excludes those children without a male head of household and these are over represented in some of the immigrant groups. However, a more important reason seems to be that we were particularly unsuccessful in interviewing immigrant families compared with the indigenous ones. Preliminary checks, in terms of sex and social class, demonstrate that those who were interviewed and included in the study were not biased, compared with those immigrants in our sample at earlier stages. But this of course does not guarantee that we have not consistently interviewed a biased group of immigrant families at each follow-up. If this is so — and we have no way of knowing — and we assume that the immigrant non-respondents, like those in the whole sample, are more likely to be disadvantaged, then our figures will tend to *overestimate* the conditions of the immigrant groups.

Turning to the actual social-class comparisons in our data, of the first-generation immigrant children, those from the West Indies are grossly underrepresented in the non-manual group together with the Irish, though the latter to a much lesser extent. In the second-generation groups those from the West Indies are again underrepresented, together with those from Ireland. There were proportionately more second-generation Asians and children born abroad to parents born in Great Britain who were in the non-manual group. Of course, the social-class categories in

Table 3.2 are extremely broad and the figures would thus mask wide variations in actual occupations.

Table 3.3 presents the family size (number of children in the household under 21) and household size (number of persons in the household) composition of the groups, and the percentage in one-parent families. The proportions with a family size greater than three children and household size greater than four people are shown. The first-generation immigrant children are more often from larger families and households than the indigenous group, except for the European group who have larger households but not larger families. For the second-generation children the differences persist for the West Indian and Irish groups (although reduced in some cases) but are no longer significant for the Asian group.

The data on the number of one-parent families should be interpreted with caution because of the small cell sizes. Of the second-generation immigrants, only the West Indian group has a significantly greater proportion of one-parent families. This is probably also the case for the first-generation West Indian and European groups but the numbers are too small for statistical testing. Although the differences between the Asian and the indigenous groups are not significant, the increase in the proportion of one-parent families from the first- to second-generation Asian groups is notable. Any simple explanation remains unclear, particularly as we do not know the reasons for the families having only one parent, and is probably explained by the small cell sizes.

The mothers (or mother figures) were asked

TABLE 3.3   *Percentages of children in families with more than three children, households with more than four members and in one-parent families*

		% with family size >3	% with household size >4	% in 1-parent families	Total
1st-generation immigrant children	Asia	56.4	88.4	5.3	113
	West Indies	58.5	79.3	17.9	56
	Ireland	43.5	81.7	13.0	46
	Europe	(16.7)	(71.7)	(27.8)	36
2nd-generation immigrant children	Asia	13.1	54.4	15.6	90
	West Indies	49.2	74.2	24.3	66
	Ireland	41.0	67.0	10.0	449
	Europe	21.4	47.9	11.7	313
Indigenous children born abroad		24.7	52.0	13.3	98
Indigenous children born GB		22.5	49.1	7.3	8 311
Total		24.3	50.9	9.0	9 583

whether they did paid work or not, and the first column of Table 3.4 shows the percentage of children in families where they did. Fewer mothers in the first-generation Asian group did paid work than in the indigenous group. Although there were no other statistically significant differences between the immigrant and the indigenous group, there is a suggestion of proportionately more second-generation West Indian mothers working.

Unfortunately, we do not have information on reasons for taking up employment and the type of work being undertaken by the mothers. However, from what emerges later on the low income and bad housing conditions of certain groups, it is probable that mothers in these groups are more likely to be working out of economic hardship and perhaps in more manual jobs (judging also by the social class of the male head of household). In any case we can be sure that the question does not have the same meaning or relevance in all the groups.

The third column of Table 3.4 indicates the proportion of male heads of households (of families with a male head) who had — due to illness or un-employment — been off work for more than ten weeks in the preceding year. None of the differences reached statistical significance (where they could be tested), except for the second-generation Asians and European groups, who had more and less time off work respectively. There might be proportionately more first-generation Asians off work but the difference is not significant statistically.

Table 3.5 presents the cumulative distribution of net weekly household income for each group. This was obtained from the mother during the home interview and would include not only earned income but any state benefits, unearned income, pensions, etc., after the deduction of tax, national insurance, etc. It can be seen that generally there are no marked differences between the groups. The exceptions are the second-generation Asian groups and those where the child was born abroad to parents born in Great Britain. These two groups have higher incomes than the total sample (although the difference for the latter group is not statistically significant). Additionally, the first-generation Europeans had a higher percentage of both high- and low-income households than the indigenous sample. However, given that the immigrant groups generally had larger households (Table 3.3) the *income per head* for the first-generation immigrants and second-generation West Indian and Irish groups are *lower* than for the indigenous group.

Table 3.6 presents two other indicators of material need. The first is whether any child in the family was in receipt of free school meals, and the second, a subjective question, was whether the parents (or parent figures) had been 'seriously troubled by financial hardship in the past twelve months'. The second-generation Irish and West Indian groups were more likely to have free school meals than the indigenous group. The differences between the latter and the first-generation groups are either statistically non-significant or could not be tested because of small cell sizes. However, there seems to be a suggestion of more first-generation West Indian, Irish and European groups receiving free school meals.

TABLE 3.4   *Percentage of children in families with mothers working and with male head of household off work for ten weeks in the year*

		% with mother working	Total	% with male head off work for more than 10 weeks	Total
1st-generation immigrant	Asia	41.4	111	14.8	108
children	West Indies	63.6	55	10.6	47
	Ireland	62.2	45	7.3	41
	Europe	(55.6)	36	(7.7)	26
2nd-generation immigrant	Asia	62.1	87	8.9	79
children	West Indies	80.0	65	7.8	51
	Ireland	67.1	440	15.3	411
	Europe	67.5	308	7.7	284
Indigenous children born abroad		57.3	96	4.6	87
Indigenous children born GB		66.5	8 187	9.3	7 810
Total		66.1	9 430	9.6	8 944

A similar pattern existed for the feeling of financial hardship except that no more of the first-generation Europeans felt hardship than the indigenous sample. Thus Tables 3.5 and 3.6 are generally consistent in showing a relative disadvantage for first-generation groups and second-generation Irish and West Indian groups compared with indigenous children.

Table 3.7 shows the housing tenure of the groups. Compared with the indigenous sample: more of the first- and second-generation Asians own their homes and fewer live in council-rented accommodation; similar proportions of both first- and second-generation West Indian immigrants rent their homes (either from the council or privately), though there is a suggestion that more of the second-generation groups own their homes and fewer of them live in council-rented accommodation; fewer of the Irish own their homes and more of the first-generation groups are in privately rented and, of the second-generation groups, in council-rented dwellings (although very marked, the differences for the first-generation group are not statistically significant); there is a concentration of first-generation Europeans in privately rented dwellings and a higher proportion

TABLE 3.5   *Total net weekly household income*

Country of origin		Net household income greater than/equal to (%)			Total
		£35	£45	£60	
1st-generation immigrant children	Asia	84.5	61.9	46.4	84
	West Indies	81.6	65.8	42.1	38
	Ireland	86.8	71.0	44.7	38
	Europe	(71.4)	(50.0)	(46.4)	28
2nd-generation immigrant children	Asia	79.1	73.1	58.2	67
	West Indies	79.2	68.8	39.6	48
	Ireland	79.7	64.5	41.5	369
	Europe	82.4	64.4	43.9	244
Indigenous children born abroad		85.9	67.6	49.3	71
Indigenous children born GB		82.6	63.3	41.0	6 507
Total		82.5	63.6	41.5	7 494

TABLE 3.6   *Percentage receiving free school meals and 'seriously troubled by financial hardship'*

Country of origin		% receiving free school meals	Total	% troubled by financial hardship	Total
1st-generation immigrant children	Asia	14.3	111	10.0	110
	West Indies	19.2	52	26.9	52
	Ireland	20.0	45	18.2	44
	Europe	(19.4)	36	(8.6)	35
2nd-generation immigrant children	Asia	9.0	89	8.0	87
	West Indies	23.4	64	33.3	63
	Ireland	16.8	446	16.2	439
	Europe	10.0	310	8.9	302
Indigenous children born abroad		7.2	97	7.3	96
Indigenous children born GB		8.5	8 194	9.2	8 119
Total		9.3	9 444	9.8	9 347

of second-generation Europeans who own their homes; a higher proportion of those where the child was born abroad to parents born in Great Britain owned their homes.

The above comparisons do not, of course, bear on the quality of the homes, and as indicators of housing conditions we have taken crowding, use of basic amenities and sharing a bed.

Table 3.8 presents the percentage of children in homes which (a) were overcrowded (> 1.5 persons per room), (b) did not have sole use of three basic amenities (hot water, indoor lavatory and bathroom), and (c) in which they had to share a bed (the percentage in the first two columns are based on slightly different totals than those indicated in the last column, due to incomplete data). It is clear that the first-generation Asians and the first- and second-generation West Indians and Irish groups are at a

TABLE 3.7   *Housing tenure*

Country of origin		House or dwelling			Total
		Owned	Council rented	Private rented	
1st-generation immigrant children	Asia	82.7	8.2	9.1	110
	West Indies	54.5	40.0	5.5	55
	Ireland	33.3	44.4	22.2	45
	Europe	(58.8)	(23.5)	(17.6)	34
2nd-generation immigrant children	Asia	75.9	18.4	5.7	87
	West Indies	67.7	27.7	4.6	65
	Ireland	41.1	54.1	4.8	438
	Europe	65.4	27.9	6.6	301
Indigenous children born abroad		69.6	25.0	5.4	92
Indigenous children born GB		52.5	42.4	5.1	7 944
Total		53.2	41.5	5.3	9 171

TABLE 3.8   *Crowding, use of amenities and sharing of bed*

Country of origin		% crowded	% without sole use of amenities	% sharing bed	Total
1st-generation immigrant children	Asia	33.0	23.6	17.0	112
	West Indies	27.5	13.5	29.6	54
	Ireland	19.6	13.0	20.0	45
	Europe	(5.6)	(8.6)	(2.9)	35
2nd-generation immigrant children	Asia	4.5	6.7	3.4	87
	West Indies	20.3	15.6	24.6	65
	Ireland	16.0	4.5	11.2	446
	Europe	4.5	7.3	6.4	310
Indigenous children born abroad		4.1	2.1	4.2	96
Indigenous children born GB		7.3	5.5	7.3	8 207
Total		8.1	5.9	7.8	9 457

considerable disadvantage on all three measures (because of small cell sizes the differences for first-generation West Indian and Irish groups and second-generation West Indians' use of amenities could not be tested but the differences are very marked). The second-generation Irish group does not differ from the indigenous group on sharing of amenities, perhaps because more of them are in council housing. Those children born abroad to parents born in Great Britain seem to be at an advantage on all the measures, though the differences are not statistically significant.

Conclusions

Here an attempt is made to summarise the preceding results to provide an overall picture for each of the immigrant groups. It is as well to point out again that the results are not of immigrants generally but of those with a 16-year-old in the household.

Asians
This was the group which exhibited the most difference between those children who were first- or second-generation immigrants.

The first-generation group had a bigger proportion of large families and households; perhaps higher proportions of male heads of household who were off work for over ten weeks in the year; a very high proportion of families in crowded conditions, without sole use of basic amenities and sharing beds; a smaller proportion of mothers doing paid work. They were as likely as the indigenous population to be one-parent families; be in non-manual occupations; have similar income distributions (although their income per head would be appreciably lower due to their larger household size); feel seriously troubled by financial hardship and claim free school meals (despite their lower income per head). They more often owned their homes and were slightly more often in privately rented accommodation than the indigenous population. Conversely, they were much less likely to be in council accommodation.

The second-generation group shared only a few of the above characteristics and were closer to the indigenous population. Thus, compared with the indigenous population: they had the same proportion of large families or households; same proportion of male heads of household being off work for over ten weeks in the year; similar or smaller proportions in overcrowded conditions, without sole use of certain amenities and sharing beds; similar proportions of mothers in paid employment; and perhaps slightly higher proportions in one-parent families. They were more likely than the indigenous population to be in non-manual occupations; own their own homes; have higher incomes (though similar proportions were

receiving free school meals and felt seriously troubled by financial hardship, which might mean that there are similar proportions of low-income families among them not shown by our categories). They were less likely to be in council accommodation and equally likely to be in privately rented accommodation.

West Indians
The differences between the first- and second-generation West Indian immigrants were by no means as great as for the Asians. Thus compared with the indigenous population *both* groups had: a bigger proportion of large families or households; higher proportion of one-parent families (similar in both groups but could not be statistically tested in the first-generation group); a far lower proportion of male heads engaged in non-manual occupations; similar income distribution (although, again, because of their larger family and household size, their income per head would be lower); a higher percentage receiving free school meals (similar in both groups but failing statistical significance in the first-generation group); more parents feeling seriously troubled by financial hardship; a much higher percentage living in crowded conditions or without sole use of basic amenities or sharing beds. Similar proportions had a male head of household being off work for over ten weeks in the year and a mother doing paid work (although there is a suggestion of more mothers in the second-generation West Indian group doing paid work). The results for the West Indian groups are not compared with the two studies mentioned in the introduction (p. 77) because these are localised and in addition do not distinguish between first- and second-generation immigrants as we have done.

Irish
There were, generally, small differences between the first- and second-generation Irish groups, except in housing. Thus, compared with the indigenous population, they had: more large families or households; a higher proportion from non-manual backgrounds (failing to reach statistical significance in the first-generation group); a similar proportion of mothers in paid employment; a higher percentage living in crowded conditions; similar income distributions (although, again, because of their larger family and household size income per head would be lower); a higher proportion receiving free school meals and feeling 'seriously troubled by financial hardship' (the difference could not be tested for the first-generation group); a higher percentage living in crowded conditions and sharing bed; a lower proportion owning their homes.

Despite the generally unfavourable housing

conditions of both Irish groups compared with the indigenous group, those of the second generation were somewhat better than the first. Thus the second-generation group did not have the higher proportion of cases in the first group who were in privately rented accommodation or without sole use of amenities. They more often were in council accommodation and owned their homes and less often shared a bed. However, they were more disadvantaged in that they more often had a male head of household off work in the preceding year.

Europe

Judging from the income distribution of the first-generation European immigrants this group is unusually heterogeneous. It seems to consist of a disproportionate number of families in both the top- and bottom-income brackets. This might be due to the great mix of countries included in the group which together with its small size make any conclusions very tentative. Thus the rather contradictory results are that they are predominantly in non-manual occupations, have small families and large households, are more often in receipt of free school meals (though no more of them say they feel financial hardship than the rest of the population) and have a very high percentage of one-parent families. Further, their housing conditions are similar to, if not slightly better than, the indigenous population. As mentioned earlier, it seems best to ignore this group because of its small size and heterogeneity.

In contrast, the second-generation Europeans are almost identical in every respect with the indigenous population. The exception is that more of them own their homes and fewer are in council-rented accommodation.

As for the group of children who were born abroad to parents born in Great Britain, it is fairly clear that they are a 'privileged' group. They are: predominantly in non-manual occupations with, perhaps, higher incomes; more often owner-occupiers; less often in crowded conditions with lack of amenities or sharing beds. They have similar-sized families and households with slightly lower proportions of mothers working or heads of households being off work for more than ten weeks in the year. They did not differ in the proportion in receipt of free school meals or in the feeling of financial hardship from the indigenous group.

It can be safely said that altogether, except for the second-generation Asians, the European groups and those born abroad to parents born in Great Britain, the picture of the conditions in which many children in these minority groups live is a very grim one indeed.

CHILDREN OF IMMIGRANTS: SCHOOL PERFORMANCE

Introduction

During the last two decades, since there have been appreciable numbers of immigrant children in schools in some areas of Britain, a considerable amount of research has been carried out on their performance in school and the difficulties they face (see Taylor, 1974; for a review, see Yule *et al.*, 1975). However, because of the concentration of immigrants in certain areas, these studies have tended to be localised, and therefore do not provide information on a national scale about the performance of immigrants. This localisation also tends to result in immigrants from only one country of origin being studied at a time, which therefore provides no opportunity to compare children from different countries. Cross-study comparisons are then hampered by variations in conditions among the different (British) locations.

The data presented here from a nationally representative sample of children can therefore contribute to the discussion by comparing the school performance of children from several countries of origin with one another as well as with indigenous children. A distinction is also made between children born in this country to immigrant parents and children who were born overseas themselves.

Two main questions are considered here. The first one concerns the importance of allowing for differences in home circumstances when comparing the school performance of immigrants and non-immigrants. An association between school performance and home background has been fairly well established previously for immigrants (for a review, see Taylor, 1974; also Giles, 1977; Yule *et al.*, 1975). Clearly both the overall differences and the remaining differences when children of similar circumstances are compared can be expected to vary with the country of origin of the children. Most previous research has found poor school performance among West Indians but not Asians (Yule *et al.*, 1975; Little *et al.*, 1968; McFie and Thompson, 1970; Taylor, J. H., 1973) though this has not been universal, as Houghton (1966) found no differences between West Indians and English primary schoolchildren in one particularly depressed area — though both groups performed less well than the national average.

Little (1978) considered the possible reasons for the difference in educational performance between West Indians and Asians, and suggested that it could be partly due to the extra effort made to accommodate Asians in schools, and partly a question of the effect on their attitudes of the two cultures: he pointed out that Asians tend to come from homes with their own language and culture, and with values which prize learning and encourage self-improvement, while West Indians' culture is a variant of the dominant (British) culture and is often disparaged by the dominant culture, which is likely to have very discouraging results.

The second area investigated here relates to differences *among* the immigrants: namely first the length of time they have spent in Britain, with second-generation immigrants at one extreme having spent all their childhood in Britain, and second the language they usually speak.

Previous research has often found a relationship between attainment and the time children have spent in the country. For example, J. H. Taylor (1973), in a study of secondary school boys in Newcastle, found that Asians who had had at least four years' education in England performed considerably better than more recent arrivals, to the extent that they were at least as good as English boys. McFie and Thompson (1970) also showed that school performance was related to length of stay in Britain, as did Yule *et al.* (1975), who in addition found that second-generation West Indians had higher test scores than first-generation West Indians. Little *et al.* (1968) showed that immigrant pupils' performance (in London primary schools) was related to length of stay in Britain, such that first-generation immigrants who had spent most of their childhood in Britain performed as well as second-generation immigrants. Little (1975) concluded that 'length of education in the UK appears to be a more important determinant of performance than length of residence'.

The present study is particularly well placed to contribute to this discussion as the subjects were at the end of their compulsory secondary schooling, which means that the time which the immigrant children have spent in British schools ranges from less than a year to more than a decade.

Reasons for the relationship between length of stay in Britain and attainment are fairly clear, namely that recent arrivals may suffer from culture shock and the difficulty of being in an unfamiliar environment, in the case of the West Indians often living with parents who are strangers (DES, 1971) and going to a strange school, where for many immigrants a foreign language is being spoken (Taylor, J. H., 1973; DES, 1971).

This leads to the final question considered here, namely that of language difficulties. Little (1975) and Dickinson *et al.* (1975) found that immigrants from non-English-speaking countries perform best on the least verbal tests. One of the aims of the present study is to contribute to this discussion by comparing the children's maths attainment and their reading attainment.

School performance is assessed here by means of tests of attainment in reading and maths. It should be borne in mind, however, in view of the well-documented cultural bias of such tests, that test results do not reflect the relative intelligence or potential of immigrants and non-immigrants, but rather reflect their attainment in the skills in question (Little, 1975; Haynes, 1971; Townsend and Brittan, 1972). This is likely broadly to represent their performance at school, which is of importance to the children as it is a major factor in determining the range of occupations and education open to them in the future.

Definition

The term 'immigrant' is defined for present purposes as 'a child born abroad with at least one parent born abroad' (first-generation immigrants) or a 'child born in Britain with at least one parent born abroad' (second-generation immigrant). The children who were themselves born abroad but whose parents were born in Britain were also included as a separate group, as they will have experienced some of the difficulties of moving to a strange country, though these are likely to be of a different nature by virtue of having British-born parents.

Both the first- and second-generation immigrants were subdivided according to their country of origin, though this subdivision had to be fairly crude in order to retain sufficient numbers in each group. The four divisions were as follows:

1. West Indies.
2. India and Pakistan, and also the rest of Asia (relatively few children) and Africa if the child's ethnic group were Asian.
3. North and South Ireland.
4. Europe — including also the USA, Australia and the USSR, but excluding Cyprus, Malta and Gibraltar.

The very small numbers of children from Cyprus, Malta or Gibraltar and those from Africa or of African ethnic origin did not fit appropriately into any of the above groups and so were excluded. The European group is clearly heterogeneous.

They will, however, be alike in that they experienced a move to a country where, for the majority, a foreign language is spoken and the customs and culture were strange to them.

Finally, a group comprising children who were born in Britain to parents who were also born in Britain (the indigenous group) was formed for purposes of comparison with the immigrant groups.

Response levels

As the analyses in the present study involved a large number of variables, the numbers in the sample were considerably reduced, as only children with almost complete data could be included. A check for bias revealed that the mean test scores of the children included in the analyses was slightly higher than the mean for the total cohort, but as this applied equally to most of the immigrant groups and the non-immigrants, the differences between them were barely affected. The only exception to this was the maths score of the first-generation Europeans included in the analyses, which was low in comparison with all first-generation Europeans. Results for this group should therefore be treated with great caution.

Results

The mean scores on the tests of attainment taken by the 16-year-olds are presented in Table 3.9. It can be seen that all the first-generation groups have lower scores on both tests than the indigenous group (although for the Irish and Asians this does not reach significance on the maths test, and the Europeans' maths test scores should be ignored — see above). Among the second-generation groups, however, it is only the West Indians who have clearly lower mean scores than indigenous children.

Each of the second-generation groups has a higher mean score than the corresponding first-generation immigrants (except the Irish maths scores) and this is particularly striking for the Asians, who become the highest scorers among second-generation immigrants. It should also be noted that there is quite a noticeable difference between first- and second-generation West Indians' test scores, particularly for reading, even

though they remain considerably lower than any of the other immigrants.

Simple comparisons of mean test scores are limited in their usefulness, as the groups tend to come from very different backgrounds which themselves are related to the children's school performance. The home circumstances of the immigrant groups in the NCDS have been shown to differ considerably both from one another and from indigenous children, in some cases to the immigrants' advantage as well as, more often, to their disadvantage.

In order to attempt to allow for this heterogeneity in background we compared the young people's school performance after adjusting for difference in their home circumstances. This of course can only be a crude endeavour to make some allowance for very complex and varying social backgrounds.

An additional aspect of this background which was of particular relevance in this study was the language which the children were accustomed to speak, which was likely to differ for many of them from the language expected by the young people's teachers. The parents of the NCDS children were asked what language was usually spoken in the home. From their responses we discovered that the West Indians, Irish and both the groups with British-born parents almost all claimed to speak exclusively English at home. Asians and Europeans varied according to whether the children were or were not born in Britain, in particular the Asians, for whom only 13 per cent of first-generation but 86 per cent of second-generation immigrants spoke only English at home.

It should be noted, however, that a Community Relations Commission study of young people of Asian origin demonstrated that 66 per cent of those who were born in Britain spoke their mother-tongue

TABLE 3.9   *Mean test scores (transformed) of immigrant groups*

			Maths test		Reading test	
			Mean	se	Mean	se
1st generation	W. Indies	(41)	−0.90	(0.11)	−1.06	(0.10)
	Asia	(87)	−0.09	(0.09)	−0.84	(0.10)
	Ireland	(41)	−0.05	(0.15)	−0.09	(0.15)
	Europe	(23)	−0.33	(0.14)	−0.07	(0.15)
2nd generation	W. Indies	(58)	−0.59	(0.10)	−0.63	(0.10)
	Asia	(71)	0.28	(0.10)	0.28	(0.11)
	Ireland	(377)	−0.05	(0.05)	0.03	(0.05)
	Europe	(266)	0.12	(0.06)	0.13	(0.06)
Child born abroad, parents born GB		(81)	0.21	(0.10)	0.37	(0.10)
Parents and child born GB		(7 185)	0.05	(0.01)	0.06	(0.01)

at home, though the study agreed with the NCDS figures for first-generation Asians (Community Relations Commission, 1976). The only differences between the two studies which could provide an explanation for these contrasting findings is that the CRC study employed interviewers who spoke the appropriate Asian language if required, and their responses were provided by the young people themselves, not their parents.

The mean test scores of the young people were then examined after allowing for their home circumstances (including the language they spoke at home), by means of analysis of variance. The results of this analysis are shown in Table 3.10, and the background circumstances included in the analysis are listed in the note to the table.

There are two main points of interest to be observed in Table 3.10: first, that the differences between each immigrant group and indigenous children are in general considerably reduced by allowing for differences in background; second, and related to the first point, when children of similar circumstances (in broad terms) are compared, some but not all of the groups differ from indigenous children in their school performance.

In order to consider the first point in more detail, the differences between each immigrant group and the indigenous children in Table 3.10 must be compared with the corresponding difference in Table

3.9. If one considers only those immigrant groups whose unadjusted mean scores are particularly low, namely the two groups of West Indians and first-generation Asians, the difference in test score between each of these groups and the indigenous group is reduced by between 20 and 40 per cent after adjusting for background circumstances. As far as the other groups with slightly low overall mean scores are concerned, namely both first- and second-generation Irish, the situation is somewhat different in that after adjustment for background factors their mean test scores are actually (very slightly) higher than the indigenous group.

The answers to the second question can be read directly from the fitted constants in Table 3.10. It can be seen that when children of similar backgrounds are compared, only the two groups of West Indians and first-generation Asians have lower mean scores than indigenous children. (As was noted in the section on response levels, the first-generation Europeans included in the analysis are a biased group, with an artificially low mean maths test score, so this figure (which has been enclosed in brackets) should be ignored.)

In general, the pattern is similar to that for overall mean scores, in that, apart from the Irish, the second generation perform better than the corresponding first generation, and, in fact, often slightly better than indigenous children. The children who were

TABLE 3.10   *Test scores of immigrants after adjusting for differences in social and home circumstances*

	Maths test		Reading test	
	Fitted constant	χ^2	Fitted constant	χ^2
1st generation				
W. Indies	−0.61	52.2 (9)	−0.75	114.6 (9)
Asia	0.05	$p < 0.001$	−0.48	$p < 0.001$
Ireland	0.20		0.18	
Europe	(−0.20)		0.19	
2nd generation				
W. Indies	−0.32		−0.34	
Asia	0.18		0.19	
Ireland	0.21		0.30	
Europe	0.20		0.25	
Child born abroad, parents born GB	0.16		0.32	
Parent and child born GB	0.13		0.14	
	Total variance = 0.93		Total variance = 0.93	
	$N = 8\ 205$; RMS = 0.78		$N = 8\ 232$; RMS = 0.76	

Note: Variables included in the analyses: sex, region of the country, family size, social class, receipt of free school meals, crowding ratio, use of amenities in the home, tenure of the home, language spoken at home.

born abroad to British parents also perform slightly better than the indigenous group. (Some caution should be adopted in interpreting the figures, as the numbers of children in each group often tend to be small.)

To summarise, the results here are in agreement with previous research (see p. 34) in showing that while many immigrant groups have lower overall mean scores on attainment tests, when children of similar financial and housing circumstances are compared only the West Indians have clearly poorer school performance than indigenous children.

In view of the findings from previous research on length of stay in Britain (see p. 35) the mean test scores of children who had been in Britain for differing lengths of time were compared. Asian and West Indian children had arrived in the country at a fairly steady rate through childhood, so were grouped by the age on arrival as 'infants' school or earlier' (0–7 years), junior school (8–11 years), and secondary school (12 or later). However, very few Europeans and Irish had arrived later than their junior school years, so all those who came after the age of 8 from these countries were combined into one group.

The relationship between age of arrival in Britain and test scores does not show a consistent pattern in all cases. For the European and Irish the differences are very small. For the Asians and West Indians there is an unexpected dip in the maths test scores of those who came during their junior school years, but again the differences are small (Figure 3.1). The only clear trend is for the Asian and West Indian reading test scores to be lower, the shorter the time they have been in Britain. This was quite marked, the difference between under 7-year-old arrivals and over 11-year-old arrivals being one standard deviation for the Asians and over three-quarters of a standard deviation for the West Indians. However, the results should be treated with some caution as the groups of children are fairly small.

Figure 3.1 also indicates that it is only the recent arrivals among the Asians and West Indians who perform worse in reading than in maths, while the children who came before they were 7 performed fairly similarly on the two tests.

At this point it seems interesting to make a comparison between the attainment of the first- and second-generation immigrant groups and the differences related to length of stay in Britain among first-generation immigrants. It seems likely that the pattern will be similar in the two cases, as both comparisons reflect differences in familiarity with the country. From Figure 3.1 it emerges that only West Indians and Asians had higher scores if they had been in the country longer, and this was only on the reading test.

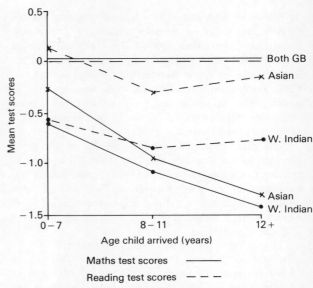

Maths test scores ———
Reading test scores – – –

FIGURE 3.1   *Test scores of first-generation immigrants (transformed)*

From Table 3.10 it appears that, again on the reading test, among the Asians and West Indians there are indeed large differences between first- and second-generation immigrants, and these differences are far greater than for the Europeans or Irish.

Both these sets of findings taken together therefore provide some support for the evidence described in the introduction (e.g. Little *et al.*, 1968) of the importance of familiarity with Britain for children's school performance.

Earlier studies found that non-English-speaking immigrant children perform less well on verbal tests (see p. 85). One would therefore anticipate that the reading test would prove more difficult than the maths test for children whose first language is not English. Comparison between the two subjects does reveal a clear difference for the first-generation Asians, who are the only group who perform on average more poorly on the reading test than on the maths test (Table 3.10) and are also the only group of whom a large proportion do not speak English at home. Further to this, Figure 3.1 showed that this difference between the reading and maths performance of the first-generation Asians was mainly among the recent arrivals, who are likely to have more language difficulties.

Conclusions

Two general conclusions can be drawn. First, overall, immigrants tend to have relatively poor attainment, but when children of similar financial and other material circumstances are compared most of the immigrant groups do as well as non-immigrants, the only main exception to this being the West Indians. Second, the poorer school performance is generally only found among first-generation immigrants, not second-generation immigrants, and to some extent is relatively short-term and language-specific. This has considerable implications for the appropriate educational provision for recent arrivals. In particular, it provides support for pleas that West Indians are often wrongly placed in ESN schools, and even more wrongly kept in these schools (Coard, 1971; DES, 1971; Taylor, 1974). The evidence suggests that more appropriate help would be of a temporary nature and related to their particular difficulties at the time, such as the strange language and the culture shock they experience on arrival in a new environment.

4   Single-Parent Families*

LIVING IN ONE-PARENT FAMILIES: RELATIONSHIPS AND ATTITUDES OF 16-YEAR-OLDS

Introduction

The research generated by the Finer Committee on One Parent Families provided a wealth of data about the prevalence and experience of living in a one-parent situation (DHSS, 1974b). Some of these studies were able to show the extent to which the composition and persistence of single parenthood varied over the years of childhood (Douglas, 1970; Gill and Stephen, 1974; Ferri, 1976).

Data on 16-year-old children in the National Child Development Study have provided an opportunity to follow up the earlier study of 11-year-old children in one-parent families in the NCDS (Ferri, 1976) and have enabled us to review the whole period from birth to 16 years. This included looking at the proportions who spent at least some part of their childhood without one of their own parents and the length of time the children tended to spend in this situation. We also considered whether, after their own unusual experience of family life, the attitudes to their own family and their aspirations for any future family of their own differed from the attitudes of children who had always lived with both their own parents.

Sample

Children living in a one-parent family are defined as those for whom it was reported at the time of any follow-up that they were living with their natural mother but no father-figure, or with their natural father but no mother-figure. This means that when a brother or sister or grandparent was reported as acting as a parent-figure it has been assumed that this person

* Original sources: Essen, J. and Lambert, L., 'Living in one-parent families: relationships and attitudes of 16-year-olds', *Child: Care, Health and Development*, 3, 1977, 301—18; Essen, J., 'Living in one-parent families: income and expenditure', *Poverty*, 40, 1978, 23—8; Essen, J., 'Living in one-parent families: attainment at school', *Child: Care, Health and Development*, 5, 1979, 189—200; Lambert, L., 'Living in one-parent families: school leavers and their future', *Concern*, no. 29, 1978.

had taken on some of the duties of that role, and that the child had, to some extent at least, two parents. Therefore, these children have not been included in the one-parent family sample. At birth, the question asked concerned the marital status of the mother rather than who was acting as the father-figure, and therefore children were regarded as living in a one-parent family at that stage if their mothers were single, divorced, separated or widowed. Children whose mothers were said to be living in a 'stable union' were not included as they will have had two parent-figures, and it was the experience of living with a lone parent which was being examined.

At the age of 16 information was obtained on 87 per cent of those children known to be in the country. An analysis was carried out to assess whether those responding were representative of their age group. This showed that those who had previously been in anomalous parental situations were slightly less likely to respond than those with both parents. This meant that the percentage of children known to have been in one-parent families by 16 years of age is likely to be an underestimation by about 9 per cent of the true figure.

Results

Before considering children who had at one time or another been in one-parent families, the proportions of children in each of the different parental situations at 16 were examined. Some comparisons were also made with the National Survey's cohort of children who were born twelve years earlier (Douglas, 1964).

Situation at 16 years

Table 4.1 shows that, altogether, 16.4 per cent of 16-year-olds were not living with both their own parents. Among these, 8.4 per cent were in one-parent families as defined above and 3.9 per cent were with a step-parent. It is interesting to note that although among those with lone parents there were over five times as many children living with their mother as with their father (7.1 and 1.3 per cent respectively), among the children with step-parents there were less than three times as many with their own mothers as with their own fathers (2.9 and 1.0 per cent), and among the families where some other relation (e.g. grandparent) was acting as the second parent-figure, there were as many with their own fathers as with their own mothers (both 0.5 per cent). This could suggest that society is more sympathetic to lone fathers, who are therefore less often left to manage by themselves than lone mothers. In addition there are economic, social and child-care pressures on fathers not to remain single for any length of time

(George and Wilding, 1972), though lone mothers will also feel these pressures to different extents.

When the proportion of children who were not living with both natural parents at 16 is compared with those in this situation at 7 and 11, it is immediately clear that the proportion has continued to rise (Table 4.2). By the age of 16 more than twice the proportion had lost at least one parent as at 7 (16.4 per cent as against 8 per cent). While at 16 there was

TABLE 4.1   *Parental situation at 16 years (NCDS)*

	Alone		+ Step-parent		+ Co-habitee		+ Adoptive parent		+ Other relation		Total	
	(%)	(N)	(%)	(N)	(%)	(N)	(%)	(N)	(%)	(N)	(%)	(N)
Natural mother	7.1	830	2.9	341	0.5	57	0.5	57	0.5	53	11.4	1 338
Natural father	1.3	152	1.0	120	0.1	14	—	1	0.5	58	3.0	346
Sub-total	8.4	983	3.9	461	0.6	71	0.5	58	1.0	111	14.4	1 684
2 adoptive parents											0.8	93
1 adoptive + 1 step-parent											0.0	3
2 relatives											0.5	59
2 foster-parents											0.1	15
2 house-parents											0.2	20
1 substitute parent only											0.4	43
Both natural parents											83.6	9 770
Total											100.0	11 687

TABLE 4.2   *Parental situation at 7, 11 and 16*

Parental situation	Children aged 7		Children aged 11		Children aged 16	
	N	%	N	%	N	%
Lost father only	737	5.0	1 067	7.7	1 338	11.4
Lost mother only	111	0.8	237	1.7	346	3.0
Lost both parents	326	2.2	277	2.0	233	2.0
Total not living with both natural parents	1 174	8.0	1 581	11.4	1 917	16.4
Total living with both natural parents	13 514	92.0	12 285	88.6	9 770	83.6
Total for whom information available	14 688	100.0	13 366	100.0	11 687	100.0

Tests:
Age by lost father only/both parents $\chi^2 = 396.8$ (2 df) $p < 0.001$.
Age by lost mother only/both parents $\chi^2 = 209.4$ (2 df) $p < 0.001$.
Age by lost both parents/both parents $\chi^2 = 0.7$ (2 df) ns.

almost no change from 11 or 7 in the proportion who had lost both parents (2.0 per cent), there was an increase from 1.7 per cent at 11 to 3.0 per cent at 16 in the proportion who had lost their natural mother, and this proportion had more than tripled from that at 7 (0.8 per cent).

The most common situation at 16 for children not living with both natural parents was to be fatherless (11.4 per cent), and this was more than twice the proportion at 7 (5.0 per cent). These figures confirm Ferri's (1976) expectation that the ratio of fatherless to motherless children is related to the age of the children, as among the 7-year-olds the fatherless outnumbered the motherless by 6.5 to 1, whereas when they were 16 the corresponding ratio was 3.5 to 1.

Comparisons with 1946 cohort
The rate of divorce has increased in the last few decades (*Social Trends 1975*, table 1.15) especially since the recent change in divorce law, so it was expected that the proportion of children in the NCDS in families broken by divorce and separation would be greater than the corresponding proportions of children born earlier. In order to find out if this were so, the findings on 16-year-olds in the NCDS were compared with those of 15-year-olds in the National Survey of Health and Development (NSHD), a study of a sample of children born in one week of 1946 (Douglas, 1970; DHSS, 1974b). The NSHD findings were based on a sample from which twins, illegitimate children and immigrants were excluded; in these comparisons the same groups were excluded from the NCDS. This has the effect of reducing the percentage in each broken-family situation. The NSHD results are the population estimates of the percentages in each group, using both 15-year-old data and additional data collected when the Survey members were 26 years of age. (For details of the sample, see Douglas, 1964.)

Overall, very similar proportions of children were in broken families in the 1946 cohort as in the 1958 cohort (13.1 and 12.9 per cent respectively: see Table 4.3). However, although similar proportions of families in each study broke up when the children were in the older age group, a larger proportion of children in the NSHD experienced a break in the family when they were under 6 than the comparable group in the NCDS. This difference could not be offset entirely by the small proportion in the NCDS for whom the age of break was not known. An explanation for this could be that the first six years of the National Survey children's lives would have been in the immediate post-war years, when the rate of divorce was temporarily increased (*Social Trends 1970*).

The figures in Table 4.4 relate to the reason for the original break-up of the families in the National Survey, whereas they describe the present situation for the 16-year-olds in the NCDS. For this reason there is an 'other' category in the NCDS which includes children living with relations or in the care of the local authority. The conclusions from this table must therefore be somewhat tentative. For example, although there appears to be a higher percentage of children in the National Survey whose mothers have died, this reason could apply to some of the NCDS children who were later received into care, thereby reducing the difference between the studies.

The overall impression from these two tables is therefore that there is little evidence of the expected differences in the likelihood of family breakdown during the twelve years.

TABLE 4.3   *Age of child at the break in the NSHD* and the NCDS*

	NSHD			NCDS			
	6 years	6–15 years	Total	7 years	7–16 years	Not known	Total
All broken families	5.9%	7.2%	13.1%	3.9%	7.9%	1.1%	12.9%
Not broken			86.9%				87.1%
Total			100.0%				100.0%
N			9 405				10 320

* Population estimates.
Broken families/cohort χ^2 = 0.2 (1 df) ns.
Age/cohort χ^2 = 37.6 (1 df) $p < 0.001$.

TABLE 4.4   *Reason for break in the NSHD* and the NCDS*

Reason	NSHD (age 15) (%)	NCDS (age 16) (%)
Father's death	4.3	3.4
Mother's death	2.6	1.4
Divorce or separation	6.2	5.4
Other	—	2.7
All broken families	13.1	12.9
N	(1 232)	(1 331)

* Population estimates.

Reason/cohort χ^2 = 18.3 (2 df) $p < 0.001$.

Children at one time or another in one-parent families

The cross-sectional analysis showed that 8.4 per cent of the cohort were with a single parent at the age of 16. The analysis described below was designed to find the extent to which the same children were reported as living with a single natural parent at each age. For this part of the analysis only those children with data at each age could be considered. In addition, as the data were collected on only four occasions, it is likely that the percentage ever having lived in a one-parent family will be an underestimate, as there will have been children who spent some of their childhood with a single parent but were not in that situation at the time of any of the follow-ups, and therefore were not included in the one-parent family sample. As will be shown later, this is especially likely, as living with a single parent often appears to be a temporary situation, and an alternative arrangement is soon found.

Figure 4.1 shows both the proportions who were ever recorded as living with either their mother or father alone, and the stage of their childhood at which this occurred: 12.2 per cent of the total cohort were living in a one-parent family during at least one follow-up. The diagram shows that over six times as many children had lived with their mothers alone as with their fathers alone (944, compared with 148). However, the ratio varied with the age of the child at the time of the break-up. Of those who had been with a single parent earlier, but were in a two-parent family by the age of 16, there were eleven times as many with their mother as with their father alone. This is partly because the former included a large number of children whose mothers had been single

at the time of their birth, but who later moved into two-parent families — often with adoptive parents. Of those with a lone parent at the 16-year-old follow-up only, there were only 3½ times as many with their mothers (31.4 per cent) as with their fathers (8.3 per cent).

Although the duration varies, lone parenthood appears to have been a transitory state for many families. A very small percentage of the one-parent family sample (2.4 per cent, or 0.3 per cent of the total cohort) were known to be with a single parent at all four ages (Figure 4.1), which means that no more than, and probably less than, this proportion of children were with lone mothers during all of their childhood. Also, over two-thirds (68.9 per cent) of the children ever in single-parent families were reported as living with one parent at only one follow-up. Nearly 40 per cent (31.4 + 8.3) were with a single parent at 16 years old only, 17.9 per cent had lone mothers only at the time of their birth, and the remaining 11.3 per cent were with one parent at either 7 years old or 11 years old.

Reasons for loss of parent

Table 4.5 shows the reasons why the children were not with both their own parents. The fatherless children are subdivided into those whose mothers were alone when the children were 16, and those whose mothers were no longer alone by then. This has not been done for the motherless, as the number involved would have been too small for many of the analyses. The table shows that for the 16-year-olds with single mothers the reason was equally likely to be marriage breakdown as death of the father, whereas among those no longer one-parent by then there were twice as many with broken marriages as widowed, suggesting that widows are less likely to remarry. The group previously with lone mothers includes children currently in a variety of situations, not necessarily with their own mother. For example, some were with relations or in care, and those who gave 'other' reasons were predominantly illegitimate children, many of whom were adopted. The reason for children not being with their mothers at the age of 16 was equally likely to be death as separation.

In the following analyses comparison have been made between the groups of children described in Table 4.5.

Relationships within the family

Most of the children in our sample who had experienced living with a single parent had also lived with both their own parents for at least part of their childhood. By the age of 16 many of those who had lost a parent had also had the experience of living with step, adoptive or other substitute parent figures. We

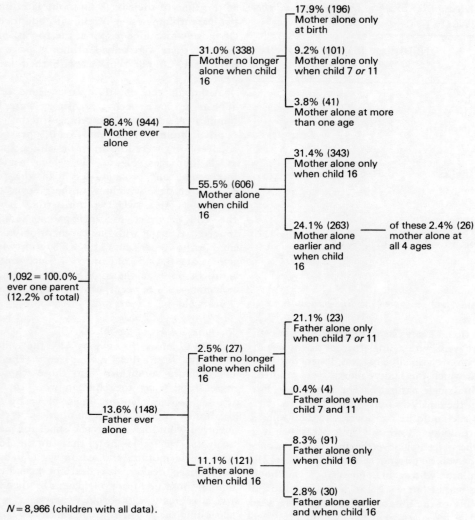

FIGURE 4.1 *Children ever in a one-parent family (NCDS)*

TABLE 4.5   *Reasons for loss of parent when child 16*

Parental situation	Reason			Total	
	Widowed (%)	Divorced/ separated (%)	Other reason or not known (%)	N	(%)
Mother alone but not when child 16	0.5	1.0	2.3	338	3.8
Mother alone when child 16	3.1	3.0	0.6	606	6.7
Father ever alone	0.8	0.8	0.0	148	1.6
Other situations, not one-parent				346	3.8
Both parents always	—	—	—	7 528	84.0
Total*				8 966	100.0

* Children with all data.

therefore expected that after these experiences, which would have differed from the experiences of parenthood of most of their peers, the children would have formed different relationships within their families as well as having different plans and hopes for their future family life than the children who had always lived with both their own parents. It was also expected that in both these respects the young people would differ in their views according to the reason for the break in their family.

Although a great deal of research has been carried out on the adjustment to society of children in one-parent families (e.g. Douglas, 1970; Ferri, 1976; Rutter, 1972), less attention has been paid to relationships within the family. Marsden (1969) and George and Wilding (1972) found that in some families the remaining parent and child were said to be closer, but in others the family's difficulties had resulted in strained relationships. George and Wilding found that in some motherless families the relationship between father and teenage daughter was strained if the daughter did not take over the duties of the absent mother. The 16-year-olds in the NCDS will have been old enough for this to have been expected of them. Glasser and Navarre (1965) discussed the possible changes in family relationships following the loss of a parent, and in particular they considered the importance of the sex of the child and the remaining parent, though this was mainly in the context of the formation of relationships in the adult world outside the family. However, Thomas (1968), in a study of a small sample of 9- to 11-year-old children, found many similarities in attitudes to their family between children in fatherless families broken by divorce and separation, and children in two-parent families. She concluded that her study provided no support for the assumption that boys would be more affected than girls by the absence of a father. Thomas expected, however, that during adolescence the child might react more strongly to the absence of one parent. In our study, therefore, the children's relationships and attitudes to family life have been examined separately for boys and girls, to find out if the responses differed according to whether or not the child was the same sex as the remaining parent.

The confidential questionnaire completed by the study children included a series of questions about their attitudes to their present family. Two of these seem of particular relevance to children with lone parents: they were asked to rate on a five-point scale ranging from 'very true' to 'very untrue' whether they 'get on well with their mother' and 'get on well with their father'.

Table 4.6 shows that each group of children in one-parent families gave a slightly higher percentage of unfavourable responses than those living with both their own parents, though for girls whose mothers were no longer alone this difference did not reach significance. Boys whose mothers were no longer alone tended to give more responses at each extreme, perhaps because the changes of parent figure that these children experienced had helped to polarise their emotions.

Those who were fatherless at the time of the follow-up differed very little from children in unbroken families in their responses concerning their relationship with their remaining parent. Similarly, those at one time or another with lone fathers hardly differed at all from unbroken families in their responses to whether they 'get on well with their father' (Table 4.7).

The children in the 'father ever alone' group whose responses to the first question referred to stepmothers

TABLE 4.6 *'Get on well with mother' and parental situation*

Parental situation		Very true	True	Uncertain	Untrue + very untrue	Total
Mother alone, not at 16	(boys)	42.1	38.4	12.8	6.7	164
	(girls)	37.1	47.4	6.3	9.1	175
Mother alone, at 16	(boys)	40.1	44.8	7.9	7.1	252
	(girls)	50.0	37.3	9.6	6.9	260
Father ever alone	(boys)	37.0	32.6	17.4	13.0	46
	(girls)	28.0	46.2	15.4	10.3	39
Both parents always	(boys)	39.5	49.3	7.8	3.4	3 183
	(girls)	42.9	44.7	7.5	4.9	3 090

Significance tests for differences between very true; true, uncertain; untrue + very untrue.
[1] Mother alone (not at 16)/both parents: boys χ^2 = 13.6 (3 df) $p < 0.01$; girls χ^2 = 7.8 (3 df) ns.
[2] Mother alone at 16/both parents: boys χ^2 = 10.6 (3 df) $p < 0.05$; girls χ^2 = 9.3 (3 df) $p < 0.05$.
[3] Father alone/both parents: boys χ^2 = 19.5 (3 df) $p < 0.001$; girls χ^2 = 14.3 (3 df) $p < 0.01$.

TABLE 4.7   *'Get on well with father' and parental situation*

Parental situation		Very true	True	Uncertain	Untrue + very untrue	Total
Mother alone, but not at 16	(boys)	36.3	33.1	18.8	11.9	160
	(girls)	20.7	39.6	24.4	15.2	164
Father ever alone	(boys)	42.5	43.8	11.0	2.7	73
	(girls)	40.3	39.0	15.6	5.2	77
Both parents always	(boys)	35.9	48.3	10.3	5.5	3 185
	(girls)	34.8	45.2	11.8	8.2	3 090

Significance tests for differences between very true; true; uncertain; untrue + very untrue.
[1] Mother alone but not at 16/both parents: boys χ^2 = 29.4 (3 df) $p < 0.001$; girls χ^2 = 40.4 (3 df) $p < 0.001$.
[2] Father ever alone/both parents: boys χ^2 = 2.3 (3 df) ns; girls χ^2 = 3.0 (3 df) ns.

or other new mother-figures reacted much less favourably than those with both their own parents. It might be expected that boys would feel differently about a new mother-figure than girls, but there was no clear difference between the sexes in this respect (Table 4.6). Table 4.7 shows that children whose mothers had been, but were no longer, alone, reacted unfavourably to their new father-figure. It is interesting to note that whereas boys and girls with both their own parents were equally likely to say it was 'very true' that they get on well with their father, among this one-parent group fewer girls gave this very favourable response to the new father-figure than boys. The reported relationships with both parents were similar whether the family had broken up through divorce or death.

It appears from these results that the young people's view of their relationship with their natural parents did not differ very much between one- and two-parent families. This is particularly encouraging as the children in one-parent families were more likely to have spent some time in the care of the local authority than those with two parents (Essen *et al.*, 1976) and it might be expected that the relationship would have been adversely affected by this temporary separation. However, when the previously single parent shared the care of the children with a substitute parent figure, the children did not feel they got on so well with the new parent figure as with a natural parent.

Aspirations for future marriage and family
Ferri (1976) found that 11-year-old children in one- and two-parent families differed in their aspirations for future family life. She examined essays written by the children describing their lives when they were 25 years old, and found that fewer fatherless children imagined either that they would be married or that they would have children of their own than did children with both parents.

At 16 years more explicit questions about their plans for families of their own were put to the young people. These were:

1. 'What do you think would be the best age to get married?'
2. 'At what age would you ideally like to start a family?'
3. 'What size family would you like to have?'

Table 4.8 shows responses to the first of these questions, namely the age at which each group of children thought it would be best to get married. One of the choices offered was 'don't wish to marry', which just under 3 per cent of all the study children selected. It was possible that a larger proportion of the children who had experienced some disturbance in their family lives than those who had not might be unwilling to get married themselves. However, although all the one-parent family groups were slightly less likely to want to marry than the two-parent families, the differences were slight enough not to reach significance, except for boys living with lone mothers, of whom 7.5 per cent did not wish to marry. This lack of differences among the groups who were shown to get on less well with their substitute parent figures than with their natural parents may either be seen as reassuring that the difficulties in relationships were only minimal or as an idealistic hope by the 16-year-olds that their future families would be different. There were no differences in the age at which the children wanted to marry between any of the groups of one-parent families and two-parent families.

The circumstances and atmosphere prior to marriage breakdown may well have been more disturbing for the children involved than the atmosphere immediately preceding the death of a parent, and might have been expected to have affected the children's plans for the future more markedly. How-

TABLE 4.8   *Ideal age to marry and reason for parental situation*

Parental situation	≤ 19 years	20—21 years	22—25 years	≥ 26 years	Uncertain	Don't wish to marry	Total
Mothers alone:							
widowed	8.6	31.3	45.7	5.4	5.0	4.0	278
separated*	11.7	26.9	41.8	7.6	6.6	5.4	316
Fathers alone:							
widowered	13.5	32.6	38.2	9.0	2.3	4.5	89
separated	12.0	36.1	33.7	7.2	6.0	4.8	83

* Including divorced.
Tests: no significant differences in (1) any age; uncertain; don't wish, or (2) age to marry.

TABLE 4.9   *Ideal age to marry and parental situation*

Parental situation		≤ 19 yrs	20—21 yrs	22—25 yrs	≥ 26 yrs	Uncertain	Don't wish to marry	Total
Mothers alone, but not at 16	(boys)	9.4	27.6	42.4	11.2	5.9	3.5	170
	(girls)	17.0	34.1	36.9	4.0	4.0	4.0	176
Mother alone, at 16	(boys)	7.1	22.4	45.3	11.0	6.7	7.5	254
	(girls)	12.5	35.5	40.3	2.9	6.6	2.2	273
Father ever alone	(boys)	9.1	37.7	27.3	14.3	6.5	5.2	77
	(girls)	16.7	32.1	42.3	3.8	2.6	2.6	78
Both parents always	(boys)	8.0	29.3	41.4	9.1	9.0	3.3	3 196
	(girls)	14.3	36.9	38.6	3.8	4.5	1.9	3 101

Tests:
[1] (Any age; uncertain; don't wish.) Girls: each one-parent situation/both parents non-significant. Boys: mother alone at 16/both parents χ^2 = 12.1 (2 df) $p < 0.01$ Other differences non-significant.
[2] Age to marry (≤ 19, < 21, < 25, ≥ 26) no significant differences.

TABLE 4.10   *Ideal age to start a family and parental situation*

Parental situation		≤ 21 years	22—25 years	≥ 26 years	Uncertain	Don't want children	Total
Mothers alone, but not at 16	(boys)	15.6	41.1	32.4	6.9	4.0	173
	(girls)	23.7	50.8	11.9	6.8	6.8	177
Mothers alone, at 16	(boys)	12.6	37.5	32.4	10.7	6.7	253
	(girls)	17.5	49.6	20.4	9.1	3.3	274
Fathers ever alone	(boys)	13.0	41.6	28.6	13.0	3.9	77
	(girls)	21.8	53.8	19.2	5.1	—	78
Both parents always	(boys)	12.6	44.7	25.7	13.6	3.4	3 188
	(girls)	16.1	56.1	17.0	7.4	3.4	3 099

Tests:
[1] (Any age; uncertain, don't want.) Girls: no significant differences between parental situations.
  Boys: mothers alone but not at 16/both parents χ^2 = 9.1 (2 df) $p < 0.05$; mothers alone at 16/both parents χ^2 = 9.2 (2 df) $p < 0.05$; fathers alone/both parents non-significant.
[2] Age/parental situation. Girls: mothers alone but not at 16/both χ^2 = 10.4 (2 df) $p < 0.01$. Boys: mothers alone at 16/both χ^2 = 6.7 (2 df) $p < 0.05$. No other significant differences.

ever, the results did not support this theory, as similar proportions of children whose parent had died and whose parents' marriage had broken down said they did not wish to remarry (Table 4.9).

Table 4.10 shows the ages at which the study children said they would like to start a family. The motherless children and girls in families with no father at 16 had fairly similar plans to the children with both parents. Boys with no father differed from children with both parents in that a larger proportion wanted to start a family at a later age, or else did not want a family at all. Boys whose mothers had been alone earlier also wanted to start a family later, on average, than those with both parents, but by contrast girls in this group were more likely either not to want a family at all, or they wanted to have children earlier than those with both their own parents. There was a slight tendency for children whose parents' marriages had broken down to be less likely to want a family than those whose parents had died, but this result did not reach significance (Table 4.11).

The third question concerned the size of the family the children would like to have. Apart from the slightly higher proportions of children in some of the one-parent families who did not want any children (as shown in Table 4.10), the proportions choosing each size of family were similar whatever the parental situation, and whatever the reason for the break-up of the family. The most popular choice among all groups was to have two children, which was selected by over half the young people (52.2 per cent).

Conclusion

Clearly there will be considerable variations in relationships within incomplete families, often reflecting the very different circumstances leading to the present family situation, as well as differing with the age at which the family broke up and the duration of one-parenthood (Marsden, 1969). However, the aim here was to find out if children in one-parent families as a group showed any more evidence of discouragement in their feelings about family life than children in unbroken families. Although some differences did emerge, none of these was very marked. In particular, there was only a small proportion of children with lone parents who were unwilling to marry and have a family of their own. This therefore differed from Ferri's results, probably because of the different way in which the responses were elicited. The 11-year-old children may not have imagined themselves as married in the future because their current experience did not include living in a family in which there were two married partners, rather than because they had definite views against marriage However, when asked explicitly at 16 years of age, only a few of the children in the NCDS who had been in one-parent families showed any such unwillingness.

These findings only reflect the young people's present intentions towards marriage and children, and do not necessarily indicate how many of them will actually marry and have children. The small proportion expressing unwillingness to marry would seem to be a positive indication that although their experiences of family life had been unusual their expressed attitudes towards future family life were not greatly affected by these experiences of living in a one-parent family.

LIVING IN ONE-PARENT FAMILIES: INCOME AND EXPENDITURE

In a society where children are customarily brought up in two-parent nuclear families, children in one-parent families are likely to suffer from there being only one adult to carry out the tasks usually shared by two people. Where the remaining parent is the mother, there may be additional problems in that she may not have received the training that would have provided her with a sufficiently well-paid job to cater for the economic needs of the family. The resultant dependence on state benefits will tend to

TABLE 4.11   *Ideal age to start family and reason for parental situation*

Parental situation	≤ 21 years	22–25 years	≥ 26 years	Uncertain	Don't want children	Total
Mothers alone						
widowed	16.5	46.0	26.3	7.2	4.0	278
separated*	15.8	43.4	24.4	10.4	6.0	316
Fathers alone						
widowered	15.7	48.3	28.1	5.6	2.2	89
separated*	18.1	48.2	18.1	12.0	3.6	83

* Including divorced.
No significant differences in (1) any age; uncertain; don't want, or (2) age to have family.

leave lone mothers, and also, to a lesser extent, lone fathers, in conditions of financial hardship, as shown by the Finer Committee on One Parent Families (DHSS, 1974b). Here we examine the financial and material circumstances of a nationally representative sample of 16-year-olds who had at one time or another lived in one-parent families.

Comparisons have been made between three sub-groups of one-parent families and the group of children who had been reported as living with both their own parents at each NCDS follow-up. The three sub-groups are:

1. Children who had been fatherless at previous follow-ups but by the age of 16 had a substitute father.
2. Children who were fatherless at the age of 16.
3. Children who had at one time or another been motherless.

Results

Although the present circumstances of one-parent families are likely to be the main determinants of their financial situation, this will probably also be affected to some extent by their backgrounds, for example their social class. In order to compare children in each parental situation who are as alike as possible in other respects, comparison has been made between children of similar social class.

The social-class distribution at birth among children ever in one-parent families differed only slightly from that of children in unbroken families. However, at the time when they are alone, the need to combine the duties of earning and child care is likely to restrict the range of jobs from which lone parents could choose, which would then be apparent either in the status of the job or in the hours worked and therefore in earnings. However, the results from the NCDS showed that lone fathers were as likely to be in a non-manual occupation when the study child was 16 as married fathers, and in general this was also the case for lone mothers.

Earnings and other sources of income

Income from earnings will be irrelevant for many lone mothers as the size of their family, age of the children and the ease with which they can find someone to care for the younger ones may prevent some mothers from going out to work. Another factor determining whether she goes to work will be her alternative sources of income, such as widow's pension and supplementary benefit. Among the mothers from non-manual backgrounds, slightly more lone mothers did go to work (69 per cent compared with 63 per cent), but among those from manual backgrounds separated mothers were less likely to work (56 per cent), though as many widowed mothers worked (67 per cent) as mothers in unbroken families (70 per cent).

A comparison of net earned incomes revealed that among those from manual social classes fathers earned similar amounts whatever their marital status. Among the non-manual social classes lone fathers and fathers in unbroken families earned similar amounts, but substitute fathers in families which were previously fatherless tended to earn less. However, there was the opposite tendency among lone mothers, who earned higher incomes than married mothers, though they were in jobs of similar status. This was particularly marked for those who were separated or divorced. This may be an indication that married women could afford to work for a low income, whereas lone mothers need to either be very selective in their jobs or work longer hours to ensure that it is financially worth while to go to work at all.

For a lone parent the alternative to working is usually to depend on supplementary benefits. Table 4.12 shows that nearly half (47 per cent) of the

TABLE 4.12 *Financial situation of one-parent families*

Parental situation	Receipt of supplementary benefit in past year (%)	Receipt of Family Income Supplement in past year (%)	Receiving free school meals (%)	Feelings of hardship in past year (%)	Total
Mother alone earlier	10	2	17	13	291
Mother alone widowed	16	3	31	24	270
Mother alone, separated/divorced	47	5	54	40	270
Father ever alone	10	2	18	18	140
Both parents always	3	1	6	7	7 385

families where the marriage had broken down and 16 per cent of the families of widows had received supplementary benefits at some time during the year, both proportions being far higher than among unbroken families (3 per cent). In addition to information about their receipt of welfare benefits, Table 4.12 shows the parents' responses to the question 'Have you felt seriously troubled financially in the past twelve months?'

Household income

Whatever are the sources of income of a household, what is important to the members of the household is the total income when all these sources are combined. Our analysis shows that there were very marked differences in their usual net weekly household income between families with each parental situation even after allowing for social class. Among those from non-manual social classes, 92 per cent of unbroken families had £35 or more per week, which was considerably higher than the percentage of lone fathers (67 per cent), widows (44 per cent) and especially separated mothers (16 per cent) with incomes above this level. The only group whose income was fairly similar to that of unbroken families were those who were no longer one-parent. These differences were considerably greater than those between manual and non-manual social classes. For example, among unbroken families, while 92 per cent of families from non-manual social classes had incomes of £35 or more per week, only slightly fewer (87 per cent) of those from manual social classes had incomes above this level. (These data were collected in 1974 so the levels of income are considerably lower than present-day levels, but this should not affect the comparisons between the groups.)

Housing

The level of income of the households gives some indication of their standard of living, but an additional understanding can be gained from a description of their living conditions, for example their housing situation, which is the largest single item of expenditure for most households. The indices used in this report to represent housing conditions are whether the child shares a bed (an indicator of space available) and the possession of certain basic household amenities: sole use of a hot water supply, indoor lavatory and bathroom.

Within each social class a higher proportion of the 16-year-olds in one-parent families shared a bed, and also lacked the sole use of the three basic amenities. However, these differences were not as great as the differences in social class: single-parent families originally from non-manual social classes were better off on both measures of housing standards than children in two-parent families from manual social classes (Table 4.13). The one-parent families' housing conditions, in particular the possession of amenities, may be better than expected from their incomes because a larger proportion of them were in council-rented property than two-parent families from the same social-class background (overall 57 per cent of one-parent families and 39 per cent of unbroken families were council tenants). However, even within the same tenure group, the children in one-parent families were at a disadvantage, most noticeably among families in private rented accommodation in which 47 per cent of fatherless families but only 32 per cent of unbroken families did not have the sole use of the three basic household amenities. In council-rented homes the difference was less marked, with 6 per cent of fatherless families and 4 per cent of unbroken families without the sole use of the three amenities.

Discussion

These results from the National Child Development Study show the considerable financial and material difficulties that lone parents with 16-year-old children, particularly fatherless families, have to face. There have been many government and independent research

TABLE 4.13   *Bed-sharing and use of amenities and parental situation*

Parental situation	Social class	Study child sharing bed (%)	Without sole use of three amenities (%)	Total
Ever one parent	Non-manual	6	4	235
Both parents always		2	2	2 054
Ever one parent	Manual	11	9	747
Both parents always		9	5	5 099

Note: Each comparison statistically significant at 5 per cent level at least.

reports showing the poverty of one-parent families, but very little action has been taken to alleviate it.

It is clearly difficult for lone parents to divide their time between earning and caring for children. George and Wilding found that this conflict placed lone fathers in their study under a great strain. The alternative is dependence on supplementary benefit. However, a comparison between this study (all widows) and a study of widows in receipt of supplementary benefits (NCDS) suggests that living on supplementary benefit may involve more poverty (Essen and Ghodsian, 1977; see pp. 101–23). Of the families who had received both supplementary benefits and widows' pensions in the year, only 4 per cent had net household incomes of £45 per week or more in 1974, whereas the analysis presented here showed that 13 per cent of all widows received £45 or more per week. In confirmation that supplementary benefits provide only a minimum standard of living, Hunt *et al.* (1973) found that fatherless families were less deprived economically if the mothers were working.

An important aspect of being short of money is the amount of anxiety felt about the situation, since this, as well as the material deprivation itself, will affect the children. The responses to the question as to whether the parents had felt in financial hardship showed disturbing numbers of families in which the children were likely to have been subjected to this anxiety (Table 4.12). It is interesting to note that in relation to the proportion in receipt of free school meals (an indicator of low income) more lone fathers than mothers were likely to feel in hardship.

There are two possible reasons for this: George and Wilding (1972) and Ferri and Robinson (1976) found that lone fathers felt they were less economical than a mother would have been, in that they were less adept at cooking economically or at mending instead of buying new clothes. The fathers may therefore have found comparable levels of income a greater strain. In addition, it has been suggested that the strain of managing a home single-handed and the accompanying anxiety about money is greater immediately after a break in the family, when the remaining parent is unused to the situation (Marsden, 1973), and our own data (see pp. 90–8) showed that most of the motherless families in the NCDS had broken up since the study child was 11, whereas nearly half the fatherless had broken up when the child was younger.

The mothers interviewed in both these studies indicated that they tended to feel their poverty through their children. They felt especially hard up when they had to refuse them toys or an outing which their friends were able to have. This could suggest that if their financial problems are accentuated by comparisons with neighbours and friends, single parents and their children may try to avoid social contact. Also, in so far as a shortage of money precludes the children and their parents from certain activities and outings, it also leads to reduced social contact. The financial circumstances of one-parent families may therefore tend to isolate them, which in itself may add to their problems.

Conclusion

This study has shown the inevitability, given the present system of state benefits, of financial difficulties when the tasks of child care and earning have to be undertaken by one person. It is already four years since the Finer Report made its recommendations, and the difficulties of single-parent families were apparent long before that time (Wynn, 1964). There is no shortage of recommendations as to the form new allowances should take (Gingerbread, 1973; Townsend, 1975), but selection of one scheme in preference to another is unlikely to be achieved until there is recognition of the principle that an urgent need exists.

LIVING IN ONE-PARENT FAMILIES: ATTAINMENT AT SCHOOL

Although there is currently in Britain a climate of general concern for children in one-parent families, it is still relatively unclear what effect living with a lone parent has on their development and, for example, on their performance at school.

Previous studies have examined the school attainment of children in broken, or specifically, one-parent families, in comparison with children in unbroken families, but the evidence has not been entirely conclusive. A very few studies (e.g. Edwards and Thompson, 1971; Rutter *et al.*, 1970) have found that children from broken homes have similar attainment to those from intact homes. More commonly, the conclusion reached is that, although children from broken homes have relatively poor school achievement overall, these differences are probably due to differences in socio-economic status (Herzog and Sudia, 1970; Gill and Stephen, 1974). Ferri (1976) presented evidence in support of this theory, using data from the National Child Development Study, by showing that the difference between the test scores of 11-year-olds in one- and two-parent families was reduced by adjusting for background factors. This could also explain the findings in Pringle *et al.* (1966), using data from the same study, that children with atypical parental situations had lower reading test scores than average (except for those in social classes IV and V), since the only background characteristic adjusted for in their study was social class. Other studies have found evidence of differences for certain groups of children with lone parents; for example, Crellin *et al.* (1971) showed that non-adopted illegitimate children had lower scores on tests of attainment than their legitimate peers, after adjusting for differences in their background.

The purpose here is to compare the school attainment of children in one- and two-parent families when they were in their last year of compulsory schooling, and to consider the extent to which differences which emerge between these groups remain, when children in otherwise similar material and social circumstances are compared. This includes a consideration of which aspects of their background are most important in explaining the differences between children in each parental situation. The analysis is essentially a follow-up of part of the study of 11-year-olds in one-parent families reported in Ferri (1976).

Data

At each follow-up health visitors completed a questionnaire in the course of interviewing the child's parents, and included in this was a question about the child's parent figures. From the responses the children living in one-parent families were identified. Children were defined as having lived in a one-parent family if they were reported at any follow-up as living with one natural parent but no other parent-figure, or if at birth their mother was single, widowed, separated or divorced. Some of these children subsequently gained a substitute parent-figure. In the course of the parental interview the lone parent was also asked the reason for the absence of the other parent. Possible responses were death, divorce, separation or illegitimacy, as well as other unspecified reasons.

In this paper comparisons have been made between children in one-parent families (subdivided into fatherless and motherless) and children who were reported as living with both their own parents at birth and at each follow-up. The fatherless families have been further subdivided, to distinguish those children who were first fatherless before they were 7, from those who lost their father later, as well as distinguishing those still fatherless at the 16-year follow-up from those who had gained a substitute father-figure by that time. The number of motherless children who had sufficiently complete data to be included in the analyses was too small to subdivide, so they have been considered in one group.

The children completed tests of attainment at each follow-up. The results presented are for tests of reading and mathematics taken at the age of 16. Scores have been transformed to achieve normality such that they have a mean of zero and a standard deviation of one.

A description of the 16-year-olds' home circumstances was obtained in the course of the parental interview. This included questions about the family's financial and housing situation. The two indicators of income used were: whether any child of the family received free school meals at present; and the range in which the normal net weekly income of the household fell. The housing indicators were: access to amenities (sole use by the household of a hot water supply, indoor lavatory and bathroom); the tenure of the home (owner-occupied, rented from the council, privately rented, or 'other'); and whether the child had a room of his own for homework (in this case reported by the study child him or herself).

Non-response

In view of the number of variables included in the analyses of variance, i.e. parental information at each of the three follow-ups as well as other home circumstances and test results, a check for bias was carried out. This showed that although those included in the analyses had a higher mean test score than the mean for all 16-year respondents, in general this applied to both those with one and two parents, so the difference between them was not significantly affected.

Results

Details of the proportions of children in one-parent families at any time, together with the reason for the absence of one parent among 16-year-olds in the NCDS is fully documented in Essen and Lambert (1977). (See pp. 91–8.) They note that among those who are motherless at the age of 16, this is equally likely to be due to the breakdown of the marriage as to the death of the father. However, among those who had gained a substitute parent-figure (of whom the majority were step-parents) there were twice as many with broken marriages as widowed. These two findings together suggest that widows are less likely to remarry. The other main point to note is that most of the illegitimate children had gained a father-figure by the age of 16. This means that over half of the group described here as 'mother not alone when child 16, but alone before the child was 7' are illegitimate children.

Background characteristics

It is clear from Essen (1978) (see pp. 98–101) that one-parent families are over-represented in the manual social classes, tend to live in poor housing and are at a considerable disadvantage financially. They are also more geographically mobile, in so far as this is reflected in the number of schools the children had attended by the age of 11 (Ferri, 1976) and a relatively high proportion have spent some time in the care of a local authority (Essen *et al.*, 1976). In addition, Lambert (1978) (see pp. 106–8) examined the aspirations and expectations for further education and work among the 16-year-olds in one-parent families in the NCDS and found that, overall, lone parents had lower aspirations for their children's further education than parents in unbroken families.

Attainment at school

The children who had lived in one-parent families at any time had statistically significant lower mean scores on both tests of reading and mathematics than children always with both their own parents. However, among the fatherless children there was very little variation in test scores, according to either the age they were first fatherless or whether or not they had subsequently gained a father-figure.

In view of the socio-economic factors associated with parental situation, which are themselves independently associated with poor school performance, it is clear that any assessment of the relationship between parental situation and attainment must make allowance for differences in background. This was done by means of an analysis of variance, which is summarised in Table 4.14. The fitted constants in Table 4.14 describe the differences in mathematics and reading test scores after adjusting (simultaneously) for all the variables listed. It is clear that the difference in mean scores between children in one- and two-

parent families was considerably reduced, such that the relationship between parental situation and attainment was no longer significant for either test. The effect of adjustment for background factors was so great for reading that the order of the fitted constants was changed, and children with both parents no longer had the highest scores. For maths, however, children with both parents still had the highest mean score.

Other variables included in the analysis were: sex, social class, family size, number of schools attended, amenities in the home, tenure of the home, whether home includes a room for homework, whether child has ever been in care, parental aspirations for future education, usual household income, receipt of free school meals and reason for the absence of one parent.

Variations among one-parent families

It can be seen that there is little variation in either maths or reading test results among the one-parent groups after adjusting for background factors. There is a very slight tendency for the groups who gained a substitute father-figure to have lower scores than the children who were still fatherless, particularly for those who were fatherless before they were 7, but the results for those still fatherless are very close to those for the motherless group. There was no consistent tendency for children to differ in their test scores according to whether their family first broke up before or after they were 7.

TABLE 4.14   *Parental situation and attainment in mathematics and reading tests*

Parental situation	Mathematics (transformed)		Reading (transformed)	
	Fitted constant	χ^2 (df)	Fitted constant	χ^2 (df)
Mother alone at 16:				
and before child 7	0.01	8.7(5) $p > 0.05$	0.05	4.2(5) $p > 0.05$
only after child 7	−0.04		0.11	
Mother not alone at 16:				
and before child 7	−0.07		−0.09	
only after child 7	−0.05		−0.04	
Father ever alone	0.00		0.03	
Both parents always	0.15		−0.06	
	N = 5 156; total variance = 0.976; residual mean square = 0.675		N = 5 181; total variance = 0.949; residual mean square = 0.659	

Reason for absence of a parent

The analysis reported in Table 4.14 was carried out twice. In the second analysis the reason for the absence of one parent was excluded, to see if this affected the differences between children in each parental situation. However, it was barely affected, as the difference in fitted constants between any two groups changed by less than 5 per cent on either test, so the rest of the analyses were carried out including the 'reason' variable.

The analysis which included the reason for absence of a parent revealed some interesting findings. Children's reading attainment was not related to the reason for the break-up, so that after adjusting for differences in home circumstances, children of widows did not differ significantly from children of divorced or separated parents in this respect. However, in the analysis of mathematics attainment, there was a statistically significant interaction between the sex of the child and the reason for the break-up of the family, such that girls of divorced or separated parents had slightly lower scores than those of widowed parents, though, as for reading, there was no such difference for the boys.

Attainment and background circumstances

However, the most striking finding from Table 4.14 is the importance of home circumstances to the difference between the attainment of a child from one- or two-parent families. It therefore seemed interesting to calculate the extent to which these differences were reduced by adjusting for home circumstances. This was carried out only for the maths test results.

Table 4.15 presents the percentage by which the overall difference in maths test scores between each one-parent group and the 'both-parents' group was reduced by adjusting for background factors. It can be seen that these differences were reduced considerably, in general by about half the initial difference. It is interesting to note that there is not a great deal of variation among the one-parent families in this respect.

The general conclusion from this part of the analysis is therefore that although children in one-parent families have relatively low test scores overall, to a large extent this reflects their poor material circumstances, rather than the absence of one parent *per se*.

Attainment and financial and housing circumstances

The purpose of the next stage of the analysis was to find out if any one aspect of background circumstances was particularly important. This was carried out by excluding certain variables from the analysis, one group at a time, to see how this affected the difference in attainment between children in one- and two-parent

TABLE 4.15   *Parental situation and social circumstances related to mathematics test scores*

Parental situation	Percentages by which difference in mean score between each one-parent group and 'both parents' is reduced by adjusting for background factors
Mother alone at 16:	
and before child 7	61
only after child 7	50
Mother not alone at 16:	
alone before child 7	49
only after child 7	44
Father ever alone	57
	N = 5 156

families. As reported above, after adjusting for differences in background most of the groups of one-parent families had higher reading test scores than those with two parents. This meant that even after excluding the variables of interest from the analysis, the differences between children in each parental situation were very small. For this reason the results for this stage of the analysis have again only been presented for the maths test.

The first column of Table 4.16 presents the unadjusted differences in maths score between each one-parent group and the group always with both parents. The second and third columns show the differences between the same groups after adjusting for all the variables in Table 4.14, except income and housing. The fourth column shows the difference between the same groups after adjusting for all the variables in Table 4.14. Thus, by comparing the difference between columns 1 and 4 with the difference between columns 2 and 4, one can assess the extent to which the relatively low test scores of children in one-parent families are accounted for by low income rather than other social characteristics. From this comparison it can be seen that for each of the fatherless groups (except those in the third group who had a substitute father-figure), low income is a substantial part of their social disadvantage. This is especially so for the two groups who were fatherless at the time of the 16-year follow-up, for whom low income accounted for half of the difference in test score associated with social characteristics. For the children who became fatherless after they were 7, but had a substitute father-figure by the time they were

16 (the fourth group), income accounted for about one-third of this difference, while for the motherless the proportion was about one-sixth.

In contrast, the effect of including housing variables in the analysis is minimal. This can be seen quite simply by comparing the figures in the third and fourth columns of Table 4.16, which are either identical or almost identical for each group. The general conclusion is therefore that income, but not housing, is an important factor in the relatively low test scores of children in one-parent families.

Discussion

The first conclusion that can be drawn from this study confirms that drawn by Ferri (1976) in her study of the NCDS children when they were 11. Although children ever in one-parent families have lower overall scores in tests taken at the age of 16 than those with both their parents, when children in similar social and financial circumstances are compared they no longer have relatively low test scores. This indicated that the depression in overall scores is related to those social and financial circumstances rather than to the children's parental situation itself.

In view of this, the study tried to distinguish the relative importance of certain factors to the children's attainment. This was carried out only for those cir-

cumstances which in principle at least are amenable to change, namely income and housing. The results clearly showed the major contribution made by low income and its associated difficulties, particularly for the families that were still without a father, though poor housing appeared to be a negligible part of the social factors associated with low maths attainment. This could be partly explained by the finding in Essen (1978) (see pp. 106–8) that although one-parent families were at a disadvantage in their housing, the extent of this (at least as indicated by our measures) was not very great.

The present analysis was also designed to contribute to our understanding of which aspects of being in a one-parent family are most harmful in terms of attainment. Previous research has found differences according to the reason for the break-up of the family. Herzog and Sudia (1970), in their review of research, concluded that boys whose fathers left following the breakdown of the marriage had lower attainment than those with widowed mothers, and Ferri's (1976) evidence agreed with this. Also Douglas *et al.* (1968) found that the test scores of 15-year-olds whose fathers had died after a long illness were lower than those whose fathers had died suddenly. Both Herzog and Sudia and Douglas *et al.* concluded that these differences probably reflected the degree of insecurity and stress in the family prior to its break-up, though Herzog and Sudia also suggested that the results could

TABLE 4.16   *Parental situation and social factors related to mathematics test scores*

| | | Differences between each one-parent group and 'both parents' group | | |
| | | After adjusting for all factors† except | | After adjusting for all factors† |
	Unadjusted	(a) Income*	(b) Housing*	
Parental situation	1	2	3	4
Mother alone at 16:				
and before child 7	0.36	0.25	0.15	0.14
only after child 7	0.38	0.29	0.19	0.19
Mother not alone at 16:				
alone before child 7	0.43	0.23	0.22	0.22
only after child 7	0.36	0.25	0.20	0.20
Father ever alone	0.35	0.18	0.14	0.15
		$\chi^2 = 11.8$ (5df) $p > 0.05$	$\chi^2 = 9.4$ (5df) ns	$N = 5\ 156$

* Income variables are 'free school meals' and 'usual household income'. Housing variables are 'access to amenities', 'tenure' and 'room for homework'.

† Listed in text (p. 103).

reflect the extent of social disapproval felt by the remaining parent.

The present NCDS results barely provided any evidence in support of this. There were no significant differences between the children of widows and of divorced or separated parents on the reading test, and on the maths test it was only among the girls that the separated had relatively low test scores.

A further aspect to consider is one which is often assumed to be of importance, namely the age of the child at the time the family breaks up. Previous research on this question has been inconclusive. Herzog and Sudia (1970) reported that most studies found that children's attainment was lower if they were under 6 years old at the time the father left the family, though some studies have presented evidence to the contrary. Carlsmith (1964) found that the younger the boy was when his father left home, the greater the depression in his quantitative ability relative to his verbal ability. However Douglas *et al.* (1968) found small differences in attainment in favour of the children whose fathers had died before, rather than after, they were 6 years old. It is possible that these results reflect other confounding factors in the situation; for example, Herzog and Sudia (1970) suggested that in so far as children are more likely to be older when a parent is widowed than when divorced, differences related to both the age of the child and the reason for the break-up of the family could be confounded by one another.

In this study this confounding effect does not arise, as allowance was made for the reason for the parental situation when looking at the age of the child at the time he or she became fatherless. The results, both of the overall difference in mean scores between each fatherless group, and of the differences after adjusting for background factors, provide no evidence of any consistent difference in attainment according to the age the child's family first broke up. The only suggestion of a consistent pattern among the fatherless group is that, after adjusting for differences in their background, the children whose mothers were still alone at the time of the follow-up were at a slight advantage over the children with a substitute father-figure.

Conclusion

The examination of variations in attainment at the end of their compulsory schooling within the one-parent group has not provided clear evidence of any particular sub-group being at a disadvantage relative to the others. The major conclusions from this research therefore applies to one-parent families as a whole: namely that, first, it is the material and other socio-economic circumstances of one-parent families which are related to their depressed educational performance, rather than their parental situation itself; second, among these circumstances, the families' financial situation plays a substantial part for the fatherless, and to a lesser extent for the other one-parent families, but there is little evidence that their housing circumstances are associated with their relatively poor performance.

LIVING IN ONE-PARENT FAMILIES: SCHOOL-LEAVERS AND THEIR FUTURE

The previous papers have reported the proportions of NCDS children living with a single parent at various ages, and how the family circumstances experienced by children frequently changed between follow-ups. Here we examine whether having lived in a one-parent family had affected the aspirations and expectations of the children, their parents or their teachers with regard to further education and plans for future work, when compared with those for children who had always lived in two-parent families. (See Tables 4.17–4.20.)

TABLE 4.17 *Age study children thought they were most likely to leave school* *

	Age most likely to leave school				
	Total (*N*)	16 (%)	17 (%)	18+ (%)	Uncertain (%)
Boys					
One parent – total	520	72	6	14	9
Both parents	3 219	62	6	23	9
One parent:					
fatherless	428	72	5	15	9
motherless	92	75	7	11	8
Girls					
One parent – total	548	68	8	16	8
Both parents	3 111	59	8	26	7
One parent:					
fatherless	455	69	8	16	8
motherless	93	62	12	17	9

* Tests: the tables included in this paper show that the differences between children in one- and two-parent families were significant at the 0.1 per cent level but differences between children in motherless and in fatherless families were not significant at the 5 per cent level.

First, about 10 per cent more boys and girls from one-parent families than those from two-parent families planned to leave school at the minimum age of 16.

Whereas one in every four of the boys and girls from two-parent families planned to stay in full-time education until at least 18, only one in every seven of the boys and one in every six of the girls from one-parent families planned to stay on till at least 18. When asked the reason for choosing to leave school, 23 per cent from one-parent families compared with 10 per cent from two-parent families said they 'needed to earn as soon as possible as my family needs the money'. Nearly a third from one-parent families thought they were 'not good enough to stay on' compared with 21 per cent from two-parent families. A higher proportion of lone parents expected that their children would leave school at 16 than did parents in two-parent families. Teachers also thought that a higher proportion of children from one-parent than two-parent families would not benefit from staying on at school.

Second, on average only 12 per cent of boys who had lived in one-parent families compared with 23 per cent of boys in two-parent families and 26 per cent

of girls in one-parent families compared with 35 per cent of girls in two-parent families planned to do full-time study on leaving school.

There was an interesting difference between boys and girls and their parents (whether lone or together) in that the proportion of boys planning to do full-time education was similar to the proportion of parents thinking this was likely, whereas a higher proportion of girls than their parents thought they would be likely to do full-time study. Teachers seemed to be the most optimistic of all in their estimation of the proportion who were suited to do full-time study, but they estimated about 10 per cent fewer from one-parent than from two-parent families to be suited to such study.

It looks as though some of the young people from one-parent families were planning to compensate either for not staying on at school or for not doing

TABLE 4.18   *Teachers', parents' and study children's views on proportions leaving school at 16 compared*

	Teachers think would not benefit from staying on (%)	Parents think likely to leave at 16 (%)	Study children think likely to leave at 16 (%)
Boys			
Fatherless	57	64	72
Motherless	55	69	75
Both parents	45	53	62
Girls			
Fatherless	47	58	69
Motherless	44	56	62
Both parents	37	46	59

TABLE 4.19   *Study children's plans for further education or work*

	Total (N)	Full-time study (%)	Job with part-time study (%)	Job with no study (%)	Don't know (%)
Boys					
One parent — total	518	12	51	23	14
Both parents	3 208	23	46	16	15
One parent:					
fatherless	426	12	51	22	15
motherless	92	12	50	27	11
Girls					
One parent — total	546	26	32	23	19
Both parents	3 107	35	30	20	16
One parent:					
fatherless	454	25	34	22	19
motherless	92	27	22	27	24

full-time study by taking jobs which would give them the chance to do part-time study (Table 4.19). Even so, higher proportions of girls and boys in one-parent families than in two-parent families planned to do jobs which involved no further study. When the social-class backgrounds of the boys and girls were taken into account some of the contrasts between those in one- and those in two-parent families were even greater, while others were less so. The only group which showed no overall difference between one- and two-parent families in their pattern of choices were girls from a non-manual background. Study of the school attainment at 16 of boys and girls in one-parent families has shown that when background factors were taken into account they were doing as well as those in two-parent families (Essen, 1978: see pp. 101–6).

TABLE 4.20 *Parents', study children's and teacher's views on proportion likely to do full-time study or to be suited to this*

	Parents (%)	Study children (%)	Teachers (%)
Boys			
Fatherless	15	12	25
Motherless	15	12	23
Both parents	25	23	34
Girls			
Fatherless	17	25	34
Motherless	18	27	35
Both parents	26	35	47

Third, the study children's choices of likely first full-time jobs (grouped into broad categories: see Fogelman, 1976, pp. 271–9) were looked at. While the proportions making choices of likely first full-time job for many categories of jobs were very similar, only 15 per cent of boys and 26 per cent of girls from one-parent families compared with 21 per cent of boys and 30 per cent of girls from two-parent families chose 'professional'-type jobs. No less than 46 per cent of all boys from one-parent families expected their first full-time job to be of a 'manual' nature compared with 38 per cent of all boys from two-parent families. A higher proportion (23 per cent) of girls from one-parent families than girls from two-parent families (16 per cent) thought they were likely to go into jobs of a service nature (shopwork, hairdressing, catering, etc.). When the young people's 'most important' reason for choosing a job was examined, the need for the job to be well paid for those from one-parent families was evident, though many of the young people from two-parent families also saw this as relevant. On the question of choosing jobs, the young people from one-parent families appeared to be relating their choices realistically to their length of education. Perhaps they had learned through experience to temper their ambitions, but the tendency to think they were 'not good enough' to stay on at school may have permeated their general attitude.

Despite the apparently realistic, or even deprecating, view of their future plans, there must be concern about how they would actually work out in practice for the boys and girls from one-parent families. Would their fewer qualifications, coupled with the greater need to earn money quickly, put them at a disadvantage and lead them to compromise more quickly? Might they, as a result, run a greater risk of lack of satisfaction, leading them to change jobs more frequently and thereby laying themselves open to unemployment, or else to sticking to their jobs and becoming bored and disillusioned? These are risks that have faced many school-leavers in recent years, but those who have lived in one-parent families are already likely to have experienced more disruption and distress in their personal lives than those in two-parent families.

The NCDS findings suggest that young people from one-parent families would be a group who would benefit from proposals to give financial assistance to pupils staying on for sixth-form education. The need to earn money to help their families has already been noted as a reason for leaving school, and the degree of financial hardship in which their families were living was found to be significantly greater than that of two-parent families. If some of these boys and girls could stay on at school longer, knowing that their families would be at less disadvantage financially, they might then have a chance of realising their potential and getting well paid and more interesting jobs later on.

5 Families on Low Incomes*

16-YEAR-OLDS IN HOUSEHOLDS IN RECEIPT OF SUPPLEMENTARY BENEFIT AND FAMILY INCOME SUPPLEMENT

Introduction

The study reported here of a nationally representative sample of children enables a comparison to be made between 16-year-olds in families who had been in receipt of supplementary benefit, family income supplement and neither of these benefits, in terms of their families, home circumstances and financial situation, as well as in terms of the young people's attitudes to their future and certain indices of their development. In addition some comparisons have been made with their circumstances when they were 11, and also groups of children have been compared according to their age at the time their families were in receipt of benefit.

Supplementary benefit is a means-tested benefit available to all people who are not in work. It is designed to bring their, or their family's, total income up to a certain minimum level. In 1974 the basic supplementary benefit scale rate for a married couple was £13.65, which was 45 per cent of the average net earnings of male manual workers (SBC, *Annual Report*, HMSO, 1976). Additional allowances are payable for rent and for children. Long-term rates, which are slightly higher, were, in 1974, available to anyone (other than the unemployed) in receipt of benefit for at least two years.

Family income supplement (FIS) is a means-tested benefit available to heads of families in low-paid full-time work. The amount of FIS awarded is half the difference between the family's gross weekly income and a specified amount appropriate to the size of the family. In 1974 that amount was £25 for a one-child family.

Data

At both the 11-year-old and the 16-year-old follow-ups health visitors completed a questionnaire in the course of an interview with a parent (usually the mother) in the child's home. The questions asked included details of the child's family, home and financial situation. The question on finance, which has been used here to define the groups of children, was 'what have been the sources of income of the household during the past twelve months?' This was a precoded question including a range of sources of earned income, unearned income and several different state benefits, including supplementary benefit (SB) and family income supplement (FIS). Any number of sources could be indicated and they could refer to any members of the household. The household is defined here as all those living and eating together, so the recipient could, for example, be a grandmother, or even a lodger.

As the question related to receipt of supplementary benefit or family income supplement at any time in the preceding year, the overall proportions of beneficiaries will be higher than if the data related to recipients at one point in time. For the same reason, our sample is likely to include a relatively high proportion of short-term recipients. Our study was carried out in 1974 shortly after the miners' strike and the three-day week. This means that an unusually high proportion of families will have been in receipt of supplementary benefit for only a few weeks, thus further increasing the proportion of short-term recipients.

From responses to the question at the 16-year follow-up and without any additional information from records, the young people were grouped according to their family's sources of income as follows (the percentages of children in the cohort in each group are also represented):

(a) SB, but not sickness or unemployment benefit or widows' pension or allowance or separated or divorced mother's maintenance (3.3 per cent).
(b) SB and unemployment benefit (0.7 per cent).
(c) SB and sickness benefit, including some who also received unemployment benefit (1.2 per cent).
(d) SB and widows' pension or allowance (0.6 per cent).
(e) SB and maintenance (0.4 per cent).
(f) FIS but not SB (1.1 per cent).
(g) Neither FIS nor SB (92.6 per cent).

* Original source: Essen, J. and Ghodsian, M., 'Sixteen-Year-Olds in households in receipt of supplementary benefit and family income supplement', in Supplementary Benefits Commission, *Annual Report 1976*, HMSO, 1977.

The above groups are mutually exclusive. Individuals in each group will often have reported other sources of income, such as earnings or pensions, in addition to those described above. Families in receipt of SB and sickness benefit have been combined with those who received both unemployment and sickness benefit, as the latter had in general had more time off sick than unemployed. Some fathers in group (b) above were said to have had time off work for sickness and some fathers in group (c) were reported as having been unemployed, so the labels do not exclusively, but do predominantly, represent each group's reasons for benefit.

Comparisons have been made between each of these groups except that, where the numbers are too small or the results are similar, all SB recipient groups have been combined.

The groups described in the second part of the paper are the children in families who have been in receipt of SB (irrespective of other benefits received) at the following ages (the percentages in each group are again presented):

(a) SB at 11 only (4.9 per cent).
(b) SB at 16 only (3.3 per cent).
(c) SB at 11 and 16 (2.6 per cent).
(d) SB at neither age (89.2 per cent).

Non-response
At the 16-year follow-up, information was obtained for 87 per cent of the relevant age group in the country. Owing to incomplete data the sample included in the present study is slightly reduced, but a further analysis showed them to be representative in terms of their background characteristics, such as social class and family size.

Results

Demographic characteristics

Table 5.1 shows the other sources of household income received during the year by each group. The first column shows that a higher proportion of the benefit-recipient groups than non-beneficiaries had received no earnings in the year. The next column shows the percentage of households whose income during the year had included the mother's or other adult's earnings, but no father's earnings. The final column shows the percentage of families whose income included the father-figure's earnings. Both these two latter groups could also include unearned income or social security. Clearly, the vast majority of non-recipients fell into the last category, but smaller proportions of the SB-recipient groups had received income from a father-figure. It is notable that a larger proportion of households on sickness benefit than on unemployment benefit had received earnings from a father-figure during the year. Table 5.2 shows a possible explanation for this, in that a higher proportion of those on unemployment benefit (51 per cent) than on sickness benefit (29 per cent) had had the whole year off work.

In addition to the families where the father-figure was out of work, another common reason for receipt of benefit was single-parenthood (Table 5.3). Some of the children whose mothers had received widows' pension or maintenance had gained a new father-figure, but about 80 per cent of both groups were fatherless at the time of the follow-up. A considerable number of FIS recipients were lone mothers (23 per cent) and nearly half (46 per cent) of the families who had received SB only were also one-parent.

TABLE 5.1   *Families of 16-year-olds in receipt of supplementary benefit or family income supplement and their other sources of income*

Source	No earned income or investments (%)	Earned income but not father's earnings (%)	Father's earnings (%)	N (= 100%)
SB only	26	42	32	390
SB + unemployment benefit	36	29	35	78
SB + sickness benefit	14	24	62	145
SB + widows' pension	35	57	9	69
SB + maintenance	44	40	17	48
FIS not SB	—	27	73	130
Neither FIS nor SB	2	7	91	10 805

Notes: The numbers on each table differ due to incomplete data. Overall tests of significance have been done for each variable in the text and tables. All differences are significant at at least the 1 per cent level unless otherwise stated.

TABLE 5.2 *Source of income of families of 16-year-olds and weeks off work for sickness or unemployment (families with male head only)*

Source	Weeks						
	0—5* (%)	6—9 (%)	10—19 (%)	20—39 (%)	40—51 (%)	52 (%)	N (= 100%)
SB only	56	3	6	5	2	28	207
SB + unemployment benefit	16	3(2)	10	14	7	51	73
SB + sickness benefit	16	9	18	21	7	29	140
FIS not SB	79	5	3(3)	6	—	7	99
Neither FIS nor SB	88	4	4	2	<1	2	10 251

* This group includes those who did not answer the questions on absence from work, who are assumed to have had no weeks absent.

TABLE 5.3 *Source of income and parental situation of 16-year-olds*

Source	Parental situation				
	Mother alone (%)	Father alone (%)	Other situations (%)	Both own parents (%)	N (= 100%)
SB only	44	2	11	42	390
SB + unemployment benefit	5	1	9	81	77
SB + sickness benefit	3	6	10	81	144
SB + widows pension	80	—	20	—	69
SB + maintenance	83	—	17	—	46
FIS not SB	23	1(1)	12	64	130
Neither FIS nor SB	5	1	8	86	10 802

* The percentages of children with no male head of household are similar to the percentages with mother alone. Recalculation of the figures in this table also shows that only 33 per cent of all fatherless families had been on SB in the past year, so the majority of fatherless families managed without supplementary benefit.

Tables 5.2 and 5.3 together give some indication of the reasons why some families received SB but none of the other sources of income, as 44 per cent were fatherless, and of those with a male head of household 27 per cent had had the whole year off work. This latter group may be long-term unemployed who were not entitled to unemployment benefit. It is possible that for the rest of this group another member of the household was the recipient.

These three tables together give some indication of the types of families in each of the benefit-recipient groups, and the possible reasons for their need for help from the state. These provide a backcloth for the following analyses of family circumstances and the children's development.

Responses to the question about the present or, if not working, the last occupation of the child's father are shown in Table 5.4 (social class has been defined by the Registrar-General's Classification of Occupations, 1966). Each of the groups in receipt of benefit had a lower proportion in the non-manual social classes than among the rest of the cohort. A similar pattern emerged from an examination of an earlier measure of the family's social background, namely the mother's educational level, in that 88 per cent of mothers in SB-recipient families and 82 per cent in FIS-recipient families but only 74 per cent in non-recipient families left school at the minimum school-leaving age.

An important consideration in examining families'

TABLE 5.4   *Source of income of families of 16-year-olds and social class (families with male head only)*

Source	Social class		
	Non-manual (%)	Manual (%)	N (= 100%)
SB	14	86	192
SB + unemployment benefit	12	88	69
SB + sickness benefit	7	93	131
FIS not SB	16	84	106
Neither FIS nor SB	38	62	9 973

TABLE 5.5   *Source of income and numbers of children in the household*

Source	No. of children under 21			
	1—2 (%)	3 (%)	4+ (%)	N (= 100%)
SB only	37	20	43	390
SB + unemployment benefit	18	27	55	77
SB + sickness benefit	36	17	47	143
SB + widows' pension	49	29	22	68
SB + maintenance	29	27	44	48
FIS not SB	33	18	49	130
Neither FIS nor SB	53	23	24	10 733

income is the number of children who must share the income. SB and FIS levels are based on the needs of the family and therefore on its size, whereas earned income is not related to need except to the extent that tax rates allow for the number of dependants. Table 5.5 shows considerable variations between the groups in terms of the number of children in the household under 21 years old, though each group receiving benefits had, on average, more children than those not on benefits. Mothers with widows' pensions had nearly as few children as those on neither FIS nor SB, and at the other extreme, those receiving unemployment benefit had more children than the other groups on SB. This does not necessarily suggest that the unemployed in general have more children, as small families on unemployment benefit are less likely to qualify for supplementary benefit. In the light of the above findings it should be borne in mind that some of the differences which follow, for example in housing conditions or school attainment, might well be affected by taking these aspects of the children's background into account.

In view of the opinion sometimes expressed in the media that immigrant families make greater demands on state benefits than indigenous families, the proportion of families of 16-year-olds in receipt of benefit from each of several countries of origin was compared. The groups were defined as those where at least one parent was born in the West Indies, on the Continent of Europe, Ireland (North or South) or Asia, or both parents were born in Britain. Table 5.6 shows that fairly similar proportions of the 16-year-olds' families from each country were in receipt of benefit. The only country with a statistically significant higher percentage on benefit was Ireland. Among the families known to have a male head of household, the proportion of beneficiaries was about 4 per cent for each country except Ireland, which had 7 per cent beneficiaries. This lack of differences is particularly notable in view of the fact that the recipient groups come disproportionately frequently from the manual social classes in which immigrant families are also found disproportionately more often.

Income levels
The measure of income used here was the usual net weekly income of the household, which does not therefore necessarily correspond to the period during

TABLE 5.6   *Source of income and country of origin of parents of 16-year-olds*

Country of origin	In receipt of SB or FIS (%)	Total
West Indies	12	120
Europe	8	351
Ireland	11	495
Asia	6	203
Britain	6	8 415

which benefit was received, which could have been at any time in the preceding year. Clearly, beneficiaries had lower income levels than non-beneficiaries, with 92 per cent of the latter, 66 per cent of FIS recipients, and only 57 per cent of SB recipients, on £30 or more. Among SB recipients the two fatherless groups were the worst off, and among the other three groups those on unemployment benefit were the worst off, though they also had larger families.

Figure 5.1 shows the difference between families in each source group subdivided by whether or not the mother was working at the time of the 16-year follow-up, as this was expected, and in fact proved to be, an important element in the household income: 68 per cent of mothers in families that had not received benefit were working, whereas 53 per cent of families on FIS (84 per cent of lone mothers, and 42 per cent of married mothers) and only 32 per cent of families in receipt of SB included working mothers. The graph shows that although each non-recipient group had higher incomes than each recipient group, the non-recipient families without a working mother had only marginally higher incomes than either the FIS or SB recipients with a working mother. There was a large difference in income between families with and without working mothers in each source group, with only approximately 10 per cent of both FIS and SB recipients where the mother did not work on incomes of over £44 whereas the corresponding proportions for households with working mothers was approximately 40 per cent. As SB is intended to supplement a family's income to a set level, one would not expect there to be a difference in income of more than the amount of the disregard, which was still £2 in 1974, between families where the mother does and does not work, among those currently

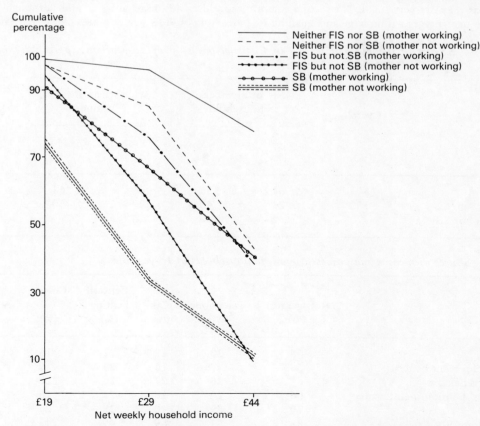

FIGURE 5.1   *Percentage of children above each income category for different groups*

receiving SB. The explanation for this difference is therefore probably that the mothers who were able to get a well-paid job were no longer entitled to, or receiving, SB, but were on a higher income level at the time of the follow-up, whereas those who were unable to get a good enough job to provide the same standard of living had remained on SB at the lower income level. This need to find a well-paid job if they want to work at all could also explain the relatively low proportion of families on SB with working mothers.

An indication of whether their income was felt to be adequate was provided by responses to a question which asked whether the parents had been 'seriously troubled by financial hardship' in the year prior to interview. Table 5.7 shows the responses. The first column shows the overall percentages who had felt troubled, and, just as in the comparison of income levels, the difference between those in receipt of benefits and those not in receipt was very marked. Fewer of those receiving FIS reported that they had been troubled than those in receipt of SB, though even among the former there were five times as many as among those not on benefit. The differences among the different SB-recipient groups have not been presented, as they are very small. The second column shows these percentages within large and small house-

holds. It is notable that over four times as many of the parents in large as in small households not in receipt of benefit felt in hardship, and among the FIS recipients the ratio was 2:1, whereas the difference for the SB groups was very small, and in the opposite direction. The third column shows a similar pattern to the findings on income, in that the families where the mothers worked were less likely to have felt financial difficulties than families with the same source of income without working mothers.

Housing conditions

The standard of living of families in receipt of benefit can be indicated to some extent by their income levels, but an additional understanding can be gained from a description of their living conditions. Information on the homes of the 16-year-olds in the NCDS included the extent to which their homes were crowded (more than 1.5 persons in the household per room), and the availability of both basic amenities and domestic goods in the home. The basic amenities selected were an indoor lavatory, a hot water supply and a bathroom, and the domestic goods are those presented in Table 5.8.

It is clear that each group of SB recipients was at a considerable disadvantage, and although those in receipt of FIS were more likely to have certain

TABLE 5.7   *Source of income and feeling of financial hardship of 16-year-olds (percentage in financial hardship)*

| Source | Overall | No. of members in household | | Whether mothers working | | N (= 100%) |
| | | 2—4 | 5+ | Yes | No | |
	(%)	(%)	(%)			
SB	57	61	55	48	61	676
FIS not SB	38	21	46	29	50	125
Neither FIS nor SB	7	2	10	6	9	10 540

TABLE 5.8   *Source of income and domestic goods in households of 16-year olds*

Source	Refrigerator (%)	Telephone (%)	Car (%)	Central heating (%)	Colour TV (%)	N (= 100%)
SB only	68	20	22	22	15	386
SB + unemployment benefit	58	7	13	24	9	78
SB + sickness benefit	64	28	27	26	20	144
SB + widows' pension/maintenance	66	20	16	23	18	117
FIS not SB	70	29	40	28	25	130
Neither FIS nor SB	88	57	69	49	43	10 747

domestic goods, there was no area in which they were as well off as those not in receipt of benefit. There were only small differences between the groups on SB, though the families also in receipt of unemployment benefit were at a slight disadvantage in many of these respects. The percentages without any television at all have not been presented, as the numbers involved were so small: less than 1 per cent of all the families of 16-year-olds did not have a television.

It is generally accepted that as families grow older they tend to become more affluent, so the families of the 16-year-olds were expected to be better off than they had been five years earlier. The housing conditions of the children were therefore examined both when they were 16 and when they were 11 (Table 5.9). Although at the time of receipt of benefit (aged 16) the beneficiaries' children were at a considerable disadvantage relative to non-beneficiaries, each of the benefit groups were even more likely to be overcrowded or lack amenities when the children were 11, which was when the families were not, for the most part, on benefit. The only exception to this were those on unemployment benefit, of whom an exceptionally high proportion were crowded at the later follow-up. These findings suggest that the families who were beneficiaries in 1973–4 may have been in long-term difficulties even though they were not necessarily in receipt of benefit five years earlier. The results presented above described the conditions in which the 16-year-olds were living. The next section examines the young people themselves, their health, pocket-money, plans for the future, attitudes to school and their performance at school.

Health and physical development
Four aspects of the health and physical development

of the young people have been selected for comparison. First, the children who had ever had asthma or had had migraine in the preceding year have been examined. However, only a slightly and non-significantly higher proportion of children in SB-recipient families (13 per cent) than non-recipient families (12 per cent) had had asthma, and the difference was similarly small for migraine.

Second, an indication of the 16-year-olds' physical development was gained from a comparison of their height and weight. As middle-class children are known to be taller than working-class children, and the SB recipients tended to come from the working classes, the differences in height were analysed both for the total sample and for each social class separately (Figure 5.2). Although the overall figures showed that the recipients of state benefit, in particular those on SB, were shorter than those not in receipt of SB or FIS, within each social class the difference between them was small and non-significant, ranging from ½cm among the non-manual groups to 1½cm for groups with no male head. There were only fourteen children on FIS for non-manual social classes so any interpretation of the findings on their physical development must be very tentative. These very slight differences were surprising, as children in large families with poor housing conditions in general have been shown to be shorter than their peers (see pp. 21–7). Figure 5.3 shows that, overall, the recipients of FIS and SB were of a similar weight to one another, but they were both lighter on average than non-recipients. However, when this was analysed within social class, although this difference remained in the manual social classes, in the non-manual social classes and in families with no male head the differences were non-significant.

TABLE 5.9 *Source of income, crowding and amenities* in families of 11-year-olds and 16-year-olds*

	11-year-olds		16-year-olds	
Source at 16	Crowded (> 1.5 persons/rm) (%)	Without sole use of 3 amenities (%)	Crowded (> 1.5 persons/rm) (%)	Without sole use of 3 amenities (%)
SB only (386)	25	26	17	15
SB + unemployment benefit (78)	38	23	41	12
SB + sickness benefit (144)	30	20	16	9
SB + widows' pension/maintenance (117)	21	17	10	13
FIS not SH (130)	33	24	23	11
Neither FIS nor SB (10 747)	11	11	8	6

* The three amenities are hot water supply, indoor lavatory and bathroom.

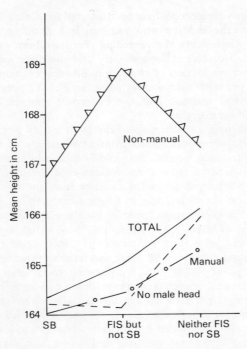

FIGURE 5.2   *Source of income and height*

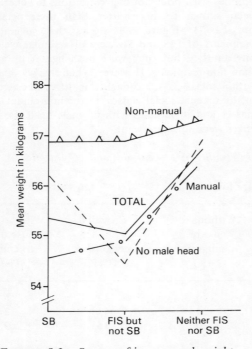

FIGURE 5.3   *Source of income and weight*

Pocket-money and spare-time jobs
In addition to living in families who are short of money and in poor housing conditions the young

people in families in receipt of benefit may be more directly affected by being given relatively little pocket-money. This was confirmed by responses by the young people when asked, in the course of a questionnaire, how much pocket-money their parents usually gave them each week, in that 49 per cent of SB recipients' children, 46 per cent of FIS recipients but only 36 per cent of non-beneficiaries received less than 75p per week. The situation was not improved by the children having a spare-time job, as only 42 per cent of SB recipients' children, compared with 52 per cent of FIS recipients' and 51 per cent of non-beneficiaries' children had a spare-time job.

Plans for the future and attitudes to school
Young people in families with low incomes may feel the need to leave school at the earliest opportunity in order to earn money. Considerably more of the 16-year-olds in the NCDS whose families were in receipt of benefit planned to leave school at the minimum leaving age (84 per cent of SB recipients' and 81 per cent of FIS recipients' children to 60 per cent of non-beneficiaries' children). The proportions were similar for each of the SB recipients' groups.

The young people were then asked their reasons for their decision to leave school. Table 5.10 shows the responses to this question. Any number of reasons could have been given by each person. As was to be expected, higher proportions of each SB group gave 'need money' as one of their reasons than did those not on SB, with the highest proportion among those on widows' pension or maintenance, who were also the group with the lowest household income. The proportions of children wanting independence varied considerably, but each of the groups in receipt of benefit were more likely to put this as a reason than the group on neither FIS nor SB. The next three columns indicate the influence friends, parents and teachers had on the young people's decisions. It is interesting to note that (apart from the fatherless children), while over twice as many of the young people in families on SB as in families not on benefit said they wanted to do the same as a friend, their parents and teachers were not reported consistently as having any more influence on the decision than children not receiving benefit. This is particularly important in the case of parents, who were therefore not felt by the young people in the SB groups to be exerting undue pressure on them to earn money. The other possible area in which differences could have emerged was in their feelings about school and their ability in school work. The last two columns of Table 5.10 show that the differences between the recipient and non-recipient groups in feeling that they were not good enough at school were larger than the corresponding differences in 'dislike of school work'.

TABLE 5.10   *Source of income and reasons given by 16-year-olds for leaving school at chosen age*

Source	Need money (%)	Want indepen-dence (%)	Same as friend (%)	Parents' advice (%)	Teachers' advice (%)	Don't like school work (%)	Not good enough (%)	N (=100 %)
SB only	33	56	15	18	10	28	35	297
SB + unemployment benefit	43	77	25	25	14	18	39	66
SB + sickness benefit	25	58	18	17	14	15	31	103
SB + widows' pension/ maintenance	46	64	10	13	5	24	36	93
FIS not SB	23	56	13	9	9	26	33	103
Neither FIS nor SB	10	47	8	20	12	18	22	8 691

The young people were also asked about their plans after leaving school, and the responses to this question are shown in Table 5.11. As expected from the high proportions leaving school early to earn money, there was a relatively low proportion of children in the families receiving benefit who expected to continue with full-time study. An interesting finding from this table was the relatively high percentage of children in the SB or FIS groups (except for the fatherless) who did not know what they would do after leaving school. This could suggest some ambivalence about leaving school, in that the differences between children of beneficiaries and of non-beneficiaries were smaller for 'dislike of school work' than for 'needing money'.

A further indication of the young people's attitude to school was provided by means of an academic motivation scale consisting of eight statements for which they were asked to indicate their level of agreement. Two examples of these statements are 'I feel school is largely a waste of time' and 'I don't like school'. After adjusting for social class, the differences in mean score between the recipient and non-recipient groups were non-significant except for the manual group, which reached significance at the 5 per cent level.

School performance

It was shown earlier that about a third of the young people in families receiving benefit gave 'not good enough at school work' as a reason for leaving school. In order to assess whether their performance in school agreed with this subjective assessment, their results on tests of mathematics and reading were

TABLE 5.11   *Source of income and 16-year-olds' plans after leaving school*

Source	Continue full-time study (%)	Job + part-time study (%)	Job, no study (%)	Don't know (%)	N (= 100%)
SB only	11	37	32	20	297
SB + unemployment benefit	7	32	32	30	57
SB + sickness benefit	12	34	22	32	107
SB + widows' pension/ maintenance	13	44	29	14	91
FIS not SB	14	39	24	23	104
Neither FIS nor SB	28	39	18	15	8 973

examined. Both the recipient groups had lower mean scores than the non-recipients on each test, even after adjusting for social class, though FIS and SB recipients' children were similar to one another in these respects.

Behaviour

The behaviour of the young people at school was assessed by means of the Rutter school behaviour scale. The teachers were asked to respond to twenty-six behavioural descriptions of the child on a three-point scale. The responses were then summed up to obtain a total score. High scores represent 'deviant' behaviour. Generally, even after adjusting for social class, children of both recipient groups were seen to be more deviant (Figure 5.4).

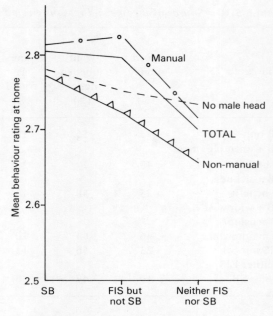

FIGURE 5.5   *Behaviour rating at home*

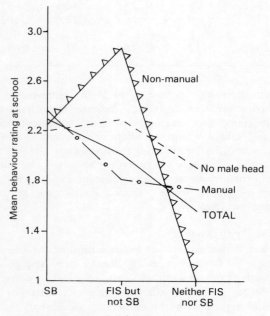

FIGURE 5.4   *Behaviour rating at school*

The complementary version of the Rutter school behaviour scale designed for the home was completed by a parent (usually the mother). As for the school ratings, within each social class, generally, the pattern was such that those whose families were on benefit were rated as slightly more deviant by their parents, though there were no differences for those with no male head of household (Figure 5.5).

It should be borne in mind that the above scales are not diagnostic instruments, but rather reflect the perceptions of the child's behaviour by the teacher and parent respectively.

Receipt of supplementary benefit at two ages

The results presented above were concerned with the young people in families in receipt of benefit in

the year they were 16. The longitudinal data in the NCDS also enable us to find out the extent to which these children's families were also dependent on benefit in the year they were 11. The figures (see p. 110) show that over 10 per cent of 16-year-olds had been in families in receipt of SB either when they were 11 or 16, and the proportion who were at one time or another on SB at any time in their childhood will be considerably larger. Recalculation of these percentages also shows that of all 11-year-olds on SB, 35 per cent were in families who were also on SB when they were 16. We also considered whether those who were on benefit at both ages differed in any respect from those only on benefit at one or the other age.

Demographic characteristics

In order to consider differences in the needs and composition of the recipient families, the children's parental situation and the weeks the male head of the family had been absent from work were compared. Table 5.12 shows considerable differences in the proportion of each group in one-parent families, with 50 per cent of the families on SB at both ages being fatherless, while 30 per cent of those on SB at 16 only and 12 per cent at 11 only were fatherless. These differences suggest that more of the families on SB at both ages may have longer-term needs than among the other SB groups. Recalculations of the figures in this table show that altogether 40 per cent of all children who were fatherless at 16 were on SB at 11, or 16, or both. A further indication of the longer-term needs of the children in families on SB at both follow-ups is shown in Table 5.13. Of those who did have a father-figure nearly half (49 per cent) had been out of work for the whole of the past year, and only 25 per cent had a father-figure who had less than a month off work in the year.

For those with a male head of household, Table 5.14 shows the percentage of each group in non-manual or manual social classes at 16. Each of the SB groups has considerably smaller proportions in non-manual occupations than non-beneficiaries, but the differences in social-class distribution among the SB groups were small and did not reach significance. This pattern was repeated in comparisons of the educational level reached by the mothers in the SB group, in that very similar proportions of each group left school at the minimum leaving age.

Other characteristics shown earlier to be associated with being on benefit are the number of children in the household and whether the mother goes to work. In the former respect there were only small differences between the groups on SB at different ages. In the case of the mother's work those only on SB at 11 were, predictably, closer to those not on SB at either age, with 55 per cent of mothers in work compared with 69 per cent of non-beneficiaries. The corresponding figures for those on SB at 16 only and

TABLE 5.14   *Age of receipt of SB and social class of families of 16-year-olds (families with male head only)*

| Source | Social class | | |
	Non-manual (%)	Manual (%)	N (= 100%)
SB at 11 only	12	88	421
SB at 16 only	11	89	216
SB at 11 and 16	10	90	112
SB at neither	39	61	8 389

those on benefit at both ages were 36 per cent and 24 per cent respectively.

Income and financial differences

The differences in parental and occupational characteristics among the SB recipients described above suggests that they would also differ in income levels. Figure 5.6 shows the proportions in each group whose usual net weekly income exceeded each of the three specified income levels. Clearly the families in receipt of SB at both ages had lower incomes than any of the other groups, and those on SB during the

TABLE 5.12   *Age of receipt of SB and parental situation of 16-year-olds*

Source	Mother* alone (%)	Father alone (%)	Other situations (%)	Both own parents (%)	N (= 100%)
SB at 11 only	12	1	17	70	492
SB at 16 only	30	2	10	58	335
SB at 11 and 16	50	3	12	35	262
SB at neither	5	1	6	87	9 022

* The percentages of children with no male head of household are very similar to the percentages with mother alone.

TABLE 5.13   *Age of receipt of SB and number of weeks father of the 16-year-olds were sick or unemployed (families with male head only)*

| Source | Weeks | | | | | | |
	0–5* (%)	6–9 (%)	10–19 (%)	20–39 (%)	40–51 (%)	52 (%)	N (= 100%)
SB at 11 only	65	6	9	5	1	14	431
SB at 16 only	43	5	12	10	4	26	226
SB at 11 and 16	25	2 (3)	10	14	6	43	125
SB at neither	89	4	3	2	<1	11	8 578

* This group includes those who did not answer the question on absence from work, who are assumed to have had no weeks absent.

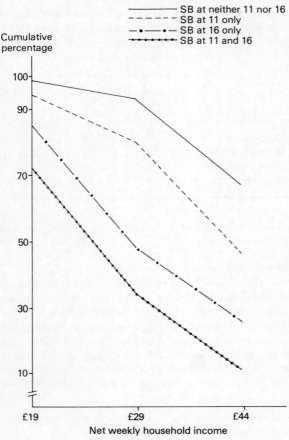

FIGURE 5.6 *Percentage of children above each income level for different groups*

of the groups on SB had felt in hardship at that time. Also, over a quarter (26 per cent) of those who were only reported as being on SB when the children were 16 said that they had felt troubled financially at that time.

TABLE 5.15 *Age of receipt of SB and feelings of financial hardship by families with 11- and 16-year-olds*

Source	Feeling in financial hardship	
	When children 11 (%)	When children 16 (%)
SB at 11 only (475)	60	30
SB at 16 only (306)	26	56
SB at 11 and 16 (245)	69	63
SB at neither (8 829)	6	6

The families who were on SB at both follow-ups may have had a better understanding of the welfare system than those who only claimed at one of the ages. Also, their needs were greater, both in terms of their lower income levels and the very small proportion of them with working fathers. For both reasons they could be expected to be more likely to have claimed for any benefits due to them, such as free school meals. The second column of Table 5.16 shows this to be so, as over three-quarters of them had received free school meals during the year, whereas only just over half of the other families who were on SB during the year had received them.

TABLE 5.16 *Age of receipt of SB and receipt of free school meals by families with 11- and 16-year-olds*

Source	Received free school meals	
	When children 11 (%)	When children 16 (%)
SB at 11 only (486)	50	33
SB at 16 only (329)	24	54
SB at 11 and 16 (261)	79	79
SB at neither (8 889)	5	5

The first column of Table 5.16 shows the percentages of families in each group who had received free school meals when the study children were 11. The

past year had lower incomes than those who had only been on SB when the children were 11. These differences could be explained by the higher proportion of one-parent families in the group on SB at both ages.

In order to gain some understanding of the extent to which the families felt their income was adequate, the responses to the question 'have you been troubled by financial hardship in the past twelve months?' were compared. The second column of Table 5.15 shows that when their children were 16 the two groups on SB at the time had a similarly high proportion of financial difficulties. Although they were not on SB at the time, nearly five times as many of the families who had been on SB five years previously as those never on SB reported feeling troubled by financial hardship. This supports the suggestion above that families in receipt of benefit may tend to be at a disadvantage generally even when not actually in receipt of benefit. The first column shows a similar pattern. The percentages are of the children in the recipient groups whose families had felt financial hardship when the children were 11. Over 60 per cent of each pattern is similar to that at 16, in that those on SB at both ages had the highest percentage (79 per cent) receiving school meals, and the second highest percentage (50 per cent) was among the other group on SB at the time in question. It is also notable that of those on SB at neither age similar proportions of families were in receipt of free school meals when the study children were 11 as when they were 16 (both 5 per cent).

Housing conditions

Families who have lived at a low standard of living for a long time may have acquired fewer household goods than other families. Table 5.17 provides some evidence for this, in that a lower proportion of families on SB at both ages had each of the domestic goods examined. The differences between those on SB at 11 only and those on SB at 16 only were small but always in the same direction, with those on SB at 11 relatively better off.

There were only small differences in the likelihood of crowding and lacking amenities between the groups on SB at different ages (Table 5.18), so that in these respects those on SB at both ages were not at a disadvantage compared with the other groups. It is notable that the group who were only on SB at 16 were more likely to be crowded or lacking ameni-

ties at the time they were *not* on SB as at the time they *were* on SB.

Physical development

The heights and weights of the children on benefit were compared to see if the relationship differed according to the age of receipt of SB. The differences were very small, but those on SB at both ages were on average 1cm shorter than those on SB at 11 only, who were in turn 1cm shorter than those on SB at 16 only. However, there were almost no differences in weight among the SB-recipient groups.

Pocket-money and spare-time job

As the households who had been in receipt of SB at both 11 and 16 were at a disadvantage financially and materially compared with the other SB groups, it was expected that the young people in these households would also be at a disadvantage in the amount of pocket-money they were given. This was found to be the case, as 53 per cent of those on SB at both ages, compared with 46 per cent of those on SB only at 11, and 47 per cent of those on SB only at 16 received less than 75p per week. As in the cross-sectional analysis, it was the group with the least pocket-money who were also least likely to have a spare-time job, with only 38 per cent of those on SB at

TABLE 5.17 *Age of receipt of SB and domestic goods in households with 16-year-olds*

Source	Refrigerator (%)	Telephone (%)	Car (%)	Central heating (%)	Colour TV (%)	N (= 100 %)
SB at 11 only	71	30	40	29	30	488
SB at 16 only	71	27	26	24	18	331
SB at 11 and 16	59	22	13	21	14	261
SB at neither	89	59	71	50	44	8 985

TABLE 5.18 *Age of receipt of SB, crowding and amenities* in families with 11- and 16-year-olds*

Source	11-year-olds		16-year-olds	
	Crowded (> 1.5 person/ room) (%)	Without sole use of three amenities (%)	Crowded (> 1.5 person/ room) (%)	Without sole use of three amenities (%)
SB at 11 only (488)	30	21	23	10
SB at 16 only (331)	27	22	20	14
SB at 11 and 16 (261)	26	24	19	11
SB at neither (8 985)	10	11	6	6

* The three amenities are hot water, indoor lavatory and bathroom.

both follow-ups but 46 per cent of both the other SB groups having a job in their spare time.

Plans for leaving school

It was expected that children whose families had been in receipt of SB earlier as well as in the past year might differ in their plans for the future from the children who had only been in this situation at one age, especially if the experience was some time in the past: 90 per cent of the children in families on SB at both ages planned to leave school at 16, as compared with 60 per cent of those not on SB. The groups of children on SB at only one age differed only slightly from each other but appreciably from those in receipt of SB at both ages (80 per cent of those on SB at 16, and 83 per cent of those on SB at 11 planned to leave at 16). There was also some variation between SB groups in the reasons given for this decision, with a higher percentage of those on SB at both ages expressing a need for money and a wish for independence than the other children on SB, though each of these groups of children in families on SB at some time were more likely to give these reasons than those not on benefit (Table 5.19). A higher proportion of the children whose families had received SB at both ages reported the influence of their friends than the children in the other SB groups, though there was little difference between any of the groups, including those

never on SB, in the proportion reporting they were influenced by their teachers or parents. The children on benefit at both ages were only slightly more likely to give dislike of school work and a feeling that they were not good enough at it as a reason for leaving than the children in families in receipt of benefit at any one age. In order to gain more understanding about their attitudes to school, the scores of each SB group on the academic motivation scale described earlier (p. 117) were compared. There was a slight trend in mean scores, with the children on SB at both ages having the highest scores (least motivated) followed by those only on SB at 11, than those only on SB at 16, and the lowest average scores belonging to those never on SB (Table 5.20). As the social-class distribution of children in each recipient group was similar, only the overall scores on each measure have been presented.

School attainment

Table 5.20 also provides a comparison of the maths and reading test scores of the children according to which age their families were dependent on benefit. Although the differences between the SB groups were small, in each case those on benefit at both ages had the lowest average score, followed by those on SB at 11 only, and the highest average scores among the recipient groups were those only on SB

TABLE 5.19   *Age of receipt of SB and reasons given by 16-year-olds for leaving school at chosen age*

Source	Need money (%)	Want independence (%)	Same as friend (%)	Parents' advice (%)	Teachers' advice (%)	Don't like school work (%)	Not good enough (%)	N (= 100%)
SB at 11 only	23	56	15	16	10	23	32	384
SB at 16 only	33	53	43	17	12	22	33	262
SB at 11 and 16	40	66	24	18	9	26	39	200
SB at neither	10	46	7	19	11	18	21	7 580

TABLE 5.20   *Age of receipt of SB and the 16-year-old — school attainment*

Source	Mean scores				
	Academic motivation scale	Maths test	Reading test	Behaviour (at school)	Behaviour (at home)
SB at 11 only (381)	21.2	− 0.56	− 0.54	2.3	2.8
SB at 16 only (256)	20.8	− 0.46	− 0.35	2.2	2.8
SB at 11 and 16 (200)	22.3	− 0.67	− 0.79	2.5	2.8
SB at neither (7 544)	19.2	0.12	0.13	1.5	2.7

at 16, though these were still lower than the non-beneficiaries. It should be remembered that these groups differed in their family and home characteristics, so these scores could be reflecting differences in their parental or home situation rather than any direct relationship with dependence on benefit.

Behaviour

Comparison of the children's scores on the Rutter scale of school adjustment revealed the same trend across SB groups as in the case of school attainment. However, the differences among them were very small, and not as great as the difference between any of the recipient groups and those never on SB. The children in families on SB at both ages were again at one extreme, with the highest (least well adjusted) scores (Table 5.20). However, this difference was not apparent in the comparison of scores on the Rutter scale of home behaviour. Each recipient group had very similar scores to each other, though they were significantly higher than the non-recipient groups (Table 5.20).

III

Health and Physical Development

6 Speech*

SPEECH PROBLEMS IN A NATIONAL SURVEY: ASSESSMENTS AND PREVALENCES

Introduction

In recent years an increasing volume of literature has appeared on the subject of language and speech problems in children. No doubt this is partly attributable to the evident connection between language and cognition (see Cromer, 1974, for a review), partly to the elucidation of brain processes underlying speech and language (e.g. Geschwind, 1970) and partly also to the controversy arising around the reputed 'codes' found in different social classes (Bernstein, 1971; Rosen, 1972). Since speech problems in children appear to be relatively common (Ingram, 1969) all this has brought an awareness of the cumulative difficulties which children with speech problems might suffer.

In our longitudinal study of a national cohort of schoolchildren it was necessary to investigate aspects of language development. The results of some of the investigations have been reported (e.g. Sheridan, 1973; Richardson et al., 1976a). One of our first priorities, however, was to define those children with speech problems in order to investigate the medical, educational and social factors associated with them. Because of the large body of data available, this seemed particularly likely to yield insights concerning the source of those problems. Additional objectives were the assessment of the apparent effects of those problems on certain growth 'outcomes', particularly scholastic attainment, and how both problems and 'effects' develop and change during the course of the

child's development. Here we present data concerning (a) the apparent prevalence of speech problems within three modes of assessment; (b) the extent of agreement between each mode of assessment regarding the identification of speech problems in each child; (c) sex, social class, birth order and family size associations with speech 'problems'; and (d) the extent and direction of parental agreement with the modes of assessment. In addition some deductions are made concerning the criteria, or the 'what exactly is being identified' aspects, of each mode of assessment. These data are from a cross-sectional analysis of the children at 11 years of age.

Method

The sources of information were as follows:

1. In answering an 'educational' questionnaire teachers of the study children were asked 'Is the child difficult to understand because of poor speech?' The responses were coded as 'certainly' or 'somewhat' or 'no'.
2. A speech test comprising the repetition of five simple sentences was administered to study children by doctors during the medical examination. The total number of mispronunciations was coded.
3. Doctors were asked in the course of medical examination if the study child had any defects of articulation. The responses were coded under the following categories: 'none'; 'stutter or stammer'; 'other speech abnormality'.

The source and definition of other variables examined will be considered in the next section.

The data were analysed in the following way. The association between each variable and each speech assessment was examined separately. Then a joint analysis was carried out with the variable in question as the dependent variable and the three speech assessments as independent variables. Thus each analysis of variance showed the relationship of the dependent variable to each speech assessment relative to the other two speech assessments. The purpose of this analysis was primarily to see what insights such knowledge would yield in terms of aetiology of

* Original sources: Calnan, M. and Richardson, K., 'Speech problems in a national survey: assessments and prevalences', *Child: Care, Health and Development*, 2, 1976, 191–202; Calnan, M. and Richardson, K., 'Speech problems in a national survey: associations with hearing, handedness and therapy', *Community Health*, 8, 1976, 101–5; Sheridan, M. D. and Peckham, C., 'Follow-up at 11 years of children who had marked speech defects at 7 years', *Child: Care, Health and Development*, 1, 1975, 157–66; Sheridan, M. D. and Peckham, C., 'Follow-up to 16 years of children who had marked speech defects at 7 years', *Child: Care, Health and Development*, 4, 1978, 145–57.

alleged problems and the 'meaningfulness' of the assessments. For example, we were able to examine the characteristics of the group of children where the speech assessments concurred and also the characteristics of the 'disparate groups'.

The statistical procedure used and the results of the statistical tests are described below (pp. 135—6).

Results

Of these 11-year-old children, teachers assessed 117 (1 per cent of the total) as having 'certainly poor speech' and 1 092 (9.5 per cent) as having 'somewhat poor speech': 1 136 (9.9 per cent) of the subjects mispronounced one word on the speech test; a further 802 (7.0 per cent) mispronounced two or more words. Doctors assessed 534 (4.6 per cent) as having defects of articulation. Of these, 469 (i.e. 4.1 per cent) were said to have 'other speech abnormality', the remainder (0.5 per cent) suffering from stammers or stutters. In all, some 2 813 (24.6 per cent) children were said to have speech problems (of whatever severity) according to at least one source of assessment.

Table 6.1 gives an indication of the extent of agreement between the modes of assessment. It shows the distributions of those children whom doctors assessed as having problems of articulation against the speech test and teachers' assessment of comprehension of the child's speech, in a variety of combinations. Before considering the results it is pertinent to ask, on the basis of the face-validity of the assessments, what sorts of agreement would be expected, and of what degree. A large measure of agreement would be expected between doctors' assessments and the speech test. Mispronunciation can be described as a type of articulation defect although all articulation defects do not necessarily involve mispronunciation. Similarly, a large measure of agreement would be expected between both of these measures and teachers' assessments: children manifesting articulation defects and/or mispronunciations would be expected to be 'difficult to understand because of poor speech'.

The results show that of the 469 children said by the doctors to have a defect of articulation, 33.1 per cent recorded no mispronunciations on the speech test, and of the same 469 children 69.9 per cent did

TABLE 6.1   *Speech test by teacher's assessment of poor speech and doctor's assessment of defect of articulation*

Teacher's assessment of poor speech and number of mispronunciations on the speech test	Doctor's assessment of defect of articulation (%)			
	None	Stammer or stutter	Other speech abnormality	Total (%)
Speech Test no mispronunciation and teacher noted poor speech	6.3	18.5	6.0	6.3
Speech Test one mispronunciation and teacher noted poor speech	1.2	9.2	3.6	1.4
Speech Test two mispronunciations or more teacher noted poor speech	1.1	15.4	20.5	2.0
Speech Test no mispronunciation and teacher noted no poor speech	79.1	33.8	27.1	76.7
Speech Test one mispronunciation and teacher noted no poor speech	8.4	8.4	10.9	8.5
Speech Test two mispronunciations or more teacher noted no poor speech	3.8	9.2	32.0	5.0
Total	100.0	100.0	100.0	100.0
N =	10 921	65	469	11 455

not have poor speech ('certainly' and 'somewhat' combined) according to their teachers. Of the 1 109 children said to have poor speech by the teacher, 726 (65.5 per cent) did not mispronounce on the speech test.

Sex differences

For each of the three speech assessments boys were significantly more likely to have speech problems than girls. Table 6.2 shows the distribution of the three speech assessments by sex. The largest sex differences were found in the group of children who mispronounced two or more words on the speech test. Large sex differences were also found in the group assessed by the teacher as having 'somewhat' poor speech.

An analysis of variance was carried out with the three speech assessments as independent variables and sex as the dependent variable (see Table A in the appendix to this section). The results of this analysis are best interpreted in combination with the estimated percentages. Table 6.3 shows the estimated percentage of boys in different groupings of the three speech assessments.

The results show that the highest percentages of

boys occur in the stammer group irrespective of whether it is in combination with the other two assessments. However, when the stammer group is excluded the largest percentages occur in the teacher's assessment. The speech test shows smaller variations than the teachers' or doctors' assessments.

Social-class differences

Children with fathers in manual occupations were significantly more likely to be assessed as having poor speech by the teacher and were also significantly more likely to mispronounce on the speech test. However, the doctor's assessment of defect of articulation was not significantly associated with social class.

Table 6.4 shows the distribution of the teacher's assessment and the speech test by social class. The results show that social-class differences increase as the child mispronounces more words. In contrast the social-class differences are small for the 'certainly' poor speech but are much larger for the 'somewhat' poor speech group.

An analysis of variance was carried out with the three speech assessments as the independent variables and social class as the dependent variable (see Table B

TABLE 6.2   *Distribution of the three speech assessments by sex*

Doctor's assessment of defect of articulation	Boy (%)	Girl (%)	No. of words mispronounced on the speech test	Boy (%)	Girl (%)
Other abnormalities	5.1	3.1	2+	12.1	5.5
Stammer or stutter	1.0	—	1	10.9	8.4
None	94.0	96.8	0	77.0	86.1
Total	100	100	Total	100	100
N =	5 879	5 577	N =	6 125	5 575

Teacher's assessment of poor speech	Boy (%)	Girl (%)
Certainly	1.5	—
Somewhat	11.2	5.0
No	87.3	95.0
Total	100	100
N =	6 217	5 814

Doctors's assessment x sex χ^2 (2 df) = 57.9, $p < 0.001$.
Speech test   x sex χ^2 (2 df) = 63.9, $p < 0.001$.
Teacher's assessment x sex χ^2 (2 df) = 189.6, $p < 0.001$.

TABLE 6.3   *Estimated percentages of boys in groupings of the three speech assessments*

	Speech test (no. of mispronunciations)								
	0 Mispronunciation Doctor's assessment			1 Mispronunciation Doctor's assessment			2 + Mispronunciations Doctor's assessment		
Teacher's assessment of poor speech	None	Stammer	Speech abnormality	None	Stammer	Speech abnormality	None	Stammer	Speech abnormality
No	48	84	53	56	88	61	54	87	59
Somewhat	68	92	72	74	94	78	73	94	77
Certainly	74	94	78	80	96	83	79	96	84

	Doctor's assessment			Speech test			Teacher's assessment		
Overall total	None	Stammer	Speech abnormality	0	1	2+	None	Somewhat	Certainly
51.3	50.6	89.2	63.3	49.5	59.0	61.6	49.2	49.2	78.6

TABLE 6.4   *Distribution of teacher's assessment and the speech test by social class*

No. of words mispronounced on the speech test	Non-manual (%)	Manual (%)	Teacher's assessment of poor speech	Non-manual (%)	Manual (%)
2+	4.5	11.5	Certainly	1.0	1.2
1	8.0	9.8	Somewhat	5.2	10.8
0	87.5	78.7	No	94.1	88.0
Total	100	100	Total	100	100
N =	4 122	7 191	*N* =	3 826	7 175

Doctor's assessment x social class χ^2 (2 df) =   5.7 ns.
Speech test   x social class χ^2 (2 df) = 192.6, $p < 0.001$.
Teacher's assessment x social class χ^2 (2 df) = 116.3, $p < 0.001$.

in the appendix to this paper). The results showed that the teacher's assessment and speech test showed similar social class variations. This is clearly shown in Table 6.5. However, it is interesting to note that the highest percentages occurred when the 'somewhat' poor speech group was in combination with the speech test.

Family size

Children living in households with five or more children were significantly more likely to have speech 'problems' according to each of the three speech assessments. However, the association between family size and the doctor's assessment of defect of articulation was weak and much smaller than the relationship between the other two speech assessments and family size. This is clearly shown in Table 6.6, which shows the distribution of the three speech assessments by family size. An analysis of variance was carried out with the three speech assessments as independent variables and family size as the dependent variable (see Table C in the appendix to this section). The

TABLE 6.5 *Estimated percentages of children with fathers in manual occupations in groupings of the teacher's assessment and the speech test*

Teacher's assessment of poor speech	Speech test (no. of mispronunciations)			
	0	1	2+	Total
No	62	69	71	62.1
Somewhat	76	80	83	78.0
Certainly	72	77	80	75.7
Total	62.9	68.8	74.5	64.3

TABLE 6.7 *Estimated percentages of children in households with 1–4 children*

Teacher's assessment of poor speech	Speech test (no. of mispronunciations)			
	0	1	2	Total
No	86	82	80	85
Somewhat	73	67	64	70
Certainly	73	68	65	69
Total	85	80	76	84

results showed that the doctor's assessment was no longer significantly associated with family size, allowing for the effects of the other two speech assessments. The teacher's assessment showed larger family size variations than the speech test (see Table 6.7). Once again the highest percentages of children from large families (5+ children) are found when the 'somewhat' poor speech group is in combination with the mispronunciation on the speech test.

Birth order

Fourth or later-born children were significantly more likely to have poor speech according to the teacher, mispronounce on the speech test and have a defect of articulation according to the doctor (Table 6.8).

An analysis of variance was carried out with the three speech assessments as the independent variables and birth order as the dependent (see Table D in the appendix to this section). The results showed that the doctor's assessment of defect of articulation was no

longer significantly associated with birth order, allowing for the effects of the other two assessments. The teacher's assessment showed larger variations in birth order than the speech test (Table 6.9). The highest percentages of children with a low birth order (fourth or more) were found when the child had 'certainly' poor speech and mispronounced on the speech test.

Parental assessment of speech difficulty

Parents were asked if their child had a speech difficulty at present. Not surprisingly, all three speech assessments were found to be significantly associated with parental assessment. As parental assessment, like the teacher's assessment and the speech test, was found to be associated with social class, the distribution of the three assessments by parental assessment was analysed within social class (Tables 6.10–6.12).

Results from these three tables showed that the largest degree of concurrence was found between parental assessment and the doctor's assessment of

TABLE 6.6 *Distribution of the three speech assessments by family size*

Doctor's assessment of defect of articulation	1–4 children (%)	5+ children (%)	No. of words mispronounced on the speech test	1–4 children (%)	5+ children (%)	Teacher's assessment of poor speech	1–4 children (%)	5+ children (%)
Other abnormality	3.9	5.0	2+	6.3	10.5	Certainly	0.8	1.9
Stammer or stutter	0.5	0.7	1	0.6	12.0	Somewhat	7.3	15.6
None	95.6	94.2	0	84.0	77.0	No	91.8	82.4
Total	100	100	Total	100	100	Total	100	100
N =	9 555	1 885	N =	9 555	1 885	N =	9 555	1 885

Doctor's assessments   x family size χ^2 (2 df) =   6.1, $p < 0.05$.
Speech test   x family size χ^2 (2 df) = 50.0, $p < 0.001$.
Teacher's assessment   x family size χ^2 (2 df) = 137.4, $p < 0.001$.

TABLE 6.8   *Distribution of three speech assessments by birth order*

Doctor's assessment of defect of articulation	1st–3rd (%)	4th or more (%)	No. of words mispronounced on the speech test	1st–3rd (%)	4th or more (%)	Teacher's assessment of poor speech	1st–3rd (%)	4th or more (%)
Other abnormality	3.9	6.4	2+	6.6	11.5	Certainly	0.9	3.0
Stammer or stutter	0.5	2.0	1	9.8	12.0	Somewhat	7.8	17.0
None	95.6	92.4	0	83.6	76.6	No	91.3	80.0
Total	100	100	Total	100	100	Total	100	100
N =	10 438	1 004	N =	10 438	1 004	N =	10 438	1 004

Doctor's assessment x birth order χ^2 (2 df) = 19.2, $p < 0.001$.
Speech test x birth order χ^2 (2 df) = 35.7, $p < 0.001$.
Teacher's assessment x birth order χ^2 (2 df) = 118.6, $p < 0.001$.

TABLE 6.9   *Estimated percentages of children with birth order 1–3*

Teacher's assessment of poor speech	Speech test (no. of mispronunciations)			
	0	1	2+	Total
No	93	91	89	92
Somewhat	84	81	78	82
Certainly	78	74	70	74
Total	92	89	86	91

stammer or stutter. Apart from this group, the teacher's assessment and doctor's assessment had similar levels of concurrence with the parents, but the speech test had a much smaller level of concurrence.

Analyses of variance were carried out with parental assessment as the dependent variable and social class and each of the three speech assessments as independent variables (see Tables E–G in the appendix to this paper). Each of the three analyses showed that all three speech assessments were still strongly associated with parental assessment allowing for social class. Similarly in all three analyses social-class differences still persisted, but these were small.

A joint analysis was carried out with parental assessment as the dependent variable and the three

TABLE 6.10   *Distribution of parental assessment of speech difficulty by doctor's assessment of defect of articulation by social class*

Parental assessment of speech difficulty at present	Doctor's assessment of defect of articulation							
	Speech abnormality (%)		Stammer or stutter (%)		None (%)		Total (%)	
	Non-manual	Manual	Non-manual	Manual	Non-manual	Manual	Non-manual	Manual
Yes	21.9	28.0	57.1	59.5	2.0	2.7	2.8	4.2
No	79.1	72.0	42.9	40.5	98.0	97.3	97.2	95.8
Total	100	100	100	100	100	100	100	100
N =	128	289	14	37	3 810	6 536	3 952	6 872

TABLE 6.11 *Distribution of parental assessment of speech difficulty by number of words mispronounced on the speech test and social class*

Parental assessment of speech difficulty at present	Speech test (no. of mispronunciations)							
	0		1		2+		Total	
	Non-manual (%)	Manual (%)	Non-manual (%)	Manual (%)	Non-manual (%)	Manual (%)	Non-manual (%)	Manual (%)
Yes	2.3	3.0	4.7	4.2	11.3	16.4	2.8	4.2
No	97.7	97.0	95.3	95.7	88.7	83.6	97.2	95.8
Total	100	100	100	100	100	100	100	100
N =	3 134	5 216	298	655	164	481	3 952	6 872

Parental assessment x social class χ^2 (1 df) = 3.9; $0.01 > p < 0.05$.

TABLE 6.12 *Distribution of parental assessment of speech difficulty by teacher's assessment of poor speech and social class*

Parental assessment of speech difficulty at present	Teacher's assessment of poor speech							
	Certainly		Somewhat		No		Total	
	Non-manual (%)	Manual (%)	Non-manual (%)	Manual (%)	Non-manual (%)	Manual (%)	Non-manual (%)	Manual (%)
Yes	30.0	29.3	11.3	10.1	2.3	3.2	2.8	4.2
No	70.0	71.0	88.6	90.9	97.7	96.8	97.2	95.8
Total	100	100	100	100	100	100	100	100
N =	20	62	107	606	3 401	5 785	3 952	6 872

speech assessments and social class as the independent variables (see Table F in the appendix to this paper). The results of this analysis showed little difference in the degree of variation between the parental assessment and the doctor's assessment and between the parental assessment and teacher's assessment.

Discussion

The expression 'speech problem' is a blanket term covering a wide variety of distinctly different conditions. Among them will be dysphasia, dyarthria, stuttering and numerous other psychological, anatomical and neurophysiological syndromes. Our crude categories of 'defects of articulation', 'mispronunciation', and 'difficult to understand because of poor speech' do not enable us to make fine diagnostic distinctions of that sort. None the less, it is probable that those data provide some indication of the extent and distribution of 'speech problems'. Considering first the overall prevalences: the proportion of children said to have speech problems by one or more sources of assessment was high (25 per cent).

Undoubtedly this value was inflated by the relatively low threshold adopted for the speech test results, namely one mispronunciation only. When the lower threshold of speech test performance is excluded (i.e. one mispronunciation only), this percentage is reduced to 16.5 per cent, which is closer to that of other calculated prevalences. For example, Wohl (1951) found that 12 per cent of children in one Scottish town had speech defects. However, Morley (1972) found that only 3 per cent of her sample of children in an English town had speech defects. Much, of course, depends on the means of assessment. The frequencies of stammering children in our group (0.5 per cent) is in closer agreement with those of Morley (0.7 per cent) and Wohl (1.3 per cent) and with frequencies from international sources (Chrysanthis, 1947). Apart from those particular data, the teachers identified 'poor speech' among a substantial proportion of the subjects: a proportion, in fact, which approached twice that of the doctors' assessments. This was probably due to a more general, 'functional' set of criteria adopted by teachers.

Of greater potential interest than the absolute prevalence, however, was the fact that there proved to be relatively little agreement between the sources of assessment concerning who had or had not a speech problem of some sort. Where a large degree of concurrence would be expected, for example between 'articulation defect' and teacher's 'poor speech', alleged speech problems according to one source remained unconfirmed, more often than not, according to the other. Even for so prominent a problem as stuttering, teachers claimed that over half of those cases diagnosed by doctors had no poor speech. This simply could be a question of severity of stuttering. Overall, these results may reflect the considerable intra-subject variability that occurs on some sounds (see Canter and Trost, 1966, for a review).

The present results concerning the sex differences of children with stammer or stutter are in accord with earlier findings reported by West (1947). Depending on the degree of concurrence, boys were three to ten times more likely than girls to be suffering from a stammer. While the aetiology of this syndrome remains controversial (see, for example, Fransella, 1970), we cannot account for the origins of this large sexual disparity. When stammer cases were excluded we still found a preponderance of boys in some of the speech-problem categories; similar findings have been reported by Woods (1960), Clark (1970) and Sheridan (1973).

Compared with the doctors' assessments, the teachers' assessments and mispronunciation on the speech test revealed appreciable social-class differences. The previous literature is ambiguous on this point. For example, whereas Morley (1972) could find no social-class differences on defect of articulation, there were social-class differences on severe defects, which agree with the findings of Sheridan (1973). Winitz (1969), in a thorough review of the literature, concluded 'more misarticulating children and more articulation errors are found in the lower socio-economic groups than in the upper socio-

economic groups although there is a low positive correlation'. It is possible that the excess of cases of 'mispronunciation' or being 'difficult to understand because of poor speech' among children from manual groups may reflect their greater use of dialect and/or non-standard English. It is becoming increasingly clear that many supposed deviances of pronunciation and articulation are in fact a normal part of some children's socio-cultural milieu (Adler, 1973). As Yoder (1970) put it: 'There is the worrisome prospect, that our testing procedures and instruments are sometimes revealing to us ethnic and social class differences in language rather than differences in speech capabilities or development of children.' The implication of this possibility is that treatment based on such misdiagnosis may be not only unsuccessful, but harmful (Adler, 1973). While the chance of children with a misdiagnosis but relatively slight disability actually receiving any treatment is extremely low in view of the great scarcity of speech therapists in Britain, being labelled, especially by a teacher, as having a 'speech problem' may in itself create difficulties for the child.

There was slight social-class difference in parental assessment of their children's speech difficulty. The overall degree of concurrence between parental assessment and the three assessments was not high, the highest degree of concurrence occurring when the doctor assessed stammer or stutter. This may reflect the fact that the doctors, at least in some cases, had obtained information concerning speech abnormality from the parents themselves during the medical examination, or the association may represent a freedom from extraneous factors like dialect or non-standard English.

There was a larger proportion of children who had poor speech according to the teachers and came from large families than with the doctors' assessments. Similar results were found for birth order. These results may reflect social-class differences; however, they may also conceal genuine family-size and birth-order differences in the prevalence of speech disorder. Morley (1972) found that severe defects of articulation were more frequent in second and later children than in first children. Butler *et al.* (1973) found that children with marked speech problems were more likely to be found in large families.

To summarise this paper. We have presented data on the prevalence of speech problems in a nationally representative group of children according to three modes of assessment. There was a large measure of disagreement between the assessments. Sex, social-class, birth-order and family-size differences were discussed. There was indirect evidence for social-class biases on the part of the teachers. Finally, we examined the relationship between parental assessment and the three modes of assessment. Overall, the degree of concurrence was low.

Appendix: analyses of variance

In all analyses of variance the three speech assessments were included in the analysis as independent variables. In Tables A–D and F all three speech assessments were included in the analysis as independent variables. Table E shows three separate analyses involving each of the speech assessments as independents. Throughout the analyses the three speech assessments were defined as follows:

1. Teachers' ratings of difficult to understand because of poor speech:
   (a) Not at all
   (b) Somewhat
   (c) Certainly
2. Doctors' ratings of any defect of articulation:
   (a) None
   (b) Stammer or stutter only
   (c) Other speech abnormality
3. Speech test results:
   (a) No mispronounced words
   (b) 1 mispronounced word
   (c) 2 or more mispronounced words

TABLE A *Dependent variable is logit transformation of the proportion of boys. Fitted constants and analysis of variance table. Main effects model (χ^2 values are adjusted for the other factors)*

Sources		Fitted constant	Standard error	df	χ^2
Overall		0.71			
Teacher	a	−0.32			
	b	0.08		2	159.2 ***
	c	0.24			
Doctor	a	−0.33			
	b	0.55		2	31.9 ***
	c	0.22			
Speech test (mispronounced words)	0	−0.09			
	1	0.06		2	30.5 ***
	2+	0.03			

Sample size = 11 455.
Test for goodness of fit of main effects model: χ^2 = 35.1*; df = 20.

TABLE B *Dependent variable is logit transformation of the proportion of non-manual children. Fitted constants and analysis of variance table. Main effects model (χ^2 values are adjusted for the other factors)*

Sources		Fitted constant	Standard error	df	χ^2
Overall		0.54			
Teacher	a	0.20			
	b	−0.15		2	76.6 ***
	c	−0.05			
Doctor	a	−0.02			
	b	−0.02		2	1.1
	c	0.04			
Speech test (mispronounced words)	0	0.12			
	1	0.00		2	33.0 ***
	2+	−0.12			

Sample size = 10 696.
Test for goodness of fit of main effects model: χ^2 = 27.8*; df = 20.

TABLE C *Dependent variable is logit transformation of the proportion of children in households with 1–4 children. Fitted constants and analysis of variance table. Main effects model (χ^2 values are adjusted for the other factors)*

Sources		Fitted constant	Standard error	df	χ^2
Overall		0.55			
Teacher	a	0.27			
	b	−0.13		2	113.3 ***
	c	−0.14			
Doctor	a	−0.04			
	b	0.00		2	1.8
	c	0.04			
Speech test (mispronounced words)	0	0.12			
	1	−0.01		2	26.3 ***
	2+	−0.11			

Sample size = 11 440.
Test for goodness of fit of main effects model: χ^2 = 24.0*; df = 20.

TABLE D *Dependent variable is logit transformation of the proportion of children with birth order 1–3. Fitted constants and analysis of variance table. Main effects model (χ^2 values are adjusted for the other factors)*

Sources		Fitted constant	Standard error	df	χ^2
Overall		0.74			
Teacher	a	0.35			
	b	−0.08		2	92.1 ***
	c	−0.27			
Doctor	a	0.08			
	b	−0.12		2	1.5
	c	0.04			
Speech test (mispronounced words)	0	0.10			
	1	−0.01		2	11.0 ***
	2+	−0.09			

Sample size = 11 440.
Test for goodness of fit of main effects model: χ^2 = 14.4*; df = 20.

TABLE E   *Dependent variable is logit transformation of proportion of parents aware of speech difficulty*

Sources		Fitted constant	Standard error	df	x^2
1. Overall		−0.7			
Doctor's rating	None	−1.1		2	398.8 ***
	Stammer or stutter	0.8			
	Other	0.3			
Social class	Non-Man				
	—Man	0.15	0.06	1	6.2 *
2. Overall		−1.1			
Teacher's rating	None	−0.7		2	141.0 ***
	Some	0.0			
	Certainly	0.7			
Social class	Non-Man				
	—Man	0.1	0.06	1	4.2 *
3. Overall Speech test		−1.4			
	0	−0.4			
	1	−0.1		2	155.7 ***
	2+	0.5			
Social class	Non-Man				
	—Man	0.1	0.06	1	4.7 *

TABLE F   *Dependent variable is logit transformation of proportions of parents aware of speech difficulty. Fitted constants and analysis of variance table. Main effects model (x^2 values are adjusted for the other factors)*

Sources		Fitted constant	Standard error	df	x^2
Overall		−0.43			
Teacher	a	−0.42			
	b	0.06		2	53.9 ***
	c	0.36			
Doctor	a	−0.96			
	b	0.78		2	226.9 ***
	c	0.18			
Speech test	a	−0.12			
	b	−0.01		2	8.7 *
	c	0.13			
Social class:	Non-Manual	−0.10	0.06	1	2.5

Sample size = 10 042.
Test for goodness of fit of main effects model: x^2 = 52.5*; df = 36.

SPEECH PROBLEMS IN A NATIONAL SURVEY: ASSOCIATIONS WITH HEARING, HANDEDNESS AND THERAPY

Introduction

In the preceding section we reported the prevalences of speech problems among 11-year-old children in the National Child Development Study, according to three modes of assessment, namely teachers' impression, speech test performance and doctors' clinical assessment. There was only a small measure of concurrence between the three assessments. The association between a number of social and biological characteristics and each of the three speech assessments was examined. An additional analysis was carried out which examined the relationship between these characteristics and the three speech assessments in combination. The purpose of this analysis was to gain an insight into the nature of the speech 'problem' being identified by each of the assessments.

In this section, further analyses examine the relationship between speech problems assessed by three assessments and hearing loss, handedness and use of speech therapy services. A preliminary report of the handedness analysis is published elsewhere (Calnan and Richardson 1976b: see pp. 204–13).

The hearing sufficiency of each child was obtained from the doctor's administration of a clinical hearing test obtained during a medical examination. The clinical hearing test consisted of the repetition of a number of words to the study child. The number of incorrect words repeated by the child was recorded. Based on this test and scrutiny of the audiogram the doctor was asked to judge whether the child had any hearing loss which would interfere with normal schooling and everyday functioning.

The hand preference of each study child was obtained from mothers during a parental interview. This criterion was found to agree fairly well with other criteria, such as which hand the child writes with and the hand used for ball-throwing (Calnan and Richardson, 1976b: see pp. 204–13).

Evidence as to use of speech therapy services was also obtained during the parental interview. The period and duration of therapy is not known.

The data were analysed in the following way. The association between each variable and each speech assessment was examined separately. Then a joint analysis was carried out with the variable in question as the dependent and the three speech assessments as independent variables. This analysis showed the association between a variable and the three speech assessments in combination. Thus we could examine the characteristics of the group of children where the speech assessments concurred and also the characteristics of the 'disparate groups'.

Results

Hearing loss

Table 6.13 shows each of the three speech assessments by doctor's assessment of hearing loss. For each of the three speech assessments, similar proportions of children suffered from hearing loss. These

TABLE 6.13 *Doctor's assessment of hearing loss by teacher's assessment of poor speech. Number of words mispronounced on the speech test and doctor's assessment of defect of articulation (percentages)*

Doctor's assessment of hearing loss	Doctor's assessment of defect of articulation			Speech test (no. of mispronunciations)			Teacher's assessment of poor speech		
	None	Stammer or stutter	Other speech abnormality	0	1	2+	None	Somewhat	Certainly
Normal	92	88	82	92	81	81	92	85	78
Hearing loss but no interference	7	8	13	7	8	13	7	11	16
Hearing loss with interference	1	3	6	1	1	6	1	3	6
N (= 100%)	10 283	60	442	9 959	1 067	638	9 655	923	105

differences persisted when sex differences were allowed for.

An analysis of variance was carried out using the proportion with any hearing loss as the dependent variable and the three speech assessments as the independent variables. The results from this analysis showed that the doctor's assessment of defect of articulation was no longer significantly associated with hearing loss when allowing for the other two speech assessments.

Results in Table 6.14 show that almost a third of the children who both mispronounced two or more words on the speech test and had 'certainly' poor speech had some degree of hearing loss. The differences in the percentage of children with hearing loss in the 'disparate' groups were small, though the percentage within these groups was still large.

TABLE 6.14 *Estimated percentages of children with hearing loss by combinations of the teacher's assessment and the speech test*

Teacher's assessment of poor speech	Speech test (no. of mispronunciations)			Total
	0	1	2+	
None	7	8	14	8
Somewhat	12	13	23	14
Certainly	17	18	30	22
Total	8	9	17	8

Handedness

We have shown (Calnan and Richardson, 1976b) that boys were much more likely to be left- or mixed-handed than girls. As a similar pattern of sex differ-

ences was found for children with speech 'problems', the relationship between handedness and speech 'pro-'problems' was considered allowing for sex differences. These results showed that none of the three speech assessments was significantly associated with handedness.

Use of speech therapy services

Table 6.15 shows each of the three speech assessments by use of speech therapy services. The percentages of children assessed as having speech problems on any of the three speech assessments and who had utilised the speech therapy services were generally low. The relationship between utilisation of the speech therapy services and each of the three speech assessments was considered allowing for sex differences. The teacher's assessment and the doctor's assessment accounted for similar differences in utilisation of speech therapy. The speech test accounted for much smaller differences. It was also interesting to note that strong sex differences in the use of speech therapy services were still found after allowing for each of the speech assessments.

Table 6.16 shows the estimated percentages for the use of speech therapy services and different groupings of the three speech assessments. These results show that the highest percentages are found when the teacher's and the doctor's assessment concur, particularly in the stammer group. Those children who only mispronounce words on the speech test showed a very low utilisation rate. These findings were derived from an analysis of variance with use of speech therapy services as the dependent variable and the three speech assessments and sex as the independents.

Discussion

In the preceding paper we stated that we expected a

TABLE 6.15   *Use of speech therapy services by teacher's assessment of poor speech. Number of words mispronounced on the speech test and doctor's assessment of defect of articulation (percentaged)*

Ever used speech therapy services	Doctor's assessment of defect of articulation			Speech test (no. of mispronunciations)			Teacher's assessment of poor speech		
	None	Stammer or stutter	Other speech abnormality	0	1	2+	None	Somewhat	Certainly
Yes	2	28	19	2	6	14	4	12	34
No	98	72	81	98	94	86	96	89	66
N (= 100%)	10 530	64	456	9 161	1 104	680	9 807	958	113

large measure of agreement between either the teacher's assessment and the speech test. In fact, the results showed that there was a low degree of concurrence between these two measures and teacher's assessment. Further analysis showed the characteristics of those children said to have defects of articulation were different from those where the child mispronounced on the speech test, or, according to the teacher, had poor speech. This evidence suggests that either the doctor and teacher are detecting different types of speech 'problems' or that they were identifying the same phenomenon through different features. Hence the teacher's assessment may be biased by educational factors because the teacher is relating a child's speech to his performance in the classroom. The doctor, on the other hand, may lay more emphasis on structural or physiological abnormality and therefore a proportion of these defects may not significantly influence the child's everyday life.

Such types of explanation cannot be made here because of the nature of the variables considered. All three speech assessments were significantly associated with hearing loss. However, the joint analysis showed that doctor's assessment was only significantly associated with hearing loss when used in combination with the speech test or the teacher's assessment. It is possible that the group of children diagnosed as having articulation disorders by the doctor may have defects which are primarily organic or structural. However, there is evidence to suggest that even children with organic defects such as cleft palate are susceptible to ear infections resulting in hearing loss.

It is generally accepted that hearing loss in young children does cause delay in speech development. Impairments in auditory discrimination of speech sound affect the development of speech perception and speech expression. Thus it is not surprising that children with hearing loss were more likely to mis-

TABLE 6.16   *Estimated percentages of children who had ever used the speech therapy services by teacher's assessment of poor speech, doctor's assessment of defects of articulation and speech test (number of mispronunciations)*

Teacher's assessment of poor speech	Speech Test (no. of mispronunciations)								
	0 Doctor's Assessment			1 Doctor's Assessment			2+ Doctor's Assessment		
	None	Stammer or stutter	Other speech abnormality	None	Stammer or stutter	Other speech abnormality	None	Stammer or stutter	Other speech abnormality
No	2	11	7	3	19	12	3	19	12
Somewhat	6	11	20	11	47	34	11	47	34
Certainly	15	56	43	26	72	60	26	72	60

pronounce on the speech test. However, it is also possible that the child's speech expression is normal for his age group but either he or she could not hear the sentences properly or exhibited a characteristic lack of confidence in that situation. Either of these would interfere with repetition leading to mispronunciation. There is a more subtle point which has been proposed by Adler (1972). He suggests that hearing tests, like speech tests, tend to use the standard English frame as the criterion measure utilised to ascertain the level of discriminatory ability. Thus children using non-standard English language systems may have problems in discriminating the required sound. He argues that

> to obtain reliable and valid discrimination scores for children of different subcultural groups necessitates the utilization of stimuli appropriate to the particular subculture being tested. The stimuli should be presented in grammatical frames relevant to the child's non-standard language code.

Similar explanations may also account for the strong association between teacher's assessments ('difficult to understand because of poor speech') and hearing loss. If so, there is a clear need for hearing loss to be adequately detected at an early age and for teachers to know that it could be the source of additional speech problems in school.

There is little evidence from the present study for the hypothesis that non-right-handedness tends to result in speech problems, though the belief is a long standing one (for a review, see Clark, 1957). Undoubtedly much positive support for the hypothesis was derived from small or selected (e.g. institutionalised; receiving speech therapy) samples of children. The present results are in close agreement with those of Douglas *et al.* (1967b), also from a large, nationally representative group of children and from evidence collected in another longitudinal study (see Rutter *et al.*, 1970).

The inadequacy of speech therapy services in Britain was clearly shown in the Quirk Report (1972). Evidence from the present study appears to support this. For each of the three speech assessments the maximum rate of utilisation was 35 per cent. The joint analysis showed that, depending on the combination of positive assessments, 72 per cent of our subjects with speech problems had at some time used the speech therapy services. By far the greatest degree of uptake of speech therapy occurred among the stammer and stutter groups, especially where these disorders were prominent enough for teachers to agree that poor speech was certainly present. However, it must be remembered that the numbers of children in the groups where the assessments concur

are small and the overall uptake of the service is low. To combat inadequacies in the staffing of the speech therapy services and to ensure that children with severe disorders receive treatment, Renfrew and Geary (1973) discuss how disorders of speech that are likely to persist could be differentiated from disorders that clear up spontaneously. Examples of this are found in the next paper, which finds that, of the group of 7-year-olds with 'marked speech defects', 31 per cent had, according to teacher's and doctor's reports, recovered normal speech. Of this 31 per cent, only 24 per cent were reported at some time to have received speech therapy.

As for the appreciable numbers of children who had received speech therapy but who were negatively assessed for speech problems on one or more counts, it is not known whether the therapy itself led to recovery from a problem. It would be interesting to examine the processes of referral to speech therapy services and also look at the characteristics of those (if any) who use the speech therapy services as a screening or preventative service and those who use the speech therapy services as a curative service.

FOLLOW-UP AT 11 YEARS OF CHILDREN WHO HAD MARKED SPEECH DEFECTS AT 7 YEARS

In earlier work (Butler *et al.*, 1973; Sheridan, 1973; Peckham, 1973; Sheridan and Peckham, 1973) we have reported our findings concerning speech defects in the whole sample of 15 490 children at 7 years of age, and a more detailed study of 215 children (144 boys and 71 girls) who were considered by both their teacher and examining doctor to have normal hearing but who showed appreciable unintelligibility of speech. We related our findings to various factors in the children's individual perinatal history and subsequent medical, social and scholastic progress. The present paper concerns a follow-up of this special study at 11 years, using the rest of the sample as controls.

Three detailed reports had been requested for every child in the sample: a social report completed by the health visitor interviewing the parent, an educational report by the child's teacher and a medical report by the examining doctor. For this inquiry we scrutinised all three reports for every 11-year-old study child traced and reviewed their records obtained at 7 years. We also rescrutinised the earlier reports of the study children for whom no information was available at 11 years.

Study children

Of the original 215 children we were able to obtain adequate information regarding health, scholastic attainments and social progress of 190. Figure 6.1 summarises our selective grouping of these children according to their educational placement at 11 years, i.e. those formally 'ascertained' for special educational treatment and those remaining in ordinary schools with or without residual speech problems. A summary of the 'missing' twenty-five children is also provided.

The sixty-six children formally 'ascertained' for special educational treatment comprised 35 per cent of the traced children. They were distributed as shown in Table 6.17.

As many as one-third of the study children for whom information was available were categorised as 'ESN' compared with 1.6 per cent of the whole sample. There was a marked preponderance of ESN boys. Three ESN children had been ascertained in a double category: one as 'epileptic', another as 'physically handicapped', and the third as 'speech defect'.

TABLE 6.17   *Children ascertained for special educational treatment*

Special school	Boys	Girls	Total
SSN	6	6	12
ESN	33	14	47
Other			
speech defect		2	2
partially hearing	2		2
physically handicapped	1	1	2
maladjusted	1		1
Total	43	23	66

The physically handicapped ESN child had a congenital heart defect and a cleft palate.

Regarding the 'other' children, two boys ascertained as partially hearing were attending appropriate special units (one of them was a twin whose originally unintelligible twin brother had now achieved satisfactory speech.) Retrospective scrutiny of these two children's medical reports at 7 years showed that although both were then considered to possess hearing levels within normal limits, the test words omitted or mispronounced in the twelve-word repetition test gave clear indications of difficulty in auditory discrimination for high-pitched consonants, indications which had obviously alerted the examining doctor to refer the children for full clinical investigation. One of the physically handicapped children had cerebral palsy, the other congenital heart disease. The maladjusted child, youngest of nine children and visually handicapped, had been committed to the care of the local authority for violent behaviour and vandalism. One of the speech-defective children was in residence at a school for children with severe language problems and the other in a residential school for autistic children.

Children attending ordinary schools
Of the 190 study children for whom we had adequate information, 124 children, or just under two-thirds (87 boys and 37 girls), were attending ordinary schools. We classified these into two sub-groups: children with residual speech problems, and those who were considered by their teacher and/or examining doctor to have achieved satisfactory speech.

Children with residual speech problems
This group, comprising 69 children, 54 boys (78 per

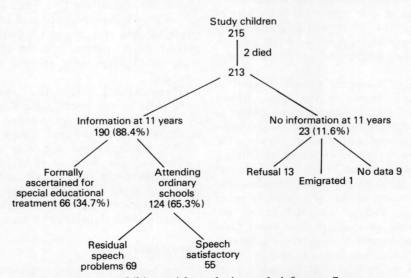

FIGURE 6.1   *Children with marked speech defects at 7 years*

cent) and 15 girls (22 per cent), included more than half the children in ordinary schools. Six of them were reported to have a stammer in addition to their residual speech difficulty. They were generally poor achievers in school: 49 per cent were receiving extra educational help compared with 8 per cent of the whole sample.

Speech therapy
Of the group with residual speech problems, 51.5 per cent had attended a speech clinic in the past and 12.9 per cent were still attending; 35.5 per cent, however, had never received speech therapy. Among the controls 0.3 per cent were currently having speech therapy, 2.3 per cent had received it in the past and 97.4 per cent had never received it.

Hearing
In addition to the doctor's clinical test, pure-tone audiograms were available for 58 of the 59 children with residual speech problems. Two of these showed moderate bilateral deafness (i.e. 35—54 dB loss on two or more of the speech frequencies) and five showed a similar loss in one ear only. The teacher noted 'poor hearing' in one child who had produced a normal audiogram and the doctor reported a moderate bilateral loss in another child with a normal audiogram. The hearing impairment in these children may have been due to a temporary condition not present at the time of the audiometric testing.

Vision
Taking our usual criterion of unaided visual acuity of 6/12 or worse in one or both eyes as constituting a visual defect, 14 per cent were noted as having defective vision; this compares with 12 per cent of the whole sample.

Associated problems
In several instances, in addition to offering further descriptions of the speech defect, e.g. multiple dyslalia, mixed word order, cluttered speech, etc., the doctors had made a brief note of the presence of associated paediatric disorders such as squint, 'slight spasticity', 'mild spina bifida', cleft palate, diabetes, congenital heart defect and behavioural problems.

Children with satisfactory speech
Of the 124 children in ordinary schools less than half, i.e. 55 children (22 boys and 33 girls), were reported to have acquired satisfactory speech, though 48 per cent were still receiving extra educational help at school. The preponderance of girls in this group contrasts markedly with the preponderance of boys in the group with residual speech problems. A point of interest is that among this group there were seven

twins, two pairs and three 'single' twins, one of the latter being the brother of the partially hearing child already mentioned. Four children were reported to have a residual stammer, one had a cleft palate and another was under treatment for grand mal epilepsy.

Speech therapy
Of the group with satisfactory speech, 24 per cent were reported at some time to have received speech therapy but only one child was still attending a speech clinic. The remaining 76 per cent had never received speech therapy.

Hearing
Moderate degrees of hearing loss (i.e. a loss of 35—54 dB on two or more of the speech frequencies on pure-tone audiogram) were reported in two children, one having bilateral and the other unilateral impairment. It was not possible to draw conclusions regarding relevance to the earlier speech defect.

Scholastic attainments
In spite of improvement in speech the scholastic achievements of the children in the group remained notably depressed compared with controls. Figures 6.2—6.4 show the scholastic attainments in the groups with residual speech problems and satisfactory speech and in the control group as reported by their teachers, regarding oral ability, literacy and numeracy. In all three areas there was a striking shortage of superior achievement among children with marked speech defects at 7 years. The scholastic performance of the children with residual speech problems and satisfactory speech was broadly similar, though a larger number of individual children with residual speech problems was reported as having little oral ability and to be very poor or non-readers.

Social behaviour at school
The Bristol social adjustment guide (Stott, 1963), which was completed for individual children by their teachers, is considered by the author of the test to assess the child's behaviour in the school situation. Stott considered that a score of 0—9 was compatible with normal adjustment, while 10—19 indicated 'unsettled' behaviour and 20 or more 'maladjustment'. Using these criteria, four times as many children with residual speech problems were considered 'maladjusted' at school compared with controls, and three times as many children with satisfactory speech (Figure 6.5).

Missing children
We have learnt from experience that children who do not attend for medical follow-up examinations usually have ongoing problems of health or behaviour

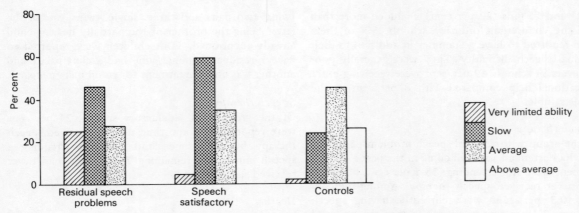

FIGURE 6.2   *Oral ability (teacher's assessment at 11 years)*

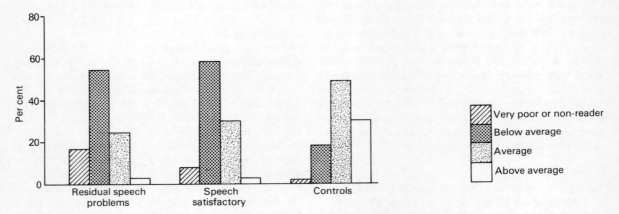

FIGURE 6.3   *Literacy (teacher's assessment at 11 years)*

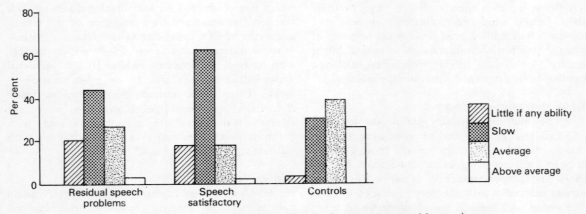

FIGURE 6.4   *Numeracy (teacher's assessment at 11 years)*

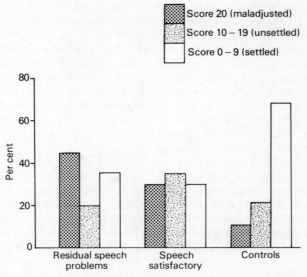

FIGURE 6.5   *Bristol Social Adjustment Guide scores at 11 years*

which, for the child's sake or their own, parents are reluctant to report. It therefore seemed worthwhile to rescrutinise the original records of the twenty-five 'missing' children. Results of this exercise were instructive.

For three 'missing' children we had final information. Two boys had died, one from a congenital metabolic disorder and the other from Hirschsprung's disease. One multihandicapped girl had emigrated. For nine children (six boys and three girls) we had no up-to-date information, but at 7 years one boy was reported to be in a residential private school for multihandicapped children, one boy was under paediatric supervision for stunted growth and other disabilities, four others (three boys and one girl) were noted to be markedly clumsy, and one girl was a member of a gipsy family. Five of the nine children (four boys and one girl) at 7 years were reported by their teachers as having poor school attainment.

The remaining thirteen children had been located but were withdrawn by their parents (eight boys and five girls). Their previous records at 7 years showed that five children had serious organic disorders: three of them (two boys and one girl) had cerebral palsy one girl congenital heart disease and one boy asthma. Four others (three boys and one girl) were reported to be 'very backward'. A further three children (two boys and one girl) were considered to be unstable, one of the boys being 'known to the police' and the parents of another noted to be 'very unco-operative'. Thus the marked speech difficulty at 7 years was in all cases associated with some other recognisably unfavourable factor.

Discussion

The above figures speak for themselves and strongly support our previous clinical experience that markedly defective speech at 7 years indicates the likelihood of continued backwardness, not only in the development of acceptable verbal communication and social maturity but also in scholastic attainments, at least until the age of 11 years. When we have had the opportunity to analyse reports of their general health, social competence and school performance at 16 it may be possible to offer a tentative prognosis regarding the ultimate effects of their disability.

There can be no doubt that more effective identification of children with speech and language difficulties at or before school entry is necessary and that this must be associated with comprehensive paediatric, audiological, visual and educational assessment, practical parent guidance, vigorous speech therapy and one-to-one teaching in favourable surroundings. We have considerable doubts, however, regarding the suitability of accommodating these handicapped children in large, noisy, visually distracting open-plan classrooms or in expecting them to benefit automatically from currently fashionable 'discovery methods' of primary education. It needs to be remembered that children learn to talk from constant listening, in reasonably quiet conditions, face to face with familiar people using adult patterns of spoken language which carry not only conceptual meaning but also an emotional halo of some sort. In other words, children with delayed speech require a similitude of mother-teaching at mother-distance. In the absence of appropriate remedial help, speech defects of any kind which have not resolved by the age of 7 years are likely to crystallise into permanency, inevitably retarding competence and scholastic achievement.

Detailed scrutiny of the study children's reports at 11 years has left us with a number of clinical impressions which will be further considered at follow-up at 16 years (see the next section). For instance, a much larger proportion of children with residual speech difficulties than children with satisfactory speech presented additional paediatric problems indicating the possibility of organic factors in aetiology. There was also evidence that the auditory competence of some of the children had not been adequately assessed. Rescrutiny of the reports at 7 years of the children 'missing' at 11 years indicated that had we been able to include them in this study, the proportion of children showing residual speech problems might have been even larger.

FOLLOW-UP AT 16 YEARS OF CHILDREN WHO HAD MARKED SPEECH DEFECTS AT 7 YEARS

Introduction

In the preceding paper we commented on the fact that few prospective studies are available concerning the scholastic progress and final accomplishments at school-leaving age of any sizeable group of children originally noted to have speech problems at infant-school age. The National Child Development Study does offer the opportunity to examine this question, and in this paper we continue to the age of 16 our examination of the progress of those children first identified as having marked speech defects at the age of 7.

Method

Analysis of the whole national sample of approximately 16 000 children aged 7 brought to light 215 children (144 boys, 71 girls) who were considered independently by both their examining doctors and their teachers to possess normal hearing but to manifest appreciable unintelligibility of speech. Cases of mild stammer which presented as the sole symptom but did not constitute unintelligibility were excluded. However, thirteen of the study children who exhibited a stammer in addition to their other problems of language and speech are included.

The study children came from local authority districts over the whole of Great Britain. The reports submitted therefore reflected widely differing arrangements for educational and social welfare. Moreover, the amount of information provided by doctors,

teachers and health visitors was uneven and sometimes incomplete so that we were obliged to write them off as 'no data', or reach an agreed judgement on the information available. Hence it has proved unprofitable to submit the material to sophisticated statistical analysis. Nevertheless, the information we have assembled is so illuminating, not to say disturbing, that we consider it desirable to provide this record for the benefit of future research workers and practioners.

Findings at 16 years

At this third follow-up, information was available for 180 (84 per cent) of the original group of 215 children (Figure 6.6). By then, three children had died. Of the 180, 54 (30 per cent) were in special schools and 126 (70 per cent) were in ordinary schools. Of the children in ordinary schools, one sub-group of 64 (51 per cent) were reported by the doctor or teacher to have a residual speech disability. For the second sub-group of 62 children (49 per cent) no speech difficulty was reported, but in some instances relevant information was sparse. No data at 16 years were available for 32 children. The parents of 17 children (12 boys and 5 girls) had refused to participate and 15 (7 boys and 8 girls) were untraced.

Children in special schools at 16 years

Table 6.18 shows the categories of 'ascertained' handicap among the 54 children receiving special education. Thirteen children were ascertained as ESN(S), 34 as ESN(M) — seven of these also had additional ascertainable handicaps, one child with Fallot's tetralogy was physically handicapped, one child was in a special residential school for speech-handicapped pupils and five boys, four of whom were in approved institutions (borstals), were maladjusted. Without exception, the four boys in approved institutes had difficult, deprived and disadvantaged backgrounds. They were all from large families and had been in the care of a local authority. One father had died when the boy was 13 and two other fathers had been unemployed for the year prior to follow-up. In two families the siblings also had police records.

Changes in categorisation between 11 and 16

Of the twelve study children classified as ESN(S) at 11 years, one child with Down's syndrome had died, the parent of one refused participation and the remaining ten were still classified ESN(S). At 16, three additional children were ascertained in this group; two had been ESN(M) at 11 and one had been a refusal at 11, but was known at 7 to have a cerebral palsy.

Of the forty-seven children classified as ESN(M) at 11, three had been reclassified (two as ESN(S) and

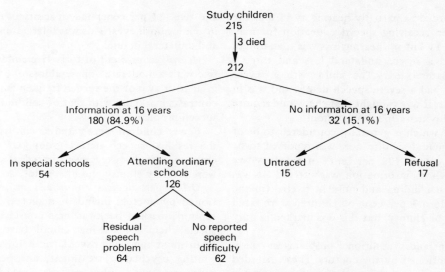

FIGURE 6.6   *Follow-up of 215 study children at age 16*

one as physcially handicapped), five were in ordinary schools, four were refusals and two were untraced.

One of the two partially hearing children classified at 11 was in a comprehensive school at 16 and the other was designated ESN(M) only. Two of the ESN(M) children at 16 years were also partially hearing, though no mention had been made of this at the 11-year follow-up. The two children who were physically handicapped at 11 were untraced at 16 and the child with Fallot's tetralogy who was classified 'physically handicapped' at 16 was also ESN(M) at 11 years. The child classified as 'maladjusted' at 11 years was in an ordinary school at 16 and all the children in this category at 16 had been ascertained since 11 years. Another child had received special education for maladjustment between 11 and 16 years but was now in an ordinary school (under NSPCC supervision).

TABLE 6.18 *Children receiving special education at 16 years*

Category of 'ascertained' handicap	Boys	Girls	Total
ESN (S)	8	5	13
ESN(M)	17	10	27
plus partial hearing	2	—	2
plus partial hearing and speech	1	—	1
plus physical handicap and speech	1	—	1
plus epileptic	—	1	1
plus physical handicap	1	—	1
plus maladjusted	1	—	1
Physical handicap	1	—	1
Speech	—	1	1
Maladjusted	5	—	5
Totals	37	17	54

The child who was in a special residential school for speech-handicapped children at 11 years was now in a comprehensive school and no longer received speech therapy. Her school progress was slow. Her twin brother was also reported at 16 years to have 'very poor speech'.

Children in ordinary schools at 16 years
Children with residual speech problems. Of the 126 children in ordinary schools, 64 (47 boys and 17 girls) were reported to have a residual speech defect. Six of them were currently having speech therapy. Information offered on 53 showed that thirteen were in remedial classes, seven were receiving extra help, but not in a remedial class, and six were not receiving extra help although the teacher considered it to be desirable.

Visual acuity. Information was available for 51 of the 64 children and fifteen (29 per cent) had visual impairment of 6/12 or worse in one or both eyes. In six the defect was unilateral (one of these children was blind in one eye) and in nine bilateral. This compared with 16 per cent in the national sample (Peckham *et al.*, 1977).

A hearing assessment was available for fifty-two children, and two children showed a serious bilateral loss (i.e. 55 dB loss or worse on at least two frequencies in one ear together with a 35 dB or worse on two or more frequencies in the better ear). One of these children was reported to have had a unilateral loss at 11 years and the other whose hearing loss was identified for the first time at 16 was reported by the doctor to be 'of grave concern'. Two additional children had a moderate bilateral loss (i.e. 35—54 dB loss on two or more of the speech frequencies). One had been recorded as partially hearing at 11 and the other had been receiving special education for maladjustment at 11 but no hearing loss was then noted. One child had a severe unilateral loss and three a moderate unilateral loss. The child with a severe unilateral loss had a severe speech defect and was in a remedial class; it was thought that she would require sheltered employment on leaving school.

Clumsiness, which is generally considered to be of neurodevelopmental significance, was reported to be present in seventeen (31 per cent) of the fifty-five children for whom information was offered. It was marked in five children and mild in twelve (in the national sample 6.7 per cent of children were rated by doctors to be clumsy, but this was marked in only 0.5 per cent).

In several instances, additional problems or conditions were mentioned by the doctors. These included psoriasis; cleft palate and hare lip; mild spina bifida injury; enuresis and scholastic retardation; severe behavioural problem (two cases, one of whom had a police record); severe speech problems which would necessitate sheltered employment (two cases); 'semi-literate' (two cases). The child who was ESN(M) at 11 was reported at 16 years to have an IQ of 75 and another child to have an IQ of 69.

Children without speech problems. Of the 126 children in ordinary schools 62 (40 boys and 22 girls) fell into this sub-group. None of them had received speech therapy in the previous year. Four children were in remedial classes, nine were in ordinary classes receiving additional help and three were not receiving extra help, though their teachers thought this desirable.

Visual acuity was tested for forty-five children,

and five (11 per cent) had an acuity of 6/12 or worse in one or both eyes. This was bilateral in five children and unilateral in one.

Hearing assessment of forty-five children identified five with a moderate unilateral loss of 35 dB or worse in at least two of the speech frequencies. This finding contrasts markedly with that of children with residual speech problems.

Fewer children were rated as *clumsy* than among the residual speech defect group. Of the forty-five children tested, twelve were rated as clumsy; three were severely clumsy and nine mildly so.

Other pathological conditions or problems mentioned by doctors included: diabetes; deviated nasal septum; marked backwardness considered to require special help on leaving school (two cases); poor adjustment requiring psychiatric help; anxiety necessitating psychiatric treatment; antisocial behaviour (two cases with police records); overdose requiring hospital admission.

Missing children at 16 years

By 16 years, of the original study group of 215 children, three had died and no information was available for thirty-two (15 per cent) of the surviving children; seventeen were refusals and fifteen were untraced (Figure 6.7). Two deaths had occurred before 11 years, one from a congenital metabolic disorder and the other from Hirschsprung's disease, and the ESN(S) child with Down's syndrome died aged 15 years. Of the refusals at 16, two were untraced at 11 (at 7 years, one was reported to be markedly clumsy and the other was under a specialist for stunted growth, clumsiness and poor speech). Three were also refusals at 11 years (at 7 years, one of the three had

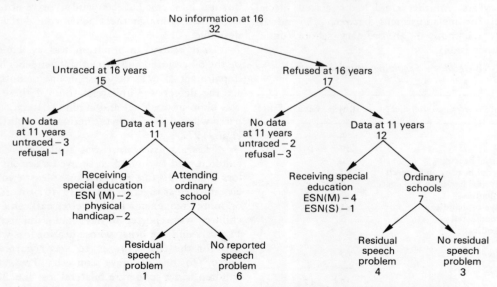

FIGURE 6.7   *Earlier information on 32 children with no information at 16 years*

severe asthma and was deemed delicate, another was maladjusted and had no speech until 4 years and the third had cerebral palsy). Of the twelve with information at 11 years, five were receiving special education and seven were attending ordinary schools (Figure 6.7).

For the fifteen who were not traced at 16 years (seven boys and eight girls), one who was a refusal at 11 years was known from information gathered at 7 years to have cerebral palsy and no speech and three had not been traced at 11 years (one having emigrated). Scrutiny of the 7-year records of the three untraced children showed that one had been reported to be markedly clumsy, the doctor of another had been 'very worried' about the child's speech and the third was a member of a large gipsy family. Of the remaining eleven children with data gathered at 11 years, four were receiving special education, two as ESN(M), and two as physically handicapped (one with cerebral palsy and another with a congenital heart defect) and seven were attending ordinary schools.

Hence, follow-up information at either 11 or 16 years was available for 206 (96 per cent) of the 215 children identified as having marked speech problems, but normal hearing, at 7 years.

Reading

For the sake of clarity, results of the test scores on the whole national sample have been grouped into three categories. Those with scores in approximately the bottom quarter of the distribution have been defined as 'low scores', those in the top quarter 'high scores' and those between the 25th and 75th centiles have been grouped together as 'middle scores'. Figure 6.8 shows the reading scores in the poor speech groups and the whole sample. Although numbers were small, the reading scores of the study children are notably depressed compared with those of the national sample, irrespective of whether or not speech had improved by 16 years. The mean score for the whole sample was 25.3 (sd = 7.1), whereas for the persistent speech defect group it was 16.0 and for the group with no reported speech problem 18.1. In the sub-group of children with persistent speech defects, fifteen were more than two standard deviations below the mean of the national sample. This also applied to eight of those with no reported speech difficulty.

Mathematics

Mathematics scores from the national sample were again grouped into three categories and Figure 6.8 shows comparisons between the study children and

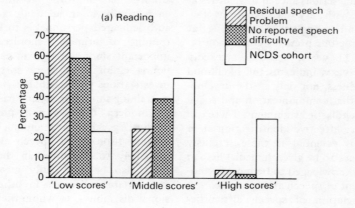

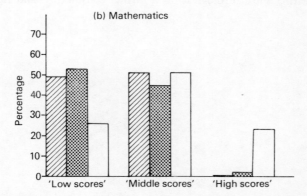

FIGURE 6.8   *Reading and mathematics scores at 16 years*

the whole sample. The mean score for the whole sample was 12.3 (sd = 7.0), whereas for both speech groups it was 7.8. Again the scores of the children with speech defects at 7 were markedly depressed, even if acceptable speech had been acquired by 16 years.

Children with high scores on the scholastic attainment tests were exceedingly rare in the study group and for interest we give further information. Only three fell into the 'high score' group on the reading test at 16 years. Two of these children had residual speech problems. One, a girl with a low arithmetic score, was in a private school; she also had poor vision. The second was a boy with 'markedly' poor speech but satisfactory school attainments. The girl whose speech was now satisfactory was sitting her O-level examinations. Only one study child had a 'high score' on the mathematics test. This boy, who had received speech therapy in the past and no longer showed a speech problem, also had an above-average reading score and was doing well at schoo; he intended to become an engineer.

Discussion

The overall results of this follow-up at 16 years of 215 children manifesting serious speech difficulties at 7 years are depressing. With very few exceptions they did badly at school and in society. The findings at age 16 strongly reinforce our previous conclusion regarding follow-up at 11 years, i.e. that markedly defective speech at 7 years indicates the likelihood of continued backwardness, not only in the development of acceptable verbal communication and social maturity, but also in scholastic attainment. There can be no doubt that more effective identification at or before school entry is essential if these seriously handicapped children are to be given remedial help at the time universally acknowledged to be most favourable for the development of speech and language.

The frequent association of speech difficulties with impairments of vision, hearing and neurological organisation, with mental retardation, psychiatric disturbance and anti-social behaviour underlines the importance of comprehensive developmental paediatric assessment, prompt treatment and continuing medical and paramedical supervision and the support of appropriate social services. The possibility of intermittent hearing impairment due to recurrent middle-ear infection must always be borne in mind. No single preliminary auditory screening test provides insurance for further continuing reliability, even though it may be acceptable on the day of testing.

There is no doubt that the frequency and significance of speech delays in pre-school and infant school-children is now increasingly recognised by parents, teachers and doctors. However, in the absence of adequate provision for remediation, this urgent problem is not receiving the attention it manifestly deserves. The number of teachers commenting that children obviously requiring speech therapy were unable to receive this help because it was not available was disconcerting.

The training of community doctors, child psychiatrists, health visitors and paramedical professionals in matters related to the physical, mental, emotional and social difficulties of normal and handicapped children has improved. It still needs to be pursued energetically if an adequate supply of experienced and dedicated personnel is to be made possible. The training of primary schoolteachers is particularly important since they are in day-to-day contact with young children of every sort. As a result of our investigations we feel that it is essential that students in training should be given a basic working knowledge of modern theories and practices regarding the medical, psychological and social implications of the various disorders of speech and language that they are likely to encounter in the classroom. Teachers must also be kept fully informed concerning the appropriate colleagues in other but related professional disciplines, to whom they can confidently turn for further consultation and advice.

7 Vision*

VISION SCREENING IN A NATIONAL SAMPLE OF 11-YEAR-OLD CHILDREN

Introduction

Reliable information on the prevalence of visual problems in the childhood population is clearly of vital importance both to practitioners and those responsible for the planning of medical services. Yet, despite the fact that defective vision is the commonest sensory handicap, there has been relatively little attempt to document the overall picture of visual acuity in British children. The National Child Development Study has provided a useful opportunity for assessing the extent to which visual handicaps are identified by screening procedures in schoolchildren. This section describes the results of tests of near and distant visual acuity in children at 11 years of age, and also the extent to which glasses were prescribed and worn.

One aspect of the survey was designed to assess the prevalence of visual impairment in childhood and, at the age of 11 years as part of the medical examination, distant and near visual acuity was screened under clinic conditions by the local health authorities. An additional investigation to test colour vision was carried out on 12 522 children by the school medical officer, using Ishihara plates.

Distant visual acuity was assessed in 12 772 children using a standard Snellen chart composed of block capital letters without serifs. Testing was carried out at a distance of 20 feet (6 metres) and instructions were given to place the chart in a good light, level with the child's eye and free from glare. Each eye was tested separately and the contralateral eye was occluded without pressure on the eyeball. The tests were performed first without glasses and

*Original sources: Peckham, C. and Adams, B., 'Vision screening in a national sample of 11-year-old children', *Child: Care, Health and Development*, 1, 1975, 93–106; Peckham, C., Gardiner, P. and Tibbenham, A., 'Vision screening of adolescents and their use of glasses', *British Medical Journal*, 1, 1979, 1111–13; Tibbenham, A., Peckham, C. and Gardiner, P., 'Vision screening in children tested at 7, 11 and 16 years', *British Medical Journal*, 1, 1978, 1312–14; Peckham, C., Gardiner, P. and Goldstein, H., 'Acquired mypoia in 11-year-old children', *British Medical Journal*, 1, 1977, 542–5.

then repeated with glasses if these were available.

Near vision was screened for 12 737 of the children using a card especially designed for the study by Sheridan and Gardiner. The letters were of the standard reduced Snellen type (Law, 1951, 1952) and readings are therefore recorded as single figures and not as fractions equivalent to the Snellen test (normal vision is 6). Instructions were given to hold the card no further than 10 inches (25 cm) from the eye. Both eyes were again tested separately, first without and then with glasses.

In order to simplify the analysis, the children have been classified into six different groups, according to the results of the Snellen test. The following criteria were used for distant visual acuity:

1. *Optimal vision*   6/6 or better in both eyes
2. *Near-optimal vision* 6/9 or worse in both eyes
3. *Unilateral impairment*
      moderate 6/6 or 6/9 in better eye, 6/12 or 6/18 in other eye
4. *Unilateral impairment*
      severe 6/6 or 6/9 in better eye, 6/24 or worst in either eye
5. *Bilateral impairment*
      moderate 6/12 or 6/18 in better eye
6. *Bilateral impairment*
      severe 6/24 or worse in better eye

Children ascertained as blind or partially sighted
By the age of 11 years eight children in the sample had been ascertained by the local authority as in need of special education for visual handicap. Two children were categorised as blind and six as partially sighted. Both blind children had cerebral palsy and had also been ascertained as severely subnormal. Two of the partially sighted children, one with bilateral cataracts and the other with Marfan's syndrome and bilateral aphakia, had also been ascertained as educationally subnormal. The remaining four children included an albino, a child with muscular dystrophy, a child with bilateral cataracts and another with optic atrophy.

Distant visual acuity was recorded for all six partially sighted children and the results are included in the subsequent analysis.

Unaided distant visual acuity

Nearly 78 per cent of the children who had both eyes tested were found to have optimal vision and a further 10 per cent to have near-optimal vision (Table 7.1). Of the 12 per cent of children with defective visual acuity 415 children (3.3 per cent) were found to have marked visual impairment with a visual acuity of 6/24 or worse in both eyes, and a further 3.3 per cent had a moderate impairment. Unilateral visual impairment, which was present in 5.8 per cent of all children, was severe in 2.0 per cent, and moderate in 3.8 per cent.

Unaided near visual acuity

Only 5 per cent of all children tested had impaired vision (Table 7.2). Twice as many of these had a unilateral defect as had a bilateral defect. A further 7 per cent had near-optimal vision and 88 per cent optimal near vision.

TABLE 7.1   *Unaided distant visual acuity at 11 years*

Vision group	Better eye	Other eye	No.		%
Optimal	6/6	6/6	9 921		77.6
Near-optimal	6/6	6/9	782 }	1 278	10.0
	6/9	6/9	496 }		
Subtotal			11 199		87.6
Unilateral impairment (moderate)	6/6 or 6/9	6/12	309		2.4
		6/18	179		1.4
Subtotal			488		3.8
Unilateral impairment (severe)	6/6 or 6/9	6/24	105		0.8
		6/36	86		0.7
		6/60	36		0.3
		<6/60	32		0.2
Subtotal			259		2.0
Bilateral impairment (moderate)	6/12	6/12	107 }		
		6/18	82 }		
		6/24	25 }	242	1.9
		6/36	22 }		
		6/60	6 }		
		<6/60	0 }		
	6/18	6/18	73 }		
		6/24	66 }		
		6/36	23 }	176	1.4
		6/60	10 }		
		<6/60	4 }		
Subtotal			418		3.3
Bilateral impairment (severe)	6/24	6/24	84 }		
		6/36	49 }		
		6/60	8 }	143	1.1
		<6/60	2 }		
	6/36	6/36	116 }		
		6/60	37 }	161	1.3
		<6/60	8 }		
	6/60	6/60	61 }	74	0.6
		<6/60	13 }		
Subtotal	<6/60	<6/60	415		3.3
Total number of children tested			12 779		100.0

Impairment of distant and near vision

By comparing the results of the near vision test with the more widely used distant vision test, it was possible to confirm the importance of the near vision test as a screening procedure (Table 7.3). Among the children with optimal distant vision, 4.3 per cent had less than perfect near vision, though six out of seven of these registered a near-optimal result. The value of near screening, however, was much greater when there was a minor degree of impairment of distant vision. Thus among the children with near-optimal distant vision, 5.5 per cent had an actual near vision defect, and 18.5 per cent had near-optimal near vision.

TABLE 7.2   *Unaided near visual acuity at 11 years*

Vision group	Better eye	Other eye	No.		%
Optimal	6	6	11 155		87.6
Near-optimal	6	9	566 }	895	7.0
	9	9	329 }		
Subtotal			12 040		94.6
Unilateral impairment (moderate)	6 or 9	12	202		1.6
		18	134		1.0
Subtotal			336		2.6
Unilateral impairment (severe)	6 or 9	24	40		0.3
		36	31		0.2
		60	31		0.2
		<60	25		0.2
Subtotal			127		0.9
Bilateral impairment (moderate)	12	12	66 }		0.9
		18	31 }		
		24	8 }	111	
		36	5 }		
		60	1 }		
		<60	0 }		
	18	18	40 }		0.5
		24	11 }		
		36	4 }	61	
		60	5 }		
		<60	1 }		
Subtotal			172		1.4
Bilateral impairment (severe)	24	24	8 }		0.2
		36	8 }	20	
		60	3 }		
		<60	1 }		
	36	36	18 }		0.2
		60	5 }	24	
		<60	1 }		
	60	60	3 }	5	0.1
		<60	2 }		
	<60	<60	3		
Subtotal			52		0.4
Total number of children tested			12 727		100.0

Over half the children with a severe unilateral impairment of distant vision also had a unilateral impairment of near vision, probably due to the presence of squint or amblyopia, which is also more often associated with a marked difference in visual acuity between the two eyes. In contrast, only about 30 per cent of children with unilateral moderate or bilateral impaired distant vision also had impaired near vision.

Prescription of glasses

Glasses had been prescribed for 1 481 children, or 11.8 per cent of children tested. The unaided distant visual acuity of nearly one in four (22.0 per cent) of the children who wore glasses to the examination was found to be optimal or near-optimal (Table 7.4). A further 26 per cent had unilateral visual impairment and the remaining 52 per cent a bilateral defect.

When the children with unaided impaired distant vision were retested with glasses, 86 per cent showed some improvement in visual acuity; this was to optimal or near-optimal vision in 64 per cent of cases. A further 14 per cent showed no improvement with glasses but it was disturbing that in seven children

TABLE 7.3   *Unaided distant and near vision in children tested at 11 years (percentages)*

Near vision	Distant vision						
	Optimal	Near-optimal		Unilateral impairment		Bilateral impairment	
		6/6, 6/9	6/9, 6/9	Moderate	Severe	Moderate	Severe
Optimal	95.7	77.0	74.3	44.8	19.4	49.6	59.1
Near-optimal							
6, 9	2.3	14.3	9.9	18.7	9.3	8.5	7.3
9, 9	1.5	3.4	9.9	6.5	2.3	10.2	6.8
Unilateral impairment							
moderate	0.3	3.9	3.2	23.7	28.3	10.9	5.8
severe	0.0	0.4	0.2	2.1	35.7	2.9	1.5
Bilateral impairment							
moderate	0.1	1.0	2.2	3.8	4.6	15.5	11.2
severe	0.1	0.0	0.2	0.4	0.4	2.4	7.8
Total							
%	100.0	100.0	100.0	100.0	100.0	100.0	100.1
N	9 870	783	481	476	258	413	512

TABLE 7.4   *Unaided distant visual acuity according to whether glasses prescribed or worn*

	Glasses prescribed and worn		Glasses prescribed but not worn		Glasses not prescribed	
	No.	%	No.	%	No.	%
Optimal	125	11.5	95	24.4	9 385	85.7
Near-optimal						
6/6, 6/9	69	6.3	38	9.9	657	6.9
6/9, 6/9	49	4.5	32	8.3	408	3.7
Unilateral impairment						
moderate	169	15.5	73	19.0	235	2.1
severe	109	10.0	45	11.7	105	1.0
Bilateral impairment						
moderate	230	21.1	69	17.9	118	1.1
severe	339	31.1	34	8.8	44	0.4
Total	1 090	100.0	385*	100.0	10 952†	100.0

* An additional six children wore glasses but vision not tested unaided.
† Sixty-two children not prescribed glasses, but visual acuity not tested.

(0.8 per cent) there was an actual deterioration in visual acuity (Table 7.5). However, the number of children with glasses who still exhibited uncorrected bilateral visual impairment was small; it constituted seventy-seven children, of whom only six still exhibited a visual acuity of 6/24 or worse in the better eye.

Among the group of children with optimal or near-optimal unaided distant vision who wore glasses to the examination, fifteen children showed a deterioration in visual acuity when tested with glasses (Table 7.5). Six children with optimal unaided vision showed a deterioration to near-optimal vision and three children exhibited a unilateral impairment when tested with glasses. Among those with unaided near-optimal vision visual acuity was worse with glasses in six children.

Glasses had been prescribed for 356 children with impaired near vision. In 206 cases (58 per cent) the near vision defect was unilateral and in 150 cases (42 per cent) bilateral. Compensation with glasses to optimal or near-optimal visual acuity occurred in 62 per cent of these children. A further 32 per cent still exhibited a unilateral visual impairment when tested with glasses and twenty-three children (6 per cent) had a bilateral impairment which was severe in six children. Glasses improved near vision in 77 per cent of children, while 22 per cent showed no improvement and two children an actual deterioration.

Children prescribed glasses but failed to bring them to examination

It was not possible to test the aided visual acuity of all children who had been prescribed glasses since 385 children (26 per cent of those prescribed glasses) failed to bring their glasses to the examination. Obviously, it is important to ascertain how visually handicapped the children are who might habitually forget or not want to wear their glasses or whose glasses were lost or needed repair. A higher proportion of children who failed to bring their glasses to the examination had optimal or near-optimal vision than did those who brought their glasses (Table 7.4). However, of those children not bringing their glasses to the examination, 27 per cent had a bilateral defect, and if glasses were to improve their visual acuity they must have been at an unnecessary disadvantage in school.

Children with impaired visual acuity not prescribed glasses

Among the children for whom no glasses had been prescribed 4.6 per cent had impaired visual acuity, which was bilateral in a third of cases (162 children) (see Table 7.4). Thus 32 per cent of all children with impaired vision were not prescribed glasses; this amounted to 53 per cent of the children who had a unilateral visual defect and 19 per cent of those who had a bilateral impairment.

TABLE 7.5   *Unaided and aided visual acuity in children who wore glasses (distant vision)*

Unaided visual acuity	Aided visual acuity												
	Optimal		Near-optimal		Unilateral impairment				Bilateral impairment				Total	
					Moderate		Severe		Moderate		Severe			
	No.	%	No.	%	No.	%	No.	%	No.	%	No.	%	No.	%
Optimal	116	92.8	6	4.8	2	1.6	1	0.8					125	100.0
Near-optimal	76	64.4	36	30.5	4	3.5			2	1.7			118	100.0
Unilateral impairment														
moderate	58	34.3	57	33.7	48	28.4			5	3.0	1	0.6	169	100.0
severe	14	12.8	13	11.9	46	42.2	36	33.0					109	99.9
Bilateral impairment														
moderate	84	36.5	81	55.2	30	13.0	9	3.9	25	10.9	1	0.4	230	99.9
severe	124	36.6	107	31.6	50	14.7	7	2.1	46	13.6	5	1.5	339	100.1
Total	472	43.3	300	27.5	180	16.5	53	4.9	78	7.2	7	0.6	1 090	100.0

Note: The areas enclosed indicate no change in visual acuity when glasses were worn. The area above the boxes indicates deterioration of vision with glasses and that below the boxes improvement with glasses.

Sex and social background
Impaired visual acuity was found to be equally prevalent among boys and girls ($p > 0.05$). However, significantly more children with defective visual acuity came from non-manual social-class backgrounds than from manual social-class backgrounds ($p < 0.001$) (Table 7.6).

As would be expected, therefore, there was no difference in the proportion of boys or girls prescribed glasses ($p > 0.05$) but significantly more of the children prescribed glasses came from non-manual backgrounds than from manual backgrounds ($p < 0.05$).

In an attempt to examine the type of children who had been prescribed glasses but who failed to bring them to the examination, it became apparent that fewer children from non-manual families were without their glasses (13 per cent) than from manual families (30 per cent), though more children in the manual group had impaired visual acuity (66 per cent) than in the non-manual group (56 per cent). This difference is significant with a probability of $p < 0.001$. A higher proportion of boys than girls were also without their glasses at the medical examination ($p < 0.05$). Among the children with impaired vision who had not been prescribed glasses there was no significant sex or social-class difference.

Colour vision
Colour vision, which was tested by the school medical officers using Ishihara plates, revealed that 6 per cent of boys and 1 per cent of girls had a red/green impairment (Table 7.7). The proportion of children with impaired colour vision who had defective near or distant visual acuity was similar to those children without a colour defect.

TABLE 7.7   *Colour vision testing by sex*

	Boys		Girls	
	No.	%	No.	%
Normal colour vision	5 957	93.5	6 041	98.9
Impairment of red/ green vision	394	6.1	66	1.1
Other colour loss	22	0.3	2	0.03
Total	6 413	99.9	6 109	100.00

Discussion

By the age of 11 years 78 per cent of children in this national sample were found to have satisfactory distant vision. These results were similar to the findings at 7 years, where 79 per cent of children were reported to have optimal distant vision (Alberman *et al.*, 1971). At 11 years, however, fewer children (10 per cent) were regarded as having near-optimal distant vision and a higher proportion (12 per cent) had visual defects. The corresponding results at 7 years were 13 and 8 per cent respectively. This change was probably mainly due to deterioration in visual acuity associated with myopia. In a national study Douglas *et al.* (1967a) reported that of 3 775 children tested at 15 years 78 per cent had optimal vision, but the proportion of children with bilateral impairment was higher than that found in the present 11-year-old sample.

It is of practical value to know that of the children with 6/6, 6/6 distant visual acuity only 0.5 per cent were found on testing to have defective near vision. The fact that a much higher proportion of children

TABLE 7.6   *Distant visual acuity by sex and social class*

Vision group	Boys				Girls				Total	
	Non-manual		Manual		Non-manual		Manual			
	No.	%	No.	%	No.	%	No.	%	No.	%
Optimal	1 614	77.6	3 010	78.2	1 588	76.9	2 744	77.0	8 956	77.5
Near-optimal	177	8.5	385	10.0	183	8.9	401	11.3	1 146	9.9
Unilateral impairment										
moderate	83	4.0	154	4.0	79	3.8	126	3.5	442	3.8
severe	45	2.2	76	2.0	39	1.1	76	2.1	236	2.0
Bilateral impairment										
moderate	80	3.8	138	3.6	71	3.4	102	2.9	391	3.4
severe	80	3.8	84	2.2	104	5.0	114	3.2	382	3.3
Total	2 079	99.9	3 847	100.0	2 064	100.0	3 563	100.0	11 553	99.9

with near-optimal distant vision (5.5 per cent) also had defective near vision emphasises the need for further investigation of children in this category.

Although a large proportion of children with defective vision had already been identified and prescribed glasses, the results of vision testing revealed that 4.6 per cent of children not prescribed glasses had a visual defect, which was bilateral (6/12 or worse in the better eye) in 1.5 per cent of children. As many as forty-four of these children had a severe bilateral defect with a visual acuity of 6/24 or worse in the better eye and had similar vision therefore to the partially sighted as at present defined. It may well be that a proportion of children had not been prescribed glasses because their defect of vision was not correctable, but a more detailed investigation needs to be carried out on this group. If the defect is unilateral, vision being good in one eye, action is less urgent, but the investigation of children with bilateral defects is a question of urgency. We have no data on whether these investigations were taking place.

It was encouraging to find that the provision of glasses produced optimal or near-optimal vision in a large proportion of children. Tested with glasses, only seven children still had a visual acuity of 6/24 or worse in the better eye, which speaks well for the ophthalmological treatment they received. Significantly more children prescribed glasses came from non-manual families, which is not surprising as impaired vision was more common in children from this group. This finding was also reported in a large-scale study carried out in the USA where 12–17-year-olds from high-income families were found to have significantly worse unaided acuity than those from families with low incomes (National Center for Health Statistics, 1973).

Also, Douglas *et al.* (1967a) found that parents of short-sighted children were more likely to be middle class. Among our children there was no significant social-class difference in children with impaired vision who had not been prescribed glasses, which might suggest that middle-class parents made more use of the available services.

Although it was shown that glasses benefit vision in a large number of children, 36 per cent of children for whom glasses had been prescribed did not bring them to the examination. The unaided visual acuity of these children, however, was markedly superior to that of children who had brought their glasses; nevertheless, 27 per cent had bilateral visual impairment which would almost certainly have benefited from wearing glasses. It is puzzling if not distressing that so many children with impaired visual acuity were without their glasses at this medical examination.

VISION SCREENING OF ADOLESCENTS AND THEIR USE OF GLASSES

Introduction

Information on the visual acuity of British school-children is scarce. The results of vision screening at 7 and 11 in the children taking part in the National Child Development Study have already been reported. We report here on visual acuity and the use of glasses in these children when they were aged 16, in their last year of compulsory schooling.

Method

Testing of distant and near vision was arranged by school medical officers. Distant visual acuity was assessed in 11 411 adolescents using a standard Snellen chart of block capital letters without serifs. The examiners were told to place the chart exactly 20 feet (6 metres) away from the child in a good light, level with the child's eyes, and free from glare. Each eye was tested separately, the other eye being occluded without pressure on the eyeball. Acuity was tested without glasses and then with glasses if they were available. Near vision was tested in 11 144 adolescents using a Sheridan–Gardiner card designed specially for the study. The card was held no further from the eye than 10 inches (25 cm). If glasses had been prescribed for use 'at the present time', the examiners recorded whether they were available for the test. No inquiries were made about the use of contact lenses, but we assumed that few adolescents would have been wearing them in 1973–4. To simplify the analysis, the children were classified into six groups according to their visual acuity: normal vision – 6/6 or better in both eyes; minor defect – 6/6, 6/9 or 6/9, 6/9; unilateral moderate defect – 6/6 or 6/9 in better eye, 6/12, 6/18 in other eye; unilateral severe defect – 6/6 or 6/9 in better eye, 6/24 or worse in other eye; bilateral moderate defect – 6/12 or 6/18 in better eye; bilateral severe defect – 6/24 or worse in better eye. Similar groupings were made for near vision using the standard reduced Snellen nomenclature.

Response levels

At the age of 16 some information was obtained on 87 per cent of the study children known to be in the country and, except for a few minority groups, these were broadly representative of the total cohort. Our sample was further reduced, as only just over 11 400 of the total cohort attended a medical examination. Analysis showed that our sample of 16-year-olds was representative in terms of sex and social class. We checked further bias in the sample by comparing (a) the proportion in each unaided distant vision group at 11 among those tested at 16 and among those not tested at 16; (b) the vision at 7 among those with data at 16 and among those with no data at 16; (c) the vision at 16 among those with data at 11 and among those with no data at 11; (d) the vision at 16 among those with data at 7 and among those with no data at 7.

Results

Acuity

Uncorrected distant visual acuity. Altogether 75 per cent of the 16-year-olds screened had normal visual acuity of 6/6 in both eyes: 9 per cent had minor defects and the remainder moderate or severe visual impairment which was unilateral in 6 per cent and bilateral in 10 per cent. In 631 adolescents (6 per cent) visual acuity without glasses was 6/24 or worse in the better eye (Table 7.8). Significantly more girls had impaired vision ($p < 0.001$), this difference being accounted for by the higher proportion of girls with bilateral defects. Visual defects were also significantly commoner among adolescents from non-manual than from manual family backgrounds ($p < 0.001$), and this social-class difference was greatest among the group with severe bilateral visual impairment. A higher proportion of girls than boys had severe bilateral defects in both the non-manual and manual social-class groupings.

Uncorrected near visual acuity. Over 85 per cent of adolescents had normal near vision: 8 per cent had a minor defect in one or both eyes, and the remainder had moderate impairment which was unilateral in 4 per cent and bilateral in 3 per cent. Only 104 children (0.9 per cent) had a severe bilateral defect of near vision.

Relation of distant to near vision. Table 7.9 shows that 83 per cent of children had normal near and distant vision, or only minor defects (group A); 11 per cent had only defects of distant vision (B); 1.5 per cent had only defects of near vision (C); and 5.5 per cent had defects of both near and distant vision (D). Only 62 (0.6 per cent) children with normal distant vision had a moderate or severe defect of near vision in one or both eyes. But 607 (5.5 per cent) children with defective distant vision (unilateral or bilateral) had near-vision defects. The four groups shown in Table 7.9 were analysed by social class, and significantly more adolescents from non-manual families (14 per cent) than from manual families (9 per cent) had defects of only distant vision ($p < 0.001$), though social classes were equally represented among the other categories of visual impairment. A higher proportion of boys had normal vision ($p < 0.001$), whereas a significantly higher proportion of

TABLE 7.8   *Unaided distant visual acuity at 16 years*

Vision group	Better eye	Other eye	No. (%) of children	
Normal	6/6	6/6	8 587	(75.3)
Minor defect	6/6	6/9	361	(8.5)
			9 552	(83.7)
Unilateral defect	6/6 or 6/9	6/12	297	(2.6)
(moderate)	6/6 or 6/9	6/18	160	(1.4)
			457	(4.0)
Unilateral defect	6/6 or 6/9	6/24	100	(0.9)
(severe)	6/6 or 6/9	6/36	95	(0.8)
	6/6 or 6/9	6/60	45	(0.4)
	6/6 or 6/9	<6.60	36	(0.3)
			276	(2.4)
Bilateral defect	6/12	6/12	108	
(moderate)	6/12	6/18	106	
	6/12	6/24	32	(2.5)
	6/12	6/36	22	
	6/12	6/60	8	
	6/12	<6/60	4	
	6/18	6/18	77	
	6/18	6/24	91	
	6/18	6/36	30	(1.9)
	6/18	6/60	13	
	6/18	<6/60	4	
			495	(4.3)
Bilateral defect	6/24	6/24	91	
	6/24	6/36	71	(1.7)
	6/24	6/60	30	
	6/24	<6/60	1	
	6/36	6/36	108	
	6/36	6/60	57	(1.5)
	6/36	<6/60	10	
	6/60	6/60	128	(1.4)
	6/60	<6/60	33	
	<6/60	<6/60	102	(0.9)
			631	(5.5)
	Grand total		11 411	(100.0)

girls had impaired distant vision but a satisfactory near vision ($p < 0.05$). More boys than girls ($p < 0.01$), however, had poor near and poor distant vision because of the higher proportion of boys with unilateral defects of near and distant vision. In contrast, similar proportions of boys and girls had defects of near vision only.

Prescription and use of glasses

Glasses had been prescribed for current use for 18 per cent of the 16-year-olds and for significantly more of the girls (21 per cent) than of the boys (16 per cent) ($p < 0.001$). Table 7.10 shows the unaided distant acuity of boys and girls prescribed glasses. There was no significant sex difference in the proportion of children with a visual defect prescribed glasses, but significantly more girls than boys with normal vision had glasses ($p < 0.001$). Overall, only a few children with 6/6, 6/6 vision had been prescribed glasses, but they did represent 15 per cent of the children ordered glasses. Nearly a quarter of the boys and one in three of the girls who had been given glasses had an unaided visual acuity of 6/9 or better in both eyes.

Although there were no regional differences in visual acuity groups, or in glasses prescribed overall, significantly fewer ($p < 0.05$) glasses had been prescribed for adolescents with 6/6, 6/6 acuity in the north of England (2.4 per cent) than in the other regions (3.8–4.5 per cent in Scotland, Wales, southern England, and the Midlands).

A higher proportion of adolescents from non-manual than manual backgrounds had been prescribed glasses ($p < 0.001$), though differences were not significant for those with normal vision, a minor defect, or a severe bilateral defect (Table 7.10). The position was reversed in the group with moderate unilateral impairment, where proportionately more manual than non-manual children had been ordered glasses ($p < 0.05$).

A third of the adolescents who had been prescribed glasses did not have them available at the examination,

and this applied equally to boys and girls. Overall, more children from manual than non-manual backgrounds had been prescribed but were not wearing their glasses ($p < 0.001$; Table 7.10).

Over a quarter (28 per cent) of glasses prescribed but not worn were for children with a visual acuity of 6/6, 6/6, and over half the children with normal vision or a minor defect who had been ordered glasses were without them. Even among the children with a severe bilateral defect sixty children (9 per cent) did not carry glasses with them and a further ten children had not been prescribed them.

As children with satisfactory distant vision may have been prescribed glasses because they had impaired near vision, the uncorrected near visual acuity of children with normal distant vision who had been prescribed glasses was reviewed. Among these children who had their glasses available, 18 per cent had a definite unilateral or bilateral near vision defect, but this applied to only 5 per cent of those who were without their glasses.

We looked at the corrected visual acuity (near and distant) for children tested with and without glasses. Among 552 with severe bilateral impairment of

TABLE 7.9 *Correlation between unaided near vision and unaided distant visual acuity at 16 (results are numbers (and percentages) of children tested)*

Near vision	Distant vision									Total
	Normal			Minor defect		Unilateral defect		Bilateral defect		
Normal vision	7 901	(71.4)	A	653	(5.9)	289	(2.6)	B	592	(5.4)	9 435
Minor defect	373	(3.4)		207	(1.9)	133	(1.2)		167	(1.5)	880
Unilateral defect	31	(0.3)	C	50	(0.5)	245	(2.2)	D	113	(1.0)	439
Bilateral defect	31	(0.3)		33	(0.3)	32	(0.3)		217	(2.0)	313
Total	8 336			943		699			1 089		11 067

TABLE 7.10 *Glasses prescribed for current use according to visual acuity, sex, and social class*

Distant vision	No. tested		No. (%) prescribed glasses		No. (%) of those prescribed glasses but not wearing them		No. tested†		No. (%) prescribed glasses		No. (%) of those prescribed glasses but not wearing them	
	Boys	Girls	Boys	Girls	Boys	Girls	Non-Manual	Manual	Non-Manual	Manual	Non-Manual	Manual
Normal	4 158	3 750	111 (2.7)	183 (4.9)	71 (64.0)	108 (59.0)	2 233	4 015	87 (3.9)	145 (3.6)	49 (56.3)	88 (60.7)
Minor defect	439	472	101 (23.0)	120 (25.4)	48 (47.5)	44 (36.7)	289	445	79 (27.3)	108 (24.3)	36 (45.6)	40 (37.0)
Unilateral defect												
Moderate	225	217	135 (60.0)	128 (59.0)	57 (42.2)	60 (46.9)	147	200	79 (53.7)	132 (66.0)	26 (32.9)	67 (50.8)
Severe	148	117	85 (57.4)	77 (65.8)	35 (41.2)	27 (35.1)	68	135	51 (75.0)	77 (57.0)	12 (23.5)	29 (37.7)
Bilateral defect												
Moderate	220	262	179 (81.4)	216 (82.4)	59 (33.0)	76 (35.1)	158	213	140 (88.6)	162 (76.1)	34 (24.3)	71 (43.8)
Severe	276	338	271 (98.2)	333 (98.5)	22 (8.1)	38 (11.4)	242	228	240 (99.2)	222 (97.4)	14 (5.8)	30 (13.5)
Total*	5 466	5 156	882 (16.1)	1 057 (20.5)	292 (33.1)	353 (33.4)	3 137	5 236	676 (21.6)	846 (16.2)	272 (25.3)	331 (39.1)
Grand total	10 622		1 939 (18.2)		645 (33.3)		8 373		1 522 (18.2)		502 (33.0)	

* We did not know whether glasses had been prescribed for 427 boys and 362 girls (of these 85% had normal visual acuity) or for 199 children from non-manual families and 396 from manual families (of these 83% had normal acuity).
† No male head, or father's occupation not known in 2 452.

distant vision 52 (9.4 per cent) were poorly corrected (6/12 or worse in better eye) and 432 (78 per cent) had an aided acuity of 6/9 or better in both eyes. The 90 children with severe bilateral impairment of near vision showed similar levels of improvement.

Discussion

Overall, our results for the 16-year-olds are comparable with those of Douglas *et al.* (1967a), who found in a national sample of 3 775 15-year-olds that 76 per cent had normal vision (6/6, 6/6), 12 per cent had an acuity of 6/9 in at least one eye, and 10 per cent had a bilateral defect (6/12 or worse in better eye). As many as 12 per cent of the NCDS children with normal vision at 11 years had a defect by age 16 (Tibbenham *et al.*, 1978b). Impaired visual acuity at 11 was equally prevalent among boys and girls, but by 16 years more girls had visual impairment. The sex differences were particularly pronounced in the group with severe defects and may be accounted for by the suggestion that myopia is more common in girls than boys (Goldshmidt, 1968) since there was a preponderance of girls with defects of distant vision only. Another aspect of the difference between boys and girls was illustrated by the higher proportion of boys with unilateral defects of near and distant vision. Although we cannot explain this, amblyopia associated with squint may be a factor. The preponderance of adolescents from non-manual families with poor vision was due to the group with defective distant vision but normal near vision. The likely explanation is again the higher occurrence of myopia in non-manual families.

Glasses had been prescribed for 18 per cent of adolescents, 6 per cent more than at 11 years, but a third of this group did not have their glasses available at the medical examination. Few adolescents seeing 6/9 or better with both eyes would welcome glasses or, arguably, would need them for medical reasons, yet 27 per cent of adolescents prescribed glasses had normal distant visual acuity or only a minor defect, and only a few of this group had defects of near vision alone. This group constituted 42 per cent of those who failed to produce their glasses at the examination. Interestingly, fewer children with normal acuity were prescribed glasses in the northern region than elsewhere, and significantly more girls than boys with normal vision possessed glasses. Distant visual acuity itself is clearly no guide to what is considered to be a need for glasses, though it may indicate whether the glasses will be worn. It might be argued that those adolescents would be better with their glasses — that is, 6/5, which we did not record — but if this is so, user rejection seems to indicate it is not desired by large numbers.

VISION SCREENING IN CHILDREN TESTED AT 7, 11 AND 16 YEARS

Introduction

To plan ophthalmological services for children it is necessary to know the proportion of children with visual defects and to assess changes in visual acuity during childhood. Ingram (1973a) recorded that three-quarters of children aged 5 to 15 who were referred to school eye clinics after routine sight tests had some ocular defect. He concluded that it was important to perform routine sight tests throughout a child's school career. Ingram's article prompted discussion on the possible role of a children's eye clinic (Gardiner, 1973; Primrose, 1973, Ingram, 1973b) and more recently the value of vision screening of children has been debated (Gardiner, 1977; Cameron, 1977; Ingram, 1977; Peckham *et al.*, 1977; Youngson, 1977). We report here data on the distant vision screening of a nationally representative sample of schoolchildren at the ages of 7, 11 and 16 years.

Screening procedure

A standard Snellen chart composed of block capital letters without serifs was used. Testing was carried out at a distance of 6 metres and instructions were given to place the chart in a good light, level with the child's eye, and free from glare. Each eye was tested separately, with the other eye occluded without pressure on the eyeball.

Vision grouping

At each age the children were categorised according to their visual acuity, when tested without glasses, into the following groups: normal vision — 6/6 or better in both eyes; minor defect — 6/6, 6/9, or 6/9, 6/9; unilateral moderate defect — 6/6 in better eye, 6/12 or 6/18 in other eye; unilateral severe defect — 6/6 or 6/9 in better eye, 6/24 or worse in other eye; bilateral moderate defect — 6/12 or 6/18 in better eye; bilateral defect — 6/24 or worse in better eye. All children with moderate or severe impairment of visual acuity, whether unilateral or bilateral, were considered to have definite defects.

Results

Only the 8 339 children on whom we have distant vision data at all three ages were included. Excluding the other children did not seem to introduce any bias; the percentage of the 8 339 who fell into each vision group at any one screening was the same as for the total sample on whom we had distant vision data at that age — that is, including those on whom we had data only at that screening or at two screenings.

The distribution of children among the various distant vision groups at each age, and the numbers changing groups between tests are shown in Tables 7.11–7.13. Substantial changes in acuity occurred between screenings. Only 86 per cent of children with normal vision at 7 years had normal vision at 11 (Table 7.11), while about 12 per cent of those who had normal distant vision at 11 had a defect at 16 (Table 7.12). Of children with normal distant vision at 7, 18 per cent showed deterioration of at least one line in one or both eyes by the age of 16 (Table 7.13). Indeed, 11 per cent of children with normal vision at 7 had a definite visual defect by the age of 16. Conversely, of the 471 children with a severe bilateral defect at 16, no fewer than 288 (61 per cent) had had normal vision at the age of 7, while

only 48 (10 per cent) had a severe bilateral defect at both ages.

More children's vision apparently improved between 7 and 11 than between 11 and 16 years. Much of the improvement was of only one or two lines in one eye, and such a change is easily explained by the technical problems of testing at an early age. Because the improvement between the ages of 11 and 16 seemed less explicable in terms of difficulties in testing, the medical records of children with severe defects at 11 who had normal vision or a minor defect at 16 were scrutinised. In nearly all these cases doctors confirmed in a supplementary question that the child had a visual defect at 11. But their comments clearly indicated that there were problems in testing children's vision even at the ages of 11 and 16.

TABLE 7.11   *Distant visual acuity of 8 339 children at 7 in relation to their distant visual acuity at 11 (results are numbers and percentages of children)*

Vision at 7	Vision at 11											
	Normal		Minor defect		Unilateral defect				Bilateral defect				Total (100%)
					Moderate		Severe		Moderate		Severe		
Normal	5 680	(85.6)	557	(8.4)	117	(1.8)	52	(0.8)	111	(1.7)	117	(1.8)	6 634
Minor defect	698	(67.5)	176	(17.0)	69	(6.7)	7	(0.7)	40	(3.9)	44	(4.3)	1 034
Unilateral defect													
Moderate	72	(26.6)	66	(24.4)	64	(23.6)	27	(10.0)	26	(9.6)	16	(5.9)	271
Severe	6	(5.0)	15	(12.6)	22	(18.5)	66	(55.5)	7	(5.9)	3	(2.5)	119
Bilateral defect													
Moderate	32	(15.3)	28	(13.4)	30	(14.4)	21	(10.0)	61	(29.2)	37	(17.7)	209
Severe	4	(5.6)	1	(1.4)	1	(1.4)	1	(1.4)	16	(22.2)	49	(68.1)	72
Total	6 492	(77.9)	843	(10.1)	303	(3.6)	174	(2.1)	261	(3.1)	266	(3.2)	8 339

TABLE 7.12   *Distant visual acuity of 8 339 children at 11 in relation to their distant visual acuity at 16 (results are numbers (and percentages) of children)*

Vision at 11	Vision at 16											
	Normal		Minor defect		Unilateral defect				Bilateral defect				Total (100%)
					Moderate		Severe		Moderate		Severe		
Normal	5 678	(87.5)	435	(6.7)	120	(1.8)	47	(0.7)	132	(2.0)	80	(1.2)	6 492
Minor defect	531	(63.0)	145	(17.2)	52	(6.2)	14	(1.7)	60	(7.1)	41	(4.9)	843
Unilateral defect													
Moderate	61	(20.1)	74	(24.4)	78	(25.7)	31	(10.2)	36	(11.9)	23	(7.6)	303
Severe	2	(1.1)	4	(2.3)	35	(20.1)	99	(56.9)	22	(12.6)	12	(6.9)	174
Bilateral defect													
Moderate	29	(11.1)	26	(10.0)	31	(11.9)	11	(4.2)	75	(28.7)	89	(34.1)	261
Severe	3	(1.1)	2	(0.8)	3	(1.1)	1	(0.4)	31	(11.7)	226	(85.0)	266
Total	6 304	(75.6)	686	(8.2)	319	(3.8)	203	(2.4)	356	(4.3)	471	(5.6)	8 339

TABLE 7.13   *Distant visual acuity of 8 339 children at 7 in relation to their distant visual acuity at 16 (results are numbers (and percentages of children)*

Vision at 7	Vision at 16											
	Normal		Minor defect		Unilateral defect				Bilateral defect			Total (100%)
					Moderate		Severe		Moderate		Severe	
Normal	5 413	(81.6)	476	(7.2)	164	(2.5)	85	(1.3)	208	(3.1)	288	(4.3)	6 634
Minor defect	722	(69.8)	132	(12.8)	47	(4.5)	20	(1.9)	50	(4.8)	63	(6.1)	1 034
Unilateral defect													
Moderate	106	(39.1)	49	(18.1)	49	(18.1)	20	(7.4)	22	(8.1)	25	(9.2)	271
Severe	13	(10.9)	7	(5.9)	22	(18.5)	60	(50.4)	10	(8.4)	7	(5.9)	119
Bilateral defect													
Moderate	46	(22.0)	19	(9.1)	33	(15.8)	16	(7.7)	55	(26.3)	40	(19.1)	209
Severe	4	(5.6)	3	(4.2)	4	(5.6)	2	(2.8)	11	(15.3)	48	(66.7)	72
Total	6 304	(75.6)	686	(8.2)	319	(3.8)	203	(2.4)	356	(4.3)	471	(5.6)	8 339

Acuity seemed to deteriorate most appreciably in the later years. For example, more children deteriorated from the severe unilateral to the bilateral groups, or from the moderate bilateral to the severe bilateral groups, or from the moderate bilateral to the severe bilateral group, between 11 and 16 than between 7 and 11. Table 7.14 shows the visual acuity at 16 of those who had normal vision at the ages of both 7 and 11: 6 per cent of these 16-year-olds had a definite defect. Among children with normal vision at 7 but a minor defect at 11 (Table 7.14) as many as 18 per cent had a definite defect at age 16, including 13 per cent with a bilateral defect.

Sex and social-class differences
There was no sex difference in changes in acuity between 7 and 11, but between 11 and 16, within the group of children from manual social-class backgrounds, more girls than boys showed deterioration from normal vision ($p < 0.01$). Differences did not reach significance within the non-manual group, possibly because of the relatively small numbers.

More children with normal vision at 7 who were of non-manual background had developed a defect by the age of 11 than those of manual background ($p < 0.01$). Much of the deterioration was probably associated with myopia, which is more common among the non-manual group (Douglas *et al.*, 1967a; Peckham *et al.*, 1977). The social-class difference was greatest among children who showed the very sharp deterioration from normal acuity to bilateral severe defect. Among children with normal vision at 11, more children from non-manual backgrounds than from manual backgrounds showed deterioration in visual acuity by the time they were 16 ($p < 0.05$).

Discussion

Our results show that visual acuity cannot be assumed to be constant between the ages of 7 and 16 and that careful, regular screening among schoolchildren is essential.

Ingram (1973a) showed that in Kettering and Corby about half of the children discovered with squint or refractive errors associated with squint and amblyopia were over 7 when first discovered. He, and others (e.g. Brown, 1975), have emphasised the need for effective pre-school screening. But even if there is effective pre-school screening, regular testing during the school years is also needed. Visual defects may occur at any stage in childhood, and a satisfactory test during the early school years should not lead to

TABLE 7.14   *Acuity at 16 of children with normal vision at 7 and 11 and of children with normal vision at 7 and minor defects at 11*

	Vision at 16							
	Normal	Minor defect	Unilateral defect		Bilateral defect		Total	
			Moderate	Severe	Moderate	Severe		
Normal vision at 7 and 11	4 997 (88.0)	359 (6.3)	102 (1.8)	40 (0.7)	111 (2.0)	71 (1.3)	5 680 (100)	
Normal vision at 7, minor defect at 11	382 (68.6)	74 (13.3)	22 (3.9)	5 (0.9)	40 (7.2)	34 (6.1)	557 (100)	

complacency about the need for tests later. Since the visual acuity of as many as one in five children deteriorated between the ages of 7 and 16, the need for regular screening extends to all children, though those with minor defects are in particular need of regular checks. Sheridan (1974) warned that among children of 5 to 7 years, 'a visual acuity of 6/9, even when occurring in only one eye, should be regarded as suboptimal distant vision requiring careful follow-up, or in some cases, immediate referral to a consultant ophthalmologist'. Altogether, 17 per cent of the children in the National Child Development Study who had a minor defect at 7 had a definite defect at 16 compared with 11 per cent of those with normal vision at age 7.

The results of a single screening cannot, however, be used for a diagnosis of permanent visual handicap: over three in five children with a minor defect at one screening had normal vision at the next (Tables 7.11 and 7.12). These improvements were probably more apparent than real, being due partly to the technical difficulties of screening children, especially young primary schoolchildren, in ordinary school settings. As children become older, they have better powers of concentration and are less easily distracted; younger children, on the other hand, may under-perform because they regard screening as a classroom proficiency test and fear making a mistake. Children who are found to have a defect at an early age probably undergo regular, subsequent tests and learn to interpret blurred images, obtaining thereby a rather better result. Also, many children with myopia learn to improve their acuity by as much as two lines by peering between half-closed lids, so that without very careful testing they 'overperform' at their later examinations.

Regular screening in the school years is therefore essential to detect the early development of visual defects. Such a system requires adequate back-up services for those identified as needing further assessment. So that children may be protected from having unnecessary treatment or glasses the specialists to whom the children are referred should have an impartial appreciation of the value of glasses, knowledge of developmental ophthalmology, and a systematic and flexible recall programme. These circumstances are not necessarily found in NHS arrangements outside the school eye service.

ACQUIRED MYOPIA IN 11-YEAR-OLD CHILDREN

Introduction

Myopia, or short sight, is an important and common cause of visual impairment which is usually acquired and nearly always progressive (Gardiner, 1964). It rarely occurs before the age of 6 years, and new cases appear throughout childhood and adolescence, particularly between the ages of 7 and 12. Karlsson (1975) has produced evidence that intellectual gain precedes the appearance of myopia and has suggested that the gene responsible for short-sightedness may have conferred an evolutionary advantage through its association with intelligence.

The National Child Development Study has presented us with an opportunity to identify, from a nationally representative sample of children, those who had acquired myopia by the age of 11 years and to examine their social background, growth and educational performance at 7 and 11 years of age. This group was compared with children who had normal unaided visual acuity of 6/6 or better in both eyes.

Assessment of visual acuity

At both medical examinations distant visual acuity was tested using the Snellen chart of block capitals under standard conditions. Each eye was tested separately. When glasses were worn, testing was carried out first without them and then with the aid of glasses. At the 11-year examination near vision was also tested using a card especially designed for the study by Sheridan and Gardiner.

Identification of myopic children

Children with acquired myopia were identified from the results of vision screening carried out at both 7 and 11 years. As such children have normal near vision and show a deterioration in distant visual acuity during childhood, they were selected if they had: (a) near-optimal or near vision, i.e. reduced Snellen 6 or 9 in both eyes, but poor distant vision, 6/12 or worse in the better eye, at 11 years; and (b) a deterioration in distant visual acuity of two or more lines in both eyes between 7 and 11 years. When both these criteria were met the children were considered to show progressive bilateral acquired myopia. Visual acuity was tested at both 7 and 11 years in 11 179 children. Of the 515 children with bilateral impairment of distant vision and satisfactory near vision at 11 years, 403 (78 per cent) showed deterioration of visual acuity of at least two lines between 7 and 11 years (Table 7.15).

These 403 children (189 boys and 214 girls; 3.6 per cent of the sample) were those whom we regarded as having progressive bilateral acquired myopia. The method used for selection meant that several people with congenital or early myopia would be missed because their visual acuity might not have deteriorated between 7 and 11 years, and hence the prevalence of myopia reported in this study is an underestimate.

A further 215 children showed a unilateral progressive acquired myopia (115 right and 100 left), but we disregarded these children. Myopia is commonly acquired in one eye before the other and several of them will probably acquire bilateral myopia; information gathered at 16 years may shed further light on this group.

There were also 73 children who had bilateral poor distant vision and good near vision whose acuity did not change by as much as two lines between 7 and 11 years. Although many were undoubtedly myopic, it is uncertain how many must have been congenitally myopic and how many had acquired myopia. In either case children with stationary myopia for four years are possibly a group with different characteristics from those with progressive myopia (Gardiner, 1964; Douglas *et al.*, 1967a), and they were excluded from this study.

Results

Sex and social-class distribution
There was no significant difference in the overall occurrence of myopia between the sexes or social classes (Table 7.16). Acquired myopia was more common in children who came from non-manual families than in those from manual families. Since the myopic children were identified by tests of visual acuity, and a representative sample of children from each social class was screened, this could not be explained by selection bias.

Family characteristics
The family background of children with acquired myopia differed from that of children with a normal visual acuity in ways other than social class. The proportion of children with myopia was highest in families with only one or two children under 21 years (4 per cent) and lowest in families with four or more children (2 per cent). Myopia was also significantly more common in first-born children (4 per cent) than in children who were fourth or subsequent children in the family (2 per cent). Both these differences persisted within social-class groups and were statistically significant ($p < 0.001$).

The proportion of myopes was higher among children whose parents were reported to the teachers to be 'very interested' in their child's school progress (5 per cent), compared with the proportion in the group whose parents showed less interest (3 per cent). These differences persisted when comparisons were made within social class ($p < 0.001$). The proportion of myopes was also higher among children whose parents wished their child to remain at school beyond the school-leaving age and who, according to the teacher, had taken the initiative to discuss their child with the school staff ($p < 0.02$, and $p < 0.01$ after adjustment for social class).

TABLE 7.15   *Identification of 11-year-old children with acquired myopia (results are numbers, and percentages, of children)*

Poor distant vision (6/12 or worse) and satisfactory near vision	Change in distant visual acuity between 7 and 11 years				Total
	Deterioration of $\geq$ 2 lines			Deterioration of < 2 lines	
	In both eyes	In right eye	In left eye		
In both eyes	403 (78.3)	20 (3.9)	19 (3.7)	73 (14.2)	515 (100)
In right eye	12 (5.5)	115 (53.0)	3 (1.4)	87 (40.1)	217 (100)
In left eye	14 (6.2)	4 (1.8)	100 (44.2)	108 (47.8)	226 (100)

TABLE 7.16   *Myopia according to sex and social class (results are numbers (and percentages))*

	Non-manual background			Manual background			Total
	Boys	Girls	Total	Boys	Girls	Total	
No. with myopia	82 (4.3)	105 (5.7)	187 (5.0)	102 (2.9)	94 (2.9)	196 (2.9)	383* (3.7)
Total no. of children	1 893	1 855	3 748	3 485	3 224	6 709	10 457†

* 20 children excluded (in 11 there was no male head of family and in nine social class was not known).
† Information on social class was not available for all children.
Test for difference in proportion of myopes, χ^2 values adjusted for the other factor — social class: non-manual *v.* manual $\chi^2 = 27.7$; 1 df; $p < 0.001$; sex: boy *v.* girl $\chi^2 = 1.6$; 1 df; $p > 0.05$. No significant interaction between sex and social class.

Educational attainment

Children with myopia had higher mean scores on the 11-year reading comprehension, arithmetic and general ability tests than the normally sighted children. The gains in mean scores were equivalent to 1.9 years on the reading test, 1.2 years on the arithmetic test, and 1.4 years on the general ability test. Since they were more likely to have fathers in non-manual occupations and to come from small families, factors which are also associated with educational performance, allowance was made in an analysis of variance for social-class background and the number of older and younger siblings in the family. After we had adjusted for these factors, the myopic children still showed striking advantages in educational performance over the normally sighted children (Table 7.17) and were 1.6 years ahead in reading comprehension, 1 year ahead on the arithmetic test, and 1.3 years ahead on the test of general ability. These advantages at 11 years are shown for each social class in Figure 7.1. The scores were expressed in terms of age-equivalent changes, and the age gain of myopes over children with normal vision was similar in each social class. No group of myopes achieved a mean attainment score below that of the overall mean.

TABLE 7.17 *Results of statistical analysis of results in reading comprehension, arithmetic and general ability tests shown in Figure 7.1*

	χ^2	df	p value
Test for difference between myopes and those with perfect vision			
Reading comprehension	136.4	1	<0.001
Arithmetic score	83.5	1	<0.001
General ability	89.6	1	<0.001
Test interaction			
Reading comprehension	0.1	1	
Arithmetic score	0.3	1	
General ability	0.3	1	
Test for difference after adjusting also for no. of older and younger sibs			
Reading comprehension	124.3	1	<0.001
Arithmetic score	74.0	1	<0.001
General ability	78.8	1	<0.001

Even at 7 years, before most affected children had become short-sighted, those who were myopic at 11 years had shown an advantage of approximately six months over their peers, as judged by the 7-year arithmetic and reading scores.

The teacher's assessment indicated that the oral ability of myopes at the age of 11 was better than

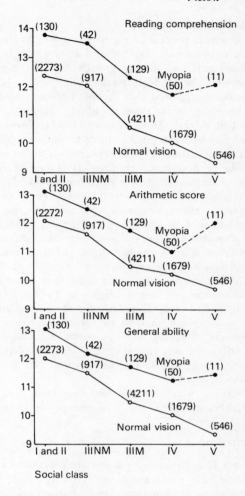

FIGURE 7.1 *Reading comprehension arithmetic score and general ability in children with myopia and those with normal vision at 11 years of age according to social class*

NOTE: Numbers of children in each social class are given in parentheses. Not all children completed all tests.

that of normal sighted children: 16 per cent of children with exceptional or above-average oral ability were myopic, whereas this applied to only 5 per cent of children with below-average or little or no oral ability. This finding persisted when adjustment was made for social class ($p < 0.001$).

In response to a question on reading habits outside school, twice as many children as normally sighted children indicated that they often read in their spare time ($p < 0.001$ after adjustment for social class). As many myopes as normally sighted children said that they often played outdoor games or took part in sport outside school hours.

Growth and development

The essential process in myopia is a lengthening of the anteroposterior axis of the eye, which is not compensated for during growth by the normal changes in the corneal and lens dimensions. It has often been suggested that myopia becomes manifest just before or at the time of puberty, during a rapid period of growth. Douglas *et al.* (1967a) showed an association between myopia and a prepubertal growth spurt and Gardiner (1964) reported an earlier onset of puberty in myopic children. It is premature to examine this question here since few of the children had reached full maturity by 11 years. There was no evidence, however, that myopia at this age was associated with an early onset of puberty. Information provided by the follow-up examination at 16 years may throw further light on the relation between puberty and myopia.

Children with myopia were taller than those with normal vision, the mean heights at 11 years being 145.4cm and 144.4cm respectively. When comparisons were made in an analysis of variance allowing for differences in family size and social class, however, this difference was almost entirely accounted for by the different social-class distribution and smaller families of myopes.

Relative weight was also examined but no differences between the two groups were found.

Discussion

We have found that myopia is more prevalent among children from non-manual family backgrounds than among those from manual family backgrounds. It is important therefore that the requisite adjustments are made for background factors in an attempt to define the physical and intellectual characteristics that may be associated with myopia. For example, the observation that myopic children are 1cm taller than children with normal vision can be explained by the social-class disparity between the two groups. Several investigators have produced evidence that myopes achieve higher academic attainments than non-myopes (Karlsson, 1975; Douglas *et al.*, 1967a). Our results add support to these observations, since 11-year-old myopic children achieved significantly higher scores on all three tests of attainment than children with normal vision, a finding that persisted even when adjustment was made for social class. Our findings, which agree with the conclusions reached by Karlsson, show that children who acquire myopia already exhibit differences in attainment before they become myopic. It was once commonly thought that short-sighted children tended to be more academic because defective distant visual acuity prevented them from pursuing active physical lives, with the result that they spent more time in reading and other sedentary occupations. The results of this study suggest that myopes participate in outdoor sports to a similar extent to children with normal vision.

We identified 215 (1.9 per cent) children with unilateral myopia. A high proportion of this group will probably develop bilateral myopia, but a few are likely to remain myopic in one eye. This throws doubt on the relevance of reading in causing myopia since reading is usually a binocular activity. Although our findings show that myopic children do read more than those with normal vision, this may be an expression of their academic tendencies. Alternatively, it might be argued that children who are academically inclined and who are avid readers would be more likely to develop myopia. This latter view was so strongly held in the 1920s and 1930s that special sight-saving schools were established at which near-work of any sort was prohibited (Ministry of Education, 1954; Ministry of Health, 1955).

Myopia has a strong genetic basis (Sorsby *et al.*, 1962). In view of the superior academic achievement of myopes and the fact that the appearance of myopia was preceded by evidence of this superiority, Karlsson (1975) postulated that the 'myopic gene had a stimulating action on the brain'. Our evidence suggests, however, that parental interest may be an important determinant of the myopic child's academic attainments. Of course, these two views are not mutually exclusive: the most practical issue is the relative importance of genetic and environmental influences. Families with a history of myopia may encourage near-work and their attitudes to education and employment might be influenced over generations.

8 Hearing*

FOLLOW-UP AT 11 YEARS OF FORTY-SIX CHILDREN WITH SEVERE UNILATERAL HEARING LOSS AT 7 YEARS

We have been unable to discover any reported information in the literature about the long-term effects on a child of unilateral hearing loss. The National Child Development Study identified severe unilateral hearing loss of 55 dB or greater on two or more of the speech frequencies in forty-six children (50 per cent boys and 50 per cent girls), a prevalence of 4 per 1 000 (Sheridan, 1972). A detailed study of these children revealed that, in addition to a hearing loss, they were reported as a group to show poor oral ability, speech difficulties and backwardness in reading as compared with children who had normal hearing (Peckham *et al.*, 1972). The longitudinal nature of the study has enabled us to re-examine the medical and educational status of these same children at 11 years of age. The related individual reports at 7 and at 11 years provided information of considerable clinical interest.

Study children

Information at 11 years was available for all but two of the forty-six children identified at 7 years. The parents of these two missing children refused to participate in the 11-year-old follow-up. One of them, who had also been reported to be clumsy, to have poor motor co-ordination, to be microcephalic and 'maladjusted', had already been formally ascertained as educationally subnormal (ESN) at 7 years. The other child had no apparent additional handicap at 7 years and speech was reported to be satisfactory.

At 11 years, two of the forty-four children for

* Original sources: Peckham, C. S. and Sheridan, M. D., 'Follow-up at 11 years of 46 children with severe unilateral hearing loss at 7 years', *Child: Care, Health and Development*, 2, 1976, 107–11; Richardson, K., Peckham, C. S. and Goldstein, H., 'Hearing levels of children tested at 7 and 11 years: a national study', *British Journal of Audiology*, 10, 1976, 117–23; Richardson, K., Hutchison, D., Peckham, C. S. and Tibbenham, A., 'Audiometric thresholds of a national sample of British 16-year-olds: a longitudinal study', *Developmental Medicine and Child Neurology*, 19, 6, 1977, 792–802.

whom information was available had, since 7 years, been formally ascertained as being in need of special educational treatment as ESN (Figure 8.1). One who was attending a special school still demonstrated a severe unilateral hearing loss. The second child, who was attending a private school, had a heart defect (Fallot's tetralogy) operated on at the age of 8, a spinal deformity, poor motor co-ordination and difficulty in visual perception. She was reported to have a permanent left hearing loss and poor speech. The one child reported to be attending a partially hearing unit at 7 years was now satisfactorily placed in an ordinary school.

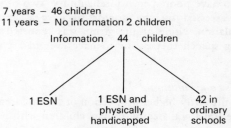

FIGURE 8.1   *School placement*

Two of the forty-two children in ordinary schools were receiving remedial help for educational backwardness. One was in a remedial class, though the teacher considered that she would benefit from attendance at a special school for ESN children. She had been in foster care and was reported to be backward at 7 years; her audiogram at 11 years was normal. The other child was the youngest of a large family. At 7 years he was reported to have poor speech, to be clumsy and unco-operative. His audiogram at 11 years revealed a continuing severe right hearing loss which was clinically confirmed.

Audiograms and hearing assessment at 11 years

We were able to obtain pure-tone audiograms for thirty-two of the forty-two children attending ordinary schools. Severe unilateral hearing loss was still present in eighteen of the thirty-two children (56 per cent), twelve in the right ear and six in the left. One child now had a residual moderate unilateral loss, and thirteen had recovered normal hearing.

No audiogram was available for ten children. Four of these were still assessed on clinical evidence as having a unilateral hearing loss, one child had a congenital absence of the right ear and no clinical or audiometric information was available for the remaining five children.

Audiometric and/or medical evidence was therefore available for thirty-seven of the forty-two children attending ordinary schools. Twenty of them were judged by the examining doctor to have a significant hearing loss. This was considered to be severe enough to interfere with everyday functioning in eleven children but none of them had ever worn a hearing aid. Parental information strongly supported the medical findings. In fact, twenty-three children (i.e. an additional three) were considered by their parents still to have a significant hearing loss.

Speech

At 7 years a higher proportion of the study group than of children with normal hearing were reported to have speech difficulties. At 11 years, however, only four of the group were reported by teachers still to have poor speech intelligibility, two of whom were assessed by the doctor to have a defect of articulation. None of the group was reported to be having speech therapy or to have ever had it in the past.

Motor co-ordination

A significantly higher proportion of the children with severe unilateral deafness than children with normal hearing was reported by their teachers at 7 years to be clumsy (Peckham *et al.*, 1972). At 11 years, this was no longer so marked, 19 per cent being rated as having poor co-ordination, whereas this applied to 14 per cent of the whole population.

Scholastic attainments

Although at 7 years the forty-six study children as a group had shown backwardness in oral ability and reading, by the age of 11 years there was little difference in test scores for reading and arithmetic between children with severe unilateral deafness and the whole sample (Figure 8.2). In addition, and contrary to our expectation, scrutiny of individual records revealed that the children with persistent severe unilateral deafness and those who had recovered normal bilateral hearing showed very similar levels of attainment, some being reported to be of outstanding academic ability and promise.

Comment

Of the children identified as having severe unilateral hearing loss at 7 years, half had recovered normal hearing by 11 years of age. This suggests that the cause of deafness at 7 years in those who had recovered was probably conductive and temporary in nature. Although at 7 years unilaterally deaf children were reported by their teachers to have more speech problems than normally hearing children, these had subsequently been resolved satisfactorily. Since none of the study children had received speech therapy this improvement apparently occurred spontaneously.

As a group, the unilaterally deaf children were reported to be doing as well as their age peers at school. This encouraging finding was confirmed by the results of educational tests used in the survey.

HEARING LEVELS OF CHILDREN TESTED AT 7 AND 11 YEARS: A NATIONAL STUDY

Subjects and methods

The subjects were those 11 370 at the 7-year NCDS follow-up and those 12 406 at the 11-year follow-up for whom audiometric data were available. At each of those ages school medical officers arranged an audiogram test for the study children. These were carried out using the audiometers, facilities and procedures locally available. This has several implications for the

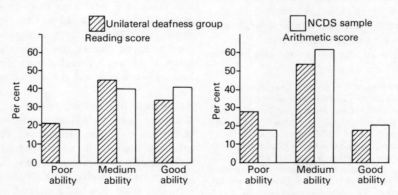

FIGURE 8.2   *Reading and arithmetic scores at 11 years*

quality of the data collected. First, audiometers were probably of variable efficiency; for example, Martin (1967) found the general standards of performance of British audiometers presented to the Royal National Institute for the Deaf for calibration to be 'poor'. Second, even audiometers that are carefully calibrated may not produce identical results if different earphones are used, though the vast majority of earphones used with British audiometers for the period in question were the TDH-39 receivers in the MX—41/AR type of cushion (Rice and Coles, 1967). Third, of the persons carrying out the audiograms, only some 60 per cent were qualified audiometricians, the remainder being mainly medical officers or nurses. Fourth, ambient conditions probably varied considerably. It has long been known that audiogram data from surveys usually diverge to some degree from those obtained under laboratory conditions (e.g. Dadson and King, 1952; Glorig, 1966). Thus although the present results would be expected to yield estimates which are biased and more variable than those obtained from standardised conditions, they do represent norms for the conditions under which testing is typically carried out. Otologically defective children (comprising about 5—6 per cent of the sample: Sheridan, 1972) were not excluded from the present estimations.

Estimation of percentile norms
Estimates have been made of the 10th, 50th and 90th percentiles of hearing loss for each frequency at each age. The estimation procedure was as follows. The raw data were available as the numbers of children in each hearing-loss category to the nearest 5 dB, these categories being grouped as follows: 0; 5 or 10; 15 or 20; 25 or 30; 35 or 40; 45 or 50; 55 or 60; 60 or more. From these distributions the cumulative percentages at the boundaries of these intervals were readily calculated and plotted on probability paper against an arithmetic scale of hearing loss. For all the frequencies this plot was very close to a straight line up to just over the 90th percentile of hearing loss, after which it departed from linearity with increasing slope. Thus a straight line fitted to those points in this percentile range should provide efficient and unbiased estimates for the 10th, 50th and 90th percentiles. The fitting was done by eye, since in all cases the plotted points were almost collinear. In order to obtain an approximate estimate of the standard errors of the estimates it was assumed that the percentiles were estimated using the mean and standard deviation calculated from a grouped normal distribution based on the cumulative sample size upon which the fitted straight line was based (just over 90 per cent of the total). By this method the 50th percentile had an estimated standard error of

about 0.045 dB and the 10th and 90th percentiles had standard errors of about 0.050 dB. Approximate 95 per cent confidence interval widths are therefore respectively 0.18 and 0.20 dB. These values are well below the sensitivity of a normal audiometer (Martin, 1967).

Comparisons of hearing-loss distributions
Two types of comparisons were made. First, the average hearing loss of different groups of children were compared, for example that of boys and girls. For this purpose the grouped distributions were arranged in a 2 x k contingency table and the average losses compared by carrying out the equivalent test for linear trend in the proportions across the k columns of the table (Armitage, 1955).

To study differential changes in distributions at 7 and 11 years (for example, between boys and girls at a given frequency) a 2 x k table of the grouped distributions at 11 years for each sex was arranged for each 7-year distribution group. A test for differences between the linear trend lines for each 7-year group was then carried out (Armitage, 1966). Significant differences therefore imply mean differences between the sexes in terms of 11-year distributions for a given 7-year group. One limitation of this analysis is that we have been unable to make any allowance for the unreliability of the 7-year estimates. The presence of large measurement error would, we believe, lead to larger sex differences than are actually present, so that our present estimates of differences should be reduced. Unfortunately, we have no data bearing on this, and the present results should be treated with a certain amount of caution.

The second comparison was that between ages and between left and right ears for the same children. In this case the grouped distributions were arranged as a k x k contingency table and the equality of the marginal distributions tested (Bhapkar, 1966).

Results

The comparison of left and right ears showed significant differences at only one frequency (1 000 cps) at 7 years and two frequencies (250 and 1 000 cps) at 11 years. Since these differences were minimal the remaining data have been presented in terms of 'better ear' only; this procedure minimises the quantity of data while representing the best possible hearing acuity of individuals in the sample.

The distributions of subjects across the categories of hearing loss at the two ages are shown in Table 8.1. The audiometric thresholds expressed in percentile standards for the total sample on the frequencies recorded at the two ages are shown in Table 8.2 and plotted in Figure 8.3. There is a paucity of audiometric data on representative samples of British children, so that comparisons are difficult. The thresholds recorded here appear to be considerably lower than those reported in a localised Scottish survey for children of this age range (Lenihan *et al.*, 1971). However, they compare favourably with the thresholds reported in a national survey of American children if we take the ISO zero-reference as very close to that of the British Standard (PHS, 1972; Davis, 1965). The results clearly indicate an improvement in hearing acuity between the ages of 7 and 11, especially in the higher frequencies, which is in line with the well-known trend leading to a peak at puberty (Reymert and Rotman, 1946; Lenihan *et al.*, 1971).

Table 8.3 shows the median audiometric losses for boys and girls separately at 7 and 11. Boys exhibited a slightly lower median loss than girls over most frequencies at 7 years. There was some evidence that the improvement between 7 and 11 was substantially greater for boys than for girls, as has been reported in other studies (Reymert and Rotman, 1946; Lenihan *et al.*, 1971). The tendency at 11 years for boys to have lower thresholds than girls in the lower frequencies (250—1 000 cps) and vice versa for higher frequencies confirms similar observation in American studies (PHS, 1975).

The median audiometric losses for social classes, grouped into manual or non-manual according to fathers' occupations, are shown in Table 8.4. These indicate a consistent superiority of audiometric performance on the part of the non-manual group at both ages. The differences at 11 years, however, were only significant in the lower frequencies, indicating a relative change between 7 and 11 years.

TABLE 8.2   *Percentiles of audiometric loss at ages 7 and 11 years[1] ***

Frequency (Hz)	Age	10th	50th	90th	χ^2 on 3 df
250	7	−0.5	9.0	19.0	32.91***
	11	0.0	9.5	19.0	
500	7	0.0	9.5	19.5	51.11***
	11	0.0	9.5	19.0	
1 000	7	−3.5	6.0	16.0	66.59***
	11	−3.5	5.0	14.0	
2 000	7	−5.0	4.0	14.0	287.27***
	11	−6.5	2.5	11.5	
4 000	7	−6.5	3.0	13.5	248.58***
	11	−8.0	1.5	11.5	
8 000	7	−5.0	6.0	18.0	713.58***
	11	−8.0	3.0	14.6	

[1] Tested for equality of 7- and 11-year distributions of hearing loss grouped as 0, 5 or 10, 15 or 20, 25 or 30, 35+.
***$p < 0.001$.

Discussion

Because of the limitations imposed by test conditions we have not intended in this section to present accurate standards of hearing levels among children. Nevertheless, the estimates obtained can be said to approximate the norms for children of this age group under the typical test conditions at that time. It is difficult to estimate the degree to which these diverge from those obtainable under laboratory conditions,

TABLE 8.1   *Data of audiometric performance at 7 and 11 years (grouped by loss in decibels re-audiometric zero for better ear: percentages)*

Frequency (Hz)	Age	0	−10	−20	−30	−40	−50	50+	Total N
250	7	11.5	42.9	37.4	7.0	1.0	0.1	0.05	11 106
	11	10.8	42.6	38.1	7.9	0.5	0.08	0.04	12 406
500	7	10.0	39.4	41.7	7.6	1.1	0.1	0.08	11 343
	11	9.3	42.8	39.6	7.6	0.5	0.1	0.01	12 398
1 000	7	21.0	49.9	25.4	3.1	0.4	0.1	0.1	11 370
	11	22.7	52.8	21.7	2.3	0.3	0.1	0.08	12 398
2 000	7	29.1	50.3	18.2	1.8	0.3	0.1	0.09	11 362
	11	37.4	48.9	12.3	1.1	0.2	0.1	0.07	12 398
4 000	7	34.0	46.1	17.0	2.1	0.5	0.2	0.1	11 358
	11	41.2	45.3	11.8	1.3	0.3	0.1	0.07	12 398
8 000	7	25.0	43.9	24.8	4.4	1.3	0.4	0.2	11 233
	11	37.4	43.5	16.3	2.2	0.4	0.2	0.12	12 386

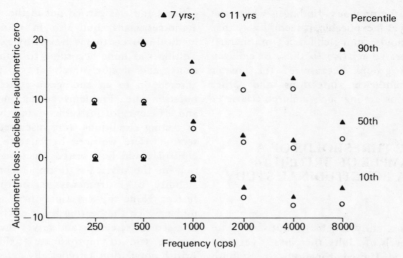

FIGURE 8.3 *Percentiles of audiometric loss in decibels for better ear of the total sample of children at ages 7 and 11 years*

TABLE 8.3 *Median audiometric loss of boys and girls at ages 7 and 11 years*[1]

Frequency (Hz)	Age	Boys	Girls	χ^2 on 1 df
250	7	8.5	9.5	43.17***
	11	9.0	9.5	46.53***
500	7	10.0	10.5	24.18***
	11	9.5	9.5	54.45***
1 000	7	5.5	6.0	17.92***
	11	5.0	5.5	42.12***
2 000	7	4.0	4.0	6.76**
	11	2.5	2.0	18.87*
4 000	7	3.0	3.5	4.04*
	11	2.0	2.0	25.76***
8 000	7	6.0	6.6	0.80
	11	3.0	2.0	21.22***

[1] Tested for linear trend boys *vs* girls, hearing loss grouped as in Table 8.2.
*$0.05 > p > 0.01$.
**$0.01 > p > 0.05$.
***$0.001 > p > 0.01$.
Otherwise $p > 0.01$.

TABLE 8.4 *Median audiometric loss of two social classes (fathers' occupation) at ages 7 and 11-years*[1]

Frequency (Hz)	Age	Non-manual	Manual	χ^2 on 1 df
250	7	9.0	11.5	30.87***
	11	9.0	9.5	20.79***
500	7	9.5	10.5	28.36***
	11	9.0	10.0	10.09*
1 000	7	5.5	6.0	30.50***
	11	4.0	4.5	1.25
2 000	7	3.5	4.0	21.98***
	11	2.0	2.5	0.00
4 000	7	3.0	3.5	19.42***
	11	1.0	1.5	0.04
8 000	7	5.0	6.0	26.37***
	11	2.0	2.5	0.04

[1] Tested for linear trend manual *vs* non-manual hearing loss grouped as in Table 8.2.
*$0.05 > p > 0.01$.
**$0.01 > p > 0.05$.
***$0.001 > p > 0.01$.
Otherwise $p > 0.01$.

but comparisons of the present variabilities (standard deviations) with those reported in an American standardised survey (PHS, 1972) on children of this age range suggests that it might not be exceedingly large. An approximation to an overall picture may also be of use to clinicians and researchers, especially in view of the paucity of national data on school-children. Our results suggest, for example, that

audiometric thresholds may be lower than those reported in a local study (Lenihan *et al.*, 1971). On the other hand, the results generally confirm the progressive improvement noted by other workers among children up to adolescence; a follow-up study on the same children aged 16 years may shed further light on this developmental pattern (see pp. 170–3). The sex and social-class differences reported here broadly agree with previous findings; while the former remain as yet inexplicable, it seems likely that audiometric thresholds among children from manual groups will be elevated relative to those of children from non-manual groups because of the greater prevalence of middle-ear infections and other otological conditions among such children (Davie *et al.*, 1972).

AUDIOMETRIC THRESHOLDS OF A NATIONAL SAMPLE OF BRITISH 16-YEAR-OLDS: A LONGITUDINAL STUDY

Introduction

Although there is a fairly reliable body of data on the audiometric levels of adults, there has as yet been no attempt in the United Kingdom to establish national estimates of the hearing levels of children such as those obtained, for example, by the US Public Health Service (1972, 1975). In the preceding section we reported audiometric data obtained from the first two follow-up studies when the children were 7 and 11 years respectively. The third follow-up enables us now to pursue the study with an assessment of hearing levels at 16 years. Although this information has certain limitations (see below), it may help to compensate for the general paucity of data on schoolchildren, until fully reliable estimates are obtained.

Material and methods

The subjects comprised those nearly 11 000 adolescents who had been audiometrically tested at the third NCDS follow-up study when they were 16 years old. The testing was arranged by the school medical officers and was carried out in the main by qualified audiometricians, but also in many cases by the medical officers themselves or by experienced nurses. Testing was done according to standardised instructions, and decibel levels at six frequencies were entered on to an audiogram attached to a medical questionnaire. Problems concerning the calibration and efficiency of instruments and the standardisation of testing conditions were discussed in the previous section. Here we need to reiterate that little direct control could be exerted on acoustical conditions, nor on the particular testing technique, or on the stability of instruments or on the motivation of testees. None the less, since these are the conditions under which the hearing levels of children are usually assessed (in screening and survey investigations), they can be said to approximate 'field norms' for the British population. Otologically defective adolescents, comprising less than 5 per cent of the 16-year-olds, were not excluded from those analyses, and changes in the composition of the sample (3 980 with data at 16 years, but not at 11; 1 166 with data at 11 years, but not at 16) were not consequential in terms of bias to overall hearing levels.

Estimation of percentile norms and statistical testing
From the data, available as numbers of children in each category of audiometric loss (in 5 dB steps from 0 to 60+), cumulative percentages were calculated and plotted on probability paper against the arithmetic scale of hearing loss. Eye-fitted curves approximated linearity up to at least the 90th percentile, so that unbiased estimates of the 10th, 50th and 90th percentiles could be obtained by interpolation. Statistical procedures for comparison of sex and social-class groups and of different ages were exactly as described in the previous paper.

TABLE 8.5   *Data of audiometric performance at 16 years, grouped by loss in decibels (re-audiometric zero* for better ear)*

Frequency (Hz)	Decibel loss							Total No.
	0 %	1—10 %	11—20 %	21—30 %	31—40 %	41—50 %	50+ %	
250	4.0	30.5	49.1	15.1	1.2	0.1	0.05	10 522
500	4.6	34.9	46.7	12.7	0.9	0.1	0.2	10 726
1 000	13.2	53.6	29.6	3.3	0.2	0.1	0.1	10 579
2 000	27.1	54.8	15.7	2.1	0.2	0.1	0.04	10 068
4 000	27.6	52.7	17.2	2.1	0.3	0.1	0.06	10 051
8 000	22.6	49.4	23.1	3.9	0.5	0.2	0.3	9 796

* 'Decibels re-audiometric zero' is an audiometric convention, decibels not being an absolute measure of sound but rather a ratio referred to an agreed standardised level thereafter called 'zero'.

Results

As at the two previous ages, the 16-year data revealed only marginal overall differences between right and left ears. Subsequent analyses were thus carried out on 'better ears' only, a procedure which minimises the quantity of data to be presented, while portraying the upper limits of hearing acuity in the sample.

Table 8.5 shows the distribution of children across hearing-loss categories (grouped in 10 dB intervals) at each frequency. Totals vary slightly from frequency to frequency, which reflects the omission of points at certain frequencies on a few of the audiograms (probably because of difficulty in obtaining firm thresholds).

Table 8.6 presents the 16-year estimates of the 10th, 50th and 90th percentiles of hearing loss at each frequency and includes the corresponding 7-year and 11-year estimates for comparison. The 50th percentiles for all three ages are shown in Figure 8.4. These data illustrate the changes of thresholds with age, as well as the thresholds at 16 years. It is evident that not only are the 16-year thresholds higher (i.e. a greater decline in hearing acuity) than might have been expected (see below for discussion) but

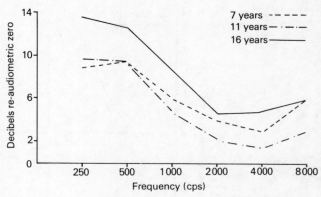

FIGURE 8.4 *Median audiometric thresholds at three ages*

they also reflect an elevation of thresholds between 11 and 16 years following a lowering between 7 and 11 years.

Table 8.7 shows that sex differences were no longer statistically significant at 16 years, except for the marginal difference at 4 000 Hz in favour of girls. Marginal differences at both 7 and 11 years were significant. The social-class differences were more interesting, however. Father's occupation was obtained in a parental interview carried out in the home by health visitors, then coded according to the Registrar-General's Classification of Occupations, and for these analyses grouped into non-manual and manual categories. Children of fathers in manual occupations had significantly higher thresholds on all frequencies than those in the non-manual category. Moreover, while this was also the case at 11 years, the 'gaps' (although small) had widened somewhat by 16 years (Table 8.8). This is illustrated further in Figure 8.5, in which the social-class medians for the three ages have been plotted together.

TABLE 8.6 *Percentiles of audiometric loss at ages 7, 11 and 16 years*[1]

Frequency (Hz)	Age	Percentiles			
		10th	50th	90th	χ^2 on 4 df
250	7	0.5	9.0	19.0	32.9*
	11	0.0	9.5	19.0	
	16	3.8	13.5	23.0	915.9*
500	7	0.0	9.5	19.5	51.1*
	11	0.0	9.5	19.0	
	16	3.0	12.5	21.6	422.9*
1 000	7	3.5	6.0	16.0	66.6*
	11	3.5	5.0	14.0	
	16	−1.2	8.7	16.5	366.3*
2 000	7	−5.0	4.0	13.0	287.3*
	11	−6.5	2.5	11.5	
	16	−5.2	4.5	13.8	202.1*
4 000	7	−6.5	3.0	13.5	248.6*
	11	−8.0	1.5	11.5	
	16	−5.5	4.8	14.8	332.2*
8 000	7	−5.0	6.0	18.0	713.6*
	11	−8.0	3.0	14.6	
	16	−4.3	6.0	16.3	468.8*

[1] Tested for equality of 16- and 11-year, and 11- and 7-year distributions of hearing loss, grouped as 0, 5 or 10, 15 or 20, 25 or 30, 35+.

TABLE 8.7 *Median audiometric loss of boys and girls at age 16 years*[1]

Frequency (Hz)	Median audiometric loss		χ^2 on 1 df
	Boys	Girls	
250	13.1	14.4	0.13
500	12.1	12.2	1.71
1 000	8.8	8.5	1.449
2 000	4.4	4.5	1.61
4 000	4.8	4.3	27.32*
8 000	6.0	5.8	2.39

[1] Tested for linear trend boys *vs* girls; hearing loss grouped as in Table 1).
*$p < 0.001$.

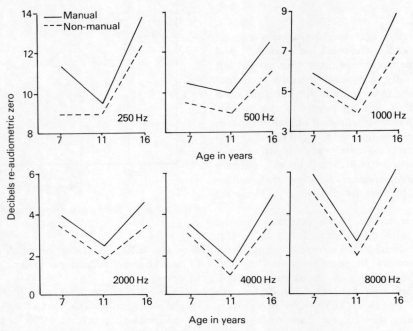

FIGURE 8.5 *Median audiometric thresholds at three ages for manual (M) and non-manual (NM) social-class groups*

TABLE 8.8   *Median audiometric loss of two social classes (father's occupation) at age 16 years*[1]

Frequency (Hz)	Social class		χ^2 on 1 df
	Non-manual	Manual	
250	12.5	13.8	33.70*
500	11.0	12.6	31.61*
1 000	7.0	8.9	30.39*
2 000	3.5	4.7	18.20*
4 000	3.6	4.9	33.24*
8 000	5.2	6.1	18.06*

[1] Tested for linear trend manual *vs* non-manual; hearing loss grouped as in Table 8.5.
*$p < 0.001$.

Discussion

The methods adopted here inevitably impose limitations on the accuracy of these data. None the less they may be of use to clinicians, researchers and screening organisers, especially as the data can be said to approximate 'field norms' for British schoolchildren. The paucity of fully reliable audiometric standards for children is a situation which perhaps deserves more attention than it has hitherto received.

The thresholds at 16 years seemed to us to be surprisingly high; they are much higher than those reported by Delaney *et al*. (1966) for a group of 16-year-olds, though lower than those reported by Lenihan *et al*. (1971) for a group of 14-year-olds in Dunbartonshire. They are also somewhat higher than those reported for 17-year-olds in a thorough American survey (PHS, 1975). As for age trends, most studies have revealed a steady increase in acuity (lowering of thresholds) up to early adulthood. This was the case with the study of Lenihan *et al*. cited above, and also in an earlier study on children by Reymert and Rotman (1946). Delaney *et al*. (1966) found a straightforward improvement at frequencies up to 3 000 Hz (and a more complex picture with higher frequencies) among children up to 17 years old, while the US National Health Survey data revealed slow and consistent falls in thresholds between ages 6 and 11 years, but a variation of less than 2 dB over the 12- to 17-year age-range (PHS, 1972, 1976: data collected in the early and mid-1960s). It follows that the present results, showing an appreciable elevation of thresholds in adolescence, after a previous improvement, are somewhat anomalous. Elevation of hearing thresholds with age (i.e. diminishing acuity) seems to be a phenomenon generally found in Western civilisation, but onset is usually thought not to occur until at least age 30. However, this decline in acuity is probably at least partly associated with acoustic insults from both industrial and non-industrial sources (Glorig and

Nixon, 1959). Ulrich and Pinheiro (1974) have pointed out that the majority of our young people have voluntarily exposed themselves to an increasingly prominent insult, namely highly amplified pop music. Lebo and Chiphant (1968) have shown that this source of noise, reaching highest levels at low frequencies, 'unmistakeably exceed those considered safe for prolonged exposure', to the extent that temporary threshold shifts and permanent cochlear damage may be inflicted (see also Dey, 1970, and Lipscomb, 1972). If it is assumed that adolescents from manual groups expose themselves in this way more frequently than those from non-manual groups, then this experience may also explain the wider social-class 'gaps' at 16 (although as far as we are aware there are no data available to support this assumption). Of course, it is possible (though it seems to us unlikely) that otological conditions, such as middle-ear infections, may explain both the social-class differences and the general elevation of thresholds. Preliminary analyses had shown hearing impairment (bilateral moderate deafness) to be more prevalent among 7-year-olds whose fathers were in manual occupation, but nearly all sufferers had recovered sufficiently to produce normal audiograms by 11 years. However, this does not rule out slight, permanent, threshold shifts at certain frequencies (Sheridan and Peckham, 1973).

9 Other Handicaps and Defects*

THE PREVALENCE AND NATURE OF ASCERTAINED HANDICAP IN THE NATIONAL CHILD DEVELOPMENT STUDY (1958 COHORT)

Introduction

The aim of this section is to present a descriptive report of handicaps among the children in the National Child Development Study. The picture is complicated by the finding that rarely do such children suffer from one clearly defined condition but rather from one major handicap associated with a number of other defects and disabilities. The findings reported here arose from a scrutiny of the records of individual children compiled by school medical officers and/or teachers at both 7 and 11 years.

From information available it is difficult to assess the effect of a given handicap on the child's life and that of his family, so we have used as a criterion of handicap any condition severe enough for the child to require formal ascertainment by the local education authority. This means that the local education authority had agreed, following a recommendation from teachers, doctors and psychologists, to provide special education suitable to the child's needs (referred to below as 'special educational treatment'). Included with those formally ascertained is a small number still awaiting ascertainment. There will, of course, be many children with defects who do not fulfil this criterion of handicap, one such example being the eight children with diabetes who were well controlled on insulin and who were satisfactorily attending ordinary schools at 11 years.

* Original sources: Peckham, C. and Pearson, R., 'The prevalence and nature of ascertained handicap in the National Child Development Study (1958 cohort)', *Public Health*, 90, 1976, 111–21; Peckham, C., Butler, N. and Frew, R., 'Medical and social aspects of children with educational difficulties', previously unpublished; Essen, J. and Peckham, C., 'Nocturnal enuresis in childhood', *Developmental Medicine and Child Neurology*, 18, 5, 1976; Calnan, M. and Peckham, C., 'Incidence of insulin-dependent diabetes in the first sixteen years of life', *The Lancet*, 12 March, 1977; Peckham, C. and Butler, N., 'A national study of asthma in childhood', *Journal of Epidemiology and Community Health*, 32, 1978, 79–85.

Also included in our definition of 'handicap' are those children who had died by 11 years with severe congenital defects. Although death usually occurred at an early age, the serious nature of the defect must have inflicted a considerable emotional and financial burden on the family.

Deaths in children under 11 years of age
There were 144 (21.5 per cent) neonatal deaths or stillbirths with serious congenital defects among 669 perinatal deaths (Davie *et al.*, 1972).

Table 9.1 shows the main categories of congenital defects among the sixty-four children who, between the ages of 4 weeks and 11 years died of a condition which, had they survived, would almost certainly have handicapped them to the extent of requiring special educational treatment (SET). A further fifteen children had died of malignancies by 11 years of age. The loss by death before 11 years due to serious handicapping conditions amounts to 223 children (12.8 per 1 000 of the sample).

TABLE 9.1 *Deaths between 4 weeks and 11 years*

Major defect	No. children
Down's syndrome	8
Cerebral palsy	8
Fibrocystic disease of the pancreas	6
Spina bifida	7
Meningo-myelococle	5
Other CNS defect	4
Congenital heart defect	20
Other defects	6
Total number of children	64

Children ascertained at 7 years
At 7 years of age 187 children or 13.3 per 1 000 had been formally ascertained as in need of SET (Table 9.2). Nearly two-thirds of these children had some physical manifestations of disease or defect and in the remainder mental retardation was the sole reported defect (Davie *et al.*, 1972). An additional thirty-two children on whom there was no informa-

TABLE 9.2   *Formal ascertainment at 7 and 11 years*

Ascertained at 7 years (population 14 032)†		Handicap category	Ascertainment at 11 years (population 15 275)*	
Number	Rate/1 000		Number	Rate/1 000
4	0.3	Blind and partially sighted	9	0.6
15	1.1	Deaf and partially hearing	20	1.3
74	5.3	ESN	266	17.1
34	2.4	SSN	51	3.3
6	0.4	Epileptic	7	0.5
8	0.6	Maladjusted	48	3.1
26	1.8	Physically handicapped	28	1.8
27	1.9	Speech defect	5	0.3
14	1.0	Delicate	22	1.4

Number of children 187
Rate 13.3/1 000

Number of children 425
Rate 27.8/1 000

*Children for whom medical and/or educational data available.
†Children for whom medical data available.

tion about ascertainment were known to be attending special classes or units.

Children ascertained at 7 years without information at 11 years
The longitudinal nature of the study made it possible to identify twenty-one children who were ascertained at 7 years but who were lost to the study at 11. This group comprised two children who died with severe congenital defects, six children whose parents expressed unwillingness to continue to participate in the survey as they did not wish to expose their children to further examinations, and thirteen children who were untraced at 11 years.

The thirteen 'untraced' children included eight children who were ESN (one was also maladjusted and had a hearing loss), three children reported to have severe speech defects and two children who had severe bilateral deafness at 7 years. The 'refusal' group of six children included three children who had severe speech defects, one of whom was asphasic and had cerebral palsy, two children who were physically handicapped − one had quadriplegia and was ESN and the other had a severe suppurative arthritis with dislocation of the left hip − and one child who was partially sighted.

Children ascertained at 7 but not requiring SET at 11 years
Thirty-three children had been 'de-ascertained' by the age of 11 years. Table 9.3 shows the categories from which they came. Of the two 'partially hearing' boys who were able to manage in an ordinary school at

11 years one suffered from a persisting severe unilateral loss and one from a severe bilateral sensorineural loss. The six 'physically handicapped' children had severe asthma (two), congenital heart disease (two), diabetes mellitus (one) and Perthe's disease (one). The five 'delicate' children suffered from chest infections (two), asthma, nephritis, and post-viral encephalitis.

Children ascertained at 11 years
By the end of their junior school career 425 children were known to be ascertained as in need of SET Table 9.4 shows how this group was built up during their infant and junior school years.

TABLE 9.3   *Children ascertained at 7, de-ascertained at 11 years*

Category of handicap	No. children
Partially hearing	2
Educationally subnormal	9*
Maladjusted	1
Physically handicapped	6
Speech defect	10
Delicate	5*

*One child in each of these groups was also ascertained as maladjusted.

Among the group of 99 children with inadequate data at 7 but known to be ascertained at 11 years, no information at all was available on 20 at 7 years, 23 were born outside the United Kingdom (eighteen

TABLE 9.4   *Children ascertained at 11 years*

Ascertained at 7	187
No data at 11	21
De-ascertained by 11	33
Ascertained at 7 and 11	133
Inadequate data at 7 but ascertained at 11	99
Not ascertained at 7 but ascertained at 11	193
Total	425

of whom were ESN), the parents of two children known to be handicapped refused to participate in the study and partial information on the remaining 54 revealed that four had been attending special schools or units at 7 years (two of them physically handicapped, one delicate and one ESN). Between 7 and 11 years the ESN group increased from 74 to 266 children and the SSN group from 34 to 51 children. As a special effort was made to trace all handicapped children at 11 years, particularly those in subnormality hospitals, this may well have accounted for the increase of severely mentally handicapped children. The speech-defect group fell from 27 to 5; 10 children were no longer ascertained, six refused to participate but the remainder were still ascertained in another category (most of them as ESN).

Children with more than one handicap at 11 years

When we reported our 'preliminary findings' on the 11-year follow-up of children in the NCDS the ascertained group included 436 known handicaps, and 29 children were known to have more than one handicap. Careful scrutiny of all individual records for this group of children has brought to light a further 19 ascertained handicaps and identified 395 individual children ascertained in a single category, 29 in two and one in three categories (Table 9.5). Even this is not the whole story, as many of the children had additional defects which, when added to the overriding handicap, all mitigate against educational progress. It is this sum total of difficulties which determines by what educational means (not forgetting further medical treatment, if appropriate)

TABLE 9.5   *Sex distribution of 'ascertained' handicaps at 11 years*

Number in each category	Category	Single ascertainment Male	Female	Double ascertainment Male	Female
2	Blind	—	—	1 SSN	1 SSN/physical handicap
7	Partially sighted	3	2	2 ESN	
4	Deaf	2	1	1 Epileptic	
16	Partially hearing	8	6	1 ESN	
				1 Delicate	
266	ESN	148	96	2 Epileptic	3 Epileptic
				5 Maladjusted	
				1 Partially hearing	2 Maladjusted
				2 Partially sighted	1 Speech defect
				3 Physical handicap	1 Physical handicap
				2 Delicate	
51	SSN	30	18	1 Blind	1 Blind/physical handicap
				1 Physical handicap	
7	Epileptic	1	—	2 ESN	3 ESN
				1 Deaf	
48	Maladjusted	37	4	5 ESN	2 ESN
28	Physically handicapped	11	8	3 ESN	1 ESN
				1 SSN	1 Delicate
				1 Speech defect	1 Blind/SSN
				1 Delicate	
5	Speech defect	2	1	1 Physical handicap	1 ESN
22	Delicate	15	2	2 ESN	1 Physical handicap
				1 Physical handicap	
				1 Partially hearing	
Number of children with handicaps		257	138	21 Double	8 Double; 1 triple

the child's best interests can be met, keeping in view the child's 'whole' life and future employment.

Table 9.2 gives the number of children in each category of handicap at 7 and 11 years together with the rate per 1 000. At 7 years those with medical data were included but an additional thirty-two children were known to be attending special schools or units (Davie *et al.*, 1972). Furthermore, at 11, teachers considered that an additional 242 children (15.8 per 1 000) would have benefited from attendance at a special school.

Children in each category of handicap at 11 years
The description of each group of handicap at 11 years includes the sex distribution, a brief description of additional ascertained handicaps and other defects, together with school placement.

Blind and partially sighted. There are nine children in this group. Details of these children are set out in Table 9.6.

Deaf and partially hearing. Four children in this group are ascertained as deaf, all attend residential special schools (one independent) and three wear hearing aids. One boy whose deafness followed pneumococcal meningitis at 1 year of age has poor vision and suffers from epilepsy, another boy has a squint and is emotionally disturbed but the boy attending an independent residential school is reported to be highly intelligent and to be doing well. The girl has a severe congenital deafness and is unable to communicate, but no further relevant details are available.

TABLE 9.7   *School placement of partially hearing children*

No. children	No. with a hearing aid	Placement
3	3	Residential special school (one independent)
1	1	Day special school for ESN children
3	1	Remedial class attached to ordinary school
2	1	Ordinary school, with teacher of the deaf
1	1	Home tuition (delicate)
3	2	Type of education unknown
3	—	Ordinary school
16		

Of the sixteen partially hearing children, two are also ascertained in another handicap category, one boy as ESN, and another, with a congenital heart defect and scoliosis, as 'delicate'. Of the remaining fourteen children, two are reported to have congenital heart defects and another poor motor co-ordination. Table 9.7 shows the type of school they are attending and whether or not a hearing aid is worn.

Successful achievement of speech is closely

TABLE 9.6   *Blind and partially sighted children*

Sex	Visual handicap	Additional ascertained handicap	Other defect	Placement
M	Blind	SSN	Cerebral palsy	Day special care unit
F	Blind	SSN and physically handicapped	Microcephaly cerebral palsy and epilepsy	Subnormality hospital
M	Partially sighted		Albino	Day special school
M	Bilateral cataracts			Day special school
M	Dislocated lenses	ESN	Marfan's syndrome	Day special school
F	Partially sighted (6/60, 6/60)		Congenital nystagmus and squint	Day special school
M	Bilateral optic atrophy		Emotionally disturbed	Residential special school
M	Bilateral cataracts	ESN		Awaiting admission to ESN school
F	6/36, 6/36 (uncorrectable)		Muscular dystrophy	Ordinary school (decision pending)

associated with the age at which deafness became apparent. Where an assessment of speech is recorded it is said to be normal in three children, limited in seven and poor in three.

Educationally subnormal (ESN now ESN(M)). This group, which comprises 266 children, is the largest category of handicap: 239 children have been ascertained to be in need of SET and twenty-seven are still awaiting a decision regarding their ascertainment. Of the 239 children, 205 are known to be receiving SET and thirty-four waiting for a place in a special school.

Seventy-four of this group (28 per cent) have associated physical or sensory defects; twenty-two have additional ascertained handicaps (Table 9.8) and the remaining fifty-two suffered from squint (eleven), poor visual acuity (ten), hearing loss (seven), cerebral palsy (six), epilepsy (five), cretinism (four), Down's syndrome (two), dislocated hip (two), cleft lip/palate (one), congenital heart disease (one), talipes (one), coeliac disease (one) and microcephaly (one).

Information is available on the educational placement of 213 of the 239 ascertained children; 57 per cent are attending day special schools or units, 7 per cent are in residential special schools and 36 per cent are in ordinary schools, receiving SET or awaiting appropriate help.

Severely subnormal (SSN now ESN(S)). There are fifty-one children in this group. Table 9.9 shows that all but eleven children are known to have obvious associated physical defects; nearly a quarter of the group suffer from Down's syndrome. Thirty-seven children attend day special schools (junior training centres), one is in a residential special school, one is receiving home tuition, ten are in hospitals for the subnormal and the placement of two is not recorded.

Epileptic. There are seven children in this group, all but one of them having a double ascertainment,

five being ESN and one deaf. Three of the ESN children also have visual defects and one a speech defect. The deaf child and the child with epilepsy as a single handicap attend residential special schools, while the remainder are in day special schools.

Maladjusted. There are forty-eight children in this group. Thirty-one are receiving SET, seven waiting for a placement in a special school and ten awaiting a decision. Of those receiving SET, three are in special schools but for five the type of schooling is not recorded.

As a group these children are known to have other handicapping conditions which would merit further study. For instance, ten were reported to have had convulsions (eight before 7 years and two after), seventeen (only one girl) to be enuretic at 11 years, six to have poor visual acuity, one poor hearing, one to be autistic, one asthmatic and four to have suffered brain damage.

Physically handicapped. There are twenty-eight children in this group, eighteen with neurological disorders, four with respiratory conditions and six with miscellaneous defects.

Of the eighteen children (eleven boys and seven girls) with a neurological disorder, twelve have cerebral palsy (eight boys and four girls), five spina bifida (three boys and two girls) and one Huntington's chorea (a girl). The clinical manifestations of the children with cerebral palsy are diverse and are shown in Table 9.10 together with their school placements.

Four of the children with spina bifida attend day special schools (two of them have urinary transplants, two are paraplegic and one word blind), and the other, who was operated on for a meningocole, attends a residential special school. The child with Huntingdon's chorea is also ESN and attends a day special school.

Of the four children with a respiratory condition,

TABLE 9.8   *Additional ascertained handicaps — ESN children*

No. of children	Handicap category	Other defect(s)
2	Partially sighted	Bilateral cataracts (1); Marfan's syndrome (1)
1	Partially hearing	Poor vision (1)
5	Epileptic	Squint (1)
7*	Maladjusted	Cerebral palsy (1); poor vision (2)
4	Physically handicapped	Cerebral palsy (2); heart defect, epilepsy, cleft palate, hearing loss and hydronephrosis (1), Huntington's chorea (1)
1	Speech defect	
2	Delicate	Cerebral palsy and squint (1); asthma (1)

* Decision pending *re* SET for two maladjusted children.

TABLE 9.9   *Handicaps and school placement of severely subnormal children*

No. children	Main additional defect or condition	Other defect(s)	Placement
13	Mongolism (7 boys, 6 girls)	Heart defect (3) Squint (2)	SH (1) TC (12)
13	Cerebral palsy (9 boys, 4 girls)	Blind (1) Blind right eye (1) Epilepsy (3) Heart defect (1)	SH (2) TC (10) NK (1)
4	Autism (4 boys)	Epilepsy (2) Partially hearing (1)	TC (3) HT (1)
3	Epilepsy (1 boy, 2 girls)	Violent behaviour (1) Hyperkinetic (2)	SH (2) TC (1)
2	Apert's syndrome (2 boys)	Hydrocephaly (1) Hydrocephaly, cleft palate, webbed fingers and toes (1)*	SH (1)
1	Phenylketonuria (girl)	Squint (1)	SH (1)
1	Cerebral agenesis (boy)	Craniostenosis (1)	SH (1)
1	Hydrocephaly (girl)		TC (1)
1	Microcephaly (girl)		TC (1)
1	Acromegaly (boy)	Heart defect and epilepsy (1)	TC (1)
11	Inadequate information (7 boys, 4 girls)		SH (2) RSS (1) TC (7) NK (1)

* This child has subsequently died.
Total number of children 51.
Placement: SH = subnormality hospital; TC = training centre; RSS = residential special school; HT = home tuition; NK = not known.

TABLE 9.10   *Placement and other defects of children with cerebral palsy*

Sex	Other ascertained handicap	Additional defect(s)	Placement
F	SSN and blind	Epilepsy	Hospital
M	SSN		Hospital
M		Emotional disturbance and epilepsy	Hospital
F		Backward	Day special school
M	ESN	Squint and defective speech	Day special school
M	Speech defect	Hearing loss	Day special school
F		Epilepsy and aphasia	Day special school
F		Defective speech	Day special school
M		Hydrocephaly	Day special school
M		Squint and nystagmus	Day special school
M		Defective speech and nystagmus	Day special school
M	ESN		Waiting for a place

one has pulmonary atresia and atrial septal defect and bronchiectasis, two children have asthma and another recurrent bronchitis. The first child attends a day special school, the two asthmatics are at residential special schools and the remaining child's school is not recorded.

Details of the six remaining physically handicapped children are set out in Table 9.11.

TABLE 9.11   *Placement of miscellaneous group of physically handicapped*

Sex	Physical handicap	Placement
M	Fallot's tetralogy cleft palate, hearing loss, hydronephrosis and epilepsy (ESN)	Day special school
M	Haemophilia (delicate)	Not known
M	Previous Perthe's disease	Special education in ordinary school
M	Muscular dystrophy	Home tuition
F	Dermatomyositis	Hospital
F	Osteogenesis imperfecta	Home tuition

Speech defect. There are five children in this group. Two children attend day special schools largely on account of additional handicaps; one girl is ESN, has severe dyslexia and is almost incomprehensible, and the other, a boy, is physically handicapped by cerebral palsy, epilepsy and severe bilateral deafness. One child with dyslalia is in a residential special school and another is receiving special help in an ordinary school. For one child information on school placement is not available.

Delicate. This is a group of twenty-two children, five of whom have an additional ascertained handicap; an ESN boy had a Wilm's tumour removed shortly after birth and is slightly spastic and another boy suffers from asthma. A physically handicapped girl has spina bifida, and a boy, haemophilia; the partially hearing boy also has a congenital heart defect.

Of the remaining seventeen children seven are asthmatic and nine have the following disabilities: nephrotic syndrome, phlyctenular conjunctivitis and keratitis, portal vein thrombosis, fibrocystic disease of the pancreas, severe burns with skin grafting, cerebral palsy (two), bowel incontinence and post-tracheotomy. A further child is reported to be emotionally disturbed.

Seventeen children are receiving SET; five attend a day special school, two are in residential special schools, one in a private school, one receives home tuition, two are in ordinary schools and for six the type of school is not recorded. Of the five remaining children, two are awaiting placement (one from hospital and the other from a special class in an ordinary school), the parents of one child have refused the recommendation of SET, one child is awaiting a final decision regarding placement, and for one there is no record of the type of school attended.

Comments

This is a descriptive paper based on detailed individual scrutiny of the records of children in the National Child Development Study for whom special education treatment is being provided (or considered) at the end of their stay in junior schools in England, Scotland and Wales in 1969. It clearly demonstrated the complex nature of each child's handicap and shows how few have a straightforward problem. We recognise that in some categories of handicap the problem is small and well met but in others we must also remember that teachers were asked for 'the number of children who, irrespective of the facilities in their area would benefit from attendance at a special school'. This figure came to 15.8 per 1 000 additional children and included, no doubt, educationally backward children which would have doubled the size of the ESN group. Furthermore, we know from our scrutiny of individual records the extraordinary provision some teachers have been able to make, with parental support, for severely handicapped children, thus retaining them in an ordinary school without SET. Parents and teacher involved in the day-to-day care of a child with a major handicap retain the hope, at least in the infant school, that his or her problems will not be so great as to require SET. Once the change to a junior school at 7 years has been made, disparity in progress between a handicapped child and his or her peers becomes more apparent, distance to school often increases, the premises may no longer be small and on one floor and other factors of a medical and social nature compel consideration of SET. If the child is to obtain the greatest possible benefit from SET, then the 'considering process' must be as short and as early as possible with, especially for physically handicapped children, review before the change to a secondary education comes at 11+.

Clearly, in some groups of handicapped children, deterioration of a medical condition, accidental injury, etc., can bring new children forward at any age, whereas in groups such as ESN failure to progress at school is the main factor in determining whether to put a child forward for SET.

There is a very fine dividing-line between 'physically handicapped' and 'delicate' children requiring SET largely depending on the availability of a suitable local school, the degree of handicap, the parents' wishes, and progress in an ordinary school, as well as the sheer multiplicity of handicaps and other defects.

Ascertainment of a child with a physical handicap does not only depend on the severity of the condition but it may be slow progress at school which tips the scale, making continued education in the ordinary school too much for both child and teacher. To be deemed 'delicate' usually means that the child finds the ordinary school routine too much for his medical condition, or is making slow progress at school perhaps due to the necessity of continued medical treatment and frequent school absence.

It is of vital importance that comprehensive assessment of the child is carried out at an early age in order to bring to light defects, many of which will add to the child's difficulties in the future and could be considered for medical or surgical treatment. Thus it is important continually to assess these children since, in some groups more than others, SET is being provided on a temporary basis and a review is particularly important at the time of transfer to a secondary school. Our scrutiny of individual records suggests that the major change in the ascertainment of handicaps between 7 and 11 years is in the group of educationally backward children, and we have reported in the previous paper that a higher proportion of the ESN children with additional physical or sensory handicaps had been ascertained by 7. It must be remembered, however, that these children were 7 years of age in 1965, and since greater emphasis is now placed on developmental screening in early childhood and fuller and more comprehensive examination at school entry (with specialist advice when necessary) we would expect a higher ascertainment rate among 7-year-old children in 1975.

A study of ascertained handicaps will never reveal the total incapacity among a group of children. While consideration for, and provision of, SET reveals the more gross physical, sensory or educational handicaps there remain many children whose handicaps, be they physical, emotional or educational, never come to the attention of the local education authorities. The nature of the study does not enable us to identify all the children whose families are coping with their disabilities supported by doctors, nurses, teachers and social workers, thus enabling them to remain in an ordinary school. We are able to conclude, however, that among one week's births of the 11-year-old population, in 1969, at least 27.8 per 1 000 children were receiving or awaiting a decision on SET in England, Scotland and Wales.

MEDICAL AND SOCIAL ASPECTS OF CHILDREN WITH EDUCATIONAL DIFFICULTIES

Introduction

Responsibility for deciding whether a child needs special education for educational subnormality requires the consideration of many factors other than measured educational performance. These include local educational policy, assessment of ability, the type and multiplicity of any associated physical or sensory handicaps, the family environment and the availability of placement in special schools and/or of special facilities in ordinary schools.

There is a considerable amount of literature about the medical and environmental aspects of children receiving special education, but much less is known about children who have educational difficulties which are not considered of sufficient severity to warrant special education. This paper reports the numbers of 11-year-old children in the National Child Development Study who were receiving or considered to require extra help for educational backwardness and compares their medical, environmental and perinatal background with those of children neither receiving nor thought to be in need of extra educational help.

Selection of children with educational problems at 11 years

Children with educational problems were identified and classified into the following three mutually exclusive groups:

1. *Educationally subnormal (ESN(M))*. This group comprised all children for whom a decision had been reached by the local education authority that the child was in need of special education for educational subnormality. The majority (64 per cent) of these children were in special schools or units. The fifty-one children categorised as ESN(S) have been omitted.

2. *Would benefit from special education ('would benefit' group)*. This group was made up of children in ordinary schools who had not been formally ascertained but whose teachers considered that they 'would benefit now from attendance at a special school', irrespective of available facilities.

3. *Receiving remedial help (remedial group)*. This group consisted of children attending ordinary schools who were receiving some form of remedial help for 'educational or mental backwardness' but were not considered by their teachers to be in need of any special provision for educational backwardness.

Throughout the subsequent analyses, comparisons have been made between these three groups and children attending ordinary schools who were not receiving or considered by their teachers to require any extra help for educational backwardness. Those children considered by their teachers to need extra remedial help for educational backwardness but who were not receiving it, together with those with incomplete data, have been excluded from this study.

Results

Prevalence

Information on educational subnormality at 11 years was obtained from both medical and educational sources and among the 15 275 children for whom these data were available 239 (1.6 per cent) were ESN(M). Teachers completing educational records for 14 148 children considered that a further 242 (1.1 per cent) would benefit from attendance at a special school and reported that an additional 964 (6.8 per cent) were currently receiving remedial help for educational backwardness (Table 9.12). Thus 10 per cent of 11-year-old children were reported to be receiving some form of special educational help for educational backwardness, or were thought to be in need of special schooling. There was a significant preponderance of boys in all three groups. An additional 160 children (1.1 per cent) were not receiving any remedial help for backwardness within the school, though their teachers thought such provision was desirable.

Regional differences

Although there were no significant regional differences in the proportion of children in the ESN(M) group or in the 'would benefit' group, the proportion of children in the educational disadvantaged group as a whole was larger in Wales and England than in Scotland ($p < 0.01$). These differences possibly

TABLE 9.12   *The prevalence of educational problems*

Group	Number of children			Rate per 1 000
	Boys	Girls	Total	
ESN(M)*	150	89	239	15.6
'Would benefit' from attending at special school	159	83	242	16.9
Receiving remedial help	601	363	964	68.1
Total	910	535	1 445	100.6

* The fifty-one children ascertained as ESN(S) (3.3 per 1 000) have been excluded from this group.

reflect the provision that schools were able to make within their normal staffing.

Environmental aspects

Social class. Previous studies have indicated that educational difficulties are closely associated with family social background, and this was amply confirmed in the present investigation. When father's occupation was categorised according to the Registrar-General's Classification of Occupations (1966), it was found that while 34 per cent of children not requiring extra educational help came from non-manual family backgrounds, this applied to 18 per cent of the remedial group, 13 per cent of the 'would benefit' group and 9 per cent of the ESN(M) children (Table 9.13). Thus in social classes I and II four per 1 000 children were ESN(M) compared with 54 per 1 000 in social class V.

Housing. Table 9.14 shows the prevalence of certain adverse social conditions among children with educational problems. Over a quarter of children in the ESN(M) and 'would benefit' groups were living in overcrowded homes (defined as a density of 1.5 or

TABLE 9.13   *Educational status at 11 years by social class*

Social class	ESN(M)		'Would benefit'		Remedial help		No help required	
	(No.)	(%)	(No.)	(%)	(No.)	(%)	(No.)	(%)
Non-manual	19	9.2	25	12.5	149	18.1	3 422	34.1
III manual	89	43.0	71	35.5	367	44.5	4 111	40.9
IV	44	21.3	54	27.0	184	22.3	1 589	15.8
V	42	20.3	29	14.5	75	9.1	475	4.7
No male head	13	6.3	21	10.5	49	6.0	451	4.5
Total	207	100	200	100	824	100	10 048	100
Social class not known	32		42		140		231	

more persons per room) and a quarter of these households did not have sole use of the three amenities of indoor lavatory, bathroom and hot water supply. This shortage of space was emphasised by the fact that a third of these children shared a bed with their siblings. No significant difference in adverse social conditions was found between the ESN(M) and 'would benefit' group, whereas there was a significant difference between these two groups and the remedial help group and between all children with educational problems and those who required no extra help. Financial hardship was also significantly more prevalent in the ESN(M) and 'would benefit' groups than in the other two groups; 32 per cent of these parents stated that they suffered financial hardship during the year preceding the interview. A similar proportion of families were receiving free school meals (Table 9.14).

Approximately three times as many children from the ESN(M) and 'would benefit' groups were fourth or subsequent children in the family compared with the group not requiring extra help, while the proportion in the remedial help group was intermediate. This was also reflected in family size (Table 9.14).

Perinatal disadvantages

Children with educational problems showed no increase in history of maternal eclampsia, ante-partum haemorrhage, abnormal delivery or foetal distress. However, they were more often below the 10th percentile of birthweight for their gestation, and significantly more children with educational problems than those not requiring extra educational help were born before the 37th week of gestation or weighed less than 2 500 grammes at birth.

Medical aspects

Analyses of medical data revealed that children with educational problems suffered more physical or sensory disabilities as well as having marked social disadvantages (Table 9.15). Whereas no significant differences emerged between the social background of the ESN(M) and 'would benefit' groups, adverse medical conditions were more common in the ESN(M) group. More ESN(M) than 'would benefit' children were found on medical examination to have articulation defects, poor motor co-ordination and a history of convulsions occurring after 7 years.

Height

The ESN(M) group was on average 4cm shorter than the group not requiring extra help, and the mean height of the 'would benefit' group and those receiving remedial help occupied an intermediate position. Height differences remained statistically significant when allowance was made for social class (Table 9.16).

Motor co-ordination

This was assessed by a heel-to-toe test in which the examining doctor rated the 11-year-old child's ability to walk backwards along a straight line with the heel of one foot touching the toe of another; nearly a quarter of ESN(M) children were rated as being 'very unsteady' on this test compared with 8 per cent of the group not requiring extra help (Table 9.15).

TABLE 9.14   *Social and family factors*

	ESN(M) (No.)	(%)	'Would benefit' (No.)	(%)	Remedial help (No.)	(%)	No help required (No.)	(%)
Home conditions								
overcrowded	138	32.6	147	27.9	689	17.8	9 125	10.5
lacks sole use of 3 amenities	52	25.4	44	22.0	148	17.9	1 096	10.8
shares a bed	71	35.0	62	30.8	205	24.8	1 614	15.9
Financial hardship	60	32.1	62	31.6	158	19.8	912	9.2
Free school meals	76	38.8	71	30.2	172	18.3	794	7.8
Fourth or subsequent child in family	89	42.3	73	36.0	219	26.2	1 504	14.8
Maximum total population	239		242		964		10 279	

Tests for differences between ESN(M) and 'would benefit' groups – not significant.
Tests for differences between all educational backward groups and no help required: $p < 0.001$ for all items.
In all cases where there is a positive association, linear trend across group is significant.

Laterality

Although the proportion of children reported by their parents to be left-handed was higher in the ESN(M) group (15 per cent) than in any of the other groups, the difference was not statistically significant.

Vision

Distant vision was tested by means of a Snellen chart and a higher proportion of children in the ESN(M) and 'would benefit' groups than in either of the other groups were found to have a visual acuity of 6/12 or worse in their better eye. The eyes were also examined for squint, which was found to be more prevalent among the ESN(M) children than any of the other groups (Table 9.15).

Hearing

Assessment of hearing was based on the results of a clinical hearing test and an audiogram (Sheridan, 1972). A higher proportion of children with educational difficulties was considered by the examining doctor to have a hearing loss sufficient to interfere with normal schooling and everyday functioning (Table 9.15).

TABLE 9.15   *Medical factors*

	ESN(M)		'Would benefit'		Remedial help		No help required	
	(No.)	(%)	(No.)	(%)	(No.)	(%)	(No.)	(%)
Poor hearing	13	7.3	6	3.6	17	2.4	100	1.0
Squint on examination	19	10.4	8	4.6	23	3.1	331	3.3
Vision 6/12 or worse in better eye	19	10.4	13	7.2	31	4.1	677	6.6
Articulation defect	45	25.0	20	11.2	49	6.6	322	3.6
Left-handed	29	14.9	16	8.3	87	11.1	1 041	10.7
Accident (causing unconciousness)	25	12.2	10	5.0	44	5.3	401	3.9
Convulsions								
ever	23	11.7	10	5.7	31	4.2	316	3.1
after 7 years	11	5.7	2	1.1	8	1.3	36	0.4
Enuretic at 11	23	11.2	25	12.4	51	6.1	422	4.1
Maximum total	239		242		964		10 279	

Tests for difference between ESN(M) and 'would benefit' group only significant for articulation defect ($p < 0.01$), poor co-ordination ($p < 0.001$), accident ($p < 0.02$).
Tests for difference between all educational backward groups and no help required significant for all items ($p < 0.001$ for all but squint: $p < 0.05$) except visual acuity and left-handedness.

TABLE 9.16   *Educational status at 11 years by height (mean height in cm)*

Social class	ESN	'Would benefit' group	Remedial help group	Controls
Non-manual	No. = 20	No. = 24	No. = 147	No. = 3 598
	143.3 sd (± 7.5)	143.3 sd (± 9.1)	144.5 sd (± 8.0)	145.8 sd (± 7.1)
	se (± 1.7)	se (± 1.8)	se (± 0.7)	se (± 0.1)
Manual	No. = 147	No. = 132	No. = 543	No. = 5 935
	140.3 sd (± 7.7)	141.6 sd (± 8.2)	142.2 sd (± 0.8)	143.9 sd (± 7.2)
	se (± 0.6)	se (± 0.7)	se (± 0.3)	se (± 0.1)
All children	No. = 183	No. = 180	No. = 748	No. = 10 201
	140.5 sd (± 7.7)	141.8 sd (± 8.2)	142.9 sd (± 7.2)	144.6 sd (± 7.3)
	se (± 0.6)	se (± 0.6)	se (± 0.3)	se (± 0.1)

Standard deviation (sd) and standard error (se) in brackets.

Speech

More children with educational difficulties than those without were considered by the examining doctor to have a defect of articulation, other than a stammer. This applied to a quarter of the ESN(M) group, but was not related to the different social-class distribution of children with educational problems and controls since no such differences were reported among the 11-year-old children in the study according to the doctors' assessment of speech (Calnan and Richardson, 1976a: see pp. 127–39). More speech therapy was reported to have been given to 11-year-old children with educational problems than those without; 16 per cent of ESN(M) children, 8 per cent of the 'would benefit' group, 5 per cent of the remedial group and 2 per cent of the controls had received therapy.

Convulsive disorders

There was a significant increase from the group with no educational difficulties through to the ESN(M) group in the proportion of children reported to have had a major convulsion. When, however, only those convulsions reported to have occurred after the age of 7 were considered, a history of convulsions was more common in the ESN(M) group than in the other two educational problem groups.

Enuresis

Bedwetting at 11 years was reported by parents twice as often among the ESN(M) and 'would benefit' groups than among children in the other groups.

Accidents

A history of scalds or burns, of flesh wounds requiring at least ten stitches and of unconsciousness following accidents was found to be significantly more common among children with educational problems than those without. Only among the reported accidents resulting in unconsciousness was there a significant difference between the educational difficulty groups, these being more prevalent among the ESN(M).

Educational aspects

A higher proportion of both mothers and fathers of children with educational difficulties, than of those without, were reported by teachers to show little or no interest in their child's educational progress (Table 9.17). Disinterest was particularly marked in the 'would benefit' group.

Children with educational difficulties were reported by their parents to have more absences from school on account of illness than those with no difficulties. This applied particularly to the ESN(M)

TABLE 9.17   *Educational factors*

	ESN group (a)		'Would benefit' group (b)		Remedial help group (c)		Controls (d)		Comments
	(No.)	(%)	(No.)	(%)	(No.)	(%)	(No.)	(%)	
Little or no parental interest in child's education									
father	(70)	51.9	(108)	65.1	(307)	48.5	(1 379)	18.9	* + 0
mother	(66)	37.9	(96)	46.8	(254)	30.9	(1 085)	12.1	+ 0
Time off school for medical reasons (+ one month)	(34)	16.6	(33)	16.3	(77)	9.2	(579)	5.7	+ 0
Reluctant to go to school	(42)	20.8	(24)	12.1	(91)	10.9	(622)	6.1	* + 0
Maximum total population	239		242		964		10 279		

Note: test for difference between groups made as follows — (a) *v.* (b), (a + b) *v.* (c), (a + b + c) *v.* (d):

    * difference between (a) and (b) significant
    + difference between (a + b) and (c) significant
    0 difference between (a + b + c) and (d) significant

In all cases where there is a positive association, linear trend across groups significant.

and 'would benefit' groups, where as many as 16 per cent had missed more than one month's schooling for medical reasons in the previous year. Nearly a quarter of the ESN(M) children and significantly more than any other group were also reported to be reluctant to go to school.

Social adjustment in school

On the Bristol Social Adjustment Guide (BASG), approximately half the children in the ESN(M) and 'would benefit' groups obtained scores claimed by Stott to indicate maladjustment in the school situation, as opposed to 10 per cent of the group with no such difficulties. The most adverse (highest) mean score was in the 'would benefit' group. There was a significant relationship between poor behaviour and educational problems after allowance had been made for social class.

Teacher's assessment

It is difficult to interpret fully teacher ratings of the educational achievement of individual ESN(M) children, as the teachers may have been making their comparisons not with normal pupils but with other handicapped children. Nevertheless, 6 per cent of the ESN(M) children, 15 per cent of the 'would benefit' group and 39 per cent of those receiving remedial help were rated as having average or above-average *oral ability*. This compared with 85 per cent of the group not requiring extra help.

Speech intelligibility was assessed by teachers, who considered that 11 per cent of the ESN(M) group and 9 per cent of the 'would benefit' group had 'certainly unintelligible' speech compared with 4 per cent of the remedial help group and 1 per cent of the group not requiring extra help.

Attainment tests

On the whole, the functional groupings of the children according to educational placement were confirmed by the results of the three attainment tests (reading, arithmetic and general ability) administered for the study at the age of 11. However, on each test a small minority of ESN(M) children achieved scores within normal limits. On the other hand, scrutiny of the data relating to forty-three ESN(M) children for whom there were no test scores revealed that a high proportion had been unable to attempt the test. It must be borne in mind that the tests were designed for normal children.

A copying-design test was specially designed for this study (Davie *et al.*, 1972) as being a possibly useful indicator of visuo-motor co-ordination. This test revealed that significantly more ESN(M) children (26 per cent) than any other group had poorer scores of less than 6. These results applied to 17 per cent of

the 'would benefit' group, 6 per cent of the group receiving remedial help and 2 per cent of the remaining group.

Further characteristics of ESN(M) children

The ESN(M) children were further divided into two groups according to whether or not an additional handicap of a physical or sensory type was present. In 29 per cent of ESN(M) children another such handicap was reported, though only a minority (eighteen out of 239) were ascertained in more than one handicap category (Table 9.18). The proportion with the other handicaps is certainly a minimal estimate as it was not possible to assess, even after scrutiny of individual records, whether in some children, reported (for example) to have clumsiness or poor co-ordination, the defect was of sufficient severity to constitute a physical handicap.

TABLE 9.18   *Physical handicaps in ESN(M) children: with additional ascertainment*

Category of ascertainment	No. children	Additional handicap(s)
Epilepsy	5	Squint (1)
Partially hearing	1	Poor vision (2)
Partially sighted	2	Bilateral cataracts (1) Marfan's syndrome (1)
Speech defect	1	
Physically handi-capped	4	Cerebral palsy (2) Congenital heart defect + epilepsy (1) Huntington's chorea (1)
Delicate	2	Mild cerebral palsy (1) Asthma (1)
Maladjusted	3*	Cerebral palsy (1) Poor vision (2)

*Two children ascertained ESN and maladjusted are omitted as they have no recorded physical handicap.
A further fifty-one children had additional handicaps or defects not ascertained. These include: cerebral palsy (6), epilepsy (5), hypothyroidism (1), Down's syndrome (1), microcephaly (1), congenital heart defect (1), cleft palate/lip (1), congenital dislocated hip (2), talipes (1), coelia disease (1), significant hearing loss (7), squint (1), poor visual acuity of $< 6/12$ in best eye (9).

There was no difference in the sex distribution of ESN(M) children with or without an additional handicap. However, 42 per cent of ESN(M) children from non-manual families had an additional handicap, compared with 31 per cent from social class III (manual) and 22 per cent from social classes IV and

V. Numbers were small in the non-manual group, but this result suggests that in ESN(M) children the higher the social class, the greater the likelihood of the child having an additional handicap.

Nearly a quarter of the children ascertained as ESN(M) at 11 years had been ascertained already by 7 years. Among those ascertained by 7 years, a significantly higher proportion had additional handicaps which could have highlighted these children's learning difficulties. The type of placement at 11 years, however, was similar for the children with or without additional handicap.

Discussion

The category of ESN(M) is one in which any administrative decision enters as much as does any accurate measure of cognitive function. The official definition of an ESN(M) child is one who, because of 'limited ability or other condition resulting in educational retardation, requires some specialised form of education'. The category of educational subnormality thus defined has been preserved here. Criteria used in other studies include psychometric assessment, where an IQ of less than 70 is usually accepted as intellectually subnormal. Intelligence level clearly plays an important part in placement, but a considerable proportion of children in ESN(M) schools have an IQ of over 70 (Chazan, 1965) and cannot therefore be regarded as intellectually subnormal.

An administrative criterion of educational subnormality gives only limited help in differentiating the problems of children ascertained from those who have educational problems but who are not specifically labelled or ascertained. The present study provides an opportunity to assess the national prevalence of children with educational problems, whether or not they have been ascertained as ESN(M). By the age of 11 years, nearly 10 per cent of all children met our own criterion of what constitutes an educational problem, namely that they were receiving some form of special help for backwardness in school. Only a small proportion of this group of backward children was receiving the attention of special educational services.

It is clear that the three groups with educational problems shared a number of common attributes to a greater or lesser degree. However, certain disabilities appeared to be commonest among ESN(M) children or those considered by their teachers to be in need of special schooling. These difficulties included poor limb co-ordination or hand control, and also visuo-motor impairment as evidenced by impaired ability to copy designs, a condition which may be associated with early learning problems and affect school progress. Convulsions and disabilities relating to the

special senses, such as hearing impairment and poor speech, were also more prevalent in the ascertained group. These additional disabilities, by increasing a child's difficulty in coping with normal school, are likely to influence a decision regarding school placement. The close association of educational backwardness with poor speech, poor co-ordination or other neuro-motor or sensory disabilities underlines the need for a full paediatric assessment to be made as early as possible to accompany the psychological and educational assessment of children with learning problems, from school entrance onwards. Clearly the earlier a child's difficulties are identified, the greater the chance that he or she can be helped to achieve maximum potential.

Boys predominated in each educationally disadvantaged group. Increased male vulnerability to educational backwardness and speech problems has been observed in other studies (Rutter *et al.*, 1970; Birch *et al.*, 1970; Stein and Susser, 1960a; Williams, 1966). Behavioural problems were also reported to be more common in boys in our study and may have affected learning, or conversely they may reflect a poor teacher—child relationship rather than anything inherent in the child. Children in the 'would benefit' group were actually more often 'maladjusted', according to the results of the BSAG test, than those who already had been ascertained as ESN(M). In a previous study of ESN(M) children in Aberdeen, five in sixteen children with IQs of 60—69 were considered to have additional psychiatric abnormalities (Birch *et al.*, 1970). In a study made in the Isle of Wight on 9- to 10-year-olds with IQs of less than 70 attending an ESN school, one-quarter had definite psychiatric problems, as compared with 6.8 per cent of the general population (Rutter *et al.*, 1970).

In the present study teachers reported a high rate of speech problems among children with educational difficulties. Spreen (1965) found that 45 per cent of children with IQs in the range 50—70 had a language handicap. Differing linguistic usage of the different social classes (Bernstein, 1961a) may partly account for this increased proportion of language difficulties in educationally backward children. Educational standards often assume the full comprehension and use of more formal language patterns.

Children ascertained as severely subnormal ESN(M) have a social-class distribution corresponding to the normal population (Frew and Peckham, 1972), whereas all three groups of our educationally backward children came more often from a manual-class family background. Among children from an unskilled social-class background the ESN(M) ascertained rate (54 per 1 000) was thirteen times higher than that from non-manual families (4 per 1 000). The 'would benefit' group showed a sixfold higher difference, between the proportion among non-manual compared with social class V families, while more than twice the proportion of social class V children were receiving remedial help in ordinary schools. This striking relationship between educational backwardness and social environment was also found in Aberdeen (Birch *et al.*, 1970), where a ninefold increase in mild mental handicap was reported among the children of unskilled urban manual workers compared with the offspring of non-manual workers.

Whereas the majority of children with IQs of 50—70 show no associated damage to the nervous system, more middle-class children show evidence of such damage (Rutter *et al.*, 1970; Birch *et al.*, 1971; Stein and Susser, 1960b). Results of the present study supported this: 29 per cent of ESN(M) children had 'additional' handicaps but the proportion was nearly twice as high among those from non-manual than those from manual family backgrounds. The reason for this must remain speculative, but clearly the origin is multifactorial. Genetic and pathological factors obviously play a part in aetiology, but the present study confirms the outstanding importance of adverse social conditions. The quality of educational facilities in poorer areas and of parental encouragement may also play a part.

NOCTURNAL ENURESIS IN CHILDHOOD

Introduction

It has been suggested that nocturnal enuresis may result from emotional disturbance (e.g. Ministry of Education, 1954), or that it may be a manifestation of development delay (Bakwin, 1971). At present, however, it seems probable that the aetiology of nocturnal enuresis is multifactorial and is related to environmental, social, developmental and psychiatric factors (Douglas, 1964; Rutter *et al.*, 1970; Miller *et al.*, 1974). We have compared the social background, medical history, behaviour and educational performance of enuretic children in a representative national sample with those who had no history of nocturnal enuresis.

Method

Information on bedwetting was gathered at the NCDS home interviews. At the 7-year follow-up the parents were asked if the child had ever been 'wet by night after 5 years of age (ignoring occasional mishaps)' and at 11 they were asked if the child had been 'wet at night in the past month'.

Enuretic group

Of the original 16 000 children, although some information was available for over 90 per cent at 7 years and again at 11 years, data relating to enuresis at both ages were complete for only some 12 000 children. Fifty-one severely subnormal children were excluded from the study. The 12 000 children were considered in the following mutually exclusive groups:

1. Children who were reported as enuretic at 11, regardless of their situation earlier.
2. Children who, though reported as enuretic between 5 and 7, were reported as dry at 11 years (subsequently referred to as 'early bedwetters').
3. Children who were reported as not being enuretic at either age.

Since information was collected at only two points of time it was not possible to draw a distinction between primary and secondary enuretics. The children reported as enuretic at both 7 and 11 years could include cases of secondary enuresis because they could have been dry at some period prior to either of these ages. Thus all children reported as enuretic at 11 years have been included in one group, irrespective of the situation at seven years.

Results

Prevalence

Of 7-year-old children in the NCDS 10.7 per cent were reported as wetting the bed between 5 and 7 years of age, but only a third of those children were still enuretic at 11 years. A further 1.3 per cent reported dry at 7 years were enuretic at 11, making a total of 4.8 per cent enuretic at 11 years. At 7 there was no statistically significant* difference between the sexes, though there were nearly twice as many enuretic boys as girls at 11 (see Table 9.19). There was no regional variation in the prevalence of enuresis.

Social class†

Enuresis at the age of 11 years was more than twice as common among children of unskilled and semi-skilled workers (social classes IV and V) than among children with fathers in professional and managerial occupations (I and II), and there was a statistically significant trend in this direction through all the social classes. This trend was also present among the early bed-wetters, but to a lesser degree (Table 9.20).

There was a preponderance of enuretic boys among the children from non-manual backgrounds at both ages. However, among the children from manual

---

* All differences and associations quoted in the text are statistically significant at a level of 0.1 per cent unless otherwise stated.
† *Social class* is defined by the occupation of the male head of the household (Registrar-General's *Classification of Occupations*, 1966).

TABLE 9.19   *Nocturnal enuresis by sex*

Group	Sex		Total	No.
	Boys (%)	Girls (%)	(%)	
Enuretic				
At 11 yrs, not at 7 yrs	1.8	0.7	1.3 }	
At 11 yrs, also at 7 yrs	4.2	2.8	3.5 } 4.8	581
At 5−7 yrs, not at 11 yrs	7.4	6.9	7.2	878
Non-enuretic	86.6	89.6	88.0	10 773
Total	100.0	100.0	100.0	12 232

Test for difference between boys and girls:
proportion enuretic at 11 yrs: $\chi^2 = 8.3$, df = 1, $p < 0.01$
proportion enuretic at 5−7 yrs: $\chi^2 = 2.3$, df = 1, $p > 0.05$.

TABLE 9.20   *Nocturnal enuresis by social class*

Group	Social class					Total
	I + II (%)	III NM (%)	IIIM (%)	IV + V (%)	No male head (%)	(%)
Enuretic						
At 11 yrs	3.0	3.7	4.7	6.3	6.0	4.8
At 5−7 yrs, not at 11 yrs	5.7	5.5	7.8	8.2	6.2	7.2
Non-enuretic	91.3	90.8	87.5	85.5	87.8	88.0
Total	100.0	100.0	100.0	100.0	100.0	100.0
No.	2 757	1 086	4 993	2 660	568	12 064

Test for difference between social classes:
proportion enuretic at 11 yrs: χ^2 (trend) = 28.7, df = 1, $p < 0.001$
proportion enuretic at 5−7 yrs: χ^2 (trend) = 22.5, df = 1, $p < 0.001$.

backgrounds, more boys were enuretic at 11 years but there was no difference between the sexes at 7.

Environment

Proportionately more of the enuretic groups at both ages were living in overcrowded homes (defined as more than 1.5 persons per room) than were non-enuretics (Table 9.21). This difference remained after allowance had been made for social class. In addition, in each social class a higher proportion of early bed-wetters (20.7 per cent) shared a bed than non-enuretics (16.3 per cent) ($p < 0.05$), though there was no difference between 11-year-old enuretics and non-enuretics. Interestingly, there was no association between enuresis and the lack of an indoor lavatory.

Family

Enuresis was twice as common among children whose position in the family was fourth or later than it was among those who were the eldest or the only child (Table 9.22). Since it is probable that the effect on a child of older siblings may differ from that of younger siblings, we have considered them separately and found an association between enuresis and both the number of older siblings and the number of younger siblings, after allowance had been made for social class.

There were proportionately more 11-year-old enuretics among one-parent families ($p < 0.05$) but this did not apply to early bedwetters. In a special study of one-parent families in the NCDS (Ferri, 1976), the proportion of enuretic girls was similar whatever their parental situation, but the boys in fatherless families were more likely to be bedwetters than those in two-parent families.

In addition, there were nearly four times as many 11-year-old enuretics among those who were in the care of the local authority at the time of the follow-up than among those who had never been in care (Table 9.23). As children in care tend to come from

TABLE 9.21   *Nocturnal enuresis by crowding*

| Group | No. persons per room | | | | Total |
	$\leqslant 1$ (%)	1.0—1.5 (%)	1.5—2.0 (%)	2+ (%)	(%)
Enuretic					
At 11 yrs	3.4	6.2	8.1	7.8	4.7
At 5—7 yrs, not at 11 yrs	6.6	7.7	9.9	6.5	7.2
Non-enuretic	90.0	86.1	82.0	85.7	88.1
Total	100.0	100.0	100.0	100.0	100.0
No.	7 467	3 321	1 114	293	12 195

Test for difference between crowding groups:
    proportion enuretic at 11 yrs: χ^2 (trend) = 63.9, df = 1, $p < 0.001$
    proportion enuretic at 5—7 yrs: χ^2 (trend) = 12.1, df = 1, $p < 0.001$.

TABLE 9.22   *Nocturnal enuresis by child's position in family*

| Group | Child's position in family | | | | | Total |
	1st (%)	2nd (%)	3rd (%)	4th (%)	5th (%)	(%)
Enuretic						
At 11 yrs	3.2	4.9	5.5	7.6	8.1	4.8
At 5—7 yrs, not at 11 yrs	6.1	8.0	7.6	7.9	7.1	7.2
Non-enuretic	90.7	87.1	86.9	84.5	84.8	88.0
Total	100.0	100.0	100.0	100.0	100.0	100.0
No.	4 606	4 058	1 905	896	717	12 182

Test for difference in position in family:
    proportion enuretic at 11 yrs: χ^2 (trend) = 53.7, df = 1, $p < 0.001$
    proportion enuretic at 5—7 yrs: χ^2 (trend) = 8.1, df = 1, $p < 0.01$.

TABLE 9.23   *Nocturnal enuresis among children who had ever been in care of local authority*

| Group | In care of local authority | | | Total |
	Yes, now (%)	Yes, in past (%)	No, never (%)	(%)
Enuretic				
At 11 yrs	16.7	12.4	4.4	4.8
At 5—7 yrs, not at 11 yrs	11.1	13.8	7.0	7.2
Non-enuretic	72.2	73.8	88.6	88.0
Total	100.0	100.0	100.0	100.0
No.	52	282	11 713	12 049

Test for difference between in care and not in care:
    proportion enuretic at 11 yrs: χ^2 = 62.6, df = 1, $p < 0.001$
    proportion enuretic at 5—7 yrs, χ^2 = 26.2, df = 1, $p < 0.001$.

the working class, this association was further analysed, and it was found that, for each social class, proportionately more enuretics than non-enuretics had been in care.

There was an association between the parents' report of having been in serious financial hardship and bedwetting, after allowing for social class. Of 11-year-old enuretics 18.7 per cent, and of early bed-wetters 12.9 per cent, but only 10.0 per cent of non-enuretics, were in families who reported that they had been in financial trouble. Although the parents' concept of financial hardship is clearly subjective and not necessarily related to the income level of the family, it is likely to be related to the degree of stress felt by the family.

Early development
At 7 years, parental information revealed that proportionately more early bedwetters of both sexes had shown other aspects of delayed development. A significantly higher proportion of early bedwetters was reported as not walking by 18 months (6.2 per cent compared with 3.9 per cent of non-enuretics) ($p < 0.01$) and not talking (i.e. joining two words) by 2 years of age (10.2 per cent compared with 5.4 per cent of non-enuretics). There were no such developmental differences between enuretics and non-enuretics at 11 years. It must be borne in mind, however, that the information collected at 7 may be subject to a 'halo' effect, since the same mothers who recorded delays in walking and talking may be more likely to report bedwetting as well.

Medical aspects
Underlying abnormalities of the urinary tract clearly did not play a major role in the aetiology of enuresis. Four children who were enuretic at 11 years were reported to have abnormalities of the kidney or bladder. One child had a duplex kidney with two ureters, one had a congenitally absent right kidney, another had an ectopic bladder with transplantation of the ureters to the sigmoid colon, and the fourth had been operated on for bladder-neck obstruction. An additional four children were reported to have had nephritis. Only three enuretic 11-year-olds were reported to have had a proven urinary infection.

Of the 11-year-old enuretics, 4 per cent had been investigated as hospital in-patients and a further 19 per cent had attended out-patient departments only. The corresponding ratios for the early bed-wetters were 2 per cent and 6 per cent respectively. There was no social-class or regional difference in the proportions attending hospital for enuresis.

Height
Children with enuresis were found to be shorter than those who were not enuretic. Because this relationship could have been explained by other factors associated with both height and enuresis (namely, social class, sex, crowding and the number of older or younger children in the household), an analysis of variance which included these factors was carried out (see Figure 9.1). The relationship between height and enuresis at 11 years remained significant after allowing for each of these factors, and when they had

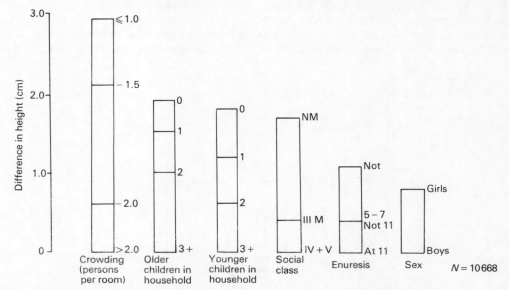

FIGURE 9.1   *Difference in height at 11 years, enuresis and home factors*

Note: Each bar represents the average difference in height between the categories shown, e.g. between boys and girls, when allowance has been made for the other variables in the analysis.

been taken into account the children who were enuretic at 11 were, on average, 1.1cm shorter than non-enuretics. Early bedwetters were, on average, 0.7cm shorter than non-enuretics.

Behaviour

On the home-behaviour scale (see statistical appendix 1), both early bedwetters and 11-year-old enuretics had higher mean scores than non-enuretics. Clearly a 'halo' effect may influence the relationship with the later enuretics, as the mothers who reported bedwetting at 11 years may have tended to report other sorts of behaviour at the same time. The association between enuresis and behaviour at home was further analysed by means of an analysis of variance. After allowing for sex, social class, crowding and older and younger children in the household — factors which are related to items of behaviour in this scale (Davie *et al.*, 1972) — enuresis at both ages remained strongly associated with a high score on the behaviour scale (see Figure 9.2). Children who had been early bedwetters had higher behaviour scores than non-enuretics, though not as high as the 11-year-old enuretics.

Enuretics also had higher mean scores on the school-behaviour scale (BSAG) than non-enuretics after allowing for the same five factors as in the analysis of home behaviour (see Figure 9.3). The difference in score between enuretics and non-enuretics at 11 years was greater than the difference in behaviour between extreme social-class groups. Although they were no longer enuretic at the time of the follow-up, early bedwetters again had higher scores than non-enuretics, but lower scores than the 11-year enuretics. However, since this scale was completed by the teacher, it will tend to reflect the relationship between child and teacher rather than provide an entirely 'objective' view of the child's behaviour.

Teachers' assessment of speech and co-ordination

At 11 years teachers reported a significantly higher proportion of enuretic boys and girls than non-enuretics to be 'difficult to understand because of poor speech', and this association persisted after allowance was made for social class. Over a quarter (25.7 per cent) of the 11-year boy enuretics from manual backgrounds were rated as having poor speech, compared with 13.9 per cent of non-enuretics from manual backgrounds.

The teachers were also asked whether the children had poor physical co-ordination. Although there was no association between co-ordination and enuresis for the boys, there were significantly more enuretic girls at 11 years who were said to be poorly co-ordinated (22.9 per cent compared with 11.9 per cent non-enuretics) ($p < 0.01$), which may reflect a different aetiology of enuresis among girls.

Educational aspects

Children in the enuretic groups at both ages had lower scores on the reading, mathematics and general ability tests than had non-enuretics. Analyses of variance showed that the association between enuresis and each measure of attainment remained after allowance had been made for sex, social class, crowding and the number of older and younger children in the household — all factors associated with educational attainment.

On the test of reading comprehension, the enuretic groups at both ages had significantly lower scores than non-enuretics (see Figure 9.4), although early

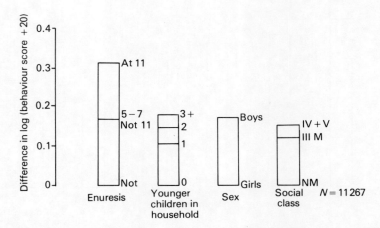

FIGURE 9.2   *Difference in home behaviour score at 11 years, enuresis and home factors*

Note: Each bar represents the average difference in home behaviour score, as described for Figure 9.1.

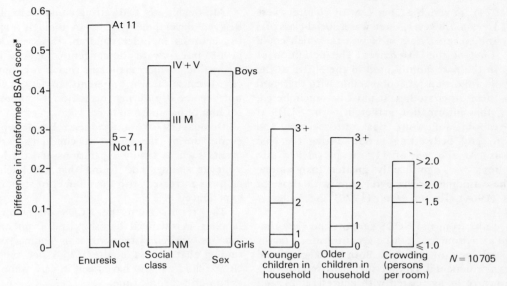

FIGURE 9.3   *Difference in school behaviour (BSAG) score at 11 years, enuresis and home factors*

Note: Each bar represents the average difference in school behaviour score, as described for Figure 9.1. Higher scores indicate 'badly adjusted' (Stott, 1963).
* Transformed score = $\sqrt{BSAG + \frac{3}{8}}$.

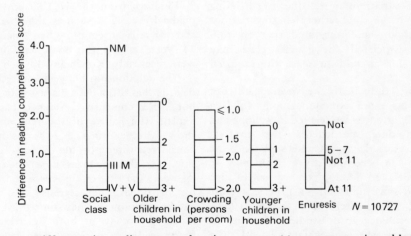

FIGURE 9.4   *Difference in reading comprehension score at 11 years, enuresis and home factors*

Note: each bar represents the average difference in reading comprehension, as described for Figure 9.1.

bed-wetters' scores were not as low as those enuretic at 11 years. A similar pattern was found for both the mathematics test and the general ability test. For all these tests, however, the difference in score between enuretics and non-enuretics at 11 years was less than half the difference between children with fathers in non-manual occupations and those with fathers in semi-skilled and unskilled occupations.

Discussion

The prevalence of enuresis among children in the NCDS was similar to that reported by Douglas (1973b) among children born in 1946, where 7.3 per cent of the 7-year-olds and 5.3 per cent of 11-year-olds were enuretic. However, NCDS figures are lower than the prevalence rates found in the study of Miller *et al.* (1974), in which 11 per cent of children were wet at 11 years. However, there was a social-class bias towards the working class in Newcastle which could explain some of the differences. The definition of 'wetting in the past month' used in the NCDS at the 11-year-old follow-up was comparable with that used in both these other studies. It must be remembered, however, that information gathered in the NCDS at the 7-year-old follow-up was retrospective and related to any bedwetting period during the past two years. At the age of 11, the prevalence rate among boys was significantly greater than among girls. These findings are in agreement with those of Douglas (1964), Rutter *et al.* (1970) and Miller *et al.* (1974).

The results from the NCDS support the view that the child's environment can be a contributory factor in the aetiology of enuresis. Both social-class and several environmental factors such as overcrowding were shown to be associated with enuresis at 11, and to a lesser extent with enuresis between 5 and 7.

Similarly, Miller *et al.* (1974) found proportionately more enuretics among the children of manual workers at comparable ages. Other studies, however, have only found a significant social-class difference among girls (Douglas, 1964; Rutter *et al.*, 1970). Stein and Susser (1967), in a study of sphincter control, concluded that social-class variations were due to differing expectations about the child rather than to variations in training methods, and suggested that environmental factors associated with social class may make it harder for a child to learn the required behaviour.

In the present study, early bedwetting, but not later enuresis, was more common among children who were also reported to be delayed in walking and talking. This finding, particularly the contrast between the two enuretic groups, adds support to the theory that delay in becoming dry at night may be part of general delayed development, which in turn may be due to environmental or genetic factors (Bakwin, 1961, 1971; Stein and Susser, 1967). Bakwin found evidence from studies of twins to support the theory that genetic factors, and their effect on rates of maturation, were important aetiological factors. However, Brazelton (1962) showed that with certain expectations, attitudes and training practices all but a very small percentage (1.5 per cent) of children can be dry at night by 5 years of age. Therefore, the necessary maturation must have occurred in at least 98.5 per cent of children by that age (MacKeith, 1972). This suggests that delayed development of sphincter control is at least in part related to an adverse environmental situation during the early years, which are also the years in which maturation of the necessary central

Although early bedwetting could be explained by delayed development, it is an unlikely explanation for enuresis in older children. However, MacKeith (1968) put forward the concept of a 'sensitive learning period', which maintains that if for some reason (e.g. because of own or parents' anxiety) a child does not become dry during this period it is more difficult for him or her to do so later.

Douglas (1970) examined several anxiety-provoking events during the study of children's early years, events such as family separations and the birth of a younger sibling, and found that the likelihood of enuresis increased with the number of stressful events experienced.

The results from the NCDS on children from families in financial hardship and from one-parent families were consistent with this finding, as was the finding that over a quarter (26.5 per cent) of the NCDS children who have been in care were reported as enuretic at some time.

Stein and Susser (1966), in a study of children in care of the local authority, found that there were more enuretics among children in institutions than among those living with their own families. However, they were unable to distinguish between the effects of the institution itself and the fact that children in care tend to come from broken families.

Findings from the NCDS showed that very few medical factors — such as abnormalities of the renal tract or renal infection — had emerged by the age of 11 years among the enuretics. Similar conclusions were reached by Kolvin and Taunch (1973).

The relationship between enuresis and psychiatric disorder has often been discussed (e.g. Shaffer, 1973), but little conclusive evidence has been found to explain the nature of the relationship, or even to show whether such a relationship exists. Shaffer considered three possible theories for such a relationship: (a) that enuresis is secondary to psychiatric disorder; (b) that enuresis is a contributory cause of psychiatric disorder, because of the embarrassment and anxiety; or (c) that some third factor is involved in the aetiology of both behaviours. Although he found evidence consistent with each process, Shaffer favoured the last explanation for most children.

In the present study there was a strong association between enuresis and behaviour difficulties both at home and at school, particularly for the 11-year-old enuretic group. It was interesting that early bedwetters had higher scores than non-enuretics, though they were dry at the time behaviour was assessed.

Rutter *et al.* (1970) also found that enuretics in the Isle of Wight study had higher scores on both home and school behaviour questionnaires than had non-enuretics, and that this association was much stronger among girls. They considered whether enuresis was primary or secondary to psychiatric disorder and found evidence for both hypotheses. Douglas (1964) also found an association between enuresis and certain symptoms of disturbed behaviour that were reported by parents.

It is likely that children would be worried about their enuresis, due in part to their parents' anxiety and to the attitude of their peers, and that this may be reflected in their school work. In the present study, enuretics had lower scores on each of the three attainment tests than had non-enuretics. These findings are in agreement with those of Douglas (1964), whose 11-year-old enuretics had lower test scores when allowance was made for social class and sex. However, Rutter *et al.* (1970) found no association between IQ and enuresis, and although there were proportionately more enuretic than non-enuretic girls among the slow readers, the same did not apply to the boys.

The findings from our study confirm that a multiplicity of factors are involved in the aetiology of enuresis, namely environmental factors such as overcrowding and delayed development, stressful events such as coming from a broken family, and factors suggesting behavioural difficulties. The study also showed that the relative importance of these characteristics varied according to whether the child was enuretic only between 5 and 7 years of age, or was enuretic at 11 years of age. Factors suggesting delayed development were associated only with early bedwetters, whereas later enuretics tended to have more behaviour difficulties and lower educational attainment.

INCIDENCE OF INSULIN-DEPENDENT DIABETES IN THE FIRST SIXTEEN YEARS OF LIFE

Introduction

The incidence rate of young-onset diabetes in the first sixteen years of life has been estimated as at least 7.67 per 100 000 population (Bloom *et al.*, 1975). When compared with maturity-onset diabetes, classical juvenile-onset diabetes is held to have a much weaker genetic component. Recent investigations have drawn attention to the possible relevance of environmental factors (Tattersall and Pyke, 1972) such as diet (Baum *et al.*, 1975; Cohen, 1971) and virus infections (Nelson *et al.*, 1974; Dippe *et al.*, 1975). If environmental factors are of aetiological importance, broadly based population studies and the detection of changes in prevalence rates over time are clearly necessary.

Subjects and methods

Twenty-two diabetic children were identified in the NCDS. In each case, the parents were sent questionnaires, and nineteen were completed and returned. The diagnosis of insulin-dependent diabetes was confirmed in all twenty-two children from their medical records. In all but one case direct contact was made with the consultant paediatrician responsible for the care of the child.

Results

Incidence

By the age of 16 years, twenty-two children with insulin-dependent diabetes had been identified. The incidence of diabetes at the three follow-ups of the NCDS using the original population of the total cohort by 7 years (15 500) was 0.13 per 1 000 population by 7 years, 0.58 per 1 000 population by 11 years, and 1.42 by 16 years (Table 9.24). This may be an underestimate, as information was not available on all children at 16 years. All of the twenty-two children were Caucasian and born in the United Kingdom. The peak incidence of insulin-dependent diabetes was 12–13 years, which is in broad agreement with other investigations.

TABLE 9.24 *Frequency of diabetes by age of diagnosis and sex*

Age of diagnosis (years)	Male	Female	Total	Cumulative prevalence per 1 000 population
2	1	1	2	—
7	0	2	2	0.13
8	1	0	1	—
9	2	0	2	—
10	2	0	2	—
11	0	1	1	0.58
12	5	0	5	—
13	1	2	3	—
14	0	2	2	—
15	2	0	2	—
Total	14	8	22	1.42

No social-class differences were found. More boys than girls had diabetes but the difference was not statistically significant, possibly due to small numbers.

Family history

Information from parents and hospital records revealed that five of the twenty-two children who had diabetes by 16 years had first-degree relatives who were diabetics. In three cases, one or other of the parents was diabetic; one of the parents had developed diabetes at 21 years, another by 30 years, and in the third case the age of onset was not known. In two other cases there was a history of diabetes in siblings.

Of the 11 692 parental questionnaires returned at age 16 in the third follow-up of the whole cohort, a history of diabetes was reported in one or other parent in less than 1 per cent of the children (Table 9.25). It must be emphasised that the population described in this table is composed of parents of 16-year-olds and is not therefore a representative sample of the adult population as a whole.

TABLE 9.25   *Distribution of diabetes in parents of 16-year-olds by reported age on onset*

	Reported age of onset (yrs)						
	15	15– 25	25– 35	35– 45	45– 55	55+	Total
Mother	2	2	10	9	5	6	34
Father	1	2	14	11	3	5	36

History of prenatal and postnatal infections

In view of the possible viral aetiology of diabetes, the child's history of prenatal and postnatal infections was examined. There were no diabetics among the children born to the eleven mothers from the total cohort who were reported in the perinatal study to have had clinical rubella in pregnancy or to the seven mothers who were reported to have been in contact with a case of clinical rubella. Among mothers of diabetics there was one case of influenza and bronchitis at twenty-two weeks' gestation and one of influenza at twenty-eight weeks. All of the diabetics

were reported by their parents to have had measles in childhood, but this was also a common illness among the rest of the cohort — i.e. 89 per cent had measles by 7 years; 55 per cent of the diabetics had had mumps in childhood compared with 42 per cent of all children in the cohort.

Discussion

The prevalence of diabetes in this national study is higher than that reported in other studies in Britain (Table 9.26). This difference may arise from a real change in morbidity rates or may reflect differences in the populations studied. As far as the definition of diabetes is concerned, the children included in this study were all insulin-dependent diabetics, whereas Wadsworth and Jarrett (1974) included diabetics who were not on insulin. Despite this, the prevalence of diabetes in the latter study was considerably lower than that reported in the NCDS. Other evidence has shown that non-insulin-dependent diabetes is not confined to the older age groups (Tattersall, 1974) and there is some evidence that maturity-onset diabetes in the young may be aetiologically different from the insulin-dependent diabetes found in the young, though whether it also differs from the non-insulin-dependent diabetes found in adults is still uncertain (Cudworth, 1976).

Other evidence suggests an increase in prevalence of young-onset diabetes over the last three decades. In 1957 the annual rate of hospital admissions for diabetes per 100 000 population in England and Wales for children under 5 was eleven for males and six for females. By 1971 this had increased to thirty-five for males and eleven for females. The 5–14 age group also showed an upward trend. Similarly, for the age group 0–14 years, patients' consulting rates from general practice in 1955–6 were 1:100 000 for males and 4:100 000 for females. By 1970–1 this

TABLE 9.26   *Prevalence of diabetes in various studies in Britain*

	Age group (years)	Sample size	Prevalence (per 10 000)
Study using selected areas in England and Wales (Henderson, 1949)	15	1 307 000	1
Northamptonshire (Beardmore and Reid, 1966)	5–16	45 500	8
Edinburgh (Falconer *et al.*, 1971)	19	73 980	5
National Survey of Health and Development (Wadsworth and Jarrett, 1974)	15	12 472	1
National Child Development Study	16	15 500	14

rate had increased to three for males and five for females (Adelstein, 1975). These figures may reflect a change in morbidity, increased efficiency of data collection, or possibly improved diagnosis, though the latter possibility seems unlikely because of the acuteness and severity of presenting symptoms in the young-onset diabetic.

Change in incidence may reflect declining mortality due to improved management. There has been no change in the mortality rate for young-onset diabetes, however, and no deaths from diabetes were reported in the NCDS. Alternatively, it may reflect changes in environmental factors, such as virus infections, which may be important in the aetiology of young-onset diabetes. Although Bloom *et al.* (1975) have shown a seasonal variation in the incidence of young-onset diabetes that coincides with seasonal variation in the incidence of virus infections, the evidence for a possible relationship between virus infections and diabetes is not conclusive (Dippe *et al.*, 1975; Gamble and Taylor, 1969).

Links between young-onset diabetes and mumps (McCrae, 1963) and also congenital rubella (Forrest *et al.*, 1971) have been suggested. We found that a higher proportion of diabetics reported a history of measles and mumps than the rest of the cohort, but the small number of diabetics makes interpretation difficult. There was no evidence to suggest an association between prenatal infections and diabetes.

In 23 per cent of the diabetics there was a history of diabetes in a first-degree relative, which is higher than the figures reported by Oakley *et al.* (1968) (13 per cent), and Bloom *et al.* (11 per cent). Oakley also reported that 2 per cent of non-diabetic children had a family history of diabetes, whereas in the present study the figure was less than 1 per cent. While there is evidence that predisposition to diabetes may be inherited, the actual pattern of inheritance is not straightforward. Thus a genetically determined predisposition to virus-induced diabetes has been suggested (*Lancet*, 1976).

Some evidence suggests that certain HLA antigens that show variations between different racial groups are also associated with young-onset diabetes (Cohen, 1971) and this may account for the variation in prevalence between countries (Wadsworth and Jarrett, 1974).

A NATIONAL STUDY OF ASTHMA IN CHILDHOOD

Introduction

Previous studies on asthma in childhood have been restricted mainly to local or selected samples from the population. The present study is an attempt to overcome the bias introduced by variations in size and characteristics of sample population by examining the prevalence of childhood asthma and wheezy bronchitis in a nationally representative sample of children.

Selection of children

The health visitor asked the parents of NCDS children at the age of 11: 'Has your child ever had attacks of asthma; of wheezy bronchitis; or neither of these conditions?' If the answer to the first two questions were 'yes', parents were then asked about the frequency of attacks, categorised as follows: at least once a week; usually less than once a week but can expect one a month; at least one attack in past year but less frequently than once a month; had attacks in the past year but do not know frequency; no attacks at all in past year but had attacks when younger. The terms *asthma* and *wheezy bronchitis* were both included in the parental questionnaire since it is often difficult to distinguish precisely between them. However, a history of asthma has been shown to be a good indicator of impaired ventilatory function (Hamman *et al.*, 1975), whereas bronchitis with associated wheezing has been less well validated, though some evidence suggests that both asthma and wheezy bronchitis constitute part of one disease entity, differing only in degree (Williams and McNicol, 1969).

Results

Prevalence of asthma and wheezy bronchitis by the age of 11
A history of asthma with or without wheezy bronchitis was reported by parents in 3.5 per cent of 13 509 children from whom information was available relating specifically to asthma or wheezy bronchitis. A further 8.8 per cent were reported to have a history of wheezy bronchitis only. The proportions in whom asthma or wheezy bronchitis had occurred in the year before the interview at the age of 11 are set out in Table 9.27. This shows that 2 per cent had suffered from asthma attacks during the previous year and a further 2.9 per cent from wheezy bronchitis. One or more attacks of asthma or wheezy bronchitis a month were reported in 102 children, of whom twenty-nine were having attacks at least once a week. Thus 7.6 per 1 000 children aged 11 were having wheezy attacks of some kind at least monthly. Eleven children were receiving special teaching because of their asthma (eight were classified as delicate and three as physically handicapped). One death had been ascribed to asthma in a girl aged 11.

TABLE 9.27   *History of asthma and wheezy bronchitis at the age of 11 years*

| Attacks in year before inquiry | No. of children | | | | | |
	Asthma		Wheezy bronchitis		Total	
At least once a week	24		5		29	
Between once a week and once a month	40		33		73	
Less than once a month	168		292		460	
Frequency unknown	38		64		102	
All attacks in year before	270	(2.0)	394	(2.9)	664	(4.9)
Attacks in the past but not in year before	199	(1.5)	801	(5.9)	1 000	(7.4)
Total	469	(3.5)	1 195	(8.8)	1 664	(12.3)

Total population = 13 509 children, of whom 11 845 had no history of either condition. Percentages of total population in brackets.

Children reported by parents to have had asthma or wheezy bronchitis in the year before the interview at the age of 11 were designated as having current attacks and comprised 4.9 per cent of the total sample. The children whose attacks were reported to have taken place before, but not during, the preceding year, are subsequently referred to as having past attacks. This group comprised 7.4 per cent of the total sample and includes twenty-nine children with a history of asthma and fifty-one with a history of wheezy bronchitis for whom there was no information about whether attacks had occurred in the past year. The remaining 11-year-old children (87.7 per cent), who had no history of asthma or wheezy bronchitis, were categorised as having neither condition.

Boys and girls
Attacks of asthma and wheezy bronchitis, both current and past, were more common in boys than girls. This difference was more marked in the asthma group, where there were nearly twice as many boys

as girls, but it was still significant in the wheezy bronchitis group (Table 9.28). Twenty of the twenty-nine children shown in Table 9.27 as having attacks at least weekly were boys.

Social class
Social class was defined according to the Registrar-General's classification of fathers' occupations when this information was available and the father was the head of the household.

The frequency of reported asthma was significantly greater in children from non-manual families than in those from manual families, and this difference was accounted for by the higher frequency of past asthma reported in social classes I and II compared with social classes IV and V ($p < 0.001$). Social class III was intermediate between these two (Table 9.29). The prevalence of wheezy bronchitis, however, showed no social-class gradient.

It was interesting to find a preponderance of manual families among those whose current attacks

TABLE 9.28   *Prevalence of asthma and wheezy bronchitis by sex*

| | Boys | | Girls | | Total | |
	No.	%	No.	%	No.	%
Asthma						
Current attacks	177	(2.6)	93	(1.4)	270	(2.0)
Past attacks	130	(1.9)	69	(1.1)	199	(1.5)
Wheezy bronchitis						
Current attacks	229	(3.3)	165	(2.5)	394	(2.9)
Past attacks	444	(6.4)	357	(5.4)	801	(5.9)
Neither condition	5 953	(85.9)	5 892	(89.6)	11 845	(87.7)
Total	6 933	(100)	6 576	(100)	13 509	(100)

Asthma (current and past) *vs* neither condition: χ^2 = 41.1 (1 df) $p < 0.001$.
Wheezy bronchitis (current and past) *vs* neither condition: χ^2 = 15.7 (1 df) $p < 0.01$.

TABLE 9.29   *Prevalence of asthma and wheezy bronchitis by social class*

	Non-manual				Manual							
	I and II		III		III		IV and V		No male head		No	Total	
	No.	%	No.	%	No.	%	No.	%	No.	%	answer	No.	%
Asthma													
Current attacks	64	(2.1)	31	(2.6)	101	(1.9)	62	(2.1)	10	(1.5)	2	270	(2.0)
Past attacks	61	(2.0)	16	(1.4)	84	(1.5)	25	(0.8)	8	(1.2)	5	199	(1.5)
Wheezy bronchitis													
Current attacks	95	(3.2)	35	(3.0)	154	(2.8)	78	(2.6)	24	(3.6)	8	394	(2.9)
Past attacks	177	(5.9)	69	(5.9)	311	(5.7)	173	(5.9)	50	(7.5)	21	801	(5.9)
Neither condition	2 610	(86.8)	1 021	(87.1)	4 795	(88.1)	2 612	(88.5)	575	(86.2)	232	11 845	(87.7)
Total	2 981	(100)	1 172	(100)	5 445	(100)	2 950	(100)	667	(100)	268	13 509	(100)

Comparison between non-manual and manual social classes:
Asthma (current and past)   *vs* neither condition: $\chi^2 = 6.3$ (1 df) $p < 0.05$.
Wheezy bronchitis (current and past) *vs* neither condition: $\chi^2 = 1.0$ (1 df) ns.

occurred more, rather than less, frequently than once a month ($p < 0.01$).

Other social factors
There was no difference in family size, or in birth order within the family, between children with a history of asthma or wheezy bronchitis (current or past) and those who suffered from neither condition. Nor was there a difference in the frequency of these two conditions according to region (northern England, southern England, Wales, and Scotland), or to overcrowding (more than 1.5 persons per room), or to financial hardship in the previous year.

Eczema and hay fever
There was a clear association between asthma and wheezy bronchitis and other atopic conditions such as eczema and hay fever (Table 9.30). Children with a history of asthma were reported by their parents to have suffered from eczema and hay fever in the year before the follow-up interview significantly more often than those with a history of wheezy bronchitis only ($p < 0.001$). Nearly one in four of

the children with current asthma had suffered from eczema, and nearly half from hay fever or allergic rhinitis.

Recurrent illness or infection
A history of recurrent headaches or migraine, vomiting or bilious attacks, and abdominal pains, was significantly more frequent among children with reported wheezy bronchitis only than among those with a history of asthma or of neither condition (Table 9.31). Similarly, a history of recurrent throat of ear infections in the year before the interview was most frequent among children with reported wheezy bronchitis. More than twice as many children with current attacks of wheezy bronchitis had suffered from recurrent infection as had those with asthma or a negative history. The percentage of children reported to have had a tonsillectomy was similar in each group (22 per cent).

Physical examination
The medical examination findings are shown in

TABLE 9.30   *Percentages of children with asthma and wheezy bronchitis reported as suffering from eczema and hay fever*

	Asthma		Wheezy bronchitis		Neither condition
	Current	Past	Current	Past	
Recurrent eczema in past 12 months	23.9***	13.7***	10.7***	4.6	3.4
Recurrent hay fever/allergic rhinitis in past 12 months	44.9***	25.4***	25.2***	8.2*	6.3
Number of children with data	268	197	384	787	11 692

Test for difference between each asthma or wheezy bronchitis group and neither condition:
χ^2 significance levels   ***$p < 0.001$
               *$0.01 < p < 0.05$
      Otherwise $0.05 < p$

Table 9.32. More than 20 per cent of children with current attacks of asthma had signs of expiratory bronchi. A 'chest deformity' (the nature of the defect was unspecified) was reported in 9 per cent of this group. By contrast, 5 per cent of those with current attacks of wheezy bronchitis had signs of bronchial spasm, and 2 per cent were recorded as having a 'chest deformity'. The parents' reports of eczema were supported by the findings of the medical examination; eczema was present most frequently in children with current attacks of asthma, and it was more frequent in those with past attacks of asthma than in those with current wheezy bronchitis. The highest proportion of children with marked nasal obstruction was also in the current asthma group.

Height and weight
Since there was no difference in mean height or weight between the asthma and wheezy bronchitis groups (allowing for sex and social class), the children with current attacks of asthma and/or wheezy bronchitis were subdivided according to whether or not attacks occurred at least once a month, or less frequently. Comparisons were then made between these two groups, the past attack group, and those with a negative history, making four groups in all. After adjustment had been made for sex and social class, because these have independent effects on height and weight, it was found that the mean height of children in the four groups did not differ significantly.

'Relative weight', i.e. the weight expected for any given height, derived from the whole sample, was examined at 11 years of age to give a crude index of nutrition (Newens and Goldstein, 1972). Children with current attacks of asthma and/or wheezy bronchitis in whom the attacks occurred at least monthly were of significantly lower mean relative weight than children in the other three groups: on average about 4 per cent lighter than expected.

Hospital attendance
Children with reported asthma, current or past, were more likely to have attended hospital as in-patients or out-patients for investigation or treatment of their asthma than children with wheezy bronchitis alone (Table 9.33). More than half the children with current asthma had attended hospital for this condition, compared with 39 per cent of those with past asthma, 27 per cent of those with current wheezy bronchitis alone, and only 17 per cent of those with a history of past wheezy bronchitis.

Absence from school
Children with current attacks of both asthma and wheezy bronchitis were frequently absent from school because of ill health in the year preceding the inquiry. Nearly 50 per cent of the children suffering more than one attack a month had missed at least four weeks of school during that year; 13 per cent of this group had been absent for more than three months. Although these children comprised only 0.8 per cent of the whole sample, they accounted for 12 per cent of the 11-year-olds who missed more than three months of school during the year before the follow-up interview. The children with past attacks of asthma and of wheezy bronchitis alone missed no more school than children with a negative history.

Educational attainments
In spite of time away from school because of illness, children with current attacks of asthma and wheezy bronchitis appeared to keep up with their school work. As there was no difference between the mean reading scores of girls and boys with asthma and those with wheezy bronchitis, comparisons of educational attainment were made between the group suffering current attacks of either condition (again subdivided according to whether attacks had occurred at least monthly or less frequently), the group with past attacks, and those who had no history of either condition. In an analysis of variance allowing for sex and social class, the mean reading comprehension test score was not significantly different in any of the four groups. Similar findings were observed from an analysis based on mean scores obtained in an arithmetic test.

Emotional and behavioural factors at home
On a modified Rutter home-behaviour scale which reflects the parental view of the child's behaviour, children with current and past attacks of asthma and wheezy bronchitis had significantly higher mean scores than those with a negative history, indicating an adverse result. This difference persisted after allowance had been made for sex and social class in an analysis of variance, and children with current attacks occurring at least monthly had the highest mean scores, followed by children who had less frequent attacks, children with past attacks, and those with a negative history.

Although behavioural disturbances such as bed-wetting have been reported more commonly in asthmatic than in non-asthmatic children, there was no evidence from the present study to support the finding.

Social adjustment at school
Social adjustment at school was measured by the Bristol Social Adjustment Guide (Stott, 1963). A high score is considered by the author of the test to be

TABLE 9.31   *Percentages of children with asthma and wheezy bronchitis reported as suffering from recurrent illness or infections*

Recurrent conditions in past 12 months	Asthma		Wheezy bronchitis		Neither condition
	Current	Past	Current	Past	
Headaches or migraine	14.6	15.4	24.7***	21.3***	15.1
Vomiting or bilious attacks	5.3	1.0*	8.8**	7.2***	4.3
Abdominal pain	10.5	9.2	14.3*	14.3**	10.7
Throat and/or ear infections	10.8	7.2	22.7***	13.7**	10.4
Number of children with data	267	195	388	788	11 711

Test for difference between each asthma or wheezy bronchitis group and neither condition:
χ^2 significance levels   ***$p < 0.001$
**$0.001 < p < 0.01$
*$0.01 < p < 0.05$
Otherwise $0.05 < p$.

TABLE 9.32   *Medical examination findings in children with asthma and wheezy bronchitis (%)*

	Asthma		Wheezy bronchitis		Neither condition
	Current	Past	Current	Past	
Bronchial spasm	20.7	3.3	4.9	0.7	—
Chest deformity	8.8	2.7	1.9	1.4	0.6
Marked nasal obstruction	7.2	5.5	6.3	1.6	1.5
Eczema	15.5	9.4	6.0	2.9	1.6
Number of children examined	251	182	366	739	10 901

TABLE 9.33   *Numbers and percentages of children with asthma and wheezy bronchitis who had attended hospital*

	Asthma				Wheezy bronchitis			
	Current		Past		Current		Past	
In-patient	54	(20.2)	25	(12.8)	28	(7.2)	52	(6.6)
Out-patient only	91	(34.0)	51	(26.0)	75	(19.4)	80	(10.2)
No attendance	123	(45.9)	120	(61.2)	284	(73.4)	654	(83.2)
Number of children with data	268	(100)	196	(100)	387	(100)	786	(100)

associated with poor adjustment in school, and a low score with good adjustment. Children with current attacks of asthma or wheezy bronchitis had significantly higher scores than those with past attacks or with neither condition ($p < 0.01$), amounting to about half the sex difference and social-class difference in adjustment. Allowance was then made, in an analysis of variance, for differences in social class, and particularly in sex, as boys generally obtain higher scores than girls. The difference in mean social adjustment score between these groups was less

marked and no longer statistically significant at the 5 per cent level.

Information about both conditions at both ages
Relevant data were accumulated for 11 914 children at the ages of 7 and 11. Table 9.34 shows the prevalence of asthma with or without wheezy bronchitis, and of wheezy bronchitis alone, at both ages.

Slightly more than 3 per cent of children were reported to have had one or more attacks of asthma,

TABLE 9.34   *Numbers and percentages of children with asthma and wheezy bronchitis at 7 and 11 years of age*

	History at 11 years of age					
	Asthma		Wheezy bronchitis		Neither condition	Total
	Current	Past	Current	Past		
History at 7 years of age						
Asthma with or without wheezy bronchitis	160 (43.0)	104 (28.0)	26 (7.0)	34 (9.4)	47 (12.6)	371 (100)
Wheezy bronchitis only	42 (2.3)	27 (1.5)	192 (10.7)	407 (22.6)	1 132 (62.9)	1 800 (100)
Neither condition	36 (0.4)	16 (0.2)	129 (1.3)	222 (2.3)	9 339 (95.8)	9 742 (100)
Total	238 (2.0)	147 (1.2)	347 (2.9)	663 (5.6)	10 518 (88.3)	11 913 (100)

with or without wheezy bronchitis, during their first seven years. At the age of 11, 43 per cent of these children were reported to be still suffering from attacks of asthma, and a further 7 per cent from attacks of wheezy bronchitis only. The remaining 50 per cent were reported free of wheezing.

At the age of 7, a further 1 800 children (15 per cent) were reported to have had one or more attacks of wheezy bronchitis, but not asthma. At the age of 11, only 13 per cent of this group were currently suffering from asthma or wheezy bronchitis and the remaining 87 per cent were free from wheezing. The parents of two-thirds of this group reported at the interview at the age of 11 that their children had never suffered from asthma or wheezy bronchitis. The attacks reported at the age of 7 may well have occurred early in life, or have been so mild that parents could not remember them, especially as four years elapsed between the two sets of interviews.

A history of asthma or wheezy bronchitis was reported at the age of 11 in 4 per cent of children who had no history of either condition at the age of 7. Of those children whose wheezing had apparently developed between the ages of 7 and 11, a total of 36 were reported to have current asthma, and 129 current wheezy bronchitis only.

Discussion

In a survey of Kent schoolchildren aged between 5 and 14, the frequency of asthma reported by parents was 3.8 per cent. Children with a positive history were found to have significantly lower peak expiratory flow rates than children with no history, showing that it is possible to detect children with impaired ventilatory function from a history of asthma (Hamman *et al.*, 1975). In the present study,

in which the diagnosis of asthma and wheezy bronchitis was also based on parental reporting, 3.5 per cent of children aged 11 had a history of asthma and 8.8 per cent a history of wheezy bronchitis.

In the year before the 11-year follow-up, 4.8 per cent of children in the present study were reported to have suffered from asthma (2 per cent) or wheezy bronchitis (2.9 per cent). A history of wheezy bronchitis at this age is likely to indicate true bronchospasm rather than a symptomatic wheeze, which may occur in young children suffering from respiratory infections. Comparable findings were reported among Birmingham schoolchildren aged 6 to 15, of whom 5.5 per cent had experienced one or more wheezy complaints in the previous six months (Smith *et al.*, 1971). Similarly, in a population of 10–15-year-old schoolchildren in Aberdeen, the prevalence of asthma was 4.8 per cent (Dawson *et al.*, 1969). In a random sample of 10-year-old school-children in Australia, 11 per cent had a history of episodes of asthma and wheezing, and 3.7 per cent had continuing asthma at the age of 10 (Williams and McNicol, 1969).

Our study confirms the increased prevalence of asthma in males (Graham *et al.*, 1967; Dawson *et al.*, 1969; Williams and McNicol, 1969; Smith *et al.*, 1971; Hamman *et al.*, 1975). The increase was more marked in children who suffered more frequent attacks, and was greater among children with a history of asthma than among those with a history of wheezy bronchitis.

The influence of social and environmental factors has been the subject of conflicting reports. In the present study, a history of asthma was more common among children from non-manual families than among those from manual families, whereas a history of wheezy bronchitis was not related to social class. Hamman *et al.* (1975) and Graham *et al.* (1967) also found an excess of children with asthma among social classes I and II. In Australia, McNicol *et al.* (1973) found no difference between asthmatic children and a control group according to father's occupation. However, Mitchell and Dawson (1973) reported an excess of severe asthma in children from social classes IV and V and they also found that children with severe attacks tended to come from large families regardless of social class.

There has been much controversy over the relationship between asthma and wheezy bronchitis. Most recent studies suggest that the two conditions are inseparable, the diagnosis most probably reflecting the severity of the symptoms (Williams and McNicol, 1969). In the present study, however, certain differences did emerge. Not only were children with a history of asthma suffering from a more severe condition, which was reflected in the findings at medical examination, but they were also more likely to have suffered from eczema or hay fever. Recurrent headaches or migraine, recurrent vomiting or bilious attacks, and recurrent ear or throat infections, however, were more common among the children with a history of wheezy bronchitis than among those with asthma. It is possible that a diagnosis of asthma is more likely to be made in the presence of an associated atopic condition which may reflect a poorer prognosis (Blair, 1977).

The personalities of asthmatic children and their reactions to emotional stress are sometimes considered to be important factors in the aetiology of asthma. Few population studies have examined this, and where a positive association has been reported between asthma and psychological disturbance, samples have been highly selective — for example, children attending hospital. In the present study, children with asthma showed poorer adjustment at school than non-asthmatic children, but this difference was not significant when allowance had been made for social class and sex. This underlines the need to make the requisite adjustments for background factors when attempting to define the characteristics of asthmatic children.

Investigation of home behaviour, which reflected the parental view of the child's behaviour, gave a different picture. The asthmatic group, and particularly those having frequent attacks, had poorer home behaviour than non-asthmatic children, even after allowing for sex and social class. This finding may be due to the greater tendency of parents, rather than teachers, to over-protect the asthmatic child. Neuhaus (1965) examined children attending public schools in New York and found that asthmatics were more maladjusted, neurotic and dependent than non-handicapped children, but no more than children with cardiac disorders. This suggests that asthmatic children have no characteristic personality patterns but show personality traits similar to those of other children with chronic illness.

Some studies have reported higher than average educational attainments among children with asthma or wheezy bronchitis (Graham *et al.*, 1967; Mitchell and Dawson, 1973). Others have found no such association (Rawls *et al.*, 1971), and this was so in the present report. However, 13 per cent of the children who had suffered from wheezing attacks at least monthly had missed at least three months schooling in the preceding year, and it is possible that their educational attainments might have been higher if they had not missed so much school.

Over half the children reported to be wheezing at the age of 11 had never attended hospital, where full investigation, including identification of allergens and assessment of respiratory function in response to therapy, should be carried out. A great deal can now be done to prevent chronic respiratory damage resulting from contact with harmful allergens: for example, regular or intermittent medication with antispasmodics or disdium cromoglycate. There is still a tendency to assume that children will 'grow out' of asthma, but this does not seem to be so, since half of the children with a history of asthma at the age of 7 were still suffering attacks four years later.

10 Other Aspects of Physical Development and Health*

DEVELOPMENTAL CORRELATES OF HANDEDNESS

Introduction

There is now considerable evidence for a high degree of lateral cerebral hemispheric specialisation, at least in right-handed subjects. The evidence comes from at least three sources:

1. Recovery or non-recovery of speech in brain-damaged subjects (e.g. Geschwind, 1970),
2. Subjects who have undergone cerebral commissuretomy (e.g. Sperry, 1967; Gazzaniga, 1970),
3. From the use of the sodium amytal injection technique (Wada and Rasmussen, 1960; Rossi and Rosadini, 1967).

The nature of the specialisation is such that the left hemisphere appears to be adapted for the processing of linguistic-analytical information, and the right hemisphere for the processing of visuo-spatial information (for reviews see Zangwill, 1960; Dimond and Beaumont, 1974).

For left-handed subjects the situation is less clear cut. There is evidence to suggest that in some of these subjects the right hemisphere is specialised for language-processing, though estimates vary (compare, for example, Milner et al., 1964; Rossi and Rosadini, 1967). Some workers have also reported a bilateral representation of speech function in left-handed subjects (Zangwill, 1960; Hecaen and Sauguet, 1971). However, it is generally agreed that such subjects have less well differentiated hemispheres with respect to

linguistic functions than right-handed subjects (Annett, 1970).

Levy (1969) believes that a reduction of lateralisation in sinistrals is detrimental due to a basis incompatibility between the neurological organisation underlying verbal and visuo-spatial types of processes (cf. Semmes, 1968); performance is reduced because of increased interhemispheric interference. Thus decrements in performance on, for example, certain visuo-spatial intelligence scales have been reported in left-handed subjects (Levy, 1969; Miller, 1971); and also on certain perceptual activities (Nebes, 1971), and image-drawing from memory (Nebes and Briggs, 1974). Others have considered the relationship between handedness, speech and language disorders (e.g. Orton, 1937; Woods, 1960; Crookes and Greene, 1963), reading (e.g. Cohn, 1961), and other abilities and attainments (Clark, 1957; Douglas et al., 1967b; Rutter et al., 1970; Annett and Turner, 1974; Newcombe et al., 1975). Many of the studies of handedness are open to criticism, mainly because of the use of small numbers of subjects or of selected samples which may, at least in part, explain the abundance of conflicting results in this area. Here we report some of the developmental correlates of handedness in a large nationally representative sample of 11-year-old children.

Method

Assessments

(1) Handedness, for this preliminary study, was assessed during the parental interview from the mother's knowledge of which hand the study child normally uses. It is appreciated that the use of a single assessment is open to criticism from several points of view, as different modes of assessment can yield different proportions of handedness within the three categories (e.g. Annett, 1970). Referring to a variety of motor tasks, Provins and Cunliffe (1972, p. 205) found that 'not only does the degree of superiority of one hand over the other vary from task to task, but also from one performance to another on all but the most highly practised and skill demanding tasks'.

* Original sources: Calnan, M. and Richardson, K., 'Developmental correlates of handedness', *Journal of Human Biology*, 3 (4) 1976; Calnan, M., Douglas, T. W. B. and Goldstein, H., 'Tonsillectomy and circumcision — comparisons of two cohorts', *International Journal of Epidomiology*, 7 (1) 1978; Peckham, C. S., Marshall, W. and Dugeon, I., 'Rubella variation in school girls: factors affecting vaccine up-take', *British Medical Journal* 1 (6063) 1977; Pearson, R. and Richardson, K., 'Smoking habits of 16-year-olds in the National Child Development Study', *Public Health*, 92 (3) 1978; Fogelman, K. 'Drinking among 16-year-olds', *Concern*, 29, 1978.

In view of the dilemmas that constantly arise as to what provides the most significant picture of laterality behaviour (cf. Oldfield, 1971), the mother's report seemed to us to provide a usable index of everyday hand usage. However, we have provided some collateral evidence in support of its discriminatory power, namely which hand the study child wrote with; which hand was used for ball-throwing in a one-shot trial during a medical examination; and the 'square-making' facility (see below) of each hand of subjects in each category of hand preference.

(2) Reading, mathematics and general ability tests scores.

(3) Teacher's reports on 'speech problems' and 'poor control of hands'.

(4) Assessment of defects of articulation and stammers were carried out by doctors during the medical examination of each child. Doctors administered a clinical speech test as part of this assessment, and recorded the number of mispronounced words in repeated sentences. Doctors also administered a 'square-making' test which consisted of pencilling diagonals across as many squares as possible in the period of one minute, using each hand in turn.

(5) Assessment of syntactic maturity and writing productivity was achieved by calculating the mean numbers of words in the written compositions of a random sub-sample of the cohort, and by calculating the mean minimal terminable unit length (MTUL) in the same essays (the latter is a measure of sentence-structuring skills — cf. Hunt, 1965; Richardson *et al.*, 1976a: see pp. 341–9).

Statistics

Analyses of variance were carried out on certain parts of the data, and these are summarised in the next section. The full tables are presented in the Appendix.

Results

The degree of concordance between the mother's report of handedness and the mother's report of which hand is used for writing is indicated in Table 10.1. For both left- and right-handed children the extent of disagreement was small, 2.52 per cent and 6.09 per cent respectively. However, children reported to be left-handed were more likely to write with their right hands than vice versa.

Table 10.2 shows the degree of concordance between the mother's report of handedness and the hand used for throwing a ball during the medical examination. This revealed that a rather greater number of sinistrals exhibited right-handed tendencies than was the case for writing, whereas dextrals were consistent on this test. Again, ambidextrous subjects exhibited greater right- than left-handed tendencies.

The differences between the handedness groups on a rough test of finger dexterity, namely square-making, are shown in Table 10.3. It can be seen that sinistrals and dextrals, as defined above, exhibited an exact inverse relationship in degree of superiority of one hand over the other on this test; the mixed-handed group occupied an intermediate position, though performing better on the average with their

TABLE 10.1   *Degree of concordance — laterality*

Mother's report of hand child writes with	Mother's report of hand normally used			
	Left hand	Right hand	Mixed	Total
Left hand	813	5	91	909
Right hand	21	5 747	363	6 131
Don't know	1	2	4	7
	835	5 754	458	7 047

TABLE 10.2   *Handedness and ball-throwing (per cent — N in brackets)*

Mother's report	R.H.	L H.	R. & L.H.	Total
Left hand	27.2 (352)	72.8 (944)	(0)	100 (1 296)
Right hand	98.7 (10 571)	1.3 (136)	0.1 (7)	100 (10 714)
Mixed	79.8 (564)	20.2 (143)	0.01 (1)	100 (707)

right hands. These relationships were statistically significant (see Table 10.6 below) and can be thought of as lending some validity to the assessment of handedness adopted throughout this study.

Table 10.4 shows that there were no substantial social-class differences in the proportion of left and mixed handedness (social class was defined according to the Registrar-General's classification of fathers' occupations).

Table 10.5 shows the distribution of three categories of handedness for each sex. From this table it is clear that relatively more of the boys (11.7 per cent) than girls (8.5 per cent) were left-handed. Similarly more of the boys (6.6 per cent) than girls (4.5 per cent) were reported as being mixed-handed. Thus 10.4 per cent of the cohort as a whole were left-handed; and 5.8 per cent were mixed-handed.

The relationships between handedness and performance in general ability (resolved into verbal and

TABLE 10.3 *Handedness and square-marking*

Hand used	Mean squares marked (N in brackets)		
	L.H.	R.H.	M.
Left hand	90.2 (1 159)	66.9 (9 621)	72.9 (634)
Right hand	68.8 (1 158)	92.0 (9 616)	86.0 (633)

TABLE 10.4   *Handedness and social class (per cent — N in brackets)*

Social class	L.H.	R.H.	M.	Total
I	10.1 (73)	83.8 (608)	6.2 (45)	726
II	10.3 (243)	84.7 (1 999)	5.0 (119)	2 361
III—NM	10.3 (124)	84.4 (1 000)	6.2 (74)	1 198
III—M	10.5 (580)	83.6 (4 639)	5.9 (325)	5 544
IV	10.0 (225)	84.7 (194)	5.3 (119)	538
V	10.6 (82)	85.2 (659)	3.8 (29)	770

TABLE 10.5   *Three categories of handedness for each sex (per cent — N in brackets)*

	L.H.	R.H.	M.	Total
Boys	11.7 (682)	81.7 (4 700)	6.6 (384)	5 800
Girls	8.5 (472)	87.0 (4 828)	4.5 (250)	5 576

TABLE 10.6   *Tests of the association of handedness and developmental variables after adjustment for sex†*

Dependent variable	Fitted constants			χ^2 on 2 df
	Left	Right	Mixed	
Verbal score	−0.6	0.4	0.2	14.0***
Non-verbal score	−0.5	0.3	0.2	12.1**
Reading comprehension score	−0.5	0.1	0.3	6.8*
Mathematics score	−0.4	0.2	0.2	5.0
MTUL	−0.02	0.5	−0.03	4.6
Composition length	−0.5	0.0	0.5	1.4
Square-marking (right hand)	−0.77	0.53	0.24	639.6***
Square-marking (left hand)	0.76	−0.55	−0.21	638.7***

† See Appendix tables for details
Significance levels: *** $p < 0.001$
                        ** $p < 0.01$
                        * $p < 0.05$
                        Otherwise ns.

non-verbal components), reading comprehension, writing productivity, syntactic maturity and square-making were investigated by means of analyses of variance that took account of the sex differences. The results of tests of association are summarised in Table 10.6 and the analyses of variance are presented in Tables A1—A8 in the Appendix. Table 10.6 shows, first of all, a statistically significant association between handedness and performance on both components of the general ability test; left-handers scored slightly below right-handers, while mixed-ability children occupied intermediate positions. Similarly there was evidence of a slight, but still significant, association between handedness and reading comprehension score. However, there were no significant differences in performance between right-handed and non-right-handed groups on the mathematics test. It must be stressed that these associations are marginal, accounting for very little of the variance of performance on these measures. Tables 10.6 also shows that there was no significant association between writing productivity and handedness, nor between syntactic maturity (MTUL) and handedness.

It can be seen in Table 10.7 that when teachers were asked whether the children in question suffered from 'poor control of hands' the responses they produced were significantly associated with handedness.

The prevalence of speech problems among our categories of handedness was also assessed by analysis of variance, the results of which are summarised in Table 10.8 and presented in full in Table A9 in the Appendix. The three different assessments reflect different social and clinical criteria (for further details and discussion see Calnan and Richardson, 1975: see pp. 127—36). However, non-right-handed children showed a greater prevalence of speech problems according to teachers' impressions (difficult to understand because of poor speech), but not according to the clinical speech test (mispronunciations) or doctors' assessments (defect of articulation or stammer).

Discussion

Estimates of the prevalence of left and mixed handedness among Western and European populations have varied a good deal. Hecaen and de Ajuriaguerra (1964), in their review of estimates, quote frequencies ranging from 2 to 16 per cent. However, it is quite likely that these frequencies decrease with older groups of subjects (Douglas *et al.*, 1967b). Even so, our estimates of 10 per cent of left-handedness and 5.8 per cent of mixed-handedness exceed those of Douglas *et al.*, 1967b). They have consistently reported about 2—3 per cent more left-handedness among Development. They quote frequencies of about 6 per cent overall for left-handedness, and almost 10 per cent for 'inconsistent' handedness. It seems likely that differences in modes of assessment would account for part of this discrepancy. An additional possibility is the reduced parental and social pressures on left-handers to transfer their preference (Levy, 1974), though only twelve years separate the National Survey and the present study. When interpreted in terms of 'non-right-handedness', however, the frequencies agree closely.

The sex differences found in the present study closely agree with those reported in many previous ones (e.g. Clark, 1957; Annett and Turner, 1974; Douglas *et al.*, 1967b). They have consistently reported about 2—3 per cent more left-handedness among boys compared with girls. Kimura (1967) believes this reflects a male developmental lag in hemispheric specialisation; if this is so, it does not appear to have the expected consequences for linguistic proficiency. An alternative explanation might be that with respect

TABLE 10.8 *Test of the association of handedness and speech problems after adjustment for sex†*

Assessment	x^2 on 2 df
Teacher	6.8*
Doctor	1.2
Speech test	4.8

† See Appendix tables for details
Significance levels: *$p < 0.05$; otherwise ns.

TABLE 10.7　*Handedness and 'poor control of hands' (per cent — N in brackets)*

	L.H.	R.H.	M.
Certainly	4.4　(56)	2.5　(263)	4.0　(28)
Somewhat	19.3 (247)	15.7 (1 649)	16.0 (113)
Not at all	76.0 (977)	81.7 (8 581)	80.0 (565)

Poor control of hands x handedness: $x^2 = 31.5$, df. = 2; $p < 0.001$.

to handedness girls conform to the 'norm', or yield to pressures, more readily.

Annett and Turner (1974), Douglas *et al.* (1967), Rutter *et al.* (1970) and Newcombe *et al.* (1975) found that left-handed subjects did not score significantly below right-handed children on attainment or ability tests. Some, however, along with Zangwill (1960) and Berman (1971), reported attainment deficits among ambidextrous or inconsistent-handed individuals, whereas Newcombe *et al.* (1975) found ambidexterity to be associated with slightly higher IQ test scores. We have found that both groups of non-right-handed subjects scored significantly below dextrals on the general ability and reading comprehension tests, though it must be stressed that the differences were marginal.

The marginal nature of these differences also fails to clarify the status of the inter-hemispheric interference hypothesis (Levy, 1969). It is true that sinistrals scored slightly below dextrals on the non-verbal component of the general ability test. It is also true that the items concerned were of a visuo-spatial type (see example, Figure 10.1a), though not of the 'performance' type on which Levy's (1969) hypothesis was based. Thus there is some support for that hypothesis. However, sinistrals also performed significantly below dextrals on the verbal component of the general ability test. This counters the hypothesis, since interference is presumed to be restricted to the right (visuo-spatial) cerebral hemisphere (Levy, 1969). On the other hand, the verbal items concerned were not of the linguistic-analytical sort common to mental ability or IQ tests; indeed, they also could be said to contain a visuo-spatial element (see example, Figure 10.1b). In fact, the items of the reading comprehension test (see example, Figure 10.1c) more approximate the conventional verbal items of IQ tests. Yet on these items, too, sinistrals scored significantly below dextrals. Again, however, it must be pointed out that the differences were small, handedness accounting for only a very small proportion of the total variance on these tests.

Gazzaniga (1970) has suggested that verbal comprehension is represented in both hemispheres (which our test results cannot refute); it is verbal production in which the hemispheres are differentiated. If sinistrals have a lower degree of cerebral hemispheric differentiation (e.g. Annett, 1970) we might expect some association between non-right-handedness and 'speech problems'. The present data offer marginal support for this hypothesis, though analysis of variance revealed no relationship between non-right-handedness and either speech-test mispronunciations or doctors' assessments. An association between left-handedness and being 'difficult to understand because of poor speech' (teachers' reports) was significant

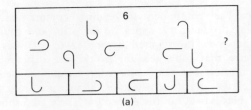

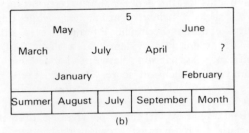

You can arrange a (money, summer, journey, job, weather) through a travel agent

(c)

FIGURE 10.1 *Examples of items comprising the (a) non-verbal general ability test; (b) verbal ability test; (c) reading comprehension test*

only at the 5 per cent level. Since the early work of Orton (1937), many workers have postulated a connection between speech disorder and hand preference, especially with respect to stuttering (for a review see Clark, 1957). The present results agree more with those of Douglas *et al.* (1967b), who found little evidence for such a connection.

With respect to writing skills there has been a general view that left-handers are 'bad writers' and suffer more from fatigue over long periods of writing (cf. Clark, 1957). In the written compositions reported on here, the subjects were timed to write for thirty minutes. The non-right-handers as a whole wrote as much as the right-handers. These results support those of Clark (1957). Shanon (1974) reviewed a number of studies suggesting that the purported effects of incomplete lateralisation are restricted to the level of phonetics, perception and recall, but also occur at the level of syntax. The syntactic measure used in the present analyses (T-unit length: an index of sentence-structuring maturity devised by Hunt, 1965) revealed no statistically significant deficiencies in the case of non-right-handers. Similarly we found that left-handers with their preferred hand were as good at marking squares as were right-handers. However, non-dextrality was quite significantly associated with teachers' reports concerning 'poor control of hands'. This is difficult to explain, unless teachers are susceptible to 'over-attribution' of suggested symptoms with 'deviant' individuals. We have found this to be so with teachers' assessments of 'speech problems' among social class V children (Calnan and Richardson, 1976b).

In summary, the frequencies of deviant hand preferences reported here are in broad agreement with previous studies, as are the sex differences. We were unable to find any strong evidence that non-right-handed individuals are handicapped relative to their right-handed counterparts, with the possible exception of 'poor speech' (as defined by teachers) and performance on certain reading and general ability attainment tests (where the average differences were very small). These results are in broad agreement with the findings of Douglas *et al.* (1967b) on a comparable, and also representative, group of subjects.

APPENDIX: RESULTS OF ANALYSES OF VARIANCE

Significance levels are denoted as follows:

***	$p < 0.001$
**	$0.001 < p < 0.001$
*	$0.01 < p < 0.05$

Otherwise $0.05 < p$

TABLE A1   *Handedness and mean verbal ability score*

Dependent variable is 11-year verbal score
Independent variables are:
1. Handedness: left, right, mixed
2. Sex
Sample size　　　　　　 = 12 851
Dependent variable mean = 22.2
Total variance　　　　　 = 87.0

Fitted constants and analysis of variance table (χ^2 values are adjusted for the other factor)

Source		Fitted constant	Standard error	df	χ^2
Overall		22.0			
	left	−0.6			
Handedness:	right	0.4		2	14.0***
	mixed	0.2			
Sex: boy—girl		−2.0	0.16	1	152.3***

Residual variance = 85.9
Test: Sex x Handedness interaction χ^2 = 0.9 (df = 2)

TABLE A2   *Handedness and non-verbal ability score*

Dependent variable is 11-year non-verbal score
Independent variables are:
1. Handedness: left, right, mixed
2. Sex.
Sample size　　　　　　 = 12 851
Dependent variable mean = 21.0
Total variance　　　　　 = 57.5

Fitted constants and analysis of variance table (χ^2 values are adjusted for the other factor)

Source		Fitted constant	Standard error	df	χ^2
Overall		20.8			
	left	−0.5			
Handedness:	right	0.3		2	12.1**
	mixed	0.2			
Sex: boy—girl		−0.2	0.13	1	2.3

Residual variance = 57.4
Test: Sex x Handedness interaction χ^2 = 0.1 (df = 2)

TABLE A3   *Handedness and reading comprehension score*

Dependent variable is 11-year reading score
Independent variables are:
1. Handedness: left, right, mixed
2. Sex
Sample size   =   12 852
Dependent variable mean   =   16.1
Total variance   =   39.5

Fitted constants and analysis of variance table
(χ^2 values are adjusted for the other factor)

Source	Fitted constant	Standard error	df	χ^2
Overall	16.0			
left	−0.4			
Handedness: right	0.1		2	6.8*
mixed	0.3			
Sex: boy—girl	−0.1	0.11	1	0.3

Residual variance = 39.5
Test: Sex x Handedness interaction χ^2 = 1.2 (df = 2)

TABLE A4   *Handedness and mathematics test score*

Dependent variable is 11-year mathematics score
Independent variables are:
1. Handedness: left, right, mixed
1. Sex
Sample size   =   12 849
Dependent variable mean   =   16.8
Total variance   =   106.9

Fitted constants and analysis of variance table
(χ^2 values are adjusted for the other factor)

Source	Fitted constant	Standard error	df	χ^2
Overall	16.7			
left	−0.4			
Handedness: right	0.2		2	5.0
mixed	0.2			
Sex: boy—girl	0.4	0.18	1	5.3*

Residual variance = 106.8
Test: Sex x Handedness interaction χ^2 = 1.5 (df = 2)

TABLE A5   *Handedness and syntactic maturity*

Dependent variable is log MTUL
Independent variables are:
1. Handedness: left, right, mixed
2. Sex
Sample size   =   520
Dependent variable mean   =   4.65
Total variance   =   0.071

Fitted constants and analysis of variance table
(χ^2 values are adjusted for the other factor)

Source	Fitted constant	Standard error	df	χ^2
Overall	4.61			
left	−0.02			
Handedness: right	0.05		2	4.6
mixed	−0.03			
Sex: boy—girl	−0.02	0.02	1	0.5

Residual variance = 0.071
Test: Sex x Handedness interaction χ^2 = 1.3 (df = 2)

TABLE A6   *Handedness and writing productivity*

Dependent variable is (composition length) x ½
Independent variables are:
1. Handedness: left, right, mixed
2. Sex
Sample size   =   519
Dependent variable mean   =   13.8
Total variance   =   13.0

Fitted constants and analysis of variance table
(χ^2 values are adjusted for the other factor)

Source	Fitted constant	Standard error	df	χ^2
Overall	13.8			
left	−0.5			
Handedness: right	0.0		2	1.4
mixed	0.5			
Sex: boy—girl	−1.6	0.3	1	25.7***

Residual variance = 12.4
Test: Sex x Handedness interaction χ^2 = 0.0 (df = 2)

TABLE A7   *Handedness and square-marking*

> Dependent variable is number of squares marked with right hand (transformed by taking square root)
> Independent variables are:
> 1. Handedness: left, right, mixed
> 2. Sex

Sample size	=	12 704
Dependent variable mean	=	9.36
Total variance	=	1.72

> Fitted constants and analysis of variance table
> (χ^2 values are adjusted for the other factor)

Source		Fitted constant	Standard error	df	χ^2
Overall		8.98			
	left	−0.77			
Handedness:	right	0.53		2	639.6***
	mixed	0.24			
Sex: boy—girl		−0.18	0.02	1	65.9***

Residual variance = 1.56

Test: Sex x Handedness interaction χ^2 = 7.0 (df* = 2*)

Fitted constants including main effects and interaction

		Handedness		
		Left	*Right*	*Mixed*
Sex	*Boy*	−0.80	0.44	0.21
	Girl	−0.76	0.64	0.27

TABLE A8   *Handedness and square-marking*

> Dependent variable is number of squares marked with left hand (square-root transformation).
> Independent variables are:
> 1. Handedness: left, right, mixed
> 2. Sex

Sample size	=	12 704
Dependent variable mean	=	8.24
Total variant	=	1.72

> Fitted constants and analysis of variance table
> (χ^2 values are adjusted for the other factor)

Source		Fitted constant	Standard error	df	χ^2
Overall		8.63			
	left	0.76			
Handedness	right	−0.55		2	638.7***
	mixed	−0.21			
Sex: boy—girl		−0.11	0.02	1	26.7***

Residual variance = 1.56

Test: Sex x Handedness interaction χ^2 = 0.1 (df = 2)

TABLE A9   *Handedness and speech problems*

Dependent variable is logit transform of proportion with mixed or left-handedness.
Independent variables are:
1. Teachers' rating of difficult to understand
   because of poor speech:
   (a) Not at all
   (b) Somewhat
   (c) Certainly
2. Doctors' rating of articulation defect:
   (a) None
   (b) Stammer or stutter
   (c) Other defect
3. Speech-test result:
   (a) No mispronounced words
   (b) 1 mispronounced word
   (c) 2 or more mispronounced words
4. Sex
Sample size = 11 466

Fitted constants and analysis of variance table: main
effects model (χ^2 values are adjusted for the other factors)

Source		Fitted constant	Standard error	df	χ^2
Overall		−0.91			
Teacher	(a)	0.09			
	(b)	−0.03		2	6.8*
	(c)	−0.06			
Doctor	(a)	0.03			
	(b)	−0.11		2	1.2
	(c)	0.08			
Speech test	(a)	−0.05			
	(b)	0.02		2	4.8
	(c)	0.03			
Sex: boy−girl		0.21	0.03	1	63.4***

Test for goodness of fit of main effects model χ^2 = 33.4 (df = 39)

TONSILLECTOMY AND CIRCUMCISION: COMPARISONS OF TWO COHORTS

Introduction

This section uses information gathered in two cohort studies — started in 1946 and in 1958 — to compare the prevalence of tonsillectomy and circumcision among children aged 11. The 1946 study started at a time when informed criticisms of both these operations were beginning to appear. The 1958 study started after a period of twelve years of intense and continuing professional criticism. Our aim is to show the changes in the proportions of children who were circumcised or had their tonsils removed in Great Britain, in different regions of the country, in different occupational groups and in different types of family.

Both tonsillectomy and circumcision were common before the war. Glover (1938) reported that in the period 1919−37 the number of children at public elementary schools in England who had their tonsils removed rose from 42 000 to 84 000. Comparable figures for circumcision are not available, though Doll and Hadley (1950) found that among males aged 15—65 circumcision was more frequent among the younger than among the older.

The evaluative studies so far published on tonsillectomy suggest that for children at ages between 5 and 7 there are some short-term benefits. For example, in the 1946 cohort, removal of tonsils between the ages of 6 and 7 was accompanied by a substantial reduction in symptoms of upper respiratory infection and nasal obstruction (Douglas, 1973c). There was, however, little evidence of long-term benefit in, for example, fewer absences from school.

The lack of even one well-planned clinical trial of tonsillectomy, according to Venters and Bloor (1974), justifies the lack of consensus that exists on the value of the operation, and this probably accounts for the widespread variations in the assessment of children as needing tonsillectomy (Bakwin, 1958; Wood *et al.*, 1972). However, as Bloor (1976) points out, even ear, nose and throat specialists who have a 'common subscription to a corpus of scientific knowledge of ENT practice, phrased in general terms' show consistent variations in their routine assessments.

Circumcision is generally performed during the first few weeks of life when there is rarely any medical indication for the operation (MacCarthy *et al.*, 1952). In this country the value of circumcision so that it is now an uncommon operation performed mainly for religious reasons or for specific medical reasons. No substantial change in this attitude of disapproval has occurred in recent or for specific medical reasons. No substantial change in this attitude of disapproval has occurred in recent years (Wright, 1967), though Bolande (1969) suggests that 'little serious objection can actually be raised against [ritualistic] neonatal circumcision since its adverse effects seem miniscule'. Richards *et al.* (1976), however, suggest that circumcision may be associated with early behavioural changes in the child which could effect early parent—child interaction and have far-reaching consequences for later development. We shall return to this suggestion briefly towards the end.

In the past both tonsillectomy and circumcision were more common among the 'well-to-do' (Glover, 1938; Gairdner, 1949), and marked regional variations were also reported (Glover, 1938) for tonsillectomy. No satisfactory explanation has been given for these differences, which may reflect variations in standards of medical assessment or in the value placed on the operation by different social groups and in different parts of Britain.

Method

The two longitudinal studies that provide the data are the National Survey of Health and Development (1946 cohort) and the National Child Development Study (1958 cohort). The former grew out of a national study of the maternity services which covered 13 687 births in Great Britain during the first week of Marsh 1946. A sub-group of 5 362 children from this cohort has been followed up at not less than two-year intervals to the age of 27. Included in the sample are all children whose fathers were non-manual or agricultural workers and one-quarter of the rest; all multiple or illegitimate births were excluded. The resulting excess of middle-class and agricultural workers' families makes a small difference in overall prevalence and in regional and birth-rank differences for both circumcision and tonsillectomy. The original population can, however, be regained by multiplying by the reciprocal of the sampling fraction.

In order to make the two cohort populations as similar as possible, multiple and illegitimate births and births in families that entered Britain after 1958 have been excluded from the 1958 cohort.

In the 1946 cohort 1 145 children had lost their tonsils by age 11. All but thirteen of these had stayed in hospital for at least twenty-four hours and the records for 90 per cent have been checked with the institutions concerned. The remaining thirteen were reported to have had their tonsils removed at home or without spending a night in hospital, and they have been omitted from this analysis. Thus the proportion who lost their tonsils by age 11 is 27 per cent (26 per cent after adjustment for sampling). Additional information from parents and school doctors is used below to check the reliability of the information that parents give. The information on circumcision comes from questions asked of the mothers at 4 years and from the school doctors' 11-year medical examination. The proportion circumcised by 11 is therefore precisely known but the age at circumcision may have been influenced by faulty recall.

In the 1958 cohort, information on both the removal of tonsils and circumcision came from the parents' answers to questions at the 11-year follow-up.

It seems from the 1946 cohort data that the reports of parents on whether their children have had their tonsils removed are reliable. For example, at 7 years the reports of both mothers and doctors were available for 4 134 children, 860 of whom had already lost their tonsils. There were only six reporting errors, all by doctors. It is by no means certain, however, that the correct age of operation is obtained from the same source. Unfortunately, we have no means of testing this and we have to bear in mind in the subsequent discussion that the ages of tonsillectomy for the 1946 study are exact, as they were obtained from hospital records, whereas in the 1958 cohort we relied on the mothers for the age of tonsillectomy and their answers will have been subject to errors of recall and possibly biased by current views on the operation (Yarrow *et al.*, 1970). In both cohorts the age at circumcision involved some element of recall.

The 1946 and 1958 cohorts use a different method of occupational classification which mainly affects the non-manual working-class group, which has therefore not been subdivided in the following analysis. The manual workers in both cohorts were classified according to skill, though the classification used in the 1946 cohort was based on the 1951 Census and that in the 1958 cohort on the Registrar-General's occupational classification published in 1966. It is, however, unlikely that the alterations in the definition of skill levels during this period were sufficient to distort the subsequent comparisons. A final problem of occupational classification was that the self-employed workers were coded as a separate group in the 1946 cohort but in the 1958 were assigned to occupational groups according to the nature of their work.

Method of analysis

The data from the two studies are first shown separately and then combined and analysed jointly in a series of analyses of variance using the proportions who had lost their tonsils by 11 years and the proportions who had been circumcised by that age as the

dependent variables in a log-linear model (see, for example, Bishop *et al.*, 1975, for an account of this model). The independent variables consist of: (a) 'cohort effect', namely whether the individual belonged to the 1946 or the 1958 cohort, (b) social group, (c) region, (d) birth rank. A further analysis tested the difference in age distribution between the studies after allowing for social class.

As already mentioned, the 1946 cohort sample is stratified by social class, and population estimates may be obtained by appropriate weighting. This has been done for many of the comparisons and the resulting figures have been asterisked. In the analysis of variance, social class is always one of the independent variables.

Results

For the study on tonsillectomy the number of children in the 1946 cohort was 4 186 (population estimate 9 916*), and in the 1958 cohort 13 479. For the study of circumcision there were 2 072 (4 895*) boys in the 1946 cohort and 6 746 in 1958.

Tonsillectomy

By 11 years 25.7 per cent (27.4 per cent in the unadjusted sample) of boys and girls born in 1946 had lost their tonsils compared with 20.1 per cent of those in 1958. This modest fall was confined to operations on children aged 6 years or less, 12.3 per cent of whom had their tonsils removed in the earlier cohort and 8.0 per cent in the later. As Table 10.9 shows, above the age of 6 years there was little change in tonsillectomy between the cohorts.

Both studies show the highest prevalence of

TABLE 10.9 *Prevalence of tonsillectomy: birth to 11 years, 1946 and 1958 cohorts*

	AGE	<4 years	4 <6 years	6 <8 years	8 <11 years	0 <11
% tonsils removed at specified age	1946 cohort	2.5* (103)	9.8* (433)	8.8* (397)	4.5*(199)	25.7*(4 186; 9 916*)
	1958 cohort	1.7 (364)	6.3 (849)	7.1 (957)	5.0 (674)	20.1(13 479)
	FATHER'S OCCUPATIONS	Non-manual	Skilled manual	Semi-skilled manual	Unskilled manual	Self-employed, retired, etc.
% tonsils removed	1946 cohort	30.7 (1 528)	27.2 (1 169)	22.9 (626)	24.1 (198)	24.6 (602)+
	1958 cohort	20.9 (4 235)	19.7 (5 476)	17.9 (2 224)	15.0 (765)	—
	REGION	North	Midlands	South	Wales	Scotland
% tonsils removed	1946 cohort	22.7*(1 038)	26.2*(1 011)	28.1*(1 406)	15.9*(234)	29.8* (497)
	1958 cohort	19.2 (3 548)	16.9 (3 263)	21.4 (3 890)	16.5 (690)	26.8 (1 328)
	BIRTH RANK	First	Second	Third	Fourth	Fifth or higher
% tonsils removed	1946 cohort	28.9*(1 724)	27.4*(1 347)	21.3* (626)	18.2*(245)	17.2* (244)
	1958 cohort	22.5 (5 294)	18.9 (4 437)	16.6 (1 827)	13.2 (718)	10.7 (383)

Notes: Figures in brackets are actual numbers, i.e. *not* adjusted for sampling in the 1946 cohort.
Percentages or numbers starred (*) = population estimates.
+ excluded from analysis of variance.

tonsillectomy in the non-manual workers' children and the lowest in the semi-skilled and unskilled workers' children, and both studies also show a declining prevalence in passing from the first born to the fifth and later-born children.

There have been only small changes in the prevalence of tonsillectomy in Scotland, Wales and the North, whereas in the Midlands, and to a lesser extent in the South, there has been a substantial fall. The regional changes, moreover, are not related to the original prevalence of tonsillectomy. Thus Scotland, with high rates in 1946, shows only slightly reduced rates in 1958, and Wales, with low rates in 1946, shows a slight increase.

These comments refer to the prevalence of tonsillectomy in the two studies when each background variable is taken in turn. They make no allowance for interaction between the variables.

The analysis of variance used 'tonsillectomy by 11' as the dependent variable and 'cohort effect', father's occupation (manual/non-manual) and any one of sex, region or birth order as the independent variables. Thus three separate analyses were done, all of which showed a highly significant fall in tonsillectomy between 1946 and 1958. There were however, no significant interactions.

A further analysis of variance to test differences in the age distribution of tonsillectomy in the two cohorts after allowing for father's occupation shows significant interactions between cohort and age. This analysis also shows that while there are social-class differences in the age distribution of tonsillectomy within studies, these differences are the same for both studies. Thus the shift away from early tonsillectomy is not accounted for by postponement of the operation among middle-class children in the 1958 cohort.

Circumcision

By 11 years 22.7 per cent of the boys born in 1946 and 10 per cent of those born in 1958 had been circumcised. Table 10.10 shows that this considerable reduction has been achieved by a fall in circumcision during the first few years of life. At later ages there has been no change — 5.2 per cent were circumcised after age 4 in the earlier study and 5.3 per cent in the later.

The decline in circumcision is proportionally greatest for children of non-manual workers, though at all occupational levels, and notably among the children of unskilled manual workers, the decline has been substantial.

In 1946 the major regional peculiarity was a low level of circumcision in Scotland and a high level in Wales — a reverse of the figures for tonsillectomy. By 1958 circumcision in Wales was much reduced, and from having the highest rate it had moved to the second lowest. Only Scotland had a lower rate.

In both cohorts the chances of being circumcised were high for the first born and decreased as birth rank increased, and in each birth rank the rates recorded in 1958 were substantially lower than those recorded in 1946.

The analysis of variance confirms both the movement away from early circumcision and the significance of the overall decline in circumcision. It also reveals statistically significant interactions between 'father's occupation and birth order' and between 'father's occupation and cohort'. Table 10.11 gives an indication of the nature of these interactions.

Table 10.11a shows that the non-manual/manual working-class differences in circumcision which were evident in the 1946 cohort have been largely eliminated by 1958. Although the incidence of circumcision

TABLE 10.10 *Prevalence of circumcision: birth to 11 years, 1946 and 1958 cohorts*

	AGE	$<$ 1 year	1 $<$ 4 years	4 $<$ 11 years	0 $<$ 11	
% circumcised at specified age	1946 cohort	17.5*	2.5*	2.7*	22.7*(2 072; 4 895*)	
	1958 cohort	4.6	2.8	2.5	10.9 (6 746)	
	FATHER'S OCCUPATION	*Non-manual*	*Skilled manual*	*Semi-skilled manual*	*Unskilled manual*	*Self-employed retired, etc.*
% circumcised	1946 cohort	29.8 (755)	20.7 (565)	18.9 (301)	21.5 (135)	25.6 (316)+
	1958 cohort	11.4 (2 160)	10.7 (2 802)	9.7 (1 115)	8.7 (404)	—
	REGION	*North*	*Midlands*	*South*	*Wales*	*Scotland*
% circumcised	1946 cohort	23.0* (545)	24.3 (485)	24.9* (664)	28.5* (117)	10.7*(216)
	1958 cohort	9.1 (1 781)	10.8 (1 665)	14.1 (1 946)	8.2 (353)	5.7 (638)
	BIRTH RANK	*First*	*Second*	*Third*	*Fourth*	*Fifth or higher*
% circumcised	1946 cohort	18.2* (858)	22.2* (656)	16.9* (315)	13.9* (133)	15.2*(110)
	1958 cohort	11.4 (2 660)	11.3 (2 288)	8.7 (904)	7.6 (313)	6.5 (201)

Notes: Figures in brackets are actual numbers, i.e. *not* adjusted for sampling in the 1946 cohort.
Percentages or numbers starred (*) = population estimates.
+ excluded from analysis of variance.

TABLE 10.11   *Prevalence of circumcision: birth to 11 years by (a) father's occupation and region and (b) father's occupation and birth rank (1946 and 1958 cohorts)*

		North	Midlands	South	Wales	Scotland
		(a) REGION – PER CENT CIRCUMCISED BY 11				
1946 cohort	Non-manual	27.1	29.7	35.4	28.4	16.0
	Manual	17.6	19.6	24.0	18.6	9.9
1958 cohort	Non-manual	9.9	11.1	14.0	10.5	5.3
	Manual	9.4	10.5	13.3	10.0	5.1

		First	Second	Third	Fourth	Fifth or higher
		(b) BIRTH RANK – PER CENT CIRCUMCISED BY 11				
1946 cohort	Non-manual	30.0	30.0	30.1	20.6	34.4
	Manual	24.7	22.3	16.4	19.5	9.6
1958 cohort	Non-manual	11.6	11.6	11.6	7.3	13.8
	Manual	11.8	10.5	7.5	9.6	4.2

dropped considerably in all occupational groups, the largest reduction occurred in the non-manual sector. This change occurred uniformly for each of the regions. Table 10.11b shows that in both studies, birth rank makes no difference to the risk of circumcision among middle-class children. But among the manual working-class children, the risk falls off steeply with increasing birth rank in both the 1946 and 1958 cohorts.

Discussion

The prevalence of tonsillectomy fell from 26 per cent in the 1946 cohort to 20 per cent in the 1958 and the prevalence of circumcision from 23 per cent* to 11 per cent. In both operations the main fall appears to have been in early life, the first six years with tonsillectomy and the first year with circumcision. However the ages given for tonsillectomy in the 1958 cohort were those recalled by the mothers, and the ages of circumcision depended on recall in both cohorts. Remembered events tend to be advanced in time and this could explain part of the age differences described. On the other hand, we have found that hospital admissions very early in a child's life are remembered with great accuracy by mothers, and it is only after children have reached the age of 2 that serious errors of recall occur. Early circumcisions are unlikely to be placed wrongly and the removal of tonsils in the pre-school years would be expected to be differentiated by mothers from their removal after 6 years. We therefore feel these age changes are not artefacts.

There was perhaps less agreement in the medical profession about the undesirability of tonsillectomy than about the undesirability of circumcision. In many respects, however, the latter has less to be said

against it as an operation and more to recommend it. It makes negligible calls on surgical resources and hospital beds, and complications are rare. It is now evident that the majority of tight foreskins retract in later life, but when there are clinical reasons for the removal of the foreskin a successful cure is the outcome. Circumcised men rarely get cancer of the penis, are less vulnerable to venereal infection, and their wives may have a reduced risk of cervical cancer.

Circumcision is usually performed at an age when there seems little need to bother about the pain inflicted. In rats, however, early painful stimuli may have long-lasting effects and it has been suggested that human infants also may be similarly affected. Richards *et al.* (1976) suggest that circumcision at birth may result in disturbances of behaviour that alter mother–child relations and could have long-term implications for development. However, in the 1946 study no difference between uncircumcised and circumcised was found for a number of developmental and behavioural indices once birth rank, country of origin, occupational group and religion were allowed for. There is thus no reason to believe that the early pain of circumcision has any long-term developmental effect even if there is evidence that suggests that circumcision may be related to early disturbance of the relationship between mother and child.

That circumcision has been so markedly reduced during these 10 years and more recently is explained by the very early age at which this operation is usually carried out so that refusal to circumcise a child immediately after birth is likely to lead to permanent retention of the foreskin unless there are later medical indications. It is clear from Table 10.10 that the decline in the operation has been solely due to the reduction of early circumcisions, i.e. within the first twelve months of life, and probably earlier than this, since 71 per cent of the circumcisions during the first year of life in the 1946 study were done in the early weeks after birth. The dramatic fall in the first year of life may therefore be attributed largely to paediatric opinion exerting itself through the hospitals.

The fall in the prevalence of tonsillectomy during this period was only half that recorded for circumcision and was mainly concentrated in the first six years of life. There have been no social-class changes in the distribution of tonsillectomy in the two studies, and this suggests that the fall has been independent of any generally disseminated views on the undesirability of tonsillectomy since these would have been expected to be best received by middle-class families. The fall in the pre-school years and the failure to find a fall in the primary school years suggests another explanation, namely the different sources of medical advice available to parents and their children in these two stages of life. In the pre-school years it was the family doctor who recommended or refused to recommend tonsillectomy, but in the school years the school medical officers also played a part. Thus, at the 6-year school medical examination of the 1946 cohort children, school doctors recommended that 7 per cent should have their tonsils removed, and during the subsequent year this is the proportion who lost them. In suggesting that the school medical officers were more resistant than family doctors to changing views in the value of tonsillectomy we should bear in mind that in the 1930s and 1940s this operation was considered valuable by school medical officers who were constantly seeing undernourished children with discharging ears, running noses and greatly enlarged tonsils who had not been under medical care in their pre-school years. Indeed, so common was the recommendation for tonsillectomy in those days that the school medical service in some areas was known as 'the tonsillectomy service' (personal comment by a retired school medical officer).

The virtual elimination of occupational group differences between 1946 and 1958 in circumcision and their retention in tonsillectomy is unexpected. A more marked reduction of these differences in tonsillectomy would have been anticipated for the following reasons. First, the advent of the National Health Service made surgery increasingly available to the poorer families, though the availability of private practice may have benefited the affluent in attempts to avoid the delays caused by waiting-lists. Second, the main reduction in tonsillectomy has been in the first six years, i.e. at the age when social-class differences in the 1946 cohort were most marked. Third, middle-class parents would have been expected to be more aware of changes in medical

views than working-class parents. This third expectation is based on the assumptions of a theory of cultural lag (Venters and Bloor, 1974). Future comparisons with the 1970 cohort may help to explain this anomaly.

Why is the prevalence of tonsillectomy in Scotland so high? It is evident that the poor housing conditions in Scotland compared with other regions would put the population at a greater risk of infectious diseases such as respiratory complaints and so increase the likelihood of tonsillectomy. Alternatively, perhaps the explanation lies with availability of surgical resources and differences in surgical procedures. First, Scotland has a larger proportion of ENT surgeons than other regions. Second, it could be argued that Scottish ENT practice is somewhat different and separate from English practice, e.g. there is a separate ENT association. If so, these differences may have led to a heavier reliance in Scotland than south of the border on examination evidence and a belief that a relatively wide spectrum of clinical signs indicate surgery. However, a difference in structure does not explain the large variation between Wales and the rest of the country.

Pre-school children in large families encounter infection brought back from school by their older siblings, and so it would be expected that a high proportion would have infected tonsils and have them removed. Yet in both studies it is the older rather than the younger who lose their tonsils. If it is the school medical services which recommend children for tonsillectomy, the low rates of tonsillectomy in later-born children might be expected since on reaching school these children are more resistant to colds and sore throats owing to their pre-school infection.

Future comparisons with a later cohort (1970) may well show a more dramatic fall in tonsillectomy and a change in the social pattern. So far only figures for 993 children are available (Osborn, 1976). They show 0.1 per cent without tonsils at 4 (the figure in 1958 was 1.7 per cent). A less dramatic change may be found in circumcision since 5.1 per cent of 508 boys in the 1970 cohort had been circumcised by the age of 4 years (7.4 per cent in 1958).

In this study we have presented statistical evidence of an association between a reduction in the prevalence of two surgical procedures and increasing professional criticism about their therapeutic or prophylactic efficacy. However, the relationships between scientific medical knowledge, medical opinion and treatment policy need closer scrutiny, for, as Richards (1975) has shown, there are problems 'involved in the acceptance and rejection of new ideas and the assessment of the value of research from judgements based on narrow scientific terms'.

RUBELLA VACCINATION OF SCHOOL-GIRLS: FACTORS INFLUENCING VACCINE UPTAKE

Introduction

Rubella vaccines became available in Britain in 1970, and in the same year a selective vaccination programme was introduced in which girls between their 11th and 14th birthdays were offered vaccine at school without preliminary serological tests for susceptibility to rubella. In the first place priority was given to the older girls — that is, those aged 13 (DHSS, 1970). Further recommendations were made by the Joint Committee on Vaccination and Immunisation to include certain 'at-risk' groups of adult women of childbearing age such as schoolteachers, nurses, and doctors, and women in the postpartum period who were identified by serological tests to be susceptible to rubella (DHSS, 1972, 1974).

The National Child Development Study provided us with an opportunity to examine the uptake of rubella vaccine by 16-year-old schoolgirls who were 12 when the rubella vaccine programme was first introduced.

Source of information and results

Vaccination of school girls is carried out through the school health service. At the follow-up of 16-year-old children in the National Child Development Study a medical examination form was completed by school doctors to indicate the results of a physical examination and details of the child's medical history, including a question on whether the child had been vaccinated against rubella. This information was obtained from interviews with the girls or their parents and from school medical records, which were available for the majority. Of the 5 541 girls with completed medical forms, information on rubella vaccine uptake was available for 5 097. For the remaining 444 (8 per cent) it was not known if rubella vaccine had been given or the question had not been answered.

The reported uptake of rubella vaccine was examined by region, social class and the type of school attended. Of the 5 097 girls, 3 621 (71 per cent) were reported to have received rubella vaccine, but there were considerable regional differences in vaccine uptake (see Figure 10.2). The highest proportion of girls vaccinated was in Scotland and the South of England, and the lowest was in the North of England and Wales.

When the uptake of rubella vaccine was examined according to the child's socio-economic background, the highest proportion of girls receiving vaccine came from social classes III and IV, whereas significantly fewer children from professional families (social

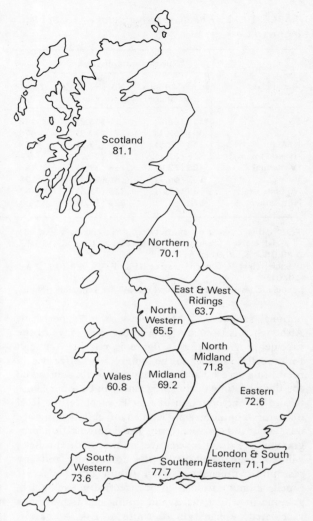

FIGURE 10.2   *Percentages of girls who received rubella vaccine by region*

classes I and II) and unskilled manual families (social class V) were reported to have been vaccinated (see Table 10.12).

The uptake of rubella vaccine was analysed by type of school, and it was reported to have been given to 2 978 (72 per cent) of the 4 118 girls attending comprehensive, grammar and secondary modern schools and 69 (68 per cent) of 102 from direct grant schools. In contrast only 77 (48 per cent) of 160 girls attending independent schools had been vaccinated. This difference is statistically significant ($p < 0.001$).

Discussion

The overall uptake of rubella vaccine reported in this

TABLE 10.12   *Rubella vaccine uptake in schoolgirls by social class*

Social class	Rubella immunisation		
	No. (%) of girls vaccinated	No. (%) of girls not vaccinated	Total
I	159 (66.8)	79 (33.2)	238
II	605 (69.1)	271 (30.9)	876
III Manual	268 (72.8)	100 (27.2)	368
III Non-manual	1 318 (71.1)	457 (25.7)	1 775
IV Manual	426 (72.9)	158 (27.1)	584
V	132 (66.7)	66 (33.3)	198
No male head	35 (61.4)	323 (38.6)	57
Not known	678 (67.7)	323 (32.3)	1 001

Test for difference in uptake between social classes (x^2; df = 1):
social classes I and II *vs* social classes III and IV 10.7 $(0.01 > p < 0.001)$;
social class V *vs* social classes III and IV   4.8 $(0.5 > p > 0.01)$;
social classes I and II *vs* social class V   0.3 (not significant).

national sample of 16-year-old girls is 71 per cent. Although this is encouraging in the early days of the vaccine programme, this figure is not high enough for rubella vaccine to be completely effective in preventing severe handicaps due to rubella contracted for the first time during pregnancy. In October 1969, before the introduction of rubella vaccines, the level of natural immunity in women of childbearing age was about 80–90 per cent. The immunisation programme in Britain is selective, so that natural rubella will continue to occur in the community and any susceptible pregnant women would be at risk. If rubella immunisation is to be effective in such a programme in which males and young children are not vaccinated, vaccination of those at risk — that is, females — must increase this figure to almost 100 per cent. The regional disparity draws attention to the areas where more intensive vaccine campaigns must be launched. In Scotland, for example, where surveys are being carried out to evaluate the long-term efficacy of rubella vaccine (Zeally, 1974), the reported uptake is the highest.

One explanation for the low uptake of rubella vaccine in girls from professional families could be that they are more likely to attend independent schools and therefore to be excluded from the vaccination programme, which is implemented through the school health services. An analysis of rubella vaccine uptake by type of school supported this hypothesis. This finding might indicate a lack of parental awareness of the problem or a lack of structure for administering vaccine in independent schools. This is of particular concern since girls in this group have a higher susceptibility to rubella (Dudgeon *et al.*, 1971). A similarly low uptake of rubella vaccine in

girls from unskilled manual families could be accounted for by a missed opportunity of vaccination owing to school absences, which are more frequent in this group (Fogelman and Richardson, 1974), or alternatively failure to obtain parental consent, which is necessary for vaccination. Although girls from this background will have a higher incidence of protection from natural infection, this is not sufficiently high for us to remain complacent.

If a selective rubella vaccination programme is to succeed, the vaccination of schoolgirls, who are a captive population, is essential. In Britain, vaccination of women of childbearing age should only be a temporary exercise aimed at protecting those who were over 14 when the school vaccination programme was introduced. Vaccination of adults is complicated by the need to carry out a preliminary test to identify those who are susceptible to rubella. It is important to do this so that appropriate advice can be given should a woman inadvertently become pregnant within eight weeks of vaccination, as the vaccine virus itself may damage the foetus (Modlin *et al.*, 1976).

Congenital rubella is preventable, but to achieve this objective the general public, particularly parents and the girls themselves, must be told of the severe complications that may result from getting rubella when pregnant. It is particularly important in obtaining parental consent to emphasise that a previous history of clinical rubella, even when it has been diagnosed by a doctor, correlates poorly with the serological state. Parents should be told that permission for vaccination should not be withheld on these grounds. Clearly if congenital rubella is to be prevented, an increased effort must be made by those responsible for implementing the vaccination programme to ensure that more schoolgirls are vaccinated.

SMOKING HABITS OF 16-YEAR-OLDS

Introduction

In 1964, and again in 1966, the Ministry of Health commissioned surveys of the smoking habits of young people. In the former, 1 161 households containing adolescents (16–19 years old) were questioned (McKennell and Thomas, 1967), and in the latter 5 601 schoolboys (11–15 years old) were questioned (Bynner, 1969). In this report we present the results of a more recent inquiry, an investigation of the smoking habits of young people in the National Child Development Study who, at the time of inquiry in 1974, were 16 years old. Although these results and those of the previous studies are not perfectly comparable, some conclusions can be drawn and the changing situation assessed.

Results

Frequencies

Frequencies will depend on how smoking is defined. In the NCDS smoking was defined as consumption of at least one cigarette per week. Table 10.13 shows the prevalence of reported smoking in the NCDS sample, with data from previous studies presented for comparison. The NCDS overall prevalence is broken down into categories of light, medium and heavy frequencies in Table 10.14, which also shows the sex differences.

TABLE 10.14 *Smoking among 16-year-old smokers in the NCDS (%)*

Cigarettes per week		Males	Females	Total
Light	(1–9)	7.7	10.2	8.9
	(10–29)	8.7	10.4	9.5
Medium	(30–49)	9.2	7.4	8.3
Heavy	(50+)	11.9	6.0	9.0
	Total (%)	37.5	34.0	35.7
	Total (N)	6 115	5 857	11 972

Tables 10.13 and 10.14 indicate: (a) that our large nationally representative sample confirms the appreciable uptake of cigarettes among adolescents, and (b) that the overall consumption has changed little in the last decade or so. It is likely that light smokers at 16 are in the intermediate stage between starting and becoming regular smokers or giving up. The general frequencies and sex differences are comparable with the GSS 2, which in 1966 found that 27 per cent of the 14–15-year-olds smoked up to thirty per week, with a further 7 per cent smoking more than

that. In the GSS 1, 38 per cent of males and 20 per cent of females were considered to be 'regular smokers'. A possible conclusion from Table 10.14 is that sex differences in smoking frequency may have narrowed considerably in this age group in the last few years, while the contrast in frequency between these 16-year-olds still at school and those of the GSS 1 further underlines the importance of transition to work in boosting cigarette uptake (Bynner, personal communication).

Social class

Table 10.15 shows the social-class differences in smoking frequencies, class being defined according to the Registrar-General's classification of fathers' occupations. In general these data indicated an appreciable progression in smoking frequency, increasing from social class I to social class V, though differences in the proportion of heavy smokers among the three working-class groups were minimal.

TABLE 10.15 *Number of cigarettes smoked per week by 16-year-olds from each social class (%)*

Social class	Cigarettes per week					Total N (100%)
	0	1–9	10–29	30–49	50+	
I	73	13	7	3	4	497
II	71	10	6	6	7	1 778
III NM	68	10	8	6	8	969
III M	63	8	10	9	9	3 822
IV	63	8	10	8	10	1 164
V	58	9	13	11	9	454

χ^2 (trend: no. smoked, 1 df) = 85.3***. Conventions regarding statistical significance in this and subsequent tables are as follows:
***$p < 0.001$; **$p < 0.01$; *$p < 0.5$: otherwise not significant.

TABLE 10.13 *Prevalences of smoking in the NCDS and other studies*

	Year	Sample size	Age groups	% smokers 15-year-olds	% smokers 16-year-olds
Cartwright Cartwright *et al.* (1960)	1959	1 578 boys	11–15	29	
TRC 1961	1961	2 340 boys	11–15	25	
TRC 1966	1965–6	1 944 boys	11–15	22	
GSS 1	1965	1 300	16–20		39
GSS 2	1966	5 601 boys	11–15	38	
NCDS	1974	11 300	16		36

TRC = Tobacco Research Council statistics, GSS 1 = Government Social Survey (McKennell and Thomas, 1967); GSS 2 = Government Social Survey (Bynner, 1967).
* 16–20 year olds inclusive and smoking defined as consumption of at least one cigarette per day.

TABLE 10.16 *Regional comparisons (%)*

Region	Cigarettes per week					Total (100%)
	0	1–9	10–29	30–49	50+	
N. England†	65	8	9	8	9	3 348
S. England††	64	10	10	8	8	4 554
Scotland	64	7	9	9	9	1 193
Wales	71	6	10	6	7	520

† Includes North-East, North-West, East and West Ridings of Yorkshire, N. Midlands (Registrar-General's Standard Regions).
†† Includes E. Anglia, London and South-East, South, South-West and Midlands.
$\chi 2$ (mean number smoked) North vs S. England (1 df) = 3.0.
$\chi 2$ (mean number smoked) England vs Scotland (1 df) = 0.9.
$\chi 2$ (mean number smoked) Wales vs Scotland (1 df) = 12.8***.

Region
Regions were grouped into four categories so that rough comparisons could be made. These data showed similar patterns of frequency for North and South England and for Scotland, while a higher proportion of 16-year-olds in Wales appeared to be non-smokers (Table 10.16). A potentially more interesting comparison of urban and rural dwellers was not possible in the present survey.

Parents' smoking and dissent over children's smoking
Information about parents' frequency of smoking was obtained during the parental interview and recorded as number per day. These were matched with those of their children to see if any association could be discerned. This was in fact the case for both mothers (Table 10.17) and fathers (Table 10.18) who smoked, and the apparent influence extended to both boys and girls. Moreover, there was some suggestion in the

TABLE 10.17 *Mothers' smoking and subjects' smoking (%)*

Mother: cigarettes per day	Sex	Subjects: cigarettes per week					Total N (100 %)
		0	1–9	10–29	30–49	50+	
0	Boys	67	9	7	7	9	2 555
	Girls	73	10	8	5	4	2 363
1–10	Boys	60	8	10	11	11	944
	Girls	52	16	15	10	7	738
11+	Boys	59	5	4	11	16	1 212
	Girls	58	9	15	10	8	1 241

Mean no. smoked (girls) mother smoking, χ^2 (trend; 1 df) = 186.6***.
Mean no. smoked (boys) mother smoking, χ^2 (trend; 1 df) = 54.4***.

TABLE 10.18 *Fathers' smoking and subjects' smoking (%)*

Father cigarettes per day	Sex	Subjects: cigarettes per week					Total N (100 %)
		0	1–9	10–29	30–49	50+	
0	Boys	71	8	7	6	8	1 789
	Girls	72	10	8	5	4	1 663
1–10	Boys	70	7	8	8	8	914
	Girls	65	12	12	8	4	733
11+	Boys	58	6	9	12	15	1 605
	Girls	62	10	12	8	5	1 530

Mean no. smoked (boys) fathers' smoking, χ^2 (trend; 1 df) = 73.7***.
Mean no. smoked (girls) fathers' smoking, χ^2 (trend; 1 df) = 55.4*.

data of the importance of sex-role modelling, boys' smoking having closer association with fathers' smoking than with mothers', and vice versa for girls. Of course, the influence of other factors such as parents' permissiveness, general attitudes to smoking and the availability of cigarettes in the home is not known, though they are probably important factors (Bynner, 1971).

In the course of an interview carried out in the home by health visitors, parents were asked to indicate how much they argued with their children specifically over smoking. The responses were broken down according to subjects' frequency of smoking and are summarised in Table 10.19. Although these data suggested that such arguing may be quite frequent, especially among the heavy smokers, and that this is so for both boys and girls, yet there still seems to be a considerable degree of equanimity. For example, approximately 40 per cent of subjects smoking at least fifty cigarettes a week claimed that they hardly ever or never argued with parents over smoking. Whether this is due to parents' acquiescence in, or ignorance of, their children's smoking is not known. Data presented in Table 10.20 suggested that the arguing was more closely related to actual frequency of smoking in the non-manual groups than in the manual groups.

Spare-time earnings and pocket-money
The subjects were asked to indicate the amounts of money at their disposal (a) from earnings from spare-time jobs, (b) from pocket-money received. Predictably, those with more money to spare also smoked more cigarettes, whether the money came from one source (Table 10.21) or the other (Table 10.22), and to a degree more or less commensurate with the quantities of money available.

TABLE 10.19 *Arguing with parents over smoking (for each sex: %)*

No. smoked per week	Often		Arguing Sometimes		Never/hardly ever		N (100%)	
	Boys	Girls	Boys	Girls	Boys	Girls	Boys	Girls
0	1	1	1	1	98	98	3 072	3 115
9	3	3	5	9	92	88	362	159
10—29	10	11	24	26	67	63	413	492
30—49	17	19	27	28	56	53	436	338
50+	25	21	32	39	43	40	552	268

Mean no. smoked by parents arguing (boys), x^2 (trend; 1 df) = 798.6***.
Mean no. smoked by parents arguing (girls), x^2 (trend; 1 df) = 948.7***.

TABLE 10.20 *Arguing with parents over smoking (for social classes grouped as manual and non-manual) (%)*

No. smoked per week	Often		Sometimes		Hardly ever/never		N (100%)	
	Non-manual	Manual	Non-manual	Manual	Non-manual	Manual	Non-manual	Manual
0	0	1	10	1	99	98	2 189	3 477
1—9	2	3	5	8	93	89	329	445
10—29	7	12	21	24	72	64	238	584
30—49	15	18	24	28	61	64	171	508
50+	28	21	35	34	37	45	205	512

Mean no. smoked by parents' arguing and social class: (i) arguing allowing for social class, x^2 (2 df) = 1 531.4***; (ii) social class allowing for arguing, x^2 (1 df) = 16.2***.

Leisure activities

It is difficult to assess the impact on smoking habits of social contacts and the way leisure time is spent. In the present study subjects were asked to indicate whether they participated in certain leisure activities 'often', 'sometimes' or 'hardly ever'. Their responses were analysed according to their smoking habits and the results for those who participated 'often' in the suggested activities are presented in Table 10.23. In this table the statistical tests relate to mean number (estimated) of cigarettes smoked by children and their frequency of participation in the listed activities. Thus these results suggested a marginal association between physical activities and smoking frequencies, but for social activities (parties and dances) the association was very marked.

TABLE 10.21 *Spare-time earnings and smoking (%)*

Earnings	Cigarettes per week			Total N (100%)
	0	1—29	30+	
£1.99	64	21	16	1 167
£2.00—£3.99	56	22	22	410
£4.00—£5.99	47	21	33	277
£6.00+	43	14	43	218

TABLE 10.22 *Pocket money received and smoking (%)*

Pocket money	Cigarettes per week			Total N (100%)
	0	1—29	30+	
99p	69	18	13	3 363
£1.00—£1.99	59	20	21	2 188
£2.00—£2.99	51	18	31	347
£3.00	48	13	39	238

Type of school

The frequencies of smoking according to types of school attended are shown in Table 10.24. These data indicated that 71.6 per cent of subjects attending grammar schools were non-smokers, a figure comparable with those of the GSSs. However, the proportion of children in secondary modern schools who were non-smokers (61.4 per cent) is considerably larger than that reported in the GSS 2 (53 per cent), perhaps indicating a decreased consumption among this group in the intervening years. Of course, at least parts of the type-of-school differences will be explained by social-class differences.

Health

Surprisingly little research had until recently been carried out on the effects of smoking on the health of adolescents. Holland and Elliott (1968), however, showed that smokers and non-smokers differed significantly in reported frequencies of respiratory symptoms (see also the discussion below). Table 10.25 shows the percentages of smokers and non-smokers in the present sample who were found to have upper or lower respiratory tract abnormalities at the medical examination.

The difference between smokers and non-smokers regarding respiratory abnormalities was not statistically significant. But this was only at the time of examination. The parents of the subjects were asked the reasons for any absence from school through illness in the previous twelve months. The responses pertaining to certain conditions, broken down according to subjects' smoking habits, are shown in Table 10.26.

The significantly greater frequencies of smoking among children who have suffered from most of these conditions supports previous evidence. The tendency for children absent from school because of 'emotional' disorders' to be above-average smokers also supports the claims of others that personality characteristics are of importance in determining

TABLE 10.24   *Type of school and frequency of smoking (%)*

Type of school	Cigarettes per week			Total N (100 %)
	0	1—29	30+	
Grammar	72	17	12	1 297
Comprehensive	64	18	18	6 439
Secondary modern	61	19	20	2 597

Mean no. smoked on type of school, χ^2 (2 df) = 59.9***.

smoking habits (Smith, 1970). We may compare our data with the impressions reported in the Government Social Surveys: in the GSS 1, for example, 29 per cent of the 16—20-year-olds believed that their coughs and catarrh were 'caused' by smoking; 58 per cent believed that breathlessness and smoking were associated, but only 2 per cent linked bronchitis with smoking.

Smoking and drinking

Given the association between involvement in social life and smoking, we might expect a close association between smoking and drinking. In the individual questionnaire those subjects who had reported having 'had an alcoholic drink in the last week' were asked to indicate its nature and quantity. This information was categorised as shown in Tables 10.27 and 10.28 and then analysed for association with smoking. Such associations were shown to exist, as expected, but were much closer for boys than for girls.

Discussion

The present analyses of information concerning the smoking habits of 16-year-olds, though inevitably

TABLE 10.23   *Leisure activities and smoking habits of those who participated 'often' (%)*

Activity	Cigarettes per week			Total N (100%)	χ^2: trend (1 df)
	0	1—29	30+		
Outdoor sport	68	18	15	4 240	24.1***
Swimming	62	20	17	5 090	11.0***
Indoor sport	67	17	16	2 788	23.6***
Going to parties	50	23	28	2 181	410.1***
Going to dance halls	51	24	26	2 798	635.5***

TABLE 10.25   *Lower (LRA) and upper (URA) respiratory tract abnormalities and smoking (%)*

Symptoms	URA		LRA	
	Abstainers	Smokers	Abstainers	Smokers
Yes	8	9	3	3
No	92	91	97	97
Total N (100 %)	6 097	3 277	6 101	3 327

TABLE 10.26   *Percentages of absentees who smoked, broken down by reasons for absence*

Reasons for absence from school	Frequency: cigarettes per week			Total N (100%)	χ^2 (1 df)
	0	1—29	30+		
Cold/catarrh	60	19	21	2 967	38.0***
Bronchitis/pneumonia	51	22	28	291	22.7***
Asthma or wheezy bronchitis	64	16	21	129	9.3
Emotional disturbance	46	18	36	213	36.0***
Cohort	64	18	17	11 972	

superficial in parts, supplement existing knowledge. They show, for example, that 36 per cent of 16-year-olds were self-reported smokers in 1974; that 9 per cent of these were 'heavy' smokers; that smoking was much heavier among working-class than middle-class children; that it was heavier among children attending comprehensive or secondary modern as opposed to grammar schools; that frequency was related to parents' smoking; that smokers frequently argued with parents over their smoking (though not to a degree commensurate with smoking frequency); that heavy smoking was closely related to money available, whether it be from pocket-money given or wages earned; that it was very closely associated with

TABLE 10.27 *Drinking in last week and no. smoked (boys) (%)*

Drink in last week	Cigarettes per week			Total N (100 %)
	0	1—29	30+	
One or more measures of wine	57	25	18	461
One or more measures of spirit	42	21	37	691
½ < 1 pint beer	65	18	17	955
Over 1 pint beer	45	19	36	1 839
None	72	14	14	3 065

Mean no. smoked by drinking, χ^2 (4 df) = 407.9***.

TABLE 10.28 *Drinking in last week and no. smoked (girls) (%)*

Drink in last week	Cigarettes per week			Total N (100%)
	0	1—29	30+	
One or more measures of wine	59.3	24.5	16.4	1 118
One or more measures of spirit	42.5	25.1	24.4	1 972
½ < 1 pint beer	53.1	36.5	20.1	838
Over 1 pint beer	43.6	23.4	25.5	187
None	73.0	17.7	9.3	3 623

Mean no. smoked by drinking: χ^2 (4 df) = 58.3***.

social activities (drinking and going to dances and parties); that children missing school over certain respiratory abnormalities were more likely to be smokers than those who did not; and possibly that girls as a group have increased their consumption of cigarettes appreciably.

Thus these data from a national sample confirm the social and demographic patterns of smoking among adolescents that have emerged from other studies, and strongly reinforce demands for increased health education. A relationship between smoking and physical debility has been generally assumed, but there is now considerable empirical evidence of an association with respiratory symptoms, and probably absence from school, among adolescent smokers (Holland and Elliott, 1968; Bewley *et al.*, 1974). Yet knowledge of these risks seems to be no deterrent. Even medical students, with special insight into these and other dangers, are not markedly influenced by the knowledge (Bynner, 1967) or smoke no less on average than do other students (Kropf and Wakefield, 1974). This reflects the social (over and above any pharmacological) functions of smoking: social pressures of siblings and friends, coupled with the media influence, are consistently among the most important factors associated with the commencement of smoking in adolescents (Bynner, 1971; Bewley *et al.*, 1974; Evans, 1976; Palmer, 1970). The situation becomes especially difficult when early smokers may not consider themselves to be 'smokers' (i.e. targets of health education) at all (Bland *et al.*, 1975). Thus a fuller understanding of the social functions of smoking now seem essential and the present results together with previous findings fully support Bynner's (1971) point that 'the need to change the image of smoking lies at the core of the problem facing health educators'.

DRINKING AMONG 16-YEAR-OLDS

Although increasing concern has been expressed about the level of drinking by adolescents, there is little firm evidence available as to its extent. Undoubtedly the statistics for drunkenness offences by young people have shown an increase in England and Wales (Home Office, 1973), in Scotland (O'Connor, 1977) and in other industrial societies. However, not only is it difficult to extricate the separate effects of a real increase and of changes in police practice but also these figures tell us little about the normal drinking behaviour of the great majority of young

people. Spasmodic outbreaks of horror stories in the news media do little to clarify the picture.

It was against a background of such concern that questions were included in the 16-year follow-up of the National Child Development Study on the drinking habits of the young people in the study. For reasons which are discussed below, we feel it necessary to be extremely cautious in the presentation of these results. Nevertheless, given the dearth of such information, and the interest of practitioners, researchers and the general public, it seems that they should be made available, provided that the uncertainties which surround them are made clear.

National Child Development Study

Included in the questionnaire, completed by the young people in the study at 16, was a group of questions on their drinking habits. These were:

1. 'How long is it since you had an alcoholic drink (beer, wine, spirits, etc.)?' To which the pre-coded options were: less than one week; two—four weeks; five—eight weeks; nine—twelve weeks; over twelve weeks; uncertain/can't remember; never had one.
2. 'If it is less than one week since your last drink, please write down the number of drinks you have had in the past week, and what they were (e.g. one whisky and two half-pints of beer).'
3. 'Where did you drink these?' To which the pre-coded options were: at home; at a friend's home; in a restaurant; somewhere else (please say where). Where the 'somewhere else' was stated to be a public house, these replies were given a further code so that they could be separately identified.

In the results section below, we examine the replies to these questions and relate them to background variables and other characteristics of the

TABLE 10.29   *Recency of drink by region and social class (%)*

		Less than 1 week	2—4 weeks	5+ weeks	Uncertain	Never	*N* (= 100%)
North England	NM	53	18	14	11	4	1 262
	M	44	19	19	12	6	2 620
South England	NM	54	20	11	10	4	1 522
	M	51	18	13	12	6	1 739
Wales	NM	44	20	20	12	4	164
	M	42	19	20	17	3	310
Scotland	NM	29	17	25	15	14	309
	M	23	16	26	19	16	790

Overall difference between social classes, $\chi^2 = 73.4$ (4 df) $p < 0.001$.
Overall differences among regions, $\chi^2 = 440.5$ (12 df) $p < 0.001$.

young people. In the discussion section we consider the vital question of whether these replies do validly reflect the actual behaviour of the young people.

Results

Region and social class

The main contrasts which appear are in relation to region and social class. Table 10.29 presents the distribution of replies to question 1 above, in relation to four broad regions and two grouped social classes (non-manual and manual).

Differences between the social classes are small, but are consistent in showing slightly more frequent reported drinking among children of middle-class backgrounds. More striking are the regional contrasts, particularly between Scotland and the rest.

Proportionately, for both social classes, compared with the English, little more than half as many of the Scots reported having a drink in the past week and about three times as many (slightly more for the non-manual, slightly less for the manual) said that they had never had a drink at all.

It might have been expected that, among those who said that they had had a drink in the past week, there were regional variations in the quantity drunk. However, there was no support for this in replies to the second of our questions.

Indeed, little of interest did appear in relation to this question. What contrasts were found were rather predictable: less wine was said to be drunk in Wales and Scotland, particularly among working-class children; more spirits were drunk by Scottish children of both social classes; working-class children reported drinking more beer, particularly in the North of England.

Rather more substantial social-class contrasts do appear in relation to where the 16-year-olds had had a drink in the past week, as shown in Table 10.30 (which is restricted to only those children who had had a drink in the past week). As can be seen, there are quite marked differences in relation to drinking at home — with middle-class children reporting this more often. Differences in having had a drink in a public house are relatively small (it should not be forgotten that 'public house' was coded only when specifically mentioned and so is likely to be under-reported).

More 16-year-olds said they had had a drink in a public house in the past week in England than in Wales and, particularly, Scotland. Whereas drinking in a friend's home was said to be more common in Scotland, this was least common in Wales, where the 'elsewhere' category was named more often than in other regions.

Sex differences

As might be expected, boys reported drinking more frequently than girls — 52 per cent of boys said that they had had a drink in the past week, compared with 40 per cent of girls. There were also fairly predictable differences in the kinds of drink: girls were more likely to drink wine (20 per cent of *all* girls had drunk wine in the past week, and 8 per cent of boys) and spirits (16 per cent of girls and 11 per cent of boys), and less likely to drink beer (20 per cent of girls and 47 per cent of boys).

Income

The 16-year-olds were asked to say how much money they received each week (a) in pocket money, (b) from part-time work, and were also asked to indicate

TABLE 10.30   *Place of any drink in the past week by region and social class (%)*

		Home	Friend's home	Restaurant	Public house	Elsewhere	N (= 100%)
North England	NM	41	24	9	37	24	663
	M	29	22	6	35	32	1 140
South England	NM	46	24	9	37	28	828
	M	37	21	6	43	30	871
Wales	NM	42	17	8	28	38	72
	M	29	18	5	30	34	126
Scotland	NM	44	34	9	22	27	97
	M	25	30	7	19	34	181

Social class x drinking at home, χ^2 = 57.9 (1 df) $p < 0.001$.
Social class x drinking in public house, χ^2 = 0.22 (1 df) $p > 0.05$.
Region x drinking at home, χ^2 = 27.9 (3 df) $p < 0.001$.
Region x drinking in public house, χ^2 = 48.5 (3 df) $p < 0.001$.

the two items on which they spent most of their money.

Table 10.31 shows the relationship between income and the proportions saying (a) that alcohol was one of their major items of expenditure, and (b) that they had had a drink in the past week.

In both cases there is a fairly clear trend, with young people more likely to say that alcohol was one of the main things on which they spent their money, and that they had had a drink in the past week, the greater their income, whether through pocket money or work.

Leisure activities

There was no relationship between reported drinking and reported participation in outdoor sports.

On the other hand, more of those who said that they often went to parties, or that they often went dancing, also said that they had had a drink in the past week. The relationship was particularly marked in the first case — 63 per cent of those saying they often went to parties claimed to have had a drink in the past week, compared with 33 per cent of those saying that they never or hardly ever went to parties.

Type of school

The differences here probably reflect the social-class and regional differences reported above: 44 per cent of 16-year-olds in comprehensives, 53 per cent of those in grammar schools and 44 per cent of those in secondary moderns said that they had had a drink in the past week.

Arguments with parents

Parents were asked, in relation to a number of topics, whether each was something about which they argued with their child 'often', 'sometimes' or 'never or hardly ever'. Included among these was 'whether or how much he/she drinks'.

Very few parents responded positively to this: 1 per cent said that they argued about drink 'often' and 5 per cent 'sometimes'. There were no social-class differences.

What little variation there was generally did relate to the frequency of drinking as reported by the 16-year-olds. Thus, of those who did say they had had a drink in the past week about 9 per cent of their parents said they argued about drinking (often or sometimes) compared with about 4 per cent of the rest. Other patterns follow very much from this — more boys' parents reported argument than girls' and least argument about drink was reported in Scotland.

Slightly more argument was reported for those who had had their drink in a public house than for those who had drunk at home.

Discussion

Intriguing as many aspects of the above results are, consideration must first be given to the question of whether they are in fact correct. Do self-reports of drinking accurately reflect actual drinking behaviour?

Certainly some reservations developed among the researchers working on these data. A few of the replies to the question on quantity of drink were so extreme as to lead one to suspect that they were fantasy. Overall the number of such replies was not large, and they have been excluded from the above analyses, but they must inevitably lead to some uncertainty about the general nature of the response.

Unfortunately there appears to be no independent

TABLE 10.31   *Income by drinking*

(a) *Pocket money*							
	−49p	*50−74p*	*75−99p*	*£1−1.49*	*£1.50−1.99*	*£2−2.99*	*£3+*
% with 'alcohol' among major expenditure	6	5	9	10	15	15	21
% having drink in past week	37	39	43	48	54	56	54
(b) *Income from part-time work*							
	−99p	*£1−1.99*	*£2−2.99*	*£3−3.99*	*£4.−4.99*	*£5−5.99*	*£6+*
% with 'alcohol' among major expenditure	8	7	11	10	15	18	19
% having drink in past week	48	48	52	59	52	55	57

data available to resolve this question. In a discussion of various measures of drinking behaviour, O'Conner (1973) is reasonably approving of the 'how much in the last week' approach, and also concludes that the validity of self-report measures is 'substantial'. However, her discussion refers to studies of adults and one could not necessarily assume that the same would be true for schoolchildren.

The few other studies which have examined school-age children have used methods similar to ours. Davis and Stacey (1972), in their study of young people aged 14—17 in Glasgow, reported general levels of drinking by their 16-year-olds that are somewhat higher than our own figures for Scotland. However, it is known that Glasgow is among the areas with the highest levels of drinking by Scottish adults (Dight, 1976) and in addition there are included in Davis and Stacey's sample 16-year-olds who have left school, so the contrast with our findings may not be so great as at first appears. Hawker (1978), in her study of 13—18-year-olds in five English local authorities, despite statements that drinking was related to age, does not present figures for individual year-groups. However, her figures for 13—16-year-olds having had a drink in the last week are very similar to ours for 16-year-olds, which would not suggest that the NCDS figures overstate the position.

Supportive as these findings are, they cannot, since they are derived from basically the same methods of data collection as the NCDS findings, dispose of our uncertainties about the validity of such methods.

As important as the question of general levels of drinking are the relationships with the other variables which are reported above. Here again, where there are comparable data from other studies, they generally support our own findings. Davis and Stacey, for example, report similar findings to our own in relation to spending power, leisure activities and smoking habits. On the other hand, contrary to the NCDS findings, they report more drinking among working-class than middle-class children, but in both studies the social-class differences are small.

For what is perhaps the most surprising of our findings, the reported lower drinking levels of Scottish children, there is no comparable information from other recent studies. Certainly, in discussing this finding with colleagues in the educational, medical and social services in Scotland, it has met with considerable scepticism. Professionals in Scotland are apparently convinced that teenage drinking in Scotland is at a higher level than elsewhere. However, while there undoubtedly is a higher reported level of alcohol-related offences by young people in Scotland, and a greater expression of public concern about the problem, these are, as far as we are aware, the first data which might enable a direct comparison between Scotland and the rest of Great Britain of the normal habits of a representative sample of young people.

What might explain these apparent contradictions? On the one hand, it could be that, because of the higher level of public discussion and concern about drinking in Scotland, those 16-year-olds felt less able to give true answers to our questions than did those in England and Wales. Given the manner in which the information was obtained, this seems unlikely, but it cannot be ruled out.

On the other hand, if our results are correct, there are several provocative possible explanations. It could be that, because of public concern about drinking problems of an extreme minority, there is effective pressure on the majority of young people not to drink. Or again, if it is true that Scottish adults drink more heavily, could it be that this is, at least in part, because they miss out on the socialising effects of being introduced to alcohol at an early age while still under the influence of their parents? Or is the heavy-drinking Scot a myth — a reflection of attitudes and perceptions rather than behaviour?

Clearly it is important that such questions be debated. For such reasons, despite our uncertainties about the data, which we hope we have made clear, we have come to feel that these results should be made available. We hope that they will contribute a little towards the debate, being based less on prejudices and assumptions than is so often the case — and at the least might stimulate further investigation into the questions surrounding drinking by young people and adults.

IV

The School

11 Ability-Grouping in the Secondary School*

ABILITY-GROUPING AND SCHOOL CHARACTERISTICS

What are the characteristics of schools which practise, or do not practise, ability-grouping? For example, do schools which employ a streaming policy tend to be of a particular size and are they more predominant in certain parts of the country? Do the schools with ability-grouping systems have pupil intakes which are characterised by a particular range of ability or social background? Is mixed-ability teaching employed only where pupil—teacher ratios are low?

Is it also true that schools that are streamed have a more 'traditional' educational philosophy, as suggested by their attitude to corporal punishment and school uniform? That is, is there any evidence to confirm the opinion that 'the fact a school is streamed or not-streamed may be regarded as just one sign of other and correlated differences in regime' (Levy and Tucker, 1972)? This question seems particularly pertinent in view of the considerable interest now shown in the attainment of children educated in schools with contrasting policies. In so far as the schools with contrasting policies differ in the respects described above, different attainment may be reflecting these other factors and not the streaming policy itself. Finally, can any information be provided on the subject which is most basic of all but on which we have 'precious little data' (Lydiat, 1977): how widespread is the practice of mixed-ability teaching?

In particular, we are concerned here with what occurs within comprehensive schools. Many educationalists argue that if comprehensive schools are to be genuinely egalitarian, there should be a policy of no selection or differentiation between pupils of different ability within schools as well as between schools. As Downey and Kelly (1975) suggest:

> Comprehensive education does not follow merely from joining several schools together nor even from abandoning selective procedures, particularly if the old divisions remain within the school . . . nor can it be undertaken without fundamental re-appraisal of the internal reorganization of the school. If we adopt a system of schools that is based on abandonment of selective procedures, we must look very hard at any such procedures it is proposed to use within the school.

Similar arguments are put forward by others: 'The desire to create a society less divisive, less intolerant, more participatory and more democratic has informed the movement towards comprehensive education. This in turn has inevitably and logically brought non-streaming in its wake' (Davies, 1975). 'To differentiate children between schools, and to differentiate children within the school are fundamentally similar practices' (Simon, 1970). 'Its [streaming] effects may be just as unfortunate and even produce a hidden tripartite system, which is no less real though contained in one building' (Young and Armstrong, 1965).

We are concerned, then, with the characteristics of schools with differing internal grouping policies. This subject is of particular interest in the case of comprehensive since grammar and secondary modern pupils are already differentiated by the external entrance procedure. There is also a very sound practical reason why we should focus our attention on comprehensives: among our representative sample of 16-year-olds the vast majority in 1974 were taught in comprehensives in Scotland (92 per cent) and Wales (83 per cent) and slightly over a half of those in England (51 per cent).

Yet while concerned primarily with comprehensive schools, some interesting comparisons in relation to the characteristics of secondary moderns ('junior secondary' in Scotland) and grammar schools (selective senior secondaries) that do not stream are

* Original sources: Tibbenham, A., Essen, J. and Fogelman, K., 'Ability-grouping and school characteristics', *British Journal of Educational Studies*, 26 (1) 1978; Fogelman, K., Essen, J. and Tibbenham, A., 'Ability-grouping in secondary schools and attainment', *Educational Studies*, 4 (3) 1978; Essen, J., Fogelman, K. and Tibbenham, A., 'Some non-academic correlates of ability-grouping in secondary schools', *Educational Studies*, 5 (1) 1979.

available, and summarised in a section before the summary. Here direct-grant schools ('grant-aided' in Scotland) are included in the same group as the grammar schools.

The data

This study is principally based on data from the 16-year NCDS follow-up but includes two pieces of information obtained at the follow-up when the children were 11 and in primary schools: the results of a reading comprehension test and of a mathematics test.

Regarding the data employed, it should be borne in mind that in a wide-ranging study such as the NCDS the priority given to a single topic, such as ability-grouping, has to be balanced against the need to investigate other topics. Therefore, information on schools' ability-grouping had to be obtained as economically as possible. This meant it was not possible to ask a number of detailed questions on ability-grouping policy throughout the school and it was therefore decided to concentrate on a single question which would provide insight into the schools' general philosophy on this issue.

It was decided that the best insight into a school's practice would be given by a question referring to the 12–13 year-group. The specific question put to the schools was:

'Which one of the following best describes how pupils in the 12–13 year-group of your school are allocated to classes?'

To this question one of the following five responses was to be indicated:

1. 'Permanent classes are formed on the basis of ability. Children take all or most of their lessons with the same class, which contains children of a restricted range of ability ("streaming", "banding").'
2. 'Permanent classes are of mixed ability but for some subjects classes are formed on the basis of ability in that subject ("setting").'
3. 'All classes are of mixed ability.'
4. 'Some other arrangement (please specify).'
5. 'Not applicable — no children of this age group in this school.'

Clearly our study has a limitation in that we are unable to identify the precise relationship between ability-grouping policy for the age-range to which the question refers and the schools' ability-grouping policies in the later years of secondary schooling. Probably many schools use mixed-ability grouping in the early years, while assessing pupils who may be later streamed or setted, particularly in the period of preparation for public examinations.

A study in Yorkshire (Lydiat, 1977) found that of forty-eight schools practising mixed-ability grouping, eleven maintained it to the end of the first year only, fourteen to the end of the second, fifteen to the end of the third and eight right through to the end of the fifth form.

Another point which must be borne in mind throughout is that, although the '12–13 year-group' will refer to the second year for most English and Welsh children, it will refer to the first year in the case of Scottish children, who generally transfer from primary to secondary schools at the age of 12.

Since it seems likely that more pupils will be grouped on a mixed-ability basis for the purpose of assessment in the first year than any other year, it is possible that as far as the whole of secondary schooling is concerned our figures may exaggerate the difference between Scotland and the rest of Britain regarding that country's tendency to practise mixed-ability grouping. (Where the Scottish situation regarding the characteristics of comprehensive schools was notably different from the rest of Britain, figures for Scotland are presented separately. No such differentiation is required for secondary modern and grammar schools as very few Scottish children attend them.)

Two more points about the basic data utilised should be taken into consideration throughout. Setting is clearly covering a broad range of situations between streaming (or 'banding') and mixed-ability grouping. In situations where many subjects are setted, pupils may be subjected to a similar degree of assessment to those in streams (see the discussion later).

Finally, it should be remembered that our data are child-based, not school-based, and therefore not strictly comparable with those studies using the school as the sampling unit. Hence discussion is phrased in terms of, say, 'the study children were more likely to be in a streamed school if they lived in Scotland', rather than the outright statement such as 'more schools are streamed in Scotland than in England', etc. In fact, our data do have a distinct and genuine advantage: they tell us directly what proportion of children — who are, after all, the object of concern — is affected by any variable.

Results

Streaming and type of school

A major study of comprehensivisation in 1968 which was followed-up in 1971–2 included a section on ability-grouping policies in schools that were already comprehensive (Benn and Simon, 1972). The data are not strictly comparable with the current study, not only because they refer to schools rather than children, but also because they refer to first-year grouping rather than the second year referred to in the current study. Additionally the definitions of streams, sets and mixed ability are not exactly the same as our own. Nevertheless the crude comparisons possible are very interesting.

The 1968 data indicated that 50.5 per cent of comprehensives were streamed or banded, with a further 14.5 per cent employing a combination of streaming and setting. By the time a sample was followed up in 1971, the level was still 49.5 per cent. From Table 11.1, it can be seen that in 1974 only 43 per cent of our study children who were in comprehensives were in schools that streamed. In so far as the data can be usefully compared, this may reflect a gradual move away from streaming in comprehensive schools. Streaming is less practised, and mixed ability more widely practised in grammar schools. However, 'mixed ability' clearly means little in the grammar school situation where only those in the higher-ability range enter in the first place.

TABLE 11.1 *Ability-grouping among children in the 12–13 age-range at schools attended by study children*

Type of school	Streamed	Setted	Mixed ability	N (100%)
Comprehensive	43.6	40.5	15.9	5 116
Secondary modern	44.1	42.3	13.6	2 226
Direct-grant/grammar	17.7	49.6	32.7	1 348

Chi-square (overall) streaming/type of school = 411.76 (4 df); $p < 0.001$.

Moreover, the fact that many grammar school pupils are not taught in streams does not necessarily indicate a change of outlook within these schools in the period since the Benn and Simon study, since a small 1971 study (Ferri, 1971) also found much less streaming in grammar schools than in comprehensives or secondary moderns.

Region
As already indicated, our teenagers were more likely to be taught in comprehensives if they lived in Scotland or Wales than in England. Further, they were slightly but significantly more likely to be at comprehensives if in the North of England (52.4 per cent) than in the South (48.9 per cent). These regional variations may reflect the pattern of political control in these areas, with the comprehensives found

in those regions which traditionally (though not necessarily currently) have a higher concentration of Labour-controlled authorities.

Not only are our study children more likely to be attending comprehensives if living in Scotland but it is also more likely, as Table 11.2 shows, that the comprehensives these Scottish children attend will employ mixed-ability teaching for the 12–13-year-olds. In fact, the regional difference is so striking that a larger number of our study children were attending mixed-ability comprehensives in Scotland than were attending mixed-ability comprehensives in the rest of Britain, despite the considerably smaller number of children in Scotland in total. On the other hand, in the two other regions where comprehensives were most prevalent, Wales and northern England, streaming was the most common type of internal grouping policy.

TABLE 11.2 *Ability-grouping among children in comprehensives by region (%)*

	Northern England	Southern England	Wales	Scotland
Streamed	52.0	41.4	63.2	18.1
Setted	38.1	50.4	29.7	32.4
Mixed ability	9.9	8.1	7.0	49.5
N (100%)	2 120	1 689	427	880

Chi-square (overall) = 68.2 (6 df); $p < 0.001$.

The much higher proportion of mixed-ability teaching and lower proportion of streaming in Scottish compared with English and Welsh comprehensives is possibly associated with the fact that we are talking about policies in the first year in Scottish secondary schools and the second in England and Wales. However, this regional difference is in line with the Benn and Simon study, which looked at first-year grouping in Scotland and England and Wales.

Size of school
A study of comprehensive schools in Yorkshire (Lydiat, 1977) claimed that 'generally school size is no predictor of willingness to use mixed-ability teaching'. Table 11.3 suggests, however, that, nationally speaking, children in the comprehensives of over 1 500 pupils were significantly less likely to be taught in mixed-ability classes.

Some of the difference could possibly be associated with the fact that often the smaller comprehensives may be old selective schools under a different name which in fact maintain their traditional regime

TABLE 11.3   *Ability-grouping among children at comprehensives by school size (%)*

	Number of pupils			
	750 or less	750– 1 000	1 001– 1 500	1 501+
Streamed	38.0	44.7	43.2	49.5
Setted	44.7	38.5	39.8	40.2
Mixed ability	17.3	16.8	17.0	10.4
N (100%)	857	1 164	2 129	914

Chi-squared: (overall) = 39.5 (6 df); $p < 0.001$.
Chi-squared: mixed ability/rest = 24.5 (3 df); $p < 0.001$.

(including streaming), whereas the large comprehensives are more likely to be purpose-built or the amalgam of several different schools.

There are several possible reasons why the situation regarding mixed-ability teaching and size of comprehensive school is different from that described by Lydiat in the Yorkshire study. First, our own data were collected two years earlier, though it seems unlikely that any major change occurred in willingness to adopt mixed-ability teaching in the two-year period between the studies. Second, our own data are national whereas Lydiat's study refers to a single area. Third, the Yorkshire study referred to first-year grouping policy. Perhaps most important, however, is the fact that this study collected data from just eighty-six schools.

If we do not consider separately the small group of schools (six) in Lydiat's survey with less than 500 pupils, we discover that there does seem to be a slight tendency for mixed-ability teaching to be less common in the larger schools in the Yorkshire study: 50 per cent of schools of 1 500 or more pupils employ mixed-ability teaching compared with 57 per cent of both those with between 1 001 and 1 500 pupils and those with less than 1 000 pupils (the latter result is obtained from combining Lydiat's 0–500 and 501–1000 groups).

Social mix
We have attempted to throw some light on the question of whether streamed and non-streamed schools tend to have rather different intakes of children, in terms of their social background.

The question used to identify the 'social mix' of the schools attended by the study children was: 'Approximately what percentage of children in your school aged less than 16 have fathers in non-manual occupations?' Possible answers were ranged in bands of 10 per cent (0–9, 10–19, etc.). A similar method

was used by Barker Lunn (1970) to identify the social mix of the schools, in her study of streaming in primary schools. This technique for identifying social mix was severely criticised by Lynn and Hampson (1971), who doubted whether head teachers' assessments could identify class background with 'complete accuracy'. This is a valid doubt. Probably the difficulties involved in this assessment account for the rather low response rate to this question. However, given that in the current study teachers were, in effect, only asked to estimate the proportion of parents in two social classes, manual and non-manual (as opposed to five in Barker Lunn's study), it seems reasonable to anticipate that this instrument serves as a broad index of social-class background.

In Table 11.4 the figures are presented separately for Scotland, as the situation there is rather different from that in England and Wales. In Scotland, overall differences do not reach significance (possibly because of the rather small numbers). However, it does seem that schools with a low proportion of children of manual background are the most likely to be streamed and those with a high proportion of manual children the most likely to employ mixed-ability teaching. In the rest of Britain streaming is clearly more associated with schools of a high manual intake and setting with a low manual intake, with no significant differences regarding mixed-ability.

TABLE 11.4   *Ability-grouping among children at comprehensives by social mix (%)*

	Percentage of parent non-manual		
	0–19	20–39	40+
Scotland			
streamed	14.8	20.5	23.4
setted	32.7	30.7	35.3
mixed ability	52.5	48.8	41.3
N (100%)	263	371	167
England and Wales			
streamed	55.2	48.5	42.4
setted	36.0	41.7	49.1
mixed ability	8.7	9.8	8.5
N (100%)	1 155	1 483	979

Chi-square: Scotland (overall) = 7.84 (4 df); not significant.
Chi-square: England and Wales (overall) = 42.6 (3 df); $p < 0.001$.
Chi-square: England and Wales, mixed ability/rest = 1.47 (2 df); not significant.

Pupil—teacher ratio

Table 11.5 demonstrates that within comprehensive schools there is a very marked trend for mixed-ability teaching to be more commonly experienced by pupils who attended schools where there was a low pupil—teacher ratio. (Our question about pupil—teacher ratio refers to the whole school and not just the 12—13 age-range.) Conversely, streaming was more commonly experienced by pupils attending schools with a comparatively high pupil—teacher ratio. If there is any element of causality in this relationship, it may have direct policy implications since it seems to indicate that mixed-ability teaching may only become more widespread with improved staff numbers, and educational policy does not seem to accommodate this possibility.

TABLE 11.5 *Ability-grouping among children in comprehensives by pupil—teacher ratio (%)*

	Pupil—teacher ratio			
	1:14 or less	1:15—16	1:17—18	1:19+
Streamed	24.1	32.0	47.6	48.6
Setted	33.9	40.1	41.5	40.7
Mixed ability	42.0	27.9	10.8	10.7
N (100%)	224	970	2 116	1 494

Chi-square: (overall) = 312.2 (6 df); $p < 0.001$.

Compulsory school uniform and corporal punishment
It has been suggested (Davies, 1975) that

> the adoption of mixed ability grouping is [thus] not merely a structural or organizational change: rather it is a total rethinking of our approach to formal education. This is perhaps why many schools which have rejected streaming have also rejected speech days or the publication of external examination results.

In the current study we have attempted to obtain some indication of whether there is any association between the schools' streaming policies and two other characteristics which are possibly indicative of the school regime (and on which data are available): corporal punishment and school uniform.

(a) *Corporal punishment*. Barker Lunn (1970) suggested that one item symbolic of the more traditional, authoritarian attitudes of pro-streaming teachers in primary schools was their greater support for physical punishment. In the current study, teachers were asked whether corporal punishment

was used in their schools 'regularly or occasionally', 'very rarely', or 'never'.

Again the data on our Scottish study children need to be presented separately. It can be seen from Table 11.6 that in Scotland there was a very high reported use of corporal punishment overall (only seven children — all in mixed-ability schools — attended comprehensives never using it) with no significant differences regarding whether or not the children were in a comprehensive organised on mixed-ability, streamed or setted lines.

TABLE 11.6 *Ability-grouping among children at comprehensives by use of corporal punishment (%)*

	Regularly or occasionally	Rarely	Never	*N* (100%)
Scotland				
streamed	91.8	8.2	0	159
setted	91.1	8.8	0	282
mixed ability	89.8	8.5	1.6	433
England and Wales				
streamed	47.6	43.0	9.4	2 052
setted	29.6	50.9	19.5	1 767
mixed ability	30.9	47.3	21.9	366

Chi-square: Scotland (reg./rare or never) = 0.65 (2 df); non-significant.
Chi-square: England and Wales (overall) = 177.31 (4 df); $p < 0.001$.
Chi-square: England and Wales (mixed ability/rest) = 19.85 (2 df); $p < 0.001$.

In England and Wales, the level of use was much lower overall, and among setted and mixed-ability schools in particular.

(b) *School uniform*. The importance of school uniform was suggested in Halsall's study (1970) of comprehensivisation by the emphasis put on it by headmasters in convincing the community that going comprehensive (but remaining streamed) did not mean a fundamental break with well-established educational traditions.

In the current study teachers were asked 'Does the school have a uniform?', with six possible responses: (1) 'No'; (2) 'Yes, but not compulsory'; (3) 'Yes, full uniform compulsory throughout the school'; (4) 'Yes, specific items only compulsory throughout the school'; (5) 'Yes, compulsory only for certain age groups'; (6) 'Other (please specify)'. For the sake of clarity some of the responses have been grouped and the few in the 'other' category omitted. Again it can be seen (Table 11.7) that the Scottish distribution is very different from that in England and Wales, with compulsory full uniform seemingly rare in Scottish comprehensives while in England and Wales it is much more widespread. The situation is further confused by the fact that the compulsory wearing of uniform is most widely experienced by pupils in streamed comprehensives in England and Wales but by pupils in schools employing mixed-ability teaching in Scotland.

Ability of 11-year-old intake

The question of streaming and ability is not a prime concern here but all the same a note is included on the ability of the intake of streamed and non-streamed schools. It would be a matter of concern to some educationalists if, for example, mixed-ability policies were apparently only adopted in comprehensive schools whose intake represented a relatively narrow ability range since in effect we would only be discussing mixed ability in a 'selective school' context.

Tables 11.8 and 11.9 present the data in terms of raw scores obtained in the 11-year-old maths and reading tests. The only significant overall difference in intake (within type of school) between schools that stream, set or employ mixed ability is that relating to 11-year-old maths scores, where it can be seen (Table 11.8) that in Scotland there is an apparent tendency for a relatively high proportion of children attending mixed-ability comprehensives to fall within the medium range of ability. (It should be noted that our results do not refer to individual schools, but to a sample of children drawn from a large number of schools of each type. Thus, although we can conclude that the combined range of schools of each kind are alike, it is still possible that individual schools of a particular kind are restricted in their ability range. Of course, if this is the case, then such schools must be distributed across the possible ability range, and cannot be more likely to be restricted to any particular part of the range.)

TABLE 11.8   *Ability-grouping among children at comprehensives by 11-year-old maths scores*

	0–12	13–19	20–35	N (100%)
Scotland				
streamed	22.5	46.4	31.1	151
setted	24.1	39.4	36.5	241
mixed ability	19.2	51.8	29.0	386
England and Wales				
streamed	35.1	40.7	24.2	1 824
setted	34.3	38.8	26.8	1 599
mixed ability	33.5	41.2	25.2	325

Chi-square: Scotland (overall) = 9.31 (3 df); $p < 0.05$.
Chi-square: England and Wales (overall) = 3.5 (4 df); not significant.

TABLE 11.9   *Ability grouping by 11-year-old reading scores (%)*

	0–9	10–22	23–40	N (100%)
Streamed	33.1	43.0	24.0	1 974
Setted	32.0	42.1	25.9	1 842
Mixed ability	30.5	46.1	23.3	711

Chi-square (overall) = 4.9 (3 df); not significant.

Summary

Using nationally representative data on Britain's 16-year-olds and the schools which they attended, an attempt has been made to outline important characteristics of comprehensive schools which do or do not practise ability-grouping. It was found that:

TABLE 11.7   *Ability-grouping among children at comprehensives by school uniform (%)*

	No uniform/ or uniform not compulsory	Uniform for certain items or ages compulsory	Compulsory full uniform	N (100%)
Scotland				
streamed	84.9	10.1	5.0	159
setted	87.0	5.3	7.7	284
mixed ability	84.6	3.2	12.2	436
England and Wales				
streamed	21.0	43.8	35.3	2 062
setted	17.9	54.8	27.2	1 755
mixed ability	19.5	54.3	26.2	370

Chi-square: Scotland (overall) = 25.94 (4 df); $p < 0.001$.
Chi-square: England and Wales (overall) = 52.48 (4 df); $p < 0.001$.

1. Pupils were most likely to attend comprehensives in Scotland and Wales, but whereas about half of the study children attending Scottish comprehensives were taught in schools employing mixed-ability grouping for the 12—13 age-range, less than 10 per cent of children in comprehensives in the rest of Britain were so grouped.

2. Pupils in larger schools were the most likely to be streamed; mixed-ability teaching was more often experienced in schools of less than 1 500 pupils.

3. On the whole, pupils were most often in streams in those comprehensive schools in England and Wales which had a high proportion of children of manual backgrounds, while setted schools more often had a relatively high proportion of non-manual children. Differences regarding Scottish children did not reach significance.

4. The lower the pupil—teacher ratio, the greater the likelihood of children being taught on a mixed-ability basis.

5. In England and Wales, within comprehensives, children who were streamed were the most likely to be in schools where corporal punishment was used (if at all). In Scotland, where the use of corporal punishment was much more common, there were no overall differences in relation to the ability-grouping policies of comprehensives.

6. Within English and Welsh comprehensives, pupils who were streamed were the most likely to have full compulsory school uniform. In Scotland a much higher proportion did not have to wear any uniform at all, with, rather surprisingly, children attending mixed-ability comprehensives the most likely to experience compulsory full school uniform.

7. Regarding 11-year-old maths scores, mixed-ability teaching was most often experienced by pupils in the middle range of ability in Scotland. There were no significant differences in reading scores in Scotland and no significant differences in either the maths or reading scores of the intake in the rest of Britain.

Streaming policy and characteristics of grammar and secondary modern schools

1. *Region*. The numbers of children in Welsh and Scottish grammar schools or secondary moderns are rather small to allow comparisons of ability-grouping policies over different types of school in these regions. However, it is interesting that in England pupils in the North were more likely to experience streaming than those in the South, in grammar and secondary modern schools as well as in comprehensives. Pupils were more likely to be taught in sets in the South in all three types.

2. *Size of school*. Although differences regarding secondary modern schools were not significant overall, it did seem that pupils were rather more likely to experience streaming in larger schools. A higher proportion of grammar school pupils were grouped on a mixed-ability basis at 12—13 in schools of less than 750 pupils (37 per cent) than in schools of 750-plus (24 per cent). Also, as with comprehensives and secondary moderns, streaming is apparently more widely practised in the larger schools (15 per cent of pupils in grammar schools of less than 750 pupils were in schools which streamed compared with 26 per cent in schools of 750-plus).

3. *Social mix*. As in comprehensives there are tendencies for mixed-ability and setting policies to be associated with high non-manual and manual intakes respectively, in both types of school.

4. *Pupil—teacher ratios*. No clear trend.

5. *Corporal punishment*. Pupils who were streamed in grammar and secondary modern schools, like those in comprehensives, were the most likely to be in schools using corporal punishment 'regularly' or 'occasionally'.

6. *School uniform*. Setted grammar or secondary modern schools seem more often to have compulsory uniform for certain ages or items than other types, while being the least likely to have compulsory full uniform throughout the school (these trends are particularly marked in setted grammar schools).

7. *Ability of intake*. There were no significant overall differences according to ability-grouping policy in the maths or reading ability at 11 of children in grammar or secondary modern schools. In the case of reading scores, however, there was an apparent tendency for streamed grammar schools to have a higher percentage (77.5 per cent) of pupils in the top-ability range than mixed-ability grammar schools (70 per cent) with the reverse being true of middle-range ability (21 and 29 per cent respectively).

Discussion

The outstanding feature to emerge is the difference between the situation in Scottish comprehensives and that in the rest of Britain. Of course, Scottish education has a different history, tradition and method of central control from education in England and Wales, and the research suggests that contemporary attitudes to streaming in Scotland, at least with regard to the early years of secondary schooling, are very different (or at a different stage) from those prevailing in the rest of Britain.

Pattinson (1963) has suggested that 'streaming, as

an organizational device, must, I think, be seen as a part of philosophy of education which is unsuited to the times in which we live'. Those who accept this may be encouraged by the low use of streaming in Scotland. Yet, as far as the educational philosophy of schools is indicated by use of school uniform or corporal punishment, there is little indication that Scottish comprehensives that are not streamed are any more 'progressive' than those that are streamed. In the case of corporal punishment there is a clear implication that its traditionally high usage in Scotland will survive the adoption of mixed-ability teaching. In England and Wales, however, there does seem to be a tendency for the streamed comprehensives to be those of the more traditional outlook, as children more commonly experience compulsory uniform and corporal punishment in them.

Educationalists who support mixed-ability teaching may also be concerned that the adoption of this policy does seem to be uncommon in two situations unlikely to be changed in current circumstances: where pupil—teacher ratios are high and where the size of the comprehensive is large. On the other hand, they may be encouraged by the fact that the adoption of mixed-ability teaching does not seem to parallel a particular pupil intake, regarding either ability or social background.

Finally, it should be noted that overall conclusions being drawn about correlates (or preconditions) of an end to streaming need to take account of the position of 'setted' schools. Some educationalists argue that setted schools are rightly classified among non-streamed schools. Ferri (1971), for example, argues that: 'While "setting" might well serve to modify the effects of a non-streaming policy, it would seem reasonable to suppose that the formation of permanent mixed-ability classes was more indicative of the school's approach to the question of organization.'

On the other hand, Thompson (1966) suggests that 'streaming' and 'setting' are virtually interchangeable: 'In effect, it is a disguised form of streaming which seriously limits attainment of all pupils except those placed in the top set.'

Our own data do suggest that, in respect of the variables we have considered, in general setted comprehensives are more like mixed-ability schools than streamed schools. For instance, pupils in setted comprehensives in England and Wales, like those attending mixed-ability schools, are much less likely to experience compulsory uniform or corporal punishment than those in streamed schools. In the case of social mix, setted schools show the reverse trend to streamed schools, with more setted schools having a high proportion of non-manual children, especially in the south of England (no trend among

mixed-ability comprehensives). On the other hand, setted schools apparently do occupy a 'middle position' between mixed-ability and streamed comprehensives in relation to pupil—teacher ratios and school size.

Our conclusion must be that while there do appear to be some substantial differences between the characteristics of comprehensives that do or do not stream the 12—13 age-range, such differences seem rather less striking than the gross differences between comprehensives in Scotland and those in the rest of Britain. Clearly any consideration of the scope and implication of the differences between streamed and non-streamed schools must take very careful account of regional variations as well as the period in pupils' lives to which the ability-grouping policies relate.

ABILITY-GROUPING IN SECONDARY SCHOOLS AND ATTAINMENT

'Already, in three-quarters of our schools, the selective system is a thing of the past.' Of course, when the Secretaries of State (DES, 1977b) wrote the above they had in mind the selection of children to go to a particular type of school, and in this narrow context the statement is true. However, the importance of this change could be illusory if divisions between schools have merely been replaced by selective systems within the schools. Downey and Kelly (1975), for example, have argued that comprehensive education cannot 'be undertaken without fundamental re-appraisal of the internal reorganization of the school. If we adopt a system of schools that is based on abandonment of selective procedures, we must look very hard at any such procedures it is proposed to use within the school.'

The case for moving towards mixed-ability teaching in schools is based on much the same arguments as the change to comprehensives. Two major types of premise can be identified. The first concerns the assumptions about children's ability and attainment which are necessary to justify assigning pupils to streams, and the second relates to the effects of streaming on the children. It is because such assumptions are believed to be invalid, and because streaming is thought to have undesirable side-effects, that, it has been argued, 'the onus is on those who use streaming as the organizational lynch pin of our schools to prove their case' (Davies, 1975).

While there clearly has been considerable re-appraisal and change in schools in recent years, reliable figures on the extent of different kinds of ability-grouping are rare, not least because of problems of definition. However, it is clear that in secondary schools the great majority of children experience being taught in classes which are restricted in their ability range, not only at the age of 16, when perhaps the examination structure makes it unavoidable, but also during the early years of secondary schooling (Fogelman, 1976).

The important point is that there is variation between schools, and there are likely to continue to be schools considering some change in their policies. Some schools opt for rigid streaming from an early age, others for setting — forming different classes for different subjects, some of them perhaps being mixed ability — and others for 'pure' mixed ability (although rarely without remedial teaching for some pupils).

When schools are faced with such choices, those affected might rightly expect to look to research results for the answer to important questions. Is it known that one method of ability-grouping is more effective than others in promoting children's educational progress?

Here we limit ourselves to attempting to pursue this question in terms of two measures of attainment: (a) reading and mathematics test scores, and (b) examination entries. It must be acknowledged that the two tests provide only a rather narrow indication of attainment. They may only be seen as indicating any relationship between ability-grouping and progress in these two basic skills, and the results may well not be generalisable to other subject-areas. Furthermore, we do not have data to test some of the most important claims for mixed-ability teaching — such as reducing social divisiveness and increasing tolerance for others. Nevertheless, many will be concerned to know, irrespective of whether such claims are justified, if they might be accompanied by adverse effects on attainment in basic skills.

Previous research on ability-grouping and attainment in secondary schools is thin. In a review, Davies (1975) was able to mention only three studies of children of secondary school age (of which only one was British). Of these, one claimed to have demonstrated 'positive academic gain' for 11- and 12-year-olds in New York who had been taught in mixed-ability groups (Goldberg *et al.*, 1966). The second, a study of the progress between the ages of 11 and 16 of children in Stockholm, found an apparent superiority after one year for restricted groupings, but this was not sustained and there were no differences in subsequent years (Svensson, 1965). The third study, an account of the experience of just one comprehensive school, found no relationship between ability-grouping methods and O-level results (Thompson, 1974).

More recently, a study of Banbury School has concluded 'that the variations in academic performance which occur at the end of the first two years are generally not attributable to differences in methods of ability grouping' (Newbold, 1977). Valuable as this research is, it is restricted to the experiences of one (rather unusual) school.

Research on secondary schools to date is thus hardly adequate to answer the question with which we are concerned. The position for primary schools is somewhat better, there being one outstanding study. Barker Lunn (1970) compared children in streamed and non-streamed primary schools on a wide range of criteria. Academic performance was by no means the sole concern of this study but on that issue it was concluded that there was 'no difference in the average academic performance of boys and girls of comparable ability and social class'.

In fact these same children were followed up into their secondary schools two years later (Ferri, 1971). As well as finding that differences in relation to primary school streaming had not appeared subsequently, the opportunity was also taken to examine the relationship between attainment and ability-grouping in the secondary school. In the event, because of small numbers, this was possible only for children in secondary modern schools. Here again, no relationship was found, except perhaps for a slight suggestion that middle-class children of below-average ability did better in non-streamed schools (but note that the majority of these were setted rather than mixed ability).

There is, then, no study of ability-grouping in secondary schools which is adequate, large, recent and relevant to this country. The study which is described here is by no means without its shortcomings — as discussed below. It is hoped, however, that it will serve as a starting-point and provide some answers to the broad question of whether different methods of ability-grouping in our secondary schools have implications for children's attainment.

Ability-grouping data

The scope and methods of a study such as the NCDS necessarily impose constraints on the kind of information which can be obtained. It was not possible to ask a large number of detailed questions on ability-grouping policy throughout the school, and our aim therefore was to find a question which would give a good indication of the school's philosophy in this area, at the same time eliciting information which was specific and therefore likely to be reliable. It was thus decided to ask about ability-grouping in one particular year-group.

It is known that many secondary schools practise mixed-ability teaching in the first year only, while assessing the children for subsequent grouping (Lydiat, 1977). On the other hand, many schools which use mixed-ability teaching will abandon this as it becomes necessary to prepare for public examinations. It would seem, therefore, that the best indication is likely to be given by what is practised in the second or third years (in a school to which children transfer at 11).

The specific question put to the schools was:

'Which one of the following best describes how pupils in the 12—13 year-group are allocated to classes?'

One of the following five responses was to be indicated:

1. 'Permanent classes are formed on the basis of ability. Children take all or most of their lessons with the same class, which contains children of a restricted range of ability ("streaming", "banding").'
2. 'Permanent classes are of mixed ability but, for some subjects, classes are formed on the basis of ability in that subject ("setting").'
3. 'All classes are of mixed ability.'
4. 'Some other arrangement (please specify).'
5. 'Not applicable — no children of this age group in this school.'

There are some obvious cautions which must be put on our use of these data. First, they will not in fact refer to the second year, but to the first, in Scotland. Certainly many more Scottish schools did indicate mixed-ability teaching in answer to this question (see previous paper). However, this difference between the two countries is in accord with other research (Benn and Simon, 1972), and it is known that the 'common course' in Scotland is generally for the first two years (Scottish Education Department, 1970). It seems therefore unlikely that this will introduce serious problems of bias. Nevertheless, our analyses are such that relationships can be identified separately for each region.

Second, there is the possibility that the school which a subject of this study was attending at 16 was not the same one as he or she had been at when aged 13. Fortunately we know how long each child had been at the present school and all analyses here are restricted to children who had been there for four years or more.

The third problem is not so easily disposed of. Our concern was with each school's current philosophy and our question was therefore about the present 12—13 year-group, but the children whose attainment we are examining were then aged 16. It is therefore possible that, because of a recent change in a school's policy, our ability-grouping measure does not in fact describe the experiences of some of the 16-year-olds. Given the unreliabilities which would have been

introduced by asking schools to remember their practices three years earlier, this problem could not be avoided. Thus it must be acknowledged that this is likely to have diluted our groups to an extent which is difficult to estimate, though what evidence there is suggests that change during the relevant period has been very slow (Benn and Simon, 1972; Tibbenham *et al.*, 1978a: see pp. 233—40).

Method of analysis

The fundamental purpose of the analysis is to make comparisons among children in the three basic ability-grouping categories ('streamed', 'setted' and 'mixed-ability') in terms of their reading and mathematics attainment at 16. However, a straightforward comparison would be likely to be extremely misleading. Most obviously, there is the possibility that the three groups of children differ significantly in their initial ability; that is, that differences found to exist at 16 simply reflect differences which were already present before the children entered their secondary schools.

It is in dealing with such problems that the power of the longitudinal approach becomes apparent. The NCDS has available the test scores of these same children at the age of 11, and these can be incorporated into the analysis so that we are in effect comparing children of the same initial ability.

The preceding paper suggested the importance of other variables which relate differentially to ability-grouping, and which could in turn bring about differences in average attainment. Of particular importance are the type of school — so-called 'mixed-ability' teaching is more common in grammar schools; region of the country — mixed-ability teaching is more frequent in Scotland; and social class — mixed-ability teaching being slightly more common in schools with a relatively more middle-class intake.

Because of the need to take such factors into account, the appropriate method of analysis is analysis of variance. This enables us to compare the average scores of children in schools with different ability-grouping policies who are similar in terms of the other characteristics incorporated in the analysis as independent variables.

Whereas this method can be used to examine scores on the reading and mathematics tests, it is not appropriate to analyse examination entries in the same way (the latter not being a continuous variable and, in this and other ways, not satisfying the assumptions of analysis of variance). As will be seen, examination entries have been investigated by a series of tables which are essentially equivalent to the analysis of variance but for which it is not possible to take into account such a wide range of other factors.

In addition to presenting the overall differences in relation to ability-grouping policy, we shall also be examining interactions. That is, do any overall differences which we find apply equally across, for example, the whole ability range? Or does mixed-ability teaching appear to be more effective for children of, say, low or average ability, while high-ability children show greater gains when streamed?

It is particularly important to emphasise that including type of school as an independent variable, and examining the interactions with ability-grouping, is, in effect, equivalent to carrying out separate analyses for different types of school. It is clear that the meaning of 'mixed ability' is very different in a selective school, where the ability range of any class must be restricted, whereas in a comprehensive school it is at least in theory possible that a class might contain children whose abilities do cover nearly the full range. It is therefore essential that the analysis does enable the separate identification of relationships within each type of school.

Sample and response level

Readers familiar with the NCDS will note that the sample used in the analysis of variance (of just over 6 000) is considerably smaller than the total number of children in the study. In part, this is due to the necessary constraints which we have introduced into the analysis (e.g. excluding children in special schools, and those in their present schools less than four years), but more substantially it is the result of needing to have information for each child on all the relevant variables — gathered from a variety of sources and at different ages — in order to be included in the analysis. There is some suggestion that this introduces a very slight bias into the groups at 16, in that the mixed-ability children with full data have slightly higher mean test scores than those excluded from the analyses. Of course, this does not matter for the full analysis of variance findings as, by including 11-year scores, this difference is automatically adjusted for, but it does mean that the unadjusted comparisons may slightly overestimate the position of the mixed-ability group.

Other variables used in the analyses

In the 'Results' section below, we shall be presenting the differences obtained in relation to ability-grouping after adjusting for all other variables included in the analysis of variance. It is important therefore to describe these other variables in some detail.

Dependent variables

1. *16-year reading test*: a comprehension test devised by the National Foundation for Educational Research for use in this study and used parallel with the Watts—Vernon test; scores on this test have been transformed to give a mean of zero and a standard deviation of one.
2. *16-year mathematics test*: a test devised by the NFER to be used with this age group; scores transformed as for the reading test.

Independent variables

1. *11-year reading test* (used in analysis of 16-year reading): same test as at 16.
2. *11-year mathematics test* (in analysis of 16-year mathematics): test devised by the NFER for use in the study.
3. *11-year general ability test* (in analysis of examination entries): see Douglas (1964).
4. *Type of secondary school*: as reported by the headteacher, categorised as direct grant, grammar, secondary modern, comprehensive, independent (including, in each case, their equivalent in Scotland); all other types excluded.
5. *Sex*.
6. *Social class*: based on father's occupation as reported in the parental interview, and categorised according to the Registrar-General's classification into non-manual, skilled manual, semi-skilled and unskilled, no male head.
7. *Region*: based on the school's local authority, classified into the Registrar-General's Standard Regions and grouped into North England, South England, Scotland and Wales.
8. *Streaming at 11*: at the 11-year follow-up each child's primary school headteacher was asked; 'Is the child's age group streamed by ability?' For this analysis just the two groups were considered — 'Yes' and 'No'. This variable has been included not only to examine whether there appears to be any relationship between it and attainment at 16, but also as it was suspected that the relationship between secondary school grouping and attainment might be affected by a child's primary school experience.

Results

Reading and mathematics test scores

Table 11.10 presents the mean reading-test scores in relation to ability-grouping — first, the unadjusted means, i.e. the straightforward comparisons before allowing for any other factors, and second, the adjusted means, i.e. after taking account of all the other independent variables listed above.

TABLE 11.10   *Mean 16-year reading score by ability grouping*

		Unadjusted mean	se	Adjusted mean	se
Streamed	(N = 2 289)	−0.11	0.06	0.04	0.04
Setted	(2 543)	0.02	0.06	0.00	0.02
Mixed ability	(1 091)	0.07	0.06	0.00	0.04
Other	(153)	0.02	0.08	−0.04	0.08
χ^2		36.7 ($p < 0.001$)		8.9 ($p < 0.05$)	

It can be seen that before adjusting for other factors, it is the children in 'mixed-ability' schools who have, just, the highest average reading scores, with those in streamed schools doing worst, and a difference of just under one-fifth of a standard deviation between the two. In view of what was said above, for example that mixed-ability teaching was more common in grammar schools, one would expect this difference to be reduced by the analysis of variance, and the 'adjusted means' show that this is the case. Indeed, after allowing for the other variables, it is the children in streamed schools who have the highest average scores.

However, it should be noticed that these differences are extremely small. Furthermore, the greatest contrast is between the 'streamed' group and the 'other' group. The latter contains a rather meaningless collection of responses which were too eccentric, or unusual, or vague to be included in one of the three main groups. It also contains relatively few children. Ignoring this group, there is really no difference at all between 'setted' and 'mixed ability' and the difference between these two and the 'streamed' is only about one-twenty-fifth of a standard deviation. There is therefore no evidence in these findings to support a relationship between reading attainment and secondary school ability-grouping.

Additionally no difference was found in relation to whether or not the child's year-group had been streamed at 11.

As mentioned above, tests were carried out for the presence of interactions. There was no significant interaction between ability-grouping and any other independent variable. In view of the importance of this finding it is worth spelling out its exact meaning: the pattern of negligible average differences found overall also holds true for each sex, for each social class, for each type of school, for each broad region, and irrespective of the child's initial reading ability, and of whether or not his or her year-group was streamed at the age of 11.

With one exception, a similar pattern is found for mathematics test scores, for which the unadjusted and adjusted means are shown in Table 11.11.

As with reading, it is the mixed-ability group that obtains the highest mean score before allowing for other factors. After adjustment, the differences reduce to the point where they are no longer statistically significant.

The exception referred to above arises from the presence of one significant interaction, between ability-grouping and whether or not the children were streamed at 11. Given the large number of interactions tested (seven in each analysis) and that this one was significant at only the 5 per cent level (χ^2 with 3 df = 9.2), it would be wrong to place too much emphasis on it, but the relevant figures are shown in Table 11.12.

Once again it can be seen that the main contribution to the interaction comes from the 'other' group. Beyond this there is a slight indication that children at mixed-ability secondary schools do less well, on average, if they were in a streamed class when they were 11. However, given the caution expressed above and the fact that the differences are rather small, the finding should be seen as no more than mildly suggestive.

TABLE 11.11   *Mean 16-year mathematics score by ability-grouping*

		Unadjusted mean	se	Adjusted mean	se
Streamed	(N = 2 281)	−0.17	0.04	0.00	0.04
Setted	(2 532)	0.02	0.04	0.00	0.04
Mixed ability	(1 088)	0.09	0.06	−0.06	0.06
Other	(153)	0.06	0.08	0.05	0.08
χ^2		71.4 ($p < 0.001$)		3.4 ($p > 0.05$)	

TABLE 11.12 *Mean 16-year mathematics score: ability-grouping by streaming at 11, adjusted for other factors*

		\multicolumn{4}{c}{Secondary ability-grouping}
		Streamed	Setted	Mixed ability	Other
Streamed	Yes	−0.02	0.01	−0.07	−0.11
at 11	No	0.02	0.00	0.01	0.17

Examination entries

In the course of the questionnaire completed by schools, teachers were asked to list for each study child all subjects which the child was studying in school at that time, and what public examination, if any, in each subject, he or she was expected to take at the end of the school year. Additionally, the schools were asked to indicate any subjects in which a GCE O level, SCE O grade (in Scotland) or CSE pass had already been obtained.

For our present purposes we have examined the relationship between ability-grouping and the proportion taking at least one O level (or O grade), for each category of the major factors in the above analyses — that is, initial ability, type of school and region.

It is particularly important in this context to take account of region. As we have reported elsewhere, there is more mixed-ability teaching in Scotland, and a greater proportion of each year-group takes SCE O grade than takes GCE O level in England and Wales.

A separate analysis (not reported in detail here) shows that, among those children who were expected to take at least one O level or O grade, there was no relationship between a school's ability-grouping policy and the *number* of such expected examination entries. Thus any contrasts are adequately described by the figures in Table 11.13, which show the proportions taking (or having taken) any O level or O grade at all.

The figures presented in Table 11.13 are for children in comprehensive schools only. When categorised by ability-grouping, initial ability and region, the numbers in direct-grant and grammar, secondary modern and independent schools are often extremely small. All such comparisons, however, have been made, and in no case reached statistical significance at the 5 per cent level.

For comprehensive school pupils, the figures in the table show neither a very marked nor a consistent pattern. Of all the possible comparisons within region and ability level, only two reach statistical significance. In the north of England, among children in the middle-ability range, those in streamed schools are more likely to be preparing for at least one O level than those in mixed-ability schools, with the setted schools' children in an intermediate position. On the other hand, among low-ability children in Scotland, it is the mixed-ability children who are more likely to be studying for O grade than the streamed, with the setted, again, between the two.

Given the contradictory direction of these two findings, and the lack of differences elsewhere, it would be wrong to make too much of them. However, the Scottish result is perhaps suggestive. Could it be

TABLE 11.13 *Proportions taking at least one O level or O grade; ability-grouping by 11-year ability by region (comprehensive schools only)*

		Streamed	Setted	Mixed ability
Bottom third of 11-year	North England	13	9	9
general ability scores	South England	11	17	*
	Wales	9	*	*
	Scotland	39	47	62
Middle third	North England	52	44	36
	South England	48	45	44
	Wales	47	48	*
	Scotland	94	88	88
Top third	North England	86	81	81
	South England	86	85	*
	Wales	89	88	*
	Scotland	100	100	100

*N is less than 30.

Significance tests: within each region and ability level all χ^2 are non-significant except:
  middle-ability children in North England, $\chi^2 = 8.4$ (2 df); $p < 0.05$.
  low-ability children in Scotland, $\chi^2 = 7.1$ (2 df); $p < 0.05$.

that mixed-ability teaching does promote the likelihood of children of below-average ability taking examinations? If this were the case, one might not expect it to show for England and Wales in relation to O levels, which are taken by a considerably smaller proportion of the age-group than are O grades in Scotland. However, if there is such an effect, then it should be expected to appear when CSE entries are examined.

The figures relevant to this hypothesis can be seen in Table 11.14. In this table there is some support for the suggestion that low-ability children in mixed-ability comprehensives are likely to take more CSEs, in that this did prove to be the case in the north of England, the only region which contained enough such children for this to be tested.

A similar result was also found for children in the middle-ability range, where, again in the north of England only, mixed-ability school pupils were taking more CSEs. Of course, this should be taken in conjunction with the earlier finding that this same group was less likely to be taking O levels.

As before, in addition to those reported in Table 11.14, other possible comparisons have been carried out, i.e. for other types of school and for high-ability children. As in the analysis of O-level entries, numbers were often small and, with one exception, no differences reached statistical significance. The exception was in the case of low-ability children in secondary modern schools in the south of England. In this group there were few children in mixed-ability schools and the contrast arose mainly from a greater number of children taking at least one CSE in setted schools than in streamed schools.

Discussion

The analyses presented here have provided no evidence for any differences among children in their reading or mathematics attainment, as measured by standardised tests, in relation to whether they attended secondary schools which reported favouring streaming, setting or mixed-ability teaching, and after taking account of their initial ability level prior to entering secondary school and other related background factors.

On the other hand, there is a strong suggestion that comprehensive schools which practise mixed-ability teaching enter more children of relatively low ability for public examinations. Although this could not be shown to be the case in southern England or Wales, mixed-ability teaching in these regions is relatively less widespread, and the number in our analyses therefore small. In the other two regions where mixed-ability teaching is more frequently practised, there is a clear indication that low-ability children in schools favouring mixed-ability teaching enter for more O-grade exams (in Scotland) and more CSEs (in northern England). For example, in Scotland, 62 per cent of the low-ability children in mixed-ability comprehensives were reported to be preparing for at least one O-grade exam compared with 39 per cent of the comparable group in streamed schools. In northern England the percentages of low-ability children taking at least one CSE were 73 per cent of those in streamed comprehensives and 84 per cent of those in mixed-ability comprehensives. Furthermore, 15 per cent of the former were said to be taking seven or more subjects at CSE, compared with 34 per cent of the latter.

There was no evidence for any differences related to ability-grouping policy in either the proportions entering for GCE O level or in the number of subjects being taken, in England and Welsh comprehensives. Neither was there any consistent association between examination entries and ability-grouping for children

TABLE 11.14   *Proportion taking at least one CSE and seven or more CSEs: ability-grouping by 11-year ability by region (comprehensive only)*

		Streamed		Setted		Mixed ability	
		Percentage taking at least one CSE	Percentage taking seven or more CSEs	Percentage taking at least one CSE	Percentage taking seven or more CSEs	Percentage taking at least one CSE	Percentage taking seven or more CSEs
Bottom third of 11-year general ability scores	North England	73	15	74	18	84	34
	South England	81	19	89	23	*	*
	Wales	60	20	64	18	*	*
Middle third	North England	89	24	89	27	94	34
	South England	90	24	91	25	96	20
	Wales	72	22	76	28	*	*

* N is less than 30.
Significance tests: within each region and ability level χ^2 are non-significant except: low-ability children in northern England, $\chi^2 = 12.8$ (4 df) ($p < 0.05$), middle-ability children in northern England $\chi^2 = 10.2$ (4 df) ($p < 0.05$).

of average and above-average ability in comprehensive schools, or for children of any ability level in schools other than comprehensives.

Of course, the findings relating to CSE entries cannot necessarily be taken to imply that comprehensives favouring mixed-ability teaching are enabling their low-ability children to reach a higher academic standard than those in schools which stream or set. First, we have only been able to describe examination entries. We do not yet have the actual results obtained by the young people in the NCDS.

Second, these contrasts may simply reflect differences in the schools' examination entry policy. This in turn could be the result of a more optimistic (perhaps more realistic) estimate of the likelihood of such children obtaining a CSE pass, or it might rather be that it is administratively easier for a child to be on a few CSE examination courses compared perhaps with an all-or-none situation in more rigidly grouped schools (but note that there were also more mixed-ability children being entered for seven or more CSEs).

That this pattern is a function of entry policy rather than attainment level is perhaps supported by the lack of any difference between the groups in tests of reading and mathematics and the finding that, among middle-ability pupils in comprehensives in the north of England, children in mixed-ability schools were entering more CSEs but fewer O levels.

Even if the explanation is of this kind, the findings should not be dismissed as trivial. If those children entering more CSEs (and O grade in Scotland) are obtaining reasonable results in them, this could prove to be of subsequent significance for the opportunities then open to them either for work or continuing education.

Turning from this specific finding to the general overall pattern, our results should perhaps offer some reassurance to those who see the lessening of rigid ability-grouping practices as a threat to standards in basic skills. Of course, we have been presenting overall averages, and there are no doubt classrooms that depart very much from these. Again, we can only report the situation as it has existed, in relation to the policies as reported by schools. We should assume neither that the situation could not be changed, nor that individual classroom practices within our three school groups are homogeneous.

Given all these cautions, we can conclude that our findings offer no evidence that the adoption of mixed-ability teaching in some secondary schools has been accompanied by any changes in reading or mathematics attainment relative to those schools which stream or set. Of course, it still remains to be shown whether it has been accompanied by the benefits for which its proponents would hope.

Conversely, if the argument put forward by Davies (1975), that it is for schools which stream to demonstrate the benefits of this policy, is justified, then these results do not contribute to such a demonstration.

SOME NON-ACADEMIC DEVELOPMENTAL CORRELATES OF ABILITY-GROUPING IN SECONDARY SCHOOLS

At the time when the practice of grouping each year according to ability was first introduced into schools its advantages were seen purely in cognitive terms (Downey and Kelly, 1975). Since then the assumption that streaming will benefit children's attainment has been questioned (e.g. Barker Lunn, 1970; Ferri, 1971), but in addition consideration has been paid to the possibility of social and emotional disadvantages associated with streaming (e.g. Barker-Lunn, 1970; Douglas, 1973a; Willig, 1963; Davies, 1975; Rudd, 1958; Lacey, 1970). In general these disadvantages are associated with the practice of selection and therefore are similar to those of concern to the advocates of comprehensivisation. Examples of the gain expected from eliminating selection are in the areas of enhanced self-respect, social integration, motivation, attitudes to school and occupational horizons of the pupils as well as flexibility in the school's organisation (Ford, 1969; Jackson, 1964; Ross *et al.*, 1972).

The studies referred to above, which compared the social development of children in streamed and non-streamed classes, were either concerned with primary schools, or only considered the practice in a single or small number of secondary schools. In the present study, however, the data have been drawn from a large, nationally representative sample of secondary schoolchildren, which has enabled a broader examination to be made of the relationship between certain non-academic aspects of the children's development and their school's ability-grouping practice.

Data

The educational questionnaire completed by schools when the young people were 16 included many questions relating to the child's progress as well as those relating to the school itself. Among these was a single question designed to provide an indication of the school's philosophy on ability-grouping. This was:

'Which one of the following best describes how pupils in the 12—13 year-group of your school are allocated to classes?'

There were four possible pre-coded responses, which can broadly be summarised as:

1. 'Streaming or banding.'
2. 'Setting (for at least some subjects).'
3. 'Mixed ability (for all subjects).'
4. 'Some other arrangement.'

In order to ensure that the children have been in the school in question a significant length of time and to increase the chance that the grouping policy which their school was practising at the time of the follow-up has been experienced by the study children, only those who had been at the school for at least four years were included in the analyses.

Four areas of the children's non-academic development were examined in the present study. The first of these were ratings made by the young people themselves, in the course of a confidential questionnaire, of their ability in certain subjects. Second, the academic motivation of the 16-year-olds was assessed by means of a scale of eight questions completed in the course of the same questionnaire. The young people's plans for their future were indicated by their expectations for leaving school, plans for further education and hopes for future occupations. The final area covered was their behaviour in school, as rated by their teachers.

Results

Self-ratings of attainment

It has been suggested that placement in a lower stream can have harmful effects on the child's self-concept (Rudd, 1958). Data from the questionnaires completed by the 16-year-olds were therefore used to compare the self-ratings of ability of children in streamed, setted and mixed-ability schools (as defined by the practice in the 12—13 year-group).

Young people's assessment of their ability in each subject is clearly related at least in part to their actual ability, so the 16-year-olds' self-ratings have been compared with others who were in the same broad band of attainment at age 11. The reason for choosing 11-year rather than 16-year attainment for this purpose is that the former was tested just before the children entered the secondary school, and therefore any changes since then are of interest in themselves as they could reflect their ability-grouping experiences. The three bands of 11-year attainment shown in the tables that follow represent approximately the top, middle and lowest thirds of the distribution of scores in reading and mathematics test results at that age.

For the most part results have only been presented for comprehensive schools, partly because the numbers became small for some of the categories in other types of school, and partly because non-selection within a school that is selective in its admissions procedure clearly has a different meaning from non-selection in a comprehensive school. The range of ability in a mixed-ability class in a grammar school may well be narrower than in a streamed class in a comprehensive.

It can be seen in Table 11.15 that the 16-year-olds' self-ratings in English are closely related to their 11-year-old ability in reading, with 10 per cent or less of each of the low-ability groups, but over 40 per cent of the high-ability groups, rating themselves above average. However, there is no such clear association between self-ratings and the school's internal grouping policy in the 12—13 year-group: in general, within each level of ability the young people were remarkably similar in their self-ratings.

TABLE 11.15   *Self-ratings in English and ability-grouping policy in comprehensives*

Reading at 11	Ability-grouping policy	Self-ratings of 16-year-olds (%)			
		Below average	Average	Above average	N (100%)
Low	Streamed	19	71	10	578
	Setted	21	72	7	522
	Mixed ability	24	67	9	191
Middle	Streamed	9	70	21	806
	Setted	8	69	23	723
	Mixed ability	10	72	18	306
High	Streamed	4	52	44	458
	Setted	3	53	44	462
	Mixed ability	6	53	41	165

Low range: overall $\chi^2 = 4.1$ (4 df) ns.
Middle range overall $\chi^2 = 3.3$ (4 df) ns.
High range: overall $\chi^2 = 3.5$ (4 df) ns.

The pattern of ratings in English were presented for Britain as a whole, as the figures broadly represented the pattern both for England and Wales, and for Scotland. However, this was not the case for the young people's self-ratings in mathematics, so these figures have been presented separately (Table 11.16).

For England and Wales the largest differences are among young people of high initial mathematical ability, who are less likely to rate themselves above average if their school practises mixed-ability grouping. There is also a tendency for more of the low-ability children in mixed-ability schools to rate themselves below average, but this does not reach significance.

For Scotland, however, there is a general wider variation between schools with different grouping

TABLE 11.16   *Self-ratings in mathematics and ability-grouping policy in comprehensives*

| Mathematics at 11 | Ability-grouping policy | Self-ratings of 16-year olds (%) | | | N (100%) | χ^2 * |
		Below average	Average	Above average		
England and Wales						
Low	Streamed	36	58	6	546	
	Setted	39	57	4	476	3.1 (4 df)
	Mixed ability	44	51	5	94	ns
Middle	Streamed	25	65	10	705	
	Setted	22	67	11	585	2.8 (4 df)
	Mixed ability	25	67	8	120	ns
High	Streamed	15	46	39	427	
	Setted	11	55	34	414	12.3 (4 df)
	Mixed ability	16	61	24	81	$p < 0.05$
Scotland						
Low	Streamed	59	41	—	27	
	Setted	59	38	3	39	1.5 (4 df)
	Mixed ability	51	44	5	57	ns
Middle	Streamed	69	22	9	54	
	Setted	52	47	1	79	12.6 (4 df)
	Mixed ability	47	47	6	155	$p < 0.05$
High	Streamed	21	34	45	44	
	Setted	29	46	24	82	7.4 (4 df)
	Mixed ability	21	39	40	105	ns

* Overall tests: ability-grouping policy by self ratings.

policies, and it tends to be in the opposite direction than that in England and Wales. At each level of initial ability fewer young people in schools practising mixed-ability grouping rate themselves below average in mathematics than those in setted schools and, in most cases, than those in streamed schools. The numbers are too small to be confident whether this is offset by more above-average ratings or not, though this does appear to be the case among the children of high initial ability. However, in view of the levels of significance, the general conclusion must be the same as for England and Wales, namely that there is very little variation between schools with different grouping policies. This can be seen particularly clearly by comparison with the much wider variation associated with the children's 11-year-old ability. It can also be seen by comparison with the surprising variation in self-ratings according to which country the children live in: in general the Scottish children rate themselves as much poorer at mathematics than children in the rest of Britain, for any given level of 11-year ability.

In support of the general conclusion for children

in comprehensives, there was only slight variation in self-ratings in mathematics and English in grammar and secondary modern schools according to the school's internal grouping policy. No consistent pattern emerged, and none of the differences reached significance.

The distribution of self-ratings in both practical subjects and science were also examined for children in comprehensives. In this case, children with scores in the same broad band on the general ability test at 11 were compared. In general there was very little relationship between internal grouping policy and self-ratings, the only exception being that, unlike the findings for self-ratings in mathematics, slightly more of the children in the middle range of ability said they were below average in science if they were in comprehensives practising mixed-ability teaching.

Academic motivation
The distribution of scores on the academic motivation scale is presented in Table 11.17. The scores range from 8 to 40, with a mean for the whole cohort of 19.4, and a standard deviation of 6.1 (for details of

the scale see Fogelman, 1976). Low scores indicate greater motivation. It can be seen that the distribution of scores is very similar whether the young person is in a school which practises streaming, setting or mixed-ability teaching.

TABLE 11.17   *Academic motivation scores and ability-grouping policy*

Ability-grouping policy	Academic motivation score (%)					
	−14	−18	−22	−26	−40	N (100%)
Streamed	22	26	21	15	16	3 782
Setted	24	25	22	14	14	4 099
Mixed ability	22	27	21	14	15	1 802

It was anticipated that the young people's motivation would vary according to their attainment and type of school as well as their sex and their home characteristics, so the relationship was re-examined (by means of analysis of variance) after adjusting for these factors. A further aim of this analysis was to see if the overall similarity in motivation masked variations among sub-groups of children, for example the pattern in grammar schools could be quite different from the pattern in comprehensives.

The analysis of variance is summarised in Table 11.20 below, where the full list of variables included in the analysis can be seen (the sample size is somewhat reduced due to incomplete data). Whether or not the child's age-group was streamed in his or her junior school was included as a variable as it could have affected the child's attitude to being streamed in the secondary school. The child's score on the general ability test at 11 was also included in order to allow for any differences in motivation associated with the child's attainment on entering the school.

The variation in mean academic motivation score between children in schools with different internal grouping policies remained very small, and did not reach significance. There were no significant interactions between ability-grouping and any other of the independent variables, which means that this overall pattern of similarity was applicable to children in each type of school, and of each initial ability level as well as for each category of the other variables. The only possible exception to this uniformity was that in Wales children in mixed-ability schools appeared slightly (but still not significantly) more motivated than children in streamed or setted schools.

Plans for future education and work
Ferri (1971) did not find any differences in aspirations for leaving school among adolescents who had, and

had not, been streamed in their junior school. It was anticipated, however, that the method of grouping in their secondary school would have closer relevance to young people's future plans. Responses to questions on the age the 16-year-olds in the NCDS expected to leave school, their plans for further education and their aspirations for future occupations were therefore examined. For further details of the measures used see Fogelman (1979: see also pp. 271−9).

Table 11.18 presents the percentages of the young people in schools with each internal grouping policy who were planning to leave school when they were 16 (i.e. within a few months). The young people have again been compared with others in the same broad band of 11-year old attainment (as measured by the general ability test) as this was expected, and proved to be closely related to their plans. However, there appears to be only a negligible (non-significant) association between the young people's school-leaving plans and their school's ability-grouping policy.

TABLE 11.18   *Percentage planning to leave school at 16 and ability-grouping policy in comprehensives*

Ability-grouping policy	General ability at 11					
	Low		Middle		High	
	%	N	%	N	%	N
Streamed	87	610	64	830	37	439
Setted	82	500	63	762	40	472
Mixed ability	87	198	70	304	36	174

It was possible that these responses reflected the young people's attitude to their school itself, rather than to further education in general. In order to gain some indication of the latter, the percentages of early leavers who planned to do only part-time or no study after leaving school were compared. However, again, there were no overall differences associated with the school's year-grouping policy, with about three-quarters of each group who were leaving at 16 planning either part-time or no study afterwards.

This general picture of little variation in plans for the future according to the school's internal grouping policy was repeated for pupils in grammar and secondary modern schools. It is, however, worth noting that although the organisation within the school was not associated with different plans, this was far from the case for the type of school attended. For example, among children in the middle-ability range at 11 the percentages of young people in secondary moderns who planned to leave at 16 and either do no more, or only part-time study, were 53 per cent (mixed-ability schools), 62 per cent (streamed schools) and 60 per cent (setted schools) — not significantly different from each other — while the corresponding percentages for young people in the same broad band of initial ability in grammar schools were only 21 per cent (mixed-ability schools), 19 per cent (streamed schools) and 23 per cent (setted schools).

It has been suggested that the occupational horizons of young people in schools practising mixed ability would be less restricted by the apparent accessibility of different jobs, because they would be less often reminded of their own ability (Ford, 1969). The study children were asked, in the course of the confidential questionnaire, what job they would like to do, and their responses to this question were therefore examined.

However, this examination revealed that, although the young people differed considerably in their aspirations according to whether they were in the top, middle or lowest range of ability at 11, at each ability level the proportions of young people in schools practising mixed-ability grouping, streaming and setting who chose each type of job were generally similar to one another. There was therefore no evidence that children in mixed-ability schools had wider occupational horizons than other children.

Adjustment to school

The final area of the young people's social development which was examined was their adjustment to school as assessed by their teachers, who completed a scale consisting of twenty-six items describing behaviour (Rutter, 1967). High scores are indicative of poorer adjustment. Clearly the resultant ratings are in no way objective, as they will partly reflect the relationship between the child and teacher as well as the teacher's expectations. The latter may be particularly important in this case, as the teacher's expectations could vary with the school's grouping policy, especially if the teacher is in accord with that policy.

Comparison of the overall mean scores of adjustment to school shows that 16-year-olds in schools which practised mixed-ability grouping among their 12—13-year-olds came in between those in streamed and setted schools in their scores, with those in streamed schools having the highest mean score (Table 11.19).

In view of the association between streaming policy and other characteristics such as type of school and region, which may themselves be related to behaviour, this relationship was re-examined after allowing for such factors. The results of this analysis are summarised in Table 11.20. It can be seen that the relationship between streaming policy and adjustment is no longer significant. It is perhaps surprising

TABLE 11.19   *Ability-grouping policy and adjustment to school of 16-year-olds*

Ability-grouping policy	Mean score (transformed)	N
Streamed	1.62	2 372
Setted	1.51	2 650
Mixed-ability	1.56	1 120
'Other'	1.56	169

$\chi^2 = 8.3$ (3 df); $p < 0.05$.

to note also that neither the type of school nor the region of the country are significantly related to adjustment, though it should be borne in mind that the comparisons have been made between children who were of similar ability on entering the school (by including general ability as an independent variable).

The only variable with which ability-grouping has a significant interaction is 'type of school'. However, there is no clear difference of importance represented by this interaction as the only large differences appear in the 'other' ability-grouping category for which the results could be distorted as it is a small and ill-defined group.

Discussion

The reasons for expecting the social development of children to differ according to their school's internal grouping policy have been clearly expressed by Rudd (1958). He described the implicit rejection likely to be felt by a child who is placed in a lower stream, and discussed how this can lead to a poorer self-concept and therefore behaviour problems and a negative attitude to school. Research on the relationship between expectations and performance has described a similar process (Pidgeon, 1970). Also, Davies (1975) discusses the non-academic correlates of streaming and concludes that 'streaming may be attacked on many grounds for its unanticipated biases and consequences'. One example of this is provided by Hargreaves (1967), who felt that the practice of streaming in his secondary school encouraged the formation of delinquent subcultures.

Although the non-academic correlates of ability-grouping have not been examined before for a large number of children in secondary schools, the evidence from studies of primary schools has tended to support these expectations. For example, social adjustment, social attitudes and attitudes to peers of different ability have been shown to be 'healthier' among children in non-streamed classes (Willig, 1963; Barker Lunn, 1970). Barker Lunn also found

TABLE 11.20   *Academic motivation scale and adjustment to school and ability-grouping policy*

Independent variables	Academic motivation scale			School adjustment*		
	$N = 5\ 836$ Total variance + 37.5			$N = 6\ 305$ Total variance + 1.78		
	Fitted constant	se	χ_2 (df)	Fitted constant	se	χ_2 (df)
Overall constant	24.01			2.77		
Ability groups:						
Streamed	−0.15		5.2 (3) ns	−0.04		3.9 (3) ns
Setted	0.10			−0.02		
Mixed ability	0.34			0.06		
Other	−0.29			0.00		
Streaming at 11						
(yes—no)	−0.28	0.17	2.8 (1) ns	−0.03	0.03	0.9 (1) ns
Type of school:						
Direct grant + grammar	−0.02		14.3 (3) †	−0.04		4.5 (3) ns
Comprehensive	0.26			0.06		
Secondary modern	−0.47			0.01		
Independent	0.23			−0.03		
Sex: boys—girls	0.90	0.15	34.5 (1) ‡	0.14	0.03	20.0 (1) ‡
Father's occupation:						
Non-manual	−1.19		75.8 (3) ‡	−0.29		100.2 (3) ‡
III-manual	0.18			−0.04		
IV + V	0.16			0.07		
No male head	0.85			0.26		
Region:						
North England	−0.09		4.0 (3) ns	−0.02		3.5 (3) ns
South England	0.14			0.02		
Wales	−0.31			0.05		
Scotland	0.26			−0.05		
General ability at						
11 years	−0.10	0.006	316.5 (1) ‡	−0.03	0.001	508.1 (1) ‡
Residual mean square	33.79			1.54		
Interactions	Ability group × each other independent variable ns			Ability group × type of school $\chi_2 = 18.2$ (9 df) $p < 0.05$ Ability group × each other independent variable ns		

* Transformation = square root.
Significance levels: $p < 0.001$‡; $p < 0.01$†; $p < 0.05$*; $p > 0.05$ ns.

more positive attitudes to school and more participation in school activities among children in non-streamed classes, particularly those of average or below-average ability. This was substantially in agreement with the co-operative atmosphere felt by Jackson (1964) in non-streamed schools. Occupational choice, however, was not found to have widened among non-streamed primary schoolchildren (Barker Lunn, 1970).

Studies of individual or small numbers of secondary schools have broadly been in agreement with these results, although less conclusively. For example, Rudd (1958) did not find any differences related to ability-grouping in the children's attitudes to school, but streamed children made fewer contributions and paid less attention in lessons, and their behaviour was more aggressive than non-streamed children. An NFER study of twelve schools also found greater participation in school life among boys who were not streamed, but not among girls, though girls were more involved in teams (Ross *et al.*, 1972). Another study, of a single school, demonstrated that children of early secondary school age were more socially integrated if they were in all-ability classes. However, other differences related to ability-grouping did not apply to children of all ability levels. For example, it was only among high-ability children that those in all-ability classes had a better academic self-image, and it was only the low-ability children who tended to have a more positive attitude to school life. Generally one conclusion reached was that the differences were as great within one system as between the systems (Newbold, 1977).

Studies of small numbers of schools are inevitably affected by the individual characteristics of the schools, which could partially explain the slightly greater likelihood of associations between ability-grouping and social development demonstrated by the above studies compared with the present study of a national sample of children.

The general conclusion from the present study was that there was barely any evidence of differences related to their school's internal grouping policy in any of the four areas of social development examined, i.e. in self-ratings, motivation towards school, plans for the future or behaviour at school. The analyses of academic motivation and behaviour provided further results of interest, namely that there were barely any significant interactions, which suggested that this pattern of only minimal differences related to grouping policy was generally applicable; for example, it applied to children of all ability levels, in each type of school and of each social class.

In view of the contrasting findings from other studies, albeit of very different samples, consideration should be given to the measure used in the present study to indicate the school's internal grouping policy. The reasons for selecting the practice in the 12–13 age-group to indicate the school's policy was described more fully earlier (pp. 233–40), where it was argued that no other single age range can more effectively indicate the school's policy. This choice means that the 16-year-olds in the study will not necessarily have experienced mixed-ability teaching themselves when they were 12 or 13, and also that many of those who were in mixed-ability classes will have been streamed or setted since then. However, the measure is not necessarily intended to describe the study children's own experience, but rather meant to indicate the school's philosophy on this issue.

The possibility that a single measure cannot adequately describe a school's policy is considered by Reid (1977). She reports that some schools in the NFER study of streaming claimed to employ mixed-ability grouping even though they had

unstreamed groups within broad bands of ability, and concluded that there is great diversity of practice among schools which claim to be similar. Also Barker Lunn (1970) found that in some mixed-ability classes in primary schools pupils were divided into small groups on the basis of their ability.

It seems likely therefore that each of the three main categories of grouping policy used here will encompass wide variations in practice, such that they overlap to some extent. However, it seems reasonable to assume that although the distinctions between the groups may be blurred, each group will broadly represent the policy it is said to represent.

It has been suggested, although little research has been done on the question, that there are factors related to ability-grouping policy other than the stated policy itself which may be of considerable importance in terms of both the children's academic and social development. Examples of these factors are teachers' attitudes to their school's policy, the quality of teaching, including the appropriateness of the method used, and whether the organisation of the school has been adapted to the change in policy (Reid, 1977; Davies, 1975). Research that has been carried out has indicated that the extent of teachers' agreement with their school's grouping policy is of more importance than the policy itself in terms of children's attainments and attitudes (Barker Lunn, 1970). This suggests that the question of how mixed-ability teaching is actually practised should be investigated more fully.

Conclusion

The present study provides evidence for educationalists and policy-makers on the question of whether to advocate a particular broad grouping policy by showing that there are only minimal variations in non-academic development between children in streamed, setted and mixed-ability schools. However, this only indicates the likely consequences of different broad policies given the present methods of putting them into practice. It does not necessarily indicate the *potential* effectiveness of different policies. Within each of the systems described here there will be considerable variation in the quality of teaching and in the teachers' attitudes which may be of more importance than the policy itself. Future research, as Reid (1977) and Davies (1975) have indicated, is now required to establish which methods of teaching and organisation are most appropriate to each practice. Following this, the effectiveness of both the broad policy and the method of carrying it out can then be tested by a re-examination of the development of children with different experiences.

12 Other School Characteristics*

THE ASSOCIATION BETWEEN SCHOOL VARIABLES AND ATTAINMENT IN A NATIONAL SAMPLE OF 16-YEAR-OLDS

Introduction

Two objectives appear to have dominated educational policy in the advanced industrial nations in the post-war era. The first, variously called 'the talent hunt', investment in 'human capital', or simply the need to train 'brains for the jobs', pinned great hopes on educational provision and attainments as a major prerequisite of economic growth. The second concerns what is known as the equality debate, the belief that education could redress social grievances surrounding differentials in status, wealth and power by the provision of 'equal opportunity for all'.

As a result of these hopes and beliefs, the schools themselves became major targets of the burgeoning educational expenditure, giving rise on the one hand to the pursuit of better facilities, more teachers, smaller classes, and so on, and on the other a liberal egalitarianism aimed at destreaming and comprehensivisation. It has always been taken for granted that improvement of school characteristics along those lines would achieve visible strides towards the desired objectives of boosted school attainments. Moreover, particularly in Britain, there has long been a spirit of freedom and experimentation surrounding school characteristics so that considerable differences exist between schools. Only fairly recently has research actually begun to evaluate these assumptions.

The best-known research is that described in the Coleman Report in the USA (Coleman *et al.*, 1966), which reached the conclusion that 'schools bring little influence to bear on a child's achievement that is independent of his background and general social context'. Since then a number of researchers, in the USA (e.g. Jencks *et al.*, 1973; Jencks and Brown, 1975; Averch *et al.*, 1975), in Ireland (Madaus *et*

al., 1979) and in Britain (Rutter *et al.*, 1978) have reached conflicting conclusions.

These studies have used a variety of 'input' measures and a variety of 'output' (school achievement) measures, together with a variety of populations and sampling methods, that has often complicated interpretation. The purpose of the present study is to present a straightforward analysis of school-effectiveness data with respect to a large, nationally representative group of 16-year-old schoolchildren.

Method

The school characteristics chosen for analysis are listed in Table 12.1 and will be described further under 'Results'.

TABLE 12.1 *School variables examined in the present analyses*

Type of school	Hours per week in English
School size	Hours per week in maths
Sex segregation	Teacher turnover
Pupil–teacher ratio	Parent–teacher meetings/
Streaming	discussions
Class size	School uniform
	Use of corporal punishment

The following procedure was adopted for analysis and presentation of data. In all analyses, school variables were first inspected for gross associations with attainments. In some cases these data have been presented directly in order to illustrate consistently weak associations. In other cases the data were subjected to analyses of variance. This enabled us to assess the 'size of effect' of each independent variable when otherwise confounding variables such as social class and type of school were taken into account. Moreover, school attainments at 11 were incorporated into the analyses so that the analyses could be interpreted as assessing size of effect of school variables after allowance was made for initial differences in attainments (the 11–16 year correlations were 0.8 for reading and 0.7 for maths). Finally, it is well known that independent variables in combination can have an effect not produced by any

*Original sources: Richardson, K., Ghodsian, M. and Gorbach, P., 'The associations between school variables and attainments in a national sample of 16-year-olds', previously unpublished; Ghodsian, M., Gorbach, P. and Richardson, K., 'Parents' and pupils' appreciation of education and schools', previously unpublished.

of them separately; this approach allowed us to test for such interactions between the variables.

Children in special and independent schools, and those in remedial classes, were excluded from these analyses in order to concentrate on the main body of schoolchildren. The analysis of variance tables are presented in the Appendix to this section in order to preserve continuity in the text; data of variables not so analysed are presented separately in the main text.

Results

Gross effects

A substantial proportion of the between-schools variation in attainments will inevitably be attributable to selective schooling and non-school characteristics. Children have been allocated to different types of school on the basis of school attainments and the latter are well known to be associated with social class (Tables 12.2 and 12.3). Thus in order to demarcate the proportion of existing variation within which *school* variables 'make a difference', it is necessary to take account of these *extraneous* variables. Tables A1 (reading) and A2 (mathematics) present the results of analyses of variance which used 16-year test scores as dependent variables and 11-year test scores, type of school and social class (Registrar-General's classification of fathers' occupations, 1966) as independent variables. The fitted constants in Tables A1 and A2 show appreciable differences in test scores to be associated with types of school (e.g. range for reading: 0.2 of a standard deviation) and social class (range for reading: 0.22 of a standard deviation). Inspection of interactions between categories of independent variables showed that, for reading, gains in test scores were greater in comprehensive and secondary modern schools than in grammar schools; there was no type-of-school interaction for maths; small social-class interactions are shown in Tables A1 and A2.

In the analyses which follow, then, we are considering the size of effect attributable to each school variable when it is known from preliminary inspection that the *total* effect of such variables is minor compared with the variables considered above. This is not done with full analysis of variance in all

TABLE 12.3 *Mean test scores for social class in each type of school (raw scores were transformed to give a normal distribution with mean 0 ± 1.0 standard deviation)*

	I & II	III NM	III M	IV & V	Total (*N*)
		(a) READING			
Grammar	1.06	0.85	0.80	0.67	980
Comprehensive	0.41	0.15	−0.17	−0.37	5 137
Secondary modern	−0.40	−0.05	−0.33	−0.49	1 852
Total	0.52	0.21	−0.13	−0.35	7 969
		(b) MATHS			
Grammar	1.18	1.03	0.91	0.67	980
Comprehensive	0.39	0.11	−0.18	−0.32	5 137
Secondary modern	−0.03	−0.25	−0.35	−0.45	1 852
Total	0.51	0.17	−0.13	−0.31	7 969

cases considered. The very repetitiveness of negative findings made this seem unnecessary, though analysis of variance data are presented in most cases. For conciseness we have collapsed all the AOVs into summary tables which exclude the three common, 'extraneous', variables, thus showing only the fitted constants associated with each 'new' variable in turn (Tables A3 and A4).

School size

School size was coded from teachers' information of number of pupils on the school register and categorised as 750, 751–1250, and 1251+. There were weak associations between school size and attainments at 16 years in both reading and maths consisting of slight decreases in test scores with increasing size. However, these associations disappeared when account was taken of the extraneous variables in analyses of variance (Tables A3 and A4). The fitted constants reflected a total difference of 0.04 of a standard deviation for reading and only 0.03 of a standard deviation for maths.

Sex segregation

Whether children were in segregated or co-educational schools did not seem to be markedly related to test

TABLE 12.2 *Social-class distributions (as percentages of the total) in each type of school*

	I & II	III NM	III M	IV & V	Total (*N*)
Grammar	48.4	13.7	30.8	7.0	980 (100%)
Comprehensive	21.2	11.0	47.7	20.2	5 137 (100%)
Secondary modern	19.2	11.3	49.1	20.4	1 852 (100%)
Total	23.8	11.3	45.8	19.2	7 969

scores. Thus the fitted constants of Tables A3 and A4 indicate differences well under one-tenth of a standard deviation in all of the four comparisons.

Pupil—teacher ratio

A pupil—teacher ratio for each school was calculated from information provided by teachers of numbers of pupils and teachers in the school. These ratios were grouped into five categories: −15.0; 15.1−16.0; 16.1−17.0; 17.1−18.0; 18.1+. The fitted constants (Tables A3 and A4) revealed no association with reading attainment and an inconsistent relationship with maths scores.

Streaming

The schools were asked to supply information on whether the English and maths classes attended by study children were 'streamed' or of 'mixed ability'. Whatever the case, the results, in terms of improvement of test performances, were minimal (Tables A3 and A4). Of course, the meaning of streaming at 16 may be somewhat obscure: even pupils in 'mixed-ability' classes may well be streamed in effect, according to examination commitments, and so on. Moreover, schools which practise streaming in that particular year may not have done so in earlier years, thus producing 'mixed effects' at 16. Accordingly we asked the schools to tell us what their present streaming policy was in the school as a whole (not specifically English and maths classes) for the 12−13 year age group. This, it was reasoned, might give some index of the influence of streaming over a period of time. Of course, a few schools may have changed their streaming policy over this period, but these are unlikely to have been great enough to obscure any large effects. The streaming policies were categorised as 'streamed', 'setted' (i.e. streamed for particular subjects), or 'mixed ability'. For obvious reasons the sample for these analyses included only those subjects who had been in the same school for at least four years, i.e. since their 12th birthday. Again, however, as the fitted constants of Tables A3 and A4 show, the effects on test performance were marginal, accounting for, on average, three-hundredths of a standard deviation for maths (in favour of mixed ability, but statistically not significant) and one-twentieth of a standard deviation for reading (in favour of streaming).

Class size

Inspection of raw data revealed the usual, and seemingly paradoxical associations with class size (i.e. in favour of *larger* classes). Our analyses of variance showed test scores to be still associated with *larger classes*, to an extent about as large as the social-class effect, for both reading and maths (Tables A3 and A4). This frequently revealed finding is of course the opposite of that expected. Our conjecture is that this result is very largely an artefact of teachers' placement of children with poor attainments in smaller classes.

Hours per week in English and maths

Teachers were asked to enter into the questionnaire how many hours per week the study subjects spent in their English and maths classes. The analyses can thus be taken to reflect effects, in terms of achievement, of time spent 'learning' in each subject area. 'English' is unlikely to be a fully satisfactory variable in the case of reading, however, as much allocated time is likely to be spent on general activities not directly related to the sorts of comprehension skills required in the test. We would expect maths activities, and thus 'hours in maths', to be more directly associated with the computational skills required in the maths test. As can be seen from the fitted constants of Tables A3 and A4, this distinction does seem to have operated. Whereas the differences in reading are very small, those in maths reflect an improvement contingent on hours per week spent in maths lessons that far exceeds the social-class effect (e.g. 0.32 of a standard deviation between less than two and three or more hours per week). Although children in 'remedial' classes were excluded from these analyses, the fall-off in test performance in the 5 hours-plus category is still probably due to the presence of a proportion of children in this group requiring extra help, and receiving it.

Teacher turnover

The index of teacher turnover adopted was the number of full-time teachers leaving the school in the last academic year, expressed as a percentage of the number of full-time teachers currently serving in the school. Distortion will be present where, for a variety of possible reasons, the school has changed in size over the discrepant one-year period, but this is likely to be either very slight and/or involve only a small minority of schools. This index can be thought of as reflecting the attractiveness of the school to the teachers (in career, professional-satisfaction or other terms) and thus the general level of morale. Whatever the factors involved in teacher turnover, however, they were not consequential since there were no strong and consistent associations between this variable and 16-year test scores. The data are presented in Table 12.4, and because of the null or weak associations evident (excepting the extreme 21+ category) no analyses of variance were carried out.

TABLE 12.4 *Test scores for rates of teacher turnover*

Type of school	% teachers leaving				
	−5	−10	−15	−20	21+
(a) READING SCORES					
Comprehensive	−0.07	−0.06	−0.04	−0.01	−0.11
Grammar	0.84	0.89	0.92	0.99	0.95
Secondary modern	−0.25	−0.27	−0.26	−0.20	−0.29
Total	−0.01	0.01	0.06	0.11	−0.08
(b) MATHS SCORES					
Comprehensive	−0.07	−0.05	−0.01	−0.02	−0.16
Grammar	1.01	1.03	1.03	1.11	1.00
Secondary modern	−0.46	−0.24	−0.33	−0.24	−0.31
Total	−0.04	0.03	0.08	0.12	−0.11

TABLE 12.5 *Frequency of parent—teacher discussion and attainments*

Type of school	Frequency		
	1/term	1/year	No regular/ not at all
(a) READING SCORES			
Comprehensive	−0.11	−0.04	−0.09
Grammar	0.93	0.93	0.75
Secondary modern	−0.20	−0.25	−0.41
Total	−0.04	0.05	−0.14
(b) MATHS SCORES			
Comprehensive	−0.16	−0.04	−0.14
Grammar	1.03	1.05	0.85
Secondary modern	−0.23	−0.29	−0.48
Total	−0.04	0.05	0.20

Parent—teacher meetings and discussions

Teachers were asked to indicate the frequency of occurrence of parent—teacher meetings organised by the school for purposes of discussing pupil progress. Of course, this is no guarantee that parents actually attended the meetings; rather, it is taken here as an index of the schools' concern about regular contacts. The data (Table 12.5) suggested a dichotomy between the two 'regular meeting' categories on the one hand and the 'non-regular' category on the other (in favour of the former). However, there was inconsistency, in that comprehensive schools organising meetings once per term were associated with reading and maths scores *lower* than those holding meetings once per year (or even 'irregularly' or 'not at all').

School uniform

The compulsory wearing of uniform may be thought of as a reflection of the corporate self-image and traditional outlook of the school. Teachers were asked to supply information about the wearing of uniform in their schools and the responses were categorised as: 'No'; 'Yes, but not compulsory'; 'Yes, compulsory'; 'Yes, but compulsory only for specific items or for certain ages'. The data of test scores are shown in Table 12.6. It was clear that a definite but slight association existed between the compulsory wearing of uniforms and school attainments that persisted within types of school, at least with regard to reading. However, the associations for maths seemed to be less consistent. Thus whatever it is about the school that compulsory wearing of

uniform represents, it does seem to have some consequences for school attainments, at least as measured here.

Use of corporal punishment

Table 12.7 shows the associations between test scores and schools' use of corporal punishment. This item may be thought of as an index of the authoritarian character of the school. Again, however, whatever this index represents in practical teaching/learning terms it did not appear to have major consequences for test performance.

Discussion

The scholastic attainments of children in school have long been chief objectives of contemporary education, especially in regard to the latter's economic and equality functions. The present research was intended as a contribution to questions regarding the effectiveness of certain school variables in promoting pupils' attainment. The method was to assess whether differences between secondary schools in certain characteristics were associated with differences in school attainments in the secondary schools, and if so to give some indication of the 'size of effect'. In some cases this was done by direct inspection of mean test score distributions; in others it was done by analysis of variance which took into account (among other things) test scores at 11 years, thus allowing estimation of 'size of effect' (differences in means) while controlling for attainments upon entry to the

TABLE 12.6   *School having uniform and attainments*

Type of school	Having uniform			
	No	Yes, not compulsory	Yes, compulsory	Specific items only/ Certain ages only
(a) READING SCORES				
Comprehensive	−0.27	−0.18	−0.02	0.03
Grammar	—	0.63	0.87	0.98
Secondary modern	−0.37	−0.33	−0.22	−0.20
Total	−0.32	−0.21	0.10	0.15
(b) MATHS SCORES				
Comprehensive	−0.29	−0.11	0.00	−0.04
Grammar	—	0.92	0.98	1.09
Secondary modern	−0.25	−0.37	−0.28	−0.26
Total	−0.27	−0.18	0.12	0.12

TABLE 12.7   *Use of corporal punishment and attainments*

Type of school	Use of corporal punishment		
	Used regularly	Used rarely	Never used
(a) READING SCORES			
Comprehensive	−0.12	−0.02	0.06
Grammar	0.89	0.94	0.93
Secondary modern	−0.26	−0.26	−0.26
Total	−0.10	0.01	0.30
(b) MATHS SCORES			
Comprehensive	−0.09	−0.04	−0.03
Grammar	1.05	1.12	0.99
Secondary modern	−0.29	−0.29	−0.40
Total	−0.07	0.01	0.26

secondary school. The results obtained can be summarised as follows:

1. *Overall effects of school variables*. The size of effect of almost all school variables was small or non-existent compared with type of school, social class and attainments at 11 years.
2. *School size*. Differences of school size were not reflected in differences in attainments.
3. *Sex segregation*. All effects on test scores were small.

4. *Pupil–teacher ratio*. There was no association in the case of reading and a statistically significant but inconsistent one in the case of maths.
5. *Streaming*. Different policies, whether considered as current (i.e. at 16 years) or retrospective (i.e. at 12–13 years), had little or no effects in terms of attainments at 16 years.
6. *Class size*. There were associations with changes in reading and maths scores, about equivalent in size to the social-class effect.
7. *Hours per week in English and maths*. Size of effects in terms of 16-year test scores were small and statistically non-significant for reading (English), but far exceeded the social-class effect for maths.
8. *Teacher turnover*. Attainments at 16 years were not markedly affected by differences in teacher turnover, except for the extreme category of over 20 per cent.
9. *Parent–teacher meetings*. There were higher attainments on the whole where schools showed 'concern' for regular meetings.
10. *School uniform*. There were slight but inconsistent associations with test scores.
11. *Use of corporal punishment*. There were small but inconsistent associations with attainments.

Before comparing these results with those of other studies it is important to be reminded of the limitations of the present study. Chief among these, perhaps, is the confinement of attainments to performance on two standardised tests. A wide variety of measures have been used in studies of this sort. Coleman *et al.* (1966) used only a verbal ability test as their achievement measure (the same data being used by Jencks *et al.*, 1973). Mayeske *et al.* (1972) used a composite score based on five standardised tests, Madaus *et al.* (1979) used curriculum-based tests, Woodhall and Blaug (1969) used numbers of GCE passes, and Brimer *et al.* (1978) used performance on GCE examinations as their 'output' measures. There is some debate at the present time as to which type of measure is the most appropriate. Standardised tests, of course, usually have high correlations with other achievement measures and are constructed on just that basis. None the less at least one study has concluded that 'curriculum-based tests are more sensitive to differences in school characteristics than are standardised tests' (Madaus *et al.*, 1979, p. 207) and the subject specificity of effects is seen in the sometimes important differences between reading and maths in our results. Moreover, it is important to note that we have only been able to examine a few of the possible school variables. In spite of these possible limitations the presentation of these data still seemed warranted, especially in view of the large, nationally representative sample of subjects covering approximately 5 000 schools. Finally, it needs to be remembered that only relatively straightforward analyses have been carried out here; further, more refined, analyses may well qualify some of the results reported.

The present study both confirms the conclusions of earlier studies, and agrees with some of the more recent dissensions. Following the pioneering investigations of the Coleman Report, Jencks and his associates concluded that 'differences between schools seem to have very little effect on any measurable attribute of those who attend them'; and few relationships were found between high-school characteristics and any measure of high school effectiveness (Jencks and Brown, 1975). Averch *et al.* (1975), in their review of all such studies in the USA, concluded that input—output studies provide very little evidence that school resources in general greatly influence student outcomes, and indeed that 'research has not identified a single variant of the existing system that is consistently related to students' educational outcomes'.

In Britain, however, the results have been a little more equivocal. Whereas Peaker (1971) drew attention to his survey data suggesting that schools 'do not appear to contribute very much', and that 'the pattern in the secondary school is largely determined by the pattern in the junior school', Byrne *et al.* (1975) have concluded that 'school system inputs are of considerable importance in explaining differences in attainment'. However, this latter study utilised an unusual measure of attainment, namely rates of 'staying on' at school. On the other hand, a British

study found the between-schools variance to be a larger proportion (20—30 per cent) of the total variance in achievement (in this case GCE performance) than was the case in either the American studies or the present study (Brimer *et al.*, 1978). That study was, of course, based on a rather homogeneous sample (i.e. those pupils pre-selected to take O and A levels) and included, moreover, socio-economic composition as a *school* variable (which would be expected to inflate the between-schools variance), but its results have been confirmed by a similar study in Ireland which claims that 'Our findings provide strong evidence for the differential effectiveness of schools: differences in school characteristics do contribute to differences in achievement' (Madaus *et al.*, 1979, p. 223; see also the small-scale study by Rutter *et al.*, 1978).

These apparent conflicts may be at least partially resolved by examining the nature of the school variables in these more optimistic reports that *are* found to 'make a difference'. As Madaus *et al.* (1979, p. 225) explain:

A further point that arises from our findings, as well as from a similar study carried out in England [Brimer *et al.*, 1978] is that the school variables that are important predictors of achievement are, for the most part, the ones that reflect the climate or activities of the school rather than its static characteristics (size, physical amenities, teacher qualifications).

In their study of twelve London schools Rutter *et al.* (1978, p. 178) also note that

differences between schools in outcome *were* systematically related to their characteristics as social institutions. Factors as varied as the degree of academic emphasis, teacher actions in lessons, the availability of incentives and rewards, good conditions for pupils, and the extent to which children were able to take responsibility were all significantly associated with outcome differences between schools.

There is perhaps some evidence in our present study to support this, in that the only school variables notably associated with attainments were the number of hours per week spent on directly relevant work (as in maths), the regularity of parent—teacher meetings and discussions, and the compulsoriness of school uniform. Perhaps future studies will consider these in greater depth.

Clearly, then, it would be hazardous to conclude from our results that schools do not, and *cannot*, make a difference. Precisely what sort of differences can be attained, and *how* they are to be attained — and, indeed, explaining in any detail the processes at work — are of course questions which generate a number of additional issues which we hope to take up in the future. In the meantime it must be remembered that studies of this sort are only a description of the status quo: they only describe what *has* been done, not what *can* be done.

TABLE A1

Dependent variable: reading score at 16, normal transformation
Independent variables: as listed

Dependent variable mean = 0.05
Total variance = 0.9018
Sample size = 7 063

Fitted constants and analysis of variance table
(χ^2 values are adjusted for other factors)

Source		Fitted constant	Standard error	df	χ^2
Overall constant:		−1.85			
Type of school	Comprehensive	−0.04			
	Grammar	0.12		2	67.9***
	Secondary modern	−0.08			
Social class	I, II	0.10			
	III, IV NM	0.06		3	114.0***
	III M	−0.04			
	IV M, V	−0.12			
Reading at 11 (gain per point about mean = 16.3, sd = 6.0)		0.12	0.001	1	9 374.5***
Residual mean square = 0.3122					

Test of interaction, adjusted for above model:
Type of school × Social class, χ^2 = 5.5 ns
Type of school × Reading at 11, χ^2 = 62.2***
Social class × Reading at 11, χ^2 = 8.8*

Interactions, adjusted for above model

READING AT 11

		Intercept	Slope	
Type of school	Comprehensive	−0.33	0.123	
	Grammar	0.58	0.088	χ^2 = 62.2***
	Secondary modern	−0.25	0.116	
Father's occupation	I, II	0.19	0.113	
	II, IV NM	0.06	0.118	
	III M	−0.10	0.122	
	IV M, V	−0.15	0.121	χ^2 = 8.8*

TABLE A2

Dependent variable: maths score at 16, normal transformation
Independent variables: as listed

Dependent variable mean = 0.04
Total variance = 0.9153
Sample size = 7 039

Fitted constants and analysis of variance table
(χ^2 values are adjusted for other factors)

Source		Fitted constant	Standard error	df	χ^2
Overall constant:		−1.00			
Type of school	Comprehensive	−0.06			
	Grammar	0.19		2	121.9***
	Secondary modern	−0.13			
Social class	I, II	0.12			
	III, IV NM	0.02		3	90.1***
	III M	−0.05			
	IV M, V	−0.09			
Maths at 11		0.06	0.001	1	5 331.5***
(Gain per point measured about mean = 17.2, sd = 10.0)					
Residual mean square = 0.4069					

Tests of interaction, adjusted for above model:
Type of school × Social class, $\chi^2 = 14.8$*
Type of school × Maths at 11, $\chi^2 = 28.2$***
Social class × Maths at 11, $\chi^2 = 5.9$ ns

Note: the standard deviation of the maths score at 11 was 10.0. Interaction, adjusted for above model:

FATHER'S OCCUPATION

Type of school		I, II	III, IV NM	III M	IV M, V
	Comprehensive	0.08	0.02	0.11	−0.14
	Grammar	0.34	0.21	0.16	−0.01
	Secondary modern	−0.05	−0.20	−0.13	−0.18

$\chi^2 = 14.8$*

MATHS AT 11

Type of school		Intercept	Slope
	Comprehensive	−0.15	0.066
	Grammar	0.22	0.061
	Secondary modern	−0.07	0.055

$\chi^2 = 28.2$*

TABLE A3

Dependent variable: reading score at 16, normal transformation.

Independent variables: each factor as listed from a separate analysis which included that factor with type of school, social class and reading at 11.

Fitted constants and analysis of variance tables
(χ^2 values are adjusted for type of school, social class and reading at 11)

Source		Fitted constant	Standard error	df	χ^2
School size	Under 750	−0.02			
	−1250	0.001		2	3.7 ns
	−3000	0.02			
Residual mean square = 0.3124					
Sex segregation	Boys in boys' schools	0.06			
	Girls in girls' schools	0.003		3	38.9***
	Boys in co-ed schools	0.01			
	Girls in co-ed schools	−0.07			
Residual mean square = 0.3110					
Pupil−teacher ratio	−15	0.001			
	−16	−0.01			
	−17	0.04		4	8.3 ns
	−18	−0.01			
	−19	−0.02			
Residual mean square = 0.3115					
Streaming in English	Yes−No	0.05	0.02	1	8.1**
Residual mean square = 0.3075					
Ability group at 12−13	Streamed	0.03			
	Setted	−0.01		2	9.5**
	Mixed	−0.02			
Residual mean square = 0.3127					
Present class size − English	20	−0.12			
	−25	0.01		3	71.8***
	−30	0.05			
	31	0.06			
Residual mean square = 0.3029					
Hours per week − English	2	−0.05			
	3	0.03		3	7.7 ns
	4	0.03			
	5	−0.01			
Residual mean square = 0.3072					

Dependent variable: maths score at 16, normal transformation
Independent variables: each factor as listed is from a separate analysis which included that factor with type of school, social class and maths at 11.

Fitted constants and analysis of variance tables
(χ^2 values are adjusted for type of school, social class and maths at 11)

Source		Fitted constant	Standard error	df	χ^2
School size	Under 750	−0.02			
	− 1 250	0.01		2	1.9 ns
	− 3 000	0.01			
Residual mean square = 0.4068					
Sex segregation	Boys in boys' schools	0.10			
	Girls in girls' schools	−0.08		3	127.5***
	Boys in co-ed schools	0.08			
	Girls in co-ed schools	−0.10			
Residual mean square = 0.4000					
Pupil−teacher ratio	−15	0.08			
	−16	−0.04			
	−17	−0.01		4	21.3*
	−18	−0.03			
	−19	0.00			
Residual mean square = 0.4061					
Streaming in maths	Yes−No	0.08	0.03	1	7.2**
Residual mean square = 0.4016					
Ability group at 12−13	Streamed	0.01			
	Setted	0.01		2	1.2 ns
	Mixed	−0.02			
Residual mean square = 0.4009					
Present class size − maths	<20	−0.13			
	−25	−0.03		3	99.9***
	−30	0.06			
	31	0.10			
Residual mean square = 0.3965					
Hours per week − maths	<2	−0.21			
	3	0.02		3	97.5***
	4	0.11			
	5	0.08			
Residual mean square = 0.3954					

PARENTS' AND PUPILS' APPRECIATION OF EDUCATION AND SCHOOL

Introduction

In any recent discussion relating to education the issue of 'consumer' — i.e. parents and pupils — rights and choices takes a prominent role (National Consumer Council, 1977a). It thus becomes important to have some idea of the attitudes of parents and pupils towards education and schools. Further, an investigation of the correlates of these attitudes might serve to identify areas of discontent and open ways for improving the relationship between the education service and parents and pupils.

This study examines the attitudes of parents and pupils to education and schools. These attitudes are then related to certain background characteristics (i.e. social class and sex), school attainment and a variety of school characteristics.

In the course of the 16-year NCDS parental interview parents were asked 'to what extent have you been satisfied with the study child's education in his/her present school?' The replies were pre-coded as 'satisfied', 'satisfied in some ways but not in others', 'dissatisfied', 'uncertain/don't know'. Parents were then asked to state their reasons for any dissatisfaction felt.

Among a number of questions which were put to the young people themselves, one asked them to respond on a five-point scale to the statement 'I feel school is largely a waste of time' by choosing one of the following categories: 'very true', 'partly or usually true', 'cannot say, no feelings either way', 'partly or usually untrue', and 'not true at all'.

Thus from the nature of the above questions we see that: (a) the questions were highly structured; (b) they are 'general' questions in two ways (first, they do not refer to any particular aspect of either education or school (Kniveton, 1969; Woods, 1976); and second, the attitude or feeling elicited is not specific, in one case being general 'satisfaction' and in the other feeling school is a 'waste of time').

Method

In the main we report the proportion of 'favourable' responses from both the parents (usually the mother) and the young people. That is, we use as our measure the proportion of parents who responded as 'satisfied' with their child's education (rather than 'satisfied in some ways but not others', or 'dissatisfied', or 'uncertain/don't know') and the proportion of children who said that it was 'not true at all' that school is a waste of time, and examine the association of these responses with characteristics of schools. The total numbers in the tables which follow vary due to missing information on some children. Furthermore, in some places we have considered only those in the three main types of maintained schools, i.e. grammar, comprehensive and secondary modern.

Results

Background information

Table 12.8 shows the distribution of the parental responses by social class (defined by the occupation of the male head of the household according to the Registrar General's classification). This table confirms the high overall rate of satisfaction (over 90 per cent being 'satisfied' or 'satisfied in some ways') found among parents by other studies (see conclusions, p. 270). Further, this feeling seems to be present to the same extent in all social classes if one combines the 'satisfied' and the 'satisfied in some ways' groups. There is, however, a tendency for a lower proportion of the non-manual social classes to express unequivocal satisfaction. The differences between social classes in the proportions expressing 'dissatisfied' are very small.

As for the young people themselves, Table 12.9 shows again that a high overall percentage gave favourable responses, in that 80 per cent of them said that it was 'not true' or 'partly untrue' — that 'school is largely a waste of time'. It is also apparent that in this case the proportions differ between the children from different social-class backgrounds, with

TABLE 12.8   *Parental satisfaction with their child's education and social class*

Parental response	Social class				
	I + II	III NM	III M	IV + V	Total
Satisfied	63.4	60.7	67.5	69.6	66.2
Satisfied in some ways	29.0	29.8	24.6	22.9	25.9
Dissatisfied	6.9	8.4	7.2	5.4	6.9
Uncertain	0.7	1.2	0.7	2.1	1.0
Total	2 270 (100%)	836 (100%)	3 824 (100%)	1 742 (100%)	8 672 (100%)

more children in the higher social classes responding 'favourably'.

Table 12.10 shows the relationship between the responses of parents and their children. As can be seen, there is a clear positive relationship between the two. Thus, for example, for the 'not true' category, whereas 62.7 per cent of the children of parents who were satisfied answered 'not true', the corresponding percentage for those parents who were dissatisfied was 43.3 per cent. At the same time, as this last figure exemplifies, there is considerable lack of concordance between the two responses.

Tables 12.11 and 12.12 show the responses for boys and girls separately. What emerges as consistent between these tables is that boys and their parents give slightly more 'unfavourable' responses and slightly fewer 'favourable' responses. About 2 per cent more of the girls' parents than of the boys' were

'satisfied'. About 6 per cent more girls than boys responded 'not true at all'.

Relationship with attainment and type of school
Parental response. Parental satisfaction was found to be clearly related to their children's school attainment as indicated by their performance on the reading comprehension test. Table 12.13 shows the results for four categories of reading attainment. The proportion of parents satisfied increases overall with reading score, and more parents in 'manual' social classes, at each different level, indicated that they were satisfied. However, as will be seen later, these results are strongly dependent on the type of school the children attended.

Figure 12.1 shows the relationship between parental satisfaction and reading score for each type

TABLE 12.9   *Pupils' responses to the statement 'I feel school is largely a waste of time'*

| Pupils' response | Social class | | | | |
	I + II	III NM	III M	IV + V	Total
Not true at all	67.4	63.7	56.6	52.2	59.3
Partly untrue	21.9	20.5	20.7	18.5	20.5
Can't say	4.9	8.3	11.2	14.2	9.9
Partly true	4.1	5.4	8.6	10.4	7.4
Very true	1.7	2.1	2.9	4.8	2.9
Total	2 246 (100%)	828 (100%)	3 738 (100%)	1 685 (100%)	8 497 (100%)

TABLE 12.10   *Parental response by their children's response*

| Parental satisfaction with child's education | Pupils' response to 'I feel school is largely a waste of time' | | | | | Total |
	Very true	Partly true	Can't say	Partly untrue	Not true	
Satisfied	2.3	6.6	8.9	19.5	62.7	6 311 (100%)
Satisfied in some ways	2.6	8.7	11.7	22.8	54.2	2 434 (100%)
Dissatisfied	8.0	14.9	12.8	21.0	43.3	663 (100%)
Uncertain	7.4	13.9	16.7	15.7	46.3	108 (100%)
Total	272	741	950	1 939	5 614	9 516

TABLE 12.11   *Parental 'satisfaction' and sex of their child*

| Sex | Parental response | | | | Total |
	Satisfied	Satisfied in some ways	Dissatisfied	Uncertain	
Boys	65.0	25.6	8.2	1.2	5 101 (100%)
Girls	67.2	25.4	6.2	1.3	4 927 (100%)
Total	66.1	25.5	7.2	1.2	10 028 (100%)

TABLE 12.12   *Pupils' responses to the statement 'I feel school is largely a waste of time' by sex*

Sex	Pupils' responses					Total
	Very true	Partly true	Can't say	Partly untrue	Not true	
Boys	3.8	9.0	10.6	21.1	55.5	6 003 (100%)
Girls	2.1	7.6	9.4	19.1	61.8	5 715 (100%)
Total	3.0	8.3	10.0	20.1	58.6	11 718 (100%)

TABLE 12.13   *Percentage of parents 'satisfied' by reading score and social class*

Social class	Reading score categories in SD units				Total
	−1	−0	0−1	1+	
Non-manual	59.2	57.1	61.5	66.2	61.4 (N = 2 762)
Manual	63.3	66.4	72.0	76.4	68.6 (N = 5 111)
Total	62.7	64.1	67.5	70.3	7 873

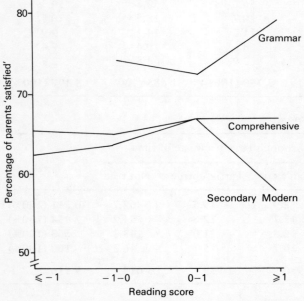

FIGURE 12.1   *Percentage of parents 'satisfied' by reading score and type of school*

ot school. Three points are immediately apparent: (a) more parents indicate satisfaction if their children are in grammar schools rather than in secondary moderns or comprehensives; (b) there is a sharp increase in the proportions of parents satisfied when their children are in grammar schools and a decrease for secondary modern schools in the higher ranges of school attainment; (c) the proportions of parents satisfied in the case of comprehensive and secondary modern pupils were very similar for a substantial part of the school performance band. In fact the proportions satisfied overall were identical in secondary modern and comprehensive schools (64 per cent).

Again, however, these results were found to be contingent on social class, and Figure 12.2 shows the relationship between parental satisfaction and reading score for different types of school and social class. For the sake of clarity comprehensive and secondary modern schools were combined for the first three categories of reading performances, as the differences between these schools in these ranges were small even within each social class (see Figure 12.1). Several points are of interest in Figure 12.2. For the first three categories of reading performance: (a) more 'manual' parents generally report satisfaction with increasing school performance of their child; (b) more non-manual parents *do not* indicate satisfaction with increasing school attainment of their children.

For the top categories of reading performance the different social classes in each type of school generally respond in a similar fashion. That is, more grammar school parents report satisfaction; there is a *decrease* in the proportion satisfied for secondary modern schools; the comprehensive school parents show a slight increase in the case of manual groups and remain constant for the non-manual groups. Overall the two groups which stand out are the 'manual grammar' parents, with a very high rate of satisfaction, and the 'non-manual comprehensives' with comparatively low proportions satisfied, which seem to be *independent* of their children's school attainment.

Young people's response. The responses of the children to the statement 'school is largely a waste of time' were again, as in the case of their parents' satisfaction, dependent on the child's attainment, social class and the type of school attended. However, though the differences between different attainment levels were generally greater in relation to the pupil's

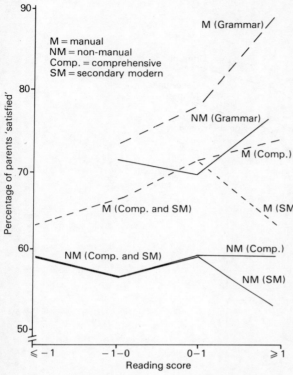

FIGURE 12.2   *Percentage of parents 'satisfied' by reading score by type of school and social class*

TABLE 12.14   *Percentage of pupils responding 'favourably' by reading score and social class*

Social class	Reading score categories in SD units				Total
	−1	−0	0−1	1+	
Non-manual	46.9	57.6	69.0	70.4	46.7 (N = 3 862)
Manual	40.3	52.0	62.3	71.7	55.2 (N = 5 036)
Total	41.2	53.4	65.1	70.9	(N = 8 898)

about 0.2 per cent for the non-manual and 3 per cent for the manual groups). What is apparent from this figure is the very high proportion of children from manual social classes in grammar schools who responded favourably, especially in the top attainment band. Furthermore, although there are differences between the children in non-manual and manual social classes in grammar schools, these differences are smaller (in the lower attainment groups) and negligible in (the higher attainment groups) in secondary modern and comprehensive schools. There seems to be a very high degree of commitment to school on the part of the children in manual social classes in grammar schools.

responses than the parents, they were usually smaller between the social classes and different types of school once the data were examined in relation to school attainment.

Table 12.14 shows the percentage of children whose response to the statement was 'not true', for each social class. There is an almost constant social-class difference of the order of 6 per cent (except in the top attainment category). However, in contrast to the parental responses, where more parents in manual rather than the non-manual social classes were 'satisfied' with their children's education, more non-manual children responded favourably to the statement than manual children.

Figure 12.3 shows the young people's responses by type of school for different attainment groups. More children in grammar schools responded favourably with very little difference between secondary modern and comprehensive schools. These data were further broken down by social class and are shown in Figure 12.4. For the sake of clarity the children in comprehensive and secondary modern schools are combined, as they were for the parents' response, as their responses were very similar even in the top attainment band (the difference between secondary modern and comprehensives for the top attainment band was

Other characteristics
Parental responses. The relation between the proportion of parents satisfied with their child's education and a number of school characteristics has been examined. This was done separately for grammar, comprehensive and secondary modern schools in order to avoid the confounding effects of the type of school. The variables chosen were: school size, sex segregation, pupil—teacher ratio, teacher turnover,* whether the child was in streamed or mixed-ability classes at the age of 16 in English or mathematics, streaming policy of the school for 12—13-year-old children, current English and mathematics class size, the number of hours per week the children had English or mathematics lessons, the frequency of parent—teacher meetings, regulations about school uniform (grouped as no uniform, voluntary, compulsory either for everyone or for certain items or certain age groups) and reported regularity of use of corporal punishment in the school.

* Teacher turnover was calculated as the ratio of the number of teachers who left in the previous academic year to the number of teachers in the school at present. Thus this does not allow for any expansion or contraction, in the number of teachers, over the two years.

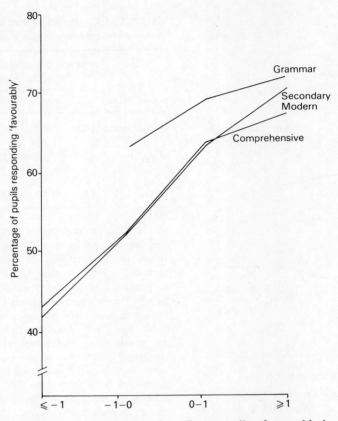

FIGURE 12.3   *Percentage of pupils responding favourably by
reading score and type of school*

For parents whose children were in grammar schools *none* of the above variables was significantly (at the 5 per cent level) related to the proportion responding as satisfied.

For those parents whose children were in a comprehensive school there were significant differences in five out of the fourteen variables. There was a higher percentage of 'satisfied' parents if their children were in smaller schools, with low teacher turnover, where punishment was not used, school uniform was voluntary and English classes were large. The latter, rather surprising, result might well be related to the higher performance of children in large classes (see the previous section).

For those parents whose children were in a secondary modern school the pattern was different yet again. Only two of the variables were significant. That is, higher proportions were 'satisfied' if their children were boys in single-sex schools rather than mixed schools and where the policy of the school was to have mixed-ability classes rather than streamed classes for children of 12—13 years of age.

It should be pointed out that all of the above differences were small, even though statistically significant, being no more than 10 per cent in the largest case.

Young people's responses. The relation between the proportion of children responding 'not true at all' to the statement 'school is largely a waste of time' and each of the same variables as above was examined.

As in the case of parents' responses, many of the variables showed no statistically significant asssociation. Where the associations were significant, the differences were again usually small.

Class size in both English and mathematics proved to be the only variable consistently related to the proportion responding favourably, i.e. 'not true', in all three types of schools. Table 12.15 shows the relationship for English class size (the results were similar for mathematics class size).

As can be seen from Table 12.15, there is an increase in the proportion of favourable responses with increasing class size. No doubt this is related to the superior performance of children in bigger classes (see the previous section) and perhaps also to the greater opportunity afforded by big classes for more social interaction (Hargreaves, 1967).

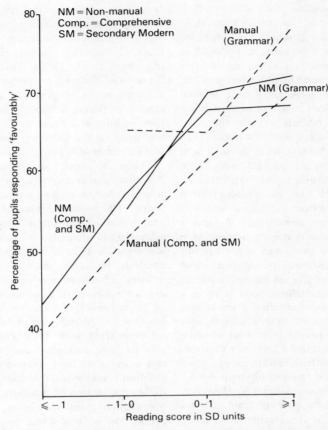

FIGURE 12.4 *Percentage of pupils responding favourably by reading score, type of school and social class.*

For children in grammar schools *none* of the other variables was statistically significant.

For those in comprehensives only three other variables were significant. That is, proportionately more children responded favourably if they were in schools which had regular parent–teacher meetings at least once per year (rather than irregular meetings); did not use corporal punishment; had either voluntary or compulsory uniform.

For young people in secondary modern schools four other variables were significant. That is, propor-

tionately more responded favourably if they were in schools; where the policy was to stream children aged 12–13 rather than have mixed-ability classes (a result opposite to that of their parents); where they had more hours per week English or mathematics; where they did not use corporal punishment.

Conclusions

A high proportion of parents reported that they were satisfied with their children's education. A greater

TABLE 12.15 *Percentage of children responding 'favourably' by type of school and size of class*

Type of school	English class size					Total
	−20	21−25	26−30	31−35	36+	
Grammar	65.0	64.3	70.5	76.2	86.7	1 274
Comprehensive	46.4	54.7	58.6	63.3	68.1	6 576
Secondary modern	44.6	54.7	58.8	62.1	60.4	2 365
Total	1 772	2 764	3 682	1 763	234	10 215

proportion of them responded favourably if they were from the manual social classes or their child was (a) a girl, (b) doing well at school (as judged by the tests described), (c) in a grammar as opposed to secondary modern or comprehensive school. To this should be added that in the case of secondary modern schools fewer parents in non-manual and manual homes whose children do well at school were satisfied than the parents whose children were in the same type of school but who did less well at school. There were very few school characteristics which were related to the proportion of parents who were satisfied, and these relationships were rather weak. The notable results were that no variables were significant for parents whose children were in grammar schools; a higher percentage of parents whose children were in comprehensive schools were satisfied if the school was small, had a low teacher turnover, did not use corporal punishment, had voluntary uniform and large English classes; a higher proportion of those parents whose boys were in a secondary modern school were satisfied if the school was a single-sex school rather than a mixed one.

A number of studies report a high level of satisfaction among parents (National Consumer Council, 1977b; Anon., 1965; Plowden, 1967), though they do not seem to examine the relationship with pupils' performance or characteristics of schools. However, the finding here, that more parents from manual social classes are satisfied, is in agreement with the Plowden Report (on primary schools, of course), though it conflicts with that of the report by the National Consumer Council.

The response of a substantial number of children to the statement 'I think school is largely a waste of time' was 'not true at all'. A higher proportion of girls and children in non-manual rather than manual social classes had this feeling towards school. Further, more children responded 'not true at all' if they did well at school, and were in grammar rather than in comprehensive or secondary modern schools. It should be added that children who did very well at school, were from manual social classes, and attended grammar schools gave the highest proportion of

favourable responses. The sex, social-class and school attainment results in this report confirm other British investigations into attitudes to school (e.g. Barker Lunn, 1970) and contrast with American findings (e.g. Berk *et al.*, 1970). Kniveton (1969), however, found no differences between boys and girls or between pupils in grammar and secondary modern school in 'liking school'. The discrepancy between these results and those presented here could be due not only to the differing questions but also to the small number of schools sampled by him.

When the proportion of young people responding 'favourably' was examined in relation to a number of school characteristics, very few differences were found. The most notable one was an increase in the proportion of favourable responses in all types of school with increasing class size. No other variable was significant for children in grammar schools. More children in both comprehensive and secondary modern schools responded favourably if their school did not use corporal punishment.

There was a clear association between the responses of parents and children. That is, those who were satisfied with their child's education tended also to have children who did not feel that school was a waste of time. In comparing the parents' and children's responses the most striking point is the higher proportion of satisfied parents in manual than non-manual social classes as opposed to the higher proportion of favourable responses by pupils from non-manual than manual social classes. Thus while children from non-manual social classes indicate more commitment to school their parents are at the same time more critical of the education they are receiving. Furthermore, parental satisfaction does not seem to be strongly related to factors which are usually the subject of much debate such as school size, pupil–teacher ratio, streaming, class size, etc. What does seem to be of most importance are the level of performance of the child and the type of school they attend, though there seems to be a fair proportion of parents satisfied with their child's education even if they are apparently doing poorly.

13 Guidance, Careers and Further Education*

EDUCATIONAL AND CAREER ASPIRATIONS OF 16-YEAR-OLDS

A study of educational and career aspirations among young people nearing the school-leaving age is relevant to many topical issues. In recent years, for example, we have frequently heard statements that young people are turning away from productive occupations in industry and are increasingly attracted to welfare-orientated jobs and others in the public sector. Another recurring issue is that of sexual equality. It is suggested that society in general, and schools in particular, have led girls to lower their aspirations and, for no good reason, to see themselves as suited to work which is of a different nature and less prestigious than that aspired to by boys (see, for example, Sharpe, 1976). Then there are changing patterns in higher education, with dramatic reductions in teacher-training, which traditionally has been predominantly female — and increases in the proportion of girls entering university; it seems, indeed, that girls are displacing working-class boys there (Hutchison and McPherson, 1976).

In general the debate on such issues is taking place amid a scarcity of relevant evidence. There is no adequate account, based on a representative sample of young people, of their hopes and intentions for their careers and education on leaving school. Several major studies in this area have been published in recent years, but each is partial. For example, Morton-Williams and Finch (1968) examined the kinds of jobs and further education foreseen by a sample of 15-year-olds, and related these to, for instance, sex differences, region and careers advice provided by schools; this study, however, was limited to children who were to leave school at the age of 15, and furthermore the data were collected in 1966, since when there have been considerable changes both in the opportunities available to school-leavers

*Original sources: Fogelman, K., 'Educational and career aspirations — findings from a national sample of sixteen-year-olds', British Journal of Guidance and Counselling, 7 (1) 1979; Lambert, L., 'Careers guidance and choosing a job', British Journal of Guidance and Counselling, 6 (2) 1978.

and (probably) in their perceptions. Again, Timperley and Gregory (1971) offer interesting observations on the relationship between career choice and personal, home and school factors, but their sample is restricted to sixth-form leavers. Rauta and Hunt (1975) did study the age group with which we are concerned — fifth-formers — but girls only; moreover, their survey was carried out in 1972, prior to changes in secondary education and to legislation on female equality. Finally, although the work carried out by Williams and Gordon (1976) is more recent and concerned with a wide range of information and hypotheses, the authors' comments make it clear that their survey was seen as a pilot study only, and for that reason their sample is small.

In this section information will be presented on the occupational and educational plans of a large and nationally representative group of 16-year-olds. Differences in their aspirations will be related to a number of background factors. The value of these data is, it is hoped, twofold. First, they should clarify some of the issues raised above and in earlier work. Second, they may serve as a base-line for future work. Williams and Gordon (1976) have argued the case for a longitudinal study relating attitudes and aspirations to eventual career patterns. Ideally, they have said, such work 'would be integrated into a major longitudinal survey from birth such as that being carried out by the National Child Development Study'. The data here are therefore presented, not only in the hope that they are of value in their own right, but also as information which could in the future be related to the actual experiences of these young people after leaving school.

Other researchers in this area have acknowledged that they are examining a situation which is far from stable, and we must do the same. The data presented below were collected in 1974, and since then the unemployment of school-leavers has increased substantially. It is difficult to estimate how different our findings would have been if the data had been collected, say, two years later. Knowledge of difficulties in obtaining employment may well have led young people to adjust their aspirations and/or expectations. Perhaps more crucially, since the major concern here is with such relationships, the changes may have been greater for some social groups than others. If our data can be compared with other people's findings and experience in subsequent years, this will enable such questions to be answered.

NCDS data

The analyses presented below centre on a group of questions included in the questionnaires completed by the young people at 16. First, they were asked: 'What would you *like* to be your first full-time job?' This was immediately followed by: 'What do you think is *in fact likely* to be your first full-time job?' Answers to these questions were coded into approximately seventy occupational categories. In order to produce comprehensible analyses, these categories have been further reduced to thirteen groups plus an 'uncertain and other responses' group. Examples of the kinds of job included in each group are given in the Appendix to this section. It should be borne in mind throughout that, for the sake of brevity, each group has been given a title which represents a wide range of occupations. Furthermore, since we were asking about aspirations and not actual jobs, it was not sensible to ask for the kind of detail such as size of business, number supervised, whether paid weekly or monthly, etc., which is usually necessary in order to classify occupations meaningfully. Such considerations warn against over-narrow

interpretations of the occupational groups in the following tables.

The data on educational plans are based on a group of three questions from the same questionnaire:

1. '*At what age do you think you are most likely to leave school?*' (for which the pre-coded options were: 16; 17; 18 or over; uncertain).
2. '*After you leave school would you like to continue with full-time study?*' (do a job that involves part-time study; do a job that requires no further study; don't know).
3. '*If you want to continue with full-time study, please ring the number against the place where you would most like to do it?*' (university or polytechnic; teacher-training college; technical school; college of commerce or secretarial college; college of art; music or drama; somewhere else; don't know).

For our present purposes, answers to these three questions have been combined to give a single composite variable.

Occupational aspirations and expectations

In relating occupational aspirations and expectations to social and other variables it is necessary to establish first whether aspirations and expectations should be considered separately. The relevant data are presented in Table 13.1. The figures in the second

TABLE 13.1   *Distribution of likely job and proportion choosing aspired job from same category by sex*

Occupational groups (see Appendix)	Boys		Girls	
	(a) % naming likely job in this category	(b) % of (a) naming aspired job in same category	(c) % naming likely job in this category	(d) % of (c) naming aspired job in same category
Outdoor	4.4	78.7	1.7	91.1
Artistic, etc.	2.0	81.4	2.4	90.2
Teachers	2.2	80.3	8.9	84.0
Professions	10.3	91.5	2.4	91.5
Other professions	7.1	76.5	3.9	80.7
Caring	0.4	80.0	12.8	90.4
Shopworkers	2.8	51.3	14.2	64.7
Other services	5.3	76.0	3.6	76.7
Clerical	3.7	60.4	30.4	80.5
Building	7.7	82.6	0	—
Engineering	20.2	86.6	0.2	83.3
Other industrial	9.9	66.0	7.0	49.1
Forces and merchant navy	8.3	88.3	1.4	69.7
Uncertain	15.8	—	11.1	—
N (= 100 %)	5 452		5 417	

and fourth columns indicate that the majority said they would like a job which was at least similar to (i.e. fell within the same broad category as) the job which they felt they were likely to do (though boys seemed to be somewhat less set in their decisions, perhaps because there was a wider range of options open to them). In other words, by this age aspirations are pretty much in line with expectations.

None the less there is considerable variation according to the type of job being considered. If popularity is defined in terms of the proportions of those *expecting* to go into an occupational group who *choose* to do so, the least popular jobs are those in shops, those in industries other than building and engineering, and (for boys only) clerical jobs. It is in relation to shopwork that there is a conflict between hopes and expectations for many girls: one in seven think they are likely to do this kind of work, but of these more than one-third would like to do something different. Similarly, of those girls expecting to go into 'other industries' (such as textiles) only about half actually would like a job of this kind.

Despite such variations, the relationship between expectations and aspirations in general seems sufficiently close to justify reducing the quantity of data to be presented here by concentrating on one of them. Furthermore, the relationship of expectations and aspirations respectively with the background variables considered below has been examined, and no dramatic differences due to using one rather than the other were found. Since the number of 'don't knows' is smaller for aspirations, it is this which has been chosen for presentation below.

Before moving on to other findings, further aspects of Table 13.1 deserve comment. Several facets of the straightforward distribution of 'likely job' are interesting. For example, the imputed limited popularity of the engineering industry is not borne out by these data, in that one in five of the boys expected to work in this area, and for most this was what they wanted to do. However, it should be noted (see the Appendix) that this group refers essentially to manual engineering occupations and not necessarily to management and professional engineering. Moreover, we can only comment on its popularity in relation to other kinds of work, not on whether it is sufficiently popular for the needs of industry to be met.

Also noteworthy is the tiny number of boys expecting to enter what we have termed the 'caring' occupations, which include, for example, social work and probation. Similarly, the proportion of boys expecting to enter teaching is only about one-quarter of the figure for girls. Indeed, if one examines the proportion expecting to enter what one might roughly term 'middle-class occupations', there is a noticeable difference between the boys' and girls' expectations, the boys tending towards the more prestigious professions and towards technical and managerial work ('other professions').

Perhaps the most striking pattern to emerge from Table 13.1 is indeed the difference between the sexes. Some are to be expected: it is very rare for a girl to go into building or engineering (no comment is offered on whether this is inevitable). But other differences, though in the expected direction, are perhaps greater than might have been anticipated, for example in relation to shopwork and clerical jobs.

Further insight into this difference between the sexes can be gained from Table 13.2, which shows the factor identified (from a precoded list) as being the most important in choosing a job. The dominant aspects of a job for a 16-year-old boy would appear to be 'good pay' and 'variety'. While good pay is not neglected by the girls, it drops in order of importance below 'variety' and 'the opportunity of helping others', a factor chosen by relatively few boys. Such differences between the sexes indicate how misleading it might be to ignore them. Accordingly, all remaining analyses treat the two sexes separately.

TABLE 13.2   *Most important factor in choosing a job*

	Boys (%)	Girls (%)
The job should involve working with your hands	11.6	4.8
It should involve using your head and need thought and concentration	11.8	7.1
It should be an outdoor job	5.5	1.6
It should be well paid	24.5	16.9
It should have convenient hours and conditions	5.8	7.5
The job should involve variety	18.6	25.4
The job should offer you chances of promotion	11.9	9.4
It should give you the chance of being in charge of other people	0.4	0.4
The job should let you be your own boss	2.4	0.8
It should be a clean job	0.8	2.5
It should give you the opportunity of helping others	4.2	20.3
It should not have too much responsibility at first	2.6	3.2
N (= 100%)	6 042	5 818

Educational plans

Table 13.3 gives the distribution of replies to the combined item on educational plans described earlier. Once again, the contrast between the sexes is immediately apparent. Although there is little difference in the proportion seeing themselves as staying on at school after the age of 16, fewer girls envisage going to a university or polytechnic, and considerably more plan to go to a college of education or into some other kind of full-time study. Among the 16-year-old leavers, the boys more commonly plan some form of part-time study; although this is also the intention of many of the girls who are planning to leave at 16, they choose full-time study, and no study at all, more frequently than the boys.

TABLE 13.3   *Educational plans by sex*

Type of study and school-leaving age	Boys (%)	Girls (%)
University or polytechnic	13.7	9.6
College of education	2.1	7.6
Other full-time study from 17/18	2.7	5.8
Part-time study from 17/18	7.5	6.4
No study from 17/18	1.7	1.5
Uncertain from 17/18	3.2	3.4
Full-time study from 16	3.5	8.4
Part-time study from 16	33.3	21.1
No study from 16	14.9	18.8
Uncertain from 16	9.8	11.6
Other (various plans with leaving age uncertain)	7.5	5.8
N (= 100%)	6 188	5 901

To establish how realistic these educational plans are, one would need to relate these statements made at 16 to what in fact happened subsequently. It is, however, possible to secure more approximate answers immediately. First, some of the figures in Table 13.3 can be compared with the actual destinations of 1974 school-leavers as reported by the DES (1976). Table 13.4 shows that the proportions of 16-year-olds planning to go to a university/polytechnic or to a college of education are somewhat higher than the proportions which actually went there in 1974, whereas the figures for 'other full-time further education' are virtually identical. But it must not be forgotten that the DES figures are for *immediate* destinations and do not take account of those who take a year or two off to work or to see the world.

A second possible comparison is with statements made by teachers as to the kind of further education to which the young people were most suited. It seems reasonable to assume that teachers are fairly accurate in their assessments of immediate future educational destinations; indeed, they are likely to be major determinants of these destinations. Apart from a slight discrepancy in relation to the proportion of boys going to a university or polytechnic, the teachers' statements are much in line with the young people's expectations as far as going to university, polytechnic or college of education is concerned. On the other hand, the proportions considered by teachers as suitable for other types of full-time further education were considerably in excess both of the 16-year-olds' expectations and of actual destinations. If one assumes that the latter under-estimate the numbers *eventually* going into further education, there is a suggestion here that not all 16-year-olds are as aware as they might be of opportunities for continued full-time education outside universities, polytechnics and colleges of education.

Of course, it is not only such overall distributions which are relevant, but also the extent of agreement on individual children. For the majority, the teachers' assessments were in line with the 16-year-olds' intentions. There were still, however, substantial numbers where they were not. For example, of those considered by their teacher to be suited to degree-level courses, just over two-thirds were planning to go to a university or polytechnic, but about 2.5 per cent planned to leave school at 16 (with no difference

TABLE 13.4   *Further education intentions, assessments and destinations*

	16-year-olds' plans		Teachers' assessments		Destinations as reported by DES (1976)	
	Boys (%)	Girls (%)	Boys (%)	Girls (%)	Boys (%)	Girls (%)
University/polytechnic	14	10	11	9	9	6
College of education	2	8	2	8	1	4
Other full-time further education	6	14	18	25	7	14

between boys and girls). On the other hand, of those whose teachers said (in response to another question) that they would benefit from staying at school beyond 16, 27 per cent of boys and 30 per cent of girls planned to leave at that age (including 4 and 6 per cent respectively without any further study).

The influence of social class

That there is a close relationship between social class on the one hand, and children's development and educational attainment on the other, is by now well known. To find a general relationship between social class and the job which a 16-year-old hopes to obtain — i.e. to find that his or her choice of job is to some extent related to father's occupation — would be unsurprising. On the other hand, there is interest in the exact nature of this relationship, and in particular in the extent of any departure from what one would expect — in other words, of potential social mobility.

Table 13.5 shows the distributions of job aspirations related to sex and social class. To make this table a little easier to assimilate, in each column the three occupational groups most frequently chosen are in **bold**. The overall pattern is much in line with expectations. For example, the 'professions' are by far the most common choice of boys of professionals and managers and the proportions in this category reduce steadily with decreasing social class. The

building-trade pattern is in the opposite direction, being most often chosen by boys from semi- and unskilled manual backgrounds. The armed forces and merchant navy figures are also in a 'working-class' direction, though the differences between the social classes here are small. The engineering industry is relatively popular with all social classes, but particularly so with children from manual backgrounds.

There is similar variation for girls, but in relation to quite different job categories. Particularly notable is the large number of girls from professional backgrounds hoping to go into teaching. Shopwork and 'other industrial' show much the same pattern for girls as did 'building' for boys, while clerical work would seem to be the female equivalent to the engineering industry.

Table 13.6 examines educational plans in the same way, and confirms the patterns which we have seen elsewhere. There is a marked contrast, even between the two non-manual groups, in the proportion intending to stay at school past the age of 16 and, within this group, in the proportion hoping to go to a university or polytechnic. By contrast, the colleges of education can apparently expect to receive applications from a group which is far more socially representative, although still by no means totally so. In all, only about one in twelve of the children of professional and managerial fathers expects to cease studying altogether at 16 as against about one in four

TABLE 13.5   *Aspired job, by sex and social class*

	Social class									
	I & II		III NM		III M		IV & V		No male head	
	Boys (%)	Girls (%)	Boys (%)	Girls (%)	Boys (%)	Girls (%)	Boys (%)	Girls (%)	Boys (%)	Girls (%)
Outdoor	5	4	3	4	3	2	5	2	4	2
Artistic, etc.	5	8	8	4	5	4	4	4	5	5
Teachers	4	18	3	8	2	9	1	7	2	8
Professions	29	10	16	4	10	2	7	1	8	2
Other professions	11	7	10	8	9	4	8	3	5	3
Caring	1	15	0.4	18	0.4	19	0.1	18	1	20
Shopworkers	2	5	2	11	2	13	2	15	2	13
Other services	4	5	5	6	7	5	6	4	7	4
Clerical	4	20	4	28	3	32	3	30	2	30
Building	3	0	5	0	9	0	11	0.2	11	0
Engineering	12	0.2	21	1	28	0.4	27	0.4	26	0
Other industrial	4	1	5	1	9	4	11	9	8	6
Forces and merchant navy	6	1	10	1	9	2	10	4	13	3
Uncertain	10	8	8	6	6	5	6	4	7	5
N (= 100%)	1 093	1 020	507	438	1 890	1 829	815	771	322	343

of those from semi- and unskilled manual back-grounds. On the other hand, it should not be overlooked that the numbers of working-class children hoping to go into higher education are far from trivial and that the great majority intend to continue with some form of study beyond 16.

Parental education

It might be expected that the relationship between parents' own educational level and their social class would be quite close and therefore produce similar relationships with children's aspirations and intentions. This is indeed the case, but categorising parents by their education produces even more extreme contrasts than did social class. Table 13.7 presents figures for selected groups only (groups

where both parents finished full-time education at about the same age are shown).

Of course, the group of children both of whose parents had stayed in education to 19 or beyond is relatively small, but nevertheless some of the figures relating to them are striking. Virtually half of the boys in this group would like to go into one of the professions, two-thirds hope to go to university and 88 per cent plan to stay at school until 17 or 18. Even within this small group there are marked contrasts between the boys and girls. The numbers anticipating staying at school are not dissimilar, but it does appear that girls from this background are somewhat less likely to go to university and more likely to opt for such jobs as teaching, librarianship, nursing, etc., rather than the more prestigious professions chosen by their brothers.

TABLE 13.6   *Educational plans, by sex and social class*

| | Social class | | | | | | | | | |
| | I & II | | III NM | | III M | | IV & V | | No male head | |
	Boys (%)	Girls (%)	Boys (%)	Girls (%)	Boys (%)	Girls (%)	Boys (%)	Girls (%)	Boys (%)	Girls (%)
University or polytechnic	31	22	16	10	7	6	6	3	7	5
College of education	3	11	3	9	2	8	2	5	2	6
Other full-time from 17/18	4	11	3	5	2	4	2	3	2	6
Part-time from 17/18	10	9	8	6	6	6	5	5	8	5
No study from 17/18	3	2	2	3	2	2	1	1	2	1
Uncertain from 17/18	6	5	3	4	2	3	2	1	3	2
Full-time from 16	5	12	4	9	4	8	4	5	2	8
Part-time from 16	19	12	34	23	40	24	38	25	28	27
No study from 16	8	8	10	16	16	21	22	26	18	21
Uncertain from 16	4	3	8	9	11	15	14	19	11	11
Other	9	6	11	7	7	5	5	6	8	8
N (= 100%)	1 148	1 143	523	454	1 976	1 885	840	793	336	353

TABLE 13.7   *Educational plans by sex and parents' full-time education (selected groups)*

| | Both parents finished education at 15 or less | | Both finished between 15 and 18 | | Both finished at 19 or more | |
	Boys (%)	Girls (%)	Boys (%)	Girls (%)	Boys (%)	Girls (%)
University or polytechnic	6	5	19	12	66	51
College of education	2	6	3	10	2	9
Leaving 17/18, all other destinations	10	12	19	23	13	19
Leaving 16, some study	44	32	35	29	5	9
Leaving 16, no study	19	25	12	13	1	2
N (= 100%)	1 867	1 758	1 300	1 314	97	92

At the other end of the scale, those whose parents left school at 15 are more likely to go into engineering and other industries (for the boys) and office and shopwork (for the girls). On the other hand, the relative size of our groups should not be forgotten. If hopes are realised, there will be substantial numbers of young men and women going into higher education whose parents did not experience this, and even left school at the minimum age in many cases.

Ability

Clearly one of the most important mediating factors in young people's occupational and educational plans will be their school attainment. By the age of 16 they are likely to have a fairly clear concept of their educational success in relation to their peers and of the general range of opportunities open to them. It is not intended here to waste paper by demonstrating that children who are doing well at school are more likely to intend to stay at school, go on to higher education, and take up middle-class jobs.

There is, however, the question of 'wasted talent'. Is it true, first, that there are significant numbers of able children who, for whatever reason, leave the formal educational system earlier than they might have done, and second, that relatively few of the more able are attracted by 'productive' occupations? To attempt to answer these questions, Table 13.8 shows the occupational aspirations and educational plans of those who scored in approximately the top 15 per cent in terms of the reading test administered at 16 to all the NCDS subjects.

In relation to work aspirations, we see the by now familiar pattern of differences between the sexes, with almost half the boys hoping to go into professional or managerial jobs, and significant numbers also hoping to go into engineering or the armed forces. Of the girls, the greatest proportion hope to go into teaching, and large numbers (though fewer than boys) are aiming for other professional and semi-professional occupations; many also see themselves going into caring professions. In addition, it is striking how many of these more able girls hope to go into 'artistic' work (though note from the Appendix that this includes a wide range of work not immediately conveyed by its title).

It appears to be true that relatively few of these children are attracted by so-called 'productive' occupations, though it should be borne in mind that some of the jobs included in the 'other professional' category, and perhaps also in the 'professions', might merit this description. Relatively few intend to stop formal study altogether at 16. Although there are substantial numbers intending to take a job which involves part-time study from 16, the great majority anticipate staying at school beyond that age. Here again there is a sex difference which cannot pass without comment: although, overall, slightly more girls plan to stay on at school, within that group boys are more likely then to proceed either to a degree course or to a job with part-time study, while girls are more likely to go into teacher-training or some other kind of full-time course.

Regional variations

The variables which have been examined so far are

TABLE 13.8   *Occupational aspirations and educational plans of children with high reading scores*

Occupational aspirations	Boys (%)	Girls (%)	Educational plans	Boys (%)	Girls (%)
Outdoor	2	3	University or polytechnic	43	38
Artistic, etc.	7	12	College of education	3	10
Teachers	5	20	Other FT from 17/18	5	10
Professions	35	18	PT from 17/18	12	9
Other professions	13	10	No study from 17/18	2	2
Caring	1	12	Uncertain from 17/18	6	5
Shopworkers	0.3	2	FT from 16	2	5
Other services	4	2	PT from 16	14	8
Clerical	4	10	No study from 16	2	5
Building	1	0	Uncertain from 16	2	1
Engineering	8	0.5	Others	8	8
Other industrial	2	0.4			
Forces and merchant navy	8	1			
Uncertain	10	9			
N (= 100%)	978	739	N (= 100%)	1 007	753

indicators of either family (social class, parental education) or personal (sex, educational attainment) influences on future plans. Such plans are of course likely to depend very much on what jobs are available to young people, not only in terms of the overall occupational structure of Britain, but also the specific distribution of local industries, etc. Although we have neither a direct nor a very local measure of this, it is interesting to examine the broad regional variation in young people's plans (although 5 per cent of them did say that they would be willing to move to get the job they wanted: Fogelman, 1976).

In the event there were considerable variations among the regions. Some contrasts undoubtedly reflect the local availability of particular kinds of work: for example, 7 per cent of both boys and girls in the South-West hoped for an outdoor job compared at the other extreme with 2 per cent of boys in London and the South-East and 1 per cent of girls in North-West England. Others are probably best explained in terms of the differing social composition of the regions: 20 per cent of boys in London and the South-East hoped to go into one of the 'professions' but only 11 per cent of boys in the East and West Ridings of Yorkshire (as they were officially known at the time our data were collected). Some contrasts are less easily explained, but perhaps arise from local traditions and the prestige of particular jobs. For example, the highest proportions of girls hoping to teach were found in Wales (16 per cent) and Scotland (13 per cent); and the highest proportion of boys hoping to enter the armed forces was found in the North of England (12 per cent).

Similar variations appear in relation to educational plans. Perhaps the least encouraging figures are those for Scottish boys. They provide the lowest proportion hoping to go to a university or polytechnic, or rather, their equivalent in Scotland — central institutions (12 per cent compared with 17 per cent for the South of England and for London and the South-East), the highest proportion intending to leave school at 16 with no further study (20 per cent compared with 11 per cent in London and the South-East), and the lowest proportion intending to leave school at 16 but continue with part-time study (26 per cent compared with 41 per cent in Yorkshire and in the North Midlands). In part this may reflect relative lack of occupational opportunity in Scotland, but it is not clear why this should necessarily produce lower educational aspirations. It may also be a function of social composition and of the lower average reading attainment at 16 of Scottish schoolchildren (see Fogelman *et al.*, 1978b: see pp. 36–42).

Although, as elsewhere, the educational aspirations of Scottish girls are lower than those of the boys, they are not so depressed relative to other parts of the country. Among girls it is the North of England which has the lowest proportion hoping to go to university or polytechnic (8 per cent as against, at the other extreme, 13 per cent in London and the South-East); the South-West which has the highest proportion intending to stop studying at 16 (21 per cent as against 16 per cent in the South of England); and Wales which has the lowest proportion aiming to continue part-time study from 16 (16 per cent as against 26 per cent in the North-West). In general, there appears to be slightly less regional variation in educational plans among girls than among boys.

Conclusions

The regional data have suggested the importance of local circumstances and traditions in describing the occupational aspirations and educational plans of young people. Bearing this caution in mind, we have nevertheless confirmed, using a large and nationally representative sample, the strong relationship found by other researchers between future plans and background variables such as social class and parental education.

It has, however, been seen that such relationships are less than exact. If aspirations and plans are in the event realised — and it has been shown that 16-year-olds' aspirations are at least related both to their own and their teachers' expectations — then there will be considerable numbers whose careers will be very different from that of their parents. In part this will be due to economic growth and a general upward shift in the occupational and educational structure. Many more of the present generation will go on to higher education, and from our own data it would appear that there are more children from working-class backgrounds likely to take up middle-class occupations than the reverse. At the same time, there is a foreshadowing of substantial social mobility (in both directions) over and above this (although of course considerable change could take place in the course of these young people's careers).

As there are no adequate comparable data available for earlier years, it is not possible to test directly the truth of statements about movement away from productive occupations in general and engineering in particular. But given the large numbers choosing jobs in our engineering group, it is clear that within the range of industrial work engineering is still extremely popular among boys. On the other hand, among more able boys the 'learned professions' appear to be much more attractive.

This leads us to perhaps the most striking and consistent pattern to emerge from the data — the sex differences. If it is really necessary to attract more young people into 'productive' jobs, then there is clearly most scope for change among girls, who at present consider such jobs rarely, if at all. If there is to be such a change, then there is not likely to be a better opportunity for it than at present. Large proportions of these 16-year-old girls hoped to go into such jobs as teaching, nursing, other medically orientated work, social work, and jobs involving working with children. Given the decline in the birth rate in recent years and current pressures on public expenditure, these are the very areas where career opportunities are, at best, no longer expanding, and often in fact contracting. They are perhaps therefore areas in which many young people are not going to be able to fulfil their aspirations, and are going to need to consider alternatives.

In this context, however, we should not forget that there are already substantial numbers of girls expecting to take jobs in our 'other industries' group, and it was in this group that the lowest proportion of those *expecting* to take such a job actually wanted to do so. If industry is to attract more young people, and girls in particular, an explanation needs to be found for this figure, together with some means of improving it. Of course, this is not simply a matter of changing images and persuading young people into factories. We must also ask ourselves if there are more fundamental changes necessary to make jobs more attractive and satisfying to an increasingly educated work-force.

Appendix: Examples of occupations included in the fourteen categories used

1. *Outdoor*: farmer, fisherman, forester, 'work with animals', gardeners.
2. *Artistic, entertainers and sportsmen*: painter, sculptor, commercial artist, actor, musician, journalist, TV producer, sportsman, model, commentator.
3. *Teachers*: all types of teacher, other than university.
4. *Professions*: university teacher or researcher, lawyer, accountant, architect, doctor, dentist, pilot, scientist, priest.
5. *Other professional and semi-professional*: export manager, production manager, bank manager, estate agent, librarian, interpreter, draughtsman, computer programmer, photographer, optician.
6. *Caring occupations*: nurse, social worker, physiotherapist, chiropodist, dental nurse, nursery nurse, probation officer, 'working with children'.
7. *Hairdressers and shopworkers*: hairdresser, beautician, shop assistant, petrol-pump attendant.
8. *Other services*: policeman, fireman, ambulanceman, postman, porter, dustman, driver, commercial traveller, demonstrator, catering worker, steward, caretaker.
9. *Clerical*: secretary, typist, cashier, filing clerk, telephonist, receptionist, bank clerk, office machine operator.
10. *Building trades*: bricklayer, plasterer, painter and decorator, carpet fitter, plumber, stonemason.
11. *Engineering trades*: mechanic, fitter, sheet-metal worker, erector, electrician, welder.

12. *Other industrial*: printer, woodworker, textile worker, packer, storekeeper, miner, labourer.
13. *Forces and Merchant Navy*.
14. *Uncertain and other replies*: includes 'don't know', unclassifiable, vague answers, and those not wanting to work.

CAREERS GUIDANCE AND CHOOSING A JOB

Introduction

There has been a rapid increase in the provision of careers guidance in schools in the last two decades. In 1964 only just over half the schools in a survey conducted by the Careers Research and Advisory Centre had a careers teacher (Carter, 1966), but by 1972 HM Inspectorate reported that an estimated 94 per cent of schools in England and Wales had one or more designated careers teachers (DES, 1973). There was a similar expansion in appointing staff in Scotland, particularly after 1971 (SED, 1976). Undoubtedly major influences on this increase in provision included preparation for the raising of the school-leaving age (which took place in 1974 after earlier postponements), and the requirement of the Employment and Training Act of 1973 that all LEAs should provide a vocational guidance service in educational institutions.

None the less, there continue to be many criticisms of the amount and quality of work that careers teachers do or can be expected to do (Carter, 1966; Schools Council, 1972; DES, 1973; National Youth Employment Council, 1974; SED, 1976; Roberts, 1977). These criticisms have usually referred specifically to the amount of time, resources, training and responsibility allowance available to these teachers. There has also been much discussion of the work and role of careers officers, and in particular their relationship with schools.

An important element in the assessment of the role and tasks of careers teachers and careers officers is the view of the consumer — the schoolchild. Some aspects of their contacts with those responsible for careers guidance can be gained from data collected in 1974 for the National Child Development Study (NCDS).

When asked at the age of 16 about where they had heard about their likely first full-time job, the answer 'at school, from a teacher or careers talk or film' came top of the sources listed by girls (mentioned by 45 per cent), and second after 'from parents' among the boys' choices (mentioned by 39 per cent). Here provisions for careers guidance in schools and contacts with careers officers are examined in relation to the young people's plans for leaving school and their choice of jobs.

School characteristics

Although the NCDS findings relate to individuals rather than to schools, and refer to Britain as a whole, they provide a useful complement to the more wide-ranging institutional survey of careers education in English and Welsh secondary schools carried out by HM Inspectorate in 1971–2 (DES, 1973) and also to surveys carried out by HM Inspectorate in Scotland in 1973–4 (SED, 1976). First, the number and training of teachers in careers guidance, and the extent of pupils' contacts with careers officers, were looked at in relation to the type of school the young people attended. This information came from the educational questionnaire completed for each study child by their teachers, and material was also taken from the confidential written questionnaire filled in at school by the young people themselves.

Only 2 per cent of the 16-year-olds were in schools where there were reported to be no teachers who had responsibility for careers guidance. The picture was, however, much less satisfactory in special schools, where 34 per cent of pupils were attending schools in which no teacher had responsibility for careers guidance; this illustrates the general lack of provision for handicapped school-leavers (DES, 1973; Walker and Lewis, 1978). Another group of teenagers who appeared to lack provision for careers guidance was the small number in 'community homes' ('list D homes' in Scotland): fifteen out of twenty-seven known to be attending such homes (which provide education on the premises) were in homes where no member of staff had a particular responsibility for careers guidance.

The number of teachers in a school who had responsibility for careers guidance was obviously related to the size of school. Big comprehensives had up to nine or more such teachers, but the average

was between one and two: 42 per cent of pupils were attending schools with one careers teacher, 33 per cent with two. In a few cases these teachers were undertaking careers guidance as a full-time appointment; in most, however, it was combined with other duties. Overall, 74 per cent of the children were in schools where a teacher was paid a special salary for this work, but this figure covered variations ranging from 79 per cent in comprehensive schools, 73 per cent in grammar schools, and 68 per cent in secondary modern schools, to only 32 per cent in special schools.

Table 13.9 shows the amount of training in careers work that teachers in different types of schools had received (if there was more than one careers teacher in a school, the answer applied to the teacher who had received most training). Pupils in comprehensive schools were more likely to have a careers teacher who had had some training than were those in other types of schools, and where the duration of training was known, comprehensive school teachers were also more likely to have received the longest period of training. Recognition of this greater amount of training is probably reflected in the higher proportion of comprehensive school teachers who were paid a special salary in respect of their careers guidance work. It will not escape notice that the relatively few careers teachers in special schools and community homes were the least likely to have received training for this work.

The somewhat lower proportion of pupils in secondary modern schools who had teachers trained for careers guidance may have led to a greater reliance on careers officers: 82 per cent were reported by their teachers to have had contact with a careers officer, compared with 75 per cent in comprehensive schools, and 66 per cent in grammar schools. Of course, this finding is also likely to have been related

TABLE 13.9 *Proportion of pupils whose teachers had special responsibility for careers guidance, related to amount of training received by the teachers and to type of school*

Type of school	N = 100%	Amount of training				
		None	< 7 days	7–15 days	> 15 days	Some, duration unknown
Comprehensive	7 133	10.5	11.8	15.1	40.3	22.3
Grammar	1 288	12.1	15.5	20.3	29.0	23.1
Secondary modern	2 561	15.4	14.2	16.2	31.0	23.2
Technical	69	23.2	7.3	21.7	34.8	13.0
Special (LEA)	135	54.8	8.9	7.4	5.9	23.0
Independent	403	18.4	13.1	15.9	20.8	31.8
Direct grant	281	12.1	12.1	15.0	28.8	32.0
Community home	11	63.6	0.0	9.1	9.1	18.2
Total	11 881	12.6	12.7	15.9	35.7	23.1

to the greater proportion of pupils in secondary modern schools who said they would be likely to be leaving school at 16, and who would thus be needing to get a job fixed up within a few months. Thus when the young people themselves were asked to say where they had heard about their likely first full-time job, pupils in secondary modern schools were more likely than those in other types of schools to name the careers officer. There was, however, no significant difference between pupils in secondary modern and in comprehensive schools who said they had heard about their likely job 'at school, from a teacher or careers talk or film'.

Regional characteristics

Welsh pupils were more likely than Scottish pupils to be in schools with teachers who had received at least some training for careers guidance and were receiving a special salary for this work; English pupils came somewhere between these two groups (Table 13.10). In Scotland a new staffing structure for secondary schools which established a system of guidance posts in all schools was still being implemented by education authorities at the time of the follow-up (SED, 1976).

When England was examined in terms of the Registrar-General's nine Standard Regions, considerable variations in the proportions of trained guidance teachers emerged. Only 7 per cent of pupils in the East and West Ridings, the North Midlands and the South were in schools where no teachers were trained in careers guidance, but this compared with 17 per cent in the North-West, and with 14 per cent in the North and in London and the South-East.

The smaller proportion of Scottish pupils reported to be in contact with a careers officer is reflected in the fact that only 14 per cent said they had heard about their likely first job from such a person, compared with over 20 per cent in England and Wales. All the findings on contacts with careers officers were, however, likely to have been affected by the reorganisation of the careers service. In

England and Wales this coincided with local government reorganisation, while Scotland was still in the process of improving its careers service to allow for the implementation in 1975 of the Employment and Training Act of 1973 (see SED, 1975).

Age of leaving school and future plans

The study children were asked at what age they were most likely to leave school, and which of the following they would like to do on leaving: continue with full-time study, do a job that involved part-time study, or do a job that required no further study; a 'don't know' category was also provided. The answers to these two questions have been combined. Since boys and girls differed in their choices, the relationship between their choice and the proportion receiving some careers guidance has been looked at separately for each sex.

Table 13.11 looks at the young people's choices in relation to three factors: first, the proportion of study children who were in schools where the teachers had at least some training in careers work; second, the proportion whom their teachers reported to be in contact with a careers officer; and third, the proportion who indicated that *teachers' advice* had been an important reason for their choice. In general there was remarkably little variation in relation to the first of these factors. This suggests that the pupils' choices for the future were not influenced in discernible ways by the presence in their schools of teachers trained in careers work. Nevertheless, although the differences are not statistically significant, there was a slight tendency for those who were uncertain about their future plans to be more likely to lack the benefit of a trained careers teacher than other groups.

The age at which pupils were likely to leave school clearly made a difference to the proportion reported by their teachers to have been in contact with a careers officer. Over 75 per cent of those likely to leave at 16 had been in contact, compared with 63 per cent of those likely to leave at 17 or 18. Those who were uncertain about when to leave were some-

TABLE 13.10   *Regional differences in careers guidance*

Region	% pupils with teachers having some training in careers work	% pupils with teachers paid a special salary	% pupils in contact with careers officer
England	87.8	74.1	75.0
Wales	90.7	86.5	76.8
Scotland	82.3	69.8	57.4
Total	87.3	74.3	73.0

TABLE 13.11   *Careers guidance related to children's plans for leaving school*

	N	% in schools having teacher with some training in careers work		% of children reported in contact with careers officer		% of children giving teachers' advice as reason for choice	
		Boys	Girls	Boys	Girls	Boys	Girls
Children likely to leave at 17/18 and planning							
University or polytechnic	(1 416)	90	89	59	61	23	18
College of education	(581)	89	88	76	67	15	17
Other full-time study (place specified)	(437)	93	85	65	65	23	17
Other full-time study (not specified)	(75)	92	95	52	70	14	23
Job and part-time study	(839)	86	86	68	67	19	12
Job with no study	(194)	86	90	50	66	15	14
Don't know	(395)	83	86	63	68	23	18
Sub-total	(3 937)	88	87	63	64	19	16
Children likely to leave at 16 and planning							
Full-time study (place specified)	(665)	88	89	81	78	11	4
Full-time study (not specified)	(47)	88	78	85	76	16	21
Job and part-time study	(3 304)	87	89	81	80	9	6
Job with no study	(2 034)	86	87	78	78	8	5
Don't know	(1 295)	85	86	82	79	9	7
Sub-total	(7 345)	86	88	80	77	9	6
Children uncertain about leaving age but planning							
Full-time study (place specified)	(122)	88	83	80	74	10	13
Full-time study (not specified)	(19)	91	—	73	75	13	25
Job and part-time study	(357)	89	89	73	77	18	16
Job with no study	(98)	89	89	58	65	13	8
Don't know	(211)	85	83	66	75	16	14
Sub-total	(807)	89	86	70	71	14	13

what less likely to have seen a careers officer than those planning to leave at 16, and there seemed to be a tendency within this 'uncertain' group, and among the 17/18-year-old leavers, for those planning to do jobs with no further study to be the least likely to have had contact.

Although the presence or absence of a teacher in the school who was trained in careers guidance did not appear to be associated with pupils' choice of leaving age and plans for the future, the advice of teachers in general appeared to have had more

influence on some groups than others. The young people were asked to say whether any of fifteen listed reasons for leaving school at their chosen age were important to them. More than one reason could be given, and the list included *teachers' advice*. Higher proportions of pupils planning to stay on at school until 17 or 18 gave this reason than of those planning to leave at 16. Girls planning to leave at 16 were even less likely than boys to say their teachers had advised this.

Job choices

The young people were asked what they would like to be their first full-time job and also what they thought was in fact likely to be their full-time job. The many different jobs have been grouped into thirteen categories which make it possible to see whether pupils choosing jobs in any particular category are more or less likely to have had the benefit of careers guidance than those making other choices.

Table 13.12 looks at the relationship between, on the one hand, children's job choices, and on the other the presence of trained careers teachers and reported contacts with careers officers. The results for the choice of 'aspired' and 'likely' jobs were very similar, so only those for the 'likely' job have been presented here. The proportions of those selecting jobs in each category who were in schools which had a teacher with some training in careers guidance were very consistent. There was, however, more variation in the proportions of those in each job category who were reported to have been in contact with a careers officer. This variation is almost certainly linked with the variation in contact according to age of leaving school, which was reported earlier. It is also probable that the specific knowledge about the availability of jobs and their requirements, as well as the general information and guidance provided by careers officers, was more likely to have been sought by some groups of young people than others in making their choices about their likely first job (see Weir and Nolan, 1977). Among those who were unspecific or did not know about their likely first job, at least one in four had not been in contact with a careers officer. For girls the numbers (28 per cent) were very similar to the overall numbers of those who did specify a job but had not been in contact with a careers officer (26 per cent), whereas for boys there was a 9 per cent difference (33 *vs* 24 per cent).

It is at the point where schools' guidance work and that of the careers service overlaps in planning talks, films and interviews at school that the influence on pupils' choices of jobs seems most likely to occur. Table 13.13 shows the proportion of pupils who said that they had heard about their choice of likely first full-time job from certain specified sources. The full list has been given, as it is interesting to see how the answers compare for different job categories and for different sources. Overall, higher proportions of the 16-year-olds said that they had heard about their jobs either from their parents or at school than from any other source. In seven job categories more boys and girls chose 'at school' than any other source: artistic; teaching; professional; semi-professional; nursing and welfare; clerical; and forces. Those choosing jobs such as farming, shopwork, building, engineering and other industrial work more often quoted the sources traditionally associated with these types of jobs — namely, parents, relatives and friends (see also Carter, 1966). Although 'careers officer' did not top the list for any of the categories of jobs, it was quoted by both boys and girls as the third source after 'school'

TABLE 13.12   *Careers guidance related to study children's choice of likely first full-time job*

Job categories	(a) % in schools having teachers with some training in careers work				(b) % of children reported in contact with careers officer			
	Boys	N	Girls	N	Boys	N	Girls	N
Farming and outdoor	87	(232)	89	(90)	77	(240)	78	(91)
Artistic and sporting	90	(105)	83	(124)	72	(110)	67	(132)
Teaching	91	(120)	87	(454)	65	(122)	64	(484)
Professional	89	(532)	91	(115)	64	(561)	63	(129)
Semi-professional	89	(374)	90	(201)	75	(390)	66	(214)
Nursing and welfare	95	(20)	88	(660)	70	(20)	74	(695)
Shopwork	85	(143)	85	(722)	85	(153)	77	(766)
Other services	88	(270)	89	(184)	80	(292)	75	(197)
Clerical	84	(196)	89	(1 564)	72	(204)	76	(1 644)
Building	90	(400)	—		78	(422)	—	
Engineering	86	(1 070)	92	(13)	81	(1 114)	62	(13)
Other industrial	86	(499)	82	(352)	76	(542)	80	(383)
Forces	85	(436)	89	(71)	72	(456)	72	(76)
Unspecific or don't know	86	(814)	88	(564)	62	(870)	72	(601)

and 'parents' for those choosing jobs of a 'semi-professional' nature, which included many administrative, managerial and business jobs, and also technical jobs such as draughtsmanship, laboratory work and photography.

Although a higher proportion of young people said that they had heard about their likely first job 'at school' than from any other source, it was possible that this was more likely to be true for those who were doing well at school. It was also possible that there would be social-class differences, as pupils from a middle-class background might be more in tune with the schools' methods of presenting information than those from a working-class background. The boys' and girls' answers were therefore looked at by scores (grouped approximately into thirds) on the reading test devised for the study by the NFER as an admittedly narrow measure of school attainment, and also within social-class categories (as defined by the Registrar-General's classification of occupation). Table 13.14 shows that the poorer readers were less likely than the good readers to quote school as the place where they had heard about their jobs. Among boys, those from a non-manual background were somewhat more likely to say they had heard about their job 'at school', but when boys of similar attainment were compared, the social-class differences among boys were not significant. Among girls, there were no overall social-class

differences, but girls from manual social backgrounds who were good readers were significantly more likely to quote school as their source of information than were good readers from a non-manual background.

The answers of those who said that they had heard about their likely first job from a careers officer were looked at in the same way, taking account of reading ability and social class. There were no overall social-class differences for either boys or girls, but for both sexes those who were good readers and whose fathers were in social classes IV and V were more likely to say they had heard about the job from a careers officer than were good readers from a non-manual background. As the young people were able to quote more than one source, some of those indicating these two sources will have been the same people. This does not, however, diminish the interest of the results. It would appear that higher-attaining pupils from working-class backgrounds were particularly likely to make use of (or at least to recall making use of) the facilities for careers guidance provided by schools and careers officers, but that these services had less impact on pupils with lower reading scores, irrespective of their home backgrounds.

The young people were also asked to choose from a list the 'thing which was most important' to them about a job. Table 13.15 shows that their choices were related to where they had heard about their likely first job: for example, higher proportions said

TABLE 13.13   *16-year-olds' choice of likely first full-time job, related to sources of information about this job*

| Likely first full-time job† | Proportion who said they heard about job* | | | | | | | | | | | | | | | | | |
| | From parents | | From relatives | | At school | | From careers officer | | From TV | | From paper/ magazines | | From friends | | Some-where else | | Don't remember | |
	Boys	Girls	Boys	Girls	Boys	Girls	Boys	Girls	Boys	Girls	Boys	Girls	Boys	Girls	Boys	Girls	Boys	Girls
Farming and outdoor	48	31	20	8	18	23	14	19	10	17	11	27	25	30	22	29	3	6
Artistic and sporting	31	35	15	12	42	39	19	17	28	22	30	28	20	17	31	33	6	8
Teaching	37	43	22	26	64	69	20	26	11	18	14	17	19	22	17	17	5	6
Professional	50	47	22	23	55	54	19	15	23	28	32	39	21	21	20	33	4	6
Semi-professional	40	36	21	21	52	58	30	25	17	11	26	25	22	18	19	16	2	2
Nursing and welfare	35	34	25	22	45	53	30	23	20	25	30	30	15	29	15	18	5	5
Shopwork	34	27	11	16	18	27	12	13	8	11	14	23	27	32	25	19	5	7
Other services	40	37	26	21	34	39	19	22	24	19	31	25	26	27	20	22	3	3
Clerical	38	35	24	23	46	48	30	25	13	13	39	39	19	27	14	11	2	3
Building	38	—	26	—	30	—	20	—	7	—	12	—	33	—	15	—	1	—
Engineering	42	—	25	31	36	8	23	15	9	8	20	31	29	31	14	15	2	—
Other industrial	44	37	23	27	27	26	17	17	9	7	13	16	33	45	11	8	2	4
Forces	34	34	24	18	55	57	22	28	39	22	47	46	25	29	30	16	3	1
Unspecific or don't know	36	34	15	18	38	51	20	18	20	16	26	26	25	22	20	15	4	4
Total	40	34	22	21	39	45	21	21	16	15	24	29	26	27	18	16	3	5

* More than one answer could be given.
† For numbers in job categories see Table 13.12, column (b).

they had heard about their job at school or from a careers officers among those who chose 'variety' or 'helping others' than among those who wanted a 'well-paid' or an 'outdoor' job.

Discussion

The finding that, in 1974, 98 per cent of 16-year-olds were in schools which said there was a member of staff who had particular responsibility for careers guidance suggests that even in the two years since the HMI survey in England and Wales (DES, 1973) there had been a slight increase in designated provision for this area of the curriculum. Thirteen years earlier, when the comparable 1946 cohort covered in the National Survey of Health and Development was aged 15 and, like the NCDS pupils, in their last year of compulsory education, it was apparently not an important enough issue for careers teachers or the formal provision of careers guidance within schools to be even mentioned in the questionnaire (Douglas *et al.*, 1968). Inevitably the rapid expansion in recent

years conceals considerable variation in practice. In a few schools careers guidance is a full-time appointment, whereas in most it is part of a range of responsibilities — particularly in Scotland, where the recommendation that guidance staff should continue to teach other subjects seems to have been widely implemented (SED, 1976). In our survey we attempted to obtain information on the amount by which the teaching load was reduced to allow for careers guidance work, but the answers proved very difficult to interpret because of the number of other responsibilities which some careers teachers were undertaking.

Our findings on the amount of training received and on whether teachers were paid a special salary for careers work suggest that, despite the increase in training schemes, a considerable proportion of careers teachers were receiving quite limited (if any) periods of training. This is reflected, too, in the absence of special responsibility allowances for these teachers. It is not possible to say whether the general brevity of training could account for the lack of any

TABLE 13.14   *Source of likely first job related to sex, social class and reading test score*

Reading scores	Proportion who said they heard about jobs							
	(a) From school/teacher/talk/film				(b) From careers officer			
	Non-manual	III M	IV M + V	All	Non-manual	III M	IV M + V	All
(1) *Boys*	(N = 1 462)	(N = 1 804)	(N = 737)	(N = 4 003)				
Low (N = 1 316)	32.5	31.0	27.5	30.3	14.6	19.9	17.1	18.0
Middle (N = 1 223)	37.2	39.2	42.7	39.2	23.5	24.1	26.2	24.3
High (N = 1 464)	46.7	49.3	42.3	47.1	19.1	22.5	29.5	21.4
All (N = 4 003)	41.5	39.0	34.9		19.4	22.1	22.3	
				χ^2 (2 df)				χ^2 (2 df)
Tests	Reading score — overall			82.2***	Reading score — overall			9.0*
	Social class — overall			9.1*	Social class — overall			4.2 ns
	Low reading/social class			2.2 ns	Low reading/social class			3.5 ns
	Middle reading/social class			1.8 ns	Middle reading/social class			0.6 ns
	High reading/social class			2.6 ns	High reading/social class			15.7***
(2) *Girls*	(N = 1 431)	(N = 1 752)	(N=1739)	(N = 3 922)				
Low (N = 1 296)	31.1	37.4	35.4	36.0	17.4	14.9	17.0	16.0
Middle (N = 1 320)	49.5	46.3	45.1	47.2	23.4	22.8	27.1	23.8
High (N = 1 306)	48.6	61.6	57.6	54.0	21.4	28.2	28.8	24.4
All (N = 3 922)	46.3	46.8	42.4		21.4	21.1	22.3	
				χ^2 (2 df)				χ^2 (2 df)
Tests	Reading score — overall			86.3***	Reading score — overall			34.4***
	Social class — overall			4.4 ns	Social class — overall			0.5 ns
	Low reading/social class			1.6 ns	Low reading/social class			1.4 ns
	Middle reading/social class			1.6 ns	Middle reading/social class			1.8 ns
	High reading/social class			18.8***	High reading/social class			9.3**

Significance levels: $p > 0.05$ ns, $p < 0.05$*, $p < 0.01$**, $p < 0.001$***.

TABLE 13.15   *The 'most important thing about choosing a job' related to sources of information about likely first jobs*

Most important thing about choosing a job	Proportion who heard about jobs at school or from careers officer	
	Boys	Girls
The job should involve working with your hands	55	49
It should involve using your head and need thought and concentration	68	72
It should be an outdoor job	52	46
It should be well paid	51	55
It should have convenient hours and conditions	60	65
The job should involve variety	72	71
The job should offer you chances of promotion	68	69
It should give you the chance of being in charge of other people	43	59
The job should let you be your own boss	55	59
It should be a clean job	41	56
It should give you the opportunity of helping others	64	76
It should not have too much responsibility at first	45	63

appreciable relationship between the amount of training received by the careers teachers and the nature of the decisions the pupils were making about their likely leaving age or first jobs. There will, of course, have been cases where the work of trained and experienced teachers will have had a profound effect on the young people, but advice to individual pupils will inevitably have led to widely differing decisions. Much will also have depended on the age at which pupils first started having contact with their careers teachers and on the frequency and content of such contacts. Information on these latter factors was not collected for this study, but the HMI surveys suggest that despite official guidelines and suggestions they vary considerably according to the priority accorded to careers work (SED, 1968; Schools Council, 1972; DES, 1973; SED, 1976).

Our findings on the proportion of pupils whom teachers reported having been in contact at any point in their secondary schooling with a careers officer give some support to the commonly held view that this contact relates mainly to school-leaving and job-finding rather than to guidance of a

more general and long-term nature (Roberts, 1977; Daws, 1977). There was a marked contrast between the proportions of pupils who had been in contact with a careers officer among those planning to leave school at 16 and among those planning to leave at 17/18. Although, on average, pupils in grammar schools were less likely than those in secondary modern or comprehensive schools to have had contact, it would appear that, even within a school, selection for interview may be governed by the pupils' intentions with regard to leaving school. This may be a deliberate attempt to regulate the numbers to be interviewed, particularly in areas where the staffing ratio is low (see National Youth Employment Council, 1974).

The assertion that 'there is no study of school leavers in Britain in which the careers service, careers teachers, or any other body offering vocational guidance has emerged as a major influence' (Roberts, 1977) is not borne out by our findings. For the young people in the NCDS, the predominant source of information regarding their likely first job was said to be 'at school, from a teacher or careers talk or film'. Our findings have, however, shown that the influence of such information on their choice was likely to be greater on those who were doing well at school. It is also relevant to note that school-leavers 'may well end up in jobs other than those at which they aim whilst at school' (Carter, 1966; see also Weir and Nolan, 1977). This is particularly likely in areas or at times of high unemployment, like the last few years (Jones *et al.*, 1975).

It will require a future follow-up of the NCDS subjects to show the full extent to which the hopes and expectations they expressed while still at school were realised on entering work. Furthermore, our data were limited to the first full-time job, and there is evidence to show that many young people change jobs quite frequently in their first years of employment (see Cherry, 1976); indeed, all can expect to change jobs a number of times in their working lives (Schools Council, 1972). Changing patterns of employment must necessarily be taken into account in any programme for careers guidance, but the choice of first full-time job is still of particular significance for the majority of school-leavers (see Hopson and Hayes, 1968, p. 159). It is the role of the careers teacher and of the careers officer as providers of information on these first jobs that has been documented here.*

---

* Although at the time of the follow-up the term 'youth employment officer' was still in official use, the current term 'careers officer' is used throughout this paper.

14 Sex Education and Preparation for Parenthood*

SEX EDUCATION, PREPARATION FOR PARENTHOOD AND THE ADOLESCENT

Introduction

Within the last three decades there has been much discussion on providing children at the right age with adequate knowledge about their reproduction processes and other related matters to enable them each to play their full part in the sexual partnership and the rearing of their children. Encouragement both to parents and teachers has been given in such documents as the Education Act 1944, the Newsom (1963), Crowther (1964) and Plowden (1967) Reports, and following the Cohen Report in 1964 when many local authorities attempted to rationalise policy within their education and health departments.

The influence of television, films and radio in providing educational programmes for schools and parents must not be forgotten. Likewise such bodies as the Health Education Council, the Schools Council, the Marriage Guidance Council and others have played an active role in this field. The sum total of thirty years' work has brought about a major change in a matter which was previously left to parents, friends or chance.

It seems that in the light of these developments and the opportunity presented by the third follow-up of the National Child Development Study (1958) when the cohort subjects were 16 years of age, the time is ripe for a reappraisal based on the teaching now provided in school and whether the recipient — the teenager — rates it a success or failure as he or she sees it within the contemporary social setting.

There is also another and long-term aspect — the

* Original sources: Pearson, R. and Lambert, L., 'Sex education, preparation for parenthood and the adolescent', *Community Health*, 9(2), 1977; Lambert, L. and Pearson, R., 'Sex education in schools', *Journal of the Institute of Health Education*, 15 (4), 1977; Lambert, L., 'Measuring the gaps in teenagers' knowledge of sex and parenthood', *Health and Social Service Journal*, 15 April 1977. (The version here is much abridged, as the original paper also contained data to be found in the other two papers in this chapter.)

health and welfare of the following generation. On the one hand there has been a steady fall in infant mortality, the introduction of developmental assessment of young children and the improved care of handicapped children, while on the other hand schoolgirl pregnancy and sexually transmitted diseases have increased. Early marriage and increasing divorce rates among young married couples give cause for concern for the nation's health and welfare.

Method

As part of the NCDS 16-year-old follow-up teachers gave information on the extent of teaching on human reproduction and allied subjects in the secondary schools which 12 764 adolescents attended, and a slightly smaller group of adolescents (12 101), while still at school, completed a confidential individual questionnaire.

Teachers in the schools attended by these adolescents were asked to record whether lessons specifically concerned with (a) the physiological aspects of human reproduction, (b) emotional or personal aspects of sexual relationships, (c) information regarding contraception, and (d) information on venereal disease, had been given to children of the study child's age at school.

The adolescents were asked whether, in school, they had learnt about 'how babies are conceived (started)', 'how babies are born', 'how people get VD (venereal disease)', 'the care of babies', 'how children grow and develop' and 'practical problems of family life (e.g. budgeting, looking after a house, etc.)'. Recognising that many of the adolescents would have been told, apart from lessons in school, about such topics, they were also asked to record where else they had obtained the most useful information on the same topics.

In an attempt to measure a very complex process the adolescents were also asked whether they 'felt they needed to know more' about these six topics and in each of them they were asked to record their view as 'yes', 'no' or 'uncertain'.

Information was also gathered on matters such as

the occupation of leisure time, relationship with parents, future marriage, and so on.

Extent of knowledge at 16

The adolescents expressed their degree of satisfaction with the extent of their knowledge on each of six topics by recording whether or not they needed to know more about it or whether they were uncertain. Their views for each topic are given in Tables 14.1 and 14.2, subdivided according to both sex and father's occupation. Accepting the limitations of this means of measuring adolescents' opinions there remains no doubt about their dissatisfaction with the extent of their knowledge. It is not easy to interpret conclusively the opinions of the adolescents on each of the six

topics. Much depends on how the respondents understood the question and how much they felt they needed to know in the light of their home surroundings, experience and general knowledge. Was it actual knowledge or its application they felt uncertain about? However, the following very general comparisons have been drawn.

Adolescents who expressed their need to have more knowledge were nearly equally divided between being quite definite in their opinion and being uncertain about their answer on the subjects of conception and birth. On the remaining four subjects, however, they were much more convinced, as a smaller proportion expressed uncertainty in each case.

Girls, more than boys, felt they required more

TABLE 14.1   *'More knowledge needed' by sex (percentaged)*

More knowledge needed	Boy	Girl	Tests for difference between sexes
(i) Conception			Overall χ^2 = 7.6* (2 df)
Yes	15	13	Yes, no χ^2 = 7.6*
No	66	68	Yes, unc. ns
Uncertain	19	19	No, unc. ns
(N)	(5 643)	(5 567)	
(ii) Birth			Overall χ^2 = 18.7*** (2 df)
Yes	15	18	Yes, no χ^2 = 18.7***
No	70	67	Yes, unc. χ^2 = 8.2*
Uncertain	15	15	No, unc. ns
(N)	(5 647)	(5 571)	
(iii) Venereal disease			Overall χ^2 = 23.0*** (2 df)
Yes	36	36	Yes, no χ^2 = 22.4***
No	47	43	Yes, unc. χ^2 = 7.0*
Uncertain	17	20	No, unc. ns
(N)	(5 762)	(5 602)	
(iv) Care of babies			Overall χ^2 = 230.5*** (2 df)
Yes	53	57	Yes, no χ^2 = 12.2**
No	23	30	Yes, unc. χ^2 = 173.3***
Uncertain	24	13	No, unc. χ^2 = 207.8***
(N)	(5 522)	(5 614)	
(v) Growth of child			Overall χ^2 = 45.2*** (2 df)
Yes	35	40	Yes, no χ^2 = 16.3***
No	40	39	Yes, unc. χ^2 = 43.6***
Uncertain	25	21	No, unc. χ^2 = 10.1**
(N)	(5 601)	(5 606)	
(vi) Family problems			Overall χ^2 = 7.1* (2 df)
Yes	58	56	Yes, no χ^2 = 7.0*
No	20	22	Yes, unc. ns
Uncertain	22	22	No, unc. ns
(N)	(5 739)	(5 682)	

knowledge about birth, the care of babies and the growth of children. Boys, however, said they needed to know more about conception and the practical problems of family life. Adolescents of both sexes from the manual social classes were more likely to wish to know more about conception and venereal disease, whereas more of those from the non-manual groups were concerned to know more about the practical problems of family life. Taking reading scores as a general indication of progress in school, those with lower scores were more likely to feel they needed to know more about conception, birth and venereal disease, while more of those with higher scores expressed their concern to know more about the care of babies, the growth of children and the practical problems of family life. More concern was expressed by adolescents living in Scotland and Wales (where fewer lessons on these subjects were given than in England) to know more about venereal disease.

Adolescents with no male head of the family or who were planning to leave school at 16 or who did not read much for leisure or who watched television often or who were proposing to marry young were more likely to express a shortfall of knowledge on the care of babies.

These comparisons have been drawn from differences found to be significant at at least the 5 per cent level. Full details of the relevant tables can be obtained from the Supplementary Publications Scheme, British Library (Lending Division), Boston Spa, Yorkshire LS23 7BO, quoting reference no. SUP 81006.

Other sources of information (outside school)

The list overleaf indicates the most frequent choice of choosing from the following sources outside school the one which they thought provided them with the most useful information (friends, brother or sister, television, books or magazines, church, parents, someone else, youth clubs or nowhere in particular). The list overleaf indicates the most frequent choice of source of useful information under each topic:

TABLE 14.2 *'More knowledge needed' within social class (percentaged)*

More knowledge needed	Non-manual	Manual	No male head	Tests for difference between social classes
Conception				Overall test x^2 = 49.4*** (2 df)
Yes and uncertain	29	39	30	NM/M x^2 = 47.7***
No	71	64	70	NM/NMH ns
(N)	(3 077)	(5 064)	(643)	M/NMH x^2 = 7.0*
Birth				Overall test ns
Yes and uncertain	31	32	29	
No	69	68	71	
(N)	(3 084)	(5 068)	(627)	
Venereal disease				Overall test x^2 = 13.1** (2 df)
Yes and uncertain	53	57	55	NM/M x^2 = 13.0**
No	47	43	45	NM/NMH ns
(N)	(3 113)	(5 147)	(634)	M/NMH ns
Care of babies				Overall test x^2 = 20.5*** (2 df)
Yes and uncertain	76	72	73	NM/M x^2 = 20.3***
No	24	28	27	NM/NMH ns
(N)	(3 074)	(5 038)	(625)	M/NMH ns
Growth of child				Overall test ns
Yes and uncertain	61	60	62	
No	39	40	38	
(N)	(3 085)	(5 071)	(625)	
Family problems				Overall test x^2 = 14.6*** (2 df)
Yes and uncertain	82	78	78	NM/M x^2 = 13.5**
No	18	22	23	NM/NMH ns
(N)	(5 153)	(5 170)	(647)	M/NMH ns

Topic	Boys	Girls
Conception	Friends	Parents
Birth	Television	Parents
Venereal disease	Television	Books
Care of babies	Parents	Parents
Growth of child	'Nowhere in particular'	Parents
Family problems	Parents	Parents

The next source most frequently chosen (usually television, books or 'nowhere in particular') was almost as common as the one listed above. Some possible sources, such as youth clubs, churches and 'someone else', were, however, rarely mentioned at all.

Lessons at school

In the educational questionnaire teachers were asked to record the lessons given to children of the study child's age. Their responses are shown in Table 14.3.

Generally, girls were likely to have fared better than boys at school, more of them were in schools which had given lessons on all four of the topics and they were less likely than boys to have been in schools giving no appropriate lessons at all. Those adolescents who came from manual home backgrounds, or who attended smaller schools (especially if 'for boys only'), were likely to have been in schools giving no appropriate lessons at all. Strangely, there was a marked regional difference for complete absence of lessons on all four (school) topics, Scotland being worst, where 22 per cent of adolescents were in schools which gave no appropriate lessons. For Wales the figure was 12 per cent and for England 5 per cent.

As already noted, the topics about which information was sought from teachers and adolescents are only strictly comparable on 'human reproduction' and 'venereal disease'. The type of school attended by each adolescent is known, though the frequency, timing and content of the lessons are not.

From the views of the adolescents on whether they felt they needed to know more, the following general comparisons have been made.

Among girls, those in mixed schools were more likely to express the view that they required instruction on conception, while if attending small schools they were short of information on the care of babies and the growth of the child.

Boys, on the other hand, if attending mixed schools, were more likely to say they lacked knowledge on conception and on venereal disease. Both sexes expressed a shortfall of information on venereal disease if they were attending comprehensive schools, and on the care of babies and the growth of the child if attending grammar or independent schools. Likewise there was a widely felt lack of information on the practical problems of family life, particularly for those in grammar schools and attending mixed schools.

Comparison with other studies

The main comparative study is Schofield's survey of 1873 children (aged 15–19) carried out in 1964 (Table 14.4). He felt it was representative of information provided and views felt in England at that time. The school-leaving age was 15 in 1964 and 16 in 1974. Schofield's information about lessons in school on various topics depended on the adolescents' memories, but in the NCDS teachers' reports were also available. In neither case was the amount of teaching recorded. In 1964 a quarter of the boys and a third of the girls preferred information from their teachers. Ten years later the impression is given from the young people's answers that, outside school, parents may now be a more frequent and more satisfying source of information (perhaps they themselves now have greater knowledge and feel more capable of expressing themselves).

When questions were put in 1964 to the 50 per cent of adolescents who were satisfied they 'knew all', considerable gaps in their knowledge of contraception and venereal disease came to light. In 1974 the 16-year-olds still felt there were considerable gaps in their knowledge of venereal disease and even more so on the topics of child growth and family problems (which a considerable number will have to face within a short period of time).

Conclusion

The information given by the teachers and by the

TABLE 14.3   *Lessons at school (each topic separately in percentages)*

	(N)	Boys' lessons	None	(N)	Girls lessons	None
Reproduction	(6 400)	89	12	(6 132)	93	7
Emotional aspects	(6 317)	65	35	(6 055)	72	28
Contraception	(6 291)	54	46	(6 009)	60	40
Venereal disease	(6 322)	64	36	(6 036)	70	30

adolescents (many of whom were about to leave school) indicates that between 1964 and 1974 there was a considerable increase in the breadth of teaching of subjects related to human reproduction. During this decade the adolescents' view of their parents' role has also changed. There are, however, still large gaps needing to be filled. Many parents in 1974 will have found it easier to discuss such matters with their children from the knowledge they themselves acquired at school as teaching on these topics increased.

In 1974, although there were small variations between the sexes, two-thirds of the adolescents expressed satisfaction with the information they had obtained by 16 years of age on reproduction and conception but slightly less than half of them were satisfied with the information on venereal disease and on the growth of children. Information on the care of babies satisfied less than one-third and on family problems less than one-quarter. Whether they were short of factual information or an understanding of its application is not known. The gaps are clear and many adolescents 'feel they need to know more'. They look to their parents and their teachers as their main sources.

There is a feeling, coming from the number of adolescents who gave answers that they were 'uncertain' on the topics on which they were questioned, that it may not only be information they require but also an opportunity to discuss it with knowledgeable and experienced adults, a role which could be filled by some, but not all, parents and teachers.

From this study of the situation as perceived in 1974 there is no wish to belittle the considerable strides made both in schools and at home since Schofield reported a decade previously, but rather to point out where, in the opinion of the adolescents, the deficiencies lie. Only a still greater recognition of the need, the use of all available manpower resources as well as interdisciplinary planning, along with the co-operation of the parents of the growing child, will achieve the objectives of sex education and preparation for parenthood. These are that those aspects of health education taught in both primary and secondary schools, and supported by knowledgeable parents, should be able to provide the maturing individuals with both the knowledge and understanding that they can apply both before and during marriage and as the parents of the next generation.

SEX EDUCATION IN SCHOOLS

Sex education evokes strong passions and strong prejudices: it challenges us to remember honestly our own childhood and adolescence and to have sympathy for young people of today, in their very different circumstances.
Lord Crowther-Hunt, House of Lords debate on 'sex education of children' (14 January 1976)

There is no *statutory requirement* laid down in the Education Act 1944 for schools to provide sex education but, in the last thirty-odd years, an increasing

TABLE 14.4   *Sex education, 1964—74*

	Schofield 1964 15—19 1 873 interviewed		National Child Development Study 1974 16 12 101 questioned			
Age group Number						
	Had teaching at school		Said they learnt at school about		Felt a need to know more*	
Subjects	Boys	Girls Percentages	Boys	Girls Percentages	Boys	Girls Percentages
Reproduction/conception	47	86	70	83	15	13
Birth	Rarely		68	81	15	18
Venereal disease	Very rarely		55	60	36	36
Contraception	Very rarely		Not asked†			
Care of babies	Not asked		19	46	53	57
Growth of child	Not asked		44	58	35	41
Family problems	Not asked		29	51	58	56

* These percentages refer to the proportion answering 'yes'. A considerable proportion were 'uncertain' (see Table 14.1).
† Secondary school teachers reported that 54 per cent of boys and 60 per cent of girls attended schools where lessons on this topic were given to pupils in the same age range.

number have included this subject in their curriculum. They have been encouraged to do this by the more flexible nature of public attitudes to sexual matters, by support from parents and by a series of government reports such as Crowther (1959), Newsom (1963), Cohen (1964) and Plowden (1967).

Michael Schofield's study (1965) showed up some gaps in young people's knowledge and a lack of teaching on sexual matters for boys (53 per cent of whom had received none), particularly in state schools. A more recent study suggests that the question may no longer be whether or not young people receive sex education in school, but whether it was presented at an appropriate stage in their development (Farrell, 1977). Both these studies used direct interview methods which enabled the topic to be examined in depth with personal questions about the young people's sexual experience.

The present study covers a much larger sample of teenagers than Schofield's and also includes Scotland and Wales. In addition it includes answers from teachers as well as from the young people themselves, which, for the first time, provides an opportunity to compare the extent of teaching on sexual and personal relationships with the degree of satisfaction about their knowledge on these topics that the young people expressed. However the wide-ranging nature of the study made it impossible to go into details about the frequency or timing of lessons. Also, as written questionnaries were used, it was not appropriate to collect very personal details about the teenagers' own sexual experiences.

One difficulty in the field of sex education lies in agreeing upon definitions. Some see the subject as biological and mechanistic, while others see it in much broader terms as including social and emotional aspects of personal relationships. Our questions included both these aspects and, in addition, we inquired into aspects of child care and development and practical problems of family life.

In the NCDS 16-year follow-up teachers were asked to provide background data about the schools the study children attended, including whether children of the study child's age had had lessons specifically concerned with:

(a) physiological aspects of human reproduction;
(b) emotional and personal aspects of sexual relation-ships;
(c) information regarding contraception; and
(d) information on venereal disease.

The study children were also asked questions relating to conception, birth and venereal disease, and in addition about aspects of child care and family life. They were asked (i) whether they had learnt about these topics in school, (ii) where they thought they had got the most useful information outside school, and (iii) whether they thought they needed to know more about each of them. Although some of the topics of the questions were comparable, the questions actually put to the pupils were not the same as those asked of the teachers. The information from both teachers and pupils resulting from questions on conception (human reproduction) and venereal disease were the most easily comparable. The pupils were not asked about contraception out of respect for some religious beliefs and it is possible that for the same reason some teachers reported that no lessons on this subject were given in their schools.

Data were presented in the preceding section (see Table 14.3) showing the proportion of boys and girls in schools which reported having received lessons on each of the four topics indicated above. Only just over half the girls and less than half the boys were in schools where pupils of their age group had been given lessons on all four topics and as many as 9 per cent of boys were in schools where pupils had received lessons on none of the topics.

The disparity between boys and girls in lessons which their age group were said to have received was even more marked for those attending single-sex schools. Whereas only one in fifty-five of girls who were in all-girl schools received no lessons, one in eight of boys in all-boy schools had had none. The position for pupils in mixed schools comes in between these two extremes (Table 14.5).

TABLE 14.5   *Boys and girls at school*

Lessons on	Mixed schools	All-boy schools	All-girl schools
All four topics	50	40	59
Reproduction only	14	17	13
Reproduction and emotional aspects only	8	10	9
All except contraception	8	6	10
All except VD	2	1	1
Other combinations	11	14	6
None	8	12	2
(N)	(9 039)	(1 460)	(1 571)

Test association between school (all boys/mixed)/lessons at school: $\chi^2 = 95.3***$ (6 df); test association between school (all girls/mixed)/lessons at school: $\chi^2 = 150.5***$ (6 df).

Young people attending secondary modern schools were more likely to be in schools which had given lessons on all four topics than pupils in comprehensive schools, though they were no less likely to have been given no lessons at all. Pupils from grammar schools were less likely to have had lessons on all four topics than those in comprehensive or secondary schools but were no more likely to have had none than pupils from comprehensive schools, though there was a difference in this respect between grammar and secondary modern schools. The pattern for pupils in independent and direct-grant schools appears to be similar to that of pupils in grammar schools. Although 26 per cent of children in LEA special schools received no lessons, it is encouraging to note that 53 per cent were said to have had lessons on all four topics (Table 14.6).

Boys in boarding schools were less likely to have been given any lessons than day-boys, though there was no difference between boarders and day-pupils among girls. There is, of course, a large amount of overlap between boarding schools and single-sex schools, and also between both these and independent schools.

On the whole there was little variation in the proportion who were not given lessons according to the number of pupils in the schools, except in the very smallest schools, which will have included the special schools, where we have already seen above that a relatively high number were given no lessons. The overlap with independent schools is reflected in pupils from smaller schools being less likely to have been given lessons in all four topics.

Although the sex ratio was essentially the same in all regions, the differences between both Scotland and Wales compared with England in the proportions of pupils who were said to be in schools giving no lessons were very marked. About one in five of the young people living in Scotland had received no lessons on any of the four topics. Although smaller than for Scotland, the proportion of Welsh pupils who had not had lessons was still twice that of English pupils, and schools in both Scotland and Wales were more likely to teach reproduction only. In England pupils in the south-eastern area (which included London) were likely to have a different pattern of teaching from those in the other regions. More of them had teaching on all four subjects than in any other regions (Table 14.7).

Learnt at school (young people's report)

Although teachers may have said that lessons on a subject had been given in their school to children of the study child's age, this is no guarantee that the study children will themselves have been present at the lessons. In some cases the lesson may not have been given to all children of the age group, in others the study child may have been absent at the time for medical or other reasons, or may even have changed schools. We therefore asked the study children whether they recalled having learnt in lessons at school about a list of six topics (Table 14.8).

When asked to indicate whether the lessons on such topics had included television or radio programmes or films, 23 per cent of those who had answered the 'learnt at school' question did not give any answer, which indicates that none of these was used. Those who did answer indicated an extensive

TABLE 14.6   *Type of school*

Lessons on	Comprehensive	Grammar	Secondary modern	LEA special school	Independent	Direct grant
All four topics	52	37	56	53	36	29
Reproduction only	13	23	11	3	26	20
Reproduction and emotional aspects only	7	12	7	8	12	25
All except contraception	8	7	4	3	5	4
All except VD	1	1	2	2	1	4
Other combinations	11	11	10	5	13	9
None	7	8	6	26	6	8
(N)	(7 138)	(1 278)	(2 563)	(195)	(435)	(274)

Test for association:
   comprehensive/grammar (all four topics, other ans. incl. none) χ^2 = 95.0*** (1 df)
   comprehensive/grammar (none of the topics, one or more topics) χ^2 = 1.2 ns
   comprehensive/secondary modern (all, rest) χ^2 = 13.7*** (1 df)
   comprehensive/secondary modern (none, rest) χ^2 = 3.1 ns
   grammar/secondary modern (all, rest) χ^2 = 123.9*** (1 df)
   grammar/secondary modern (none, rest) χ^2 = 4.7* (1 df)

TABLE 14.7   *Region and sex education (percentages)*

	Registrar-General's Standard Regions					
	North-West, North East & West Ridings	Midlands, North Midlands, East	South & South-West	London and South-East	Wales	Scotland
All four topics	50	58	57	60	31	19
Reproduction only	13	11	13	10	21	26
Reproduction and emotional aspects only	10	8	10	7	7	8
All except contraception	8	7	7	7	13	10
All except VD	2	1	1	1	1	2
Other combinations	11	11	4	10	16	13
None	6	4	3	6	12	23
(N)	(3 329)	(3 126)	(1 597)	(1 981)	(683)	(1 400)

Test for association:
    lessons (all four topics, other ans. incl. none)/region χ^2 = 861.1*** (5 df)
    lessons (none of the topics, one or more topics)/region χ^2 = 457.7*** (5 df)
    lessons/region (London & South-East, other regions) χ^2 = 97.9*** (6 df)

TABLE 14.8 *Learnt at school (each topic separately)*

	Boy		Girl	
Learnt about	(N)	%	(N)	%
1. How babies are conceived	(4 342)	70	(4 916)	83
2. How babies are born	(4 204)	68	(4 758)	81
3. How people get VD	(3 406)	55	(3 543)	60
4. The care of babies	(1 165)	19	(2 727)	46
5. How children grow and develop	(2 739)	44	(3 424)	58
6. Practical problems of family life	(1 808)	29	(3 022)	51
None of the above*	(846)	14	(246)	4
Total in sample	(6 191)	100	(5 905)	100

* These did not give a positive response to any of the six topics.

TABLE 14.9   *Use of films, television and radio in lessons*

Lessons included	Boy		Girl	
	(N)	%	(N)	%
Films	(3 416)	64	(4 061)	72
Television	(1 620)	30	(1 420)	25
Radio	(244)	5	(184)	3
na (none)*	(1 314)	25	(1 212)	21
Total †	(5 345)	100	(5 659)	100

† Total is total who said they had 'learnt at school' about these topics — more than one answer could be given.
* na is those who answered question on 'learnt at school' but did not say that these included films, etc.

use of films (Table 14.9). One in five said that both films and television had been used.

Although we have not combined the topics in the same way as was done for the teachers' reports of lessons given at school, we looked at proportions of young people who reported that if they had learnt about one topic they had also learnt about the other topics. As might be expected, this showed that some topics went together more than others, and also that there were variations between boys and girls. For example, 88 per cent of the boys and 91 per cent of the girls who had learnt about conception also said they had learnt about birth, but 51 per cent of girls

and only 25 per cent of boys had learnt about the care of babies.

As the study children may not have been in the class at the time, and also as the questions asked of the teachers and the young people were phrased differently, it was not possible to make direct comparisons between the two on the amount of concurrence over teaching given and learning recalled, but some of the topics were sufficiently close for some indication of agreement to be gained: 69 per cent of the boys and 79 per cent of the girls in the total sample who were in schools reported by the teachers to have had lessons on reproduction said they had learnt about 'how babies are conceived', 62 per cent of boys and 66 per cent of girls who were in schools reported by the teachers to have had lessons on venereal disease said they had learnt about 'how people get VD' in lessons at school. As might be expected, the measure of agreement between lessons and learning was closer when only the answers of those who said they had learnt at school were looked at. This was especially true for conception, where over 90 per cent of both boys and girls who said they had learnt about this topic were in schools which had had lessons on reproduction at school. Less than 5 per cent of boys and 4 per cent of girls said they had had lessons on topics such as conception or VD when their teachers had given lessons on none of the four subjects they were asked about. These results suggest that there was a broad but not total measure of agreement between teachers and pupils about whether lessons had been given on these topics.

More knowledge needed (young people's view)

There are likely to have been wide variations in the number and depth of lessons that schools provided. In addition, sex education is a subject which is not confined to the classroom and, indeed, debates continue about its appropriateness for that setting (Rogers, 1974). However, it should be of interest to teachers to know the areas in which young people feel most ignorant.

The young people's reports of whether they felt they needed to know more about each of the six topics discussed above made it clear that even for widely taught subjects such as conception and birth there was a need for more knowledge. When we came to the more practical subjects, such as the 'care of babies' and 'practical problems of family life', a large proportion of teenagers in the study felt that they needed to know more about them (Table 14.10).

Girls were more likely than boys to know more

about birth, care of babies, growth and development, and how people get VD, while boys were more likely to want to know more about conception and family problems. There were no social-class (Registrar-General's classification, 1966) differences in the proportions wanting to know more about birth or growth. Young people from manual social-class backgrounds were more likely than those from non-manual homes to want to know more about conception and venereal disease, while those from non-manual homes wanted more information on baby care and family problems. When mean reading test scores were looked at, the young people with lower scores were more likely to want information on conception, birth and venereal disease, while those with higher mean reading scores wanted more information on growth, baby care and family problems.

The type of school attended appeared to make no difference to the proportions who felt they knew enough about birth, but there were differences for the other topics. Pupils from comprehensive and secondary modern schools wanted more information on conception and pupils in comprehensives also wanted to know more about venereal disease than those in other types of schools. Grammar school pupils wanted more information on growth, baby care and family problems. Pupils from independent schools were mainly similar to those from grammar schools except that they felt less need for information on family problems than pupils from maintained schools. Whether pupils were boarders or day-pupils made no difference to feeling they knew enough about any of the six topics.

There was some variation for boys and girls according to whether they attended single-sex or mixed-sex schools. Boys attending mixed schools were less likely than those in all-boys schools to feel they knew enough about venereal disease and family problems. Girls in mixed schools were less likely than those in all-girl schools to feel they knew enough about conception, while girls in all-girl schools were

TABLE 14.10 *More knowledge needed (percentages)*

Topic	Boy				Girl			
	(N)	Yes	No	Uncertain	(N)	Yes	No	Uncertain
Conception	(5 643)	15	67	19	(5 567)	13	68	19
Birth	(5 647)	15	70	15	(5 571)	18	67	15
Venereal disease	(5 762)	36	47	17	(5 602)	36	43	20
Care of babies	(5 522)	53	23	24	(5 614)	57	30	13
Growth of child	(5 601)	35	40	25	(5 606)	40	39	21
Family problems	(5 739)	58	20	22	(5 682)	56	22	22

more likely than those in mixed schools to say they knew enough about baby care, growth and family problems. There were no differences for boys or girls in mixed- or single-sex schools with regard to knowing enough about birth itself. In general, the size of the school made little difference except that pupils in smaller schools were less likely to feel they knew enough about birth.

In view of the marked differences found in the pattern of lessons given in Scotland and Wales, the regional variations in which topics the young people felt they knew enough about are of particular interest. Young people in Scotland and Wales were more likely to feel they needed to know more about venereal disease than those in England, while those in London and the South-East were the least likely to want more information on this topic (though 49 per cent were not sure they knew enough). Those from London and the South-East were also the least likely to want more information on birth, though they did want more information than young people in other regions on conception. On both conception and birth Welsh and Scottish young people did not differ markedly from those in regions other than London and the South-East. Although the great majority of young people in all regions did not feel they knew enough about baby care, those in Scotland seemed somewhat more confident on this topic than others. There were no regional differences in the need to know more about growth and the great need for knowledge about the practical problems of family life was shared by young people in every part of Britain.

Discussion

There has clearly been an increase in the provision of lessons on sex education in all types of schools, and particularly in state schools, since Schofield's study in the mid-1960s. In 1974 teachers reported that over 90 per cent of both boys and girls in the NCDS were in classes where children of their age-group had been given lessons on one or more aspect and such lessons were recalled by at least 70 per cent of boys and 80 per cent of girls. But there is no room for complacency. Even though subjects such as conception and birth were widely taught, one out of three of the 16-year-olds in the sample did not feel confident that they knew enough about these subjects, and as many as 80 per cent wanted to know more about some of the less frequently taught subjects. Probably some will always feel this way, even when they are married and parents themselves. But for many of them there was little time left for them to learn more about such topics while at school, as 67 per cent of the young people planned to leave at the end of that school year. It is also useful to remember that these were the first year of pupils since the school-leaving age was raised to 16, and a number of schools may have included lessons on sex education and family life in the final-year curriculum which the previous years of school-leavers would not have had.

Girls still tended to be more likely to have been in classes having lessons on sex education topics than boys, and boys in single-sex schools were the least likely of all to have been given lessons. However, boys were not always more likely to feel a need to know more about the various topics. Sometimes, as in the case of 'the care of babies', they were more likely to be uncertain about the state of their knowledge, which perhaps reflects a realisation that they did not know how much they would be likely to be involved in this situation.

Although there were not many schools where venereal disease had been the only topic left out of a teacher's syllabus, there were many teenagers who were not getting lessons, and more who did not recall lessons on the subject and did not feel they knew enough about it. It was also a subject which both boys and girls appeared to have found difficult to discuss with their parents, as boys were more likely to say they got their most useful information outside school from television, and girls from books (see the next section).

Our findings echo those of other researchers and educationists (Rogers, 1974) in suggesting that venereal disease is still a topic that tends to be neglected. The same may also be true of contraception, but as we did not question the young people on this topic, and as some schools may have had religious reasons for not teaching the subject, the picture we are able to give on this topic is incomplete.

Clearly, from our evidence there was a felt need for opportunities for teenagers to learn more about the growth and development of children, and about the practical aspects of child care and family life. As we did not ask teachers about these subjects, we could not compare their statement of provision with the young people's, but it would appear that although approximately half the girls and fewer boys were learning something on these topics there was a near universal opinion that they did not know enough about them. Girls were more definite that they needed to know more about growth and development and baby care, and boys about family problems.

The demand for teaching in basic subjects and the complexity and ever-changing needs of modern society mean that schools are always under pressure to do better and to do more. Sex education and preparation for parenthood are topics which require careful and imaginative planning and plenty of time for discussion, preferably at home as well as at school, if lessons are to provide teenagers with knowledge that they will find useful as they grow older, marry, and become parents themselves. It will probably still be some time before total coverage in sex education is achieved (Rogers, 1974) and the findings of this study suggest that the contents of such lessons is even more important than the numerical extent.

MEASURING THE GAPS IN TEENAGERS' KNOWLEDGE OF SEX AND PARENTHOOD

Although there has been an increasing provision of lessons on sex education and preparation for parenthood, it was neither intended nor expected that schools should be the only source of information on such topics. Parents have traditionally been considered to be the main providers, though several research studies have shown that their role in this aspect is not as widespread as had been thought.

The peer group continues to be a primary source of information, though this is often garbled or inaccurate. The growth of television and the other media has also provided an increasingly available source, either incidentally or specifically.

In addition to the data described in detail in the two preceding sections, the NCDS 16-year-olds were given a list of sources of information outside school and were asked to say which one they found to be 'the most useful'. The nine sources listed were: friends or a brother or sister; television and films apart from ones shown at schools; books or magazines; church; parents; 'someone else'; youth clubs; 'nowhere in particular'.

Choices

When questioned about the most useful out-of-school sources of information on sex and parenthood it was clear that although there were differences between boys and girls in the order of their reported 'most useful' source, the three most popular choices for each of the six topics were confined to five out of the nine possible sources: films (non-school), 'someone else', youth clubs and church were mentioned by less than 10 per cent of respondents.

The three most popular choices of useful sources of information are shown in Table 14.11. Girls more frequently put their parents as the most useful source for each topic with the exception of venereal disease (for this topic parents were not among the first three choices at all). For 'family problems', one in every two girls answering the question put their parents as the most useful source of information. Among the other most useful sources for girls, books were mentioned among the first three choices for five out of six topics, family problems being the exception.

Parents

Boys only put their parents more often than any other source for 'care of babies' and 'family problems'. It is noticeable that 'nowhere in particular' features among the top three choices by boys for all six topics and television is among the first three for every topic except 'conception'. Boys were less likely than girls to say they had learnt in lessons at school about each of the six topics and their sources of information outside school appeared to be mainly impersonal or vague.

Although friends (or brothers and sisters) are mentioned by both boys and girls among the first three most popular choices of sources of useful information about conception and venereal disease, they do not feature in this way for the other four topics.

If 'sex education' is interpreted in a strictly limited way as relating to sexual intercourse, then these results may be taken to corroborate the view of Gagnon (1974) on the importance of the peer group. But in the wider context of childbirth and child-rearing, and the practical problems of family life, it is not surprising to find that the teenagers' friends feature very little as a source of useful information.

We looked to see whether the 16-year-olds' reports of having learnt in lessons at school about these topics or their feelings about whether they needed to know more about them made any difference to their choices of 'most useful source of information'. In general, this did not prove to be the case, and the overall pattern showed that neither the receipt of lessons in

TABLE 14.1 *Choices of the most useful source of information*

	Boys						Girls					
Conception	Friends*	23%	Nowhere*	22%	Books	15%	Parents	31%	Friends	19%	Books	17%
Birth	Television	25%	Nowhere	19%	Parents	15%	Parents	30%	Television	18%	Books	16%
VD	Television	25%	Friends	19%	Nowhere	17%	Books	24%	Television	17%	Friends	16%
Care of babies	Parents	28%	Nowhere	28%	Television	19%	Parents	42%	Books	17%	Nowhere	11%
Growth of child	Nowhere	26%	Television	23%	Books	17%	Parents	27%	Books	23%	Nowhere	18%
Family problems	Parents	42%	Nowhere	21%	Television	18%	Parents	51%	Nowhere	14%	Television	11%

* Friends could include brothers or sisters, and 'nowhere' = 'nowhere in particular'.

school nor the extent of knowledge made much difference to the young people's choice of most useful sources of information when these factors were looked at in conjunction with one another.

In conclusion, the expectation that girls will talk to their parents (probably mainly their mothers) and boys will pick up information in a more casual manner about sexual matters, babies, parenthood, and family life continues to be true for some, but by no means all of today's teenagers. For the majority, parents, books, television, and friends are likely to be important sources outside school of useful information.

It is equally clear that the majority of teenagers feel that institutions such as youth clubs and the churches play virtually no part in providing them with useful information. The term 'someone else' (other than parents, siblings or friends) probably included a wide range of adults, among them doctors and social workers, but they were also a minority source of information.

The vague nature of the phrase 'nowhere in particular' makes interpretation of this choice difficult. It may be seen by some as a very natural response, especially by adolescents who do not like to be pinned down too much, but may be seen by others as a cause for concern.

Needs

The lack of knowledge about all these topics which the teenagers expressed makes it very important that teachers and those sources which the young people said they found useful outside school should provide information that is as beneficial as possible. Parents, friends, television, books and magazines appeared to be the sources that young people were most likely to consult in order to amplify or reinforce teaching given in schools, or as alternatives if lessons were not available.

Professionals

There is much that medical staff, social workers and other advisers can do in this situation, by supporting and advising parents, and by helping to provide the information that appears in television programmes, books and magazines. Ideally the process of learning about sex and parenthood should be an ongoing one in which knowledge and understanding are built up and lead to personal autonomy and maturity and the ability to care for others.

15 Other Aspects of Schooling*

LONG-TERM CHANGES IN THE SCHOOL ATTAINMENT OF A NATIONAL SAMPLE OF CHILDREN

Introduction

It is now well established that children of all ages differ in their school attainment according to certain background characteristics such as social class and family size, and in general the same characteristics have been found to be associated with attainment whether the children are aged 7 (Davie *et al.*, 1972), 11 (Douglas, 1964; Fogelman, 1975; see pp. 21–7) or 15 (Douglas *et al.*, 1968). Additionally, studies of relative progress through the school years have shown that the gap between children of different backgrounds widens as the children progress through school (Douglas, 1964; Douglas *et al.*, 1968; Fogelman and Goldstein, 1976: see pp. 27–36; Ross and Simpson, 1971).

Using data from a nationally representative sample, constancy of attainment through school and the characteristics associated with change have been examined in a different way. First, we have considered the extent to which the same children performed relatively well or poorly at different stages of their school life, and therefore how well the study children's performance at the end of their compulsory schooling could have been predicted by their earlier attainment. Among those who did not perform consistently, the question of whether change was most likely to take place in the primary or secondary school years is examined. Second, the background characteristics of certain groups whose performance changed between various stages of their school career

are compared with the rest of their age group, in particular the groups who performed consistently (i.e. were in approximately the same band of attainment) throughout their school years.

From the results on tests administered at 7, 11 and 16 the NCDS children have been grouped according to their performance at each age in relation to their peers. At each age, for each test, those with scores in approximately the top third of the distribution have been defined as 'high scorers' (H), those in the second third 'middle' (M), and those in the lowest third 'low scorers' (L).

It is possible that the extent of movement has been slightly increased by the fact that the same tests were not used at each age, so that exactly the same type of skill may not have been required at each age. This possibility is discussed more fully in Fogelman *et al.* (1978b: see pp. 36–42).

Response levels

The sample was reduced as the analyses required test data at all three ages to be available, but an analysis showed that the sample was representative in terms of social class, sex and family size, though those from the North-West and the South of England are slightly underrepresented.

Results

The first part of this paper is concerned with the extent to which children's performance levels change relative to that of their peers between the ages of 7 and 16, and the stage at which this is most likely to occur. The amount of change in the primary school years is indicated in Table 15.1, which shows the 11-year attainment of children in each range of performance at 7.

Several points are apparent from this table. First, the extent of change is similar for maths and reading. Second, movement in the middle range is quite large, in that those in the middle range at 7 are almost as likely to have moved to either the top or bottom third at 11 as to have remained in the middle range.

The most interesting conclusions that can be

*Original sources: Essen, J., Fogelman, K. and Ghodsian, M., 'Long-term changes in the school attainment of a national sample of children', *Educational Research*, 20 (2) 1978; Hutchison, D., Prosser, H. and Wedge, P., 'The prediction of educational failure', *Educational Studies*, 5 (1) 1979; Fogelman, K. and Gorbach, P., 'Age of starting school and attainment at 11', *Educational Research*, 21 (1) 1978; Ghodsian, M. and Calnan, M., 'A comparative longitudinal analysis of special education groups', *British Journal of Educational Psychology*, 47, 1977; Fogelman, K., 'School attendance, attainment and behaviour', *British Journal of Educational Psychology*, 48, 1978.

TABLE 15.1   *Percentage of children in each band of attainment at 7 and 11*

	At seven					
	Maths			Reading		
	High	Middle	Low	High	Middle	Low
At eleven						
High	61	31	9	63	34	9
Middle	29	38	27	28	39	24
Low	10	31	64	9	27	67
	100%	100%	100%	100%	100%	100%

$N = 12\,771$

drawn from Table 15.1 are from comparisons with Table 15.2, which shows the extent of movement between 11 and 16. The likelihood of change in attainment during the primary school years is greater than during the secondary school years. The only respect in which they are similar is that there are practically as many in the low range for maths at 7 and 11 (64 per cent) as at 11 and 16 (65 per cent). Apart from this, each of the groups composed of children in the same range at 7 and 11 is smaller than the corresponding group in the same range at 11 and 16. Similarly, the proportions moving from one extreme at 7 to the opposite extreme at 11 are much larger than the corresponding figures between 11 and 16. These latter figures are particularly low, the highest being 5 per cent of high maths scorers at 11 who became low scorers when they were 16, while only 2 per cent moved from either low to high or high to low on the reading test.

TABLE 15.2   *Percentage of children in each band of attainment at 11 and 16*

	At eleven					
	Maths			Reading		
	High	Middle	Low	High	Middle	Low
At sixteen						
High	77	20	3	76	25	2
Middle	18	45	32	22	53	23
Low	5	35	65	2	22	75
	100%	100%	100%	100%	100%	100%

$N = 10\,368$

Tables 15.1 and 15.2 provide a simple indication of stability of attainment, but by only considering

two ages at a time some of the available information on the pattern of changes is not presented, for example the extent to which the same children changed in the secondary and in the primary school years is not apparent.

The children have therefore been grouped for each test according to their relative performance at each of the three ages, and from among all the possible combinations groups of particular interest have been selected. These are presented in Table 15.3 and consist of:

1. The children who remained in the same range at 7, 11 and 16 (the first three groups).
2. Those who moved from one extreme at 7 to the opposite extreme at 16, subdivided according to their performance at 11 (the next six groups).
3. The remainder, who in general showed moderate changes in attainment. These have all been combined into one group, and as they include children with many different patterns of performance have been omitted from most of the analyses.

TABLE 15.3 *Percentage of children with each pattern of attainment at 7, 11 and 16 (H = high, M = middle, L = low)*

7	11	16	Maths %	Reading %
H	H	H	16.5	17.7
M	M	M	7.3	7.1
L	L	L	11.7	17.5
H	L	L	1.5	1.5
H	M	L	2.3	1.3
H	H	L	0.6	0.2
L	H	H	1.6	1.8
L	M	H	1.6	1.3
L	L	H	0.4	0.4
Remainder			56.6	51.2
Total			100.0% (N = 9 402)	100.0% (N = 9 482)

Several interesting conclusions can be drawn from Table 15.3. First, a smaller percentage of children were consistently low scorers at maths (11.7 per cent) than at reading (17.5 per cent), though there was a similar proportion of consistently high scorers on each test (16.5 per cent and 17.7 per cent).

Second, it is of interest to know whether children are as likely to move from the low group to the high group as to move to this same extent in the opposite direction. Combination of the groups shows that altogether 4.4 per cent move from high to low and 3.6 per cent from low to high on the maths test, and the corresponding percentages for the reading test are 3.0 per cent and 3.5 per cent. There is therefore only a slight tendency for children to move in one direction more than another on each test. However, there is some difference between the tests in that although the proportions who improve are similar on the two tests, a smaller proportion of good readers become poor readers (3.0 per cent) than good mathematicians become poor mathematicians (4.4 per cent).

The most striking finding from this table, already indicated in Tables 15.1 and 15.2, is the contrast between the extent of substantial change in attainment before, and after, 11. The proportions moving from low to high by 11 and remaining 'high' scorers at 16 are 1.6 per cent for maths and 1.8 per cent for reading, whereas only 0.4 per cent on each test remain 'low' at 7 and 11 and then become 'high'. The contrast is similar in the opposite direction.

Characteristics of groups

It can be calculated from Table 15.3 that altogether 35 per cent and 42 per cent scored in the same third of the maths and reading distributions respectively at each age. This section will compare the background characteristics of these children with the groups whose performance relative to their peers changed substantially and the population as a whole. As some of the groups are small, the 'change' groups have been combined for a few of the comparisons. The characteristics relate to the children's circumstances when they were 7 years of age.

The largest difference between the sexes on the maths test is that there is a smaller percentage of boys than of girls in the HHL group. However, this is only a small group, and the difference did not reach significance. On the reading test there are more differences between the sexes, with boys over-represented in each of the three groups which moved from low scores at 7 to high at 16 (LHH, LMH and

LLH) and underrepresented in the three groups whose attainment level falls (HLL, HML and HHL), though not all of these results reached significance (Table 15.4).

The differences in the percentages in non-manual social classes in each of the constant groups is very striking, and in the expected direction (Table 15.5). For maths, and barely for reading, the group whose performance improved considerably before the age of 11 (LHH) includes a relatively high proportion of children from non-manual social classes, though not as high as the constantly high attainers. On the other hand, among those who did not improve until after 11 (LLH) there appears to be an underrepresentation of non-manual social classes for both tests. Each of the groups whose performance deteriorated (HLL, HML and HHL) includes a smaller proportion from non-manual social classes than the total sample (except HHL, which has a similar proportion on the maths test). Thus on the whole the groups whose relative performance deteriorated are likely to be from the manual social classes but those who improved are more likely to be from non-manual classes.

It is also of interest to know whether children from a particular social class were more likely to change in their attainment (irrespective of direction) than children from other social classes. However, there appeared to be little tendency for the social classes to differ in this respect, except that children from non-manual backgrounds were slightly more likely than other children to perform consistently in maths while those from semi- and unskilled social classes were slightly less likely to do so than the average. It was also notable that although many of the children with no male head of household will have experienced changes in their life-style due to their parental situation, they were no more likely to

TABLE 15.4 *Percentage of boys in each group for maths and reading (H = high, M = middle, L = low)**

	Groups									
	HHH	MMM	LLL	HLL	HML	HHL	LHH	LMH	LLH	Total
Maths (N = 100%)	55 (1 552)	51 (684)	47 (1 100)	48 (140)	51 (212)	38 (58)	51 (150)	58 (153)	45 (33)	51 (9 402)
Reading (N = 100%)	48 (1 677)	51 (673)	56 (1 661)	25 (146)	43 (125)	36 (22)	72 (167)	72 (123)	65 (37)	51 (9 482)

(% boys)	Maths: all comparisons ns	LMH/rest χ^2 = 26.2 (9 df) $p < 0.01$
	Reading:	HLL/rest χ^2 = 31.6 (9 df) $p < 0.001$
	LHH/rest χ^2 = 31.1 (9 df) $p < 0.001$	HML/rest, HHL/rest and LLH/rest ns

* Significance levels reported for Tables 15.4 to 15.9 have been adjusted to take account of multiple comparisons by increasing the number of degrees of freedom (Gabriel, 1966).

TABLE 15.5   *Percentage in non-manual social class* in each group for maths and reading*

	Groups									Total
	HHH	MMM	LLL	HLL	HML	HHL	LHH	LMH	LLH	
Maths (N = 100%)	54 (1 479)	26 (650)	14 (1 032)	15 (136)	18 (202)	33 (57)	47 (146)	38 (148)	22 (32)	31 (8 957)
Reading (N = 100.%)	56 (1 607)	28 (649)	12 (1 545)	13 (142)	22 (119)	10 (20)	35 (159)	31 (112)	21 (34)	32 (9 034)

(% NM)   Maths: LHH/rest χ^2 = 17.0 (9 df) $p < 0.05$ HHL/rest and LLH/rest   ns
HHL/rest χ^2 = 17.2 (9 df) $p < 0.05$ Reading: HLL/rest χ^2 = 23.6 (9 df) $p < 0.01$
HML/rest χ^2 = 17.2 (9 df) $p < 0.05$ all other change groups/test   ns

* Social class is defined according to the Registrar-General's Classification of Occupations (1960).

change in their attainment than the rest of their age group.

A further indication of the child's social background is provided by his parents' educational level. The percentages of children whose fathers stayed on at school after the minimum school-leaving age are shown in Table 15.6. The corresponding figures for mothers staying on at school showed a similar pattern, and so have not been presented. Due to the small numbers, the change groups have been combined to ignore their 11-year performance.

For both attainment tests the group whose performance substantially improved in comparison with their peers included a slightly, but not significantly, higher proportion than average of children whose fathers stayed on at school, while the group whose performance deteriorated relatively included a low proportion with fathers who stayed on at school. The group which improved therefore tended to be similar to the constantly high attainers in this respect, while the group who deteriorated tended to be more like the constantly low attainers.

The regional distribution of the children in each change in reading group is shown in Table 15.7. The most striking findings are those for Scotland, which was overrepresented in the group whose performance dropped from the 'high' range to the 'low' range and considerably underrepresented in the group which moved in the opposite direction. However, the constantly low performers did not include a disproportionately high percentage of Scottish children. The children whose reading performance improved substantially were more likely to be found in the South of England, and the reverse was also true, i.e. those whose performance deteriorated were less likely to be in the South of England. The only marked difference in the regional distribution of the three constant groups was also in the South, which included relatively few poor attainers.

The regional distribution for change in maths results was less marked, and on the whole the pattern was similar to that for reading so it has not been presented. However, there were a few contrasts between the results for maths and reading, in that Scotland was overrepresented in the group whose performance substantially improved, and among the

TABLE 15.6   *Percentage of children in each group whose fathers stayed on at school after the minimum school-leaving age*

	Groups					Total
	HHH	MMM	LLL	H → L	L → H	
Maths (N = 100%)	42 (1 444)	17 (635)	8 (987)	15 (383)	30 (313)	24 (8 720)
Reading (N = 100%)	47 (1 486)	21 (665)	8 (1 055)	11 (391)	29 (330)	24 (8 795)

(% stay on)   Maths: H → L/rest χ^2 = 15.4 (5 df) $p < 0.01$
L → H/rest χ^2 = 6.4 (5 df)   ns
Reading: H → L/rest χ^2 = 18.5 (5 df) $p < 0.01$
L → L/rest χ^2 = 5.1 (5 df)   ns

TABLE 15.7   *Percentage of children in each change-in-reading group in each region*

	Groups					Total
	HHH	MMM	LLL	H → L	L → H	
North	28	27	31	27	26	28
Midlands	26	25	28	20	29	26
South	31	29	24	18	37	28
Wales	4	6	6	7	6	6
Scotland	11	13	11	27	2 (N = 7)	12
(N = 100%	(1 677)	(673)	(1 661)	(293)	(327)	(9 481)

Regions based on Registrar-General's Standard Regions.

Overall test (reading)   H → L/rest χ^2 = 71.0 (20 df) $p < 0.001$
                               L → H/rest χ^2 = 39.5 (20 df) $p < 0.01$

group whose performance deteriorated the proportion of Scots was similar to that of the total sample. The only other differences were that among the group whose attainment level dropped there was a relatively high proportion from the North, and a low proportion from the Midlands.

It can be seen in Table 15.8 that in general there is a fairly consistent pattern in relation to family size in that for each test each of the groups whose performance improved includes a higher than average proportion of children in small families (i.e. less than three children in the household) such that there is as high a proportion of small families in almost all of these groups as in the constantly high attaining group. Also, each of the groups whose performance became relatively poor has a lower than average proportion of small families (except the HHL-reading and HML-maths groups which include a similar proportion of small families to that in the total sample). The differences are particularly marked, and consistent for both tests, for the groups whose attainment changed before they were 11 (the HLL and LHH

groups), though, as the table shows, only one of these comparisons reached statistical significance.

Comparison of the change groups in terms of the study child's position among the children in the household showed a similar pattern in that the first-born children were overrepresented in the groups whose performance improved and among the constantly high attainers, and underrepresented in the groups whose performance deteriorated and the constantly low attainers.

Table 15.9 shows the percentages of children whose mothers were recorded by the teachers at the 16-year-old follow-up as either 'over-concerned' or 'very interested' in their child's progress (the other possible responses were 'show some interest', or 'show little or no interest'). The teachers also recorded the interest shown by the fathers, but the pattern was similar for both parents, so it has only been presented for the mothers. There is a very striking difference in the percentage of children in each of the constant groups whose mothers were said to be interested in their progress. The differences

TABLE 15.8   *Percentage of children in each group in small families* for maths and reading*

	Groups									Total
	HHH	MMM	LLL	HLL	HML	HHL	LHH	LMH	LLH	
Maths	53	50	32	29	39	23	65	52	52	38
(N = 100%)	(1 485)	(655)	(1 020)	(133)	(202)	(57)	(147)	(149)	(31)	(8 966)
Reading	55	46	27	36	40	45	56	48	56	44
(N = 100%)	(1 617)	(652)	(1 524)	(144)	(120)	(20)	(160)	(173)	(34)	(9 042)

* Small families defined as one or two children under 21 in the household.

(% small families)   Maths: LHH/rest = 28.3 (9 df) $p < 0.001$
                               Each other change group/rest   ns
                               Reading: each change group/rest   ns

TABLE 15.9   *Percentage of children in each group (maths and reading) whose mothers were reported by teachers as interested in the child's progress when they were 7*

| | Groups | | | | | |
	HHH	MMM	LLL	H → L	L → H	Total
Maths (N = 100%)	70 (1 464)	39 (623)	18 (994)	35 (382)	46 (312)	43 (8 736)
Reading (N = 100%)	71 (1 591)	39 (622)	16 (1 512)	34 (269)	41 (308)	43 (8 802)

(% mothers interested) Maths and Reading: each change group/rest   ns.

between the change groups and the total cohort were much smaller, in particular for the group which improved. However, it is interesting that fewer mothers were reported as interested at 7 among those whose attainment was high at the time and then fell, than among the group which also performed well at the time but continued to do so at 11 and 16.

Discussion

The examination of the characteristics of the children whose performance changed substantially during their school years showed that in most respects, for example in social class, family size, parental education and mother's interest in the child's education, the groups which improved were closer than average to the consistently high performers, while the groups whose attainment dropped tended to be more like the group always at the low level of performance. The constantly high attainers differed very markedly from the constantly low attainers in terms of each of these variables, always in the direction expected from previous research (see the Introduction).

The analyses reported here, by selecting for comparison only those children whose performance changed substantially, cannot be generalised to describe the characteristics of all children whose school performance changes in relation to their year group. However, an analysis which considered this question, using the NCDS data, has been reported elsewhere (see pp. 36—42). This showed that, after allowing for 7-year and 11-year test results, the mean 16-year maths and reading test scores were higher for those children who were already relatively advantaged in terms of attainment, namely boys, children from non-manual social classes, with fewer older siblings and to a small extent fewer younger siblings and children from the south of England. In almost all respects our results are therefore in agreement, which shows that the characteristics of the children whose attainment substantially improved or deteriorated are

similar for the most part to the characteristics associated with overall change. For example, children in Scotland showed considerably poorer performance in reading at 16 after adjusting for earlier performance. Similarly the results presented here showed that Scottish children were particularly over-represented in the groups whose relative reading attainment dropped considerably, and those showing substantial relative improvement included a strikingly small proportion of Scottish children.

However, there are two areas in which there is an interesting difference in emphasis. Fogelman *et al.*'s results showed that although boys have higher 16-year scores for given earlier scores than girls on both tests, the difference is greater for maths. However, the results of the present analysis showed that boys were not significantly more likely to be in the groups which substantially improved in maths (or less likely to deteriorate substantially), though they were in reading. This suggests that in maths the overall relative drop in level attained by girls is due to a slight deterioration among a large number of girls, rather than large changes in performance by a few. Conversely, in reading, the two sets of results taken together suggest that the overall improvement by boys is composed at least in part by a few boys showing a marked improvement in performance.

The second interesting contrast is in the social class of the children whose relative attainment improved substantially during the secondary school years. Although the result was non-significant, the present study showed that this group included an underrepresentation of non-manual social classes, which is contrary to the pattern of an overall widening gap between social classes demonstrated by Fogelman *et al.*

Tables 15.1 to 15.4 have provided an indication of the extent to which children who are performing particularly well, or poorly, in comparison with their peers at an early stage of their school careers, are no longer performing so well, or badly by the minimum school-leaving age, and, for those who do change, the stage in their schooling at which this is most likely to occur.

Approximately two-thirds of the groups at each extreme at 7 were in the same range at 11 for each test, and about 10 per cent moved from one extreme to the other between these two ages. The likelihood of children moving from one extreme to another between 11 and 16 was very small. However, on the whole, three-quarters of the extreme groups at 11 were in the same range at 16, which means that considerable numbers of children moved into and out of the middle ranges between these two ages.

In general, therefore, the extent of movement during the primary years was far greater than during the secondary school years. It is the extent of this latter change which is of most practical importance, as it is at about 11 that selection within, if not between, schools may be made, on the assumption that little change in relative performance will take place after that age.

The extent of this movement is clearly particular to the conditions existing in the country at the time of the study, and will be determined by many factors both inside and outside the education system. Certain practices within the education system are designed to facilitate change, such as comprehensive rather than selective schools, or schools which favour mixed-ability teaching rather than streaming. Further work is now in hand in order to find out whether the likelihood of change in performance does vary with those aspects of the education system.

THE PREDICTION OF EDUCATIONAL FAILURE

A considerable amount of evidence now exists to show that at any given age there are differences in average attainment between children from different backgrounds. A number of studies have demonstrated that differences in social class and family size are associated with differences in children's test scores; it is also well known that children from homes with fewer basic amenities and higher levels of living density tend to have poorer attainments at school (Davie *et al.*, 1972).

Further evidence has shown that changes in attainment between the ages of 7 and 11 years are associated with social class, family size, crowding and amenities — the children in the more disadvantaged groups falling behind their peers at 11 (Fogelman and Goldstein, 1976, see pp. 27–36).

It is hoped here to show how and to what extent educational 'failure' (identified at 16 years) may be predicted at an earlier stage using both educational and socio-environmental factors at ages 7 and 11.

Over the past half century, administrators and research workers have sought an effective method of predicting academic achievement, both at secondary and tertiary levels. Eysenck (1971), for example, has argued the case for IQ tests as predictors of success or failure in school or university, and IQ tests and other standardised tests have been used in determining allocation to type of secondary school and entrance to university.

Walker (1957) introduced the concept of success ratios in investigating the prediction of academic achievement in Scottish secondary schools. Powell (1973) attempted to assess the effect of various predictors of success at university with a view to possible introduction of standardised achievement tests (SATV and SATM) as the university selection criterion in Scotland. McPherson (1971) examined the effect of introducing non-academic factors to improve prediction.

The aim of such projects has in general been the prediction or explanation of success rather than the prevention of failure, though in many ways the statistical problems are conceptually similar. In general the emphasis has not been on intervention programmes to help those adjudged likely to be unsuccessful, though Wilson (1971) has shown that the supportive services provided by universities can reduce failure rates if those requiring the resources can be identified in time. If an intervention programme is to be mounted, then it is important to know to what extent academic success or failure can be predicted and to consider as wide a range of possible predictors as may be convenient.

From another approach, Alberman and Goldstein (1970) looked at the performance of an 'at risk' register of children who are felt, because of perinatal circumstances, to be disproportionately susceptible to certain handicaps, concluding that such a register could be an efficient method of using resources to identify children with handicaps not visible at birth.

Predicting educational failure has one major difference from this, since it is at least conceptually easier to define an outcome of handicap than of educational failure.

Prediction of failure

Preliminary analyses of NCDS data (not shown here) compared low achievers with average and successful children. The relationship between social factors and school attainment has been well established by previous studies, and our findings confirm that social class, large family size and poor accommodation all tend to be associated with children's poorer attainment. As expected, it was also found that the lower the child's achievement, the less likely were the parents to have shown interest in their child's education, to have been longer at school themselves and to wish their children to stay beyond the minimum leaving age. Although the majority of parents were satisfied with their child's education, no matter what his or her attainment, in general the parents of lower-achieving children tended to be less satisfied.

In this project we were concerned with being able to use information gathered at an earlier stage to predict what we might expect educational performance to be at a later stage in the educational system as constituted at present. This was to enable us to identify an 'at risk' group with whom intervention strategies could most fruitfully or most urgently be pursued. We should emphasise that our analyses relate to prediction of 16-year-old attainment rather than explanation and that while the 11-year (or 7-year) characteristic may be a very strong predictor of 16-year attainment, it does not necessarily imply that it can be taken as an equally strong causal factor. For example, if we were to find that 11-year attainment was the strongest predictor of 16-year attainment, this would not be a complete explanation, since we are still left to ask what causes 11-year attainment. Fuller longitudinal analyses of attainment are described elsewhere.

We shall consider the prediction of reading and mathematics separately, and try to identify predictors which will be simple but effective and easy to apply; there is little benefit in developing a highly effective prediction formula which is so complex that it needs a professional statistician to apply it, if a much simpler formula can be nearly as effective.

The method of procedure adopted was as follows. Certain variables seemed good candidates as predictors. We used the technique of analysis of variance to introduce them all simultaneously as predictors, and to estimate their relative efficacy, carrying out this analysis separately for 11-year and for 7-year values of the predictor variables. We also considered the variables in isolation as predictors. From this we selected the most effective predictors and then estimated the predictive efficacy for the selected 11- and 7-year predictors alone and in combination.

The technique of analysis of variance enables us to investigate the predictive effectiveness of a number of variables simultaneously. In a simple (main-effects) model we assume that a dependent variable (for example, the reading score at 16) can be predicted as a simple sum of effects based on the categories of the predictor variables. Thus reading score could be predicted as a sum of so many points for being of a given social class plus so many points for the size of family. Analysis of variance attempts to produce the 'best' predictor scores, taking as a measure of

predictive impact of a variable the difference between the highest and lowest values of the fitted constants for the categories of that variable in the analysis of variance (see note 1 on page 311).

The 16-year scores for reading and mathematics have been transformed to give a mean of zero and a standard deviation of one. For ease of reference the fitted constants in the analyses of variance are expressed diagrammatically in Figures 15.1–15.4. The first set of analyses (Figures 15.1 and 15.2) were conducted using 7-year characteristics only, while Figures 15.3 and 15.4 refer to the influence on 16-year scores of 11-year-old characteristics.

From these it can be seen that school performance at 7 and 11 years, as indicated by test scores and by teacher's rating of ability, appears to be the strongest predictor of attainment at 16, and that in comparison the social factors describing social class, housing conditions, family size and income have relatively little importance.

Figures 15.1 and 15.2 relate to the influence of 7-year variables on 16-year transformed reading and mathematics scores. The most effective predictor in both reading and mathematics is the teacher's rating of the child's ability. In each case the difference between the highest and lowest rating is of the order of 1.1 to 1.2 points of transformed score (standard deviations) at 16. Figures 15.1 and 15.2 show further that a child's test scores at 7 represent the second most important predictor of his or her attainment at 16, the difference between the highest and lowest scores accounting for 0.95 points of transformed reading score and 0.92 points of transformed mathematics score. On the other hand, the analyses of 11-year variables shown in Figures 15.3 and 15.4

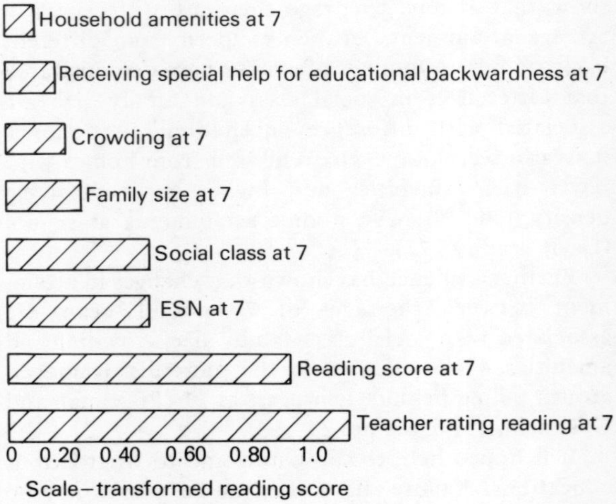

Household amenities at 7

Receiving special help for educational backwardness at 7

Crowding at 7

Family size at 7

Social class at 7

ESN at 7

Reading score at 7

Teacher rating reading at 7

0   0.20   0.40   0.60   0.80   1.0

Scale—transformed reading score

FIGURE 15.1   *Reading: 16-year achievement predicted by 7-year characteristics*

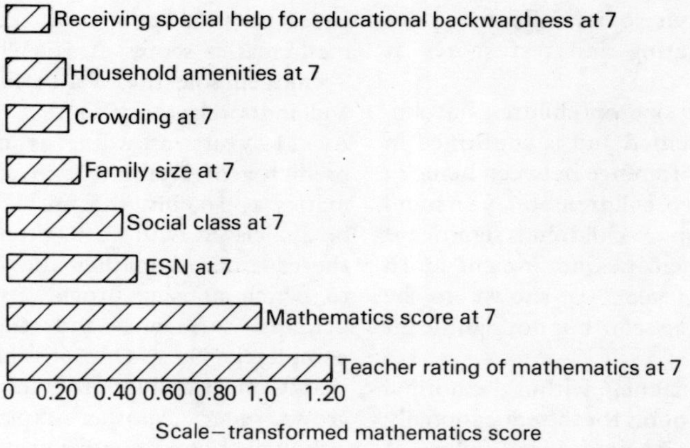

Receiving special help for educational backwardness at 7

Household amenities at 7

Crowding at 7

Family size at 7

Social class at 7

ESN at 7

Mathematics score at 7

Teacher rating of mathematics at 7

0   0.20   0.40 0.60   0.80 1.0   1.20

Scale—transformed mathematics score

FIGURE 15.2   *Mathematics: 16-year achievement predicted*
by 7-year characteristics

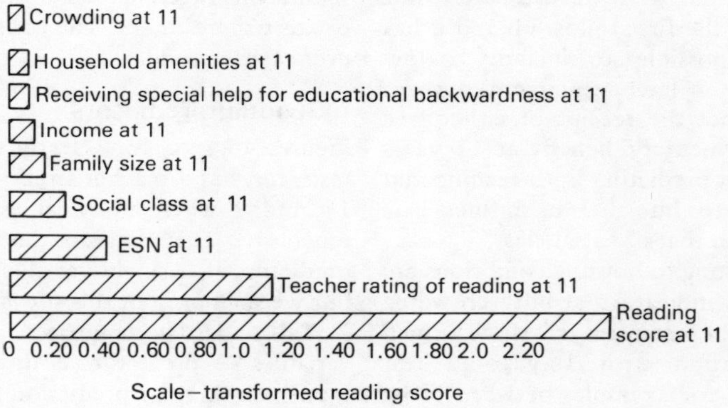

Crowding at 11

Household amenities at 11

Receiving special help for educational backwardness at 11

Income at 11

Family size at 11

Social class at 11

ESN at 11

Teacher rating of reading at 11

Reading score at 11

0   0.20 0.40 0.60 0.80 1.0   1.20 1.40 1.60 1.80 2.0   2.20

Scale—transformed reading score

FIGURE 15.3   *Reading: 16-year achievement predicted*
by 11-year characteristics

Household amenities at 11

Crowding at 11

Family size at 11

Receiving special help for educational backwardness at 11

Income at 11

ESN at 11

Social class at 11

Teacher rating of mathematics at 11

Mathematics score at 11

0   0.20 0.40 0.60 0.80 1.0 1.20 1.40   1.60 1.70 1.80 1.90 2.0

Scale—transformed mathematics score

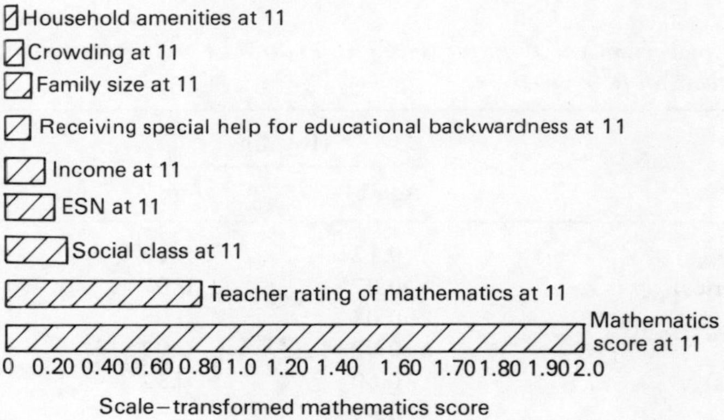

FIGURE 15.4   *Mathematics: 16-year achievement predicted*
by 11-year characteristics

indicate that test scores at 11 are better predictors of 16-year scores than are teacher ratings, the difference between the highest and lowest scores representing approximately two points of transformed score on both reading and mathematics tests.

Factors associated with socio-environmental background are shown to be poorer predictors of 16-year scores than those relating to early attainment. Among the social factors examined, social class appears to be the most important discriminator of educational success or failure, but even so its influence pales besides that of teacher rating and test scores at 7 and 11.

The influence of family size on children's attainment has been well documented and is confirmed in this study in so far as the difference between being in a small family of one or two children at 7 years and being in a family of five or more children is significant for both reading and mathematics attainment at 16 years. Family size at 11 years is shown to be significant for 16-year reading score but not significant for mathematics.

Of course, receiving special help within the normal school or being in special schools for the educationally subnormal (ESN) will be associated with failure at 16, particularly for the small number already classified as ESN at 7 years.

Data on family income were unfortunately not available at the time of the first follow-up and it has therefore only been possible to include a 'low income' variable at 11 on later attainment. Figures 15.3 and 15.4 show that the receipt of either free school meals or supplementary benefit at 11 years is a significant factor in predicting both reading and mathematics score at 16 but that its influence is considerably smaller than that of social class.

As far as factors relating to housing conditions are concerned, the findings indicate that both crowding and the use of household amenities at 7 show a small but significant association with 16-year-old test scores. The difference, for example, between living in overcrowded conditions at 7 (i.e. more than 1.5 persons per room) and living in homes where there is a smaller degree of density is shown to be equal to 0.18 points of transformed reading and mathematics scores at 16. Whether or not a child at 7 enjoyed sole use of a bathroom, hot water supply and indoor lavatory in the home is also significant. At 11 years crowding is no longer a significant predictor of attainment in either reading or mathematics at 16, but the use of amenities continues to be associated with both, though to a lesser extent in the case of the mathematics score. The small extent to which housing provides a stronger prediction is perhaps surprising and the explanation is not completely clear. One possible explanation could be that home variables grow less important as the child grows older. Another explanation could be that although home condition variables might still be effective, their continuity was such that its effect after 11 might be in line with that before and no significant difference would be noticed after allowing for test scores at 11. The housing measures are in any event fairly crude.

Individual predictors

Figures 15.1 to 15.4 clearly show the superiority of test scores and teacher's ratings as predictors at both 11 and 7 when all variables are considered simultaneously. This suggests that these will be the best predictors if a single variable is used for prediction, but we shall present this specifically.

Table 15.10 compares the strengths of the variables as predictors both for reading and mathematics, looking at prediction from 11 to 16 and from 7 to 16 years. As a measure of strength of prediction we have used the squared multiple correlation R^2 (see note 2 on page 311). We discuss later the practical

TABLE 15.10   *Strength of certain variables measured at 11 or 7 as predictors of educational performance at 16 (squared multiple correlation R^2)*

	Reading		Mathematics	
Predictors	Age 11	Age 7	Age 11	Age 7
Social class (three categories)	0.12	0.12	0.11	0.11
Family size (three categories)	0.07	0.07	0.04	0.04
Overcrowding	0.04	0.05	0.03	0.03
Amenities	0.02	0.02	0.01	0.03
Test score (five categories)	0.60	0.32	0.50	0.20
Income (poverty)	0.04	—	0.03	—
Teaching rating (three categories)	0.42	0.33	0.40	0.27
Receiving special help for backwardness	0.09	0.04	0.06	0.02
ESN	0.05	0.01	0.03	0.01
Age father left school		0.09		0.10
Age mother left school		0.09		0.09

Notes: R^2 values may be very slightly different from those quoted in Table 15.11. This is presumably because of the slightly different samples which arise as a result of excluding missing data on different sets of variables.

meaning of the coefficient for prediction, but at present it is sufficient to note that test score and teacher's rating are much more effective than any others. Thus for reading at 16 the best 11-year predictors are test scores (R^2 = 0.60) and teacher's rating (R^2 = 0.42) and the next best is parental social class (R^2 = 0.12). Poverty measures at 11 come a long way behind and are scarcely correlated (R^2 = 0.04) with achievement at 16. These findings are the same for both reading and mathematics and for prediction from 7 and from 11. No measure of parental income is available at age 7.

Predictive efficacy of test scores and teacher's rating

In view of the clear superiority of test scores and teacher's ratings as predictors at both 11 and 7, we decided to concentrate on these four criteria for both reading and mathematics, both alone and in various combinations. Table 15.11 compares these and gives as a measurement of predictive efficiency the squared multiple correlation, R^2. Several observations can be made. Predictions of 16-year scores are of course much better when based on 11-year characteristics than on 7-year characteristics; and predictions for reading are somewhat better than those for mathematics. Particularly at 11 the optimal predictive efficacy seems to be somewhat 'flat'; little is added to the R^2 obtained with the strongest single predictor when other variables are brought in. Thus R^2 focusing on 11-year score only for reading is 0.60; including 11-year teacher's rating increases R^2 only as far as 0.65, while including all Table 15.10 11-year variables

only pushes up R^2 to 0.66; nor does longitudinal information seem to be of much help as far as general predictive value is concerned: including 7-year score with 11-year score only increases R^2 to 0.63. The introduction of other predictors at age 7 has a greater effect but it is still not particularly marked. Although teacher's rating is a better predictor than test score at 7, test score is considerably better both for 11-year-based prediction and joint 7- and 11-year-based prediction, though 11-year test score plus 7-year teacher's rating provide a stronger joint 7- and 11-year prediction.

As stated in the previous paragraph, good predictions (R^2 = 0.60 and 0.51 respectively for reading and mathematics) are obtained when the 11-year test score is taken as the sole predictor. The correlation for this single variable is very nearly as great as that for all 11-year predictors simultaneously and considerably greater than that obtained with any other single variable. This simple and significant result can be viewed from two perspectives. First, it may appear dispiriting that in the British educational system as presently constituted, in general, pupils' final school performance should apparently be so settled by the end of primary school, though this is perhaps less determinate than might at first appear: R^2 of 0.6 reduces the (residual) standard deviation to 0.63 of its original value, thus a pupil's 'headroom' is only restricted by about a third. On the other hand, for those who wish to engage in positive intervention, it may be quite encouraging to know that prediction is a relatively straightforward and successful procedure and that an 'at risk' group can be readily and effectively identified.

TABLE 15.11   *Prediction of 16-year attainment from 11- and 7-year test scores and teacher assessments*

	Reading		Mathematics	
	R	R^2	R	R^2
7 + 11 score + teacher rating	0.810	0.657	0.745	0.555
11 score	0.777	0.604	0.711	0.505
11 rating	0.659	0.434	0.632	0.400
11 score + rating	0.805	0.648	0.735	0.541
7 score	0.569	0.324	0.451	0.203
7 rating	0.581	0.338	0.512	0.262
7 score + rating	0.620	0.384	0.549	0.300
score 7 + 11 score	0.791	0.625	0.718	0.516
rating 7 + 11 rating	0.697	0.486	0.662	0.438
rating 7 + 11 score	0.793	0.629	0.723	0.522
11 − variables only (all)	0.815	0.664	0.747	0.559
7 − variables only (all)	0.655	0.429	0.609	0.371

How accurate are the predictions?

So far we have been quoting multiple correlations (R^2) as evidence of predictive efficacy but without attempting to estimate what would be their success on average. If we wanted to catch at 11, say 90 per cent of the 16-year 'education failure' group, what percentage of the total age group should be our 'at risk' group? Conversely, if we took as our 'at risk' group the lowest 20 per cent at 11, what proportion of them would we expect to be in the 'education failure' group at 16? Knowledge of the answers to such questions is certainly very important in consideration of such a project. These are of course also strongly influenced by the proportion of the population who constitute the 'education failure' group.

Figures 15.5 and 15.6 show this for actual results, using 11-year test score as the sole predictor for reading ($R^2 = 0.60$; $R = 0.78$) and for mathematics ($R^2 = 0.51$; $R = 0.71$) and taking the arbitrary failure-point as near as possible in the two subjects

(lowest 15.4 per cent in reading and 18.6 per cent in mathematics). Each group shows two curves: the rising one (the 'netted' curve) shows the percentage of the 16-year 'failure' group who would be netted by a 11-year 'at risk' group comprising a given percentage of the total population; and the falling curve (the 'composition curve') indicates the percentage of the 'at risk' group who will actually be in the 'education failure' group at 16.

For reading, the steep upward shape of the 'netted' curve remains relatively straight up to 70–80 per cent. One can net 75 per cent of the potential 'failure' group by taking an 'at risk' group of about the same size as the 'failure' group, i.e. 18 per cent. For mathematics, however, the prediction is less effective and to locate 75 per cent of the 'failure' group an 'at risk' group needs to be almost double that size (34 per cent).

Conclusions

Several studies (Douglas *et al.*, 1968; Coleman *et al.*,

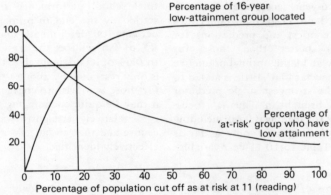

FIGURE 15.5   *Reading (note: low-attainment group arbitrarily defined as those scoring up to raw score 16 (i.e. lowest 17.6%))*

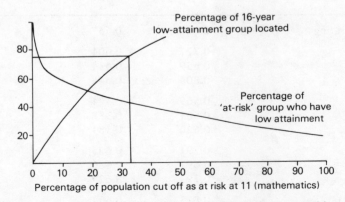

FIGURE 15.6   *Mathematics (note: low-attainment group arbitrarily defined as those scoring up to raw score 6 (i.e. lowest 18.5%))*

1966) have shown that differences in educational attainment are cumulative over time. The less successful groups are inferior in performance at an early stage, and fall still further behind over time, while those individuals more successful at the outset in general maintain and increase their lead. If we are not merely passively to accept this state of affairs, then there must be some attempt to intervene in this process at an earlier stage before large groups of children are condemned to educational failure. In particular, it would be necessary to be able to devise some measures to identify at an early stage those 'at risk' so that greater resources might be directed to them. Such a measure would have to be simple, so that it would readily be applied, yet sufficiently effective so that those employing it could be sure that they could pick up a large proportion of the potential failure pupils with as small an 'at risk' group as possible.

Comparison of possible 11- and 7-year predictors has shown that those predictors which are education-based (performance on a standard test or teacher's assessment) are, perhaps not surprisingly, considerably more effective as predictors than are factors relating to home circumstances, with indicators of poverty in particular having little value. We have stressed that a high predictive correlation is not necessarily an indication of a strong causal connection. However, it does provide a first step, though perhaps the simplest one, in a three-stage strategy to combat educational failure. Knowing what are the indicators, at an earlier age, or prospective failures enables us to identify an 'at-risk' group. Having identified those 'at risk', it is then possible to investigate and isolate those of their characteristics that contribute to their lack of success. The third stage will then be to find ways to overcome the effect of these characteristics.

The measures which have shown the greatest success in prediction at the beginning of secondary or junior school are a standardised achievement test and the teacher's rating of pupils' ability. Prediction from 11-year information is relatively accurate ($R^2 = 0.50-0.64$) and the standardised test score is the best predictor. At age 7, the prediction is not quite so strong but is still far from negligible and the best predictor we found was teacher's rating. The success of the standardised test as a predictor, measuring as it does highly similar qualities at the different ages, is not surprising, but that of the teacher's rating, which is widely considered to be a fairly subjective quantity, is more unexpected. Our results show that a relatively good identification of those at risk of becoming education's failures can be achieved at 11 (although less so at 7), using quite simple predictors.

Notes

1. Many other well-known educational surveys (e.g. the Coleman Report (1966), *Equality of Educational Opportunity*) have used the analogous technique of regression analysis, with different measures of impact. The Coleman Report ordered variables according to their hypothesised causal priority and took as a measure of impact the increment in R^2 when the variable is added to an equation after the 'causally prior' ones. This method has the effect that the first variable entered in an equation will usurp all the effect (often quite large) that is common to it and subsequent variables. Other writers have suggested the use of the 'unique contribution', i.e. for each variable the increment in R^2 when the variable is entered last in an equation. Such a procedure means that the 'common effect' is not allocated to any variables. We believe that our approach is superior because the measure is more easily visualised; it is generally less affected by changes in other variables entered in the equation and it avoids the problem of allocating causal priority among variables.

The measure of importance of a variable (spread of fitted constants) will depend to some extent on how fine a division of the variable is used. It is unlikely, however, that this will seriously affect the results since the two variables with the strongest prediction have nearly the same number of categories (4 and 5) and these two variables are considerably stronger in impact than any others. Another factor which might affect the apparent strength of a variable as a predictor is the fact that the same test was used for 11- and 16-year reading. We are unable to make any accurate assessment of the effect of this, but it is probable that it will not be too large since results are very similar for mathematics, and patterns are similar although weaker at 7 where the tests used were different.

2. The proportion of variance is determined by regression using dummy variables for the categories of the predictor variables. The measure of impact of variables is therefore the square multiple correlation R^2 even for a single variable.

AGE OF STARTING SCHOOL AND ATTAINMENT AT AGE 11

The relationship between date of birth and school attainment is well established. It has been shown, for example, that an above-average proportion of summer-born children are to be found in lower streams and in ESN classes, and also obtain poor O-level results. The explanation for this is more a matter of controversy. Such children will have spent on average a shorter period in school, but alternative explanations offered include: being the youngest in a class where teaching levels are geared to the average; problems arising from joining an already established class; the effect of teachers expecting more from older children.

Data from the National Child Development Study allow a more direct test of the association between length of schooling and attainment at the age of 11. After certain exclusions (such as those children who had received any nursery education, which was relatively rare at that time), the NCDS provides a sample of some 10 300 children, all born in the week of 3—9 March 1958. These divide approximately equally into two groups: (i) those who started their infant schooling between the age of 4 years 6 months and 4 years 11 months ('early starters'); (ii) those who started between the age of 5 years and 5 years 6 months ('late starters').

Age of starting school was found to be related to a number of background and school variables. For example, 'early starters' were more likely to be from middle-class homes, were most common in Wales and least common in Scotland, and were likely to be attending smaller schools and to be in smaller classes.

To take account of such relationships, analysis of variance has been used to examine the association between age of starting school and measures of attainment and behaviour administered when the children were 11, and generally in their final year of primary schooling. These dependent measures were: a general ability test score; a reading comprehension test score; a mathematics test score; and school behaviour (Bristol Social Adjustment Guide).

Independent variables included in each analysis of variance were: age of starting school, social class, family size, region, parents' education, teacher's rating of parental interest in the child's schooling, tenure and crowding ratio of the home, class size and child's attendance rate.

The mean difference between the 'early' and 'late' starters on the behaviour measure was small and reduced to non-significance by the analysis of variance. The findings for the other three dependent measures are summarised in Table 15.12. This shows the unadjusted differences between the means of the two groups, and then the remaining differences after taking into account the other independent variables listed above. The scales of the dependent measures are expressed in very approximate age equivalents so that differences are reported in 'months'. It can be seen that, although somewhat reduced by the analysis of variance, statistically significant differences remain in favour of the 'early' starters.

TABLE 15.12   *Differences in test scores in months — 'early' starters minus 'late' starters*

	Unadjusted	Adjusted	95% confidence interval
General ability	4.9	2.6	1.4 to 3.8
Reading	4.4	2.3	0.9 to 3.7
Mathematics	4.3	2.6	1.4 to 3.8

The nature of the sample — all being born in one week — excludes the kinds of alternative explanations previously offered for this relationship. This, together with the large number of related background variables which it was possible to take into account, suggest strongly that the differences found are the result of length of schooling.

Consideration should perhaps be given to the question of a single school-entry date, as recommended by the Plowden Report on primary schools in 1967. At least, those responsible for admitting children to schools at a particular age should be aware of the likely implications of their decisions.

A COMPARATIVE LONGITUDINAL ANALYSIS OF SPECIAL EDUCATION GROUPS

Introduction

There has been mounting controversy, both in the United Kingdom and the USA, about whether children labelled as 'educationally subnormal' should remain in ordinary schools or be placed in 'special' schools. The arguments generally hinge on the detrimental effects of special schools on the emotional, social or intellectual development of the children attending such schools (Ross *et al.*, 1971b; Meyers, 1973; Miller, 1973). However, there has been surprisingly little systematic research to evaluate the efficacy of these or other types of provisions. The results of the American studies seem to be inconclusive (Hammons, 1972) and the British studies (Stein *et al.*, 1960; Green, 1969; Ascher, 1970; Rutter *et al.*, 1970) also emerge with conflicting results (Tizard, 1966; Pilling, 1973).

This paper presents the results of a longitudinal analysis of the school performance of four groups of children, not all of whom were necessarily labelled ESN. However, they are children who at some point (or points) in their school careers, before the age of 11, were judged to have educational needs different from those of the majority of children. Some of these children were in special schools, some were receiving help within ordinary schools and others had been recommended for special schools but were in ordinary schools.

Throughout this discussion, unlike almost all previous studies in this field, account is taken of both earlier performance and placement in comparing the different groups. However, it must be pointed out that we have not taken into consideration the whole range of personal and social factors (e.g. motivation, environmental stress) which may differentiate between our groups and directly or indirectly affect their school performance.

Method

At the ages of 7 and 11 each child in the NCDS underwent a medical examination and completed a number of educational tests, their schools completed a questionnaire, and their parents were interviewed.

On the basis of information from teachers and the local authority medical officers the following groups were delineated separately at 7 and 11:

1. Children ascertained as ESN(M) and attending special schools for educationally subnormal children (referred to as 'ESN special school').
2. Children ascertained as ESN(M) and attending ordinary schools (referred to as 'ESN ordinary school').
3. Children not ascertained as ESN(M) but for whom the teachers said that, irrespective of the facilities in the area, they 'would benefit now from attendance at a special school' (referred to as 'recommended').
4. Children who were receiving help for educational backwardness within the normal school and who were not recommended by their teachers for special school placement (referred to as 'receiving help').

The above groups are mutually exclusive except for groups (3) and (4): that is, some of the children in the 'recommended' group were also receiving help for educational backwardness.

The children not falling into any of the above groups comprised the comparison group and were:

5. 'Normal' children attending ordinary schools (referred to as 'non-SE' — non-special education).

The above groups were formed on the basis of information at the two ages. Thus it must be remembered that there is no information about intermediate placements which might have occurred between the two ages.

Children who were also ascertained as having a neuro-physiological defect were excluded as they seem to represent a separate group in terms of etiology, prognosis, etc. (Williams and Gruber, 1967; Zigler, 1966). Nevertheless, there may still have been some with such disorders which were undetected, or were not severe enough to lead to ascertainment, who remained in our sample groups.

As measures of school performance, tests of reading and arithmetic attainment at the ages of 7 and 11 have been used.

Method of analysis

The simplest way of detecting change between two or more groups across time is by comparing averages for each group. However, due mainly to the problems of interpreting scores which have been separately transformed and standardised at two ages, this method is unsatisfactory (Fogelman and Goldstein, 1976: see pp. 27—36). The method used by Fogelman and Goldstein (and also adopted here) is designed to identify whether, for children with the same given initial test score, the average at a later stage is different for the various groups they belong to. The problem can be formulated as one of the regression of performance at one age on that of an earlier age for the different groupings of children. This method avoids the above problems and has the additional advantage of providing more detailed information about changes which may occur. Specifically, one can see whether differences between groups at the final stage vary over the range of initial scores.

The problems of measurement error in the 7-year tests have been considered by Fogelman and Goldstein (1976), who concluded that for the tests used the measurement error was small and could reasonably be ignored in the analysis.

Results

Results are presented in two sections. Section A contains the descriptive statistics for the different groups included in the analysis, and section B presents the findings of the analysis of variance

TABLE 15.13   *Numbers of children in each group at 7 and 11*

| Groups at 7 | Groups at 11 | | | | | |
	ESN special school	ESN ordinary school	Recommended	Receiving help	Non-special education	Total
ESN special school	15	2	—	—	1	18
ESN ordinary school	18	10	2	1	10	41
Recommended	44	23	19	31	108	225
Receiving help	4	6	20	88	449	567
Non-special education	31	48	81	520	11 153	11 833
Total	112	89	122	640	11 721	12 684

TABLE 15.14   *Means at 7 for reading and (in parentheses) mathematics for groups of 4 or more children*

Groups at 7	Groups at 11					
	ESN special school	ESN ordinary school	Recommended	Receiving help	Non-special education	Total
ESN special school	5.0 (0.4)	— —	— —	— —	— —	5.0 (0.4)
ESN ordinary school	5.8 (0.3)	7.4 (1.5)	— —	— —	11.3 (2.4)	7.3 (1.1)
Recommended	6.5 (0.8)	7.9 (1.3)	9.8 (1.7)	8.5 (1.6)	10.4 (2.7)	9.1 (2.0)
Receiving help	14.0 (3.0)	10.3 (3.0)	12.0 (2.0)	12.8 (2.7)	17.4 (3.6)	16.4 (3.4)
Non-special education	9.8 (1.7)	12.0 (2.1)	12.3 (2.8)	16.8 (3.9)	24.7 (5.4)	24.1 (5.3)
Total	7.4 (1.0)	10.2 (1.9)	11.7 (2.4)	15.8 (3.6)	24.3 (5.3)	23.5 (5.2)

TABLE 15.15   *Means at 11 for reading and (in parentheses) mathematics for groups of 4 or more children*

Groups at 7	Groups at 11					
	ESN special school	ESN ordinary school	Recommended	Receiving help	Non-special education	Total
ESN special school	1.7 (0.1)	— —	— —	— —	— —	1.7 (0.1)
ESN ordinary school	2.3 (0.8)	4.6 (2.3)	— —	— —	9.1 (3.3)	4.8 (2.1)
Recommended	2.7 (0.3)	5.4 (1.5)	5.7 (1.5)	8.4 (3.7)	8.9 (4.8)	7.0 (3.2)
Receiving help	3.3 (1.0)	6.7 (3.2)	6.4 (3.3)	8.9 (6.6)	12.0 (9.3)	11.2 (8.6)
Non-special education	2.3 (0.6)	6.3 (3.1)	7.6 (4.3)	10.4 (8.0)	17.0 (18.7)	15.7 (17.6)
Total	2.3 (0.5)	5.5 (2.5)	6.9 (3.7)	10.2 (7.6)	16.7 (17.8)	16.0 (16.7)

designed to assess the relationship between attainment and the provision.

A. Basic results

Table 15.13 presents the numbers of children in each group at 7 and 11. The actual analyses were carried out on very slightly different numbers as not all the children in Table 15.13 had test information at both ages. Table 15.14 presents the means at 7 for reading and (in parentheses) mathematics, for each category containing four or more children. Table 15.15 presents the corresponding figures at the age of 11.

It can be seen from Table 15.15 (for example, by looking at the means for the row and column totals) that there is a clear gradation in mean scores from the

'non-special education' to the 'ESN special school' group for both the 7- and 11-year groupings. However, taking the 11-year groups, for instance, one difficulty is that we do not know how much these differences are due to difference in initial performance and group membership and how much to the educational provisions of the children at 11.

The focus here will be to compare between groups over particular ranges of scores at 7 years. Table 15.16 presents the reading and Table 15.17 the mathematics distributions for the 7- and 11-year groups. These are only shown in detail for the range of scores falling roughly below the mean, as this is the effective score range over which the special education children are distributed.

TABLE 15.16 *Cumulative percentages of reading score at 7 for 7- and 11-year groups*

Reading score at 7	ESN special school		ESN ordinary school		Recommended		Receiving help		Non-special education		Total	
	7	11	7	11	7	11	7	11	7	11	7	11
0	50.0	12.4	5.4	4.6	4.6	1.7	0.4	0.6	0.03	0.03	0.2	0.2
1—2	50.0	15.3	5.4	6.9	10.2	3.4	0.5	1.2	0.08	0.1	0.4	0.4
3—4	56.3	23.9	24.9	14.9	18.0	7.5	2.1	3.4	0.4	0.4	0.9	0.9
5—6	62.6	42.0	51.3	27.5	31.9	19.1	7.9	7.9	1.4	1.4	2.4	2.4
7—8	75.1	62.0	67.5	47.0	46.6	34.0	16.0	15.9	3.1	3.0	4.5	4.7
9—10	75.1	74.4	71.0	63.1	63.7	50.5	25.2	26.2	5.3	5.1	7.3	7.5
11—12	87.6	86.7	73.7	69.7	75.7	58.8	34.7	37.3	8.3	7.9	10.7	10.8
13—14	93.9	94.3	84.5	78.6	84.0	72.0	43.5	45.0	11.3	10.8	14.0	14.1
15—16	93.9	95.3	87.2	84.3	89.1	79.4	52.6	53.9	14.9	14.4	17.9	18.0
17—19	93.9	98.0	87.2	87.7	93.3	88.5	65.5	68.0	21.6	20.9	24.8	24.8
20—22	93.9	98.0	87.2	90.0	97.5	93.5	76.8	78.8	30.3	29.7	33.5	33.5
23—25	100.0	99.0	87.2	96.9	100.0	97.6	89.3	88.8	42.6	42.1	45.6	45.6
26+		100.0	100.0	100.0		100.0	100.0	100.0	100.0	100.0	100.0	100.0
N =	16	105	37	87	216	121	559	638	11 712	11 624	12 540	12 575

TABLE 15.17 *Cumulative percentages of mathematics at 7 for 7- and 11-year groups*

Mathematics score at 7	ESN special school		ESN ordinary school		Recommended		Receiving help		Non-special education		Total	
	7	11	7	11	7	11	7	11	7	11	7	11
0	81.2	51.0	50.0	23.9	26.0	9.2	6.3	6.3	1.1	1.2	2.1	2.1
1	93.8	70.2	63.2	38.6	47.0	31.7	20.2	19.1	4.6	4.6	6.3	6.4
2	93.8	89.5	78.9	65.9	67.9	58.3	36.1	36.2	13.4	13.0	15.6	15.6
3	100.0	93.3	89.5	84.1	79.5	73.3	53.3	52.2	25.2	24.9	27.7	27.7
4		96.2	97.4	94.3	87.4	88.3	72.5	68.2	39.2	38.9	41.8	41.8
5		99.0	97.4	97.7	95.8	93.3	85.3	79.3	53.3	53.3	55.7	55.7
6+		100.0	100.0	100.0	100.0	100.0	100.0	100.0	100.0	100.0	100.0	100.0
N =	16	104	38	88	215	120	559	638	11 682	11 582	12 510	12 532

B. Analysis of variance results

The purpose of the analyses which follow is primarily to take into account the differences among the groups of 11-year-olds which stem from their initial performance and group membership.

Separate analyses of variance were carried out with reading and mathematics scores at 11 as dependent variables and 7-year score and the groupings at both ages as independent variables. A simple additive 'main-effects' model was used at first which assumed that the relationship (specifically, the slope of the regression line) between the 11- and 7-year score is the same for each 7- and 11-year group (i.e. there are

no 'interactions' between 7-year score and the groupings at 7 and 11). It also assumes that the differences in average attainment at 11 between, say, the 7-year groups are the same for each 11-year group (i.e. there are no 'interactions' between the groups at 7 and 11). However, it was apparent in the light of further analyses that this model was inadequate and the results of these analyses are not presented. There were interactions between 7-year score and the groups at each age, and, also, interactions between the groups at the two ages which had to be added to the above simple 'main-effects' model.

Comparison of 11-year groups for each 7-year group. Appendix A contains the results of those analyses that include the first set of interactions described above, i.e. those between 7-year score and 7- and 11-year groups. Two analyses of variance were carried out: one for reading and one for mathematics. Taking reading, for example, the 11-year score was used as dependent variable with 7-year score, 7-year groupings, and interaction terms between 7-year score and the groups at both ages as independent variables. Figures 15.7 and 15.8 present, graphically, the results for the group who at 7 were 'non-special education'. As the model includes only the interactions mentioned, the gap between the 11-year groups is the same for each 7-year group and thus the interpretations drawn here apply also to the other 7-year groups, i.e. the special education groups.

As can be seen from Figures 15.7 and 15.8, the regression lines do not cover the same range of 7-year score. This is because, for each group, these lines can only be assumed to be reasonable descriptions of the data over the range where the majority of children score in that group (see Tables 15.16 and 15.17). Thus comparisons can only be made over these ranges.

Although these figures do not portray a clear picture, the following general interpretations are offered:

(1) *Reading.* For the same score at 7, the children

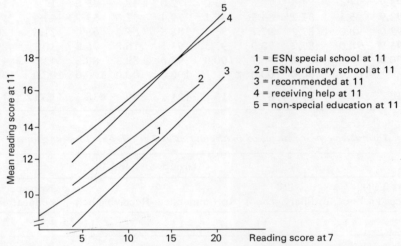

FIGURE 15.7   *Mean reading at 11 against reading at 7 for the 'non-special education at 7' group (model including 'main effects' plus 7-year score by group interactions)*

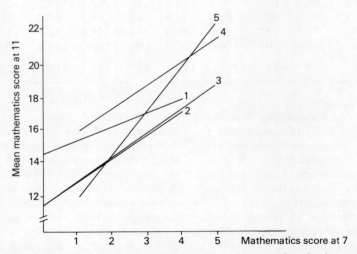

FIGURE 15.8   *Mean mathematics at 11 against mathematics at 7 for the 'non-special education at 7' group (model including 'main effects' plus 7-year score by group interactions)*

who were in the 'non-special education at 11' or 'receiving help at 11' group had similar attainments at 11. Both these groups were doing better than the remaining three (i.e. 'ESN special school at 11', 'ESN ordinary school at 11' and 'recommended at 11'). These latter groups perform about equally well (again for the same score at 7) except for the 'recommended at 11' group, who do particularly badly at low 7-year scores.

(2) *Mathematics*. For the same score at 7, the children who were 'receiving help at all' or were in the 'ESN special school at 11' group do better than the others but are overtaken, in the higher ranges, by the 'non-special education at 11' group. Over a considerable range of 7-year score the 'non-special education at 11' group perform worse than the 'receiving help at 11' group.

The next stage of the analyses was to test the assumption, in the above model, that the differences between the 11-year groups were the same for each 7-year group and vice versa. That is, 'interactions' between the groups at the two ages were added to the above model. For this purpose the two ESN groups at 7 were combined so as to obtain larger groupings. These interactions were not significant for reading (and are not presented) but were so for mathematics. Appendix B contains the results.

The regression lines from this Appendix were plotted and the following points can be made:

1. On the whole the results confirm those of the earlier and simpler model.
2. For the same 7-year score, the gap between the 'receiving help at 11' and the 'non-special education at 11' groups (with the latter doing worse) is smaller for children who had been 'non-special education' at 7 than for other 7-year groups.
3. For the 'receiving help at 7' or 'recommended at 7' groups the 'receiving help at 11' do particularly well by being consistently superior (for the same 7-year score) to all the other 11-year groups.

For these same 7-year groups, the 'ESN special school at 11' children do better (for the same 7-year score) than those in the 'non-special education at 11,' 'recommended at 11' or 'ESN ordinary school at 11' groups over a wider range (compared with the other 7-year groups) of 7-year score.

Comparison of 7-year groups for each 11-year group. In this section the 7-year groups are compared for each 11-year category. The very restricted range of 7-year score (Tables 15.16 and 15.17) obtained by the two 7-year ESN groups, though not surprising, makes any interpretations relating to these very tentative, and applicable only over narrow ranges. The small size of the groups in this section further restrict the interpretations. These comments, which apply particularly in the case of ESN children who were in special school at 7, must be borne in mind in reading the following.

(1) *Reading*. The regression lines from Appendix A were plotted. Figure 15.9 presents the reading results for the 'ESN special school at 11' group. The following descriptions apply to the other 11-year groups as well: the 'recommended at 7' group do better, at 11, than the children in the 'ESN ordinary school at 7', 'receiving help at 7', 'non-special education at 7' and 'ESN special school at 7' groups for the same 7-year score. These groups do progressively worse in the above order. The gap between the groups tends to decrease with increasing 7-year score.

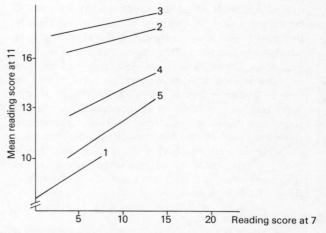

FIGURE 15.9 *Mean reading at 11 against reading at 7 for the 'ESN special school at 11' group (model, including 'main effects' plus 7-year score by group interactions)*

(2) *Mathematics*. In this case the results proved to be extremely complex. Not only were the pictures presented by including the first and the second set of interactions complex, they also differed from each other substantially in some cases. In view of this, only the results for the two ESN groups at 11 are discussed as they are probably of most importance and interest. Further, the results of the two models described above (the first model consisting of the 'main effects' plus 7-year score by-group interactions, and the second being the first model plus group-by-group interactions) will be discussed in conjunction with each other.

Figure 15.10 presents the results for the children who were in the 'ESN special school at 11' group. The results are similar for the other ESN group, i.e. those in ordinary schools at 11. The following points can be made: for the same 7-year score, the 'ESN at 7' and 'recommended at 7' groups do equally well and both do better than the 'receiving help at 7' and (especially) the non-special education at 7' groups. The evidence from Appendix A (i.e. the model not including group-by-group interactions) indicates that the ESN children in ordinary schools at 7 do much better than those in special schools. The gap between the 7-year groups generally narrowed with increasing 7-year score.

Discussion

Here an attempt is made to draw together the rather fragmentary results presented so far.

Reading

Among children whose attainment had been comparable and low at 7, the ESN children in special and ordinary schools at 11 do about equally well at the later age (those in ordinary schools doing slightly better at higher scores). However, the type of school which they had been attending at 7 seems to be quite important. Those who were ESN and had been in ordinary schools at 7 made better progress than those who had been in special schools at 7. Perhaps what is important here is that those children who were in some way 'receiving attention' within the ordinary school at 7 (i.e. by receiving help, being recommended or being ascertained ESN) were, for the same 7-year score, doing better at 11 than the two extremes (i.e. those who, at 7, were 'non-special education' and those who were ESN in special schools).

Mathematics

The pattern of results almost always seemed to be more complex for mathematics than for reading. This might be partly due to the fact that mathematics may be a more diverse task than reading, thus making it perhaps more difficult to tap a common mathematics ability. Another reason might be the limitations of our data (namely, small group sizes and using tests designed for the general population which lack sensitivity in the lower ranges with which we are concerned). Nevertheless, some overall remarks can be made.

For the same score at 7, ESN children in special schools at 11 do better than ESN children in ordinary schools. There does again seem to be tendency for those who were recommended, ESN in ordinary schools or receiving help (i.e. those receiving some 'attention') at 7 to do better at 11, for the same 7-year score, than the two extremes (non-special education and ESN special school at 7).

What is particularly impressive is that for the same score at 7, for both reading and mathematics, on the whole those receiving help at 11 do better than other 11-year groups, especially for low 7-year score. Although it is not known for how long the children were receiving help, this does seem to indicate that receiving special help in the ordinary school without being ascertained or placed in special schools in beneficial. There is additional support for this proposition from the fact that in mathematics

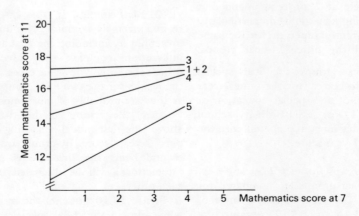

FIGURE 15.10   *Mean mathematics at 11 against mathematics at 7 for the 'ESN special school at 11' group (model including 'main effects' plus 7-year score by group interactions plus group-by-group interactions)*

for the same score at 7 the children who were receiving help both at 7 and 11 do better than all other groups. In the case of reading this applies to those who received help at 7 and were either 'non-special education' or 'receiving help at 11'. (All this of course only applies in the ranges considered above.)

Further, the fact that ESN children in special schools at 7 make less progress than others by 11 argues against early placement in special schools. At the same time, the poor relative performance of those who were 'non-special education at 7' argues for the early detection of need.

While research of the type reported here is badly needed to establish, at a general level, the relationship between attainment and different provisions, it would be more valuable if it were accompanied by investigations into the reasons and mechanisms giving rise to the results. Thus we do not really know why, for given initial performance, the ESN children in ordinary schools do about as well in reading as those in special schools, but perform less well in mathematics. This is unlikely to be due to different methods of teaching, as the children were distributed nationally. Could it be due to a general bias in emphasis towards one subject?

Nor do we know why those who were at a special school or were 'non-special education' at 7 performed relatively worse than others at 11. Perhaps we can make some obvious reasoned guesses about the latter group, i.e. 'they did not receive enough appropriate attention at an earlier age when they "needed" it'. But why is being at a special school at 7 a disadvantage at 11? Is it a consequence of the 'stigma' of going to special school? Is it a function of the school organisation? Is it that in early years these schools emphasise other aspects of development?

These questions lead us to two further and crucial points. The first is that the actual criteria used (or the factors involved) in allocation to different provisions are not clearly known and may vary from one local authority to another (Presland, 1970; Williams, 1965). It might well be that the differences obtained are due to the fact that particular types of children with particular circumstances are allocated to each provision.

This brings us to the second point, which bears on the limited scope of studies which just investigate scholastic achievement. There is a growing awareness of the cultural relativity associated with 'diagnosing need' in this area (Mercer, 1968). While this concept can easily become an excuse for 'non-action', it has the merit of drawing attention to the child's total life experience and social background (see, for example, Zigler, 1966, for a discussion of experiential and motivational factors). In addition, there is the awareness of environmental 'handicaps' or 'deficiency' as a concomitant, if not the cause, of 'subnormality'. While, again, there is a danger of confusing 'deficiency' with 'relativity', this warns against an emphasis on schooling when the problem is 'societal': witness the remarkable difference in social-class distribution between ESN children with and without organic defects (Williams and Gruber, 1967; Stein and Susser, 1960b). However, all this is not to detract attention from those relatively few cases (Rutter *et al.*, 1970) who display organic deficiencies.

Considerations such as the above, plus the complexity of the results presented here, show the futility of 'all-or-nothing' solutions to the debate about special education. Instead, they underline the need for much more subtle distinctions to be made if evaluation, let alone innovation of provisions, is to be attempted (Keogh, 1975).

SCHOOL ATTENDANCE, ATTAINMENT AND BEHAVIOUR

Introduction

In discussions of school attendance and truancy, it seems rarely to be considered necessary to justify one's concern. There is now a sizeable body of evidence on attendance and truancy levels and their relationship with personal, social and school variables. However, it is usually assumed, understandably perhaps, that the children not attending school do less well scholastically than their peers. Furthermore, when this assumption is made explicit, this can involve somewhat contradictory claims about the direction of causality, as the following quotations exemplify:

> His absences caused him to be educationally backward and socially poorly adjusted; on return to school he could hardly fail to notice, and be affected by, his poor attainment and lack of friends; a vicious circle could all too easily be established (Galloway, 1976).

> Fear of being seen as illiterate or semi-illiterate is a cause of truancy among the older secondary pupil (Hopwood, 1975).

Whichever is the primary cause, or whether there is a causal relationship at all, both kinds of argument contain the assumption that children who are frequently absent from school show poor attainment and adjustment to school. In the event, what little evidence there is suggests that this relationship is by no means as straightforward and may not hold for all groups of children.

Text for this paper cont. p. 321

APPENDIX A

Analyses of variance findings using a model with 11-year score as dependent and 7-year score, groups at 7, groups at 11 and interactions between 7-year score and groups at both ages as independent variables

| | Dependent variables | | | |
| | 11-year reading score Mean = 16.11 Variance = 38.72 N = 12 619 | | 11-year mathematics score Mean = 16.87 Variance = 106.08 N = 12 510 | |
Independent variables				
Overall constant	4.46		2.08	
Education at age 7	Intercept	Slope	Intercept	Slope
ESN special school	−1.43	0.28	−0.90	1.15
ESN ordinary school	0.51	0.07	0.45	−0.59
Recommended	0.99	0.04	0.54	−0.28
Receiving help	0.20	0.18	−0.41	0.48
Non-special education	−0.24	0.28	1.40	1.15
Education at age 11				
ESN special school	−2.71	0.07	−1.58	−0.35
ESN ordinary school	−0.75	0.14	−1.31	0.28
Recommended	−1.03	0.24	−1.17	0.32
Receiving help	1.69	0.15	1.31	0.21
Non-special education	2.77	0.25	2.75	1.45
Residual mean square	22.60		67.08	

All variables are significant at the 0.001 level.

APPENDIX B

Analysis of variance findings using model with 11-year mathematics score as dependent variable and 7-year score, groups at 7, groups at 11, interactions between 7-year score and groups at both ages and interactions beween 7 and 11-year groups as independent variables.

Dependent variable = 11-year mathematics score, mean = 16.87, variance = 106.08 (N = 12 510), overall constant = 2.19.

| Education at age 7 | ESN special school at 11 | | ESN ordinary school at 11 | | Recommended at 11 | | Receiving help at 11 | | Non-special at 11 | |
	Intercept	Slope	Intercept	Slope	Intercept	Slope	Intercept	Slope	Intercept	Slope
ESN	−1.58	0.14	−0.50	0.73	0.54	0.83	3.74	0.66	−1.76	1.77
Recommended	−1.49	0.07	−0.81	0.66	−0.95	0.76	1.44	0.59	−0.45	1.70
Receiving help	−1.35	0.62	−0.90	1.21	−0.32	1.32	2.93	1.14	1.22	2.25
Non-special education	−2.61	1.14	−1.76	1.73	−1.26	1.83	1.62	1.66	4.23	2.77
Residual mean square = 66.94										

All variables are significant at the 0.001 level.

Note: The relationship between 11-year mathematics score and 7-year arithmetic score is adequately described by a straight line, whereas that for reading becomes markedly non-linear for high 7-year scores. This, at least in part, reflects the fact that the 7-year reading test discriminated poorly between good readers and resulted in nearly one-third of children obtaining the top scores of 29 and 30. In order to simplify the analysis, the scale of the 7-year reading score has therefore been transformed to give an approximately linear relationship.

Douglas and Ross (1965), for example, related composite scores on reading, vocabulary, intelligence and arithmetic tests, taken at the age of 11 by their sample of children born in 1946, to attendance records over the previous four years. Although in general they did find a relationship between average scores and attendance, this did not hold for their 'upper middle class' group. Among the latter even those who had averaged about eight weeks' absence per year obtained test scores no lower than the best attenders.

A not dissimilar result was reported by Fogelman and Richardson (1974). Again at the age of 11, the reading comprehension, mathematics and general ability tests scores of the National Child Development Study children born in 1958 showed an overall relationship with attendance level in the current year, but when the social-class background of the children was taken into account the relationship reached statistical significance only for the children whose fathers were in manual occupations.

The purpose here is to extend this analysis of the NCDS data to the age of 16. Additionally, we shall be examining the relationship between attendance and adjustment to school, and attempting to assess the relative importance of poor attendance early and late in the child's school career. It must be stressed that throughout we shall be looking at actual reported attendance rate. Absences will be due to a variety of reasons and should not be equated with 'truancy'.

The following variables are utilised:

1. *School attendance at 7*: calculated as a percentage from information provided by the teacher on the number of possible half-day attendances and of actual half-day absences in that school year (i.e. from September 1964 to the date of completion of the questionnaire, which, for almost all children, fell between March and July 1965).

2. *School attendance at 15*: calculated as above but referring to the autumn term, 1973 (questionnaires were completed in the spring or summer term of the same school year).

3. *Social class*: father's occupation as reported in the 16-year parental interview, and classified according to the Registrar-General's (1966) Classification of Occupations. The following categories and abbreviations are used:

    | I and II | Professional and managerial |
    | III NM | Other non-manual occupations |
    | III M | Skilled manual |
    | IV | Semi-skilled manual |
    | V | Unskilled manual |
    | NMH | No male head of household |

4. *Region*: the local authority of the child's home at

16 categorised into the Registrar-General's Standard Regions, and further combined here to give North England, South England, Scotland and Wales.

5. *Overcrowding*: calculated from information provided during the parental interview at 16, the classification of 'overcrowded' being ascribed to children living in homes with a ratio greater than 1.5 persons per room.

6. *Reading comprehension test score at 16*: from a test constructed by the National Foundation for Educational Research (NFER) for this study and designed to be parallel to the Watts–Vernon reading test. In order to satisfy the assumptions of analysis of variance, scores have been transformed to give a normal distribution with a mean of zero and a standard deviation of one.

7. *Mathematics test score at 16*: also from a test constructed by the NFER for use with this age group and transformed to the same scale as the reading test. (Neither of the above tests has been published, but copies and technical details are available from the NCB.)

8. *School behaviour at 16*: as assessed by the Rutter School Behaviour Scale (Rutter, 1967), transformed, to achieve normality, to a scale which has a mean of 1.7 and standard deviation of 1.4. On this scale, higher scores indicate 'poorer' behaviour.

Results

The simple relationships between attendance at the two ages and scores on the attainment tests and behaviour scales are summarised in Tables 15.18 and 15.19, which show the fitted constants from the regression of the scores on grouped attendance rates, without adjustment for any other independent variables. It can be seen that in all cases there is a marked and significant relationship. For all three measures the difference in means between those with 70 per cent or less attendance at 15 and those with better than 95 per cent attendance is roughly one standard deviation of the total sample score.

As might be expected, the relationship between these measures and attendance at 7 is, though still highly significant, less marked – the contrasts being about half as great for reading and maths and even less for school behaviour.

Tables 15.18 and 15.19 give only the crudest assessment of the relationship with which we are concerned. Previous studies (e.g. Fogelman and Richardson, 1974) have demonstrated the relationship between school attendance and various factors in the child's background. Such relationships continue to be found within our most recent data.

TABLE 15.18   *Fitted constants for 16-year attainment and behaviour in relation to 15-year school attendance*

15-year attendance rates	Reading score	Maths score	School behaviour score
Up to 70%	−0.49	−0.49	1.01
Up to 85%	−0.19	−0.25	0.24
Up to 95%	0.19	0.17	−0.42
Up to 100%	0.49	0.57	−0.83
N	7 670	7 634	7 962
χ^2 (3 df)	901.0***	1 187.6***	1 818.3***

In this and all subsequent tables significance levels are indicated: *** $p < 0.001$; ** $p < 0.01$; * $p < 0.05$; otherwise $p > 0.05$.

TABLE 15.19   *Fitted constants for 16-year attainment and behaviour in relation to 7-year school attendance*

7-year attendance rates	Reading score	Maths score	School behaviour score
Up to 70%	−0.24	−0.17	0.29
Up to 85%	0.00	−0.06	0.07
Up to 95%	0.10	0.09	−0.16
Up to 100%	0.14	0.14	−0.20
N	7 670	7 634	7 962
χ^2 (3 df)	39.8***	45.0***	61.0***

For example, Table 15.20 shows the relationship between social class and school attendance at 15 separately for each sex. Social-class differences are in the expected direction, with a clear progression from those in professional families to those with fathers in unskilled manual occupations. The overall slight sex differences are more surprising, and perhaps due to a greater incidence of illness among adolescent girls.

It will be noticed that the total number of children included in Tables 15.20 and 15.21 differs from that reported in the analyses of variance (Table 15.22) and Tables 15.18 and 15.19 which are based on the sample used in the analyses of variance; as the latter incorporate data collected from a number of sources, and in particular at more than one age, there are inevitably children with incomplete information who cannot be included. Dependent variable means for the reduced sample do not differ greatly from those for

TABLE 15.20   *15-year attendance by sex and social class (percentaged)*

Social class	Sex	Attendance rate Up to 70%	→ 85%	→ 95%	→ 100%	N
I and II	B	4	7	26	63	1 134
	G	4	9	32	56	1 145
III NM	B	6	10	31	53	533
	G	6	13	38	43	470
III M	B	11	16	33	40	2 021
	G	11	18	37	31	1 922
IV	B	11	18	29	41	614
	G	16	20	31	32	592
V	B	24	21	26	24	247
	G	22	24	33	20	243
NMH	B	15	20	29	36	352
	G	14	25	28	28	369
Total	B	10	14	30	46	4 901
	G	11	17	34	38	4 741

the total sample, so it seems reasonable to conclude that the former is still a representative sample.

Table 15.21 represents the distribution of attendance rates for the three home countries with England divided into North and South. The contrasts in this table are marked. About one in twelve of 16-year-olds in the South of England were absent for 30 per cent or more of the time in the autumn term of 1973, whereas the figure for Wales was just over one in five.

TABLE 15.21   *15-year attendance by region*

Region	Attendance rate Up to 70%	→ 85%	→ 95%	→ 100%	N
North England	11	16	31	42	5 305
South England	8	14	32	45	4 391
Scotland	13	17	33	37	1 375
Wales	20	20	29	31	663

A further factor demonstrated to be related to attendance rate is the child's housing circumstances, and a discussion of the NCDS findings on this topic (Tibbenham, 1977) has demonstrated, in particular, the relevance of whether or not the child lives in an overcrowded home.

Thus an adequate account of the relationship between attendance and attainment must take account of such background variables as the above, by means of a multivariate analysis. Additionally, it is informative to include both 7-year and 15-year attendance in these analyses as independent variables, as it is then possible to compare the relative strength of their relationship with attainment and, by inspection of the interactions, assess the remediability of any effects of early absence.

Analysis of variance results

Main effects
The results of the three analyses, i.e. with reading, mathematics and behaviour scores as dependent variables, are summarised in Table 15.22.

The analyses reported in Table 15.22 enable us to estimate the mean differences associated with the various levels of attendance, once allowance has been made for the other independent variables included in the analysis. For example, in reading test scores there is a mean difference of 0.72 (of a standard deviation) between those with 70 per cent or less attendance at 15 and those with between 95 and 100 per cent, and this figure is adjusted to take into account any differences between these two groups in their attendance at 7, their sex, social class and regional distribution and whether or not they lived in an overcrowded home.

It will be noted that 'region' has not been included

TABLE 15.22 *Analyses of variance summary*

		16-year reading score		16-year mathematics score		16-year school behaviour scale	
Independent variables		Fitted constants	χ^2 (df)	Fitted constants	χ^2 (df)	Fitted constants	χ^2 (df)
Attendance at 7:	$<$ 70%	−0.13		−0.05		0.11	
	Up to 85%	0.04		−0.01		0.01	
	Up to 95%	0.04	7.6 (3)	0.02	2.4 (3)	−0.05	4.8 (3)
	Up to 100%	0.05		0.03		−0.05	
Attendance at 15:	$<$ 70%	−0.36		−0.38		0.94	
	Up to 85%	−0.14	477.0 (3)***	−0.20	711.9 (3)***	0.22	1 424.1 (3)***
	Up to 95%	0.14		0.13		−0.38	
	Up to 100%	0.36		0.45		−0.78	
Sex:	(Boys−Girls)	0.02	1.1 (1)	0.14	51.2 (1)***	0.29	112.3 (1)***
Social class:	I & II	0.46		0.48		−0.27	
	III NM	0.27		0.20		−0.18	
	III M	−0.06	621.0 (5)***	−0.05	598.0 (5)***	0.00	112.7 (5)***
	IV	−0.19		−0.14		−0.02	
	V	−0.42		0.33		0.22	
	NMH	−0.06		−0.16		0.21	
Region:	North	−0.02		−0.06			
	South	0.06		0.01			
	Wales	−0.04	14.7 (3)***	−0.05	31.1 (3)***		
	Scotland	0.00		0.11			
Overcrowding:	(No−Yes)	0.39	98.0 (1)***	0.23	33.3 (1)***	−0.26	26.3 (1)***
	Residual mean square	0.777		0.766		1.42	
	Significant interactions	Attendance at 15 × sex $\chi^2 = 8.09$ (3)*		Attendance at 15 × social class $\chi^2 = 31.7$ (15)***		Attendance at 15 × sex $\chi^2 = 19.1$ (3)*** Attendance at 15 × social class $\chi^2 = 28.0$ (15)***	
	Total variance	0.966		0.972		1.80	
	Sample size	7 670		7 634		7 962	

as an independent variable in the analysis of school behaviour scores. This is because no initial relationship was found between those two variables, even before allowance for other factors.

The effect of the analyses of variance is to reduce the contrasts associated with different attendance levels, but not very markedly in the case of 15-year attendance. In comparison with Table 15.18, the contrasts between children at the two extremes of attendance are reduced by about 25 per cent in the case of reading and mathematics, but only by about 6 per cent for the school behaviour scale. In this last case, then, the difference between the best and poorest attenders, as categorised, still amounts to nearly one standard deviation.

A further estimate of the importance of these differences associated with attendance can be gained by comparing them with the differences in the analyses associated with social class. In each case the extreme social-class comparison is between children of fathers in professional or managerial jobs and those in unskilled manual jobs. On the reading test the adjusted mean difference between these two groups is only very slightly larger than that between the two extreme 15-year attendance groups. On the mathematics test it is slightly smaller, and on the behaviour scale it is less than one-third the size. In general, scores on the behaviour scale appear to be less closely related to social factors than do the attainment test scores, which suggests than an even greater importance could be attached to the strong relationship between attendance and school behaviour, though it should be noted that the behaviour scale does contain two items — truants and absence for trivial reasons — which will apply, by definition, to some of the absentees. Furthermore, there may be a 'halo' effect with teachers more likely to give adverse ratings to frequent absentees.

A further point worthy of note is that the relationship between 15-year attendance and each of the dependent variables is reasonably linear. To some extent this must be due to the way we have categorised attendance levels, but it may also suggest that there is not a threshold relationship between the two — i.e. that decreases in school attendance are associated with reasonably regular decrements in attainment.

The differences associated with 7-year attendance which, as we saw in Table 15.18, were already considerably smaller when unadjusted for other factors, have now decreased to the extent that they do not reach statistical significance at the 5 per cent level. This finding is discussed further below in the section specifically concerned with the relationship between attendance at 7 and at 15.

Interactions

The preceding paragraphs have summarised the overall differences associated with different attendance rates. However, it is important to know whether such differences are similar among, for example, boys and girls or children from different social-class backgrounds. In particular, as already mentioned, previous work has suggested a different relationship for working-class and middle-class children at the age of 11.

Such relationships have been examined by testing for the presence of significant interactions, in each of the analyses summarised in Table 15.22, between attendance at 15 and each of the other independent variables in the analyses. Those reaching significance are indicated in the table. It will be seen that in no case is there a significant interaction between attendance at 15 and attendance at 7, region or overcrowding. Thus the overall differences reported above can be taken as being reasonably constant for different parts of the country and for children in different housing circumstances (at least as measured by overcrowding), and neither do they seem to be related to the child's earlier attendance level at the age of 7.

For reading test scores there is no evidence of an interaction between attendance and social class, and the only significant interaction which does appear is with sex. However, inspection of the fitted constants obtained when this interaction is fitted shows this finding to be relatively trivial. It arises from the fact that, within the poorest and the best attendance group, the girls obtain slightly higher reading scores, whereas in the intermediate groups the reverse is true. However, in each case the difference is extremely small, and this interaction is probably best ignored.

On the mathematics test no interaction was found between attendance and sex, but one does appear between attendance and social class. However, it can be seen from Figure 15.11 that this does not offer support for any real differentiation between the social classes. The relationship between attendance and mathematics attainment is slightly less marked for the skilled manual (III M) group than for the other social-class groups, but clearly the main contribution to the interaction arises from the pattern of those children in families with no male head. Among these children the poorest attenders obtain the lowest mathematics scores of all the groups, but instead of the reasonably steady improvement with increased attendance shown by other groups, there is a much more marked increase in scores to the point where the mean score of the best attenders is higher than those of any of the working-class groups. This may suggest a strong dichotomy between those fatherless families experiencing severe problems, failing to get the child to school and the child doing extremely poorly at mathematics, and those who are able to cope well.

For the school behaviour scale, significant interactions appear between attendance and both sex and social class. Again they are not such as to have any major effect on our interpretations. Boys obtain constantly higher scores (i.e. exhibit more deviant behaviour) for all attendance groups but one, the group having between 70 and 85 per cent attendance, where the mean scores of the two sexes are virtually identical. It is difficult to offer even a most speculative explanation for this.

The social-class patterns are shown in Figure 15.12. The behaviour score differences between the best and poorest attenders are really very similar and no clearly consistent patterns appear, except that there is

once again an indication of the children with no male head of the family improving their relative position as their attendance increases. Also, the relatively good behaviour ratings of the best attenders among the skilled non-manual group is worthy of note.

Attendance at 7 and 15

As Table 15.23 shows, although there is an obvious association between attendance at the two ages, there is a substantial number of children who were poor attenders at 7, but whose attendance was at acceptable levels at 15.

Conversely, and in absolute terms the number of children concerned is far larger, there are many whose attendance was good at 7 but who were frequently absent when they were 15.

Given, then, that there are considerable changes in

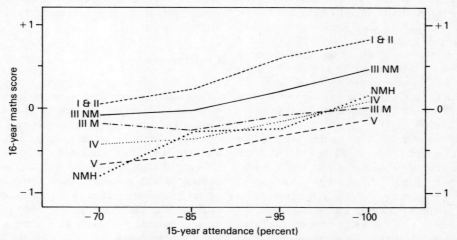

FIGURE 15.11   *16-year mathematics score: attendance at 15 × social-class interaction*

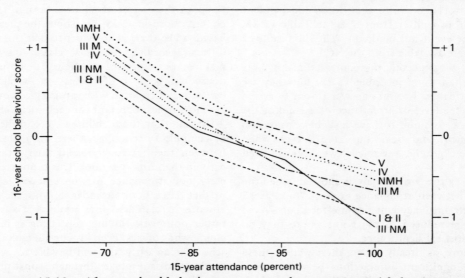

FIGURE 15.12   *16-year school behaviour score: attendance at 15 × social-class interaction*

TABLE 15.23   *A comparison of attendance at ages 7 and 15*

Attendance at 7	Attendance at 15				
	Up to 70%	Up to 85%	Up to 95%	Up to 100%	N
Up to 70%	26	21	26	28	330
Up to 85%	18	21	33	28	1 600
Up to 95%	10	16	33	41	4 430
Up to 100%	9	12	31	48	4 523

TABLE 15.24   *Comparison between attendance at age 7 and 16-year attainment and behaviour: fitted constants from analysis of variance*

Attendance at 7	Reading	Mathematics	Behaviour score
Up to 70%	−0.17	−0.10	0.23
Up to 85%	0.00	−0.05	0.08
Up to 95%	0.07	0.06	−0.13
Up to 100%	0.10	0.09	−0.18
χ^2 (3 df)	24.8***	24.9***	47.8***

many pupils' attendance record in the course of their school career, the question that arises naturally is whether those children whose attendance is poor at the age of 7 show a lasting deterioration in attainment and behaviour, or whether this is offset by good attendance later on. To a certain extent this can be answered on the basis of data already presented in Tables 15.19 and 15.22. From Table 15.19 we see that there certainly is a significant simple relationship between 7-year attendance and the 16-year outcomes with which we are concerned; in each case the poorest attenders' scores are on average approximately one-third of a standard deviation worse than those of the best attenders.

To take the answer a stage further we need to know to what extent these would be reduced if the relevant background variables, but not 15-year attendance, were taken into account. This can be established by repeating the analysis reported in Table 15.22, omitting 15-year attendance from the independent variables. Table 15.24 presents the fitted constants associated with 7-year attendance from such an analysis. (Note that of course the fitted constants associated with the other independent variables will also differ from those in Table 15.22, though in the event not markedly. The full results of this analysis are available from the NCB.)

As would be expected, the contrasts in this table are greater than those in Table 15.22, but they are still not very large. The first answer to our question then is that the level of attendance of a child at the age of 7 does continue to have a slight relationship with attainment and behaviour at 16, even when associated background variables have been allowed for.

However, as the earlier analysis showed, when the relationship between attendance rates at 7 and at 15 is also taken into account, any effects of 7-year attendance are reduced to the point where they do not reach statistical significance.

Furthermore, as already stated, there were in these analyses no significant interactions between attendance levels at the two ages. Thus the relatively high

attainment of the good attenders and the low attainment of the poor attenders, and the size of the contrast between the two groups of children at 16 would appear to hold irrespective of their earlier attendance rate.

Conclusions

From these findings a fairly clear, straightforward relationship between school attendance and attainment and behaviour appears, in that children with high attendance levels obtain on average higher scores on tests of reading comprehension and mathematics and are less often indicated by their teachers as showing deviant behaviour. Although we have been concerned with actual attendance rates irrespective of causes of absence, rather than truancy, this last result is consistent with Tyerman's (1968) suggestion that truancy should be taken as a warning of possible emotional problems.

Contrary to what has been found at the age of 11 for both the cohort of children born in 1946 and the children born in 1958, on whom the present study is based, at 16 there is no evidence that this relationship differs according to social class. Apart from the mathematics scores of children with no male head of household, the differences in attainment and behaviour of children with varying levels of attendance are more or less constant for each social class.

By the time these children were in their final year of compulsory schooling, there was little relationship between their attainment and their attendance rate early in the primary school. This is not to suggest that early non-attendance can be ignored (since it does predict later poor attendance, and such continued absence is related to low attainment). It is in fact a rather optimistic finding, suggesting as it does that a child who misses even a considerable amount of school at an early age will be able to overcome any resulting disadvantage through subsequent regular attendance.

V

Measuring Behaviour in the School and Home*

* Original sources: Ghodsian, M., 'Children's behaviour and the BSAG: some theoretical and statistical considerations', *British Journal of Social and Clinical Psychology*, 16, 1977; Ghodsian, M., Fogelman, K., Lambert, L. and Tibbenham, A., 'Changes in behaviour ratings of a national sample of children', *British Journal of Social and Clinical Psychology*, 19, 1980.

CHILDREN'S BEHAVIOUR AND THE BSAG: SOME THEORETICAL AND STATISTICAL CONSIDERATIONS

This paper critically examines and analyses the structure of a widely used instrument — the Bristol Social Adjustment Guide (BSAG)* — intended nominally for 'detecting and diagnosing maladjustment, unsettledness or other emotional handicap in children of school age' (Stott, 1969, p. 7).

There have been relatively few studies of the structure of behaviour ratings. There does not appear to be any study which, at the same time, uses a national sample, studies the structure across social class and sex and avoids using a special population, e.g. children attending a clinic. The data presented here overcome all these limitations. They should therefore help to clarify the discrepancies in this field, due perhaps to the idiosyncracies of other studies.

The prime motive is to emerge with a simple indicator of the behaviour of the child at school. This, when taken within certain essential theoretical considerations, referred to below, might be of use in future research in the developmental aspects of children.

The BSAG

The BSAG consists of 146 'items of behaviour' each designated as belonging to one of 12 separate 'syndromes'. The teacher is asked to underline the items which he/she thinks 'describes the child's behaviour or attitudes' (Stott, 1969, form BG1/2). Each underlined item contributes a score of 1 (there are also 29 additional items representing 'normal' behaviour that are not scored). Hence any one child will have 12 'syndrome' scores (one for each syndrome) and a total score made up of the addition of the 'syndrome' scores.

General considerations

The methodology used by Stott in arriving at his items and the final guide, though difficult to unravel, was quite simple and conventional (Stott, 1969, pp. 35–55). The initial items were arrived at by discussion with house parents of children's homes. These were also 'grouped into what *prime facie* seemed behaviour of more or less similar types'

(Stott, 1969, p. 40). The children were divided into 'maladjusted', 'unsettled' or 'stable' groups and the wordings of the items and their groupings were progressively altered, using successive samples, to achieve clustering of items in a group and differentiation between the 'maladjusted' and 'stable' children.

However, nowhere in the handbook to the 1969 (or indeed the 1970) edition is Stott in any way explicit as to how the validating groups (i.e. 'maladjusted' versus 'stable') were selected. Stott is not insensitive to the difficulties involved in arriving at such a categorisation. He states that 'when it comes to finding some external . . . validation for tests of social adjustment there is no such (as compared to intelligence tests) easily available canon' (Stott, 1969, p. 21).

This cul-de-sac is mainly a result of a common theoretical orientation in the field of deviance or adjustment. By assuming, as Stott seems to do, that one is trying to reach in the child a 'thing' called maladjustment which has arisen from 'the possession of common instinctual response patterns, from certain types of neural impairment, or through the cultural transmission of certain forms of aberrant behaviour' (Stott, 1969, p. 17) one is adopting a 'medical model' (Albee, 1969) and might be looking for something which might not exist (Szasz, 1960; Sarbin, 1967). (See Schneider, 1953, Pervin, 1960, for alternative formulations; Scheff, 1963, Rotenberg, 1974, for discussions of relevant processes; and Hersch, 1968, Kittrie, 1971, for social implications.)

As far as we are concerned here we assume that in compiling the guide (as outlined above) Stott has asked and obtained a reasonable answer to the following question: what are the behaviours which are defined as deviant in the school setting by its dominant members (i.e. teachers)? The items are thus taken to be indications of these behaviours. Later on (see the Discussion), further comments will be made, using indirect evidence, to bear on this point. In addition the validity of the individual syndromes will be discussed.

The data presented here were collected in 1969 as part of the second follow-up of the National Child Development Study. Teachers completed BSAG forms for some 14 000 children. The social-class categories used are based on fathers' occupations and are classified according to the Registrar-General's classification of 1966.

Method

Factor analysis using principal factoring (Nie *et al.*, 1970, p. 219) was used. Restriction of space does not allow a thorough discussion on the important problem of deciding on the number of factors to be

* All comments and analyses presented pertain to the 1969 edition unless specifically noted otherwise. Although this has been superseded by a revised edition in 1970, most of what is presented is relevant to the 1970 edition and should be helpful for those researchers who have already collected data using the 1969 edition.

extracted. This is influenced by technical considerations (Vaughan, 1973), theoretical orientations and empirical limitations of the type of method and data. The assumption that behaviour is due to some inherent, finite and invariant characteristic of the individual leads some to the quest for measuring and quantifying all the intricate aspects. Related to this is the belief that the method and data can identify all such aspects. All this ignores the notions that factor analysis is no more than a way of summarising a set of data (and providing simple measures) and that this type of method and data (i.e. behaviour ratings) can at the most only isolate major dimensions in any situation (see Peterson, 1960; Becker, 1960).

In the present analysis never more than three factors appeared as significant (using the criterion of a minimum eigenvalue of unity). Where two factors appeared as significant, the third factor was also extracted and studied. Similarly two-factor solutions were tried in all cases when three were significant to seek out the solution which provided the most meaningful, clear and stable result.

Frequency distributions of each syndrome were also plotted. These exhibited the expected J-shaped characteristic typically found in behaviour ratings. (A normalising transformation was also tried but it yielded a similar factor structure.) Regression lines were plotted between several of the syndromes. They all displayed linear trends (where there was an appreciable correlation) except for syndrome 6 ('writing off adults'). This showed a linear relationship with syndromes from one cluster (see below) but with syndromes from the other cluster the linearity was restricted only to the lower range of syndrome 6. This syndrome was nevertheless included in the analysis and will be discussed again later.

Results

Table V.1 shows the varimax rotated factor loadings of the syndromes in the two-factor solution. Quartimax and oblique rotations were also tried but they did not add to the clarity of the factors. Only loadings equal to or greater than the arbitrary, though conservative, figure of 0.4 are presented except for syndromes 4 and 9 (discussed below). The three-

TABLE V.1   *Rotated factor loadings of the syndromes (decimal points omitted)*

Syndromes	Social class						Sex		Total sample	C
	I	II	III NM	III M	IV	V	M	F		
Factor 1: restless, outgoing, anxious										
4. Anxiety for acceptance by adults	363	380	279	430	422	421	493	411	420	177
5. Hostility towards adults	662	617	657	651	625	616	653	621	639	463
6. 'Writing off' adults	447	400	447	440	478	432	410	441	447	441
7. Anxiety for acceptance by children	634	683	680	697	695	664	664	694	685	469
8. Hostility towards children	572	618	628	672	690	626	673	646	653	452
9. Restlessness	338	512	552	507	527	485	501	521	530	299
10. 'Inconsequential' behaviour	656	748	791	765	767	883	724	779	770	646
Factor 2: withdrawn, inhibited, anxious										
1. Unforthcomingness	704	672	712	700	707	695	721	695	706	510
2. Withdrawal	657	668	712	684	706	688	680	706	692	481
3. Depression	611	625	620	632	652	705	657	648	652	525
6. 'Writing off' adults	433	502	500	492	470	455	492	501	491	441
11. Miscellaneous symptoms	553	505	518	562	523	625	599	524	533	396
N =	665	2 179	1 109	5 162	2 064	700	7 202	6 816	14 018	

Notes:
(a) Only loadings equal to or greater than 0.4 are shown except for the four exceptional cases explained in the text.
(b) The group totals do not add up as the number of children with information for each analysis differed.
(c) *C* is the communality for the whole sample.

factor solutions explained an additional amount of total variance ranging from 5.4 to 9.4 per cent; the first two factors explained together between 45.7 and 50.6 per cent.

The two-factor solutions provided better factor invariance across the groups plus a clearer interpretation of the factors. The major specific drawbacks of the two-factor solution (other than the general one of loss in variance explained) were with syndromes 4 in the three non-manual classes and syndrome 9 in social class I.

Although in the three-factor solution the communalities of syndromes 4 and 9 were higher than in the two-factor solution, they were still low (0.142–0.206). Further, as the loadings of these syndromes on the second factor in the two-factor solution were very low (0.001–0.169), it is not unreasonable to include them in factor 1 despite their small contributions.

The other 'peculiarity' which is apparent from Table V.1 is the appreciable loading of syndrome 6 on both factors in all groups. This implies that this syndrome is mixed. This was to be expected from the shape of the regression lines described above. On face validity the items making up this syndrome also tend to confirm this. This is further discussed below. In all the groups syndrome 12 ('miscellaneous nervous symptoms') did not load appreciably on any factor and was disregarded.

It can be seen from Table V.1 that two very clear and stable clusters seem to emerge from the analysis across all the social-class and sex categories. This indicates that, in the case of the BSAG at least, the structure of teachers' perception which it elicits is quite stable. Statistical measures of factor similarity do not seem to be needed as the resemblances between the groups are very clear.

Inspection of the items contributing to the syndromes indicates that the first factor represents what seems like anxious, aggressive restless, outwardly expressed behaviour, while the second denotes anxious, withdrawn inhibited behaviour. However, if no rotation or other rotations were undertaken, different factors would have emerged. For instance, if the axis were not rotated, we would have obtained one general anxiety factor common to all of the syndromes and another 'outgoing–ingoing' factor orthogonal to it.

Factors similar to these have appeared consistently in research on behaviour ratings (Jenkins and Glickman, 1946; Himmelweit, 1960; Peterson, 1960; Pimm *et al.*, 1967; Phillips, 1968; Arnold and Smeltzer, 1974; Herbert, 1974). (Some of these studies extract more than two or three factors. There is considerable lack of factor similarity between studies other than for two or sometimes three of the factors. The references above regarding limitations of this kind of study become pertinent here and should provide a major reason for the divergence found.) However, the two common labels, 'conduct' and 'personality' problems, used by many researchers to denote these factors will not be adopted here. They appear inappropriate for several reasons, the most obvious being that they help to attribute an endemic problem to the child and that they are both in fact concerned with conduct. Failing to find one suitable adjective for each they are best referred to as factors 1 and 2 with a few explanatory words when needed.

Factor scores were computed using (a) simple summation of the major syndromes (loading of 0.4 and above) on each factor; (b), as (a), but with syndrome 6 omitted from both factors; (c) using a multiple regression model whereby estimated regression weights are attached to the syndromes to produce factor scores for each child on each factor (Nie *et al.*, 1970, p. 226). The correlation coefficients for (ab), (ac) and (bc) were extremely high (between 0.942 and 0.973). However, the intercorrelations between the factors for each method of scoring were 0.523, 0.296 and 0.093 respectively.

Method (a) can be discarded at once in view of the strong evidence that syndrome 6 (as indicated by its regression with other syndromes and its high loading on both factors) is a 'mixed' syndrome producing a high intercorrelation between the two factors. The choice between method (b) and (c) ultimately depends on the purpose of the research. However, the factors explain almost the same proportion of variance in both methods and (b) has the advantage of being simpler.

Discussion

On the whole it seems that the analyses presented here have shown that two factors emerge with very good stability across the six social classes and the two sex categories. They should provide us with a simple and economic measure of behaviour at school as seen by the teacher which can be used in other research. This is not to say that behaviour in the classroom is simple enough to be represented along these two dimensions but that we have to face the inherent limitations of this type of method and data. There are clearly many intricate aspects to classroom behaviour — to be teased out by more intensive and less structured methods. These two factors only represent summaries of what might be major aspects of classroom behaviour as seen by the teacher.

Despite the fairly low level of abstraction of the items and Stott's claim of using 'bits of behaviour' or 'emotional expressions' which are 'interpretable at the level of animal instinct' (Stott, 1969, p. 46), it is likely that several factors influence the interpretation of the BSAG by teachers. For example, there is considerable research evidence about biases in ratings by teachers and others (see Vernon, 1964, pp. 58–69). Apart from such factors as sex, age, IQ and specificity of items (Paxson, 1968; Datta *et al.*, 1968; Lambert and Hartsough, 1973), teachers also seem to perceive children along quite broad and general dimensions (Hallworth, 1962).

Such considerations of course detract from the validity of the individual syndromes as being distinct and distinguishable dimensions (Ryan, 1958) and warn against exaggerated emphasis on, for example, 'profile analysis'. However, it does seem that the items forming a syndrome are quite homogeneous, as indicated by the finding that generally the syndromes only load heavily on one factor (with the exception of syndrome 6). An analysis using the individual items would have thrown more light on this but it was precluded on the grounds of data-processing considerations.

There is also evidence regarding the discrepancy between teacher's ratings and those by mothers or other professionals. For example, Schanberger (1968) found very low and barely significant correlations between teachers and psychologists. For the sample of the National Child Development Study a correlation of 0.21 was obtained between the total score on the BSAG and a home behaviour scale completed by mothers (see Lambert and Hartsough, 1973).

Indeed, it can be argued that the factors or the ratings represent the teacher. Though possible, this is as extreme a view as assuming that they are characteristics of the child. It is unlikely that a teacher's perception of a child is wholly a 'projection of himself'. It seems more reasonable that, at least partly, we are looking at the child's behaviour through the eyes of the teacher.

A more important point is whether we have been asking the right questions, and if so have we gone about them in the right way? One test of 'rightness' is whether they help in understanding anything about other aspects of the child's behaviour.

CHANGES IN BEHAVIOUR RATINGS OF A NATIONAL SAMPLE OF CHILDREN

Introduction

It is of considerable interest and importance for those involved in research into, and the development and use of, children's behaviour ratings to have some information on the *constancy* of such ratings over time. In particular, this might throw some light on questions such as the prediction of later disturbance from earlier behaviour (Graham *et al.*, 1973; Liem

et al., 1969) and the planning of services for intervention by professionals (Shepherd *et al.*, 1966).

We here present data on the behaviour ratings of a large and nationally representative sample of children at the ages of 7, 11 and 16. First, the relationship between the ratings at successive ages is considered. Second, six groups of interest are delineated across the three ages. Third, certain characteristics of these groups are examined. The findings are presented separately for ratings of behaviour at home and school.

It should perhaps be added that we are leaving aside the whole question of the validity of the behaviour ratings used. At any one time an extreme score might represent a serious condition (however brought about), causing suffering for the child and/or the people around him or her, a temporary reaction to transient life situations, the acceptance by different groups of different behaviours regarded as 'normal', the differing standards of raters as to the 'rarity' of occurrence of a behaviour, the familiarity of the child to the rater, and so on. To quote Rutter *et al.* (1975a):

> the questionnaire is a *statistical* measure, whereas psychiatric disorder is a measure of disability which implies *impaired function* rather than departure from society's norms. The mere presence of deviant behaviour is not enough for a psychiatric diagnosis. The age appropriateness of the behaviour in terms of the child's life circumstances and socio-cultural setting must be considered, but besides this the behaviour must be evaluated in terms of its persistence, its spread . . . its effect on the child's developmental course and its association with impaired function.

At home

In the course of the National Child Development Study, a modified version of the Rutter Home Behaviour Scale (Rutter *et al.*, 1970b) was completed by a parent (usually the mother) during the home interview when the children were aged 7 and 11. At the age of 16 a different version of the same scale was again completed. On each occasion the mother was asked to respond to a number of behavioural descriptions of the child on a three-point scale (in addition there was a 'don't know or inapplicable' category at 7 and two separate categories for 'don't know' and 'inapplicable' at 11).

At school

At the ages of 7 and 11 the Bristol Social Adjustment Guide (Stott, 1969) was completed by teachers. This consists of 146 descriptions of behaviour which the teacher is asked to underline if he/she thinks they are applicable to the child in question. At the age of 16 teachers completed the Rutter School Behaviour Scale (Rutter, 1967), which is the complementary version of the Home Scale mentioned above.

Comparability of ratings across surveys

1. *Home ratings.* As mentioned above, the same ratings were used at home at the ages of 7 and 11. The 16-year Home Scale had all but two of the items on the earlier scales (although not always with exactly the same wording) plus an additional nine items. The question of comparability is further discussed under 'conclusions'.
2. *School ratings.* As in the case of the home ratings, the scales used at 7 and 11 were identical. However, in this case the 16-year scale consisted of different behavioural descriptions as well as having a format different from those at 7 and 11. Evidence for comparability exists from a study reported by Yule (1968) in which he found a very high (i.e. 0.92) correlation between the BSAG and the Rutter School Behaviour Scale.

Method

We have decided to focus mainly on 'high' scores, as these represent 'deviant' behaviour, and have taken roughly the top 13 per cent on each rating to represent this group. Any figure is necessarily arbitrary. This figure is higher than those selected by Rutter *et al.* (1970b) but is similar to those reported by Rutter *et al.* (1975a) for the school ratings and was found to give adequate sample sizes when comparing across the three follow-ups. It also corresponds to a score of 25 or more on the BSAG, which is well within the category Stott designates as 'maladjusted'. This group is referred to, quite generally, as the 'deviant' (D) group rather than 'disturbed' or 'psychiatrically disordered', which might imply illness when this is not warranted.

We have also taken a 'low' group (L), comprising the substantial proportion of children scoring roughly in the lowest 50 per cent, to represent the 'non-deviant' or 'normal' group for the purpose of comparison with the 'deviant' group. Again, this figure is arbitrary but it seems reasonable to take this substantial group of children to contrast with those in the deviant category.

The ratings were transformed using logarithmic and square-root transformations for the home and school ratings respectively. This was to improve the linearity of the relationship between the ratings at successive ages. These transformations also had the effect of producing a roughly normal distribution for the 16-year ratings in anticipation of future work on these scales. In the analyses that follow, the

numbers of children vary from one table to another as well as from home to school ratings. This is because of incomplete information for some children. Furthermore, it was found that between certain ages (11 to 16 at home and school, 7 to 16 at school) there was a disproportionate number of high-scoring children with missing behaviour ratings at a later age. Our figures for proportions remaining in the deviant groups will be underestimates if these children were more likely to be in the deviant group at the later age than were other children in the deviant group at the earlier age. However, we have no reason to believe this to be so. The differences between children without ratings at one or more ages and the total sample were very small in relation to sex, social class, family size and birth order.

Results

Simple correlations

Tables V2 and V3 present the means, standard deviations and simple product moment correlation coefficients for the home and school ratings. In the cases where comparisons are possible (i.e. between 7 and 11) there seem to be little or no differences in the means and standard deviations between the ages. The correlations among home ratings are higher than those for the school ratings even though they contained less items per rating, thus making a high correlation less likely. To a certain extent, however, this is to be expected, as in the majority of cases the same people, namely mothers, would be completing the home ratings, whereas three different teachers would have completed the school ratings. Furthermore, a different scale was used at school at the age of 16. The latter point, however, is unlikely to be a major factor as the correlation between the school ratings at 7 and 11, when the ratings were the same, is very similar to that between 11 and 16, when they were different. These correlations point towards some stability between the follow-ups, though, as expected, the relationships are closer for adjacent follow-ups than between 7 and 16.

TABLE V.2   *Means and standard deviations*

Age at follow-up	Ratings at:			
	Home		School	
7	2.87±	0.20	2.66±	1.41
11	2.87±	0.20	2.55±	1.44
16	2.70±	0.26	1.60±	1.35

TABLE V.3   *Product moment correlations among home ratings (lower triangle) and among school ratings (upper triangle)*

Age at follow-up	Age at follow up:		
	7	11	16
7		0.41	0.31
11	0.48		0.39
16	0.38	0.46	

Movement between two ages

It is difficult to interpret these correlation coefficients as either 'low' or 'high'. An alternative way of looking at the constancy of the behaviour represented by these ratings is to ask what happens, at a later age, to the children who at an earlier age were in the 'deviant' group: that is, to look at the distribution, at a later age, of children who were roughly in the top 13 per cent category at an earlier age.

Tables V.4 to V.7 show these distributions (cumulatively) for the home and school ratings between the ages of 7 to 16 and 11 to 16. The distributions for 7 to 11 were virtually identical to those for 11 to 16 and hence are not shown. Thus we can see the percentage of the deviant group at an earlier age which falls within any top category of the ratings at a later age. A corresponding column for the bottom 50 per cent or so of the children is also presented to provide a comparison.

Taking Table V.4 for example, we can see that about 43 per cent (third column) of the children who were in the 'deviant' group at the earlier age of 7 fell

TABLE V.4   *Change between ages of 7 and 16 in home ratings*

% bands at 16	% of children above each 16-year band who, at 7, were in the:	
	Bottom 50%	Top 13%
100	100 (N = 3 912)	100 (N = 1 254)
90	85	97
80	70	93
70	57	89
60	46	83
50	35	76
40	27	67
30	18	58
20	12	43
13	7	30
10	6	25

TABLE V.5   *Change between the ages of 11 and 16 in home ratings*

% bands at 16	% of children above each 16-year band who, at 11, were in the:	
	Bottom 50%	Top 13%
100	100 (N = 3 816)	100 (N = 1 419)
90	83	99
80	70	96
70	57	92
60	45	88
50	33	82
40	24	74
30	16	65
20	9	51
13	5	38
10	4	31

TABLE V.6   *Change between the ages of 7 and 16 in school ratings*

% bands at 16	% of children above each 16-year band who, at 7, were in the:	
	Bottom 50%	Top 13%
100	100 (N = 5 475)	100 (N = 1 437)
90	86	96
80	74	92
70	63	87
60	50	80
50	40	73
40	29	64
30	20	53
20	13	41
13	8	30
10	6	25

within the top 20 per cent (first column) of children at 16. From the same table we can see that only about 12 per cent of the children who were in the bottom 50 per cent group at the earlier age (second column) were in the top 20 per cent group at 16 (first column). We can also see what proportion of the children previously in the 'deviant' group were still in the 'deviant' group at a later follow-up. For example, from Table V.7 it can be seen that the top 13 per cent category at the age of 16 for the school rating (first column) contained about 35 per cent of those in the deviant group at 11 (third column) and only 7 per cent of those who were in the bottom 50 per cent at the age of 11 (second column). Thus, although a disproportionate number of children who

TABLE V.7 *Change between the ages of 11 and 16 in school ratings*

% bands at 16	% of children above each 16-year band who, at 11, were in the:	
	Bottom 50%	Top 13%
100	100 (N = 5 561)	100 (N = 1 309)
90	85	99
80	73	95
70	61	91
60	49	87
50	38	80
40	28	73
30	19	62
20	11	48
13	7	35
10	6	28

were in the deviant category stayed there by the later age, 65 per cent of them moved out of that category. However, it must be appreciated that the children in this latter group did not necessarily move into the group we have designated as 'low'. Thus in Tables V.4—V.7 about 44 per cent of those in the deviant group at an earlier age moved to the band between the 'low' group (bottom 50 per cent) and the deviant group (top 13 per cent) at a later age. The corresponding figure for those who were in this band at a later age and were in the 'low' group at the earlier age is about 30 per cent.

From Tables V.4—V.7 it can be seen that the proportions of each deviant group which are no larger in that category at a later age are as follows:

At home:	between 7 and 16	70%
	between 11 and 16 or 7 and 11	62%
At school:	between 7 and 16	70%
	between 11 and 16 or 7 and 11	65%

Thus there is clearly a lot of movement out of the deviant categories between follow-ups.

Movement across three ages
The last section considered the position of children

at a later follow-up who were in the 'deviant' groups at an earlier age. In this section certain special groups are delineated across all *three* follow-ups, i.e. between 7, 11 and 16, and certain of their characteristics are examined.

The groups of interest are:

1. Children who were in the 'low' (L) (bottom 50 per cent) group at all three ages (LLL).
2. Children who were in the 'deviant' (D) (top 13 per cent) group at all three ages (DDD).
3. Children who changed position sharply at an earlier age:
   (a) 'low' at 7 and 'deviant' at 11 and 16 (LDD)
   (b) 'deviant' at 7 and 'low' at 11 and 16 (DLL).
4. Children who changed position sharply at a later date:
   (a) 'low' at 7 and 11 and 'deviant' at 16 (LLD)
   (b) 'deviant' at 7 and 11 and 'low' at 16 (DDL).
5. The remainder of children (R).

In what follows tests of statistical significance have been carried out between each group of interest and the total sample (leaving out that group). Furthermore, the significance levels have been adjusted to take account of the multivariate comparisons (Gabriel, 1966).

Table V.8 shows the proportions of children falling into each group for the home and school ratings. What is most striking about this table is the very low number (i.e. about 2 per cent) of children who remain in the 'deviant' groups at all three ages. Furthermore, the number in each group (except in the LLL group) is very small and hence caution is needed in interpreting the findings which follow.

Table V.9 shows the proportions of each group who were boys for the home and school ratings. There is a clear underrepresentation of boys in the LLL group for both home and school ratings. The reverse is true for the DDD group for school, while for home there is no sex difference.

On the whole, there is a slight suggestion that, at later ages, more boys enter the 'low' groups both for the home and school ratings. As a partial corollary, more girls seem to move into the deviant groups at later ages, at least after the age of 11.

TABLE V.8 *Proportion in each 'change' category over three follow-ups*

Ratings at	Change groups							Total
	LLL	DDD	LDD	LLD	DLL	DDL	R	
Home	20.94	2.28	0.36	0.77	1.22	0.60	73.82	100% 7 144
School	22.93	2.09	0.66	1.66	1.32	0.68	70.67	100% 5 862

Table V.10 shows the percentage of children from non-manual backgrounds (defined by the occupation of the male head of household at the age of 7, categorised according to Registrar-General's classification of 1960) in each group.

Apart from the home DDL group, there is an underrepresentation of non-manual children in all groups who were in the deviant category at least once. These differences are not significant (except for the school DDD and LDD groups) but there seems to be a suggestion that proportionately more manual children are in the change groups and the 'always deviant' group. There are proportionately more non-manual children in the LLL groups for both home and school.

Table V.11 shows the percentage of children from 'small' families (defined as ≤ 3 children in the family when the study children were 7 years old) in each group. There are no significant family-size differences for the home ratings except for the overrepresentation of children from bigger families in the LLD group. For school, however, there was an underrepresentation of children from small families in the DDD group. That is, proportionately more children from bigger families joined the deviant group at a later age at home and more stayed in the deviant group, at

TABLE V.9   *Percentage of boys in each change group for home and school ratings*

Ratings at	Change groups							Total
	LLL	DDD	LDD	LLD	DLL	DDL	R	
Home	45.1***	52.8	38.5	43.6	57.5	58.1	52.1	50.6
N = (100%)	1 496	163	26	55	87	43	5 274	7 144
School	39.4***	71.8***	60.0	39.0	57.7	62.7	53.9	50.9
N = (100%)	2 261	206	65	164	130	67	6 969	9 862

***p < 0.001.

TABLE V.10   *Percentage of children from non-manual backgrounds in each group*

Ratings at	Change groups							Total
	LLL	DDD	LDD	LLD	DLL	DDL	R	
Home	40.2***	23.4	8.0	24.1	26.0	34.2	32.0	33.3
N = (100%)	1 465	154	25	54	83	41	5 092	6 914
School	42.5***	10.1***	8.57*	20.0	24.2	16.7	27.0	29.9
N = (100%)	2 136	178	59	150	180	60	6 412	9 116

***p < 0.001.
*p < 0.05.

TABLE V.11   *Percentage of children from 'small' families at the age of 7 (≤ 3 children) in each group*

Ratings at	Change groups							Total
	LLL	DDD	LDD	LLD	DLL	DDL	R	
Home	70.6	67.5	61.5	40.7***	72.4	73.8	70.4	70.1
N = (100%)	1 494	163	26	54	87	42	5 261	7 127
School	78.2***	43.4***	51.6	62.8	77.2	64.1	66.8	68.9
N = (100%)	2 185	189	62	156	123	64	6 645	9 424

***p < 0.001.

school. There were also proportionately more children from smaller families in the school LLL group.

Tables V.12 and V.13 present the birth-order composition of the groups for home and school ratings respectively. There is a suggestion that there are proportionately more first borns who are in the deviant group at home at the three ages, though the difference does not reach significance. Also for home, there seem to be proportionately fewer first borns and more later-born children in the groups who become deviant later on (LDD and LLD) (although the LDD differences are not significant).

At school the picture is quite different. There is an underrepresentation of first borns and an overrepresentation of later borns in the groups which are deviant at the three ages or who become deviant after 7 (DDD, LDD). (However, the difference for the LDD group is not significant.) There is also an underrepresentation of later borns in the groups which remains 'low' at three ages.

Conclusions

Using behaviour ratings on a large and nationally representative sample of children in three follow-ups at the ages of 7, 11 and 16 the following results have been found:

1. There are moderate (0.31–0.48) correlations between the ratings at different ages, these being higher the closer the time interval between the sweeps. The relationships between ratings from 7 to 11 were very similar to those from 11 to 16.

2. The majority of children (62–70 per cent) in the extreme groups labelled as 'deviant' (the top 13 per cent at any age) have moved out of that group by a later follow-up, i.e. four, five or nine years later. By the same token, similar proportions of those children who were in the deviant group at a later age were not so at an earlier age. The proportions here correspond very well with those reported by the ILEA (1975) despite differing time intervals. However, about 44 per cent of those in the deviant group at an earlier age move to the band between the groups we have defined as 'low' (bottom 50 per cent) and 'deviant' (top 13 per cent). The same percentage for those who were in the 'low' group at an earlier age was about 30 per cent. The results were again very similar for the 7 to 11 and 11 to 16 follow-ups.

3. Only very small groups of children remain in the deviant groups at all three ages (2.28 per cent for home and 2.09 per cent for school ratings).

4. There were more girls in the groups which were 'normal' (the 'low' groups) at all three ages, especially at school.

5. For school only, there was a preponderance of

TABLE V.12   *Change groups by birth order — home ratings*

Birth order	Change groups							Total
	LLL	DDD	LDD	LLD	DLL	DDL	R	
1	34.9	47.2	23.1	14.5	49.4	41.5	39.8	38.8
2–3	49.9	41.0	61.5	54.5	44.6	48.8	46.7	47.4
4+	15.2	11.8	15.4	30.9	6.0	9.8	13.4	13.8
Total	1 478	161	26	55	83	41	5 192	7 036

*$p < 0.05$ for first borns/others.

TABLE V.13   *Change groups by birth order — school ratings*

Birth order	Change groups							Total
	LLL	DDD	LDD	LLD	DLL	DDL	R	
1	41.5	25.7	25.5	38.2	48.1	43.9	37.8	38.6
2–3	49.3	47.1	46.8	44.7	41.7	35.1	46.7	47.1
4+	9.2***	27.1	27.7	17.1	10.2	21.1	15.5	14.3
Total	1 874	140	47	123	108	57	5 525	7 874

***$p < 0.001$ for 4+ borns/others

boys in the group which was defined as 'deviant' at all three ages.

6. There is a suggestion that more girls join the 'deviant' groups and more boys join the 'normal' ('low') groups at a later age at both school and home.

7. There is a tendency for more children from manual backgrounds to be in the change groups and the 'always deviant' group. The differences are not statistically significant except for the children who remain in the deviant group at all three ages or who move to and remain in the deviant group for the school ratings.

8. There are proportionately more children from non-manual backgrounds in the groups which were 'normal' ('low') at all three ages.

9. More children from bigger families (> 3 children in the family at the age of 7) joined the deviant group (on the home rating) and more stayed in the deviant group (on the school rating). At all ages there were fewer children from bigger families in the group which was defined as 'normal' on school but not on home ratings.

10. There were proportionately fewer first-born and more later-born children who were in the deviant group on the school ratings, at the three ages. There was also a suggestion of a higher proportion of first-born children in the deviant group at home, at all ages. More later-born and fewer first-born children join the deviant group, for the home rating, at a later age.

One consideration in interpreting these results is the question of comparability of scales across the follow-ups. In addition to the earlier comments made, the results presented go a little further to support the comparability of ratings. Thus the correlation co-efficients and the distribution of 'deviant' groups between 7 and 11 (when the ratings were strictly comparable) and between 11 and 16 (when they were not) were very similar. Another important consideration when relating combinations of ratings at different ages to background factors is any bias which might arise by the virtue of each rating being individually biased in relation to these factors. Thus the finding that more children from non-manual backgrounds are in the 'low' groups at the three ages is to a certain extent tautological given that, usually, there are more non-manual children whose scores are low on each rating. Similar and more subtle processes might be at work in the other groups.

Altogether, what is perhaps most interesting is the high degree of movement from the extreme categories. Between the ages of 7 to 11 or 11 to 16 something like 4.6 per cent (35 per cent of the top 13 per cent) of the sample as a whole remain in the deviant (top 13 per cent) category. By chance alone as many as 1.7 per cent would be in this group. Between the three ages, 2.28 per cent at home and 2.09 per cent at school remain in the top 13 per cent category. Only about 22 per cent of children remain in the 'normal' (lower 50 per cent) category at all ages.

To what extent these behaviour ratings reflect meaningfully on the children and how much the movements across time reflect real changes in behaviour rather than the efficiency of the ratings cannot be answered here. What is needed is comparison of these ratings with data gathered independently by other means. What can be said with assurance from these results is that, in interpreting research studies, they give considerable warning against assuming a static and pathological stage for the children identified as deviant.

VI

Written Language*

*Original sources: Richardson, K., Calnan, M., Essen, J. and Lambert, L., 'The linguistic maturity of 11-year-olds', *Journal of Child Language*, 3 (1) 1976; Richardson, K., 'The writing productivity and syntactic maturity of 11-year-olds in relation to their reading habits', *Reading*, 11 (2) 1979.

THE LINGUISTIC MATURITY OF 11-YEAR-OLDS

Introduction

Previous NCDS reports have presented results of analyses relating to certain linguistic variables, namely reading and speech defects. Here we present the results of some analyses relating to the syntactic development of these children as evidenced in written composition. We particularly wanted to examine the relationship between this aspect of development and several other variables which preoccupy educational and child development theorists, especially scholastic attainment, as well as the sex, social-class and regional distributions.

Method

Hunt (1970) points out how teachers have always been aware that older children write sentences which are different from those of younger children — different not only in vocabulary and subject-matter but also in syntax. Researchers have tried for decades to describe such differences in objective, quantitative and revealing terms (McCarthy, 1954). The early work (i.e. from 1920 to 1960) in this area typically concentrated on one or more well-tried measures — parts of speech, types of sentence, sentence or utterance length, ratios of subordinate to main clauses, or 'weighting scales' for simple, compound, complex and compound—complex sentences (for reviews, see Heider and Heider, 1940; McCarthy, 1954, O'Donnell *et al.*, 1967). Because these measures were not altogether objective (e.g. in identifying clauses) or revealing (in the sense of showing significant and consistent developmental changes), more refined procedures of analysis were continually demanded, and the changing perspectives in language theory since 1960 helped to provide them. Thus more recent studies of syntactic development have employed modes of analyses suggested by the transformational grammar developed by Chomsky (1957, 1965) and his associates.

Hunt (1965), in analysing the writing of schoolchildren (9-, 13- and 17-year-olds), had observed an age-dependent increase in both clause length and subordination. On these grounds he suggested an entirely new linguistic unit. This consisted of segmenting the body of writing into each main clause with attached subordinate clauses, and calculating their mean length in words. Since these segments constituted the shortest units which it is grammatically allowable to punctuate as sentences, Hunt called them *minimal terminable units* — later shortened to T-units. In comparison with other measures, including sentence length, clause length and subordination index, the mean T-unit length (MTUL) was found to correlate best with age (Hunt, 1965). Hunt's findings have been replicated and affirmed by O'Donnell *et al.* (1967), Mellon (1967) and Smith (1974). The index has been applied and its utility confirmed for a variety of purposes, including comparison with multiple marking (Potter, 1967), assessment of immigrant children (Gipps and Ewen, 1974), and as the basis for transformational analysis (Peltz, 1973). O'Donnell *et al.* (1967, p. 99) concluded that 'the mean length of T-units has special claim to consideration as a simple, objective, valid indicator of development in syntactic control'.

Hunt's study showed that T-units are somehow linked to maturity — but what makes them longer? On the basis of further research into this question it became evident that older writers use progressively more sentence-embedding transformations per T-unit (Hunt 1970; see also O'Donnell *et al.*, 1967). Thus the crucial quality of this dimension of development is 'the ability to pack a greater density of ideas into a single sentence by embedding one sentence in another' (Cazden, 1972, p. 83). This cognitive aspect of syntactic development had been speculated upon by earlier workers. For example, La Brant (1933) had taken increasing use of subordination to indicate the development of judgement and the understanding of relations between judgements. Harrel (1957) suggested that subordination demonstrated the perceiving and understanding of relationships between objects, ideas and events. Hunt (1970), following Miller (1956), interpreted the phenomenon of increased embedding of elementary sentences in terms of a recoding process: 'As the mind matures it organises information more intricately and so can produce and receive more intricately organised sentences' (Hunt, 1970, p. 58).

We have used the T-unit in the present study because it is an easily used and seemingly valid index of syntactic development, as well as one which makes sense in terms of cognitive growth. However, it has been subject to certain criticisms. First, it has long been known that a writer's sentence structure is affected by the kind of task set and the mode of discourse used in response. Rosen (1969) compared the MTULs produced in a variety of writing tasks by the same pupils in the course of a school year. Dramatic differences were found as pupils moved from one composition to another. Rosen's subjects were between 15 and 16; a similar finding was reported by Anderson (1939) for a subordination index for a group between 17 and 22. Thus older pupils at least can exercise a degree of flexibility in their use of syntactic resources; in certain contexts better 'linguistic effect' is obtained with deliberately shorter rather than longer T-units. Somewhat related points are made by Read (1971) and by Christensen (1968), though in general they are in favour of the T-unit. It is fairly clear, however (Rosen, 1969; Hunt, 1965), that younger subjects such as ours (i.e. 11-year-olds) would use these special devices rarely, and then only in special places in particular kinds of writing (e.g. fiction) so that they are unlikely to influence the *mean* T-unit length to any marked degree. Second, the MTUL provides only a *summary* of syntactic development and may obscure important differences (e.g. frequency of use of different transformations) in the sentences of different groups of children. It is probably for these reasons that Cazden (1972, p. 252) believes the T-unit to be a superficial index of structural complexity (but we believe she is quite wrong to liken it, as she does, to mean utterance length). Third, Van der Geest *et al.* (1973) speculate on the appropriateness of splitting up *all* co-ordinated sentences into smaller segments (and note that it may be a particular problem for languages other than English). It should be pointed out, however, that this raises all the problems of objectivity, prevalent in some previous indices, which the T-unit was intended to surmount (Hunt, 1965, 1970).

The subjects and sampling procedure

The subjects were 521 11-year-olds randomly selected as a sub-sample from the 16 000 children in the National Child Development Study. The sub-sample is a nationally representative group in terms of sex, social class and region of education. The scripts analysed consisted of written composition collected from all the children during the second follow-up study when they were aged 11 (Davie, 1973). At that time the children were asked by their teachers in school to complete a general ability test (which approximates the conventional intelligence test, with verbal and non-verbal items), a reading comprehension test, a mathematics ability test, a copying designs test, and to provide the sample of writing in question. The tasks were administered in the form of a 'test booklet' requiring a total time of three hours (it was recommended that the testing be spread over two days). The writing task was the last in the series and a set time of thirty minutes was allowed for its completion. The protocol provided was as follows: 'Imagine that you are *now* 25 years old. Write about the life you are leading, your interests, your home life and your work at the age of 25. (You have 30 minutes to do this.)' This approach has been used successfully by Veness (1962) and by Gooch and Pringle (1966). It was requested that a quiet room be set aside for the purpose; the pupils were supervised by their class teacher, by whom the timing was controlled. While this procedure allowed the sampling of all the children in the cohort, it should be clear that the researchers could exercise no direct control over the conditions. Obviously variations in time of year, time of day, preparedness and mood of individuals, and suitability of test conditions, are inevitable and teachers could only be taken on trust as to stringency over timing, and so on. It should be appreciated that these factors could have some bearing on the results and their interpretations.

An important point to have in mind is that most researchers in this area have emphasised the necessity of an adequate writing sample from each individual for analysis to be accurate. The individual passage lengths in the present study ranged from less than 50 words to over 600 words (mean 204.9 ± 106.7 (sd)). We have therefore made some check on the relationship between MTUL and passage length (see below under Results).

Procedure for T-unit marking

The procedure was exactly that of Hunt (1965), but incorporating the systematising refinements used by Rosen (1969). In addition, scripts containing direct speech were excluded since its syntactic form often deliberately departed from that in the remainder of the script (these constituted less than 2 per cent of the initial sample). Each script was segmented into T-units, each of which consisted of one main clause plus any subordinate clause or non-clausal structure attached to or embedded in it. For these purposes a clause was defined as any expression containing a subject (or co-ordinated subjects) and a finite verb (or co-ordinated verbs). The total number of T-units was then counted and entered on record sheets. The total number of words in the script was also counted and entered on the record sheets. The number of words was divided by the number of T-units to obtain the mean T-unit length. Each script was marked once and then checked by at least one other member of the research team. We estimate that at least 90 per cent immediate concurrence was obtained. Doubtful cases were resolved by group discussion or, as in the case of about a dozen scripts beyond resolution, excluded from the initial sample and from further analysis. In addition to the use of the T-unit, the 'composition length in words' was used in the analyses as an index of writing productivity.

Statistics
Differences or associations mentioned in the test are statistically significant except where otherwise stated or qualified. Details and results of statistical analyses are presented in the Appendix (p. 348).

Results

The mean T-unit length for the whole sample was 10.8 ± 4.4 (sd). This conforms very closely to the value expected for 11-year-olds, as deduced from previous studies. Figure VI.1 shows that this value was between the value reported by Hunt (1965), O'Donnell *et al.* (1967), each on three different age groups, and by Rosen (1969) and Potter (1967) on 15- to 16-year-olds. Frequency distributions are shown in Figures VI.2 and VI.3. Figure VI.4 is presented in order to show the relationship between composition length and MTUL. Although the plot conveys the impression of a trend, this is only weak, although statistically significant. Thus, given the composition length for any individual, it would be possible to predict the MTUL with only a small degree of confidence. There are two inferences to be drawn from these data. First, there is little evidence that MTULs on passages of short length are being constrained *by virtue* of their being short samples. It did not seem to be the case that as compositions became longer the MTUL became significantly greater. The second inference, then, is that mere production, or 'fluency', does not necessarily imply syntactic maturity, as reflected in our measure.

The relative performances of boys and girls in terms of composition length and MTUL are shown in Table VI.1. The girls showed a clear 15 per cent superiority in 'productivity', or amount written, but the slight difference in MTUL was not statistically significant. Differences in favour of girls in terms of productivity of writing have been a consistent finding in previous research (e.g. La Brant, 1933; Harrel, 1957; Myklebust, 1965, 1973). Sex differences in

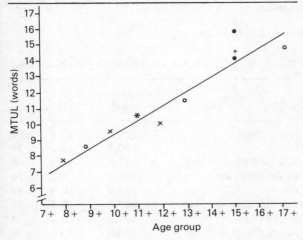

FIGURE VI.1   *Plotted data of MTUL against age group for five studies*

○, Hunt (1965) — an American study of average ability children; x, O'Donnell *et al.* (1967) — an American study of average-ability children; ●, Potter (1967) — a British study of 'good writers' and 'bad writers' of the same age, + Rosen, (1969) — a British study of boys who 'were top 25 per cent of the ability range': *, the present study.

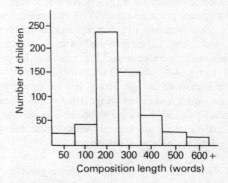

FIGURE VI.2   *Frequency distribution for composition length*

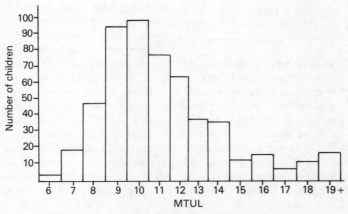

FIGURE VI.3   *Frequency distribution for MTUL*

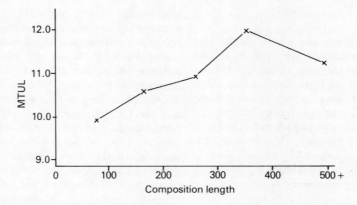

FIGURE VI.4   *Plot of composition length against MTUL*

syntactic measures seem somewhat more equivocal in the literature. For example, although Sampson (1964a, 1964b) reports a higher subordination index for girls, as does Smedley (1968), no sex differences were found by La Brant (1933), Harrel (1957), Menyuk (1963) and O'Donnell *et al.* (1967), among others. The well-known precocity of girls relative to boys on a variety of linguistic/verbal measures has received much attention but little theoretical underpinning; explanations proffered range from socialisation phenomena to differential rates of maturation (myelination, hemispheric lateralisation) in the central nervous system. The discrepancies between the two measures in our study led us to conjecture that sex differences in linguistic/verbal measures (i.e. verbal productivity) are explicable in socialisation terms rather than biological ones, since the latter would probably affect *all* measures.

TABLE VI.1   *Sex differences on the linguistic variables*

	Word length	MTUL	N
Boys	180.7	10.7	257
Girls	228.8	11.4	264

Table VI.2 shows that there was no pronounced regional variation in either composition length or MTUL, at least none that analysis of variance could reveal. It might be expected to detect *some* regional variability in syntax. Speaking of the USA, Griffin (1968) claims that 'A series of studies of syntax of children in various parts of the country gives grounds for identifying some features that may be regional and some that appear to be common in language behaviour.' Either our regional barriers are too crudely drawn or we are measuring those features which are regionally common. A potentially more

TABLE VI.2   *Regional analysis of linguistic variables*

Region	Composition length	MTUL	N
North West	195.2	10.4	50
North	200.3	10.3	38
East and West Riding	211.0	11.0	66
North Midlands	204.8	9.8	26
East	207.9	10.9	48
London and South-East	205.4	10.6	79
South	207.7	10.5	24
South-West	210.0	10.3	29
Midlands	228.1	11.1	49
Wales	201.3	11.9	42
Scotland	187.9	10.5	65

informative comparison of urban, sub-urban and rural children was not within the scope of the present study.

Table VI.3 shows the social-class analysis of composition length and MTUL. Differences in composition length are in the expected direction (i.e. favouring the non-manual groups); children from social class I produced essays which were about 25 per cent longer than those from children from social class V, and the trend was statistically significant. In MTUL there were no significant differences: that is, there were no apparent differences in syntactic maturity between the social-class groups. Harrel (1957) found his subordination index correlated only slightly with the socio-economic level of his subjects. Similarly, Lawton (1968) found that middle-class boys wrote significantly longer essays at all ages, but he could detect no social-class differences on the subordination index. On the other hand, Smedley (1968) found significant social-class differences in his subordination index in favour of the middle-class children. Bernstein (1961a and b) claims that there are differences in subordination and sentence structure between his 'restricted' and 'elaborated' codes which are class-related: for example, public language (working class) — 'Little use of subordinate clauses to break down the initial categories of the dominant subject'; formal language (middle class) — 'logical modifications and stress are mediated through a grammatically complex sentence construction, especially through the use of a range of conjunctions and subordinate clauses'. It might be expected that such reputed differences would be reflected in our data, but this is not the case. It is interesting that Robinson (1965) could find no grammatical differences between the social classes on formal and informal letters written by 12-year-olds. It is possible on the other hand that our instrument may be too blunt, at least in some respects, to detect genuine social-class differences in syntax. For example, when Lawton (1968) went on to apply Loban's weighted index of subordination to his writing samples, significant social-class differences were found. The Loban index takes account of second- or third-order subordination (e.g. a subordinate clause modifying or placed within another subordinate clause). Hunt (1965), on the other hand, claimed that higher-order subordination was so rare among young children as to make it an unlikely index of maturity. Superficial inspection of our own samples confirms this. The issue, however, demands a more systematic investigation.

The relationship between our linguistic measures and other conventional indices of cognitive/scholastic development is shown in Figures VI.5—VI.8. These figures show first of all a clear and highly significant association between composition length and each of the variables, reading comprehension score, and

TABLE VI.3 *Social-class distribution of composition length and MTUL*

Social class†	Composition length	MTUL	N
I	232.5	10.7	21
II	228.9	11.4	114
III Non-manual	203.9	10.3	32
III Manual	196.0	10.7	250
IV	196.4	10.4	80
V	179.9	10.4	18

† Defined according to the Registrar-General's classification of fathers' occupation

components of the general ability test. MTUL, on the other hand, showed a much weaker association with these variables; the association with the reading comprehension score was not statistically significant; those with the components of the general ability test were statistically significant but not pronounced.

These interesting findings raise several questions. Let us first examine the results of previous research. With regard to productivity, Percival (1966) found a substantial correlation between composition length and IQ, as did Hunt (1970). Rosen (1969) found large differences between 'high-ability' and 'low-ability' groups on composition length, whereas differences on MTUL were slight. Similarly, Menyuk (1963) could make no significant differentiations in use of transformations on the basis of IQ scores. Indeed, it is only rarely that we find an association between a syntactic measure and IQ/mental ability in the literature. These results have led us to suggest that whatever it is that is responsible for the lower reading scores of the 'poor readers' it does not seem

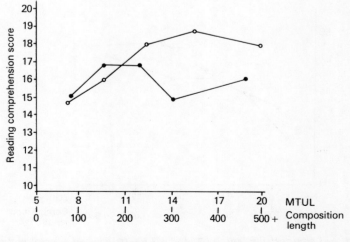

FIGURE VI.5 *Plot of composition length (○) and MTUL (●) against reading comprehension scores*

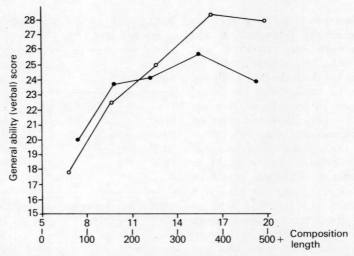

FIGURE VI.6   *Plot of composition length (○) and MTUL (●) against scores on the verbal component of the general ability test*

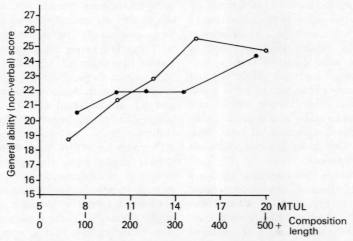

FIGURE VI.7   *Plot of composition length (○) and MTUL (●) against scores on the non-verbal component of the general ability test*

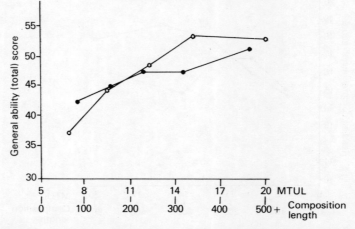

FIGURE VI.8   *Plot of composition length (○) and MTUL (●) against general ability (total) scores*

to be the individual's degree of syntactic maturity. We shall return to these questions later (see under Discussion, p. 351).

Teachers' assessments of pupils' mental development are often said to have considerable validity, at least regarding the prediction of scholastic attainment. Indeed, many of the traditional standardised test instruments are validated against teachers' assessments as criterion. At the same time as the children in our sample were producing these compositions, their teachers were asked to rate them on five-point scales for several parameters of scholastic aptitude. These included 'number work', 'general knowledge', 'oral ability' and 'use of books'. The ratings were compared with our indices of linguistic maturity and productivity.

Table VI.4 shows that there are clear and statistically significant relationships between all of these ratings and composition length. This is especially so for 'oral ability' and 'use of books', but it also holds for 'number work' and 'general knowledge'. Those children placed in the 'exceptional' category produced particularly long compositions. However, there was little association between MTUL and teachers' ratings, only reaching statistical significance in the case of 'number work' (Table VI.5).

Discussion

In this broadly exploratory study we have been concerned with obtaining some objective index of the syntactic development of a nationally representative group of children and with relating this to several factors and variables which preoccupy educational and child-development theorists. We reasoned that such comparison might yield additional insights and deductions about children's mental growth and its differentiation. Our first finding was that the degree of syntactic maturity (as represented in the MTUL) of 11-year-olds corresponded closely with the findings from other studies in this country and the USA. Linguistic competence seemed to have only a weak association with linguistic productivity as measured by composition length. The disparity between these two measures was particularly evident when boys and girls were compared: a clear, statistically significant difference in productivity in favour of the girls appeared, but there was no sex differences in MTUL. We suggested that this reflects the well-known 'conformism' of young girls relative to boys. Such social factors seem to us more likely explanations than, say, differences in neurobiological maturation processes, though their source originates from beyond the school and family in the nature of our society and its role pressures.

Our results relating to social class are not so clear cut. Although children from non-manual groups wrote significantly longer compositions on average than did those from manual groups, there were no overall difference in MTUL. Much has been written on the subject of language and social class. Our results certainly offer some evidence to support the view that all but a few socio-cultural environments provide adequate contexts for the syntactic aspects of language development (see Labov, 1969; Rosen, 1972; and Ginsberg, 1970).

The fact that reading comprehension scores are more closely associated with productivity than with MTUL is rather puzzling. One possibility is that the test used contained syntactic idiosyncrasies which are more familiar to particular subjects, i.e. those who are also most productive and come from higher social classes. Several researchers (e.g. Peltz, 1973) have suggested that readability may be influenced by elements of syntactic patterning, and Siler (1973, p. 600), after comparing the effects of variations of such patterning, concluded that 'syntax appeared to have a greater effect than semantics in oral reading performance'. In so far as there is 'something, as yet unknown, in syntactic construction' (Callary, 1974, p. 190) which differentiates the social groups, then it is possible that standardised reading comprehension tests contain a concealed, and (from a reading point of view) unintended bias. This may be reminiscent of the culture-loaded/culture-fair controversy in IQ testing, but it at least seems worthy of further

TABLE VI.4   *Mean composition length (words) and teachers' ratings*

Ratings	Number work	General knowledge	Oral ability	Use of books
Exceptional	243.4	256.3	284.4	280.1
Above average	257.9	242.0	254.8	237.9
Average	202.2	200.3	200.1	199.9
Below average	171.1	173.3	168.1	159.4
Little	157.8	125.3	79.9	72.6

TABLE VI.5   *Mean MTUL (words) and teachers' ratings*

Ratings	Number work	General knowledge	Oral ability	Use of books
Exceptional	10.7	11.2	12.4	11.0
Above average	11.2	10.9	10.8	10.9
Average	10.8	10.7	10.7	10.8
Below average	10.4	10.5	10.5	10.3
Little	9.6	10.4	11.6	10.6

research. Lack of syntactic development (at least within the limits of our measure) does not seem to be responsible for the relatively low reading scores of 'poor readers'.

With respect to the general ability test we have noted that both verbal and non-verbal components show a much stronger association with productivity than with MTUL. Many other workers have failed to detect a clear and consistent relationship between IQ and aspects of syntactic maturity (see the references cited under Results). In the 1930s La Brant (1953, p. 472) wondered: 'Is the sense of relation as indicated by use of dependent clauses not measured by mental tests?' The test used in that study employed items demanding what we might call 'logico-deductive' thinking. Linguistic expression of the sort sampled here probably demands creative, *inductive* thinking. It is interesting that when mental ability tests are constructed from items *requiring* inductive thinking, many familiar differences (including social-class differences) disappear or even reverse (Pask and Lewis, 1964). But all we are suggesting is that a combination of factors, from class culture to the nature of standardised test items, might explain the sort of relations we have reported.

Some of the most intriguing results in our view are those relating productivity and MTUL with teachers' ratings of their pupils' 'oral ability', 'general knowledge', 'number work' and 'use of books'. All ratings showed striking, statistically significant associations with composition length (indeed, these were the strongest associations to emerge from the whole analysis). Only 'number work' showed a statistically significant association with MTUL, though even this was weak. An important factor here may be the influence of knowing the characteristically co-operative and hard-working pupils in the class-room. A 'halo effect' generalised over all ratings would pick out those pupils who are also typically productive in writing tasks, irrespective of their syntactic maturity. It also seems possible — at least in the context of 'oral ability' — that teachers over-emphasised the conventional yardstick of standard English expressed in formal ways. It has been shown that supposed 'aberrant' speech, including dialect and colloquialisms, is none the less well articulated and syntactically rich (Labov, 1969; Rosen, 1972).

Finally, the approach used in the present study (especially the anonymity of the researchers) may have had some bearing on these results. Rosen (1973) has shown how the 'context of situation' and 'sense of audience' can affect language production. An interested/trusted adult as audience can transform individuals' writing because they now feel free to write what they feel. In addition Harrel (1957) and O'Donnell *et al.* (1967) have shown that pupils of this age typically demonstrate greater use of syntactic resources in writing than in speech.

Appendix

Statistical analyses

Before proceeding to the main analyses, a study was made of the distributions of MTUL and composition length. Neither had a normal distribution and the relationship between them was non-linear. It was found that the following transformations both created approximate normality and gave an approximate linear relationship between the transformed variables, and also between each transformed variable and the reading comprehension, verbal ability, non-verbal ability and general ability test scores. The latter four scores all have approximately normal distributions. Hence all the following analyses use the transformed variables. The transformations are: (a) $\log_e\{$mean T-unit length$\}$; (b)$\{$composition length$\}^{1/2}$.

Analyses of variance

We summarise here the results of significance tests using the transformed variables. Tables using the untransformed variables are given in the main text where appropriate. Since the degrees of freedom for the residual mean square in the F statistic are large (between 450 and 510) the χ^2 statistic is quoted for simplicity. Significance levels: ***$p < 0.001$; **$p < 0.01$; *$p < 0.05$.

Composition length as independent variable

Simple linear regression analyses and significance tests of the null hypothesis that the coefficient of composition length is zero.

(i) Dependent variable mean *T-unit length* χ^2 (df = 1) = 23.75***

(ii) Dependent variable *reading comprehension* χ^2 (df = 1) = 30.1***

(iii) Dependent variable *verbal ability* χ^2 (df = 1) = 60.2***

(iv) Dependent variable *non-verbal ability* χ^2 (df = 1) = 37.8***

(v) Dependent variable *general ability* χ^2 (df = 1) = 56.4***

Mean T-unit length as dependent variable

(i) Independent variable *sex* χ^2 (df = 1) = 0.4

(ii) Independent variable *region* (categorised into 11 Standard Regions: see text) χ^2 (df = 10) = 12.5

(iii) Independent variable *social class* (6 categories, I, II, III NM, III M, IV, V) χ^2 (df = 5) = 7.1

Mean T-unit length as independent variable

(i) Dependent variable *reading comprehension* χ^2 (df = 1) = 2.4

(ii) Dependent variable *verbal ability* χ^2 (df = 1) = 11.7***

(iii) Dependent variable *non-verbal ability* χ^2 (df = 1) = 3.5

(iv) Dependent variable *general ability* χ^2 (df = 1) = 9.6**

Composition length as dependent variable

(i)   Independent variable *sex* χ^2 (df = 1) = 25.6***
(ii) Independent variable *region* χ^2 (df = 10) = 4.5
(iii) Independent variable *social class* χ^2 (df = 1) = 3.9*

(For definition of the categories of the independent variable see text.)

General knowledge rating
    Dependent variable *mean T-unit length* χ^2 (df = 4) = 1.8
    Dependent variable *composition length* χ^2 (df = 4) = 44.1***

Number work
    Dependent variable *mean T-unit length* χ^2 (df = 4) = 12.8*
    Dependent variable *composition length* χ^2 (df = 4) = 57.8***

Oral ability
    Dependent variable *mean T-unit length* χ^2 (df = 4) = 6.3
    Dependent variable *composition length* χ^2 (df = 4) = 62.7***

Use of books
    Dependent variable *mean T-unit length* χ^2 (df = 4) = 5.4
    Dependent variable *composition length* χ^2 (df = 4) = 74.1***

THE WRITING PRODUCTIVITY AND SYNTACTIC MATURITY OF 11-YEAR-OLDS IN RELATION TO THEIR READING HABITS

Introduction

It is well known that after the acquisition of reading most children engage in it to a considerable extent, not only as exercises in school, but also for leisure purposes in their own time. For instance, there is evidence for the use among schoolchildren at home of a wide variety of reading matter and that a very large proportion of parents buy books for their children (Taylor, J. J., 1973). A survey of children's reading interests carried out by the Schools Council suggests that not only is leisure reading fairly extensive among a majority of schoolchildren but also that it has a powerful influence in the handling of reading matter in schools as well as on general ability and attainment assessments (Whitehead *et al.*, 1975). One question which naturally arises is whether leisure-time reading is at all reflected in children's writing, either in productivity or in grammatical structure. The present section presents some data from the National Child Development Study which have some bearing on this question.

Method

The subjects of the present inquiry were 521 11-year-old boys and girls who comprised a random sub-sample of the approximately 16 000 children in the NCDS. The data were derived from three sources during the 11-year follow-up. First, teachers were asked, in the course of answering an educational questionnaire, to rate each study child's use of books as one of the considered 'aspects of ability and attainment'; rating was estimated on a five-point scale (see below). Second, study children completed a questionnaire at school concerning their own leisure interests and activities, among which were two items involving reading:

(a) reading books (apart from school or homework);
(b) reading newspapers, magazines and comics.

Frequencies of engagement in these activities were categorised as 'often (nearly every day)', 'sometimes', and 'never or hardly ever'. In addition, the children were asked whether or not they borrowed books from a public library. Finally, study children were asked to write a composition in school on what they imagined their life to be like at the age of 25 years. Thirty minutes were allowed for this task.

We concentrated on two aspects of interest in these compositions. First, it seemed important to know the volume of children's writing; we thus used 'composition length in words' as a measure of writing productivity. Second, it was desirable to have some indication of the syntactic richness, or structural complexity, of the language written. Syntax is a major aspect of linguistic development; for example, it has been shown how schoolchildren use progressively more sentence-combining transformations in their speech and writing as they get older (Hunt, 1965). Moreover, this trend would seem to be part of a more general cognitive capacity: namely, 'the ability to pack a greater density of ideas into a single sentence by embedding one sentence in another' (Cazden, 1972). A major problem, however, is how this ability can be represented meaningfully and quantitatively. We have adopted the T-unit devised by Hunt (1965). The T-unit, which is the length in words of units consisting of each main clause together with attached subordinate clauses and non-causal structures, inevitably conceals a lot of interesting information. However, it has the advantage of exhibiting an increase in length as a direct function of syntactic complexity (O'Donnell *et al.* 1967; Hunt, 1970; for full details of sample, data collection and analysis see pp. 341–8 above).

Results of statistical tests carried out are shown in the appendix (p. 352)

Results

Figure VI.9 is a plot of composition length and MTUL against teachers' ratings of 'use of books'. Differences in the ratings were reflected in substantial differences in composition length, and the differences were highly statistically significant. However, MTUL did not appear to be significantly associated with these teachers' ratings.

The plots of composition length and MTUL against reported frequency of 'reading books for leisure' are shown in Figure VI.10. In this case both

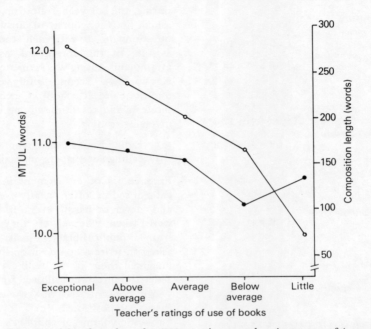

FIGURE VI.9   *Plot of composition length and MTUL against teachers' reports of 'use of books'* (● *MTUL,* ○ *composition length*)

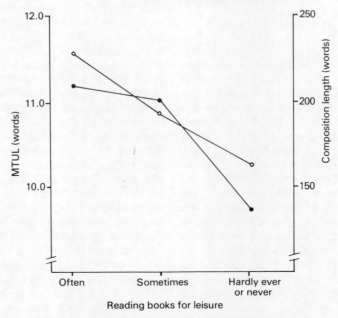

FIGURE VI.10   *Plot of composition length and MTUL against children's reports of reading books for leisure* (● *MTUL,* ○ *composition length*)

MTUL and composition length exhibited statistically significant differences between the frequency categories.

Interestingly, although about one-third of study children claimed to borrow books from a public library, doing so had only a marginal relationship with composition length (only just reaching statistical significance at the 5 per cent level) and none at all with MTUL (Table VI.6).

Finally, Figure VI.11 shows the plot of composition length and MTUL against reported frequencies of 'reading newspapers, magazines and comics'. Differences in these frequencies were not reflected in composition length. A suggestive association between frequency of reading newspapers, etc., and MTUL failed to reach statistical significance on analysis of variance. However, a trend analysis (Gaito, 1965) revealed a significant linear association for these data.

TABLE VI.6   *Mean composition length and MTUL in relation to borrowing library books*

Response	Mean composition length (words)	MTUL (words)	N
Yes	212.7	11.0	353
No	189.5	10.6	163

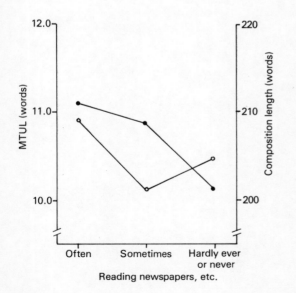

FIGURE VI.11   *Plot of composition length and MTUL against children's reports of reading newspapers, magazines or comics (● MTUL, ○ composition length)*

Discussion

Written composition has certain advantages over speech as a medium of linguistic assessment. Harrel (1957), O'Donnell *et al.* (1967) and others have demonstrated that pupils of age 11 use a greater variety of syntactic resources in writing than in speech. Furthermore, it seems likely that the unstructured nature of the subject chosen, as well as the familiarity of context and audience would have facilitated maximum exercise of writing skills among the study children (see, for example, Rosen, 1973). The questions we have asked here concern the extent to which those skills are a reflection of different reading habits.

As regards productivity, the data have shown a strong association between composition length and teachers' assessments of use of books. Reading books for leisure also seems to be clearly reflected in productivity. This would suggest that, at the very least, reading gives children more to write about. However, there was no significant association between productivity and reading newspapers, magazines and comics.

The association with borrowing books was slight. Of course, it might be that many children who borrow library books do not read them very much, and that the terms 'often' and 'newspapers, etc.' will mean different things to different children. However, there do seem to be grounds for further research in this area.

Turning to what is often called 'syntactic maturity', there is some evidence in the present data that children who read books for leisure most often, and children who read newspapers, comics and magazines most often, also write longer than average T-units. Conversely, children who receive good teachers' assessments on 'use of books' or who borrow library books do not write longer than average T-units. There are at least three possible explanations for this seeming paradox. First, merely being seen handling or looking at books does not necessarily imply effective use; for example, Neville and Pugh (1975) found wide differences among schoolchildren in the efficient use of books. Teachers may have based their assessments on rather superficial visible criteria. A second possibility is the well-known 'halo effect', i.e. teachers may well have attributed above-average use of books to those children who (among other things) were generally productive, regardless of grammatical complexity. The third possible explanation is that self-motivated leisure reading, as opposed to enforced reading, really does have consequences in terms of enchanced syntactic development. This would support Beardsley and Wright's (1974) argument that

Much of the reading of junior and secondary level is done as an integral part of the timetable, silently for enjoyment or the acquisition of information. However, this gives little opportunity for verbal involvement and interaction, which is a valuable part of children's increasing awareness and understanding of what is read.

Although we need to remember the limitations of the measures used, at least the present research gives some indication that self-motivated reading may not be peripheral to written expression but rather that it has an important contribution to make. It thus supports the contentions of Whitehead *et al.* (1975) that schools should make more books available for leisure-time reading.

Appendix: statistical analyses

The following transformations were applied to the dependent variables to achieve approximate normality of distribution, before proceeding to the analysis of variance: (a) $\log_e$ {MTUL}; (b) {composition length} $^{1/2}$.

Below are summarised the results of significance tests using the transformed variables:

Significance levels: *** $p < 0.001$; ** $p < 0.01$; * $p < 0.05$ (otherwise not significant).

(a)   DEPENDENT VARIABLE: COMPOSITION LENGTH
(i)   Independent variable *'use of books'* χ^2 (df = 4) = 74.1***
(ii)   Independent variable *'reading for leisure'* χ^2 (df = 2) = 25.6*
(iii) Independent variable *'reading newspapers, magazines or comics'* χ^2 (df = 2) = 1.7
(iv)   Independent variable *'do you borrow books from a library?'* χ^2 (df = 1) = 5.8*

(b)   DEPENDENT VARIABLE: MTUL
(i)   Independent variable *'use of books'* χ^2 (df = 4) = 5.4
(ii)   Independent variable *'reading books for leisure'* χ^2 (df = 2) = 9.5**
(iii) Independent variable *'reading newspapers, magazines or comics'* χ^2 (df = 2) = 3.3 (trend: F (df = 1) = 5.6*)
(iv)   Independent variable *'do you borrow books from a public library?'* χ^2 (df = 1) = 0.9

Overview

It is a daunting task to attempt to bring together in any way the findings which have been presented in the previous pages. They have in common that they are derived from a single study of a large group of young people growing up, but within that structure the studies presented have addressed themselves to a wide-ranging and disparate set of topics. Nevertheless, it is important to ask whether there are any general conclusions or patterns which emerge from the overall picture. Further, given their quantity, are there any findings which appear to be of particularly greater importance than the others, or to have particularly urgent implications?

Any attempt to answer such questions must inevitably be largely personal. Not only would someone else attempting an overview no doubt lay emphasis on different aspects, but someone with a specialist interest in a particular area might well seize on some detail as being of most importance even though it may be overlooked here. Thus it is hoped that this overview will act at least as a stimulus; certainly, it cannot serve as a substitute for reading individual sections.

Change and stability

A particular contribution of cohort studies is their ability to study change, and it has been possible to do so from several contrasting points of view. These are mainly concerned with change over time, but before discussing this it is important to note how in some areas it is difficult to disentangle change over time from changes in context and/or in perception. The findings regarding speech assessment and, in particular, behaviour ratings demonstrated very clearly that many children received very different ratings from different people even at about the same time. This in itself warns against making overgeneralised predictions about a child's future characteristics based on a single measure — on one occasion, in one context and as perceived by one individual.

Turning to the question of change over time, the general picture emerging from the NCDS is of considerable turbulence; at the same time, this is not incompatible with numbers of children, not always

small, experiencing continuing and long-term disadvantages or problems. For example, the housing conditions of children in the study generally improved as they grew older, and considerable numbers were in poor housing conditions at one or two follow-ups but not at the others. On the other hand, 4 per cent (equivalent in Britain's total population to about 30 000 children in each year-group) lived in overcrowded conditions at 7, 11 and 16.

A second very fundamental example of change is the family circumstances of these children. About 12 per cent had by the age of 16 been reported as living in a one-parent family at the time of at least one follow-up (others may have experienced this *between* follow-ups), whereas, in the entire sample, just twenty-six children were with one parent at *all* follow-ups (i.e. about 2 per cent of those ever with a single parent).

A similar pattern of change is reflected in the children themselves, in terms of:

1. *Physical measures.* There were considerable changes in visual acuity, with, for example, only 10 per cent of those with a severe bilateral defect at 16 having had such a defect at 7,
2. *Behaviour.* Although there is undoubtedly a core group of children with persistent problems, the general relationship between behaviour ratings at 7, 11 and 16 was low, with large numbers of 'deviant' children at one age moving into the normal category by the next follow-up,
3. *Attainment.* Only about 40 per cent of children were in the same broad band (i.e. the top, middle or bottom third of the total distribution) at 7 and 16, and about one-quarter of those in the top third at 16 had not been there at 11.

This last finding demonstrates most clearly the practical implications of this pattern of change. At the very least it suggests that educational selection, whether for a particular type of school or for streams within a school, must allow for these marked and common contrasts in rates of development. Many will no doubt feel that they are incompatible with early selection.

Furthermore, we are describing the pattern which existed in a system which entailed, in many areas, children still going to selective secondary schools and, in the majority of non-selective schools, some kind of grouping by ability. Advocates of mixed-ability teaching might well suggest that more comprehensive schooling and more mixed-ability teaching would be accompanied by more movement between attainment bands at various ages.

The NCDS data offer only the most broad indications of how it might be possible to predict what kinds of children are most likely to change in their attainment, behaviour or health. In general, those children who did change shared many of the characteristics which predominate among those children towards whom they moved. For example, just as middle-class children on average did better on tests of educational attainment than working-class children, so were the former overrepresented among those whose relative attainment improved, and the latter among those for whom it deteriorated.

The social contrasts to which this leads can be seen in the study of social factors associated with change in attainment. The NCDS data have shown an increasing gap throughout the school years between children of different social class and family size.

The natural question to ask is whether this pattern of social change provides any pointers as to how to foster change, if, for example, there is the objective of reducing such inequalities. One aspect of NCDS analyses is, in a limited way, relevant to this, and it is not optimistic. Where changes in a family's social circumstances did occur, such as in the social class, due to a change in the father's occupation, or in the family size, there is no evidence that this resulted in any improvement (or deterioration) in the child's development. Indeed, it has been suggested in many of the discussions above that educational inequalities are inherent in the structure of our society, and it could not be expected that they might be reduced by, for example, general improvements in material circumstances or changes in the educational system alone.

The importance of the 'early years'

Another question, on which one would expect a longitudinal study to be especially well placed to suggest answers, concerns the importance of the earlier years in a child's life as determinants of subsequent development, and indeed several of the analyses reported in this book are relevant to this.

By way of preface, it should be made clear that the timing of NCDS follow-ups means that our information on the early years is usually restricted to the knowledge that some event or circumstance took place or affected the child at some time during the period up to the age of 7. This is a rather longer

(and later) time span than some people would describe as 'early'. Our evidence does not allow us to comment on whether, within this period, the first two or three years of life, for example, are generally more crucial than the subsequent four or five.

Two particular sets of analyses were designed with the question of the relative importance of the early years in mind. The analyses of the relationship between housing circumstances and children's attainment found, as has been shown in earlier NCDS work and elsewhere, that there was a strong association between such factors as crowding, amenities and tenure and educational attainment at 16. However, it was found that this relationship was very much the same for housing circumstances at 7, at 11 or at 16. In other words, although children in poor housing conditions did show poor school performance, this was no less the case if they had first come into those poor conditions after the age of 11 than if they had experienced them at the age of 7.

The second analysis of this kind was in relation to children in one-parent families, and the question asked was whether those children whose families had broken up when they were relatively young showed evidence of poorer progress than those for whom the break-up had occurred at a later age. This was not found to be the case (although once background factors were taken into account the fact of being in a one-parent family did not relate to the child's development, and it would perhaps be least misleading to say that this factor was equally unimportant, irrespective of the age at which it happened). Of course, this conclusion is restricted to the particular developmental measures available. It remains possible that more sensitive measures, of personal relationships and other affective aspects, for example, would produce a different picture.

Although the analyses concerned were not designed to examine such ideas so directly, two other findings are relevant. In the study of school attendance and educational attainment it was found that although there was an association between school attendance at the age of 7 and attainment at 16, this was reduced to non-significance when attendance rate at 15 was taken into account. In other words, although early school absence does matter if it is compounded by continued poor attendance, any effects it may have can be offset, and possibly even overcome altogether, if subsequent attendance is high.

Against such findings as these, there is evidence from one analysis of greater motility in the early years, in that changes in relative attainment were found to be greater in the primary school years than in the secondary, though considerable changes were found in the later period also.

Taken overall, although of course the early years are important as a foundation, and are a period of more rapid development and greater relative change, these findings suggest that adverse circumstances, whether enduring such as poor housing or traumatic such as the loss of a parent, are of equal importance for a child's development whether experienced early (that is, in this context, before the age of 7) or later in childhood.

Family size

The strong association between children's development and their family size, persisting when other background factors such as social class are taken into account, is now well known and is confirmed by our latest work (although the degree of relationship between family size and height did seem to have diminished by 16). The major question which still remains to be answered by research on this issue is whether family size has a direct causal effect (and if so, this leads to further questions as to whether this is due to shared material resources or shared time with parents, etc.), or whether the relationship is due to some attitudinal correlate(s) whereby parents who have small families are also most effective in fostering their children's progress.

It is, in fact, unlikely that the truth is to be found totally in one or the other of these explanations. NCDS data do not in the event provide a clear exclusion of either. For example, if shared resources (of whatever kind) were the explanation, then one might hypothesise that a child's development would be more affected by the number of older siblings, with whom he or she has been sharing throughout his or her life, than by the number of younger siblings. However, on the one hand, at 11 it was found that the relationship of these two factors to attainment was similar, while on the other hand the number of older siblings was much more strongly related to progress between 11 and 16.

More clearly compatible with the 'attitudinal correlate' kind of explanation is the finding that *change* in family size was not related to progress between 11 and 16.

It is at the same time unlikely that observational data can altogether resolve this question or that experimentation in this area would be acceptable. Nevertheless, the balance of our findings do warn against too easy an assumption that family size does have a direct effect. If it does not, then it becomes misleading to hope that a reduction in the number of large families, encouraged perhaps by family planning policy or the structuring of child benefits, would be directly beneficial to the development of the children in those families.

Regional differences

Some of the most intriguing findings have been in relation to regional differences, and particularly the contrast between Scottish children and others. At the age of 7 the average reading attainment of Scottish children was found to be outstanding (even *before* allowing for the disproportionate numbers in lower social-class groups) and provoked much discussion of the quality of family life in Scotland and the attitude of Scottish parents to education.

At 16 the picture was somewhat different. In reading the Scots had made less progress than the English and Welsh children (even *after* allowing for the differing social composition of the regions). In mathematics the pattern was more complex, in that among middle-class children the Scots made the greatest average progress, the unskilled manual did less well and the other Scottish working-class children were in an intermediate position. Furthermore, the Scottish 16-year-olds expressed the lowest aspirations for continued education.

Whatever the explanation for these findings, they are unlikely to be due to administrative differences between schools. Mixed-ability teaching, for example, is more common in Scottish secondary schools, but this has not been found to be related to children's attainment. Other school characteristics examined have also been found to have at most very weak relationships with attainment.

Although we have reservations about these particular data, the regional contrasts which were found in relation to the consumption of alcohol were surprising. Scottish 16-year-olds reported considerably less drinking than those in other regions. This is quite contrary to expectations. Among those who did say that they had had a drink in the past week, the Scots were least likely to report having had a drink in their homes. These findings should lead to further investigation. If they are correct, and if Scotland has the worst rates of adult alcoholism, as is generally believed, then this may well have important implications for identifying the cause of the latter problem.

Other regional differences confirm those found both elsewhere and at earlier stages of the NCDS, showing the relatively favoured position in many respects of the South of England over the rest of Britain.

Sex differences

At 7 girls had on average been slightly ahead in their reading test score, with little difference in mathematics. At 11 differences were very small on both tests. By 16 boys had moved ahead, especially in mathematics. However, these differences were, though statistically significant, still small, and the contrasts were by no means as striking as the differences in occupational and educational plans and aspirations.

Although girls were as likely as boys to plan to stay at school beyond 16, they were then less likely to see themselves as going to universities or polytechnics (or the equivalent in Scotland), and more likely to choose colleges of education or some other kind of further education. Even among those of high ability these differences persisted.

Similarly, job aspirations differed between the sexes in ways that were to some extent predictable, but perhaps are in some respects no longer acceptable. By 1974, at least, and to the limited extent that it can be seen as their responsibility, schools seemed to have been unsuccessful in broadening the career outlook of girls, and industry unsuccessful in attracting them. On the contrary, girls were continuing to regard as most popular those job sectors which are currently contracting, such as teaching and other areas of public employment.

There is one area where it is less welcome to find that sex differences are reducing: 16-year-old girls reported smoking very little less than their male counterparts.

Some findings with possible practical implications

It is unrealistic to expect research findings necessarily to lead directly and immediately to unequivocal implications for practice or policy. Policy decisions stem from a complex process in which research information is only one element. The points which are made below are therefore not intended to provide suggested policy directives, but are rather seen as information which is relevant to policy, which seems to merit assimilation by those concerned with policy, and which policy decisions should take into account. In some cases they amount to recommendations for further research, in that there are findings which certainly seem to be relevant, but about which more needs to be known before their practical implications can be identified.

The multidisciplinary approach to the NCDS continues to demonstrate how inextricably intertwined are those aspects of a child's life which, for policy and professional purposes, often tend to be seen as separate. Thus the division below into three categories — health, education and social policy — should not be taken too literally. Professionals and government departments will find matters of interest to them under headings which they might not see as their immediate responsibility.

Health

1. *Medical services.* 16-year-olds have been shown to make frequent use of medical resources — hospital admissions, out-patients' attendance and GP visits were all unexpectedly high. Consideration might be given to the special health problems of adolescents and preventive measures that might reduce their use of expensive services.
2. *Hearing.* There is evidence of hearing loss by many children between the ages of 11 and 16. At the very least there should be continued monitoring and concern about this and its possible effects. There may be a need for educational measures or other publicity to make young people aware of the dangers which may be to a large extent self-inflicted in discos, dance-halls, etc.
3. *Vision.* One-third of the children for whom spectacles had been prescribed did not have these with them for the NCDS medical examination. This may point to the need to impress on children, parents and teachers the importance of wearing glasses when they have been prescribed (although it should not be forgotten that of those who did not have their glasses, one-half proved to have normal vision, or only a minor defect, on testing). Many children develop vision defects relatively late in childhood and adolescence. It should not be thought that pre-school vision screening will obviate the need for subsequent regular screening.
4. *Smoking.* Although there is an indication that smoking by adolescents is decreasing, this appears to be less true for girls. The need for continued health education on this topic is thus reinforced. Furthermore, it has been shown that even by 16 smoking is associated with increased respiratory illness.
5. *Rubella.* Vaccination of girls in 1974 was still well short of the 100 per cent target which is needed in order to be effective. The campaign has been more effective in Scotland than in England and Wales. Groups which give particular cause for concern, because uptake was low, include girls in independent schools and daughters of fathers in unskilled manual occupations.
6. *Diabetics.* There is evidence of an increase in insulin-dependent diabetics among 16-year-olds. Among this group there was no relationship found with perinatal infections. However, a history of this condition among first-degree relatives was higher than reported by other studies.

Education

1. *Guidance.* Almost all schools now have teachers with special responsibility for careers guidance. However, few such teachers had received more than minimal training in this work. A minority

of special schools had teachers specifically responsible for careers guidance. There is evidence that 16-year-olds are not as aware as they might be of routes through further/higher education outside the universities, polytechnics and colleges of education.

2. *Sex and health education*. There were in 1974 still 9 per cent of 16-year-olds in schools that reported providing no sex education at all. Although most schools gave instruction on the physiological aspects of sex, only half of the 16-year-olds (slightly more girls, slightly fewer boys) had additionally learnt about such topics as child care and family life. The majority of the young people themselves expressed the desire to learn more about such topics.

3. *Absenteeism*. Perhaps surprisingly, the overall attendance rate for 16-year-olds was found to be only a little lower than that found in this and other studies for younger children. However, the number said by their teacher to have truanted (in the past year) was disquietingly high. Contrary to some previous studies, it was demonstrated that poor attendance is associated with decrements in attainment for all social groups.

4. *Ability-grouping*. The average attainment, behaviour and attitudes of 16-year-olds was not found to be associated with the ability-grouping policy of their secondary schools. Although the broad categories used do not allow for detailed indications of what kind of ability-grouping policies might be implemented, and how, the results should serve as reassurance that a change in ability-grouping policy is unlikely, *per se*, to lead to changes in attainment, etc. On the other hand, there is some indication that schools which favoured mixed-ability teaching entered more children of relatively low ability for public examinations. This finding merits further investigation. As a first step one would wish to know whether these children do in fact obtain worthwhile results in the extra examinations taken.

5. *Education of the handicapped*. Although this should be regarded as no more than suggestive, there were significant numbers of children with severe defects who had not been ascertained as in need of special attention, and who were apparently coping well within normal schools (although we cannot know whether they might have been able to do even better than this).

Social policy

1. *Adolescent drinking*. We have already mentioned our reservations about these data, but we hope that our findings will stimulate others to check, first, whether the consumption of alcohol by this age group is as high as our figures may indicate, and second whether this relates to problems at a later age.

2. *Housing*. The NCDS data continue to show the strong association between housing circumstances and children's development, and the large number who experienced adverse conditions (overcrowding, lack of amenities) during childhood. However, there are some indications that the housing stock available for families with children has improved to the point where some of the grossest effects of the worst housing conditions no longer appear in sufficient numbers to produce significant findings (which is not to belittle their importance for the relatively small numbers which may still be affected). For example, there was little evidence of a relationship between housing circumstances and health in adolescence or physical growth. Again, it does not appear that the slightly poorer housing circumstances of children in one-parent families were such as to explain their developmental disadvantages — financial problems appeared to be more important.

3. *Sex and health education*. Although parents, friends and school were given as the main sources, television and magazines were also reported as important for information on these issues. Thought should be given to how such sources might be better and more systematically exploited.

4. *Immigrants*. Perhaps the most important role which these findings can play is in the education of public attitudes. They demonstrate the adverse circumstances with which first-generation immigrant children in particular have to cope: their poor housing and other social circumstances, and the financial problems which in turn influence young people's educational and career aspirations. It is not surprising that in general the first-generation group were doing relatively poorly at school (although their reading test scores improved quickly with their length of time in Britain). The picture for second-generation immigrants (i.e. children born in this country to parents from abroad) was somewhat different. All groups showed markedly higher attainment than the first-generation groups, to the point where only the 'West Indian' children were doing worse than 'indigenous' children. Children from Asian families were particularly successful. However, the problems experienced by immigrant children do not disappear altogether within a generation. The West Indian children continued to do less well at school, and together with the Irish their general social circumstances remained relatively disadvantaged in the second generation.

5. *Children in one-parent families*. One of the most

important aspects of the findings has been to illustrate the nature of this group. Although about one in eight of 16-year-olds had experienced life with a single parent, only a tiny fraction of these had done so throughout the sixteen years. Children who had experienced being in a one-parent family were doing less well in school at 16 than they had been doing at 11 but there was no evidence of any particular problems appearing in adolescence, as might have been predicted. Both parents and children had lower aspirations for continued education, often for financial reasons. Teachers shared this view but were often more optimistic than both child and parent(s). The 16-year-old analyses confirmed earlier findings that although overall these children were progressing less well at school, they were doing no worse than children who were with both their parents and came from similar backgrounds and circumstances. Moreover, it was possible to take this question a step further and demonstrate that, among the disadvantages experienced by this group, their financial difficulties appeared to be more crucial than their housing circumstances for children's development. The financial difficulties of these families are severe. Divorced or separated mothers had particularly low incomes, and widows did little better, but even those families where there was a new father-figure were not so well off as the unbroken families. It is perhaps reassuring to find that the attitudes and expectations of those young people for their own future family lives did not appear to have been affected, though one cannot predict whether attitudes will be borne out by reality. The large number referred to above which had a substitute parent, the financial disadvantages even of families that had gained a new father-figure, and the suggestion that children with substitute parents were doing less well than those

whose parents had remained alone, indicate strongly the need for further research into children with step-parents.

A concluding note

We hope that the studies that have been presented, and that comprise only a part of what the National Child Development Study has produced since its inception, continue to demonstrate the value of large-scale longitudinal studies such as this one. The 1946 cohort, referred to in many of our papers and which in many respects provided a template for the NCDS, continues to study a sub-sample of its subjects — and their children. A further cohort study was embarked upon in 1970 and has carried out follow-ups at the ages of 4 and 11.

Only by means of such a series of studies can we hope to monitor adequately the health and development of our young people and relate these to changing patterns in our society.

Our own work continues. Further analyses of the data described in this book have been undertaken and reported (a full publications list can be obtained from the National Children's Bureau). In 1978/9 we were able to collect and add to our information the public examination results of the young people in the study.

In 1981 a further full follow-up was mounted. About 12 500 interviews took place and information was collected on employment and training, family formation, housing, further and higher education and many other aspects of life.

Thus there is a sense in which all the analyses and findings in this book are preliminary. In the coming years we shall be able to add to this picture of young people in Great Britain and relate their adult lives to the details of their childhood and schooldays which have been presented here.

Statistical Appendix*

Analyses of continuous variables

Many of the results in this book were produced by examining the differences in outcome variables such as children's attainment or physical development associated with differences in factors such as sex, social class or previous attainment. These data were analysed using the general linear model (analysis of variance) to fit as main effects all the variables which were thought to be important in explaining the outcome, testing each one as 'last one in' — that is, by comparison of the total main effects model and the 'main effects minus test variable' model. (If it were suspected that two or more variables might have non-additive effects, the interaction term was fitted and tested in addition to the main effects model.)

This meant that the effect of each variable could be considered, not in isolation, but when all the other important factors had been taken into account. This is particularly important when independent variables are related to one another. Testing independent variables singly, one would be unable to say how much of the effect was accounted for by the variable itself and how much was due to its relationship to other important variables not included in the analysis. For example, to investigate the effects on attainment of growing up in a single-parent family, one could compare children from single-/two-parent families after allowing for differences in income, housing, social-class and other variables. This enables one to see whether children from one-parent families fare worse simply because as a group they tend to be in low-income families with poor housing, etc., or whether, when the low income and poor housing have been taken into account, there is any extra disadvantage attributable to having only one parent.

It is important to be clear what is implied by this method of testing and what hypothesis and what order of causality we are in fact investigating. If we feel (as we may well do) that as a result of their sole responsibility lone parents will be able to devote less time and attention to their careers and thus be poorer paid and live in poorer housing, and we wish to describe the position *in our society* of children of lone parents, then we should not adjust for such variables as income, housing, tenure, and so on. On the other hand, if we wish to investigate whether children appear to have an inherent need for two parents, or, looked at in a policy-orientated way, whether the drawbacks can be overcome by the provision of suitable help and financial allowance, then it would be appropriate to allow for income, tenure, and so on.

The model fitted was, for two variables:

*Prepared by Douglas Hutchison.

$$y_{ijk} = a + b_j + c_k + d_{jk} + e_{ijk}$$

where

y_{ijk} = outcome for ith individual in category j of the 1st variable and category k of the 2nd variable

b_j = effect on outcome of category j of the 2nd variable

c_k = effect on outcome of category k of the 2nd variable

d_{jk} = interaction (or non-linear) effect on outcome of the 1st and 2nd variables

e_{ijk} = error term, with mean zero and constant variable

with the constraints:

$$\sum_j b_j = \sum_k c_j = 0$$

$$\sum_j d_{jk} = \sum_k d_{jk} = 0$$

Dummy variables were used to include categorical independent variables. The technique used (effect coding) fits $n - 1$ constants for an n-category variable, with the constant for the nth category being equal to one minus the sum of these $(n - 1)$ (Kerlinger and Pedhazur, 1973).

Test statistics quoted from the analyses of variance are in terms of χ^2 rather than the conventional F-statistics. This is because the number of degrees of freedom associated with the residual variation is so large, because of the sample size, that the test statistics follow a very good approximation to the distribution of a multiple of chi-square random variable, since

$$\chi_k^2 = k \cdot f(k, n) \text{ for large } n$$

Transformations

Reading, mathematics and behaviour scores were transformed where necessary to follow the normal distribution so that statistical techniques such as analysis of variance could be applied without violating the assumptions of normality on which these techniques depend.

Reading and mathematics scores were transformed empirically to follow the normal distribution except for reading at 11 and mathematics at 7 when the raw scores were used.

The transformation for Rutter Home Behaviour Scores was the same at all 3 ages: log (total score + 10). BSAG scores at 11 and 7 were transformed using $\sqrt{\text{BSAG} + 3/8}$, while at 16 for the school Rutter scale, the square root of the total score was used.

Age corrrections

Because the data for each survey were collected over a period of months, this meant that, for some variables, it was necessary to correct the data for the age of the child at the time of recording.

In the case of height, $u - bt$ was analysed, where t is the difference between the 'desired' age and the actual age of the child when height was measured, and b is the stop of the regression of y on t.

Analysis of two-way tables

When two-way tables were produced and *post hoc* analyses of subsections of the tables were carried out, the test statistic was compared with the same initial value as for the whole table (Gabriel, 1966). For example, if the original table was $n \times m$ and, say, it was decided to test r rows $(r < n)$ the test statistic was compared with the chi-square distribution with $(n - 1) \times (m - 1)$ degrees of freedom.

If the sub-analysis had been specified before the table had been produced, the degrees of freedom in the chi-square would be calculated in the normal way, i.e. $(r - 1) \times (m - 1)$.

References

Acheson, R. M. and Hewitt, D. (1954) 'Oxford child health survey: Stature skeletal maturation in the pre-school child', *British Journal of Preventative and Social Medicine*, 8, 59–65.

Adelstein, A. M. (1975) 'National statistics', *Postgraduate Medical Journal*, 51, supp. 2, pp. 57–67.

Adler, S. (1972) 'Dialectal differences and learning disorders', *Journal of Learning Disabilities*, 5 (6) June, 344–50.

Adler, S. (1973) 'Articulatory deviances and social class membership', *Journal of Learning Disabilities*, 6 (10) 650–4.

Albee, G. W. (1969) 'Emerging concepts of mental illness and models of treatment: the psychological point of view', *American Journal of Psychiatry*, 125, 870–6.

Alberman, E. D., Butler, N. R. and Sheridan, M. D. (1971) 'Visual acuity of a national sample (1958 cohort) at 7 years', *Developmental Medicine and Child Neurology*, 13 (1).

Alberman, E. D. and Goldstein, H. (1970) 'The "at risk" register: a statistical evaluation', *British Journal of Preventative and Social Medicine*, 24, 123–5.

Anderson, J. (1939) 'An evaluation of various indices of linguistic development', *Child Development*, 8, 62–8.

Annett, M. (1970) 'Handedness, cerebral dominance and the growth of intelligence', in Bakker, D. and Satz, P. (eds), *Specific Reading Disability* (Rotterdam; Rotterdam University Press).

Annett, M. and Turner, A. (1974) 'Laterality and the growth of intellectual abilities', *British Journal of Educational Psychology*, 44, 37–46.

Anon. (1965) 'Parents and the primary school: a survey of parental opinion', *Educational Research*, 7, 229–35.

Armitage, P. (1955) 'Tests for linear trends in proportions and frequencies', *Biometrics*, 11, 375–86.

Armitage, P. (1966) 'The chi-square test for heterogeneity of proportions after adjustment for stratification', *Journal of the Royal Statistical Society*, series B, 28, 150–63.

Arnold, L. E. and Smeltzer, D. J. (1974) 'Behaviour checklist for children and adolescents', *Archives of General Psychiatry*, 30, 799–804.

Ascher, M. A. (1970) 'The attainments of children in ESN schools and remedial departments', *Educational Research*, 12, 215–19.

Averch, H. A., Carroll, S. J., Donaldson, T. S., Keisling, H. J. and Pincus, J. (1975) 'How effective is schooling: the input–output approach', in Levine, D.M. and Bane, M.J. (eds), *The Inequality Controversy: Schooling and Distributive Justice* (New York, Basic Books).

Bakwin, H. (1958) 'The tonsil-adenoidectomy enigma', *Journal of Pediatrics*, 52, 339.

Bakwin, H. (1961) 'Eneuresis in children', *Journal of Pediatrics*, 58, 806.

Bakwin, H. (1971) 'Eneuresis in twins', *American Journal of Diseases of Children*, 121, 222.

Barker Lunn, J. C. (1970) *Streaming in the Primary School* (Slough, NFER).

Baum, J. D., Ousted, M. and Smith, M. A. (1975) 'Weight gain in infancy and subsequent development of diabetes mellitus in childhood', *Lancet*, 2 (7940) p. 866 (letter).

Beardmore, M. and Reid, J. J. A. (1966) 'Diabetic children', *British Medical Journal*, 2, 1383–4.

Beardsley, G. and Wright, E. (1974) 'Comparative reading', *Reading*, 8, 27–32.

Becker, W. C. (1960) 'The matching of behaviour rating and questionnaire personality factors', *Psychological Bulletin*, 157, 201–12.

Belmont, L., Stein, Z. A. and Susser, M. W. (1975) 'Comparisons of associations of birth order with intelligence test score and height', *Nature*, 255, 1 May.

Benn, C. and Simon, B. (1972) *Halfway There* (London, McGraw-Hill).

Berk, L. E., Rose, M. H. and Stewart, D. (1970) 'Attitudes of English and American children toward their school experience', *Journal of Educational Psychology*, 61, 33–40.

Berman, A. (1971) 'The problem of assessing cerebral dominance and its relationship to intelligence', *Cortex*, 7, 372–86.

Bernstein, B. (1961a) 'Social class and linguistic development: a theory of social learning', in Halsey, A.H., Floud, J. and Anderson, C. A. (eds), *Education, Economy and Society* (New York, Free Press) 288–314.

Bernstein, B. (1961b) 'Social structure, language and learning', *Educational Research*, 3, 163–76.

Bernstein, B. (1971) *Class, Codes and Control*, vol. 1 (London, Routledge & Kegan Paul).

Bernstein, B. (1972) 'A sociolinguistic approach to socialisation: with some reference to educability', in Gumpez, J.J. and Hymes, D. (eds), *Directions in Sociolinguistics* (New York, Holt, Rinehart & Winston).

Bewley, B. R. and Bland, J. M. (1976) 'Smoking and respiratory symptoms in two groups of school children', *Preventative Medicine*, 5, 63–9.

Bewley, B. R., Bland, J. M. and Harris, R. (1974) 'Factors associated with the starting of cigarette smoking by primary school children', *British Journal of Preventative and Social Medicine*, 28, 37–45.

Bhapkar, V. P. (1966) 'A note on the equivalence of two test criteria for hypotheses in categorical data', *Journal of the American Statistical Association*, 61, 228–35.

Bhapkar, V. P. (1968) 'On the analysis of contingency tables with a quantitative response', *Biometrics*, 24, 329–38.

Birch, G., Richardson, S.A., Baird, D., Morobin, G. and Illsley, R. (1970) *Mental Subnormality in the Community: A Clinical and Epidemiologic Study* (Baltimore, Williams & Wilkins).

Bishop, Y. M. M., Frienberg, S. E. and Holland, W. P. (1975) *Discrete Multivariate Analysis* (Cambridge, Mass., MIT Press).

Blair, H. (1977) 'Natural history of childhood asthma', *Archives of Disease in Childhood*, 52, 613—19.

Bland, J. M., Bewley, B. R. and Day, I. (1975) 'Primary school-boys: image of self and smoker', *British Journal of Preventative and Social Medicine*, 29, 262—6.

Bloom, A., Hayes, T. M. and Gamble, D. R. (1975) 'Register of newly diagnosed diabetic children', *British Medical Journal*, 3 (5983) 580—3.

Bloor, M. (1976) 'Bishop Berkeley and the adenotonsillectomy enigma; an exploration of variation in the social construction of medical disposals', *Sociology*, 10; 43.

Blythman, M. (1975) 'Truants suffer from the disadvantages of life', *Scottish Education Journal*, 58, 80—4.

Bolande, R. P. (1969) 'Ritualistic surgery — circumcision and tonsillectomy', *New England Journal of Medicine*, 280, 591.

Bormouth, J. R. (1966) 'Readability: a new approach', *Reading Research Quarterly*, 1, 79—132.

Brazelton, T. B. (1962) 'A child-oriented approach to toilet-training', *Pediatrics*, 29, 121.

Brimer, A., Madaus, G. F., Chapman, B., Kellagan, T. and Wood, R. (1978) *Sources of Difference in School Achievement* (Windsor, NFER).

British Medical Journal, (1975) 'Heritability of diabetes', *British Medical Journal*, 4 (5989) 127—8.

Brown, M. A. (1975) 'Vision screening of pre-school children', *Clinical Pediatrics*, 14, 968—73.

Butler, N. R. and Alberman, E. D. (eds) (1969) *Perinatal Problems* (Edinburgh, Livingstone).

Butler, N. R. and Bonham, D. G. (1963) *Perinatal Mortality* (Edinburgh, Livingstone).

Butler, N. R., Peckham, C. S. and Sheridan, M. D. (1973) 'Speech defects in children aged 7 years', *British Medical Journal*, 1, 253—7.

Bynner, J. M. (1967) *Medical Students' Attitudes Towards Smoking* (London, HMSO).

Bynner, J. M. (1969) *The Young Smoker* (London, HMSO).

Bynner, J. M. (1971) 'The dilemma facing health education', in Pearson, G. R. (ed.), *The Second World Conference on Smoking and Health* (London, Pitman).

Byrne, D. S., Williamson, B. and Fletcher, B. (1975) *The Poverty of Education: A Study in the Politics of Opportunity* (London, Martin Robertson).

Callary, R. (1971) 'Syntactic correlates of social stratification', unpublished doctoral dissertation, Louisiana State University.

Callary, R. (1974) 'Status perception through syntax', *Language and Speech*, 17, 187—92.

Calnan, M. and Richardson, K. (1976a) 'Speech problems among children in a national survey — 1 Assessments and prevalences', *Child: Care, Health and Development*, 2, 181.

Calnan, M. and Richardson, K. (1976b) 'Developmental correlates of handedness in a national sample of 11-year-olds', *Journal of Human Biology*, 3, 4.

Cameron, H. (1977) 'Vision screening in preschool children', *British Medical Journal*, 2, 701—2.

Canter, G. J. and Trost, J. E. (1966) 'The speech handicapped', *Review of Educational Research*, 36, 56—74.

Carlsmith, L. (1964) 'Effect of early father absence on scholastic aptitude', *Harvard Educational Review*, 34, 3—21.

Carter, C. O. (1964) 'Review of the home and the school', *Eugenics Review*, 56 (2) 93.

Carter, M. P. (1966) *Into Work* (Harmondsworth, Penguin).

Cartwright, A. *et al.* (1960) 'Young smokers — an attitude study among school children touching also on parental influence', *British Journal of Preventative and Social Medicine*, 14, 28—34.

Cazden, C. B. (1972) *Child Language and Education* (New York, Holt, Rinehart & Winston).

Central Advisory Council for Education (England) (1967) *Children and their Primary Schools* (Plowden Report) (London, HMSO).

Central Statistical Office (1970) *Social Trends*, 1 (London, HMSO).

Central Statistical Office (1975) *Social Trends*, 6 (London, HMSO).

Chamberlain, R., Chamberlain, G., Howlett, B. and Claireaux, A. (1975) *British Births 1970* (London, Heinemann).

Chazan, M. (1965) 'Factors associated with maladjustment in educationally subnormal children', *British Journal of Educational Psychology*, 35 (3), 277—85.

Cherry, N. (1976) 'Persistent job changing — is it a problem?', *Journal of Occupational Psychology*, 49, 203—21.

Chomsky, N. (1957) *Syntactic Structures* (The Hague, Mouton).

Chomsky, N. (1965) *Aspects of the Theory of Syntax* (Cambridge, Mass., MIT Press).

Christensen, F. (1968) 'The problem of defining a mature style', *English Journal*, 57, 4—11.

Christiansen, N., Mora, J. O. and Herrera, G. (1975) 'Family social characteristics related to physical growth of young children', *British Journal of Preventative and Social Medicine*, 29, 121—30.

Chrysanthis, K. (1947) 'Stammering and handedness', *Lancet*, 252, 270—1.

Clark, M. M. (1957) *Left Handedness* (University of London Press).

Clark, M.M. (1970) *Reading Difficulties in Schools* (Harmondsworth, Penguin).

Clayson Committee (1973) *Report of the Departmental Committee on Scottish Licensing Law* (Edinburgh, Scottish Home and Health Department, HMSO).

Coard, B. (1971) *How the West Indian Child is made Educationally Subnormal in the British School System* (London, New Beacon Books).

Cohen Report (1964) *Health Education* (London, HMSO).

Cohen, T. (1971) 'Juvenile diabetes in Israel', *Israel Journal of Medical Science*, 7, 1558—61.

Cohn, R. (1961) 'Delayed acquisition of reading and writing ability of children', *Archives of Neurology*, 4, 153—62.

Coleman, J. S., Campbell, E. Q., Hobson, C. J., McPartland, J., Mood, A. M., Weinfield, F. D. and York, R. L. (1966) *Equality of Educational Opportunity* (Washington DC, US Government Printing Office).

Committee on Housing in Greater London (1965) *Report* (Chairman: Milner-Holland) (London, HMSO).

Community Relations Commission (1976) *Between Two Cultures: A Study of Relationships between Generations in the Asian Community in Britain* (London, CRC).

Cook, J., Altman, D.G., Moore, D.M.C., Topp, S.G., Holland, W. W. and Elliot, A. (1973) 'A survey of the nutritional status of school-children: relation between nutrient intake and socio-economic factors', *British Journal of Preventative and Social Medicine*, 27 (2).

Craft, M. (1970) *Family, Class and Education* (London, Longman).

Crellin, E., Pringle, M.L.K. and West, P. (1971) *Born Illegitimate* (a National Children's Bureau report) (Slough, NFER).

Cromer, R. F. (1974) 'The development of language and cognition', in Foss, B. (ed.), *New Perspectives in Child Development* (Harmondsworth, Penguin) 184—251.

Crookes, T. G. and Greene, M. C. L. (1963) 'Some characteristics of children with two types of speech disorders',

British Journal of Educational Psychology, 33, 31—49.

Crowther Report (1959) *15 to 18* (London, HMSO).

Cudworth, A.G. (1976) 'The aetiology of diabetes mellitus', *British Journal of Hospital Medicine*, 16 (3) 207—16.

Cullingworth, J. B. (1965) *English Housing Trends* (London, G. Bell & Sons Ltd).

Dadson, R. S. and King, J. H. (1952) 'A determination of the normal threshold of hearing and its relation to the standardisation of audiometers', *Journal of Laryngology and Otology*, 66, 366—78.

Datta, L., Schaffer, E. and Davis, M. (1968) 'Sex and scholastic aptitudes as variables in teachers' ratings of the adjustment and classroom behaviour of negro and other seventh grade students', *Journal of Educational Psychology*, 59, 94—101.

Davie, R. (1973) 'Eleven years of childhood', *Statistical News*, 22.

Davie, R., Butler, N. R. and Goldstein, H. (1972) *From Birth to Seven* (London, Longman in association with National Children's Bureau).

Davies, R. P. (1975) *Mixed Ability Grouping* (London, Temple Smith).

Davis, H. (1965) 'The ISO zero-reference level for audiometers', *Archives of Otology and Laryngology*, 81, 145—9.

Davis, J. and Stacey, B. (1972) *Teenagers and Alcohol* (London, HMSO).

Daws, P. P. (1977) 'Are careers education programmes in secondary schools a waste of time? — A reply to Roberts', *British Journal of Guidance and Counselling*, 5 (1).

Dawson, B., Horobin, G., Illsey, R. and Mitchell, R. (1969) 'A survey of childhood asthma in Aberdeen', *Lancet*, 1, 827—30.

Delaney, M.E., Whittle, L.S. and Knox, E.C. (1966) 'A note on the use of self-recording audiometry with children', *Journal of Laryngology and Otology*, 80, 1135—43.

Department of Education and Science (1971) *The Education of Immigrants*, Education Survey 13 (London, HMSO).

Department of Education and Science (1973) *Careers Education in Secondary Schools*, Education Survey 18 (London, HMSO).

Department of Education and Science (1976) *Statistics of Education, 1974: School Leavers* (London, HMSO).

Department of Education and Science (1977a) *Statistics of Education, 1975: School Leavers* (London, HMSO).

Department of Education and Science (1977b) *Education in Schools: A Consultative Document* (London, HMSO).

Department of the Environment (1975) *Housing and Construction Statistics*. 13 (London, HMSO).

Department of Health and Social Security (1970) *Circular 9/70* (London, DHSS).

Department of Health and Social Security (1972) *Circular 17/72* (London, DHSS).

Department of Health and Social Security (1974a) *Circular 1/74* (London, DHSS).

Department of Health and Social Security (1974b). *Report of the Committee on One-Parent Families* (Finer Report) (London, HMSO).

Dey, F.I. (1970) 'Auditory fatigue and predicted permanent hearing defects from "rock-n-roll" music', *New England Journal of Medicine*, 282, 467—70.

Dickinson, L., Hobbs, A., Kleinberg, S. M. and Martin, P. J. (1975) *The Immigrant School Learner* (Slough, NFER).

Dight, S. E. (1976) *Scottish Drinking Habits* (London, HMSO).

Dimond, S. J. and Beaumont, S. G. (eds) (1974) *Hemisphere Function in the Human Brain* (London, Elek).

Dippe, S. E. *et al.* (1975) 'Lack of causal association between coxsackie B4 virus infection and diabetes', *Lancet*, 1 (7920) 1314—17.

Doll, R. and Hadley, A. L. (1950) Correspondence, *British Medical Journal*, i, 181.

Donnison, D. V. (1967) *The Government of Housing* (Harmondsworth, Penguin).

Douglas, J. F. (1973) 'A study ot streaming at a grammar school', *Educational Research*, 15, 140—3.

Douglas, J. W. B. (1964) *The Home and the School* (London, MacGibbon & Kee).

Douglas, J. W. B. (1970) 'Broken families and child behaviour', *Journal of the Royal College of Physicians*, 4, 203.

Douglas, J. W. B. (1973b) 'Early disturbing events and later enuresis', in Kolvin, I., MacKeith, R.C. and Keadow, S.R. (eds), *Bladder Control and Enuresis: Clinics in Developmental Medicine*, No. 48/49 (London, SIMP and Heinemann).

Douglas, J. W. B. (1973c) 'Prospective study of effectiveness of tonsillectomy in children', in Davies, A. M. (ed.), *Uses of Epidemiology in Planning Health Services*, Proceedings of the Sixth International Scientific Meeting, International Epidemiological Association, Savremena Administracija, Belgrade.

Douglas, J. W. B. (1976) 'No end to inequality', *Times Educational Supplement*, 23 July.

Douglas, J. W. B. and Ross, J. (1965) 'The effects of absence on primary school performance', *British Journal of Educational Psychology*, 35, 18—40.

Douglas, J. W. B., Ross, J. M. and Simpson, H. R. (1967a) 'The ability and attainment of short sighted pupils', *Journal of the Royal Statistical Society*, 130, 479—503.

Douglas, J. W. B., Ross, J. M. and Cooper, J. E. (1967b) 'The relationship between handedness, attainment and adjustment in a national sample of school children', *Educational Research*, 9, 223—32.

Douglas, J.W.B. and Simpson, H.R. (1964) 'Height in relation to puberty, family size and social class', *Millbank*

Douglas, J. W. B., and Simpson, H. R. (1964) 'Height in relation to puberty, family size and social class', *Millbank Memorial Fund Quarterly*, 42, 20—35.

Downey, M. E. and Kelly, A. V. (1975) *Theory and Practice of Education: An Introduction* (London, Harper & Row).

Dudgeon, J. A. *et al.* (1971) 'Immunisation against rubella', *Practitioner*, 207, 782—90.

Edwards, H. and Thompson, B. (1971) 'Who are the fatherless?', *New Society*, 17, 192—3.

Epstein, W. (1961) 'The influence of syntactic structure on learning', *American Journal of Psychology*, 74, 80—5.

Essen, J. (1978) 'Living in one-parent families: income and expenditure', *Poverty*, 40, 23—8.

Essen, J. and Fogelman, K. R. (1979) 'Childhood housing experiences', *Concern*, 32.

Essen, J., Fogelman, K. and Head, J. (1978) 'Childhood housing experience and school attainment', *Child: Care, Health and Development*, 4, 41—58.

Essen, J. and Ghodsian, M. (1977) 'Sixteen year olds in households in receipt of supplementary benefit and family income supplement', Appendix to Supplementary Benefits Commission, *Annual Report 1976* (London, HMSO).

Essen, J. and Lambert, L. (1977) 'Living in one-parent families: relationships and attitudes of 16-year-olds', *Child: Care, Health and Development* 3, 301—18.

Essen, J., Lambert, L. and Head, J. (1976) 'School attainment of children who have been in care', *Child: Care, Health and Development*, 2, 339—51.

Essen, J. and Parrinder, D. (1975) 'Housing for children — further findings from the National Child Development Study', *Housing Review*, 24, 112—14.

Essen, J. and Peckham, C. S. (1976) 'Nocturnal enuresis in

childhood', *Developmental Medicine and Child Neurology*, 18, 577—89.

Evans, R. I. (1976) 'Smoking in children developing a social psychological strategy of deterrence', *Preventative Medicine*, 5, 122—7.

Eysenck, H. J. (1971) *Race, Intelligence and Education* (London, Temple Smith).

Fairbairns, Z. and Wintour, J. (1977) *No Place to Grow Up* (London, Shelter).

Falconer, D. S., Duncan, L. J. P. and Smith, C. (1971) 'A statistical and genetical study of diabetes. 1   prevalence and morbidity', *Annals of Human Genetics*, 34, 347—69.

Farrell, C. (1978) *'My mother said . . . the way young people learn about sex and birth control'* (London: Routledge & Kegan Paul).

Ferri, E. (1971) *Streaming: Two Years Later* (Slough, NFER).

Ferri, E. (1976) *Growing Up in a One-Parent Family: A Long-Term Study of Child Development* (Slough, NFER).

Ferri, E. and Robinson, H. (1976) *Coping Alone* (Slough, NFER and National Children's Bureau).

Floud, J. E. (1961) 'Social class factors in educational achievement', in Halsey, A. H. (ed.), *Ability and Educational Opportunity* (Paris, OECD).

Floud, J., Halsey, A. H. and Martin, F. M. (eds) (1956) *Education, Economy and Society* (London, Heinemann).

Fogelman, K. (1975) 'Developmental correlates of family size', *British Journal of Social Work*, 5, 43—57.

Fogelman, K. (ed.) (1976) *Britain's Sixteen-Year-Olds* (London, National Children's Bureau).

Fogelman, K. (1979) 'Educational and career aspirations — findings from a national sample of sixteen-year-olds', *British Journal of Guidance and Counselling*, 7 (1).

Fogelman, K., Essen, J. H. and Tibbenham, A. (1978a) 'Ability grouping in secondary schools and attainment', *Educational Studies*, 4, 201—12.

Fogelman, K. R. and Goldstein, H. (1976) 'Social factors associated with changes in educational attainment between 7 and 11 years of age', *Educational Studies*, 2, 95—109.

Fogelman, K., Goldstein, H., Essen, J. and Ghodsian, M. (1978b) 'Patterns of attainment', *Educational Studies*, 4 (2), 121—30.

Fogelman, K. and Richardson, K. (1974) 'School attendance: some results from the National Child Development study', in Turner, B. (ed.), *Truancy* (London, Ward Lock).

Fogelman, K., Tibbenham, A. and Lambert, L. (1980) 'Absence from school', in Berg, I. and Hersov, L. (eds), *Out of School: Perspectives on Truancy and School Refusal* (London, Wiley).

Ford, J. (1969) *Social Relations in a Secondary School* (London, Routledge & Kegan Paul).

Forrest, J. M., Menser, M. A. and Burgers, J. A. (1971) 'High frequency of diabetes mellitus in young adults with congenital rubella', *Lancet*, 2, 332—4.

Fransella, F. (1970) 'Stuttering: not a symptom but a way of life', *British Journal of Disorders of Communication*, 5 (1) 22—9.

Frew, R. and Peckham, C. S. (1972) 'Mental retardation in a national study', *British Hospital Journal and Social Services Review*, 16 September.

Gabriel, K. R. (1966) 'Simultaneous test procedures for multiple comparisons on categorical data', *Journal of the American Statistical Association*, 61, 1081—96.

Gagnon, J. H. (1974) *Sexual Conduct: The Social Services of Human Sexuality* (London, Hutchison).

Gairdner, D. (1949) 'The fate of the foreskin', *British Medical Journal*, II, 1433.

Gaito, J. (1965) 'Unequal intervals and unequal *n* in trend analysis', *Psychological Bulletin*, 63, 125—7.

Galloway, D. (1976) 'Persistent unjustified absence from school', *Trends in Education*, 4, 22—7.

Gamble, D. R. and Taylor, K. W. (1969) 'Seasonal influence of diabetes mellitus', *British Medical Journal*, 3, 631—3.

Gardiner, P. A. (1964) 'The relation of myopia to growth', *Lancet*, 1, 476—9.

Gardiner, P. A. (1973) 'School eye clinics', *British Medical Journal*, 1, 552—3 (letter).

Gardiner, P. A. (1977) 'Vision screening in preschool children', *British Medical Journal*, 2, 577 (letter).

Gazzaniga, M. S. (1970) *The Bisected Brain* (New York, Appleton-Century-Crofts).

General Register Office (1961). *Census 1961, England and Wales Housing Tables* (London, HMSO).

General Register Office (1966) *Classification of Occupations* (London, HMSO).

George, V. and Wilding, P. (1972) *Motherless Families* (London, Routledge & Kegan Paul).

Geschwind, N. (1972) 'Language and the brain', *Scientific American*, 226, 76—83.

Ghodsian, M. and Essen, J. (1982) 'Children of immigrants: I. Social and Home Circumstances', *New Community*, 8 (3), 195—205.

Gill, D. G. and Stephen, R. (1974) 'Anomalous family circumstances in Aberdeen', in *Report of the Committee on One-Parent Families*, 2, 13 (Chairman: Sir Morris Finer) (London, HMSO).

Gingerbread (1973) *One Parent Families — A Finer Future?* (London, Association for One-Parent Families).

Ginsberg, H. (1972) *The Myth of the Deprived Child* (Englewood Cliffs, N.J., Prentice-Hall).

Gipps, C. and Ewen, E. (1974) 'Scoring written work in English as a second language: the use of the T-unit', *Educational Research*, 16, 121—5.

Glasser, P. and Navarre, E. (1965) 'Structural problems of the one-parent family', *Journal of Social Issues*, 21, 98—109.

Glorig, A. (1966) 'Audiometric reference levels', *Laryngoscope*, 76, 842—9.

Glorig, A. and Nixon, J. (1959) 'Music as a source of acoustic trauma', *Laryngoscope*, 78, 1211—18.

Glover, J. A. (1938) 'The incidence of tonsillectomy in school children', *Proceedings of the Royal Society of Medicine*, 31, 1219.

Goldberg, M. L., Pascow, A. H. and Justman, J. (1966) *The Effects of Ability Grouping* (New York, Teachers' College Press).

Goldshmidt, E. (1968) 'On the ecology of myopia: an epidemiological study', *Acta Ophthalmologica*, sup. 98.

Goldstein, H. (1971) 'Factors influencing the height of seven-year-old children — results from the National Child Development study', *Human Biology*, 43 (1).

Goldstein, H. (1972) 'Statistical appendix', in Davie *et al.* (1972).

Goldstein, H. (1976) 'A study of the response rates of 16-year-olds in the National Child Development study', in Fogelman, K. R. (ed.), *Britain's Sixteen-Year-Olds* (London, National Children's Bureau).

Goldstein, H. and Fogelman, K. R. (1974) 'Age standardisation and seasonal effects in mental testing', *British Journal of Educational Psychology*, 55 (2) 109.

Goldstein, H. and Peckham, C. (1976) 'Birthweight, gestation, neonatal mortality and child development', in Roberts, D. F. and Thomson, A. M. (eds), *The Biology of Human Fetal Growth* (London, Taylor & Francis).

Gooch, S. and Pringle, M. L. K. (1966) *Four Years On* (London, Longman).

Goodman, L. A. (1976) 'The relationship between modified and usual multiple regression approaches to the analysis of dichotomous variables', *Sociological Methodology*, 83–110.

Graham, P., Rutter, M. and George, S. (1973) 'Temperamental characteristics as predictors of behaviour disorders in children', *American Journal of Orthopsychiatry*, 43, 328–39.

Graham, P. J., Rutter, M. L., Yule, W. and Pless, T. B. (1967) 'Childhood asthma: a psychosomatic disorder? Some epidemiological considerations', *British Journal of Preventative and Social Medicine*, 21, 78–85.

Grant, M. W. (1964) 'Rate of growth in relation to birth rank and family size', *British Journal of Preventative and Social Medicine*, 18.

Green, L. F. (1969) 'Comparison of school attainments', *Special Education*, 58, 9–12.

Griffin, W. J. (1968) 'Children: development of syntactic control', in Rosenberg, S. and Koplin, J. H. (eds), *Developments in Applied Psycholinguistics Research* (New York, Macmillan).

Guttman, L. (1941) 'The quantification of a class of attributes: a theory and method of scale construction', in Horst, P. (ed.), *The Prediction of Personal Adjustment* (New York, Social Sciences Research Council).

Hallworth, H. J. (1962) 'A teacher's perception of his pupils', *Educational Review*, 14, 124–33.

Halsall, E. (1970) *Becoming Comprehensive: Case Histories* (Oxford, Pergamon).

Hamman, R. F., Halil, T. and Holland, W. W. (1975) 'Asthma in schoolchildren', *British Journal of Preventative and Social Medicine*, 29, 228–38.

Hammons, G. W. (1972) 'Educating the mildly retarded: a review', *Exceptional Children*, 38, 565–70.

Hargreaves, D. H. (1967) *Social relations in a Secondary School* (London, Routledge & Kegan Paul).

Harms, L. S. (1963) 'Status areas in speech: extra-race and extra-region identification', *Lingua*, 12, 300–6.

Harrel, L. E. (1957) 'A comparison of the development of oral and written language in school-age children', *Monographs of the Society for Research in Child Development*, 22(3).

Hawker, A. (1978) *Adolescents and Alcohol* (London, Edsall).

Haynes, J. M. (1971) *Educational Assessment of Immigrant Pupils* (Slough, NFER).

Healy, M. J. R. and Goldstein, H. (1976) 'An approach to the scaling of categorised attributes', *Biometrika*, 63, 219–29.

Hecaen, H. and de Ajuriaguerra, J. (1964) *Left-Handedness* (New York, Grune & Stratton).

Hecaen, H. and Sauguet, J. (1971) 'Cerebral dominance in left-handed subjects', *Cortex*, 7, 19–48.

Heider, F. K. and Heider, G. M. (1940) 'A comparison of sentence structure of deaf and hearing children', *Psychological Monographs*, 52, 42–103.

Henderson, P. (1949) 'Incidence of diabetes mellitus in children and need for hostels', *British Medical Journal*, 1, 478–9.

Herbert, G. (1974) 'Teachers' ratings of classroom behaviour: factorial structure', *British Journal of Educational Psychology*, 44, 233–40.

Hersch, C. (1968) 'The discontent explosion in mental health', *American Psychologist*, 23, 497–506.

Herzog, E. and Sudia, C. E. (1970) *Boys in Fatherless Families* (Washington DC, US Department of Health, Education and Welfare).

Himmelweit, H. T. (1960) 'A factorial study of children's behaviour problems', in Eysenck, H. J. (ed.), *The Structure of Human Personality* (London, Methuen).

Holland, W. W. and Elliott, H. A. (1968) 'Cigarette smoking, respiratory symptoms and anti-smoking propaganda', *Lancet*, 1, 41–3.

Home Office (1973) *Offences of Drunkenness, 1972* (London, HMSO).

Hood, C., Oppe, T. E., Pless, I. B. and Apte, E. (1970) *Children of West Indian Immigrants* (London, Institute of Race Relations).

Hopson, B. and Hayes, J. (eds) (1968) *The Theory and Practice of Vocational Guidance* (Oxford, Pergamon).

Hopwood, R. (1975) 'It depends what you mean', *Youth in Society*, 11, May–June, 11–12.

Houghton, V. P. (1966) 'Intelligence testing of West Indian and English children', *Race*, 8(2) 147–56.

Hunt, A., Fox, J. and Morgan, M. (1973) *Families and their Needs with Particular Reference to One Parent Families* (London, HMSO).

Hunt, K. W. (1965) *Differences in Grammatical Structures written at Three Grade Levels*, National Council for Teachers of English; Research Report No. 3 (Champagne, Illinois).

Hunt, K. W. (1970) 'Syntactic maturity in school children and adults', *Monographs of the Society for Research in Child Development*, 35(i), 134.

Hutchison, D. and McPherson, A. (1976) 'Competing inequalities: the sex and social class structure of the first year Scottish university student population, 1962–1972', *Sociology*, 10, 1.

Ingram, R. H. (1973a) 'Role of the school eye clinic in modern ophthalmology', *British Medical Journal*, 1, 278–80.

Ingram, R. H. (1973b) 'School eye clinics', *British Medical Journal*, 2, 548–9 (letter).

Ingram, R. H. (1977) 'Screening children for visual defects', *British Medical Journal*, 2, 890 (letter).

Ingram, T. (1969) 'Disorders of speech in childhood', *British Journal of Hospital Medicine*, 10, 1608–25.

Inner London Education Authority (1975) *Literacy Survey: 1973–4 Follow-up Preliminary Report* (London, ILEA).

Institute for the Study and Treatment of Delinquency (1974) 'Truancy in Glasgow', *British Journal of Criminology*, 14, 248–55.

Jackson, B. (1964) *Streaming: An Education System in Miniature* (London, Routledge & Kegan Paul).

Jackson, P. W. and Lahaderne, H. M. (1967) 'Scholastic success and attitude toward school in a population of sixth graders', *Journal of Educational Psychology*, 58, 15–18.

Jackson, W. S. (1955) 'Housing and pupil growth and development', *Journal of Educational Society*, 28, 370–80.

Jencks, C. *et al.* (1973) *Inequality* (New York, Basic Books).

Jencks, C. and Brown, M. D. (1975) 'Effects of high schools on their students, *Harvard Educational Research*, 45, 273–324.

Jenkins, R. L. and Glickman, S. (1946) 'Common syndromes in child psychiatry: I deviant behaviour traits', *American Journal of Orthopsychiatry*, 16, 244–61.

Jones, P., Smith, G. and Pulham, K. (1975) *All Their Future* (Oxford, Department of Social and Administrative Studies, University of Oxford).

Karlsson, J. L. (1975) 'Influence of the myopia gene on brain development', *Clinical Genetics*, 8(5) 314–18.

Kendall, M. G. and Stuart, A. (1961) *The Advanced Theory of Statistics* (London, Griffin) II, ch. 29.

Keogh, B. K. (1975), 'Social and ethical assumptions about

special education', in Wedell, K. (ed.), *Orientations in Special Education* (London, Wiley).

Kerlinger, F. M. and Pedhazur, E. J. (1973) *Multiple Regression in Behavioural Research* (New York, Holt, Rinehart & Winston).

Kimura, D. (1967) 'Functional asymmetry of the brain in dichotic listening', *Cortex*, 3, 163–78.

Kittrie, N.N. (1971) *The Right to be Different* (London, Johns Hopkins Press).

Kniveton, B. H. (1969) 'An investigation of the attitudes of adolescents to aspects of their schooling', *British Journal of Educational Psychology*, 39, 79–81.

Kolvin, I. and Taunch, J. (1973) 'A dual theory of nocturnal enuresis', in Kolvin, I., MacKeith, R. C. and Meadow, S. R. (eds), *Bladder Control and Enuresis: Clinics in Developmental Medicine*, No. 48/49. (London, SIMP and Heinemann).

Kropf, A. and Wakefield, J. (1974) 'Effects of medical education on smoking behaviour', *British Journal of Preventative and Social Medicine*, 28, 246–51.

Kuchlick, A. and Cox, G. (1973) 'The epidemiology of mental handicap', *Developmental Medicine and Child Neurology*, 15, 748.

La Brant, L. L. (1933) 'A study of certain language developments of children in grades four to twelve inclusive, *Genetic Psychology Monographs*, 14, 387–491.

Labouvie, E.W., Batisch, T.W., Nesselroade, J.R. and Baltes, P. B. (1974) 'On the internal and external validity of simple longitudinal designs', *Child Development*, 45, 282–90.

Labov, W. (1969) 'The logic of non-standard English', *Georgetown Monographs of Language and Linguistics*, 22, 1–31.

Lacey, C. (1970) *Hightown Grammar – The School as a Social System* (Manchester University Press).

Lambert, L. (1977) 'Measuring the gaps in teenagers' knowledge of sex and parenthood', *Health and Social Service Journal*, 77, 15 April, 668–9.

Lambert, L. (1978) 'Living in one-parent families: school leavers and their future', *Concern*, 29, 26–30.

Lambert, N. M. and Hartsough, C. S. (1973) 'Scaling behaviour attributes of children using multiple teacher judgements of pupils' characteristics', *Educational Psychology Measurement*, 33, 859–74.

Lambert, R. (1964) *Nutrition in Britain: 1950–60*, Occasional Papers on Social Administration (Welwyn, Codicote Press).

Lancet (1976) 'Inheritance of virus-induced diabetes mellitus', *Lancet*, II, 28–9.

Law, F. W. (1951) 'Standardization of reading types', *British Journal of Ophthalmology*, 35, 765–73.

Law, F. W. (1952) 'Reading types', *British Journal of Ophthalmology*, 35, 689–90.

Lawton, D. (1968) *Social Class, Language and Education* (London, Routledge & Kegan Paul).

Lebo, C. P. and Chiphant, K. P. (1968) 'Music as a source of acoustic trauma', *Laryngoscope*, 78, 1211–18.

Lenihan, J. M. A., Christie, J. F., Russel, T. F., Orr, N. M., Hamington, H. D. and Knox, E. C. (1971) 'The threshold of hearing in schoolchildren', *Journal of Laryngology and Otology*, 85, 375–85.

Levy, J. (1969) 'Possible basis for the evolution of lateral specialization of the human brain', *Nature*, 224, 614–15.

Levy, J. (1974) 'Psychobiological implications of bilateral asymmetry', in Dimond, S. J. and Beaumont, J. G. (eds), *Hemisphere Function in the Human Brain* (London, Elek).

Levy, P. and Tucker, J. (1972) 'Primary school attainment

and streaming', *British Journal of Educational Psychology*, 42(1).

Liem, G. R., Yellott, A. W., Cowen, E. L., Trost, M. A. and Izzo, L. D. (1969) 'Some correlates of early-detected emotional dysfunction in the schools', *American Journal of Orthopsychiatry*, 38, 619–26.

Lindgren, G. (1976) 'Height, weight and menarche in Swedish urban school children in relation to socio-economic and regional factors', *Annals of Human Biology*, 34 (6).

Lipscomb, D.M. (1972) 'The increase in prevalence of high frequency hearing impairment among college students', *Audiology*, 11, 231–7.

Little, A. (1975) 'Performance of children from ethnic minority backgrounds in primary schools', *Oxford Review of Education*, 1 (2) 117–35.

Little, A. (1978) *Educational Policies for Multi-Racial Areas* (Goldsmiths' College, University of London).

Little, A., Mabey, C. and Whitaker, G. (1968) 'The education of immigrant pupils in Inner London primary schools', *Race*, 9 (4) 439–52.

Lydiat, M. (1977) 'Mixed-ability teaching gains ground', *Comprehensive Education*, 1 (1).

Lynn, R. and Hampson, S. L. (1971) 'Streaming in the primary school: a critique', *Educational Research*, 13 (2).

McCarthy, D. (1954) 'Language development in children', in Carmichael, L. (ed.), *Manual of Child Psychology* (New York, Wiley).

MacCarthy, M. D., Douglas, J. W. B. and Mogford, C. (1952) 'Circumcision in a national sample of 4 year old children', *British Medical Journal*, 2, 755.

McCrae, W. M. (1963) 'Diabetes mellitus following mumps', *Lancet*, I, 1300–1.

McFie, J. and Thompson, J. (1970) 'Intellectual abilities of immigrant children', *British Journal of Educational Psychology*, 40(3) 348–51.

MacKeith, R. C. (1968) 'A frequent factor in the origins of primary nocturnal enuresis: anxiety in the third year of life', *Developmental Medicine and Child Neurology*, 10, 465.

MacKeith, R. C. (1972) 'Is maturation delay a frequent factor in the origin of primary nocturnal enuresis?', *Developmental Medicine and Child Neurology*, 14, 217.

McKennell, A. C. and Thomas, R. K. (1967) *Adults' and Adolescents' Smoking Habits and Attitudes* (London: HMSO).

McNicol, K. N., Williams, H. E., Allan, J. and McAndrew, I. (1973) 'Spectrum of asthma: psychological and social components', *British Medical Journal*, 4, 16–20.

McPherson, A. F. (1971) 'Survey of Educational and Occupations', Final Report to the SSRC (unpublished).

Madaus, G. F., Kellaghan, T., Bakow, E. A. and King, D. J. (1979) 'The sensitivity of measures of school effectiveness', *Harvard Educational Review*, 49, 207–30.

Marsden, D. (1969) *Mothers Alone: Poverty and the Fatherless Family* (London, Allen Lane).

Marsden, D. (1973) *Mothers Alone* (Harmondsworth, Penguin).

Marshall, W. A. and Tanner, J. M. (1969) 'Variations in pattern of pubertal changes in girls', *Archives of Disease in Childhood*, 45 (239).

Marshall, W. A. and Tanner, J. M. (1970) 'Variations in the pattern of pubertal changes in boys', *Archives of Disease in Childhood*, 45 (239).

Marshall, W.C. (1969) 'Discussion on the disease in various counties', *Symposium Series in Immunological Standardisation*, 2 (68).

Martin, A. E. (1967) 'Environment, housing and health', *Urban Studies*, 4, 1–21.

Martin, M. C. (1967) 'The RNID audiometer calibration scheme', *Journal of Laryngology and Otology*, 81, 833–47.

Mayeske, G. W., Cohen, W. M., Wisler, C. E., Okada, T., Beaton, A. E., Proshek, J. M., Weinfeld, F. D. and Tabler, K. A. (1972) *A Study of Our Nation's Schools* (Washington DC, US Department of Health, Education and Welfare).

Mellon, J. C. (1967) *Transformational Sentence – Combining: A Method for Enhancing the Development of Syntactic Fluency in English Composition* (Cambridge, Mass., Office of English Education and Laboratory for Research in Instruction).

Menyuk, P. (1964) 'Syntactic rules used by children', *Child Development*, 35, 533–46.

Mercer, J. (1968) 'Mental subnormality', in Rubington, E. and Weinberg, M. S. (eds), *Deviance: The Interactionist Perspective* (London, Collier-Macmillan).

Meyers, C. E. (1973) 'The school psychologist and mild retardation – report of an ad hoc committee', *Mental Retardation*, 11, 15–20.

Miller, A. (1962) 'Some psychological studies of grammar', *American Psychologist*, 17, 748–62.

Miller, E. (1971) 'Handedness and the pattern of human ability', *British Journal of Psychology*, 62, 111–12.

Miller, F. J. W., Billewicz, W. Z. and Thomson, A. M. (1972) 'Growth from birth to adult life of 442 Newcastle-upon-Tyne children', *British Journal of Preventative and Social Medicine*, 26(4).

Miller, F. J. W., Court, S. D. M., Knox, E. G. and Brandon, S. (1974) *The School Years in Newcastle-upon-Tyne* (Oxford, Oxford University Press).

Miller, G. A. (1956) 'The magical number seven, plus or minus two: some limits on our capacity for processing information', *Psychology Review*, 63, 81–97.

Miller, P. (1973) 'All children are special', *Association of Educational Psychologist Journals*, 3, 40–6.

Milne, J. S. and Lauder, I. J. (1975) 'Pure tone audiometry in older people', *British Journal of Audiology*, 9, 50–8.

Milner, B., Branch, C. and Rasmussen, T. (1964) 'Observations on cerebral dominance', in de Reuch, A. V. S. and O'Connor, M. (eds), *Disorders of Language* (London: Churchill).

Ministry of Education (1954) *Health of the School Child*, Report of the Chief Medical Officer for the Years 1952 and 1953 (London, HMSO) ch. 9, 78.

Ministry of Health (1955) *An Historical Sketch of the Origins, Development and Present Organisations of the School Health Service*, Report of the Chief Medical Officer of Health and Principal Schools Medical Officer for 1954 (London, HMSO) 24.

Ministry of Health (1968) *A Pilot Survey of the Nutrition of Young Children in 1963* (London, HMSO).

Mitchell, R. G. and Dawson, B. (1973) 'Educational and social characteristics of children with asthma', *Archives of Disease in Childhood*, 48, 467–71.

Modlin, J. F. *et al.* (1976) 'Risk of congenital abnormalities after inadvertent rubella vaccination of pregnant women', *New England Journal of Medicine*, 1, 972.

Morley, M. (1972) *The Development and Disorders of Speech in Childhood* (Edinburgh, Churchill Livingstone).

Morton-Williams, R. and Finch, S. (1968) *Schools Council Enquiry I: Young School Leavers* (London, HMSO).

Moser, C. A. and Kalton, G. (1971) *Survey Methods in Social Investigation* (London, Heinemann).

Moyes, C. D. (1976) 'Adverse factors affecting growth of school children in St Helena', *British Journal of Preventative and Social Medicine*, 51(6).

Mulholland, W. V. (1977) 'Screening children for visual defects', *British Medical Journal*, 2, 1083 (letter).

Myklebust, H. R. (1965) *Development and Disorders of Written Language, Vol. I* (New York, Grune & Stratton).

Myklebust, H.R. (1973) *Development and Disorders of Written Language, Vol. II* (New York, Grune & Stratton).

National Centre for Health Statistics (1973) 'Visual acuity of youths 12–17 years', *Vital Health Statistics*, 11(127).

National Consumer Council (1977a) *Advise and Consent* and *Question Marks for Schools* (pamphlets) (London, National Consumer Council).

National Consumer Council (1977b) *When did you last see your teacher?* (press release) (London: National Consumer Council).

National Youth Employment Council (1974) *Final Triennial Report* (London, HMSO).

Nebes, R. D. (1971) 'Handedness and perception of part–whole relationships', *Cortex*, 7, 350–6.

Nebes, R. D. and Briggs, G. G., (1974) 'Handedness and the retention of visual material', *Cortex*, 10, 209–14.

Neligan, G.A. and Prudham, D. (1976) 'Family factors affecting child development', *Archives of Disease in Childhood*, 51, 853.

Nelson, P. G., Pyke, D. A. and Gamble, D. R. (1974) 'Viruses and the aetiology of diabetes: a study in identical twins', *British Medical Journal*, 4 (5991) 249–51.

Neuhaus, E. C. (1965) 'A personality study of asthmatic and cardiac children', *Psychosomatic Medicine*, 20, 181–6.

Neville, M. H. and Pugh, A. K. (1975) 'Reading ability and ability to use books', *Reading*, 9, 23–31.

Newbold, D. (1977) *Ability Grouping: The Banbury Inquiry* (Slough, NFER).

Newcombe, F. G., Ratcliff, G.G., Carrivick, P.J., Hiorns, R.W., Harrison, G. A. and Gibson, J. B. (1975) 'Hand preference and IQ in a group of Oxfordshire villages', *Annals of Human Biology*, 2, 235–42.

Newens, M. E. and Goldstein, H. (1972) 'Height, weight and the assessment of obesity in children', *British Journal of Preventative and Social Medicine*, 26, 33–9.

Newsom Report (1963) *Half Our Future* (London, HMSO).

Nie, N. H., Bent, D. H. and Hull, C. H. (1970) *Statistical Package for the Social Sciences* (New York, McGraw-Hill).

Nisbet, J. D. (1953) 'Family environment and intelligence', *Eugenics Review*, 45.

Nisbet, J. D. and Entwistle, N. (1967) 'Intelligence and family size 1949–64', *British Journal of Educational Psychology*, 37(2) 188.

Oakley, R. (ed.) (1968) *New Backgrounds* (London, OUP, for Institute of Race Relations).

Oakley, W. G., Pyke, D. A. and Taylor, K. W. (1968) *Clinical Diabetes and its Biochemical Basis* (Oxford, Blackwell).

O'Connor, J. (1973) 'The measurement of levels of drinking', *Economic and Social Review*, 4, 2.

O'Connor, J. (1977) 'Normal and problem drinking among children', *Journal of Child Psychology and Psychiatry*, 18, 279–84.

O'Donnell, R. C., Griffin, W. J. and Norris, R. C. (1967) *The Syntax of Kindergarten and Elementary School Children: A Transformational Analysis* (Illinois, National Council of Teachers of English).

Oldfield, R. C. (1971) 'The assessment and analysis of handedness: the Edinburgh inventory', *Neuropsychologia*, 9, 97–113.

Orton, S. T. (1937) *Reading, Writing and Speech Problems in Children* (London, Chapman & Hall).

Osborn, A. (1976) Personal communication.

Palmer, A. B. (1970) 'Some variables contributing to the

onset of smoking among junior high school students', *Social Science and Medicine*, 4, 349–65.

Parrinder, D. (1972) 'Housing for children – a second look', *Housing Review*, 21, 3.

Pask, G. and Lewis, B. (1964) 'Communications in problem-solving groups', in Jones, C. and Thornley, D.G. (eds), *Conference on Design Methods* (Oxford, Pergamon).

Pattinson, W. (1963) 'Streaming in school', *Educational Research*, 5(3).

Paxson, W. M. (1968) 'The teacher's perception of the pupil', *Dissertation Abstracts*, 29, 1728–9.

Peaker, G. F. (1971) *The Plowden Children Four Years Later* (Slough, NFER).

Pearson, P. D. (1974) 'The effects of grammatical complexity on children: comprehension, recall and conception of certain semantic relations', *Reading Research Quarterly*, 10, 155–92.

Pearson, R. and Lambert, L. (1977) 'Sex education, preparation for parenthood and the adolescent', *Community Health*, 9.

Pearson, R. and Richardson, K. (1978) 'Smoking habits of 16-year-olds in the National Child Development study', *Public Health*, 92, 3.

Peckham, C. S. (1973) 'Speech defects in a national sample of children aged 7 years', *British Journal of Disorders of Communication*, 8(1) 2.

Peckham, C. S., Gardiner, P. A. and Goldstein, H. (1977) 'Acquired myopia in 11-year-old children', *British Medical Journal*, 1(6060) 542–5.

Peckham, C.S., Sheridan, M.D. and Butler, N.R. (1972) 'School attainment of 7-year-old children with hearing difficulties', *Developmental Medicine and Child Neurology*, 14, 592.

Peckham, C. S. and Tibbenham, A. (1977) 'Vision screening in older children', *British Medical Journal*, 2, 958.

Peltz, F. K. (1973) 'The effects upon comprehension of repatterning based on students' writing patterns', *Reading Research Quarterly*, 9, 602–21.

Percival, E. (1966) 'The dimension of ability in English composition', *Educational Review*, 18, 205–12.

Pervin, H. R. (1960) 'Existentialism, psychology and psychotherapy', *American Psychologist*, 15, 305–9.

Peterson, D. R. (1960) 'The age of generality of personality factors derived from ratings', *Educational Psychology Measurement*, 20, 461–74.

Phillips, B. N. (1968) 'Problem behaviour in the elementary school', *Child Development*, 39, 895–903.

Pidgeon, D. A. (1970) *Expectation and Pupil Performance* (Slough, NFER).

Pilling, D. (1973) *The Handicapped Child: Research Review, vol. III* (London, Longman, National Children's Bureau).

Pimm, J.B., Quay, H.C. and Werry, J.S. (1967) 'Dimensions of problem behaviour in first grade children', *Psychology in Schools*, 4, 155–7.

Plowden Report (1967) *Children and Their Primary Schools* (London, HMSO).

Pond, M. A. (1957) 'The influence of housing on health', *Marriage and Family Living*, 19, 154–9.

Potter, R. R. (1967) 'Sentence structure and phrase quality: an explanatory study', *Research in the Teaching of English*, 1, 17–28.

Powell, G. F., Brasul, J. A. and Blizzard, R. M. (1967) 'Emotional deprivation and growth retardation simulating idiopathic hypopituitarism', *New England Journal of Medicine*, 276(23).

Powell, J. L. (1973) *Selection for University in Scotland* (Edinburgh, SCRE).

Presland, J. (1970) 'Who should go to ESN schools?', *Special Education*, 59, 11–16.

Primrose, J. (1973) 'School eye clinics', *British Medical Journal*, 2, 117–18.

Pringle, M. L. K., Butler, N. R. and Davie, R. (1966) *11,000 Seven Year Olds* (London, Longman).

Prosser, H. (1973) 'Family size and children's development', *Health and Social Services Journal*, 10 March.

Provins, K. A. and Cunliffe, P. (1972) 'The reliability of some motor performance tests of handedness', *Neuropsychologia*, 10, 199–206.

Quirk Report (1972) *Speech Therapy Services*, Report of the Committee under Randolph Quirk, appointed by the Secretary of State for Education and Science (London, HMSO).

Rauta, I. and Hunt, A. (1975) *Fifth Form Girls: Their Hopes for the Future* (London, HMSO).

Rawls, D. J., Rawls, J. R. and Harrison, C. W. (1971) 'An investigation of six to eleven year old children with allergic disorders', *Journal of Consulting and Clinical Psychology*, 36, 260–4.

Read, C. W. (1971) *The Learning of Language* (New York, Appleton-Century-Crofts).

Reid, M. (1977) 'Mixed feelings', *The Times Educational Supplement*, June.

Renfrew, C. E. and Geary, L. (1973) 'Prediction of persisting defect', *British Journal of Disorders of Communication*, 8, 37.

Reymert, M. L. and Rotman, M. (1946) 'Auditory changes in children from ages 10 to 18', *Journal of Genetic Psychology*, 68, 181–7.

Rice, C. G. and Coles, R. R. A. (1967) 'Comments on the lack of standardisation in calibration of the audiometer earphones most commonly used in Great Britain', *Journal of Laryngology and Otology*, 81, 829–32.

Richards, M. P. M. (1975) 'Innovations in medical practice: obstetricians and the induction of labour in Britain', *Social Science and Medicine*, 9, 595.

Richards, M. P. M., Bernal, J. F. and Brackbill, Y. (1976) 'Early behavioural differences: gender or circumcision?', *Developmental Psychobiology*, 9, 89.

Richardson, K., Calnan, M., Essen, J. and Lambert, L. (1976a). 'The linguistic maturity of 11 year olds: some analysis of the written compositions of children in the National Child Development study', *Journal of Child Language*, 3, 99–115.

Richardson, K., Peckham, C.S. and Goldstein, H. (1976b) 'Hearing levels of children tested at 7 and 11 years: a national study', *British Journal of Audiology*, 10, 117–23.

Robbins Report (1963) *Higher Education* (London, HMSO).

Roberts, K. (1977) 'The social conditions, consequences and limitations of careers guidance', *British Journal of Guidance and Counselling*, 5(1) January.

Robinson, H. and Gorbach, P. (1977) 'Urban regional differences in children's educational attainment', unpublished mimeo (National Children's Bureau).

Robinson, W. P. (1965) 'The elaborated code in working class language', *Language and Speech*, 8, 243–52.

Rogers, R. S. (ed.) (1974) *Sex Education: Rationale and Reaction* (Cambridge, Cambridge University Press).

Rosen, H. (1969) 'An investigation of the effects of differentiated writing assignments on the performance in English composition of a selected group of 15–16 year old pupils', Ph.D. thesis (University of London).

Rosen, H. (1972) *Language and Class: A Critical Look at the Theories of Bernstein* (Bristol, Falling Wall Press).

Rosen, H. (1973) 'Written language and the sense of audience', *Educational Research*, 15, 177–87.

Ross, J. M., Bunton, W. J., Evison, P. and Robertson, T. S. (1972) *A Critical Appraisal of Comprehensive Education* (Slough, NFER).

Ross, J. M. and Simpson, H. R. (1971) 'The national survey of health and development 2: rate of school progress between 8 and 15 years and between 15 and 18 years', *British Journal of Educational Psychology*, 41, 125—35.

Ross, S. L., De Young, H. G. and Cohen, J. S. (1971) 'Confrontation: special education placement and the law', *Exceptional Children*, 38, 5—12.

Rossi, G. F. and Rosadini, G. (1967) 'Experimental analysis of cerebral dominance in man', in Millikan, C. H. and Darley, F. L. (eds), *Brain Mechanisms Underlying Speech and Language* (New York, Grune & Stratton).

Rotenberg, M. (1974) 'Self-labelling: a missing link in the societal reaction theory of deviance', *Sociological Review*, 22, 355—54.

Rudd, W. G. A. (1958) 'The psychological effects of streaming by attainment', *British Journal of Educational Psychology*, 28, 47—60.

Russell, J., Fairweather, D., Millar, D., Brown, A., Pearson, R. C. M., Nelligan, S. and Anderson, G. (1963) 'Maternity in Newcastle upon Tyne: a community study', *Lancet*, 1.

Rutter, M. (1967) 'A children's behaviour questionnaire for completion by teachers', *Journal of Child Psychology and Psychiatry*, 8, 1—11.

Rutter, M. (1972) *Maternal Deprivation Reassessed* (Harmondsworth, Penguin).

Rutter, M., Cox, A., Tupling, C., Berger, M. and Yule, W. (1975a) 'Attainment and adjustment in two geographical areas. I — the prevalence of psychiatric disorder', *British Journal of Psychiatry*, 126, 493—509.

Rutter, M., Grahame, P. and Yule, W. (1970a) 'A neuropsychiatric study in childhood', *Clinics in Developmental Medicine*, 35—6 (London, Spastics International Medical Publications with Heinemann).

Rutter, M., Maughan, B., Mortimore, P., Ouston, J. and Smith, A. (1979) *Fifteen Thousand Hours: Secondary Schools and their Effects on Children* (London, Open Books).

Rutter, M., Tizard, J. and Whitmore, K. (1970b) *Education, Health and Behaviour* (London, Longman).

Rutter, M., Yule, B., Morton, S. and Bagley, C. (1975b) 'Children of West Indian immigrants — III home circumstances and family patterns', *Journal of Child Psychology and Psychiatry*, 16, 105—23.

Ryan, F. J. (1958) 'Trait Ratings of high school students by teachers', *Journal of Educational Psychology*, 49, 124—8.

Sampson, O. C. (1964a) 'Written composition at 10 years as an aspect of linguistic development', *British Journal of Educational Psychology*, 24, 243—50.

Sampson, O. C. (1964b) 'A linguistic study of the written compositions of 10 year old children', *Language and Speech*, 7, 176—82.

Sarbin, T. R. (1967) 'On the futility of the proposition that some people be labelled "mentally ill"', *Journal of Consulting Psychologists*, 31, 447—53.

Schanberger, M. C. (1968) 'An investigation of interrelationships of ratings of classroom teachers and school psychologists of selected physical learning and behavioural characteristics of children', *Dissertation Abstracts*, 28, 4960—1.

Scheff, T. J. (1963) 'The role of the mentally ill and the dynamics of mental disorder; a research framework', *Sociometry*, 26, 436—53.

Schmidt, R. (1966) 'Density, health and social disorganization', *Journal of the American Institute of Planners*, 32, 38—40.

Schneider, E. V. (1953) 'Sociological concepts and psychiatric research', in Milbank Memorial Fund, *Interrelations between the Social Environment and Psychiatric Disorders* (New York, Milbank Memorial Fund).

Schofield, M. (1965) *The Sexual Behaviour of Young People* (London, Longman).

Schools Council (1972) *Careers Education in the 1970s*, Working paper No. 40 (London, Evans/Methuen).

Schorr, A. L. (1964) *Slums and Social Insecurity* (London, Nelson).

Scott, J. A. (1961) *Report on the Heights and Weights of School Pupils in the County of London in 1959* (London, London County Council).

Scottish Education Department (1968) *Guidance in Scottish Secondary Schools* (Edinburgh, HMSO).

Scottish Education Department (1970) *Staffing of Secondary Schools in Scotland* (Edinburgh, HMSO).

Scottish Education Department (1975) *Education in Scotland in 1974* (Edinburgh, HMSO).

Scottish Education Department (1976) *Guidance in Scottish Secondary Schools* (Edinburgh, HMSO).

Seglow, J., Pringle, M. L. K. and Wedge, P. J. (1972) *Growing up Adopted* (Slough, NFER and National Children's Bureau).

Semmes, J. (1968) 'Hemispheric specialisation: a possible clue to mechanism', *Neuropsychologia*, 6, 11—26.

Shaffer, D. (1973) 'The association between enuresis and emotional disorder: a review of the literature', in Kolvin, I., MacKeith, R. C. and Meadow, S. R. (eds), 'Bladder control and enuresis', *Clinics in Developmental Medicine*, 48—9 (London, SIMP with Heinemann) 118.

Shanon, B. (1974) 'Lateralisation effects on reaction time to simple sentences', *Cortex*, 10, 360—5.

Sharpe, J. (1976) *Just Like a Girl* (Harmondsworth, Penguin).

Shepherd, M., Oppenheim, A. N. and Mitchell, S. (1966) 'Childhood behaviour disorders and the child-guidance clinic: an epidemiological study', *Journal of Child Psychology and Psychiatry*, 7, 39—52.

Sheridan, M. D. (1972) 'Reported incidence of hearing loss in children of 7 years', *Developmental Medicine and Child Neurology*, 14, 296.

Sheridan, M. D. (1973) 'Children of 7 years with marked speech defects', *British Journal of Disorders of Communication*, 8, 9—16.

Sheridan, M. D. (1974) 'What is normal distance vision at 5 to 7 years?', *Developmental Medicine and Child Neurology*, 16, 189—95.

Sheridan, M. D. and Peckham, C. S. (1973) 'Hearing and speech at 7', *Special Education*, 62, 16—20.

Sheridan, M. D. and Peckham, C. S. (1975) 'Follow-up at 11 years of children who had marked speech defects at 7 years', *Child: Care, Health and Development*, 1, 157—6.

Siler, E. R. (1973) 'The effects of syntactic and semantic constraints on the oral reading performance of second and fourth graders', *Reading Research Quarterly*, 9, 588—602.

Simon, B. (1970) 'Streaming in the comprehensive school', *Secondary Education*, 1, 1.

Smedley, D. A. (1968) 'Language and social class among grammar school children', *British Journal of Educational Psychology*, 39, 195—6.

Smith, G. M. (1970) 'Personality and smoking: a review of the empirical literature', in Hunt, W.G. (ed.), *Learning Mechanisms and Smoking* (Chicago, Aldine).

Smith, J. M., Harding, K. and Cumming, G. (1971) 'The changing prevalence of asthma in school children', *Clinical Allergy*, 1, 56—61.

Smith, W.L. (1974) 'Syntactic recoding of passages written

at three levels of complexity', *Journal of Experimental Education*, 39, 195–6.

Sorsby, A., Sheridan, M. and Leary, G. A. (1962) *Refraction and its Components in Twins* (London, HMSO).

Southgate, V. (1962) *Southgate Group Reading Tests: Manual of Instructions* (London, University of London Press).

Sperry, R. W. (1967) 'Brain bisection and consciousness', in Eccles, J. C. (ed.), *Brain and Conscious Experience* (New York, Springer-Verlag).

Spreen, O. (1965) 'Language function in mental retardation: a review 1. Language development, types of retardation and intelligence level', *American Journal of Mental Deficiency*, 69 (4) 482–94.

Start, K. B. and Wells, B. K. (1972) *The Trend of Reading Standards* (Slough, NFER).

Stein, Z. and Susser, M. (1960a) 'Families of dull children: part III social selection by family type', *Journal of Mental Science*, 106, 1304.

Stein, Z. and Susser, M. (1960b) 'The families of dull children: a classification of predicting careers', *British Journal of Preventative and Social Medicine*, 14, 83–8.

Stein, Z. A. and Susser, M. (1966) 'Nocturnal enuresis as a phenomenon of institutions', *Developmental Medicine and Child Neurology*, 8, 677–85.

Stein, Z. and Susser, M. (1967) 'Social factors in the development of sphincter control', *Developmental Medicine and Child Neurology*, 9, 692–706.

Stein, Z., Susser, M. and Lunzer, E. A. (1960) 'Reading reckoning and special schooling among the mentally handicapped', *Lancet*, II, 305–7.

Stott, D.H. (1963, revised 1969) *The Social Adjustment of Children*, 3rd edn (London, University of London Press).

Svensson, N. E. (1965) 'Ability-grouping and scholastic achievement', *Stockholm Studies in Educational Psychology*, 5 (Stockholm, Almqvist & Wiksell).

Szasz, T. S. (1960) 'The myth of mental illness', *American Psychologist*, 15, 113–18.

Tanner, J. M. (1962) *Growth at Adolescence*, 2nd edn (Oxford, Blackwell).

Tanner, J. M., Whitehouse, R. H., Marabuni, E. and Resele, L.F. (1976) 'The adolescent growth spurt of boys and girls of the Harpenden growth study', *Annals of Human Biology*, 3 (2).

Tanner, J. M., Whitehouse, R. H. and Takaishi, M. (1966) 'Standards from birth to maturity for height, weight, height velocity and weight velocity: British children 1965', *Archives of Disease in Childhood*, 41.

Tattersall, R. B. (1974) 'Mild familial diabetes with dominant inheritance', *Quarterly Journal of Medicine*, 43, 339–57.

Tattersall, R. B. and Pyke, D. A. (1972) 'Diabetes in identical twins', *Lancet*, 2, 120–5.

Taylor, F. (1974) *Race, School and Community* (Slough, NFER).

Taylor, J. H. (1973) 'Newcastle upon Tyne: Asian pupils do better than whites', *British Journal of Sociology*, 24 (4) 431–47.

Taylor, J. J. (1973) 'The voluntary reading habits of secondary school pupils', *Reading*, 7, 11–18.

Thomas, M. M. (1968) 'Children with absent fathers', *Journal of Marriage and the Family*, 30, 89–96.

Thompson, B. L. (1975) 'Secondary school pupils' attitudes to school and teachers', *Educational Review*, 18, 62–6.

Thompson, D. (1966) 'Streaming in the secondary school', *Educational Review*, 18.

Thompson, D. (1974) 'Non-streaming did make a difference', *Forum*, 16 (2) 45–9.

Tibbenham, A. (1977) 'Housing and truancy', *New Society*, 39, 501–2.

Tibbenham, A., Essen, J. and Fogelman, K. R. (1978a) 'Ability-grouping and school characteristics', *British Journal of Educational Studies*, 26, 8–22.

Tibbenham, A., Peckham, C. S. and Gardiner, P. A. (1978b) 'Vision screening in children tested at 7, 11 and 16 years', *British Medical Journal*, 1 (6123) 1312–14.

Timperley, S. R. and Gregory, A. M. (1971) 'Some factors affecting the career choice and career perceptions of sixth-form school leavers', *Sociological Review*, 19, 1.

Tizard, J. (1966) 'Schooling for the handicapped', *Special Education*, 44, 4–7.

Tobacco Research Council (1966) *Statistics of Smoking in the United Kingdom* (London, TRC).

Topp, S. G., Cook, J. A., Holland, W. W. and Elliot, A. (1970) 'Influence of environmental factors on height and weight of school children', *British Journal of Preventative and Social Medicine*, 24.

Townsend, H. E. R. and Brittan, E. M. (1972) *Organisation in Multi-Racial Schools* (Slough, NFER).

Townsend, P. (1975) 'Problems of introducing a guaranteed maintenance allowance for one-parent families', *Poverty*, 31.

Trémolieres, J. and Boulanger, J. J. (1950) 'Contribution a l'étude du phenomene de croissance et de stature en France de 1940 à 1948', *Recueil de Travaux — Institut National de l'Hygiène*, 4 (cited in Tanner, 1962).

Tuckman, T. and Regan, R. (1967) 'Size of family and behavioural problems in children', *Journal of Genetic Psychology*, 3.

Tyerman, M. J. (1968) *Truancy* (London, University of London Press).

Ulrich, R. F. and Pinheiro, M. L. (1974) 'Temporary hearing losses in teenagers attending repeated rock-n-roll sessions', *Acta Otolaryngologica*, 77, 51–5.

US Public Health Service (1972) *Hearing levels of Children by Demographic and Socio-Economic Characteristics*, DHEW Publication, No. (HBM) 72–1025 (Washington: US Government Printing Office).

US Public Health Service (1975) *Hearing Levels of Youths 12–17 Years*, DHEW Publication No. (HRA) 75–1025 (Washington: US Government Printing Office).

Van der Geest, T., Gerstel, R., Aspel, R. and Tervoort, B. T. L. (1973) *The Child's Communicative Competence* (The Hague, Mouton).

Vaughan, D. S. (1973) 'The relative methodological soundness of several major personality factor analyses', *Journal of Behavioural Science*, 1, 305–13.

Veness, T. (1962) *School Leavers* (London, Methuen).

Venters, G. and Bloor, M. (1974) 'A review of investigations into tonsillectomy', *British Journal of Preventative and Social Medicine*, 28, 1.

Vernon, P. E. (1964) *Personality Assessment: A Critical Survey* (London, Methuen).

Wada, J. and Rasmussen, T. (1960) 'Intra-carotid injection of sodium amytal for the lateralisation of cerebral speech dominance', *Journal of Neurosurgery*, 17, 266–82.

Wadsworth, M. E. J. and Jarrett, R. J. (1974) 'Incidence of diabetes in the first 26 years of life', *Lancet*, 2 (7890) 1172–4.

Walker, A. (1982) *Unqualified and Underemployed* (London, Macmillan).

Walker, A. and Lewis, P. (1978) 'School and post-school experiences of severely mentally handicapped young people', unpublished mimeo.

Walker, D. A. (1957) 'The theory and use of the success

ratio', *British Journal of Statistical Psychology*, 10, 105—12.

Warren, R. D., White, J. K. and Fuller, W. A. (1974) 'An errors-in-variables analysis of managerial role performance', *Journal of the American Statistical Association*, 69, 886.

Wedge, P. J. (1969) 'The second follow-up of the National Child Development study', *Concern*, 34—9.

Wedge, P. J. and Petzing, J. (1970) 'Housing for children', *Housing Review*, 19, 165—6.

Wedge, P. J. and Prosser, H. (1973) *Born to Fail?* (London, Arrow Books).

Weir, D. and Nolan, F. (1977) *Glad to be Out?* (Edinburgh, Scottish Council for Research in Education).

West, D. J. and Farrington, D. P. (1973) *Who Becomes Delinquent?* (London, Heinemann).

West, R. (1947) 'The pathology of stuttering', *Nervous Child*, 2(2) 97—106.

Whitehead, F., Capey, A. C. and Maddren, W. (1975) *Children's Reading Interests*, Schools Council Working Paper No. 52 (London, Evans/Methuen).

Williams, G. and Gordon, A. (1976) 'Why teenagers decide on further study or look for a job', *The Times Higher Educational Supplement*, 7 February.

Williams, H. E. and McNicol, K. N. (1969) 'Prevalence, natural history and relationship of wheezy bronchitis and asthma in children: an epidemiological study', *British Medical Journal*, 4, 321—5.

Williams, P. (1965) 'The ascertainment of educationally subnormal children', *Educational Research*, 7, 136—46.

Williams, P. (1966) 'Some characteristics of educationally subnormal children', *British Journal of Psychiatry*, 112, 79.

Williams, P. and Gruber, E. (1967) *Response to Special Education* (London, Longman).

Willig, C. J. (1963) 'Social implications of streaming in the junior school', *Educational Research*, 5, 151—4.

Wilner, D. M., Walkey, R. P., Pinkerton, T. and Tayback, M. (1962) *The Housing Environment and Family Life: A Longitudinal Study of the Effects on Morbidity and Mental Health* (Baltimore, Johns Hopkins University Press).

Wilner, D.M., Walkey, R.P. and Tayback, M. (1956) 'How does the quality of housing affect health and family adjustment?', *American Journal of Public Health*, 46, 736—44.

Wilson, J. D. (1971) 'Predicting levels of first year university performance', *British Journal of Educational Psychology*, 41, 163—70.

Winitz, H. (1969) *Articulatory Acquisition and Behaviour* (New York, Appleton-Century-Crofts).

Wiseman, S. (ed.) (1964) *Environment and Education* (Harmondsworth, Penguin).

Wohl, M. T. (1951) 'Incidence of speech defects in the population', *Speech*, 15, 13—14.

Wood, B., Wong, Y.K. and Theodoridis, C.G. (1972) 'Paediatricians look at children awaiting adeno-tonsillectomy', *Lancet*, 2, 645.

Woodhall, M. and Blaug, M. (1969) 'Variation in costs and productivity of British primary and secondary schools', in Hupnes, K. and Janmann, J. (eds), *Economics of Education in Transition* (Stuttgart, Ernst Klett).

Woods, N. E. (1960) 'Language development and language disorders: a compendium of lectures', *Monographs of the Society of Research in Child Development*, 25(77).

Woods, P. (1976) 'Pupils' views of school', *Educational Review*, 28, 126—37.

Wright, J. E. (1967) 'Non-therapeutic circumcision', *Medical Journal of Australia*, I, 1083.

Wynn, M. (1964) *Fatherless Families* (London, Michael Joseph).

Yarrow, M. R., Campbell, J. D. and Burton, R. V. (1970) 'Recollections of childhood: a study of the retrospective method', *Monographs of the Society for Research in Child Development*, 138(35).

Yoder, D. E. (1970) 'Some viewpoints of the speech clinician', in Williams, P. (ed.), *Language and Poverty* (New York, Markham).

Young, M. and Armstrong, M. (1965) 'The flexible school — the next step forward', *Where?*, Autumn.

Youngson, R. M. (1977) 'Screening children for visual defects', *British Medical Journal*, 2, 1221—2.

Yudkin, J. (1944) 'Nutrition and size of family', *Lancet*, II.

Yule, W. (1968) 'Identifying maladjusted children', in *The Child and the Outside World*, 29th biennial conference of the Association for Special Education, Coventry, August.

Yule, W., Berger, M., Rutter, M. and Yule, B. (1975) 'Children of West Indian Immigrants II: intellectual performance and reading attainment', *Journal of Child Psychology and Psychiatry*, 16(1) 1—17.

Zajonc, R.B. and Marcus, G.B. (1975) 'Birth order and intellectual development', *Psychological Review*, 82, 74—88.

Zangwill, O. L. (1960) *Cerebral Dominance and its Relation to Psychological Function* (Edinburgh, Oliver & Boyd).

Zeally, H. (1974) 'Rubella screening and immunisation of schoolgirls: a long term evaluation', *British Journal of Preventative and Social Medicine*, 28(1), 54—9.

Zigler, E. (1966) 'Mental retardation: current issues and approaches', in Hoffman, M. L. and Hoffman, L. W. (eds), *Review of Child Developmental Research*, vol. 2 (New York, Russell Sage Foundation).

Index